ALSO BY JONATHAN ALTER

The Defining Moment:
FDR's Hundred Days and the Triumph of Hope

Between the Lines:
A View Inside American Politics, People, and Culture

THE
PROMISE

President Obama, Year One

JONATHAN ALTER

SIMON & SCHUSTER
NEW YORK   LONDON   TORONTO   SYDNEY

Photo Credits

AP Photo/Pablo Martinez Monsivais: 1
David Katz/Obama for America: 2
Official White House Photo by Pete Souza: 3, 4, 5, 6, 7, 8, 9, 10, 11, 12, 13, 14, 15,
16, 17, 18, 19, 20, 21, 22, 25, 26, 27, 28, 29, 30, 31, 32, 33, 34, 35, 36
Official White House Photo by Chuck Kennedy: 23, 24

Simon & Schuster
1230 Avenue of the Americas
New York, NY 10020

First Simon & Schuster hardcover edition May 2010

SIMON & SCHUSTER and colophon are
registered trademarks of Simon & Schuster, Inc.

For information about special discounts for bulk purchases,
please contact Simon & Schuster Special Sales at 1-866-506-1949
or business@simonandschuster.com.

The Simon & Schuster Speakers Bureau can bring authors to your live event.
For more information or to book an event contact the Simon & Schuster Speakers
Bureau at 1-866-248-3049 or visit our website at www.simonspeakers.com.

Designed by Level C

Manufactured in the United States of America

10   9   8   7   6   5   4   3   2   1

Library of Congress Cataloging-in-Publication Data is available.

ISBN 978-1-4391-0119-3
ISBN 978-1-4391-5408-3 (ebook)

For Emily, with all my love

Author's Note

The Dutch historian Pieter Geyl wrote, "History is an argument without end." The argument over Barack Obama's presidency is only beginning, and it's too early to draw definitive conclusions about him. My aim is to offer a narrative of his first year in office as a basis for future arguments. This is journalistic history, a melding of old-fashioned reporting with a few commonsense assessments of what might be of lasting historical interest. For this reason I've written it in the past tense without first-person references or the polemics of punditry.

Washington in 2009 was a confusing blur of activity. You might catch something here or there about health care or Afghanistan or the Obamas' new dog, but no one could possibly keep up with the Niagara of news coming out of the new administration. Even reporters assigned to cover the White House found themselves overwhelmed. Amid endless Web deadlines, few had time for more than an occasional glimpse behind the curtain.

My goal was ambitious: to cover the important and compelling dimensions of the Obama story across a broad front, not snip off a piece; to push my sources for information that had not been published before; and to write in real time about a moving target—history on the fly.

I offer a few judgments of where I think the president succeeded and where he fell short of his promise. But mostly I'm trying to give readers more information to make their own judgments—to discover for themselves where their assessments are based on the historical record and where they are not.

This book cannot tell you if Obama and the Democrats will suffer big setbacks at the polls. The answers depend on the state of the economy and the state of the world at election time. Obama's leadership will look good if he succeeds in bringing down unemployment and flawed if he fails to do so, with foreign policy a political loser only if the wars in Iraq and Afghanistan drag on or he mishandles a crisis. The political repercussions of the enactment of health care reform could take years to play out.

From Franklin Roosevelt to Lyndon Johnson to Ronald Reagan, American presidents have done much of their domestic scoring in the first quarter. Whatever their important new initiatives or midcourse adjustments in later years, they set the tone for the rest of their presidencies in Year One. My last book was called *The Defining Moment: FDR's Hundred Days and the Triumph of Hope,* but it actually covers about twelve months of Roosevelt's political life. A year strikes me as the right amount of time for an assessment.

The Promise addresses three questions.

First: What happened? I trace as much as I can of the backstory and hidden history of one of the most momentous and difficult presidential debuts of modern times. Starting on the day after he was elected, Obama was forced to grapple with the worst set of problems of any incoming president since Roosevelt in 1933. Because this book is being published while Obama is in office, sources don't always talk as openly as they would when they know a campaign or administration will end by the time the book is out. But most were surprisingly candid.

Second: What's the president like? Never before have we known so little about someone so intensely observed. I used my access to Obama and his circle to assess his leadership style and how he operates in private. The book explores his temperament, his approach to decision making, and his analysis of his ambitious first year. I approach these sections with a humble appreciation of how little journalists and historians can know about any human being. Whether he succeeds or fails, the world will be arguing over Barack Obama for a long time. I doubt future historians will find him to be a dramatically different individual than he appears in these pages, but I can offer no guarantees.

Third: How well did he do? Obama came to office facing two wars and a cratering economy. I begin by arguing that he essentially took charge in Washington even before being elected in November 2008 and made historic and necessary economic decisions (the most ever by a president-elect) before being inaugurated in January 2009. Just as his long first year started early, it ended late—on Sunday, March 21, 2010, with the big victory on health care. In that sense, this book covers more like a year and a half of Obama's political life.

I chronicle his performance on the huge and underappreciated stimulus package, the auto bailouts, bank rescue and regulation, reaching out to the Muslim world, advancing nuclear nonproliferation, communicating (or miscommunicating) with the public, sending sixty-one thousand more troops to Afghanistan, and a health care bill that repeatedly came back from the dead. The topic of every chapter could be its own book—and probably will.

I learned hundreds of new things about the Obama White House, but a couple of big stories stand out. The president decided to pursue major health care reform in 2009 over the objections of his vice president, his chief of staff, and Senate leaders. This was a risky and historically significant decision he made all alone and it nearly wrecked his first year on the domestic side of his presidency. On the national security side, Obama did more than drive a deliberative process on Afghanistan, another risky policy that could end badly. Facing what the White House considered insubordination from the Pentagon, he angrily dressed down the brass and grabbed control of his own government, a moment described within the National Security Council as reminiscent of President Truman's confrontation with General Douglas MacArthur in 1951.

WRITING CONTEMPORARY HISTORY is tricky, like pulling pottery out of the kiln before the glaze has hardened. Certain decisions that loom large now could look less important later, and what I've downplayed might become central to our politics, depending on events.

Whatever its shortcomings, a journalistic account can be history too. The memoirs and oral histories that historians often rely on are usually completed years afterward, when memories have faded; most of my more than two hundred interviews were conducted a few weeks at most after events took place, when memories were fresh. Of course historical perspective is harder, and I hope the reader will forgive that mine has not yet been deepened by time.

If journalism is the first rough draft of history, as Philip Graham, onetime proprietor of *Newsweek* and the *Washington Post,* put it, then this book might be considered a second draft, with dozens more versions to come.

Contents

Preface

Barack Obama's political fate in 2009 turned on a paradox that comes not from politics but the world of philosophy and physics: What happens when an irresistible force meets an immovable object? The irresistible force was Obama, who came to office on a wave of hope and excitement beyond that of any president in modern memory. The immovable object was official Washington, D.C., a bulwark of business-as-usual.

After being sworn in on January 20, 2009, Obama dented more immovable barriers than any president since Ronald Reagan. He took action to prevent another Great Depression, reordered national priorities, led by example in the White House with his family, and restored American prestige abroad. The Recovery Act alone was the equivalent of five or six major pieces of legislation, and it was followed by more than a dozen bill signings and scores of executive orders. To widespread surprise, the banks stabilized enough to reimburse the taxpayers for almost all of the $700 billion they borrowed. Most important, by the beginning of his second year, what Obama called his "philosophy of persistence" paid off with the first major reform of the nation's health care system since the enactment of Medicare in 1965.

Despite these achievements, Obama's debut was rocky by any standard. For most of what he called a "rough year," the official unemployment rate stood at a grim 10 percent, but that didn't even include discouraged workers no longer in the job market or those seeking longer hours. A "deficit of trust," as Obama put it in his 2010 State of the Union Address, grew rapidly. If the immovable object was dented, the force sent to pierce it was deflected, or at least slowed. The expectations of Obama had been wildly inflated all along, as he knew. But they came from a deep and sincere place in the American character, and their dashing would complicate his task.

The damage was inflicted from all quarters. Republicans developed a simple narrative—Obama as radical—that the White House never managed to match with an easily understood message of its own. Independents were particularly contemptuous of the president's congressional focus. And Democratic voters, fatigued perhaps from the campaign, decided that they weren't the ones they'd been waiting for after all. They largely left the battles of 2009 to Obama, a man who had insisted from the start that he couldn't bring change by himself.

Obama's plan for his first year was to build a stripped down legislative race car to roar through his early presidency. But the strategy was built on speed. When health care reform took much longer than expected, it threw a monkey wrench into the engine. Instead of the first year being the story of just Barack Obama, it became the story of Max Baucus and Ben Nelson and a bunch of other unloveable "process" characters. The GOP, by contrast, had a tight and effective strategy of obstruction.

It was easy at first—and fully justified—for the new president to blame the old one. "We knew that we were going to have this huge mess to clean up and it was going to require really difficult decisions," Obama said later. The president didn't want to spend all of his time and political capital in a shovel brigade cleaning up after the elephants. But he didn't have any choice. Memories are short, and by midyear he owned the wreckage left him by George W. Bush.

Beyond the attacks from the right, Obama's mainstream critics complained all year that he was too ambitious; he loaded too much freight on the Washington train. But the Slow Down crowd failed to take account of the rapid evaporation of any president's political capital. Obama was right to at least try to "put points on the board" in Year One. As he said in a year-end interview, if he didn't tackle health care right away, it would never happen. So he doubled down on a reform bill with a gambler's instinct that is rare in cautious Washington. The president ended in March 2010 about where he predicted he would be when he launched reform efforts almost exactly a year earlier—with a bill that left no one completely satisfied but accomplished a lot nonetheless, most notably ending America's status as the only advanced nation in the world that discriminated against sick people.

The president had big wins before health care. Many critics paid too little attention to the huge public investments of the stimulus and the first budget and to the dozens of specific campaign promises Obama quickly kept, from education reform to clean energy to stem cell research.

The stimulus, officially called the American Recovery and Reinvestment Act, was poorly framed politically and too slow in creating jobs. But without it, the country would have likely stayed mired in a deep recession or even slipped into a depression. Certain signs of dramatic progress were hiding in plain sight. In January 2009, when Obama took office, the American economy was losing seven hundred forty-one thousand jobs a month and the economy was shrinking by nearly 6 percent annually. At the one-year mark, the January 2010 job-loss figures had been cut to twenty thousand and the economy was growing at nearly 6 percent. Ironically the president's early success in stopping the free fall had the effect of lessening appreciation for what he had accomplished. The global economy didn't melt down; unemployment didn't double to 20 percent. But this achievement was, in Obama's description, an abstract "counterfactual" that no amount of explaining could possibly make stick.

Better communication would have helped. The great irony was that a candidate who came to office in part because of his silver tongue was unable until 2010 to explain convincingly why the country should follow him on health care. The president had trouble mastering the persuasive powers of the office. He failed to give voice to public anger or to convince the middle class that he was focused enough on their number one concern: jobs. He failed to persuade his fellow Democrats to use their fleeting sixty-vote supermajority in the Senate to enact more of his program. And he failed to attach more conditions to the bank bailouts, which cost him leverage he might have exercised to restructure the financial industry and lessen the likelihood of another grave economic crisis.

From the start Obama was boxed in not only by the mess that Bush left him but by the contradictions at the center of his appeal. He had promised something that he couldn't deliver—a capital culture where Democrats and Republicans worked together. It wasn't just that the rhetoric of campaigning and the reality of governing were at odds; that's always true in politics. The difference this time was that millions more people than usual took the rhetoric to heart, then turned on the television to see the ugly reality more vividly than they expected. Fulfilling Obama's campaign promises required getting bills passed, which in turn required working inside the same broken system he was pledging to reform. The congressional sausage making stank so bad that for a time it spoiled everyone's appetite for the meal.

Obama thought he could simultaneously transform the long "arc" of American politics and get specific things done in Congress, the latter a process often described as akin to "herding cats." He kept saying, "Change is difficult," but he underestimated how difficult. That was a sign of overconfidence not just in himself but in the public.

It was understandable why he would be overconfident in the good sense of the country, considering that it had just elected a man with a first name (Barack) that meant Muslim blessing, a middle name (Hussein) that conjured the enemy of the United States in two recent wars, and a last name (Obama) disturbingly close to that of the most evil man in the world. Because he had such faith in the judgment of the American people, the president viewed the 2008 election as a mandate for seriousness, for building what he called "a New Foundation" for long-term growth, when his victory was more properly explained as a repudiation of the previous eight years and a reflection of his personal appeal.

Serious was good, but it didn't have a lot to do with the political universe he now inhabited, a place of cable blowhards and bumper-sticker attacks. Obama was more comfortable in the private, less political part of the presidency, chewing over policy. Some advisors said that his greatest talent wasn't giving a speech but chairing a meeting, where he balanced Socratic dialogue with a hardheaded search for rational, if less than ideal, solutions. The best example of these skills came in the twenty hours of meetings he held in the fall of 2009 about Afghanistan and Pakistan, the most sustained deliberation on a national security threat since the Cuban Missile Crisis in 1962. Again and again the president, with Vice President Joe Biden's help, pushed back against tired assumptions before settling on a new policy. Whether the new approach would prove the least bad option or end in disaster remained to be seen.

For years Obama had been quietly measuring himself against the men who had held the office before him. Abraham Lincoln was his favorite. In his 2006 book *The Audacity of Hope* Obama wrote that he admired "that self-awareness, the humility" of Lincoln. He knew, too, that Lincoln often frustrated his supporters by reaching out to adversaries.

During the transition Obama read up on Franklin Roosevelt, who was faced with a more dire economic crisis upon taking office. But FDR arguably had an easier task politically in 1933 than Obama in 2009. Taking action to get out of a major depression was less controversial than taking action to prevent one. And Obama liked to point out that in 1933 FDR didn't yet have to worry about fighting a war.

Roosevelt and Obama responded to their predicaments in similar ways. Both refused the pleas of liberals to nationalize the banks and chose at first to continue the banking policies of their conservative predecessors, before eventually moving leftward. But they differed on the timing of their major social legislation. FDR waited until 1935, two years after taking office, to introduce Social Security; Obama pressed forward with major health care reform immediately, even though during the campaign he had simply promised to pursue it "before the end of my four-year term." Less well-known was that Obama actually pumped much more money (in constant dollars) into the economy in his first hundred days than Roosevelt had dared. Coincidentally, both presidents in their first months authorized the same number of young people—two hundred fifty thousand—to take part in national service, but Roosevelt's Civilian Conservation Corps was enormously popular, while Obama's expansion of AmeriCorps was barely noticed.

On foreign policy Obama's pragmatism was reminiscent of John F. Kennedy, who described himself to Jackie when they were courting as "an idealist without illusions." In 1961 JFK had a much worse first year than Obama, with a disastrous CIA landing at Cuba's Bay of Pigs and his humiliation by Soviet Premier Nikita Khrushchev at a summit in Vienna. Kennedy recovered in Year Two.

Lyndon Johnson's success enacting Medicare, voting rights, immigration reform, antipoverty programs, and education funding in 1965 was a model for Obama, whose achievements already put him in LBJ's company as a legislative success. Obama hoped to avoid being swamped by bad foreign policy and economic news like Jimmy Carter and looked to Ronald Reagan for lessons in changing the trajectory of American politics. He hired a large number of veterans of Bill Clinton's administration, but advisors who have served both men stressed so many differences between them that this book includes a chapter on the subject.

Beyond comparisons to individual presidents, the activism of the Obama administration in 2009 suggested that he and his team believed in Arthur M. Schlesinger Jr.'s cycles of American history. Just as Roosevelt's ascension in 1932 marked the end of laissez-faire economics (without finishing off capitalism) and Reagan's landslide in 1980 ended the era of confiscatory taxation and overregulation (without shredding the New Deal safety net), so they hoped that Obama's victory in 2008 would prove historic for reasons beyond the color of his skin. In cyclical terms his triumph would bring down the curtain on the Reagan era. It would ease the politics of fear, end the postponement of difficult solutions to festering problems, and renew the ability of the United States to compete globally—all without sacrificing national security and social stability.

Unfortunately for Obama, the means of achieving that vision— pragmatism and a long-term horizon—did not yet add up to a coherent governing philosophy. Obama's policy prescriptions were complex and defied easy summation, which made it harder for him to explain them than it was for Reagan, Clinton, and even Bush. The rocket fuel of his campaign was his personal story; developing a powerful story about America and where it was going proved more elusive.

As Schlesinger knew, history doesn't always conform to broad cycles. Before long, Obama found himself buffeted by an array of domestic forces: conservative Republicans who proved expert cable news knife fighters; liberal Democrats with little conception of the mechanics of real change; Wall Street bankers ungrateful for being saved and bent on scuttling reform; the Pentagon, determined to never again be silent about its troop requests; and frustrated voters, battered by the recession, with no patience for anyone in charge.

That didn't even cover the most worrisome external challenges: rogue regimes in North Korea and Iran racing toward nuclear capability; a confident China flexing its muscles for the first time; and the resurgence of al Qaeda, which had found a foothold along the Afghanistan-Pakistan border, in Yemen, in parts of Africa, and even in the minds of a few desperate people living in the United States.

"This is not a normal presidential situation that I find myself in," Obama said one day toward the end of 2009. "I mean, we have the most difficult set of challenges facing the country since the Great Depression. And that's not hyperbole—it's subject to objective proof." Here the president, seated by the fireplace in the Oval Office, began to chuckle slightly. "When a [H1N1] pandemic ranks fourth or fifth on my list of things to do—you know you've got a lot of stuff on your plate."

How Barack Obama confronted at least some of those challenges is the subject of this book. His early leadership holds invaluable clues to his promise—and to ours.

THE PROMISE

Prologue

A mile above sea level the thin Denver air refreshed the throngs as they waited in the summer darkness for their man to ascend. It was an electric evening for a nation yearning to believe in something or someone again. Barack Obama accepted his party's nomination for president on August 28, 2008, the forty-fifth anniversary of Martin Luther King's "I Have a Dream" speech at the Lincoln Memorial. As he bathed in the adulation of eighty thousand Democrats gathered in a football stadium, Obama touched on the themes that would bring him to the presidency.

He began by reminding the country of his breakout convention speech four years earlier: "I told you my story of the brief union between a young man from Kenya and a young woman from Kansas who weren't well-off or well-known, but shared a belief that in America their son could achieve whatever he put his mind to."

"It is that promise that's always set this country apart," Obama said, firmly in the American grain now, using the word *promise* the first of nineteen times.

"The promise of America," Obama exulted, "[is] the idea that we are responsible for ourselves, but that we also rise or fall as one nation, the fundamental belief that I am my brother's keeper, I am my sister's keeper. That's the promise we need to keep. That's the change we need right now."

Obama lashed Washington's lack of compassion—"a government that lets veterans sleep on our streets and families slide into poverty . . . that sits on its hands while a major American city drowns before our eyes." In Washington, he said, they call trickle-down economics "the Ownership Society, but what it really means is you're on your own. Out of work? Tough luck. No health care? The market will fix it. Born into poverty? Pull yourself up by your own bootstraps even if you don't have boots. You're on your own."

He spoke less than three weeks before the American economy

nearly vaporized, and some of the promises he mentioned (to "keep our toys safe") would soon recede from public view.

But many of his words would resonate—or clang—through the first year of his presidency. "We measure progress by how many people can find a job that pays the mortgage," he said, pledging to cut taxes for 95 percent of working families, encourage equal pay for women, invest in renewable energy, "higher standards and more accountability in education," research and technology, new roads, fuel-efficient cars, and clean water, and to fulfill "the promise of affordable, accessible health care for every single American."

"Individual responsibility and mutual responsibility—that's the essence of the American promise," he said.

This was a fighting speech, designed in part to show that the former community organizer, less than four years out of the Illinois State Senate, was tough enough to be president. "When John McCain said we could muddle through in Afghanistan, I argued for more resources and more troops to finish the fight against the terrorists who actually attacked us on 9/11," Obama said of his Republican opponent. "John McCain likes to say that he'll follow bin Laden to the gates of Hell, but he won't even follow him to the cave where he lives."

Pivoting from his partisan shots, the nominee returned to his familiar red state–blue state theme with "the promise of a democracy where we can find the strength and grace to bridge divides and unite in common action."

As he built toward the end, Obama deftly wrapped the promise he embodied with that of the nation he hoped to lead: "It's a promise that I make to my daughters when I tuck them in at night and a promise that you make to yours. . . . Let us keep that promise, that American promise, and in the words of scripture hold firmly, without wavering, to the hope that we confess."

1

Obama Takes Charge

3-D chess, some of his friends called it. Barack Obama was always thinking a few moves ahead. His aim was to position himself on the board before anyone else—and checkmate his adversaries. The man was more cunning than anyone knew. On the Tuesday flight to Tampa to prepare for three days in private for the all-important first presidential debate, scheduled for Friday, September 26, he hatched an idea.

In the week after Lehman Brothers imploded, Obama had offered himself as the calm, steady, and well-informed future president appearing to set aside politics as the nation plunged into crisis. More than 80 million voters who hadn't taken part in the primaries were just tuning in. The way to win the 2008 election, less than six weeks away, was to get them comfortable looking at an inexperienced 47-year-old black man and seeing a president. That meant mixing shrewd political tactics with a head start on governing.

A mere two weeks earlier, the political world had been arguing over which candidate first used the expression "lipstick on a pig." Now it was in a state of shock. Over the fateful weekend when Lehman fell, Obama, briefed by Treasury Secretary Henry Paulson, alerted his staff that something cataclysmic was happening that he couldn't tell them about. As details emerged, the watchword in the Obama camp was *caution.*

John McCain took a different tack. Campaigning in Jacksonville, Florida, on Monday, September 15, the very day of Lehman's demise, McCain started rambling about unemployment. He noted that Americans were struggling but added fatefully, "The fundamentals of our economy are strong." Afterward he claimed to have been quoted out of context, but coming only weeks after his top economic advisor said the country was filled with "whiners" suffering merely a "mental depression," it hurt him badly.* When he heard the news of McCain's remarks, David Plouffe, Obama's normally phlegmatic campaign manager, shouted, "No fucking way!" McCain was a modern-day Edward John Smith, captain of the *Titanic*. He'd hit an iceberg and didn't know it.

The global economy was in free fall, with a run on banks around the world that was more terrifying than anything since 1933. In some ways the 2008 bank runs were even scarier than those of seventy-five years before, when most depositors were forced to line up outside the banks to take their money out. Now investors withdrew trillions of dollars with a few mouse clicks, sending even healthy financial institutions thousands of miles away reeling within minutes.

The height of the Great Panic was the forty-eight-hour period between Wednesday, September 17, and Thursday, September 18, as the yields on short-term Treasury bills actually went below zero. Withdrawals from money market funds topped $400 billion overnight, when $5 billion was the norm. With Lehman's collapse, the international insurance giant AIG was suddenly gasping for air, the victim of $440 billion in now worthless credit default swaps. Jeff Immelt, the CEO of General Electric, later told friends that he wasn't sure that night if GE Capital could survive. Its failure, he feared, could bring down the industrial giant. On Friday, September 19, the director of the International Monetary Fund, Jacques de Larosière, said the world was "on the brink of a systemic meltdown."

A few elderly Americans remembered the 1929 Crash as teenagers. For everyone else, September 2008 brought the most frightening market turmoil in their lifetime, with the values of homes, investment portfolios, and life savings declining by a quarter, a half, or more. By the following spring, when the economy began to stabilize, it was almost hard to remember the fear—what it felt like to hear the fevered chatter about the nation plunging into another Great Depression.

OBAMA WAS A gifted campaigner, but he didn't much like running for president. He missed his family on the road and loathed the pettiness and stupidity of the process, the constant focus on trivial campaign issues that had nothing to do with the real decisions he would face in office.

Being president was a different story. "The weird thing is, I know I can do this job," he told David Axelrod over the summer. "I like deal-

------

* That advisor, Phil Gramm, whom McCain had supported for president in 1996, was the principal architect of the financial deregulation of the 1990s. He would likely have been McCain's treasury secretary.

ing with complicated issues. I'm happy to make decisions, I'm looking forward to it. I think it's going to be an easier adjustment for me than the campaign. Much easier."

Now, with the crisis, the job was looking harder—much harder. "The good news is we're gonna win," the candidate chuckled to his senior staff on one of their evening conference calls. "The bad news is the world's falling apart."

The crisis was good news for him in another way. Suddenly there was a clear and historic purpose to the first year of an Obama presidency: to stop the bleeding, return the patient to health, and place the nation on a sharply different course. Instead of letting go of his big campaign promises on energy, health care, and education, he now sought to connect them to the recession. He knew immediately that the old bubble economy fueled by financial speculation and real estate was dead and that figuring out what came next would occupy much of his time in office. This was intellectually invigorating for him.

In the meantime Obama leapt at the chance to make the banking meltdown work for him politically. He made sure to be photographed as often as possible with supporters Warren Buffett and Paul Volcker, giant figures of financial success and rectitude whose very presence won him votes among more affluent (or formerly affluent) middle-aged and older Americans. Even when no one was looking he was often on conference calls with Buffett, Volcker, and other experts who could help him become conversant on the complexities.

Obama was sideswiping President Bush almost daily, but Bush took it in stride. He thought that Obama was likely to be the next president, and he instructed Paulson to keep him fully briefed. Soon Paulson and Obama were speaking on the phone as often as several times a day, more frequently than Paulson talked to McCain. The treasury secretary told friends that the Democrat had a firmer grasp of the details. The difference between McCain and Obama in their understanding of the crisis, he said, was like "night and day."*

Paulson's three-page plan for a $700 billion bailout of the insolvent banking system was so sketchy as to be insulting, but Obama was fairly sure he would have to support some sort of monster bailout. The Bush administration was boxing the Democrats in, forcing them to sign off on the rescue plan or get blamed for a depression, but there wasn't much they could do about it. The main thing for Obama was to learn

---

* In his 2010 book, *On the Brink*, Paulson wrote that "I was impressed with [Obama]. He was always well-informed, well-briefed, and self-confident. Throughout the crisis, he played it straight. He genuinely seemed to want to do the right thing."

as much as he could as fast as he could—and to look like a responsible and even-tempered future president.

Obama's advisors thought their man was on track to win the election if he could prevail in the first debate. McCain's bounce in the polls from selecting Sarah Palin as his running mate had worn off; in fact the Palin choice was helping solidify Democrats and independents for Obama. And the "optics"—the word du jour in politics—were looking good. As John Weaver, McCain's 2000 campaign manager, put it, Obama was speaking economic English and his old boss "angry Greek." All Obama had to do, his aides figured, was win that first debate.

But the candidate himself wasn't satisfied. Obama saw an opening to "change the dynamic," as he often put it: to seal his victory by forcing an error. He had done it before. After he lost the New Hampshire primary to Hillary Clinton in January, he told one of his best friends from Chicago, Marty Nesbitt, that it was time to shake things up. So he gave an interview to a Nevada newspaper saying that Ronald Reagan, not Bill Clinton, had "changed the trajectory of American politics." He knew this was like waving a red cape in front of the Clintons. Sure enough, Hillary overreacted by running ads portraying Obama as a Reaganite. When the press roundly denounced the ads, Obama's stature rose. Nesbitt figured this may have been the most brilliant move of the entire Obama campaign.

Now it was time to force McCain to compound his mistakes. Tom Coburn, the right-wing senator from Oklahoma who struck up an odd friendship with Obama when they were both freshmen senators in 2005, called to suggest that Obama and McCain issue a joint statement in support of Paulson's bailout.* Obama liked the idea and wanted to propose it first, before McCain (who had also heard from Coburn) got the chance. If McCain jumped with him, it would take the issue off the table. He knew that if McCain agreed to a joint statement, it would prevent him from campaigning against the bailout, which was McCain's last, best hope for winning. It would "lock him up," as a senior Obama aide put it, and confirm Obama's message of transcending partisanship.

Obama later told a friend that he thought McCain would reject his offer. A joint statement originated by Obama would make it seem as if Obama was the alpha male and McCain just following along, and he was almost certain McCain wouldn't play that way. In fact he sensed that McCain wouldn't be able to resist one-upping him, which was fine

---

* In the Senate in 2006, Obama and Coburn cosponsored the so-called Google-for-Government bill that required the posting of federal contracts on the Internet. They and their wives had dinner together and liked to joke that Obama could muss Coburn's hair, but Coburn had no way to muss Obama's.

with him. He figured that if he couldn't "lock McCain up," he could "set McCain up," as a member of Obama's inner circle put it, to overreact and maybe do something to reinforce his image as erratic.

Obama wasn't a tennis player, but he mulled a tennis metaphor offered by a friend: his opponent was like one of those guys in white shorts running from the baseline to the net, then from sideline to sideline, all over the court trying to hit the ball. With a bit of luck, Obama might make him run right out of the match.

The candidate didn't mention the possibility of a joint statement to anyone outside his staff. But on the way to a rally in Clearwater he talked to Buffett about getting Paulson to agree to limits on executive compensation, more transparency, and other ways to reach a deal with Democrats.* That way Obama would feel better about the bailout. If McCain joined him in supporting a bipartisan rescue plan, it could help stabilize markets and ease the crisis. His advisors were lukewarm; some argued that the one day of attention they received for making the futile offer of a joint statement wasn't worth identifying Obama more closely with the unpopular bailout he would likely have to support.

Obama disagreed. On Wednesday, September 24, two days before the debate in Oxford, Mississippi, he placed a call to McCain in New York, where the senator was having a bad day after reports surfaced that his campaign manager, Rick Davis, had been receiving $15,000 a month to lobby for the embattled mortgage giant Freddie Mac.

Calling McCain was a highly unorthodox move in the middle of a campaign, and the Obama camp had every reason to believe that McCain would either come on the line immediately or call back within minutes. McCain did neither. From his debate prep quarters at the Morgan Library on Madison Avenue, he was weighing a final decision on a bold plan.

Six hours later McCain finally called back and, just as Obama hoped, tried to trump him. When Obama proposed a joint statement, McCain agreed and then vaguely suggested that both men should maybe do something more, like suspend their campaigns or even postpone the debate and fly to Washington to take charge together. Obama told him that he didn't think the two presidential candidates dropping everything and injecting themselves into the delicate negotiations would be helpful, but they agreed that Plouffe would talk to Davis about where things stood. McCain went quiet, and then they each hung up.

McCain tried to one-up him much faster than even Obama hoped.

---

* In the end Paulson's Troubled Asset Relief Program (TARP) included nothing about compensation.

Just minutes after hanging up, as his campaign arrived back at the Belleview Biltmore Resort near Clearwater, Obama was surprised to receive word that McCain was about to publicly announce that he was temporarily suspending his campaign and postponing the first debate in order to fly back to Washington. He hadn't said on the phone that he'd do this alone if Obama didn't join him, but that was okay with Obama. "I think this is absolutely nuts," he told his staff. In Washington Paulson thought McCain was "playing with dynamite" and told him so in testy phone calls.

Later that afternoon Obama went before the cameras to announce that he would go to the debate regardless of McCain's plans and that a president "must be able to multitask." Obama argued that this debate, on national security, was now more important than ever.

During one of the many internal campaign conference calls that day, David Axelrod, Obama's chief strategist, was late; he was on the phone talking to his friend Rahm Emanuel, the campaign's connection to the House leadership. "Just put Rahm on the call and we'll get it straight from him," Obama instructed. It was the first time the future White House senior staff all got together on the same conference call.

Then President Bush called and, in terms Obama described as "almost apologetic," told him that at the behest of John McCain he was inviting him to a big meeting at the White House the next day, Thursday, September 25, to deal with the crisis. Obama said yes, then phoned House Speaker Nancy Pelosi and Senate Majority Leader Harry Reid and asked to be the point man for the Democrats in the meeting. Recognizing that their nominee was already in effective command of their party, they readily agreed. Campaign aides were upset that Obama would miss his third and final debate prep session in Florida, which they thought he needed. But all in all, it was a great news day for him.

And the news just kept getting better. It turned out that in New York that day McCain was ticking off David Letterman by giving an interview to Katie Couric (who had just eviscerated Palin) when he was supposed to be on Letterman's show on the same network. Letterman and his guest, MSNBC anchor Keith Olbermann, savaged McCain. As Obama predicted, his opponent had overreacted to his gambit and was now zigzagging wildly. Obama figured McCain would eventually have to reverse himself and show up at Ole Miss for the debate, which would inevitably contribute to the impression of fecklessness. (In fact McCain never canceled his hotel rooms there or actually suspended any campaign operations.) Things were looking up in Obama World. Obama and Marty Nesbitt "just looked at each other and said, wow, man, this is good for us," Nesbitt remembered.

In Washington the Democratic congressional leadership finally started getting serious about Paulson's TARP plan. TARP stood for Troubled Asset Relief Program, though one Wall Street executive said it should have stood for "Total Abdication of Responsibility to the Public." The plan called for the government to buy hundreds of billions of dollars in toxic assets. This was impractical because no one knew what anything was worth; within weeks Paulson would revise the plan into a more classic bailout, but in the meantime legislators with any sense of responsibility knew they had to do something to confront the crisis. A week earlier, as the damage from Lehman's collapse cascaded through the global economy, Pelosi said she had to leave town for the weekend but would be back Monday. "We may not have an economy on Monday," Federal Reserve Chairman Ben Bernanke told her. The Democrats were prepared to set aside their misgivings and bail out the banks.

It was the Republicans who balked. Free-market conservatives, particularly on the House side, began an active rebellion. On Wednesday, Barney Frank, the chairman of the House Financial Services Committee, got word that the GOP was going back on the deal. Frank had stuck his neck out for the Democrats by working with a deeply unpopular administration on a deeply unpopular bailout. He and Paulson had developed a decent, even friendly working relationship in the two years since Paulson became treasury secretary. Now Frank was angry and getting angrier about the prospect of Republicans double-crossing Democrats and opposing the bailout. Thursday morning he called Paulson, by now practically a daily ritual, and asked, "What the fuck is going on here?" Paulson didn't know.

Frank made sure that he and the other relevant committee chairmen came along with the leadership to that afternoon's big White House meeting, scheduled for 4 p.m. Harry Reid, who arrived a little early, told his spokesman, Jim Manley, to make sure Obama met with the Democrats before the meeting, so they would have a chance to talk separately. When Obama and his campaign press secretary, Robert Gibbs, arrived at the White House they went to the Roosevelt Room, where the other Democrats had gathered. Pelosi and Frank reported that House Minority Leader John Boehner planned to blindside them with a new conservative proposal. It's a setup, they agreed. Obama urged everyone to stay cool.

President Bush, who had finally addressed the nation the night before on the crisis (just as Washington Mutual collapsed—the biggest bank failure in U.S. history), opened the September 25 meeting in the Cabinet Room by conjuring a global depression. "If money isn't loosened up," he said, "this sucker could be going down." He showed almost no knowledge of the specifics of the crisis and quickly turned the floor over to Paulson, who said little but urged that a deal to save the banking system be approved quickly. When recognized by the president, Pelosi and Reid designated Senator Obama to speak for the Democrats.

Obama gave a lengthy and well-informed overview explaining that Democrats were close to agreement with Paulson on a deal. He stressed a couple of important Democratic concessions and agreed with Paulson that speed was essential. Having been told of dissension in the House Republican caucus, he said archly that some in Congress were willing to take their time, but he and the Democrats were not among them.

Obama sensed that while Democrats were united, Republicans were in disarray. So he boldly turned to McCain and said, "What do you think, John?" If this were all a GOP setup designed to isolate Democrats as the party of billionaire bailouts, now was the time to find out.

But McCain wasn't ready to talk. He said he believed in seniority and would go last. It was a feeble attempt at a joke (seniority allows senators to ask questions first), and no one laughed. He seemed in a foul mood, offended by Obama's showy display of his command of the complex issues. "I'll just listen," McCain said, which didn't go over well with anyone in the room. He was supposed to lead, not listen. That was the whole point of postponing the debate, flying back to Washington, and getting everyone together in the Cabinet Room to confront the grave crisis. Instead McCain was "mute," as Obama later put it.

The Arizonan deferred to House Republican Leader Boehner, who began retreating from TARP. He proposed an alternative under which Wall Street firms would create a fund to insure mortgages. This was an idea out of right field that Paulson thought irrelevant to the current crisis. When GOP Senator Richard Shelby produced a list of 192 conservative economists and other academics who opposed Paulson's plan, Bush got snippy. "I don't care what somebody on some college campus says," the president said, looking irritated. "I trust Hank."

Paulson was in a tight spot at the meeting. He seemed to be indulging Spencer Bachus, the ranking Republican on Barney Frank's House Financial Services Committee, who made it sound as if he was there as a representative of other House conservatives who wanted an alternative to TARP. The treasury secretary was treating Bachus as a power player rather than an obscure backbencher.

Paulson had already indiscreetly told a few people in the room that he thought Obama had a stronger grasp of the crisis than McCain did, and here he was face-to-face with the Republican nominee. Even as both Obama and McCain proceeded to confirm everything Paulson had been whispering about them, the exhausted treasury secretary radiated worry that Republicans would find out that he preferred dealing with the Democrats, who had, after all, given him more support for his plan than had many congressional Republicans.

By this time the molecules of power in American politics were in a rapid state of realignment. McCain's absence from the discussion was stark. Bush, who was supposed to be leading the meeting, was poorly informed and detached. "He's already in Crawford," whispered one Republican. That left the skinny African American guy who had crashed into their world only three and a half years earlier. He was the only one of the big dogs who seemed to know what he was talking about. Obama was taking charge of the meeting—and the crisis—peppering the others with detailed questions.

The Republicans clearly wanted to scotch Paulson's plan, but they weren't quite willing to say so explicitly. Their own mortgage insurance plan was completely unworkable, as Obama showed when he questioned them about it at length. He noticed that the lead Republican still hadn't spoken. "I'd like to hear what Senator McCain has to say, since we haven't heard from him yet," Obama said loudly.

Finally, forty-three minutes into the meeting, McCain took the floor. He slouched back in his chair and spoke in a monotone, which those who knew him recognized as a sign that he was going through the motions. He was clearly restraining himself in a way that left him subdued and less articulate than normal. McCain later told Paulson he'd said little "because it's pretty hard to say anything with Barney Frank screaming at you." More likely, the Democratic nominee's ability to take over the meeting left him depressed.

At 72, exhausted by the grueling pace of the campaign, the one-time naval aviator was lost at sea. Members of both parties were astonished by his performance. He was the one who had brought them all here—and for what? McCain, holding a single notecard, mentioned almost no specifics at all. The self-styled straight-talking maverick was reduced to a series of platitudes about how House Republicans had "legitimate concerns" and everyone needed to "work together" and "move forward" until they reached an acceptable compromise. When he was asked explicitly what he thought of Paulson's plan, he said he hadn't read it.

This was astonishing. He hadn't read a three-page plan to spend $700 billion dollars, which was more than all the money already spent in Iraq? A Republican sitting some distance down the long table whispered to a pair of Democratic senators, "Everyone here is ready to vote for Obama, including the Republicans." Barney Frank was even more disgusted than usual. "This was about as unpresidential as it gets," he said later.

Bush's expressive face said it all. When Obama spoke, he paid careful attention, as if he knew that here was his successor. When McCain spoke, Bush's face was quizzical and unconvinced, as if he'd eaten something sour. Dick Cheney offered his closed-mouth crooked half-smile, a sign of his skepticism. Obama chuckled softly.

From there the meeting spiraled out of control. Bachus loathed Frank; he later claimed to have a secret list of seventeen socialists in the House, and it was hard to imagine that Frank's name wasn't on it. Frank believed right-wingers like Bachus had practically wrecked the country. The two men started squabbling over whether the Democrats had been blindsided that morning. Cross talk rang through the Cabinet Room. Bush tried to bring some order before standing and announcing, "Well, I've clearly lost control of this meeting. It's over."

After the meeting broke up, the Democrats huddled with their aides in the narrow and crowded hallway just outside the Cabinet Room. They were angry and confused. Should they go to the microphones and blast the deal right then?

"Shhh! This place may be bugged," Obama said, referring to the White House he would occupy four months later. He was joking, but the point was serious. "We need to go back there," he said, gesturing across the hall to the Roosevelt Room, which was fortuitously unoccupied.

Back inside the Roosevelt Room, the Democrats resumed their conversation over what to do next, when there was a knock at the door. In walked a highly agitated Henry Paulson. He started in right away: "Please. I'm begging you—begging you!—don't go out and attack the plan."

"That's bullshit, Hank," Pelosi said.

Now Paulson was down on one knee, pleading with the Democrats not to "blow up" the deal. It was hard to know how serious he was, but others in the room found it scary to see the treasury secretary pathetically praying in the middle of a crisis.

"I didn't realize you were Catholic," Pelosi deadpanned. (Paulson is actually a Christian Scientist.)

Barney Frank muscled his way past Harry Reid and started yelling. "Fuck you, Hank! Fuck you! Blow up this deal? We didn't blow up this deal! Your guys blew up the deal! You better tell Bachus and the rest of them to get their shit together!" When Paulson tried to equivocate, Frank threw in another "Fuck you, Hank!"—his third of the day.

Everyone knew Frank had a temper, but no one had seen anything like this. For a moment it struck Robert Gibbs and Jim Manley that this little scene really could get physical: the pudgy congressman versus the gawky treasury secretary, right here in the White House. As a former Dartmouth football player, Paulson was the favorite, but maybe Frank had a shot.

The only person standing between Frank and Paulson was Barack Obama, who bent his arms and spread his palms to keep the two men apart. "Okay, guys," Obama said, like a teacher preventing a playground brawl.

But Frank wasn't about to back down. "Your problem is with the Republicans who want to torpedo this, not us!" he yelled. "You go back and tell the president his problem is with his own fucking party!"

Obama took control of the conversation, cool as usual. "Calm down, Barney. Let's sort this out," he said. "Hank, you've got to go back and talk to Spencer and put this thing back together."

Paulson seemed apologetic. "I know, I know," he said.

McCain had already left the White House. If the Republicans weren't going to comment, Obama figured, the Democrats shouldn't either. It was wrong to get partisan on the premises. Obama suggested that Pelosi's and Reid's spokesmen go before the microphones and say very little except that Obama would hold a press conference when he returned to the Mayflower Hotel in half an hour. That would give the candidate a chance to think a bit before opening his mouth, a practice he generally preferred. He would tell the press little more than that McCain's idea of injecting presidential politics into the delicate negotiations had not been helpful. But first he vented to staff.

"That was surreal," Obama said on the speakerphone from the car on the short ride back to the hotel, with several campaign aides on the call. "Guys, what I just saw in there made me realize, we have *got* to win. It was crazy in there."

"Maybe I shouldn't be president," he said in his familiar wry tone, only with more amazement than usual. "But *he* definitely shouldn't be."

Obama was struck by how disengaged both Bush and McCain seemed. All day the campaign had been convinced that McCain and Bush were in cahoots to sandbag Obama. But now it was clear that there was no strategy and McCain was just freelancing.

Obama couldn't get over it. "Bush said, 'Whatever Hank says.' But Paulson wouldn't talk either." He was incredulous. "I've never seen a meeting like that in my entire life."

Nor had any of the older and much more experienced politicians in the room. That's because for nearly thirty years, through Republican and Democratic administrations, a conservative worldview on both economics and national security had dominated American politics. Democrats could chip away at the edifice, but the structure did not belong to them. Now the old order, like the one represented by Herbert Hoover in an earlier era, seemed to be crumbling.

"We *can't* lose this election," Obama said on the conference call shortly before arriving at the Mayflower. "Because these guys can't run the country."

But could Barack Obama? Could he confront the crisis, rebuild the economy, and restore the country's promise? Could he prove, as he claimed, that good judgment was more important than experience?

After the White House meeting his already phenomenal self-confidence ratcheted even higher. As Nesbitt and others attested, the experience of that day powered him through the critical first debate. The next two debates were almost anticlimactic, and he went on to win the election by the widest margin of any Democrat in nearly half a century.

"In the ten days between the Lehman collapse and the first debate, everyone suddenly saw him as the next president," said Anita Dunn, his campaign communications director. Longtime aide Pete Rouse called that September week a "dry run for being president."

The Obama administration wouldn't occupy the White House for another four months. But what the Chinese for centuries have called the "mandate of heaven"—the legitimacy mysteriously but unmistakably bestowed upon a leader—had shifted. Barack Obama's first year in power had already begun.

2

White House–in-Waiting

When the Democratic nominee called advisors in September and October to talk about the future, he didn't superstitiously say, "If I'm president . . ." He confidently said, "When I'm president . . ."

In truth, he had been thinking about his presidency for months, even years. During the campaign he and the legislative director of his Senate staff, Chris Lu, shared a running joke about the classic 1972 Robert Redford movie, *The Candidate,* in which an appealing empty suit named McKay runs for the Senate. In the last scene, McKay, having just won, turns to an aide in the car and says, "What do I do now?"* Obama told Lu, "That's not going to be us."

Back in May, when it was clear to Obama that Hillary Clinton couldn't catch up, Obama asked Lu to launch early transition planning. But he warned him to tell no one, not even his wife. Clinton hadn't conceded yet, and if word leaked she would no doubt bludgeon Obama with the news (even though Clinton had started her own transition planning much earlier). Lu quietly rented a small office above a Subway shop on Massachusetts Avenue in Washington and, immediately after Hillary quit, began meeting with the core of the transition team. He took the budget prepared in 2004 by David McKean for John Kerry's transition, tweaked it, updated the numbers, and made it Obama's. Then it grew wildly. By the time of the election more than six hundred Democrats were consulted on the transition, and more than 150 were granted security clearances. Conversely, John McCain was so worried that leaks would make him look presumptuous that he asked for no security clearances for his people before the November election.

The Obama transition was run by John Podesta, Bill Clinton's last chief of staff, whose credibility was enhanced by his decision not to seek a job in the administration. Podesta was a supremely well-organized guy and ran the operation as if it were a corporation. All

---

* Redford's actual line is "What do we do now?" but it has gone down in political lore as "I."

members of the team signed a strict ethics statement attesting that they weren't lobbyists, and all received what was called the "No Ego, No Glory" memo pointing out that they were volunteering for the good of the country and should not expect a job in return.

If it ever came out that so many people were involved in the transition before the election, Obama knew he would have been creamed for "dancing in the end zone." So Podesta demanded confidentiality agreements and rigid compartmentalization. "We consciously decided to separate the campaign from the transition," Podesta said, "so that if anything came out, the campaign could say, 'We don't know what those doofuses are up to—they're not authorized to do anything.'"

One early memo told Obama that Democrats were generally bad at transitions and Republicans good at them because Democrats focused on policy and Republicans on management. Obama vowed privately that his transition would be more Republican: more disciplined, organized, and secretive. It was no coincidence that the progressive think tank that Podesta founded, the Center for American Progress, was at least loosely patterned on the Heritage Foundation, the conservative think tank that stocked the Reagan administration in 1981.

In mid-October Obama held a secret meeting in a dingy Reno hotel room to talk about the White House staff. McCain had been hitting him for "measuring the drapes" at the White House and it was important that no word of the meeting leak. Two of Bill Clinton's chiefs of staff, Podesta and Erskine Bowles, flew out for the meeting, and a third, Leon Panetta, was on the phone. Everyone agreed that it was critical to hire the White House chief of staff right after the election, before selecting the Cabinet, a sharp reversal of the way Clinton did it.

The best advice Obama got in this period was to leave as many friends at home as possible. Eight of Jimmy Carter's nine top presidential aides in 1977 came from Georgia. Clinton's early White House was full of Arkansans, including his first chief of staff, Mack McLarty, an amiable Arkansas energy executive whom Clinton knew from kindergarten. McLarty didn't get the job until the week before the Inauguration, which made it impossible for the Clinton administration to hit the ground running. There would be no kindergarten friends in senior positions at the Obama White House, though Obama was hardly prepared to rule out Chicagoans.*

More important, Obama decided that the old Democratic habit of

---

* Obama's kindergarten became an issue twice in the campaign, first when he was falsely accused of attending a madrassa when a young boy in Indonesia, and later when Hillary Clinton's campaign spread the word that Obama had wanted to be president since kindergarten, which he denied.

favoring "Cabinet government" at the outset must be broken. The only way to run a successful administration was out of the White House, though of course he wouldn't say that when he wooed potential Cabinet members in the weeks ahead.

Unlike the Clintons, Obama had little history in the Democratic Party. He had come from nowhere—the fastest, farthest journey in modern American political history—largely by himself. All he had with him were his family and friends from Chicago and a small handful of contacts in Washington, a city he dropped by occasionally for a Senate vote and a place to crash.* "Most of my good friends are not in politics and are not in the political world," he said.

———

OBAMA'S UNIVERSE CONSISTED of a series of concentric circles. His innermost ring included the families that vacationed with the Obamas every Christmas in Hawaii: his younger sister, Maya Soetoro-Ng, and Michelle's brother, Craig Robinson, and their families; his closest male friends, Marty Nesbitt, who ran a company that offered extra parking at airports, and Dr. Eric Whitaker, an executive at the University of Chicago Medical Center, and their families (Nesbitt's wife, Anita Blanchard, an obstetrician, delivered the Obama children); and Valerie Jarrett and her college-age daughter. Along with Obama's mother-in-law, Marian Robinson, these were the only Untouchables. The hard truth, as one senior White House official put it, was that everyone else was dispensable.

As the only political advisor who was also an intimate family friend, Jarrett enjoyed a special perch that sometimes fueled resentment from other aides, who envied her direct access. Four years older than Obama, she acted almost as a wise older sister, with an uncanny ability to anticipate just how both Obamas would—and should—react to any situation. She was often the contact when someone wanted to reach them (especially from the business community), she knew just how assiduously to watch their backs, and she could tell them bluntly when they weren't being true to themselves.

They met in 1991, the year Barack and Michelle were engaged. Michelle was up for a job with Mayor Richard M. Daley at Chicago City Hall. Jarrett, already a formidable business executive, was to be her boss, and Barack wanted to make sure that working for Daley was right for his fiancée. After Valerie reassured them, they fell into easy conversation. Michelle and Valerie hit it off immediately, and Valerie

———

* Obama kept a one-bedroom apartment on Capitol Hill that had what he described as a "vintage college dorm, pizza feel to it." Michelle refused to stay there.

found she had much in common with Barack too. They both had been raised partly abroad, Obama in Indonesia and Jarrett in Iran, where her father had worked as a doctor. She thought that Barack was smart and a good listener, a real catch for her new friend. A strong three-way friendship began that night, and over the years Jarrett became a valued counselor to both.

Beyond family and close personal friends, Obama relied on a few longtime advisors, starting with David Axelrod. "Ax," as he was often called, met Obama around the same time Valerie did. Bettylu Saltzman, the well-connected "lakefront liberal" who worked with Obama in 1992, when he registered an astonishing 150,000 black Chicagoans as the head of Project Vote, called Axelrod and said, "I want you to meet this guy because I think he's going to be the first black president."* So Axelrod met him, found him warm and impressive, and agreed that he'd probably be the first black something. But it wasn't until 2003 that he took him on as a client.

Axelrod was a former reporter and columnist for the *Chicago Tribune,* already the top political consultant in Illinois and one of the best regarded nationally. He managed to represent both reformers like the late Mayor Harold Washington and regulars like Daley, quite a feat in Chicago. In national politics, he played important roles in the presidential campaigns of Paul Simon in 1988 and John Edwards in 2004.† Ax was a full-service political professional who could devise strategy and message, produce TV and radio ads (his specialties were man-on-the-street testimonials and grainy attack ads using newspaper headlines), write speeches, and spin reporters, though he was so absentminded that his colleagues didn't trust him with anything involving logistics. David Plouffe joked that he could fill the back of a pickup with all the BlackBerrys and cell phones that Ax had lost.

The son of a New York psychologist who committed suicide when David was nineteen, Ax mixed soulful liberal idealism with Chicago street smarts in a way that Obama considered both decent and hardheaded. When he first agreed to run Obama's 2004 Senate campaign, Obama was thrilled; this was a big break. Axelrod felt the same; Obama was the candidate he'd been hoping for since he had first gone as a boy to see Bobby Kennedy speak in New York. The two became

---

* When he ran for president Obama downplayed Project Vote, in part because it was focused on African Americans and he was trying to expand his base. But it previewed the organizational gifts on display in 2008. It was Saltzman who asked Obama to speak at a 2002 Chicago rally protesting the Iraq War that gave Obama important early stature as the antiwar candidate.

† Axelrod quit the Edwards campaign after clashing with Elizabeth Edwards.

good friends. Over time Ax became Obama's political sounding board, droll sidekick, and the self-described keeper of his flame—reminding everyone why he ran for president in the first place.   .

The final and least well-known member of the high command was Pete Rouse, a modest Japanese American sometimes called "the 101st senator" for his subtle knowledge of the Senate. A thirty-year veteran of Capitol Hill, Rouse had been chief of staff for Majority Leader Tom Daschle and before that for Illinois Senator Dick Durbin. After Daschle lost reelection in 2004, Obama shrewdly hired Rouse to run his Senate operation. Rouse schooled the freshman from Illinois in the peculiar folkways of the Capitol and became something resembling a management consultant for him, especially on critical matters of personnel. Later Obama would tell his senior staff and Cabinet that they should imitate Rouse and "manage down as well as up." Some colleagues considered him a sweeter version of Winston ("I Solve Problems") Wolf, the character played by Harvey Keitel in the movie *Pulp Fiction*. Revered by a large network of underlings for his gentle interest in their lives, Rouse lived alone in Washington with his cats, oblivious to the trappings of power. On January 20, 2009, he chose to watch Obama's Inaugural Address at home on television instead of from the podium.

Just a notch below Valerie, Ax, and Pete was Robert Gibbs, the crafty Alabaman who had come aboard during the Senate campaign and forged a close bond with Obama during four years of constant travel. Gibbs, a soccer goalie at North Carolina State University in the early 1990s, was a fierce protector of his boss, famous for not returning emails from the press. Below Gibbs were Dan Pfeiffer and Bill Burton, two disciplined young spokesmen who joined the campaign on Day One and would play important roles in the White House Communications Office, and Jon Favreau, the talented 27-year-old speechwriter. Over time Anita Dunn, a Daschle veteran and pioneer for women in political consulting, and her husband, Bob Bauer, Obama's personal lawyer, turned into important confidantes. A handful of friends from Harvard Law School and the University of Chicago would also join the administration, but their numbers were small compared to the collection of Rhodes Scholars, party operatives, and other FOBs ("Friends of Bill") in the Clinton years.

Reggie Love, 25, became the younger brother Obama never had.* Love was a basketball and football star at Duke and had NFL tryouts. He weighed an offer from the Arena Football League against an entry-

---

* In fact Obama has two younger half-brothers on his father's side, whom he never lived with and barely knows: Mark, who lives in China, and George, who lives in Kenya.

level job in the mailroom of Obama's Senate office, well before the presidential campaign. Duke's legendary "Coach K" recommended he "learn the fundamentals" of politics in the Senate. Before long Love proved so friendly and efficient that Rouse promoted him to be Obama's traveling aide. He ably juggled dozens of tasks, providing the candidate with bottled water, Nicorette gum, and personalized cell phone service. He stayed up late watching ESPN in the hotel suite with Obama, joined the group of basketball regulars, and along with Marvin Nicholson, the lanky trip director, became a golfing buddy. Obama told people, "Reggie is the coolest guy I know."

———————

ON OCTOBER 21, just two weeks before the election, Obama surprised the political world by taking time out from politics to fly to Hawaii to visit his terminally ill grandmother for the last time.* He had often said that the greatest regret of his life was not returning to Honolulu when his mother was dying in 1995, and he wasn't going to make the same mistake with Toot. The long flight to Hawaii and back proved to be helpful for the organization of the White House. He took a fat three-ring binder and organization charts from Podesta and Rouse and had eight hours each way to make some key decisions when he wasn't napping.

The subject of Rouse's memo was who would report directly to whom inside the White House, and it was an important decision. Under one flowchart, a dozen senior staff would report directly to the president. This was the way disorganized Democrats always seemed to do it, going back to JFK and Jimmy Carter. Clinton followed the pattern and it contributed to the "college bull session" nature of his early tenure. Obama chose Pete's other chart, the one labeled "collaborative hierarchy." This centralized all power in the chief of staff's office so that there was no confusion on lines of authority. The new chief of staff would have much more power on paper than many of his predecessors.

A week before the election Obama asked his inner circle, "Who should I pick?" The candidates were Tom Daschle and Rahm Emanuel.

Obama was clearly leaning to the man everyone in Washington called "Rahm." Over the summer he had sent him an email: "Heads up, I'm coming for you." Then, after TARP passed the House on the second try with Rahm's help, he sent one saying, "I told you we made a great team."

———————

* Rush Limbaugh, anticipating the next right-wing attack line, made the outlandish claim that he was returning to doctor his birth certificate.

But Obama also liked Daschle immensely and knew that Daschle's continuing stature with his former Democratic colleagues in the Senate, where he had served as majority leader before his defeat in 2004, would be a big asset in the White House. It was hard to know how many Democrats would be in the Senate after the election—fifty-five? fifty-six?—and Obama would need them all. Daschle was also a good judge of talent. The several aides Obama had shrewdly hired from Daschle's orbit in 2004 and again in 2008 had served him well. If chosen, the soft-spoken South Dakotan would manage the White House staff with his usual gracious competence. Temperamentally he was almost identical to Obama: smart, calm, and tougher than he looked. Had Obama wanted to continue molding his organization in his own image, as he had during the campaign, Daschle would be perfect.

Daschle's shortcoming, which had hurt him in the Senate and in South Dakota politics, was that he wasn't hard-charging enough. He didn't get up every day ready to run through a wall. This was not a problem that anyone ever associated with Rahm, with one exception.

During the campaign, Rahm, normally so confident, had been turned into the mushy man in the middle, describing himself as hiding under his desk so as not to confront the choice between Hillary Clinton and Obama. He took refuge in his title as chair of the House Democratic caucus, though that hardly required him to avoid intraparty fights. The Clintons had given him his start in national politics when he was just a *pisher* (Yiddish for "an irritating squirt"). He didn't feel right betraying them, even though Hillary had once tried to fire him from the White House.

At the same time he was from Chicago, knew Obama, and was close friends with Axelrod, who had signed the *ketubah*, the Jewish marriage contract (a role at Jewish weddings reserved for a close friend of the groom) when Rahm married Amy Rule. In 2007 Obama trusted him in part precisely because Rahm *didn't* endorse him. When Marty Nesbitt asked Rahm to support Obama and Rahm said no, Marty reported back that this was the right answer. If he had sold out his patrons, the Clintons, he might one day sell out Obama too. This was cold comfort to Obama at a time when he could count on one hand the number of elected officials who had endorsed him, but he accepted it.

Obama and Rahm already had a teasing relationship based on Rahm's legendary profanity. At a 2005 roast of Rahm, Obama joked about how Rahm had lost part of his middle finger in a teenage accident, which "rendered him practically mute." Rahm played along. At the 2006 Gridiron Dinner in Washington, Rahm said, "Senator Obama and I don't just share a home state. We also share exotic names that were given to us by our fathers—Barack, which in Swahili means 'blessed,' and Rahm, which, roughly translated from Hebrew, means 'go screw yourself.' "

When Ted Kennedy ended his neutrality in February 2008 and endorsed Obama, Rahm joked privately that since Kennedy was coming out from under the desk, he would be all alone. "I hope he'll at least leave me his blankie," Rahm added. He provided quiet advice all spring through Ax, but he didn't endorse until the primaries were over in June. Rahm was impressed that the average donation to Obama was $109, but he didn't think the campaign was in close enough touch with Rahm's own "people in the bungalows" on Chicago's North Side, a lament that would later be heard in the Obama White House. All summer Rahm told Ax, "It's all about reassurance," and that reassurance meant offering a specific number of new jobs that Obama's recovery program would create. The actual number was less important than that there was a number in the first place.

Because job creation would be hard, the campaign settled on four million jobs created *or saved*. The latter was a gaping rhetorical loophole they would use throughout 2009: How could any reputable statistician count someone who *didn't* get laid off? But it got them to a higher number they could sell politically.

By October Rahm had become an important part of the campaign. Obama depended on him for a lot more than a read on how Congress was reacting to Paulson's plan. He was always a step ahead on the politics and knew how to integrate the crisis into what Obama was saying on the trail. More important, he fit in with at least some of the senior staff he hadn't known before. Even Pete Rouse, who was devoted to his old boss Daschle, thought in the end that Rahm was the stronger candidate for chief of staff, mostly because, while Daschle was a "principal" (Washington-speak for a powerful elected representative or someone of Cabinet rank) and would have done the job capably, Rahm was "half-staff, half-principal," for a job that was just that. Before long Pete grew so friendly with Rahm that Rahm's children recorded the voice mail on Rouse's cell phone.

In the end Obama saw that having a full principal as chief of staff was probably a bad idea. Some of the other chiefs of staff over the years who had also been principals—Eisenhower's Sherman Adams, Reagan's Donald Regan, and George H. W. Bush's John Sununu—had blown up for one reason or another. Leon Panetta, soon to be Obama's CIA director, had been a White House staffer and member of Congress before successfully running Clinton's White House. That was a better model.

Rahm was chosen, Axelrod said, because he straddled two worlds: he had unmatched knowledge of the White House and Congress but also a gut instinct for the thinking of middle-class Americans. It was true that in 2006 he had been a highly partisan figure, but he had cultivated Republican friendships with South Carolina Senator Lindsey Graham and Illinois Congressman Ray LaHood, among others, and could find more. Old Chicago friends like Bettylu Saltzman believed Rahm had matured and would handle the job well. Others wanted some insurance. Lynn Cutler, a Chicagoan and former vice chair of the Democratic National Committee, thought Rahm was a good choice but told Axelrod that the White House staff should know that after Rahm ripped their skin off, Ax would be there to give them a hug.

Obama made his final decision a couple weeks before the election and was happy with it. After he heard the choice Daschle himself thought that he had dodged a bullet. He worried that the job would have consumed his life.

Now the soon-to-be president just had to convince Rahm Emanuel to give up his dream of being the first Jewish speaker of the House.

———

RAHM WAS IN all the early meetings, but nailing down a commitment from him to be chief of staff taxed Obama's persuasive powers. In the days before and after the election, the two men spoke in person about the job at least half a dozen times. Obama made the case that this was a unique moment and that Rahm could get a lot more accomplished in the White House than on the Hill. You could stay caucus chair and wait your turn as speaker, or you could play at a higher level, Obama told him. If he took the job, Obama said, he'd be his "right-hand man" on everything. Obama leaned on him hard.

Rahm was not just pretending to be torn. He confided to friends that if it had been a relatively normal year, like 2000, he would have definitely said no. The job wasn't worth the family stress and the sacrifice of his longtime dream of being speaker. Relinquishing a seat he had worked so hard for was tough. He told a reporter, "You guys [in the press] will never understand what it means to give it up. It's just very hard. You have to give up your independence and your own identity and subsume it. And that's a lot."*

Rahm's decision to be so open about his ambivalence and to

---

* A week or two after taking the job Rahm called John Fritchey, an Illinois state representative who planned to run for his seat, and felt him out about being a placeholder so Rahm could return to Congress at some point. Fritchey said no, and he lost the primary anyway.

dawdle over the decision struck some Obama partisans as disrespect-ful. It seemed as if Rahm asked practically everyone he knew whether he should take the job. But he later said there was a method to it: he was deliberately signaling to other potential appointees that if he could sacrifice the House speakership, they could set aside their busi-nesses and law practices, take a pay cut, and come serve their country. He was using his own reluctance as another instrument of pressure. When people complained about not getting the positions they wanted, he reminded them that Obama was the only one in the country who did.

After Rahm took the job Obama was a bit worried about what his new chief of staff would do with all his power. He later said that, left to their own devices, Rahm and Ax, who talked five or six times a day even before the transition, might "go charging down a path" he wasn't "comfortable with." He envisioned Valerie and Pete as counter-weights. They would each, like Axelrod, carry the title senior advisor to the president. The new White House would have a quadrangular structure at the top. The Big Four would all advise, anticipate, inform, and initiate. Barack Obama was headed into the choppiest economic waters of any president in seventy-five years. He needed all hands on deck.

———

IT WAS NO coincidence that three of the Big Four were from Chicago, although only one (Emanuel) had been born there. Since shortly after graduating from Columbia, Obama had marinated in the tangiest local political culture in the nation. Where New Yorkers knew the identi-ties of top investment bankers and Angelinos kept track of Hollywood studio executives, Chicagoans could tell you the names of their alder-men and even sometimes of their state senators as if they were local athletes.* Even at its most bitter, the spectacle was entertaining. Which politician was the boodler and which the reformer? Which big-talking supporter was full of it and which could actually make something hap-pen downtown? Obama's experience in local politics helped him learn to read people better.

Mayor Richard J. Daley, the last of the great city bosses, died in 1976, long before Obama got to town, and he wasn't particularly close to

---

* This was partly because patronage had been sewn into neighborhood life for longer than in other cities. For instance, Michelle Obama's father, Fraser Robinson, held his job as a worker in the city water department in part because of his political work as a precinct cap-tain in the Regular Democratic Party organization.

Daley's son, the current mayor, known as Richie, who had backed an opponent in the 2004 Senate primary. Obama was never a real part of the Daley machine. Instead he was what Chicagoans used to call a "blue-ribbon" candidate, a classy gentleman-politician like Adlai Stevenson and Paul Simon.* The blue-ribbon candidate got to have it both ways: staying above politics while benefiting from it. But Daley was skeptical of Obama seeking the presidency. "What's he done?" He privately complained in 2007, even as he felt compelled to endorse him.

Obama had a lot of Chicago in him, but it was a different Chicago than the stereotype. "It's a rough-and-tumble place where you learn how not to take things personally," Jarrett said. "The 'Midwestern values' thing is real. We take it down a notch here and it makes us more forgiving." Or at least more straightforward. When David Wilhelm returned to Chicago from Washington after a stint in the 1990s as chairman of the Democratic Party, he said, "I'm going back to Chicago, where they stab you in the front."

Chicagoans had long suffered from a "second city" complex that left them jealous of other cities. But the deeply ingrained we-try-harder ethic also made them especially proud of where they lived. For all its tortured racial past, the city was more beautiful and peaceful than it had been in previous decades. Beginning in the 1990s prominent Chicagoans set aside differences to focus, at least some of the time, on common goals. To put it mildly, not everyone in Chicago "disagrees without being disagreeable," one of Obama's favorite descriptions of how he viewed his own approach. Local rogues still made good copy. But in recent years there was something less nasty than New York, Washington, or Los Angeles about the place—and certainly less pretentious.

The scandal surrounding Illinois Governor Rod Blagojevich reinforced the city's image as an ethical sinkhole.† Obama responded by noting that politicians came in two flavors: those who went into politics to make money and those whose motive was to serve the public. It was a simple and valid distinction. The latter category—represented in the late twentieth century by inspiring public servants like Harold Washington, Paul Simon, and Congressman Abner Mikva—had a major

---

* In 1948, Daley, as party boss, slated Stevenson for governor and University of Chicago economist Paul Douglas for Senate. Simon, who also received machine backing for much of his career, died shortly before Obama's 2004 Senate primary. His daughter Sheila appeared in an ad supporting Obama that helped greatly.

† Blagojevich was arrested on December 9, 2008, on federal corruption charges stemming from his role in "pay to play" fund-raising schemes and an effort to win favors in exchange for appointing a replacement for Obama in the Senate.

influence on Obama. But even the cleanest politicians in Chicago rev-
eled in their toughness and could be found quoting Hyman Roth's line
from *The Godfather:* "This is the business we have chosen."

After Obama became president it was easy for critics to say he was
surrounded by "the Chicago mafia." If so, they hadn't properly learned
how to dump a body, as their handling of New York Governor David
Paterson and White House Counsel Greg Craig would later attest. In
truth, the White House would not be filled with Chicagoans. This reflected a misunderstanding of the way Obama operated; he was in
constant interaction with a couple dozen aides who were from "Chicago" only if that meant the experience that they had of working there
during the campaign. And Jarrett, Axelrod, and Emanuel were hardly
the Chicago hacks of fevered imagination.

They did, however, bring a certain attitude about how politics and
government interact. "Barack's thing is, do the stuff you think is best,
do what's most important, do the governing right and the politics
will take care of itself," Axelrod said, before launching into a famous
quote from the late Mayor Daley. " 'Good government is good politics,' Daley said. Obama really believes that." This was a critical point
about Obama and the way he would handle his early presidency. He
disdained efforts to win cable brawls or find the perfect pictures for the
photo-ops or craft sound bites that cut through the clutter. He thought
these staples of Washington politics were ephemeral if the government
delivered jobs and health care for people, just as Chicago politicians
delivered at home.

Of course Daley's line didn't mean simply that doing the right thing
was good politics; it meant that politics and government in Chicago
were essentially indistinguishable. The same was increasingly true in
the capital. Washington didn't run on patronage (nor Chicago anymore),
but the system was greased every day by old-fashioned Chicago-style
deals. Obama would come to office believing that those deals—not
his speeches—were the way things got done. A legendary Chicago al-
derman named Paddy Bauler was known in the 1950s for exclaiming,
"Chicago ain't ready for reform!" For all his talk of transparency, Barack
Obama, former state senator from the 13th district, wasn't sure Washington was either.

EVER SINCE THE Pennsylvania primary, Anita Dunn had run a 7 a.m.
conference call for Obama's senior staff and a 10:15 p.m. call with the
candidate after he'd said goodnight to his kids. The calls were relatively short; the only time one had gone for a full hour was after the

Reverend Jeremiah Wright fiasco, when the campaign hung in the balance.*

By mid-September the perilous state of the economy dominated the calls, just as it would dominate the early days of the Obama White House. With the exception of his work in the Illinois State Senate curbing predatory lending, Obama hadn't looked closely at the financial system until he started giving speeches about it early in the campaign. But he was a quick study and now eagerly dug into the complex details. This was homework that he much preferred to political chores, and he spoke about the economy with confidence-inspiring fluency.

Soon enough Ben Bernanke's trillion dollar Fed guarantees and Henry Paulson's $700 billion bailout proposal cooled the meltdown. The specter of a conservative Republican administration investing massively in the private economy shocked the system enough to stop the panic selling. But now Paulson had to get his TARP bill through Congress. His first efforts to do so were seen as laughable. Paulson, dubbed "King Henry" by *Newsweek,* had offered a three-page September 19 plan that contained the eye-popping Section 8, which stipulated that the secretary's actions would be "non-reversible . . . and may not be reviewed by any court of law or any administrative agency."

If the "systemic risk" that Paulson worried about was plenty real, the response was disturbingly indiscriminate. A big question that would persist for years was whether Bernanke and Timothy Geithner, chairman of the New York Fed (which handled the details), could have figured out a way to structure some of the early deals so that the government got better terms. Even by late 2009, when every major bank except Citigroup had paid back its TARP money, the impression of a colossal injustice remained—that fabulously wealthy bankers would be made whole, but ordinary Americans would not. This impression would weaken faith in government and complicate Obama's efforts in 2009.

The politics of the bailout were brutal. Early polls showed only 22 percent of the public supporting the government's efforts. Nancy Pelosi received forty thousand calls, letters, and emails on TARP—almost all against. Every day brought frightening news: jobless claims surging to

---

* Wright, the pastor at Chicago's Trinity United Church of Christ, had performed the Obamas' marriage, baptized their children, and inspired the title of Obama's book *The Audacity of Hope.* When tapes circulated in March 2008 of Wright's inflammatory sermons, it threw the Obama campaign into crisis. Obama defended Wright in a famous speech he delivered on race in Philadelphia, but when Wright ranted before the National Press Club in April, Obama disassociated himself from him.

modern highs; home sales plummeting to modern lows; bank failures surged to levels not seen since the Depression.

On September 29 the Dow closed down 777 points after the House voted down the bank bailout. This was a shocker. "You're sitting there thinking, did we finally put Humpty Dumpty together only to have him fall down again?" Robert Gibbs remembered. "That period cemented [for Obama] that this is not a problem that's going to get solved by the time you get sworn in, and if you win, your life is going to be different." All the later critics seemed to forget what had happened when Congress, for a moment, decided not to approve bailouts: a catastrophic Wall Street collapse.

By this time John McCain's campaign was doomed. Eventual passage in early October of the first installment of the TARP bailout ($350 billion) did little to assuage fears. Americans had lost 30 to 40 percent of their net worth on paper—several trillion dollars just evaporated—and they weren't about to vote for four more years of the same economic policy.

As the crisis deepened Obama asked his young campaign economic advisors, Austan Goolsbee of the University of Chicago and Jason Furman of the Brookings Institution, to assemble a team of eight to ten big thinkers for conference calls every five days or so. These calls were mostly intended to help the candidate get a handle on fast-moving events. Three former treasury secretaries were on the list: Robert Rubin, the self-effacing senior advisor (and former chairman) at ailing Citigroup, soon to be reduced to a ward of the state; Larry Summers, the brilliant economist and Rubin protégé, who had been pushed out as president of Harvard; and Paul O'Neill, the quirky former Alcoa chairman who had been fired by President Bush and was now supporting Obama. Two former chairs of the Council of Economic Advisers, Nobelist Joseph Stiglitz and Laura D'Andrea Tyson, also took part, as well as the usual complement of senior campaign aides.

Warren Buffett and Paul Volcker were often on the line. The second richest man in the world had met Obama in 2004 and been impressed. His endorsement gave the candidate a boost with independent and even Republican voters. Volcker, who had known Obama since mid-2007, helped convince him to support TARP. When Volcker said he had to miss a meeting in Miami with Obama and other economists because of a scheduled trip to Europe, the campaign implored him to make a brief appearance before leaving. He stayed long enough to have his picture taken.

Rubin didn't have a close relationship with Obama, who decided during the transition that it wouldn't look good to be seen talking to a man whose bank had just laid off seventy-five thousand people. Even after he resigned from Citigroup in January 2009, Rubin had almost no contact with the president. But he would play the same role for the Obama administration that Harvard Law School professor Felix Frankfurter did under Franklin Roosevelt: stocking the government with his protégés. During his years at the top of Goldman Sachs, the Clinton administration (where he ran the National Economic Council and then served as treasury secretary), Citigroup, and the Hamilton Project (a think tank of moderate Democrats and deficit hawks), Rubin mentored scores of bright young policy types. More than a dozen of them eventually worked in important positions under Obama and maintained their relationships with Rubin.* The difference between Frankfurter and Rubin was that the U.S. government didn't have to spend $29 billion (with guarantees of up to $306 billion) bailing out Harvard Law School, as it did Citigroup.

Summers quickly became Obama's dominant economic advisor. He knew a lot more about economics than the political advisors, and at least a little more about politics than the other economic advisors. And he proved exceptionally good at framing the central questions in ways that everyone could understand. In a series of influential columns for the *Financial Times* dating back two years before the crisis, Summers had nimbly moved away from the deregulatory policies he supported as treasury secretary in the 1990s and warned in 2007 of trouble to come.

At this stage Obama also made time in his campaign schedule to hear from advisors on the progressive side, a view he would hear less of when president. Former Labor Secretary Robert Reich, Andy Stern of the Service Employees International Union, and Jared Bernstein of the liberal Economic Policy Institute were all encouraged to weigh in. As usual, Obama employed the Socratic method with the economists and business experts, probing for new perspectives. It was hard to tell what his own views were beyond what he said publicly, but he tried to keep at least some of the conversation focused on the folks identified by Leo Gerard, head of the United Steelworkers Union, as "the people who take showers after work, not before."

Of course the inner group of advisors, the ones Obama listened to most, was hardly unshowered in the morning, and few with any connection to Wall Street had completely clean hands. Buffett, with his

---

* Tim Geithner, Larry Summers, Peter Orszag, Michael Froman, Philip Murphy, Gene Sperling, Jason Furman, Jacob Lew, Gary Gensler, Diana Farrell, Lewis Alexander, Lael Brainard, and David Lipton.

famous foresight, had for years called derivatives "financial weapons of mass destruction," but even he had invested heavily in them, and in Moody's, one of the corrupted ratings agencies that gave cover to the reckless. As treasury secretary, Rubin had warned of the dangers of un-regulated derivatives but later admitted he didn't fully understand the exotic products that were taking Citigroup down. Summers had taken a more hands-off view than Rubin of regulating derivatives while at the treasury department in the 1990s and as late as 2008 made more than $5 million consulting on them for the hedge fund D. E. Shaw and Co.* Of the nation's financial titans now surrounding the Democratic nomi-nee, only Volcker remained largely unstained by the Bubble Economy, though even he had his share of investments in it.

For vice-presidential candidate Joe Biden, the conference calls were "an epiphany." This was not the Barack Obama he thought he knew from the Senate. Biden had been lukewarm on Obama—he thought he was wrong to run in 2008—right up until Obama told him in August that he wanted him for the ticket. In fact after dropping out of the pres-idential contest following the Iowa caucuses, Biden, though ostensibly neutral, secretly advised Hillary's campaign all winter and spring.

Obama knew about the Hillary connection before he chose Biden and couldn't care less. Politically he liked Biden's appeal to working-class voters (especially in his native Pennsylvania, a swing state), but he also picked him because he thought Biden's many friendships on Capi-tol Hill and his foreign policy experience would be helpful in the White House. Everyone in Washington knew that Biden was a motormouth, but you had to be made of stone to avoid liking the guy. And the more you talked to him, the smarter and better informed he seemed.

Obama expected that Biden would make a gaffe or two during the campaign (he had called Obama "articulate and bright and clean" in 2007), but he was surprised and angry when his vice-presidential can-didate seemed to say something stupid every few days. After Biden said on the stump that Obama would be immediately "tested" overseas, a comment that pointed up the nominee's lack of experience, the run-ning mates had a chilly conversation on the phone.

Biden wasn't accustomed to being reamed out, and he hated being "handled" by Obama's Chicago headquarters, but he had to admit that Obama had some chops he hadn't noticed before. By the time of the financial crisis the vice-presidential candidate felt Obama was inhabit-

---

* The *New York Times* revealed that Summers was a consultant for Taconic Capital Advisors as early as 2004, when he was still president of Harvard and lecturing faculty members on why they shouldn't moonlight.

ing the role of president on the conference calls. "Barack says, well, folks, sorry I'm late. I've got four questions. Bang. Bang. Bang. All deep and on point. He was in total friggin' command!" Biden marveled in October 2008. "Here's a forty-seven-year-old guy confronting one of the most complicated economic dilemmas anyone has had to face since 1929 to '33. If the subject had been Iran or Russia I could have said I'd be as good, but not on this. I was truly impressed."

The next day Biden called Obama and said, "You sold me, sucker."

He wasn't alone. The financial experts who took part in the meetings smelled power, but they were also tough judges of political talent. Obama and his economic advisors met in Miami on September 19. The conversation became extremely detailed—too detailed, some thought, for a candidate who was not yet president. But Obama more than held his own. Walking out of the hotel, Rubin asked Summers what he thought. "I think he was an A-plus," Summers said. Rubin agreed. The nominee had been calm and knowledgeable even if several of those consulted still found his ideological orientation a mystery.

In retrospect, some remedies they discussed looked puny. The House of Representatives had passed $150 billion in stimulus earlier in the year, which went nowhere in the Senate. This amount seemed huge at the time, especially to those who recalled that the last stimulus package, Bill Clinton's in 1993, was for $16 billion—and it lost. To be bold, Obama's advisors were talking in September 2008 about doubling the House number to $300 billion, a figure that seemed outlandishly high at the time but would prove to be much lower than the final figure.

For all the big talk on stimulus, Obama and his preelection transition team could also seem timid. Volcker suggested that the ad hoc responses to Bear Stearns, Fannie and Freddie, Lehman, AIG, and soon the auto companies weren't going to work. "We can't keep doing this over a weekend," he said. Volcker favored a new Reconstruction Finance Corporation, the Depression-era institution that made loans to companies. Summers wasn't interested; he thought Volcker was yesterday's news. Some of the Obama people thought it was *Summers* who seemed like a rerun. He and the other Clinton people kept comparing 2008 to 1993, when Clinton had inherited an ailing economy. It sounded like a comparison between a hurricane and a drizzle. And Summers's abrupt manner made many in the Obama universe fear that he didn't understand the friendly campaign culture they had created over the past two years.

Volcker told Obama that in some ways he would be worse off than FDR when he took office. When Roosevelt came in, Volcker explained, he closed the banks and announced that the government would reopen only the healthy banks. A week later, when he began opening some banks, Americans figured those were the good ones; everyone put their money in them and the banking crisis (though not the Depression) ended. Today's depositors were institutional investors and much more sophisticated. They wouldn't assume the reopened banks were safe. Obama would not have the luxury of a bank holiday to save the system.

———

BY ALL ODDS, big ideas like health care reform that were not directly connected to the crisis should have been abandoned or downplayed at this point. Doing so would have been fine with Obama's political aides, who cited numbers provided by lead pollster Joel Benenson that showed the public favored moving forward on energy first because it might create jobs. Health care was a big issue with activist Democratic primary voters and a nonissue (or even a negative) for everyone else, especially people who worried that their hard-earned tax dollars would go to the poor. More than 95 percent of voters had health insurance, and their interest in those who lacked it was limited.* Mostly they were anxious about what might happen to them if the system changed. The hard political truth that would shadow the debate for months was that the uninsured simply don't vote in large numbers.

For three decades activist Democrats had their hearts set on a dream—universal coverage—that wasn't a political winner, which was the main reason they hadn't won it. Obama thought the only answer was to shift the parameters of the debate. If the issue was framed around cost, access, and heartless insurance companies telling people with preexisting conditions to fend for themselves, perhaps the public response might be more positive.

Obama was always interested in the polling on health care, but he was more focused on the connection between what he said on the stump and how much room he'd have to maneuver if he won. "If I don't talk about this during the campaign then I can't do it in the first year—and I want to do this," he told his policy team over the summer. "So figure out how we win the argument [with McCain]."

The unveiling of Obama's latest version of his health care reform was scheduled for September 20. When Lehman collapsed, the rollout was delayed and a few of the political strategists argued in vain that it should not be rescheduled. Obama answered this on the campaign

———

* The Obama White House liked to cite this figure, though it is an estimate.

trail: "Some say we can't afford to reform health care now. I argue, how can we afford not to?"

Making the connection between the economy and health care would continue to be tough, but Obama was game to educate the public on why the country couldn't get control of the budget until it controlled health care costs. Framing it as a cost issue had the additional benefit of shifting the conversation away from the uninsured and toward fiscal responsibility, where there were more independent voters.

Whatever the specifics, this new passion for health care represented a hugely significant shift in the candidate's thinking. An internal memo from his Senate office showed that as recently as 2006 he had listed his policy priorities in the Senate as energy, education, and nonproliferation; there was no mention of health care. Even in the presidential campaign he at first seemed less interested in the subject than his Democratic rivals were. He pandered to younger voters by opposing a mandate requiring everyone to buy health insurance. Mandates were politically unpopular (and unlikely to pass, he said privately), but he knew they were critical to making any reform work. Hillary fumed as the press let him off the hook for a half-baked health care plan, which Obama promised to enact only "by the end of my four-year term."

But the financial crisis helped Obama focus on the long-term fiscal future of the country, which was grim without some control of health care costs. And somewhere along the campaign trail the stories he heard of families selling their homes to pay for a child's cancer treatment; of small businesses crushed by the high cost of health insurance; of laid-off workers losing their coverage along with their jobs, reached him and worked a change in his ambitions for his presidency. Now a confident candidate was ready to go for a big health care program in his first year, while he had the political capital. Soon it would be clear that he was virtually the only one in his inner circle who felt that way.

3

Grant Park

Obama and Robert Gibbs had a ritual after every debate. When Obama came off the stage at the end, Gibbs would give him a fist bump to signify that he had done well, not "the terrorist fist jab" of Fox News's fevered imagination, just a nice tap. After the Nevada and New Hampshire primary debates, where Obama had not done well, there was no bump. But when Obama finished his first debate with John McCain at Ole Miss, Gibbs was so happy that he gave him a two-fisted bump.

"He walked into the first debate as a candidate and walked out as president," Anita Dunn said later. "The campaign was over right then." The final two debates and the vice-presidential debate did nothing to change that judgment, as the campaign moved forward with what Axelrod described as a "nervous confidence."

The final week brought a weird limbo. Those who weren't in the field operation felt as if their work was done. Axelrod and Joel Benenson went over the polling numbers again and again to see if they could find some weakness, something they had overlooked. They could not. The campaign, flush with cash, bought a half hour of national television time just to keep up the interest level and ensure a big turnout. And superstition ruled. If anyone dared to mention a job in the new administration, other staffers shouted, "Don't talk that way!"

Starting when Palin spooked the Democrats in early September, Marty Nesbitt showed every nervous supporter he met an email he received. Over a picture of Obama giving his acceptance speech in Denver someone had written, "Chill the Fuck Out. I Got This." Obama loved it, and when his friend Mike Strautmanis poured out his anxieties in a long late-night email, Obama replied simply, "I got this."

For bigger audiences Obama played a coach worried about sitting on his lead. "I don't want to hear that any of you are jockeying for jobs or looking for apartments in Washington," he said sharply to "Obama for America" senior staff and fund-raisers by conference call, threatening to fire anyone who did. "We haven't won yet. Don't leave anything on the field!"

All the signs from the field were good. Even the racists seemed to be coming around. For weeks reports flowed into the campaign of chagrined canvassers in swing districts finding voters who said, "I can't believe it, but I'm pulling the lever for the black guy," or even "Things are so bad I'm voting for the nigger."

On the last weekend of the campaign the field organization exceeded the wildest dreams of the onetime community organizer. American politics had never seen a get-out-the-vote operation like this one. A new "online call tool" allowing phone calls from home computers yielded more than a million calls into swing states. Volunteers placed another three million calls from the campaign's "Last Call for Change" phone banks. All the calls were placed from states that were not in play. The idea was to free up volunteers on the ground in swing states to get their Obama voters to the polls.

Even as he moved toward victory, Obama introduced a note of pessimism. Aboard the plane he mused to aides that with all the controversial things he planned to do in office there was a "decent chance" he would be a one-term president. This was the kind of thing that candidates and presidents like to say, and almost nobody believes them. From afar it had an especially phony ring from a man who despised the conventional artifice of politics and derived some of his authenticity and self-regard from that sense of separation from the process. Obama was too competitive to consign himself to being a one-termer. He knew that in the modern era one term is synonymous with failure, and that his being defeated for reelection would be especially humiliating for African Americans.

But the musings stuck in the minds of his staff because their man was not given to pieties, especially in private. Over the next several months he made the point repeatedly to signal to Axelrod, Gibbs, and others that he was not going to be a cautious president who played all the careful political angles just to get reelected. They should get used to his taking political risks.

THE FINAL DAY of the campaign opened with word that Toot would not live to see her grandson elected president. Early that morning she had died peacefully in her sleep, with Maya at her side. After announcing the news to a crowd in Charlotte, North Carolina, Obama struggled to keep his composure. A few cameras caught tears rolling down his grieving face, but his voice never broke—the most visible sign yet of his deep determination to keep his emotions in check.

That evening he held an election-eve rally with one hundred thousand people in Manassas, Virginia, site of the Battle of Bull Run. The candidate made no mention of the Civil War, but he didn't have to. A black man was poised to carry the cradle of the Confederacy, and carry it comfortably. The candidate was spent. On the flight back to Chicago he told Axelrod, "I think we're going to win, but if we don't I'll be at peace. We've run as good a campaign as you could run, and if it isn't there, it isn't there."

Just to be extra sure it was there, Obama flew to Indiana to campaign on Election Day. He had narrowly lost the primary in the Hoosier State and made it a personal project to drag it back into the Democratic column for the first time since 1968. He brought his best friends along. On the plane he spotted his Chicago friend Eric Whitaker looking at Valerie Jarrett and shaking his head. "What's the matter with you?" Obama asked.

"You may be the frickin' president of the United States," Whitaker said.

"And I still may lose," Obama replied.

"On the other hand, you may be the frickin' president of the United States," Whitaker said. "That's crazy."

Obama spent most of the short flight working with Nesbitt on a top priority: the rosters for the four teams for that afternoon's basketball games, to be held at the Attack Gym on Chicago's West Side. Basketball on election days had been a superstition ever since the New Hampshire primary, where Obama skipped playing and lost to Hillary Clinton in an upset. This time he had the youngest team but was convinced that Nesbitt had the best players and had rigged the lineups.

It was a great honor to be asked to play, a sign that you were good enough on the court and that the soon-to-be-president liked you. Senator Bob Casey, who had bonded with Obama during the Pennsylvania primary, flew in, as did Julius Genachowski, a new-media expert and basketball buddy from Harvard Law School who would soon head the Federal Communications Commission. Alexi Giannoulias, the Illinois state treasurer, had special jerseys made up labeled "This One" and "That One," a sly reference to McCain calling Obama "that one" in the first debate.

In the first game Obama's team lost on a three-pointer, but they won the second game against the team captained by Arne Duncan, the Chicago schools superintendent and future education secretary who had played professionally in Australia. It was the first time Obama, a lesser

player than most of the others, had beaten Duncan's team, and it gave
him such satisfaction that he was still talking about it two weeks later.
Nesbitt's team won the tournament on a shot at the buzzer and Obama
mock-complained, "See, Nesbitt, I told you you rigged it!"

The games were hard-fought as usual, but the skinny point guard
was given an extra couple of inches when he drove to the basket. "It
was the only time we all backed off a little bit—nobody wanted to give
him a black eye," Duncan said. Obama, who had suffered a broken
nose playing basketball in law school, took nothing off his own game,
though he did joke at one point after colliding with Reggie Love that
he was badly injured, which threw a scare into the others. Obama kept
playing and risked looking beat-up for a speech that would be seen by
hundreds of millions of people around the world.

OBAMA SPENT MOST of the day at home in Kenwood, a once Jewish neighborhood of large homes that bordered Hyde Park. He and
Michelle voted that morning at a school down the street. The media
throng saw that Bill Ayers, the 1960s radical who became a household
name during the campaign, cast his ballot in the same precinct (though
not at the same time).* But no one in the press noticed that another
neighbor, Louis Farrakhan of the Nation of Islam, was moved to the
front of the line so he wouldn't bump into the Obamas.

Obama had butterflies of course. In the afternoon Tom Daschle
called to share some of the favorable early exit polls. It looked as if the
Democrats might finally win this time, Daschle said. Obama reminded
him of 2000 and 2004, when they thought the same thing. When his
chief speechwriter, Jon Favreau, congratulated him, he told him not
to jinx it. But he was confident enough to work on the "If We Win"
speech and send back the "If We Don't Win" speech without notes. "I
don't even want to look at that damn thing," he said. After a steak dinner at home the Obama family headed downtown to the Hyatt Regency
on Wacker Drive, where they gathered with the Bidens in Suite 3605 to
watch the returns. Lane Evans, an early supporter forced to leave Congress after his Parkinson's disease worsened, was invited by for a chat.

---

* Ayers, a onetime leader of the Weather Underground, a 1960s radical group connected to
a series of bombings, was a Chicago neighbor of Obama. In 1996 Ayers hosted a small fund-
raiser for him, and they served on a nonprofit board together. Ayers's well-respected work
as an educator brought him into close contact with Mayor Daley and other local leaders,
until he published a book in 2001 showing little remorse for his actions as a Weatherman.
Although both Obama and Ayers denied they were more than acquaintances, their relationship became a campaign issue in 2008.

Axelrod knew they'd won at 6:30, when he cracked open the first sample precincts from Indiana, where Obama was outperforming the campaign's expectations. Obama called him around 8:30. "It sounds like we're going to win," he said. Axelrod agreed, but remembering that Democratic strategist Bob Shrum called John Kerry "Mr. President" on election night in 2004, he added, "I'm not going to congratulate you prematurely." Later, up in the hotel suite, they watched McCain graciously concede. "Can you congratulate me now?" Obama joked.

When the television screen flashed Obama's picture and the words "President-Elect Barack Obama," Michelle turned to her husband and said, "You are the forty-fourth president of the United States. Wow. What a country we live in."

Obama was at ease, his feet propped up on the coffee table. He felt his mother-in-law, Marian, take his hand, then squeeze it. He wondered, *What's she thinking?* A black woman who grew up in the 1950s in segregated Chicago is watching her daughter become first lady of the United States.

Axelrod's thoughts went back four years, to Obama's election to the Senate. That night he had gone to look up the ward and precinct of St. Pascal's Catholic Church on Chicago's Northwest Side. In 1983 former vice president Walter Mondale visited the church to campaign for Harold Washington for mayor and was jeered by racists in an ugly scene. Washington received almost no votes there. In 2004 Axelrod learned that Obama had won both the ward and the precinct of St. Pascal's and told the new senator that Harold was smiling down on them, grateful for the progress they had made in two decades. This night, with the presidency in hand, he thought of a meeting in his conference room in late 2006, when Obama said he was running for president in part so that millions of kids would look differently at themselves. Now something that those kids thought was absurd—that a black man could be elected president of the United States—had come to pass.

Malia gave her father a fist bump. "What's the first thing you're going to do as president?" she asked. "I'm going to get you guys a dog," Obama said. Malia pressed: "I'm serious, like the first political thing?" Obama rolled his eyes. "Malia's working for the school newspaper now," he explained.

But Obama was thinking about a related question as the news sunk in—not the first thing he'd do on Day One, but the big thing he'd do in Year One. He later told aides that in a quiet moment on Election Night he had asked himself, *What's the single achievement that would most help average Americans?* His answer was health care reform, though he hadn't emphasized it during the campaign.

It was time to give his speech. Backstage Obama summoned Axelrod, who jogged to catch up to him in the tunnel as he strode toward the stage. "I just wanted you to know," Obama said, "there was a good fireworks display planned, but I killed it. Too frivolous for the times."

Within minutes he and his family stepped forward, separated from the entire world by two-inch-thick bullet-proof glass. He began by savoring the historic "defining moment":

> If there is anyone out there who still doubts that America is a place where all things are possible; who still wonders if the dream of our founders is alive in our time; who still questions the power of our democracy, tonight is your answer. . . .
>
> It's been a long time coming, but tonight, because of what we did on this day, in this election, at this defining moment, change has come to America.

But he made a point of emphasizing the long struggle to come:

> I know you didn't just do this to win an election and I know you didn't do it for me. You did it because you understand the enormity of the task that lies ahead. For even as we celebrate tonight, we know the challenges that tomorrow will bring are the greatest of our lifetime—two wars, a planet in peril, the worst financial crisis in a century.

Out in Grant Park 250,000 people were more interested in the history than the challenges ahead. They celebrated with no arrests, which was almost unheard-of on festive occasions in the city. For older Chicagoans the location had a special resonance. In 1968 police had clubbed antiwar demonstrators across Michigan Avenue from the Conrad Hilton Hotel, the same area of Grant Park where Obama now gave his victory speech. The violence at that year's Democratic National Convention split the Democratic Party and helped elect Richard Nixon, who came to personify an ugly chapter in the American story. Forty years later the party's wounds seemed finally healed and some of Chicago's tortured racial history joyously transcended, at least for one night. Retired cops and long-ago hippies and their children and grandchildren all gathered in the park, this time on the same side of the barricades.

Across the country most Democrats, many independents, and even some Republicans considered this the sweetest presidential victory of their adult lives, as years of bitterness and even despair over the state of American politics gave way to at least some measure of hope. In October in Guilford, North Carolina, Sarah Palin said she was glad to be back in the "real America." On Election Day John McCain and Palin lost Guilford County and North Carolina and their party lost its claim to a curiously persistent and noxious idea; the night marked the end of a four-decade stretch during which conservatives got to define what being a patriotic American meant. Republicans might soon rise again, and their talent for fierce opposition would continue to shape national politics, but the culture wars that once lay at the touchy center of the national debate would now be waged more often at the fringe. A new generation of elites felt no embarrassment over displays of love for their country. In Harvard Square students stopped traffic and sang "God Bless America" and "America the Beautiful" for the first time since World War II.

The nations of the world greeted news of Obama's election with relief and even exultation. For years their people had liked Americans as individuals but felt contemptuous toward the American government; now perhaps that would change. There was hope too that a new day might be at hand for race relations in their own countries. "Obama's election is the ratification of the American dream," a Cabinet minister in South Korea told a visiting American dignitary. "If a first-generation minority can become president of the most powerful nation on earth, anything is possible." Commentary reflected an instant surge in prestige for the United States as television carried images of cheering crowds from Iraq and Israel to India and Indonesia, plus London, Beijing, Athens, Stockholm, and, of course, the coincidentally named Obama, Japan, among many other cities. Foreign heads of state began telephoning congratulations to Chicago before the returns were complete. In Kenya, government officials declared a national holiday in honor of the new American president, grandson of a goatherd on the shores of Lake Victoria.

The joy of the African American community knew no bounds. John Lewis, the civil rights hero whose skull had been fractured by Alabama police near Selma in 1965, said he "never imagined, never had any idea" he would see this day: "We have witnessed tonight in America a revolution of values, a revolution of ideals. There's been a transformation of America, and it will have unbelievable influence on the world." Obama himself had never promised a revolution of values, and within months some of the same old racial attitudes would be back. But Lewis could be excused for getting carried away on a night like this.*

---

* The longtime civil rights leader Andrew Young, who supported Hillary in the primaries, was happy ("This is the America we love") but more jaundiced. Young figured that the election of an African American president was made possible only by the screwups of Bush. He compared Obama's election to the advent of black mayors in the 1960s: "The world got so

Jesse Jackson stood with the media in the park, musing about Obama and Martin Luther King. In June he'd been caught on tape in a jealous fit saying he wanted to "cut [Obama's] nuts off" for "talking down to black people." Now Jackson recalled that, as a student at Columbia University in 1983, Obama saw one of the debates when Jackson was running for president: "He told me later, 'That's when I realized this was possible.' " Jackson ticked off the names of forgotten civil rights activists: "I'd like for those nameless, faceless martyrs to show up for just one night, to know they were redeemed tonight." Jackson was subdued; he was on the wrong side of the rope line, far away from the tents where Obama's important supporters were gathered. But by the time the president-elect spoke, he was in tears.

On Chicago's LaSalle Street a working-class African American who grew up in Chicago stopped a white reporter. "Congratulations!" he said.

"Congratulations to you," the reporter replied.

"No, it's you folks, the Caucasians, who did this, who should get the credit. We knew we'd vote for Barack today, but we just weren't sure y'all would."

In the National Finance Committee tent, the big donors, the ones whose early money had made it possible for him to win, climbed up on tables and chairs to get a glimpse of the president-elect as he thanked them. Penny Pritzker, the formidable Chicago businesswoman who spearheaded his record fund-raising, sat on the cold ground, out of view. Obama expected to see her there, and when he didn't he emailed her at 2 a.m. asking where she'd been. Pritzker replied, "Mr. President-elect, I am short and my mother told me it was inappropriate to stand on furniture."*

For Valerie Jarrett the evening brought one of the great nonverbal moments of her life. Backstage Obama approached her wordlessly and they just stared at each other for perhaps ten seconds. All the pride and emotion of the journey were contained in the look. Then they shook their heads slightly, smiled, and hugged. Jarrett still couldn't get any words out.

Andy Stern of the Service Employees International Union, head of the only big labor union still growing, caught up with Obama in the

---

messed up that no one really wanted to tackle it. So they turned it over to us. That's what happened to the cities."

* The Obama fund-raising juggernaut was often seen as a social-networking phenomenon, but it was actually more like an Internet startup. Obama and Pritzker knew that they needed the equivalent of venture capitalists to put in seed money before their enterprise could "go public."

tent. "I guess they're not going to make fun of community organizers anymore," Obama told him with a smile. "It's going to be a hallowed profession."*

The speech had gone over well and Jon Favreau got the president-elect to pose for a picture with him and his parents. "Well, Favs," Obama said, "now you've got the Inaugural [Address] and the State of the Union."

"Don't I get a break?" Favreau protested.

"Yeah, you get a little break," Obama replied. "And then you're really screwed."

Many young staffers ran around the park wearing T-shirts reading "Let's Go Win This Fucking Thing" and all day had signed their fevered emails "LGWTFT," homage to David Plouffe's line after New Hampshire. At 12:30 a.m. Plouffe, whose wife was about to give birth, sent out an email to the staff: "We won this fucking thing."

Mike Strautmanis's nervous September email flashed in Obama's mind when he saw him. "I told you, 'I got this.' I told you to tell your people—'I got this,' " Obama said. Strautmanis stammered that the next time he'd be sure to give him the benefit of the doubt.

Obama got it and then some. The election returns told a striking story of a changing and more engaged America. With nearly a hundred electoral votes to spare, Obama beat McCain 53 percent to 46 percent, the biggest Democratic victory since Lyndon Johnson's in 1964. Virginia, North Carolina, Indiana, and other states that had long been comfortably Republican fell to the Democrats as motivated liberals flocked to the polls and discouraged conservatives stayed home. The 63 percent turnout of eligible voters was small by international standards but the highest in nearly half a century in the United States.

More important were the demographics of the 131 million Americans who voted. The gender gap persisted, with Obama carrying women by 13 points and men by 1. McCain won 55 percent of white men nationwide (nearly 90 percent in Louisiana and Alabama), which in the 1980 election would have been enough to win. But the Arizonan was running in a different country than the one Ronald Reagan knew. For the first time more than a quarter of the electorate was non-white. Obama carried 95 percent of African American voters (100 percent of black women in North Carolina, according to exit polls), and they made up 13 percent of voters, up 2 points since 2004. The Latino vote, which had nearly doubled in a decade to 9 percent of the elec-

---

* Not quite. By summer 2009 conservatives grew agitated over a few abuses at ACORN, a network of community activists that had worked with Obama in Chicago during the 1990s.

torate, went 2–1 for Obama, an ominous sign for a Republican Party that showed no sign of pulling back from its opposition to immigration reform.

Obama easily carried voters earning less than $100,000 a year and making more than $200,000; McCain won narrowly among those in between. The breakdown was similar for education level, with Obama crushing McCain among Americans who didn't finish high school (63 percent) and those with postgraduate degrees (58 percent) and splitting the voters in between.

The scariest figure for the GOP was the breakdown by age. The only age group McCain carried was his own, those over 65, voters more resistant to change and, in some cases, to the idea of a black man as president. But among 18- to 29-year-old voters Obama won 66 percent, up twelve points from John Kerry's showing in 2004. He won 54 percent of young white men, a cohort that hadn't given a majority to a Democrat since the 1960s.

The headline for those who followed politics closely was *generational realignment*. All the canvassing and college organizing and cool new web videos had paid off. But young people were fickle; their permanent allegiance to the Democrats was hardly assured. Still, those about to run the country had chosen a new path, one that they, not their parents and grandparents, would tread. Obama hadn't just prevailed in the present; he had carried the future in a landslide.

Yet the question remained: How much change did the country truly want? Like all presidential elections, 2008 was a referendum on the status quo, not a mandate for every policy prescription that the winner proposed. The returns were at bottom a stunning repudiation of the cowboy presidency of George W. Bush, with its ideological preoccupations and failure to honor what the Declaration of Independence called "a decent respect to the opinions of mankind." Weakened by his incompetent response to Hurricane Katrina, a quagmire in Iraq, and a wrenching recession, Bush was a deadweight on his old rival McCain, especially among self-described moderates (44 percent of the electorate), who went 60–39 for Obama. Independents (29 percent of voters) went 52–44 for the winner. Many of these swing voters liked to strike a blow against incumbents and could easily turn on the new president. Obama in 2008 was like Franklin Roosevelt in 1932 and Ronald Reagan in 1980: the beneficiary of failure. The size of each of their victories depended on the intensity of the rejection.

But no one knew if, like FDR and Reagan, Barack Obama could convert disgust with the incumbent into faith in a new order. He would bring many advantages to his search for the elixir of great leadership: a crisis to focus public attention, a significant new Democratic majority in Congress to advance his program, a rare gift for oratorical inspiration. His supple mind, Zen temperament, and forward organizational thinking would all help.

Yet none of this could assure successful navigation of the treacherous currents of the American presidency. The expectations were immense, as people around the world held up Obama's promise as their own—the promise that leadership mattered, that Washington could be changed, that a skinny black man on TV could make a difference in their lives. Mario Cuomo, a former governor of New York and one of the great orators of the twentieth century, liked to say that politicians campaign in poetry and govern in prose. This was the reality of hope.

4

The Cabinet Maker

On the morning after the election Barack Obama left his house shortly after 8 a.m. in a sweatshirt and baseball cap and headed to a friend's apartment building to exercise. Then he got to work on running his government.

With the Chicago transition headquarters not yet available, a 12:30 meeting was scheduled at the sleek Randolph Street offices of Ariel Capital Management. Since he founded his firm in 1983 as a Warren Buffett protégé, John Rogers had festooned his office and prospectus with pictures of turtles and adopted as his investment philosophy "Slow and steady wins the race." Now his old friend Barack was going to use his conference rooms for a few days to plot what he hoped would be a fast and steady transition.

The man suddenly being addressed as "Mr. President-elect" was greeted by what he later described as "gallows humor." Ax told him, "I really feel bad that we've done this to you."

Obama didn't waste much time reviewing the previous night's historic event or his historic predicament. He went right to the group's progress on the transition "work-flow plan." John Podesta thought the meeting would last about forty-five minutes, but the president-elect kept it going for more than four and a half hours.

Obama had been thinking much more about the transition than even his team realized. On Day One he was ready to narrow down his Cabinet to two or three names for each post. He had some people in mind for big jobs, but the striking thing was how few top Democratic policymakers he knew well personally; one former Clinton aide working on the transition guessed they would all fit on a single index card.

Obama understood the legislative process in Washington better than governors like Ronald Reagan and Bill Clinton, who had never served there before becoming president. But he had run no state or local government, chaired no Senate committees, and made few high-level connections beyond his campaign supporters, his Harvard Law and

Chicago circles, and the group of former Daschle aides who helped him when he first arrived in Washington in 2005. His short lists weren't collections of friends, like Clinton's in 1992; they were wish lists of acquaintances he had met briefly or heard good things about, like the fantasy football league draft he put together with his Chicago buddies. He told the November 5 meeting that he would conduct job interviews with most of the top candidates.

When names began to leak almost immediately, Obama was quietly furious. He suspected Biden aides and made sure they were excluded from future high-level meetings. The gabby vice president himself was left out of many important conversations on personnel.

Now that he wasn't campaigning, Obama was turning out to be an insistent taskmaster. Within thirty-six hours of winning he was on the phone to Anita Dunn complaining that he had no communications strategy. "I know we just won, but we can't drift like this," the president-elect said.

Dunn thought, *Drift? Give me a break.* What she said to Obama was "We were focused on the election." Obama wanted to move rapidly with a communications strategy that would take them to the Inauguration. He said so lightly, even lightheartedly, but Dunn knew that with Obama he absolutely meant it.

By the weekend Axelrod, Dunn, and the others had broken the transition into three communication phases. Phase One would extend from the election to Thanksgiving. It would emphasize how quickly Obama was selecting his Cabinet, put an intense focus on the economy, and validate the voters' choice by repeatedly demonstrating that Obama was up to the job. Phase Two, which went from Thanksgiving to the end of the year, would strike a bipartisan, "team of rivals" tone while filling out the rest of the Cabinet and some other top jobs. Phase Three included the run-up to the swearing-in on January 20, plus securing TARP funding from Congress that would come up for a vote before the Inauguration. No one could really plan that far ahead, or anticipate the velocity of the economic downturn, but they knew they'd be busy.

Obama made it clear to senior staff that he wanted to lengthen the time horizons they had all grown accustomed to during the campaign. Instead of trying to win the day in the media, they should think more about coming out ahead at the end of the week. And policy success should be measured in years or even decades. "We've got to be about the long term," he told them.

On Friday, November 7, Obama held his first press conference as president-elect. The location was the Conrad Hilton Hotel on Michigan Avenue, scene of the demise of the Democratic Party in 1968. There he set the confident yet realistic tone for everything to follow. He would "confront the crisis head-on," he said: "It is not going to be quick, not going to be easy. But America is a strong and resilient society and I know we will succeed."

———

EVEN BEFORE HE had decided his own fate, Rahm Emanuel was at work staffing the White House. Because he couldn't hire lobbyists—whatever their qualities, they were too toxic—it sometimes seemed as if Obama was staffing his administration through a single Washington think tank, the Center for American Progress, founded and run by John Podesta. Eventually more than fifty people from CAP would join the administration.

As it turned out the backgrounds and policy preferences of the staff didn't mean much because Obama himself was going to be such an active president. When he interviewed Patrick Gaspard, a Haitian American political operative from New York, for the job of political director, Obama told him, "I'll hire you, but you should know that I'm going to be my own political director."

Beyond Obama's appeal, it was hard times—and the promise of making history—that closed the sale with everyone from Rahm to the lowliest aide. "You never want a serious crisis to go to waste," Rahm told a *Wall Street Journal* conference of CEOs the week after the election, in a line that would characterize the Obama administration's approach. "Things that we had postponed for too long, that were long-term, are now immediate and must be dealt with. This crisis provides the opportunity for us to do things that you could not do before."

That opportunity made Washington feel like it did when FDR was elected in 1932 or Kennedy in 1960. It was hard to walk up Connecticut Avenue without running into some lawyer or policy entrepreneur wearing a big smile, position papers spilling out of his briefcase. While Obama occupied the Chicago transition headquarters until January, a separate transition team began to assemble in a nondescript federal office building at 6th and D in Northwest Washington. Before the election most of the contacts had been by phone or email. The first meeting of those who had been selected to run different parts of the transition took place in the basement of the building and felt like a festive Clinton reunion. After soberly reciting the strict ethics standards the transition team would work under, Norm Eisen, an impish lawyer and Obama classmate from Harvard Law School, suddenly let out a war whoop. It captured the mood. Obama was president, and life for Washington Democrats was about to get good again.

FOR MONTHS OBAMA had worked through Senator Jack Reed (a West Point grad and early supporter) to convince Robert Gates to stay on as secretary of defense.* After he offered Gates the job at a secret meeting held at a fire station on the grounds of Reagan National Airport, he was even more sure that the decision was right. It worked on at least four levels: Gates provided continuity on Iraq, where he agreed with the Obama policy of withdrawal; he was a veteran of three Republican administrations, which lent an impression of bipartisanship that Obama considered essential; he offered political cover for tough decisions on canceling weapons systems and otherwise standing up to the military brass; and he was known as a decent, nonideological guy who had learned something from his mistakes as a cold war hard-liner in Republican administrations.†

Gates had a deceptive personal appeal. On first impression he reminded one defense transition official of "the guy at P. C. Richard's who sold microwave ovens." He quit work at the Pentagon at 5 p.m. and, unlike Donald Rumsfeld, gave broad latitude to his staff. But Gates was formidable in meetings and in public, where he said all the right things about how the country needed more diplomacy and less use of conventional military power. This sophisticated "tool box" approach was belied by the fact that the *increase* he proposed in the defense budget was more than the entire State Department budget for diplomacy. But it sounded good. Soon some White House staffers started calling him "Yoda," after the wizened character in *Star Wars*.

THE OTHER MAJOR Cabinet posts would not be as easy to fill. Secretary of state was important of course, but with the onset of the crisis in September, secretary of the treasury became the most critical appointment.

Unlike George W. Bush, who leaned heavily on Dick Cheney, Obama was fully in charge and making all the key decisions himself. He resolved to break precedent and announce his economic team before his national security team. While Larry Summers was itching for a

---

* If Gates had declined, among those on the list for secretary of defense was Hillary Clinton.
† Nobody in the Obama circle much cared that Gates had been tarnished by the Iran-Contra affair in the 1980s and by his record as George H. W. Bush's CIA director, where on his watch the CIA added to an already long list of intelligence failures by not predicting the collapse of the Soviet Union. A bigger hurdle was that in 2008 he gave a speech saying he wouldn't push the Comprehensive Test Ban Treaty without upgrading the warheads on U.S. missiles, thereby undermining the treaty.

return to his old job as treasury secretary, Obama wanted to widen the circle. He knew that as president of the New York Fed, Tim Geithner was right at the center of the bailout action, consulting closely with Paulson. In fact he was the only one other than Paulson and Bernanke who had a handle on the details.

Obama and Geithner had met for the first time during the fall campaign, in a secret meeting at the W Hotel in New York. They hit it off immediately, and not just because they were almost exactly the same age (born two weeks apart in August 1961) and both prided themselves on their unpretentiousness. Like Obama, Geithner had grown up abroad, in Zimbabwe, Zambia, India, and Thailand. They took a tour of the horizon together and delved immediately into the complexities of the global recession. Afterward both discovered that during the early 1980s Geithner's father, Peter Geithner, oversaw the Ford Foundation's micro-credit program and had even met once with one of its Indonesian program officers, S. Ann Dunham-Soetoro, Obama's mother. Obama loved stories like this.

Trained well by his years under Henry Kissinger in the consulting business, Geithner played hard-to-get when Obama edged toward offering him Treasury. He listed the reasons he was wrong for the job (especially that his appointment wouldn't represent Obama's theme of change), recommended Summers for a return engagement at Treasury, and insisted that he didn't want to move to Washington. All of this, of course, was the surest way to make Obama interested. Obama believed that the most appealing characters in public life were the ones who took what they were doing seriously, but didn't take themselves too seriously. "He's our kind of guy," he told Axelrod after the meeting.

Several people suggested Paul Volcker as an interim one-year treasury secretary to get through the crisis. The six-foot-seven former chairman of the Federal Reserve had the stature to calm markets; his policies had helped rescue the economy in the early 1980s. Volcker, who wanted the job, met with Obama to discuss it. But Volcker would have been a lame duck, and the idea never got traction. Besides, Volcker's adversaries inside were beginning to whisper that he "wasn't up to it." This was their way of saying that they wouldn't be able to control what he might say publicly. A prestigious loose cannon was the last thing the Obama camp wanted. At 81, Volcker wasn't under any illusions about his age. He noticed that people called everyone else by their first name or last name, but only he, and now Obama, were accorded a "Mr." He knew that if he took a position inside the White House as a senior counselor it would be awkward for other aides—like having your father around telling you what to do.

Sure enough, Summers wasn't happy about Volcker's setting up a competing power base. Volcker sent Obama a memo that asked at the bottom, "Do you agree or not agree?" He was bluntly told that he couldn't send such memos to the president-elect unless they were properly vetted. This was standard in the government, but Volcker decided that if someone else was going to decide whether his memos were important enough for Obama, he wouldn't send any more.

SO THE SHORT list for Treasury, the most crucial post in the early Obama administration, would be exceptionally short from the start. It was a choice between two supremely well-credentialed members of the establishment: a Council on Foreign Relations–bred chairman of the Federal Reserve Bank of New York versus a prodigy economist and former treasury secretary and Harvard president who lacked the social graces but had a proven track record dealing with the Mexican debt crisis and other challenges.

To the president-elect neither choice was perfect. On the one hand, Obama worried that Geithner might not be ready for the Cabinet in terms of his public profile, a concern that proved correct. On the other, he remembered that he had privately supported Harvard's decision to fire Summers in 2005, not over the substance of his politically incorrect statements about women and the sciences but, as one friend from the time recalled Obama saying, because Summers clearly lacked the "diplomatic skill set" for the Harvard presidency.

In making his decision Obama, as usual, listened patiently to advocates on both sides. Michael Froman, a former Treasury official and Citi banker and one of the transition chiefs, was pushing hard for his old friend Geithner. Froman had become close friends with Obama at Harvard Law School, and they drew closer still in the waning days of the campaign as the Fromans' young son, Jake, lay dying of cancer. Froman had more influence with Obama than did Rubin, his boss at Citigroup. As a member of the board of the Harvard Corporation, Rubin had recruited Summers to run Harvard in 2001, then stuck with him even after most of the rest of the board resolved to fire him. Now he and Rahm Emanuel were championing Summers's return to the helm at Treasury.

Obama bonded with Geithner personally; they had the same "no drama" style. And Obama thought that Geithner's work over the previous eight months made him just about the only one in the country who possessed the right technical experience to confront the complex financial crisis. He knew he would get slammed for continuing with the same crowd, but he didn't think breaking with TARP and starting over was the way to go. He would opt for the guys, especially Bernanke and Geithner, who had saved the system in September.

This was ironic because for all their heroic work, the triumvirate—Bernanke, Paulson, and Geithner—made colossal mistakes in 2008, starting in March with their letting Jamie Dimon's JP Morgan buy the ailing Bear Stearns with taxpayer money. Volcker, who had saved the American economy by slaying inflation in the early 1980s, didn't think he was being particularly clairvoyant when he predicted that every bank, car company, and insurance company that ran into trouble would now come to the Fed with a tin cup in hand. But neither Geithner nor Bernanke called Volcker to ask his advice and they scrambled as Lehman collapsed in September and made the wrong decision in not saving it.

The very week in November when Obama was elected and making his decision about who should run Treasury, Geithner was paying AIG's counterparties at par, 100 cents on the dollar, in part because French banks convinced him with dubious arguments that it was illegal not to do so. Goldman Sachs alone got at least $13 billion from the taxpayers this way, yet later claimed—to Obama's and Geithner's chagrin—that it hadn't needed it to avoid ruin.

Neil Barofsky, the inspector general for TARP, was harsh on Geithner. The Fed "refused to use its considerable leverage," Barofsky wrote in a report a year later. Spooked by European banks threatening collapse, Geithner gave what critics called "backdoor bailouts" of tens of billions to some of the wealthiest financial institutions in the world. He failed to negotiate, to use the power he had, though Geithner later said this analysis (made popular by former New York governor Eliot Spitzer) was completely wrong. He said he had no options and would do "the exact same thing" if he had it to do all over again.

"You gotta understand the context," Geithner's counselor at Treasury, Gene Sperling, said later. No one relished rescuing such an irresponsible company, but AIG was financially structured so that a rating downgrade (inevitable if counterparties weren't paid in full) could send the healthy parts of the insurance giant into a dangerous meltdown that would wreck the global economy. Sperling called it the equivalent of "a guy standing in Times Square with explosives strapped to his body yelling at police, 'Tell me you love me! Say it or everyone dies!' " Default, in this telling, was not an option.

It was true that Geithner and company averted a catastrophic meltdown of the financial system, and that was apparently good enough for Obama. He apparently never considered appointing a banker or Fed governor from outside the East Coast who knew finance but was less connected to the policies that caused the crisis. Had he done so, he might have avoided some blowback down the road.

Up close the crisis was so frightening that it tended to obliterate memories of what any of the players had done before. The president-elect knew only secondhand that Summers, Geithner, and Gary Gensler (another Goldman alum, who became head of the Commodity Futures Trading Commission) had been advocates of financial deregulation when they served under Clinton in the 1990s, but he didn't care as long as it didn't threaten a confirmation fight. Like Barney Frank, Obama subscribed to the FDR/Joe Kennedy theory of supervising Wall Street: hire people who know from the inside how the scams work.* And he was opting for experience across the board.

Obama's preference for experience came with a price in insularity. He was surrounded by advisors infused with the values of Wall Street, even if they had only studied the market from academia or regulated it in government, not made money there. Geithner and Summers knew the market's limitations and favored financial regulatory reform, but at bottom they believed their role was to rescue the system, then rationalize it. They offered sophisticated explanations for every decision at a level of complexity that easily bamboozled reporters and were impatient with what they called "populist" arguments on bonuses, conspiratorial cracks about "Government Sachs," or even more cultural (and inevitably personal) observations about a group of smart people who all knew one another and all looked at the world through nearly identical eyes. It was the last of these, not feverish left-wing fantasies, that posed the most subtle and substantial challenge. Obama was inside that cozy group now, and it would be increasingly difficult for him to see beyond its borders.

———

BY THIS TIME Obama worried that his Cabinet would smack too much of the Clinton era. While Geithner had served at Treasury in those years, he wasn't identified as a Clinton person, as Summers was. When Podesta, a major link to the Clintons, favored Geithner, he brought some others off the fence. Obama decided to work on getting both men in his government. Geithner insisted that he didn't want to resign as chairman of the New York Fed to be an advisor in the White House. That meant putting him at Treasury might be the only way to hire him.

———

* FDR appointed Kennedy, a Wall Street trader, as the first chairman of the Securities and Exchange Commission.

Summers, by contrast, was in the private sector and could perhaps be lured in with the right offer. Okay, Obama said, let's go with Geithner.

Summers wasn't happy. Obama asked him to come to the White House as a senior advisor with daily access; he wanted Summers close by. Summers said no, he would go in only as head of the National Economic Council, where Rubin had served before becoming treasury secretary, a job already promised to Jack Lew, a former budget director under Clinton. Summers knew that absent an exceptionally close relationship with the president, staff equals clout in Washington, and the NEC had the staff. He also hoped that when Bernanke's term as Fed chairman expired in 2010, he would be in position to get the job. The president-elect couldn't promise anything on the Fed chairmanship (Bernanke ended up being reappointed), but he wanted Summers and accepted most of his demands. Jack Lew took the top management post at the State Department in compensation.

At first glance Geithner and Summers got the wrong jobs. The director of the National Economic Council is supposed to be an honest broker who efficiently coordinates policymaking between agencies. The treasury secretary is supposed to be a commanding presence whose very appearance on TV calms markets. Geithner was an efficient coordinator; Summers, as a former treasury secretary, had the requisite gravitas. But Obama's personal instincts moved him toward Geithner, and his political instincts also told him a fresh face like Geithner's was needed at Treasury. Even after the vetters discovered disturbing tax problems on Geithner's record—problems that would cause Obama considerable embarrassment six weeks later—he stuck with his choice.

To no one's surprise it didn't take long for Summers to escalate his demands. He was a former Cabinet secretary agreeing to be a mere staffer—a patriotic and perhaps unprecedented step down—and he wanted more power in return. Summers tried to get responsibility for energy and health care. When that failed, he insisted that anything related to the economy from any agency be routed through him. Summers rightly said that he was just asking for the NEC to have the same powers that it did when Bob Rubin and Gene Sperling ran it during the Clinton administration. The problem was, Summers wanted it both ways—to use his authority as NEC director to be the gatekeeper and simultaneously to serve as the president's lead thinker on the economy. In foreign policy terms, he planned to be the equivalent of a Henry Kissinger or Zbigniew Brzezinski, not Brent Scowcroft. Because Clinton had modeled the NEC job on Scowcroft and first filled it with the self-effacing Rubin, this was going to be quite a change.

Among those unhappy about it was Peter Orszag, the young former head of the CBO who had been named Obama's budget director. He thought the OMB director should be able to talk directly with the president without going through the NEC, a point on which he ultimately prevailed. Summers found that Orszag was a shrewder infighter than he looked. A tennis buddy warned him (in a story Summers denied), "Watch out for the guy with the cowboy boots and the bad toupee."

———

FOR HUNDREDS OF thousands of Democrats, getting a job with Obama was the impossible dream. The so-called plum book, published every four years by Congress, lists only about seven thousand political positions available for a new president to appoint, out of a federal workforce of around 15 million. Every other government position is filled by the civil service, not the president. Eight years earlier the Bush transition received about forty thousand résumés. Obama's office stopped counting when they got to five hundred thousand. Working for Obama became even cooler than being a movie star. Kal Penn, costar of the *Harold and Kumar* movies, arranged to have his character die in the TV show *House* so that he could quit show business and work in the White House in a midlevel position in Valerie Jarrett's Office of Public Engagement.

Mathematically an applicant for a plum book job had a 1-in-70 chance of winning a position in the federal government. The chances of working in the White House were 1-in-600. Anyone hoping for a job was required to post a résumé on the website Change.gov; beyond a tiny handful of Cabinet members and White House aides, there were no exceptions. Michael Froman and his team didn't actually review the posted résumés; they had their own short lists for senior positions, assembled with the help of Podesta, Axelrod, Emanuel, Rouse, Jarrett, and the president-elect. But the database was helpful for staffing the next levels down.

To actually get a chance to move to Washington, take a pay cut (most did), and work for Barack Obama required contacts of course, but also a willingness to subject oneself to a political colonoscopy. The probing was more intrusive for positions in the agencies, which required Senate confirmation (not necessary for most jobs in the White House—yet another reason to want to work there). Even the spokespersons for Cabinet secretaries were usually subjected to Senate hearings and the full investigative treatment. At the time, the vetting process was a mere hassle; eventually it became one of the great headaches of the early Obama administration.

———

THE JOY THE Obama campaign workers felt about November 4 was soon tinged with worry and even resentment. As one not-so-funny joke had it, the best way to get a job with Obama was to have supported Hillary Clinton. "We spent the last six months winning an election," said one Obama campaign staffer. "They spent the last six months getting in position." Another early Obama supporter complained that the Obama high command "reaches out to their adversaries and tolerates their friends." It was understandable why so many Clinton people got the good jobs; they had the experience. But there was a trade-off that was not unlike the one Obama exploited against Clinton during the campaign. More experience might also mean less change.

The Clinton retread story was true enough for the sub-Cabinet and other positions requiring Senate confirmation, where about 40 percent of the Obama appointees had worked for the Clinton administration. This was where much of the real work of government got done. But the Cabinet itself was only partially a Clinton sequel, with five Cabinet-rank appointments out of twenty-two counting as true Clinton-era veterans. The rest had a mix of backgrounds, ranging from a Nobel Prize winner in physics (Steven Chu at Energy, who quoted Faulkner at his announcement), to a Latina congresswoman (Hilda Solis at Labor), to a former four-star army general who had been forced into retirement by the Bush administration (Eric Shinseki at the Veterans Administration).

In the Cabinet and among White House staff, experience and diversity usually trumped longtime loyalty to Obama. For instance, Austan Goolsbee, who had been Obama's economic advisor since 2003, lost out as chair of the Council of Economic Advisers to Christina Romer, a Berkeley economics professor and expert on the Depression who had the advantage of being a woman. At 39, Goolsbee had academic tenure at the University of Chicago and a devil-may-care attitude toward Washington, so he let it be known that he wouldn't be joining the administration. When Obama called, Goolsbee said he had enough housing problems as it was without looking for a place to live in Washington, which would be his fourth residence. The author of Obama's campaign promises on housing had bought a new house in Chicago without being able to sell his old house and was currently renting a third house while the new house was fixed up. He was a walking housing crisis.

Obama called again and said, "I insist you come. This is the biggest crisis since the Great Depression. Do you want to sit on the sidelines?"

"It seems like I'd be on the sidelines in Washington," Goolsbee replied. He knew Obama well and felt he could be honest with him.

Obama was incredulous. "What are you saying, that if you can't be chairman of the Council of Economic Advisers, you're not coming?"

Goolsbee said he wasn't saying that at all. He would come for any meaningful role, but he wondered if it was possible to make a difference with the same old Clinton mafia dominating the upper reaches of policymaking. Afterward Goolsbee was torn, but his wife thought that if the president of the United States called him twice he really didn't have a choice.

Obama didn't seem to take offense at Goolsbee's temerity. Remembering Goolsbee's role in bringing in Volcker, he assigned him to be the White House point man for a new economic advisory board he convinced Volcker to chair. Goolsbee also became a member of the CEA.

Through all the personnel complexities, Obama's goal, as he said publicly, was to "combine experience with fresh thinking." He saw the latter as connected to diversity. At his insistence his administration was much more diverse by race, ethnicity, and sexual orientation than any before it. But he said several times that he didn't want the personnel teams settling for less qualified people. He insisted that they try harder to find candidates who were both qualified and diverse. When Congresswoman Barbara Lee, chair of the Congressional Black Caucus, complained that not enough of the caucus's recommendations were getting hired, Obama was attentive but unmoved. "If they're giving us a bunch of people who are just the usual suspects, I want you to go out and get others," he told his staff. Though Hispanics weren't as well represented as African Americans in the uppermost positions, Obama made a special effort to place them in second-level jobs where they could get the experience necessary to move up later in his term.

For Obama diversity cut both ways. He liked the idea of breaking the tradition of appointing a minority to head the Department of Housing and Urban Development, opting instead for Mike Bloomberg's innovative New York City housing chief, Shaun Donovan, a white guy. Other departments got a lower priority. Rahm was eager to find a place in the Cabinet for Ray LaHood, a savvy hale-fellow congressman from Peoria. LaHood was up for agriculture secretary, but when transition researchers discovered that he had a fondness for agriculture earmarks, he was switched to Transportation. LaHood was a straight affirmative-action pick: he was a Republican.

The president-elect's decision memos on personnel were simple enough; they contained boxes to be checked off labeled "Approve," "Deny," and "Discuss." Early on most came back marked "Discuss." The president-elect wanted to be deeply involved in every major personnel decision. He interviewed more than forty people in person and perused the files on scores more. He was determined not to micromanage his administration any more than he had his campaign, but choosing the right people was critical to being successful. Now that he was in one place for more than a few hours, he could give free rein to his inquisitive nature about policy and personnel.

Obama spent much of November and early December reviewing candidates. For two years on the campaign trail he had argued that what mattered most was judgment, not experience. But with little chance to assess the judgment of hundreds of applicants for the top jobs, he now opted heavily for the very quality he had once devalued. Though no particular experience could qualify someone for the presidency, the same was not true for jobs below that level. And as the financial crisis worsened, the political environment changed; the public was now looking for a few seasoned hands to get the country out of the mess.

The result was a strikingly conventional series of choices at the sub-Cabinet level, with Clinton administration officials tending to move up one step from where they had been a decade before. Former deputy assistant secretaries were now candidates for assistant secretary, and former heads of small agencies had a shot to run something a little bigger. These were often the best-qualified appointees in a narrow sense, but choosing them for important sub-Cabinet posts over those with less traditional résumés meant fewer creative thinkers would make the trek to Washington. It wasn't long before "Change We Can Believe In" was lampooned as "Change We've Unsuccessfully Tried Before."

One transition official who had worked in the Obama campaign circulated a policy memo to a large group. Her boss, a Clinton veteran, told her sternly that she should have directed the memo just to him so he could have sent her ideas out under his signature. "[That] isn't the way we operated during the campaign," she said, clearly taken aback. His reply sent a chill through Obama World: "Welcome to the NFL."

Many disappointed applicants from the campaign didn't understand that most of the good jobs required particular experience or expertise. The exceptions were ambassadorships and membership on various prestigious boards and commissions. For those political spoils (a tradition Obama never promised to change) a Chicago lawyer named David Jacobson (soon joined by Donald Gips, director of presidential personnel) identified a small handful of standouts among the five hundred members of the campaign's National Finance Committee, sending the others into what sometimes became hysterics. When they submitted lists to the president-elect, he invariably scrawled in the margins "not diverse enough" or "better mix," the latter meaning that he wanted to see more noncontributors, Hillary supporters, or Republicans considered.*

Occasionally Obama would make a rookie mistake. He thought the consul-general to Bermuda, for instance, had to be a lawyer (confusing *consul* with *counsel*). But for the most part he was remarkably well-informed about the functioning of the U.S. government, especially for a man who, if one subtracted all the time he was out of town campaigning in 2006 (for other candidates), and in 2007 and 2008 for himself, had spent only one full year, 2005, in Washington, and for most of that time he was distracted by writing a book.

Obama was a big reader as well as writer and actually read most of the memos he received, which surprised newer aides who had grown accustomed in other jobs to sending their written work into the void. "Agency review" transition teams prepared three different documents: a book-length binder jammed with information for those who had been designated to run departments or agencies, a twenty-five-page version of the briefing book for senior staff, and a three-page memo about each agency that went directly to the president-elect. Before interviewing candidates for major positions Obama always read the three-page memo and often the twenty-five-page version as well.

In the interviews Obama's questions were open-ended. He wanted to know why the candidates cared about the issues they would handle and how they thought those issues fit in with the responsibilities of other agencies. The process favored contextual and subtle thinkers who would be more than mere advocates for their agency's narrow interests. He rarely asked for specific positions on contentious policy matters, though his questions often showed much deeper knowledge of their fields than the interviewees expected. He impressed even the also-rans as low-key and unpretentious, "the least puffed-up politician I ever met," as one disappointed candidate put it.

Decency, equanimity, intelligence, analytical rigor. An ability to inspire, set goals, and execute. Every organization absorbs the character it discerns in its leader, and Obama's nascent administration was no different. He hoped his appointees would look for the same qualities of leadership in the people they hired, and that those officials would in turn take on talented subordinates, and so on down the line. That was the idea, anyway.

---

* Jacobson and Gips got so tired of their thankless jobs that they accepted ambassadorships themselves, Jacobson to Canada and Gips to South Africa.

FIGURING OUT THE Cabinet was like working a jigsaw puzzle. Should Eric Holder be White House counsel or attorney general? Obama decided on the latter, and only partly because he liked the idea of appointing the first African American to be the nation's chief law enforcement officer. As a popular former deputy AG, Holder could be expected to restore morale in the battered department faster than other candidates. He had been tarred by his association with Bill Clinton's last-minute pardon of fugitive financier Marc Rich; it soured him on the Clintons and he broke with them in 2007 to support Obama even earlier than another of Obama's favorites, Arizona Governor Janet Napolitano, the other strong candidate for Justice. Napolitano, a former prosecutor whose crisp competence made her popular even with Arizona Republicans, would get the job of running the sprawling Department of Homeland Security and later made the short list for the Supreme Court.

Tom Daschle wanted to run all of health care policy. The former Senate majority leader remembered that First Lady Hillary Clinton had cut Donna Shalala, Clinton's secretary of health and human services, out of the action on her 1993–94 health care plan. So Daschle convinced Obama to let him wear two hats, as secretary of HHS but also as the White House czar on health care policy. No one had managed that since the early 1970s, when Henry Kissinger was national security advisor and secretary of state simultaneously, an arrangement that Kissinger himself later admitted was awkward. Daschle didn't realize it yet, but he was making himself a fat target.

Obama had hoped that Al Gore would serve as the climate change czar and drive the world toward a new agreement on greenhouse gases. But Gore was happier on the outside using his own brand (and new fortune, the product of some smart tech investments) to advance the cause. When Gore went to Chicago to meet with Obama and Biden on December 9, he came away extremely impressed. Perhaps it was a measure of his checkered relationship with Bill Clinton,* but Gore said afterward that the meeting with Obama went better substantively

---

* The Clinton-Gore relationship went sour during the Lewinsky scandal and grew worse at the 2000 Democratic Convention, where Gore, the nominee, was miffed by Clinton's trying to steal the show. He also believed that Hillary had snubbed Tipper as a friend. The relationship improved around the time of 9/11, and Gore stayed neutral in the 2008 primaries, in part because he depended on the largesse of Clinton Global Initiative donors for his own climate change activities. Gore was grateful to Clinton in August 2009, when Clinton traveled to North Korea to bring back two reporters who had been jailed while working for Gore's TV network. Upon Clinton's return the two men embraced at the airport.

than a similar one twelve years earlier when, as vice president-elect, he traveled to Little Rock to meet with President-elect Clinton. Obama signed off on Gore's protégé, Carol Browner, as climate change czarina. Browner came out of the old command-and-control world of top-down government regulation, but she became a convert to market-based solutions, including a cap-and-trade system. Rahm thought that Browner would work out as long as she understood that she worked for Obama, not Gore. "When Gore comes and chains himself to the White House Gate, it will be Carol's problem," he told colleagues.

With the economy reeling, secretary of commerce was a post worth having. Penny Pritzker, who helped run her family's multibillion-dollar conglomerate, was ambivalent about Obama's offer, which would mean leaving her corporate and civic obligations in Chicago. It turned out that Obama was ambivalent too. Pritzker's support had been critical to Obama since he first decided to run for the Senate, but there were appearance problems. While Axelrod liked Pritzker personally, he argued that it sent exactly the wrong signal for Obama to appoint his campaign finance chair to the Cabinet when he was trying to change the culture of Washington. Obama agreed and called Pritzker on November 20 to tell her that although the transition lawyers said her tangled business dealings wouldn't prevent her confirmation, the Senate hearings would be unpleasant and distracting. They agreed that the timing was wrong for her to take a Cabinet post. This was highly unusual for a president-elect or a president, most of whom leave the delivery of bad news to subordinates. Pritzker, who would continue to stay in close touch with Obama, saw the honesty as another example of his straightforward way of doing business and a sign of their friendship.*

Pritzker's absence from the Cabinet meant that there would be no one in Obama's government with big-time business experience. Pritzker and some of Obama's other friends from the corporate world thought this was a problem. Commerce would have been the natural place for a captain of industry, but the appointments there became almost a joke. After Pritzker, Bill Richardson got the call. When the New Mexico governor turned out to be deeply implicated in an investigation of the state bond business, he was cut loose without a second thought.

Later Harry Reid suggested Republican Senator Judd Gregg, who was eager to leave the Senate and take the job. Obama was intrigued by the idea of sending a splashy signal of bipartisanship. The appointment

---

* Similarly Obama delivered the word personally to Michael Froman that he would have to voluntarily give up his Citigroup bonus if he wanted to join the government. Froman did.

was announced, but Gregg backed out, claiming that he hadn't realized until then that he agreed with Obama on virtually nothing. (By the end of 2009 Gregg would become a leading obstructionist, cataloguing for Republican senators all the parliamentary tricks they could use to slow Obama's health care plan.) Obama finally settled on former Washington State governor Gary Locke, an Asian American who, he hoped, could help manage bilateral trade with China. There would be no one inside the councils of government who had ever run a publicly traded company.

Tom Vilsack, the former governor of Iowa and a major Hillary supporter, went in as the underdog for Agriculture to Kansas Governor Kathleen Sebelius, who had supported Obama early. Vilsack, who had been abandoned at birth and adopted out of a Roman Catholic orphanage, connected immediately with Obama, especially when they started talking about the 28 million Americans on food stamps. At one point Obama exclaimed, "Wow, you're passionate about this stuff!" In the end, after a detailed conversation about biofuels, he said simply, "Well, you got it." Obama told him that the top priority of his department should be that American children be well fed. Like so many other moves Obama had made, this was a strikingly different emphasis for the department: simple, even obvious, but significant. Since its founding in the Lincoln administration, the USDA had always been focused on serving (or pandering to) farmers. Now it was to have another central mission. Unfortunately for Vilsack, the USDA computers seemed to be from the Lincoln administration too. When he asked how many employees worked in the department, nobody knew; the place lacked the software to keep track.

After Colin Powell turned down secretary of education, the assumption was that Arne Duncan, the much-admired Chicago schools superintendent and Obama's longtime basketball buddy, would get the position. But Rahm wasn't yet convinced that Duncan was an ardent enough reformer (this impression would soon change), and Obama wanted to make sure that his judgment hadn't been clouded by friendship. Of the other hard-charging superintendents, Joel Klein of New York was too controversial and Michelle Rhee of Washington, D.C., too new in her job. So he considered Michael Bennet, the reformist Denver schools chief. Obama and Bennet hit it off in the interview, but because Obama intended to choose another Coloradan, Senator Ken Salazar, as interior secretary, he decided he couldn't take Bennet too.* It was

---

* Bennet was later appointed to the Senate seat that Salazar vacated, and Obama supported him in the 2010 Democratic primary.

a new day for reformers in the Democratic Party, long hidebound on education. George Miller, the leading voice on education in the House, advised the president-elect that the most important thing was that the new education secretary be a "disrupter" instead of an "incrementalist."

Bill Gates, who spent much of his time on education projects after leaving Microsoft, called to tell him the same. Gates and Obama found they were in near-complete agreement on accountability issues. The president-elect strongly believed that disruptive reform of the status quo was required, which meant overcoming the teachers unions that blocked charter schools, merit pay, and the firing of poorly perform- ing teachers. But the unions were still enormously powerful inside the party, so some finesse was required. It took Obama a while to figure out that his good friend Arne was as well respected nationally as he was in Chicago. Duncan, who as a kid had managed to win acceptance as the only white guy allowed to play basketball with South Side street gangs, was perfect. He was a bomb-thrower who was so diplomatic that he didn't seem to be throwing a bomb. He got the job.

————

EARLY ON OBAMA started playfully referring to his economic team as "the propeller heads." Peter Orszag even distributed colorful little bean- ies with plastic propellers on top. In truth Obama's preference in per- sonnel wasn't for number-crunching nerds but for what might be called policy mandarins, savvy pragmatists with government experience and big brains.* He favored broad-gauged, integrative thinkers who could both absorb huge loads of complex material and apply it practically and lucidly without resorting to off-putting jargon.

Some were foreign policy types, some economists, some health care specialists. Almost all had advanced degrees from Ivy League schools, proof that they had aced standardized tests and knew the shortcuts to success exploited by American elites. A few were bombastic, but most had learned to cover their faith in their own powers of analysis with a thin veneer of humility; it made their arguments more effective. But their faith in the power of analysis remained unshaken. Obama believed, as Ron Klain, Biden's chief of staff, put it, that knotty public policy questions "had right answers and wrong answers and that if you put enough smart people on the problem, you could usually get to the right answer."

Having so many extraordinarily smart men and women around cer-

————

* From the seventh century to the twentieth, Chinese mandarins were scholar-officials who held important bureaucratic posts based on scoring well on difficult imperial examinations.

tainly beat the alternative: the Bush White House, with its legions of second-raters.* And yet the potential for hubris would always be there. The incoming members of the Obama administration bore at least some resemblance to their predecessors in the Kennedy and Johnson administrations, the ones author David Halberstam ironically dubbed "the best and the brightest" for their folly in embroiling the United States in the Vietnam War. Those mostly WASP Ivy Leaguers were among the early policy mandarins, known in the 1960s as "action intellectuals." Their successors in government four decades later came from more varied ethnic backgrounds but shared the Ivy League as well as a certain arrogance and a detachment from the everyday lives of most Americans. Over time, many in OMB, NEC, and other parts of the White House often proved better at killing ideas for putting people back to work than at creating them.

Having faith in these intellectuals didn't mean Obama bore any animus toward business leaders; he was close to Pritzker and to Robert Wolf of UBS, and he had friendly enough relationships with another dozen or so, including Warren Buffett, Jeff Immelt of GE, Eric Schmidt of Google, and Howard Shultz of Starbucks. He relied on Valerie Jarrett to keep him in touch with corporate America. But next to the highly credentialed policy mandarins favored by the president, business executives did not command his special respect. Obama didn't believe he needed them close by, and fewer of them served in his White House than at any time in recent decades. The word *entrepreneurship* was used only once in his big Georgetown speech on the economy in April 2009 and rarely thereafter. When job creation finally became Topic A, the absence of more business owners in his circle became a handicap. Axelrod's consulting firm, Jarrett's time as CEO of a real estate company, and Summers's experience running Harvard didn't help much.

Obama was conflicted about Wall Street and conventional definitions of worldly achievement. His own career was built on faith in a different path. In his early 20s he had an unhappy experience working for a corporate advisory firm in New York before becoming a community organizer. He picked Joe Biden (and Rahm Emanuel, for that matter) in part because they had a closer connection to middle-class people than some others he could have chosen. The late House speaker Sam Rayburn had famously said that he would trust the men surrounding JFK more if just one had "run for sheriff." Obama got the point.

But that was a conscious approach connected to only one part of his

* In his book *Speech-less* former Bush speechwriter Matt Lattimer writes that large numbers of Bush aides were selected for their ideology, not their intelligence.

personal experience. The parts of his life he didn't write about much in his books—Punahou, Columbia, and Harvard—also left their mark. Because he didn't flaunt these elite associations and celebrate them in print (it was politically unwise to do so, even in private) their effect on his thinking may have been less conscious. But it's safe to say that at some level Obama bought into the idea that top-drawer professionals had gone through a fair sorting process, the same process that had propelled him and Michelle to the Ivy League, and were therefore in some way deserving of their elevated status. Eventually a full quarter of Obama appointees would have some connection (as alumni or faculty) to Harvard, just one of several elite universities represented en masse in the government. More than 90 percent of early appointees had advanced degrees, and only one (whose identity was never released) lacked at least a college degree. "This is the only place I've ever worked in my life where I'm aware of the inadequacies of my own degree," Ron Klain said later, only half-joking. "I went to Georgetown and then Harvard Law School as opposed to Harvard and then Harvard Law."

It was a short step from faith in the Ivy League to faith in any of the other glittering institutions that signified great achievement for a certain class of ambitious Americans. For Obama huge personal wealth was not a necessary ingredient for prestige; over and over in his career, often to Michelle's chagrin, he had turned down chances to make more money. Obama's faith lay in cream rising to the top. Because he himself was a product of the great American postwar meritocracy, he could never fully escape seeing the world from the status ladder he had ascended. He surrounded himself with the best credentialed, most brilliant policy mandarins he could find, even if almost none of them knew anything about what it was like to work in small business, manufacturing, real estate, or other parts of the real economy.

Obama's own success in the meritocracy had its psychological benefits. He bore no traces of the status anxieties that afflicted Lyndon Johnson, Richard Nixon, or even George W. Bush. Obama's thin shoulders carried no discernible chips. He usually resisted any temptation to prove he was the smartest guy in the room, a crippling shortcoming for other politicians. But assessing people, consciously or unconsciously, by whether they had met certain markers of intelligence and success shaped his personnel choices.

The quintessential policy mandarin may have been Orszag— Princeton summa, Marshall Scholar, PhD from the London School of Economics—whose complicated personal life in 2009 would keep Washington simultaneously entertained and confused over where he got the time for so many extracurricular activities.* Orszag filled the Office of Management and Budget with a new breed of "behavioral economists" trained to argue that, contrary to conventional economic models, human beings don't always do what's in their rational self-interest. These thinkers believed that with the proper government rules and incentives, society could be dramatically improved.† To supervise all government regulation Obama hired his Chicago friend Cass Sunstein, a wide-ranging and frighteningly prolific law professor who cowrote a book titled *Nudge* that popularized behavioral economics.‡ OMB's health care maven was the noted oncologist and bioethicist Ezekiel Emanuel, who might well have won the post even if his brother were not the incoming White House chief of staff. Even the OMB spokesman, Ken Baer, had a PhD from Oxford. The policy mandarins were everywhere.

————

THE EARLY TRANSITION seemed to be a success. Obama knew what he wanted and made decisions crisply. Podesta possessed an encyclopedic knowledge of policy and politics and was extraordinarily well organized. It didn't hurt that the Bush administration, from the president and outgoing chief of staff Josh Bolton on down, proved enormously cooperative. This was especially true on national security, where the Obama team learned early on that the later Bush policies were quite different from the immediate post-9/11 period. (Waterboarding, for instance, had ended in 2005, and Bush was on record supporting the closure of Guantánamo Bay.) On December 1 Obama met with his national security team and reported afterward to the global media gathered in Chicago that the challenges they discussed—two wars, the threat of nuclear weapons, American dependence on foreign oil—were "just as grave" as the economic crisis.

As he presented himself to the world, Obama indulged a bad old habit of manufacturing trappings. To make himself seem more presidential, his staff arranged for a contrived if official-looking seal reading "The Office of the President-elect" to be hung on the podium before

---

* The divorced father of two, Orszag faced news reports that his former girlfriend gave birth to their daughter not long before he announced his engagement to a TV reporter.

† The classic example is requiring workers to opt out of 401k savings plans or be automatically enrolled, thereby sharply boosting national savings and investment.

‡ Sunstein and Orszag were both behavioral economists, but they differed on whether government should force changes in behavior (Orszag) or merely encourage it voluntarily (Sunstein). The debate applied most immediately to whether government guidelines that identified effective medical treatments should be mandatory.

him, though no such office formally existed. The eight American flags surrounding him helped only a little.

Faced with questions about what would happen if his team clashed, Obama had a ready answer. They wouldn't have joined his administration if they didn't all "share a core vision," he said. Part of that vision was a clear understanding that there would be no freelancing: "I'm a strong believer in strong personalities and strong opinions. I did not ask for assurances that they agreed with me at all times." But "differences in tactics" (the only differences he seemed to anticipate) were manageable as long as there was no confusion about the lines of authority: "I will be setting policy in the White House. As Harry Truman said, the buck stops with me." There would be times in the months ahead when Obama would have to remind certain officials of the point.

Harrison Wellford, who had worked on several Democratic transitions, called Obama's team "the most mature, moderate, sensible I've ever seen." Early on, before the vetting headaches, it looked as though many of the personnel picks were a cut above the norm, people of accomplishment who didn't depend on Obama for their professional identity. One such person of accomplishment stood above the rest. Her inclusion in the Obama Cabinet at the end of 2008 said more about the new president than practically anything he had done all year.

5

Picking Hillary

All Obama's Cabinet picks were important; it mattered who was at the helm of every department driving change. But only one choice grabbed the attention of the public: Hillary Clinton.

The idea of choosing Clinton for secretary of state was first raised by John Podesta in small meetings over the summer. Obama had already been thinking about it. Few remembered that when he was elected to the Senate in 2005 he gravitated to Clinton. She was the one who best understood how to arrive as a celebrity and still be effective with colleagues. When Obama said publicly in 2007 that they began the race as friends, he was being sincere. He found Bill Clinton exasperating but Hillary formidable, even when she was delivering low blows.

His staff took a dimmer view of her. A senior aide in the communications office once half facetiously described Clinton as "the enemy of all that is good for America." Obama true believers weren't so ready to forgive her for the pandering, petty distortions and mock outrage ("Shame on you, Barack Obama!") of the 2008 campaign. They were still steamed that she had dragged out the campaign after Obama's eleven straight primary and caucus wins in February 2008, wins that, had they been Clinton's, would have almost certainly led her supporters to demand that Obama withdraw from the race in the name of party unity. Their man was more chivalrous, they thought, but when he took the stage in St. Paul on the night in June when he clinched the nomination and said a few nice words about his vanquished opponent, they assumed he was simply mouthing platitudes. They should have listened more closely. "I'm a better candidate for having had the honor of competing against Hillary Rodham Clinton," he said, and he meant it.

Obama knew she was smart and disciplined, but her toughness and fortitude were what most impressed him. The selection, he said later, "was not a light-bulb moment," but it dawned on him that her stature abroad meant she could carry his message faster and farther than anyone else. He simply was not going to have time to travel to as many places and meet as many foreign leaders as he would like. Clinton was not just formidable; she was an international superstar who could advance American interests overnight. Then there was the "team of rivals" concept that Obama borrowed from Doris Kearns Goodwin's book about Abraham Lincoln and his Cabinet. The frontrunner for the 1860 Republican nomination was William Seward, a senator from New York who derided Lincoln's lack of experience. He became Lincoln's secretary of state and soon his biggest defender.

The politics of picking Clinton were shrewd. It would unify the party after a divisive year, signaling the end of hostilities not just to the Clinton partisans but to Obama's own supporters. If he accepted Clinton, they couldn't very well reject her and the other Clinton-era veterans' coming aboard. An added benefit, which Obama's people refused to acknowledge at the time, was that picking Clinton would get her out of the Senate. Had she stayed, the press would have asked her about every Obama initiative; the continuing story line would be about whether she had veto power over health care and other parts of his program. Without any allegiance to the president beyond the ties of party she would have been generally supportive but probably willing to speak her mind often enough to throw Obama off his game. A repeat in 2012 of Ted Kennedy's mutiny against Jimmy Carter in 1980 was not likely, but not impossible either. The tension in the Obama-Clinton relationship might well have resurfaced, to the detriment of both. The old LBJ line got a workout: Better to have your rivals inside the tent pissing out than outside the tent pissing in.

For weeks before the election, Obama's talk of choosing Clinton rankled the campaign senior staff. Plouffe, Gibbs, Jarrett, and Jim Messina (a Capitol Hill operative who had joined the campaign in a senior role) essentially asked, How can you do that? Axelrod struck the others as quietly against, but he played it down the middle by stressing only his qualms about the role Bill Clinton would play. Rouse saw some logic in the idea, and as she listened to Obama, Jarrett came around.

At a meeting on October 31 the high command aired Clinton's shortcomings. Finally Obama broke in and said forcefully, "You guys are missing the fundamental point—she's the most qualified candidate."

As the discussion over Clinton progressed in November Obama said certain conditions would have to be met if she were to become secretary of state. First, he was concerned about Bill Clinton freelance globetrotting as a "secondary" secretary of state. Hillary and Bill would have to come to an understanding on that. Second, they would need an agreement that all contributions to the Clinton Global Initiative (for which Bill raised billions for cutting-edge global projects) would be disclosed and that the former president would scratch plans for overseas affiliates. Finally, Obama said, "[Hillary has] some anger issues with me that she's going to have to work out." When a Clinton administration veteran suggested that things were better and she was over the bitterness of the campaign, Obama smiled and said, "Believe me, she's not. It may be better, but believe me, she's not over it."

Obama's team came to understand that Barack and Hillary were like two prizefighters who had developed grudging respect after a fifteen-round title bout. Obama himself naturally preferred the Magic Johnson and Larry Bird analogy, with Magic and the Los Angeles Lakers taking two out of three NBA finals from Bird's Boston Celtics. He respected Hillary as a talented and disciplined competitor and never worried about her loyalty. "He always understood the upside," Podesta said.

———

THE UPSIDE OF Bill Clinton was a little harder for Obama to see. Since the summer Rahm Emanuel had been urging Obama to spend more time talking to the former president. The club of men who held the office was tiny, Rahm reminded him, and he had a lot to learn from Bill Clinton. Obama resisted. The history was still too raw.

The bad blood began in 2006, when Obama had the temerity to plan a challenge to Hillary's coronation. It got worse in 2007, when Bill received some poor advice; he made the mistake of believing his close friend and biggest fund-raiser, Terry McAuliffe, who told him practically every day that the race was over. McAuliffe sincerely thought that Obama was finished, but he also thought that the Democratic Party could be intimidated into believing that it was no contest. By several accounts this overconfidence had a deep effect on the psyche of the former president, who came to believe that he would finally be able to repay his debt to Hillary, whom he had so publicly humiliated in the 1990s.

The old Bill Clinton would have been a master at making his new dream come true. But at 62 he was politically rusty, like a veteran Hollywood studio executive who had lost his fingertips for the box office. When Hillary publicly shed tears in New Hampshire describing the stress on her, Bill told her that crying was a mistake and would turn off male voters. He was wrong.

The former president had a complex relationship with Ted Kennedy. He knew that Kennedy's best friend in the Senate was Chris Dodd and that the Massachusetts senator wouldn't endorse Hillary until Dodd dropped out. But he kept calling Kennedy anyway. Kennedy was a terrific mimic and even though Clinton's Arkansas twang was a long way from his Boston accent, he had it down. "I love you, Ted," Kennedy would say merrily, imitating Clinton's transparent efforts to ingratiate himself with him.

Over the first three weeks of 2008 Bill Clinton and Kennedy had several tense telephone conversations, each a little worse than the one before. The day after the Iowa caucuses, with Dodd and Joe Biden dropping out, Clinton phoned Kennedy to close the deal for his endorsement of Hillary. This was a sign of how out of touch he had become. Kennedy was indeed on the verge of breaking his neutrality—to endorse Obama. As Kennedy lavishly praised Obama's Iowa victory speech the night before, an angry Bill Clinton interjected, "Gimme a break!" He was enraged at Obama's nerve—that he thought he could just drop his bags off at the Senate and run for president. All his self-pity and entitlement came pouring out in a torrent of abuse. The guy had done nothing! "Nothing!" Clinton said. It was in this context that he made a comment about how Obama "used to get us coffee," which may not have been racial but struck Kennedy as arrogant and belittling.

Soon race entered their arguments more explicitly. The week before the January 19 Nevada caucuses they spoke twice more, and the second conversation nearly became a shouting match. Kennedy bluntly told Bill that he was at least partly to blame for race becoming an issue in the campaign. He was upset over separate comments by Hillary's New Hampshire campaign chairman and the founder of Black Entertainment Television that dredged up Obama's youthful drug use. "I've seen this [code] language before. I know what it means," Kennedy told the former president. "Too much blood has been shed [in the civil rights movement] to go back to all that."

Bill Clinton replied heatedly that it was the Obama campaign that was introducing race, by accusing him and Hillary of doing so. He was furious that David Axelrod had made what the Clintons interpreted as a causal link between Hillary's support for the Iraq War and the assassination of former prime minister Benazir Bhutto of Pakistan. Apparently forgetting who he was talking to, Bill tried to feed Kennedy his line that Hillary had not favored the Iraq War in 2003; she merely voted to grant the president the authority. Kennedy, who had led the antiwar forces in the Senate at the time, didn't appreciate the snow job. "Everyone knew it was a vote for war," he told the former president.

Kennedy and his niece Caroline had decided that Obama, not Hillary, was the true heir to the Kennedy legacy. On Sunday, January 27, the day after Obama's big victory in South Carolina, Caroline Kennedy published an eloquent op-ed piece in the *New York Times* saying that Obama reminded her of her father. Axelrod later said that a widely aired Obama TV ad featuring Caroline reached enough middle-aged women voters to help get Obama through Super Tuesday.

That Sunday morning Ted Kennedy phoned both Clintons to inform them that he too would be endorsing Obama.* Bill, who had already heard the news, called back first. As he began to outline his decision Kennedy heard nothing at the other end of the phone. "Mr. President, are you there?" Kennedy asked. "Okay, thank you, good-bye," Bill said sullenly and hung up. Moments later he called back and said, "I want to know why." Kennedy explained that it wasn't about Hillary, but about a new chapter in history, a unique time and a unique individual suited to the times. Kennedy could hear Bill's pen scratching down everything he said. After that conversation Kennedy predicted, accurately, that the former president would tell people privately that Kennedy had chosen race over gender and endorsed Obama mostly because he was black.

Bill Clinton knew that other Democrats were upset with him too. Word got back to the Obama and Clinton camps in February that Rahm Emanuel had phoned the former president and told him to "stop acting like the fucking hack-in-chief." Rahm was the only one other than Hillary who dared talk to Bill Clinton that way, which was one reason Bill liked him so much.

By this time Bill's relations with Hillary's campaign had deteriorated. Bruce Lindsey, Clinton's longtime aide, received a plaintive call from the Hillary forces on the front lines. The message was clear: *You've got to calm him down. This is really hurting us.* Bill went quiet for the rest of the primaries, but by then the damage was done. He campaigned hard for Hillary but talked to no reporters. The former president had been muzzled, though Obama was convinced he was still spreading rumors about him. When the liberal talk show host Ed Schultz asked him off the air who was stirring up opposition in the Jewish community, Obama replied, "It's the fucking Clintons."

It's not clear which rumors Obama was tracking back to the Clintons. They didn't have to do much to get their Jewish supporters riled up about Obama, whom some mistrusted for no other reason than his middle name. Feelings ran especially high in California, where Clinton fund-raisers told undecided Jewish donors that Obama was "unreliable" on Israel, whatever that meant.

Bill's bitterness remained after Obama finally wrapped up the nomination in June. He was offended that "the Chosen One," as he had taken to calling Obama, visited John Edwards in North Carolina and

---

* This was a courtesy that Bill Richardson did not extend, which led Clinton and James Carville to start calling Richardson "Judas."

visited Hillary twice, but he never made the trip to Chappaqua to pay his respects. Obama and Bill didn't have a proper one-on-one meeting until September 11, when they had lunch alone at Bill's Harlem office: "my first conversation with him in my entire life," Bill called it.

Four days before the election Bill and Obama campaigned together at a midnight rally of thirty-five thousand in Kissimmee, Florida. Bill focused not on Obama the Man but on Obama the Executive, who had proven himself with a brilliant campaign. The former president's way with words escaped him. "He can be the chief executor of good intentions as president," Bill Clinton told the crowd.

————

AS USUAL, BARACK Obama was looking ahead. To him, the past wasn't a source of grievance but merely raw material for future books he hadn't yet had time to contemplate. For now he needed the best secretary of state he could find.

Once he made up his mind Obama courted Hillary intensely. They talked by phone before and after the election on a variety of subjects. Without saying why, Obama asked her to come to his transition office in Chicago on November 13.

Philippe Reines, Hillary's press secretary, kept telling his boss that Obama wanted her for secretary of state. "Philippe, that is ridiculous! It is *absurd*. Not going to happen," she responded. When she arrived for their one-on-one at the Kluczynski Federal Building in downtown Chicago, Obama offered her the job. He laid it on thick, insisting that she was the only one who could restore American prestige abroad, that she had to do this for her country. Clinton was stunned. Her first reaction was to say she didn't think she was interested. She immediately began talking about other candidates (including former UN ambassador Richard Holbrooke). But she didn't close the door.

Although the trip was supposed to be secret, the Obama team made only perfunctory efforts to keep it that way. The meeting wasn't held at a secret location, and Clinton flew commercial. Obama's press pool saw Clinton's Secret Service detail enter the underground garage, and lower-level transition personnel saw Huma Abedin, one of Clinton's closest aides, on the premises.

Clinton was flattered but leaned strongly against accepting. After the meeting she described Obama's sincerity in making the case to her. In the words of one of her friends, she compared the session with him to "having her arms, legs, fingers, and toes twisted in a nice way." That day she gave Bill, her staff, and her friends all the arguments against accepting: that she would lose her autonomy, that she loved the Senate, that she would not be a player in health care reform. Three of her close friends were sure that she would have turned down the job if the offer had stayed secret.

Sensing this, the Obama team leaked the story that "a contingent offer" had been made. By the time she landed back at LaGuardia, the wires were reporting it. The Clinton forces considered the leak inspired, at least from the Obama perspective. If she said no, she would look like she wasn't helping her country in a time of crisis. News of the offer also generated pressure from many of her supporters to take the job. After their anger that she had not been offered the vice presidency, they were relieved that Obama had offered such a plum and made it clear that they would feel better about him if he had her on board.

Over the next week Clinton wavered. She phoned Obama at night and told him no; her latest reason was that as secretary of state she couldn't retire her $10 million campaign debt. Obama talked her through that. The technicalities of campaign finance law made it difficult to pay off, but he pledged his help. He was determined to take away every excuse she offered. She was still leaning against and had even prepared a statement explaining that she was staying in the Senate. Her staff was divided along gender lines. Reines and her foreign policy advisor, Andrew Shapiro, were in favor; old friends and aides Cheryl Mills, Capricia Marshall, and Maggie Williams were against.

Clinton's diminished power in the Senate was a big factor in helping her make up her mind. She called Harry Reid and pushed for an enhanced role in health care in the new Congress; Reid reminded her that there were several senators ahead of her in seniority. Her real beef was with Ted Kennedy, with whom she had tangled in 2002 over the No Child Left Behind education bill. She was a member of his Committee on Health, Education, Labor and Pensions and wanted a subcommittee to chair with jurisdiction over some part of health care. Kennedy had turned her down cold, which raised eyebrows even with his own staff considering her long commitment and expertise. Clinton was always wonderfully attentive when someone she knew got sick, but Kennedy's cancer didn't prevent her from complaining to friends about what he was doing to her. Hadn't he already inflicted enough damage when he endorsed Obama? She no longer knew what Kennedy really thought of her and realized that she probably never would.

Getting snubbed in the Senate on health care after the election was a bitter coda to a Senate career that Clinton otherwise considered one of the happiest periods of her life. She cared about reforming health care more than she cared about North Korea or Syria, and now she would be a mere spectator in the push for reform. Friends later detected in her a note of schadenfreude when Obama's health care policy hit early speed bumps. She was happy enough, and immersed in her new job, but disappointed that history would likely be made without her.

Bill Clinton didn't push his wife. It was her turn and her call. But he ultimately wanted her to take the job, and not just because he thought it her due and agreed with Obama that she would be outstanding, one of the great secretaries of state. The former president's philanthropic efforts in recent years had been largely international and dependent on his unparalleled list of global contacts. Out of office, his only remaining authority was what he called "convening power." But his Rolodex was aging; his old high-level friends at home and abroad—people like Bob Rubin, Tony Blair, and Nelson Mandela—had long since moved offstage. The truth was that he no longer knew many world leaders, only "formers." Although complying with Obama's strict disclosure guidelines would hurt him with his donors in the short term (which he was sensitive to), he was confident that the new relationships Hillary would establish as secretary of state could keep what would someday be known as the William Jefferson Clinton and Hillary Rodham Clinton Foundation vital for another fifteen years or more. "With this move, he figured their good work could continue," as one Arkansas associate put it.

Even so, the former president was having a hard time letting go of his hurt. The man who liked to say that he needed to forgive his enemies because he himself had so much need for forgiveness was no longer taking his own advice to heart. He could forgive Bob Dole and Newt Gingrich a lot faster than he could forgive Bill Richardson and Jim Clyburn, the African American congressman from South Carolina who suggested he was introducing race into the campaign. Well after the election it still didn't take much to set him off on a tear about how the Obama folks played dirty pool in the primaries, how Obama didn't work hard enough, how Obama still thought he was the Messiah. A Democratic senator who overheard some of this was flabbergasted by the level of immaturity in Bill's rants. It was reminiscent of the Lewinsky scandal, when a brilliant man stopped using his brain in favor of another organ, only this time he was thinking with his spleen.

———

THE FIRST PUBLIC sign that the Hillary Clinton deal was done was the appointment of Greg Craig as White House counsel. The Clintons still considered him a traitor from the campaign, when he was quoted by name in *Newsweek* saying that if Hillary couldn't control Bill during the campaign, she wouldn't be able to control him in the White House. He later cowrote a pointed op-ed alleging that Hillary's years as first lady didn't constitute true foreign policy experience. Had he been granted his wish for a national security position, most likely as NSC advisor or deputy secretary of state, it would have meant that Hillary was not taking the job. But the counsel's office was distant enough from foreign policy to cause no worries. Or so it seemed at the time.

Other national security appointments also seemed tailored to Hillary. Retired (and retiring) Marine Corps General Jim Jones, recipient of the Silver Star and onetime supreme allied commander, would get the NSC job. The taciturn Jones was no Henry Kissinger or Zbigniew Brzezinski, and he was at a stage of his life where he no longer felt the need to impress people with the hours he put in at the office. But he offered an impressive strategic overview (especially on the role of energy in geopolitics), and as the only senior aide to come out of the military he gave Obama an important window on that culture. Hillary could work with him, and even better with Jones's deputy, Tom Donilon, a veteran of the Clinton State Department, whom many considered to be the de facto NSC advisor. Military officers understood Jones's delegating to Donilon as nothing out of the ordinary, just a general letting his colonel do the hard work.

Hillary would continue to have a good relationship with Leon Panetta, President Clinton's former chief of staff, who was slated to run the CIA, and with Dennis Blair, the director of national intelligence. John Brennan had the inside track for CIA, but when his name leaked (which made Obama furious) liberals claimed he was implicated in the Bush interrogation policies and he was switched to homeland security advisor, which did not require Senate confirmation. Susan Rice, Obama's top campaign advisor on foreign policy, had been squeezed out in the early maneuvering for NSC advisor, which prompted a polite protest from blacks and women on the transition team. After agreeing to move to New York as UN ambassador, she was soothed by a call from Obama and had no problem with Hillary, who promised to keep her in the loop, and would.

Hillary tried to get a pledge that the White House would let her name all her own deputies at the State Department. Obama agreed (the source of many staff squabbles to come), but gave himself some wiggle room. He wanted one of his own people to help him at Foggy Bottom, Jim Steinberg, who had advised Democrats on foreign policy going back to Michael Dukakis's 1988 campaign and had accompanied Obama to Berlin over the summer. Steinberg got a helpful push from Podesta and won the number-two job at State. Hillary made it clear that she wanted a role for Richard Holbrooke. With Holbrooke designated as a "special representative" for Afghanistan and Pakistan, former senator George Mitchell for the Middle East, former ambassador Stephen Bosworth for North Korea, attorney Todd Stern for climate change, and Retired General Scott Gration for Sudan, the most critical areas seemed to be covered—more evidence of the "all hands on deck" philosophy.*

John Kerry was granted a Chicago interview with Obama, but it was mostly for the president-elect to tell him he favored Hillary. (Bill Richardson's interview was even more of a formality.) Ted Kennedy and some others called Obama to recommend Kerry, but in the end there was no one inside the Obama camp arguing for him. After all he'd done for Obama in 2004 (offering him the historic convention keynote address) and 2008 (his early endorsement was announced just after Obama's loss in New Hampshire, softening the blow at a critical time), an angry Kerry was sure that he deserved better treatment, more of a chance to make his case before the deed was done. Hillary Clinton had no experience in foreign policy! The choice, he thought, was bizarre.

More like brilliant. By choosing Hillary, Obama could benefit from her intelligence and celebrity and bionic ability to master the briefing books without much worry of being undercut, for she would have no leverage over the president. Any threat to quit would have to be backed up by a willingness to go into early retirement, a fate she was not ready to contemplate. In the meantime she would approach the complexities of foreign policy with her trademark energy and tenacity, and that could only be good for the country. She would likely stay as secretary of state for five or six years, and after that, who knew? She would be 69 in 2016, three years younger than John McCain in 2008, and she seemed to look better with age. When asked in interviews whether she ever thought that far ahead, she always said no, but not many people believed her.

---

* Not everyone was brought on deck. Anthony Lake, President Clinton's first national security advisor, had been for Obama early. Though he said he didn't want to go back into government, he watched in amazement as his old rival Holbrooke, a strong Hillary supporter, got a plum. Lake was only one of several early Obama supporters in the foreign policy and national security arena who saw Clinton supporters get jobs they might have wanted.

6

Instant President

It didn't take long for Obama to realize he had inherited a nightmare—much worse than even the most partisan Democrats charged in 2008. He would need to act boldly not just for his own political reasons but to keep the country from being swamped by its problems.

Events were moving too swiftly for the public to absorb the enormity of Obama's early moves. Never before in American history did a president-elect make so many presidential-level decisions before being sworn in. Obama signed off on the largest public investment since World War II and lobbied a huge bank rescue bill through Congress while he was still technically a private citizen. (He had resigned from the Senate shortly after the election.) If, in John F. Kennedy's words, "to govern is to choose," then Obama was governing right away.

And he did it with a decisiveness that impressed Hillary Clinton, Joe Biden, and just about everyone else who came into contact with him. After one conference call in early December the vice president–elect and two-time presidential candidate leaned across his desk in Wilmington, Delaware, and admitted to his aide Ron Klain, "We got this ticket in the right order."

Obama kept stressing, "We only have one president at a time." (Barney Frank quipped, "This overstates the number of presidents we have.") The line sounded good, but it wasn't accurate. During the 1932–33 transition, as the banks collapsed and the nation slid deeper into the Great Depression, Franklin Roosevelt said something similar. But his strategy was to spurn efforts to cooperate with Hoover and enter stage left on Inauguration Day. Obama consciously chose a different course, at least on the banks. While he didn't presume to compare himself to FDR or the 2008 recession to the Great Depression, he was clear in his own mind where Roosevelt had gone wrong. "I explicitly rejected FDR's strategy of not taking any ownership of what needed to be done during the transition and I think that was the right decision," he said later. "If we had played games—if, for example, I had refused to weigh in on TARP, which we knew was politically radioactive, prior to my being sworn in—we would not have hit the ground running. And I think the situation could have spiraled out of control much more severely."

The problems, David Axelrod said, were simply too serious to settle for bashing Bush and hoping for the best.

OBAMA COULD NOT yet sign bills, issue executive orders, or sleep in the White House, but he was otherwise already discharging many of the functions of office: announcing personnel, receiving daily briefings on national security and the economy, negotiating with Congress, and holding as many as five press conferences a week.

Even many Democrats charged that he erred by letting Congress draw up the huge stimulus package, but there was little choice given the urgency Obama had created. The president-elect didn't have enough staff in place to do more than indicate policy preferences and dollar ranges on the fly. Besides, he knew something about the vanity of legislators. If a bill didn't seem to be coming from them they would slow everything down and pick it to death. By letting Congress take the lead, he gave lawmakers the ownership necessary for genuine action. One of the oldest adages in civics is that people support what they help create. Had Obama not applied that idea to the stimulus and health care, he would have had much less to show for 2009.

But Obama took this logic too far. The irony was that an enormously self-confident president may have underestimated his own clout. Throughout both the stimulus and health care debates, even many turf-conscious member of Congress would have welcomed a little more guidance from the White House. Obama showed a few cards early, but he liked to stay flexible on his bottom line until the House and Senate were resolving their differences at the end of the process. This made strategic sense but infuriated people all year long.

At least he was focused on the mechanics of getting stuff done. For decades Democratic presidents had made the same foolish mistake—downgrading the White House Office of Legislative Affairs.* That would change now. Obama and Rahm Emanuel knew the history and made a point of hiring top-flight former congressional staff—Phil Schiliro (Henry Waxman), Jim Messina (Max Baucus), Pete Rouse (Tom Daschle), Ron Klain (Joe Biden), Melody Barnes (Ted Kennedy), Rob

---

* Jimmy Carter's new administration stupidly stiffed House Speaker Tip O'Neill when he wanted some Inauguration tickets. Bill Clinton's first liaison with the Hill was a former lobbyist.

Nabors (David Obey), among others—to coordinate with longtime colleagues and former bosses under the direction of a tireless chief of staff who still had great relationships with many of his old House colleagues. It was back to the world of Lyndon Johnson, who told his staff that whatever job they held, everyone in the White House—from the typing pool secretary with a brother on the Hill to the president himself—worked in congressional relations.

At an all-day transition meeting Rahm explained the game plan: to connect quick early successes to long-term victories. Every effort had to relate to three connected goals: (1) use victories to add to existing strengths, while avoiding distractions; (2) stimulate the economy while making progress on long-term initiatives in health, energy, and education; and (3) bring real, not cosmetic, change to the way Washington does business.

The "No Distractions" theme would be critical to shaping 2009. It meant that divisive issues requiring the approval of Congress, like comprehensive immigration reform, the Employee Free Choice Act (a priority of organized labor, better known as "card check," that would make it easier for unions to organize), and repealing the ban on gays in the military would all be set aside temporarily while Democrats focused on Obama's first-tier agenda. Those priorities that made the cut for 2009 would be advanced relentlessly. Instead of hoarding their political capital, Rahm said, they would leverage the capital earned on early wins to build more for the tougher struggles down the road. Unlike some politicians, he didn't borrow such lingo from the business world just to add a corporate patina to the meeting. The concept of leveraging capital was central to the president's mission, he said.

Obama himself was jaundiced about how much political capital he had. He thought it was already being spent down, starting with his commitment before the election to lobby Congress to free up the second tranche of TARP. "At that point everyone knew [backing another $350 billion for TARP] was political suicide," Obama said later. That and the prospect of further unpopular bailouts made it obvious "pretty quickly that this was going to be a rocky year."

The only option, he thought, was to power through with their issues. They might disagree on the size of the programs (e.g. major health care reform versus one-bite-at-a-time) but no one counseled caution on the domestic policy front. The plan was for "action and action now," as FDR put it in his first inaugural. Rahm, in overdrive, assigned one of his deputies, Mona Sutphen, to troll the government for dozens of possible new laws and executive orders. Then the team worked out a schedule for the first thirty days.

The plan for a rapid series of bill signings and executive orders worked; the ambitious personnel goals fell short. Obama was supposed to sign nomination papers for his thirty-four top appointees on Inauguration Day and all thirty-four were to be confirmed by the Senate the next day. That proved to be wishful thinking. Only a handful were approved right away.

———

ONE OF RAHM'S early priorities was to get Valerie Jarrett appointed to fill Obama's Senate seat. He wanted her out of the White House, where he worried that her long and close relationship with the Obamas would threaten his authority. Dick Durbin, who was close to the Obama circle, thought Jarrett would make a fine senator from Illinois. Who could object to Valerie's being the president-elect's replacement? Well, four people, actually: the Obamas (especially Michelle), who made it clear they needed her at the White House; Jarrett herself, who was briefly intrigued by the idea of a Senate seat but ultimately angry at Rahm for throwing her name into a messy situation where she was identified as "Senate Candidate B" on federal wiretaps; and Governor Rod Blagojevich, who quickly found out that the only thing Rahm would offer in exchange for his appointing Jarrett to the Senate was the administration's "appreciation."

In 2002 Rahm had won the congressional seat vacated by Blagojevich when he ran for governor. The two worked closely in 2004 to push for the reimportation of less expensive pharmaceuticals from Canada, a winning issue for Democrats. Rahm, Obama, Durbin, and other prominent Illinois Democrats overlooked Blagojevich's sleaziness and backed him for reelection in 2006. Within months they abandoned him amid signs that his "pay-to-play" fund-raising had become too flagrant and his behavior erratic. Obama barred him from the Democratic National Convention, avoided him at governors conferences, and made sure he wasn't invited to Grant Park on election night.

When Blagojevich was arrested in early December for trying to sell Obama's now vacant Senate seat to the highest bidder, cable news analysts speculated on Rahm's getting indicted. Camera crews staked him out around the clock, making him a virtual prisoner in his own house. They shouldn't have bothered. To Obama's annoyance, Rahm was freelancing, talking with Blagojevich much more than Obama realized and recommending that he pick Jarrett without the president-elect's approval. But Rahm didn't trust Blagojevich, and he knew the governor was under investigation by the feds. In more than a dozen conversations with Blagojevich about the Senate seat, all caught on a federal wiretap, he was exceptionally careful. After seeing the transcripts, Rahm bragged, "I didn't drop the fucking 'f bomb' once!"

———

IN LATE **2009**, when health care reform was bogged down in the Senate, Obama was inclined to look skeptically at Congress's ability to move major legislation. He catalogued the evolution from the old days: "Congress is just much more complicated. There is much less party unity. There's much more freelancing. The filibuster creates a supermajority on every piece of legislation." But he was also lucky enough to come in at a time of upheaval on Capitol Hill—change that went beyond strong new Democratic majorities in both houses.

The Senate was tough. Its rules, almost certainly unconstitutional, required sixty votes to break the filibuster and get anything done, which meant, in essence, minority rule.* Unlike his predecessor as Democratic majority leader, Tom Daschle, Harry Reid usually deferred to committee chairmen. But in the new House Nancy Pelosi was in full command and committee chairmen were powerful only if they had a strong relationship with her, as her fellow Californians Henry Waxman and George Miller did. Scheduling endless hearings, delaying markup, all the old ways of gumming up the works were no longer acceptable in the House. And the new leadership thought that the tradition of waiting five years between big authorization bills on energy, agriculture, science, and other issues made no sense. "You don't just get to wall off hundreds of billions of dollars anymore and say, 'Not till 2020,'" said Miller, the chairman of the House Education and Labor Committee. In a chat with Obama they agreed that the old sequence of when education bills could be considered was also outdated.

Miller, the wry, white-haired draftsman of much of what went through the House on domestic policy, was saying things in December that would have been unimaginable for a committee chairman in the past, such as "If we have the same old jurisdictional battles, if we do that to Barack Obama, hopefully he'll roll over us." His colleagues didn't disagree. Pelosi told her caucus, "We're going to *do* it, not just talk about it and posture."

The first big bill, destined to be one of the most important but least appreciated pieces of legislation of modern times, was the stimulus, later to be called the Recovery Act. For all the complexities to come, the outlines of where the money would go were simple enough: one

———

* In the Federalist Papers, Alexander Hamilton and John Jay clearly limit supermajority rule to treaties, veto overrides, and other specific exceptions.

third for middle-class tax cuts, mostly in the form of tax credits and re-bates; one third for "state stabilization" (to make sure states didn't have to lay off teachers, firefighters, and bureaucrats or interrupt unemploy-ment insurance, food stamps, COBRA payments, and parts of the safety net); and one third for infrastructure, most of which wouldn't flow into bridges, tunnels, and the rest for a year or so because of the slowness of American contracting.

The House Democratic leadership was determined to get it right on the stimulus. Under prodding from Obama, Pelosi made a decision un-popular with her colleagues and banned all earmarks from the recov-ery bill, which meant that little projects in various districts could not be attached as amendments. But the money would be so immense and reach so far into every area of the country that it was hard for members to believe their constituents wouldn't get plenty of pork.

It was striking that neither Martin Feldstein, who had been Reagan's top economic advisor, nor Mark Zandi, chief economist for Moody's and an advisor to McCain's presidential campaign, favored loading up the stimulus with tax cuts. Like other prominent economists, they ar-gued that expanding programs like food stamps and unemployment benefits, which were spent immediately rather than saved, was the fastest way to revive the economy. Zandi, a widely respected fore-caster, scared the hell out of the congressional leadership in December. "When Mark Zandi said the U.S. economy was, quote, 'shutting down,' unquote, it's like you see Three Mile Island. Clang! Clang! The reactor is shutting down," remembered Miller, referring to the near meltdown of the Pennsylvania nuclear power plant in 1979. Axelrod later said that no one would ever know just how chilling the economic briefings of November and December felt at the time.

————

THE ANSWER TO all the scary talk on the economy was stimulus and more stimulus, and Rahm set as a goal that Obama would sign the Recovery Act on his first day in office. The early political fight would be over the aggregate size of the package. In early December Penn-sylvania Governor Ed Rendell suggested a pie-in-the-sky stimulus of $165 billion and was amazed when Obama didn't bat an eye. In fact the president-elect and his team had already doubled that figure, then more than doubled it again, to around $800 billion, so that the cost went past what the United States had spent over five years in Iraq and Afghanistan.

Later the figure looked too small to some, but at the time the num-bers they were talking about internally seemed impossibly large. "I was shocked it was as big as it was," recalled labor leader Andy Stern, who was accustomed to progressives being disappointed in the commitment of Democrats to public investment. Ron Klain recalled sitting around the transition office and joking with other veterans of the Clinton administration about how in 1998 and 1999, when the government was running the largest budget surpluses ever, they would fight for hours over an extra $20 million or $30 million. Now they were running the largest deficits ever and were discussing adding, with the bipartisan endorsement of economists, hundreds of billions in investments. The group found it surreal.

Obama was certain on one point: instead of starting with an assessment of what the political system would bear, he began with an assessment of what the economy required. After two years of nonstop campaigning he was tired of playing the political angles. Now he prided himself on getting to the "right" answer on the merits before delving into the politics.

There were political limits of course. The Democratic congressional leadership and Rahm agreed that $1 trillion was the ceiling. (Republicans cited much lower figures.) The *New York Times* columnist and Nobel Prize winner in economics Paul Krugman and other progressives might want more, but they didn't have to round up the votes. Of course the trillion-dollar line had already been breached. An $800 billion stimulus combined with a $700 billion TARP bailout would mean that Obama and the country would be $1.5 trillion in the hole at the beginning of his presidency. That didn't even include the $8 trillion in guarantees from the Federal Reserve and FDIC since 2007, which was money not actually spent but a frightening figure nonetheless. In the 1960s Senator Everett Dirksen had memorably said, "A billion here, a billion there and pretty soon you're talking about real money." Now that *billion* had become a *trillion*. Would the taxpayers see any of it again? At the time, no one knew.

But only fringe economists thought there was any other choice. With hundreds of billions of dollars sucked out of the economy in a deflationary cyclone, the government had to pump in huge sums or the whole world would fall into a depression. This was straight out of the work of the midcentury British economist John Maynard Keynes, who suddenly enjoyed a broad revival even among those who normally scorned government spending. Free-market economists, who had ridden high for thirty years on the theory of self-correcting markets, found themselves discredited even within the confines of the University of Chicago and their other longtime citadels of influence.

When the recovery began in mid-2009 conservatives and many

independents would wonder why Barack Obama had to spend "like a drunken sailor." The answer was to keep the world's passengers from drowning.

———

THE OBAMA PEOPLE were still trying to find the restrooms at the transition headquarters at 451 6th Street NW when the bill was being written on Capitol Hill. Rahm and Podesta told Obama that he had to let the House leadership draft the legislation and "run the traps" on potential problems. The transition team simply didn't have the horses to write a monster bill, so the task fell to the speaker's office and the Appropriations Committee, chaired by fiery Wisconsin liberal David Obey, with some help from the committees run by Miller and Waxman. The resulting bill became the largest economic recovery program in American history, far bigger, in constant dollars, than anything FDR did in his storied first hundred days.

Republicans began lashing out wildly and flung the Democrats' early 2008 description of a "timely, temporary, and targeted" stimulus back in their faces. Miller reminded his Republican colleagues that the triple-*t* line was written *before* the financial collapse, when everyone thought there would be a short, shallow recession. Now the odds favored a long and deep recession, or, if the economists were to be believed, possibly another depression. It was time to retire the slogan, but Minority Leader John Boehner and House GOP Whip Eric Cantor declined to do so. Boehner, who once stunningly passed out checks from the tobacco industry on the House floor, counseled obstruction from the start.

For Obama the choice was simple: stimulus or bust. Spend now or spend the next decade in a recession like Japan's. The longer Congress dawdled, he reasoned, the harder it would be to win approval for the measure. With the notion of signing a bill on Day One of his presidency clearly unrealistic, Obama set a deadline of February 16, Presidents Day.

For the Obama transition teams and their allies on the Hill, three questions loomed large in designing the package. The first was whether the proposed spending was economically stimulative: Did it save or create jobs, and thereby put money in people's pockets? It turned out that economists believed almost any spending met this criterion. In a recession even the worst kind of boondoggle is stimulative, a fact that critics had a hard time comprehending. The second, more parliamentary but still critical question was whether a particular stimulus idea entailed any new authorization or new agencies, because new programs would require hearings and lots of other reviews that would slow the whole process down. So nothing that required a new law or structure of government could be included. Finally came the question of whether the spending achieved any larger, long-lasting purpose. The New Deal had left a legacy of state parks, bridges, roads, schools, and other permanent contributions to American life. Could Obama's program do the same?

Apparently not. With precious little time for innovative policymaking, it became a trade-off of speed over impact, speed over creativity, and, no doubt, speed over competence. Obama believed there was a steep cost to delay; if talks on the stimulus dragged into the spring or summer the recession would get much worse. But had the Democrats taken a bit more time they might have been able to think harder about job growth, which eventually became the big economic challenge of 2009.

The president-elect's lack of experience in the bowels of the federal bureaucracy didn't help. The Department of Energy, for instance, got $40 billion even though its loan guarantee office hadn't managed to sign a single contract in its two-year existence. The department was dysfunctional—it simply couldn't spend money—and it didn't begin to perform until the White House made good on its threat to shift some of the money to other agencies in late 2009.

The biggest frustration involved infrastructure. Obama said later that he learned that "one of the biggest lies in government is the idea of 'shovel-ready' projects." It turned out that only about $20 billion to $40 billion in construction contracts were truly ready to go. The rest were tied up in the endless contracting delays and bureaucratic hassles associated with building anything in America.

This drove Rahm nuts. He loved to talk about the 1994 Northridge, California, earthquake, where a dynamo named C. C. Myers had repaired four bridges on the Santa Monica Freeway in an unheard-of sixty-six days. Or the I-35 bridge that had collapsed in Minneapolis and was already open again, months ahead of schedule. The aim now was not to finish early (which meant that people would lose their jobs), but at least to start early so the money would get out there. Where was C. C. Myers? Rahm wanted to know.

OTHER JOBS IDEAS also foundered. Obama failed to persuade congressional Democrats to offer tax credits to employers for each new person they hired. Their argument was that businesses would just pocket the tax credit for workers they were going to hire anyway, thereby gaming the system for billions. That may have been true, but it left Obama without a credible jobs program.

His advisors rejected WPA-style direct government hiring, an idea that had fallen out of fashion in the 1970s, when the Carter administration's CETA jobs program ran into trouble and contracting-out services became the rage. Government jobs would have attacked unemployment immediately. (In 1934 FDR and his relief administrator, Harry Hopkins, created four million jobs in two months.) It was true that the twenty-first-century economy was different from the twentieth century's—it contained millions of middle-aged white-collar workers who didn't want jobs picking up trash and weren't qualified to work construction—but there were plenty of Americans who just wanted to work. Unemployment for low-wage workers was 30 percent in some areas; any job would do. The failure to think more boldly about creating jobs fast would haunt the administration in the months ahead.

In the meantime all the talk of quick spending was misleading. When officials said money had been "spent," all they meant was that a contract had been signed. Most of the actual job creation under the Recovery Act wouldn't take place until 2010 or 2011. In their planning the Obama advisors figured that as long as unemployment stayed under 10 percent for the year, they could slide through until the stimulus jobs started flowing. On that one, they famously bet wrong.

In December Christina Romer and Jared Bernstein, soon to be top White House economists, projected 2009 unemployment figures using the only data available to them: third-quarter GDP for 2008. What they didn't know was that the GDP numbers for the quarter they were in, the fourth, had "fallen off the cliff," as Bernstein later put it. So their projection of 8 percent unemployment turned out to be more than two points low, and Obama was soon pummeled for double-digit joblessness.

———

THE FIRST TASK was triage. Even much later, after all the publicity, many voters still didn't understand the economic logic of sending $175 billion to the states: if hundreds of thousands of state and local employees were laid off, they wouldn't pay taxes, which would worsen the state budget shortfalls, and they wouldn't go shopping, which would send retail sales down even further. This was the vicious cycle the stimulus was designed to ease.

Not every effort to boost consumer spending passed muster. Summers fought hard for a state sales tax rebate to inject liquidity into the system. Podesta, among others, hated the idea and brought Obama around to rejecting it. It was technically tough to execute, but the big problem was that it didn't meet the test of doing something big with a trillion dollars. They were already offering one-time tax cuts. Putting a few more dollars into consumers' pockets for a quick boost at the mall seemed shortsighted.

Contrary to public perception, the vast bulk of stimulus spending went to worthy programs, mostly long-neglected infrastructure projects such as local sewage systems and sensible investments in future productivity such as clean energy, scientific and medical research, and electronic hospital records.* Science got a huge boost because both Obama and the congressional leadership figured that jobs might as well be created where they could do the country the most long-term good. And Obama later said that they intentionally put "some tail" on the stimulus—jobs created in 2010 and 2011—to help sustain the recovery.

The most conspicuous middle-class tax cut was a $400-per-taxpayer break spread out over many paychecks. Democrats got the worst of both worlds on this part of the package: the voters didn't notice the extra $17 a week in their paychecks, and the Republicans didn't praise them as tax cuts because they came in the form of tax credits, not permanent cuts in the marginal rates paid by the wealthy.

Everyone agreed on the need to fund things fast, but figuring out the details was an immense task under an impossible deadline. Democrats on the Obama transition team were accustomed to having no authority to spend a nickel in Republican Washington. Now they were being asked to spend hundreds of billions of dollars overnight—and do so long before they moved into their White House offices. Congressional Democrats had at least been in the majority for two years, but even they and their staffs felt the world moving at warp speed. "This period was the mother of all cluster fucks," remembered one transition official.

Members of Congress complained that Washington was a drifting boat with no one at the tiller. But in some ways this made it easier to get decisions made quickly. Transition officials could walk down the hall of the Washington transition headquarters on 6th Street and speak to four or five Cabinet nominees, then call the Hill with a consensus. The action moved faster than anyone imagined possible. It's not the

---

* In an example of poor planning, the bill failed to incentivize hospitals to use the Veterans Administration's open-source Vista software, which can be installed for a fraction of the price of commercial software. After much hype, there was no evidence to suggest huge long-term cost savings for the medical system from electronic record keeping.

"first hundred days" anymore, an exhausted Phil Schiliro emailed a reporter at 1:45 one morning in early January. "It's the pre-70 days."

— — —

OBAMA KNEW THAT he was locking himself into record spending increases before he even took the oath. The big debate on the size of the stimulus and the budget took place at a long meeting at the Chicago transition headquarters on December 16, a day so snowy that Geithner, Summers, Orszag, and the rest of the economic team that would guide the country wisely decided to take the El instead of fighting traffic around O'Hare.

For a status report on how bad things were, Summers turned the floor over to Romer, who had written her PhD dissertation on FDR's failure to spend enough government money to end the Depression in the early 1930s. Romer said that this recession was sure to be the greatest downturn since that time. The numbers were grim across the board, with unemployment—5 percent a year earlier—headed into double digits. Every one point of unemployment meant 1.3 million Americans lost their jobs. Reports were surfacing of Chinese investors getting cold feet about investing in the U.S. economy. The message was clear: 2009 hadn't begun yet, but the whole year was shot and the economy could head further south in 2010.

The campaign had called for $150 billion in stimulus, and Senator Chuck Schumer had just raised eyebrows by saying on TV that $300 billion might be required. Orszag said the number sounded about right but was willing to go higher. Romer favored $1.2 trillion and insisted that the minimum amount needed to prevent another depression was in the range of $800 billion, which would represent the greatest share of GDP of any public investment in American history. Summers thought that sounded fine. Rahm listened with a pained expression. Schiliro said nothing but noted afterward that getting something of that size through Congress would be awfully tough.

Romer was about to turn 50 and was the picture of scholarly respectability, but she said Axelrod had told the economic team to make sure this briefing was "a holy shit moment," so here it was. Obama shook his head and smiled. "I can't believe she just said 'shit,' " he remarked. Romer pressed on, insisting, "We have to hit this with everything we have."

Afterward Austan Goolsbee told Obama, "That must be the worst briefing any president-elect has ever had." Obama, who had just attended one meeting on al Qaeda's presence on the Afghanistan-Pakistan border and another on the aftermath of terrorist bombings that claimed 173 lives in Mumbai, said that it wasn't even his worst briefing of the week.

The long Chicago meeting had long-term consequences. The president-elect and the group settled on between $700 billion and $800 billion in stimulus, which is where Congress eventually ended up too. "Unlike [Bill] Clinton in such situations, Obama didn't worry about the politics," said an aide who worked for both men and speculated that if Clinton were president he would have settled for a stimulus half as large. "It was an expert-driven decision."

Orszag turned 40 that day and Obama, as was his habit, brought in a cake. But that wasn't his only gift for Orszag. After overruling him on the stimulus, the president-elect agreed to a budget deficit of about 3 percent of GDP, though he was willing to see it drift a little higher if the budget was stripped of the usual gimmicks designed to make the deficit appear smaller. For weeks the budget director had argued that holding to what experts considered to be the magical 3 percent figure was essential to preventing myriad other economic problems over the next five years. By agreeing to 3 percent Obama was simultaneously admitting that the budget wouldn't be balanced for years and condemning himself to tight budgets for every year of his presidency after 2009.

When Obama was informed that it was also Carol Browner's birthday (her 53rd), he apologized for not giving her a cake too, but playfully offered the climate change czarina a present: billions more in the stimulus for construction of the so-called smart grid. Obama agreed with Al Gore that boosting clean energy wouldn't mean much without building a new network of modern national transmission lines for electricity. The real goal, he thought, should be to make the grid akin to the Interstate Highway system in the 1950s or the Internet in the 1990s: a prime engine of growth for the economy. He liked to talk about thousands of miles of transmission lines and 40 million "smart meters" across the country.

But reality soon intruded. In early January top transition staffers in Washington held a video phone conference with Obama in Chicago. The topic was the NIMBY ("not in my backyard") problem (at work in everything from the siting of nuclear waste to the imprisonment of terrorists in supermax prisons) that now afflicted the smart-grid debate. The regulatory hurdles to modernizing the grid were beyond belief; it turned out that no fewer than 231 different state and local regulators had to sign off on modernization. Obama was appalled. "We went to the moon!" he said. "We can do better than this! Go back and talk to more people and see whether it [the grid funding] can be bigger." To say that Obama was getting worked up might be an exaggeration, but he was adamant: "Let's not play small ball. Let's make this a national priority—it's gonna create lots of jobs!"

The exhortation went over well in the room in Washington. One aide felt she had witnessed the president-elect's first "leadership moment." So they went back to the experts and repeated Obama's message: We can do better!

But they couldn't. In the end the stimulus included about $11 billion for smart-grid development, which was more than ever before but not much of a down payment on a project with a $2 trillion price tag (most of that to be raised someday from the private sector). Obama couldn't do more because big investments in power grids would have required tackling the issue of eminent domain. When the Supreme Court had ventured into that area in 2005 it proved enormously divisive. Americans don't like the government condemning their land—for anything. And fighting jurisdictional issues would slow the stimulus. So Obama's dream of a huge new project that would simultaneously promote clean energy and create hundreds of thousands of new jobs would have to wait.

Even so, the stimulus contained billions in tax credits, loan guarantees, and weatherization funds (for low-income jobs that could not be exported) and more money for alternative energy research right away than Obama had originally promised in ten years. The enviros were happy about that.

Obama did even better on education. During the campaign he was booed when he talked about merit pay in front of the National Education Association—a favorable sign to reformers. But it wasn't clear until after the election how thoroughly he was committed to the goals of transformative change in the schools. When Arne Duncan went to see Obama in Chicago the president-elect said he had two principles. First, all education policy should revolve around what was best for kids, not adult interest groups. With this perspective, every divisive question in education was much clearer. Higher teacher pay? That was good for kids because it would attract better teachers to the profession. Contracts that barred paying effective teachers more than those with seniority? Bad for kids. Using federal dollars to incentivize states to lift the caps they placed on the number of charter schools allowed? Good for kids. Pressuring states to tear down the firewalls some had erected between student evaluation and teacher evaluation? Good for kids. Obama's second principle was to avoid putting a stick in anyone's eye. "Let's engage, not attack," he said.

Like Nixon going to China,* Obama felt he had enough credibility with the "adult interest groups" to transform American education policy. (It helped the reformers' cause that the teachers unions had unanimously supported Hillary Clinton in the Democratic primaries, which meant he owed them little.) Though Obama was sometimes annoyed by the pressure he felt from reformers, it turned out that he and George Miller were in exactly the same place, a place where Democrats, long in the pocket of teachers unions, had never been before. They both wanted to use the stimulus to drive better performance in schools, even if it offended one of their party's most loyal interest groups. The idea was to offer states what Miller called "applesauce," more money, to force them to resist entrenched interests and swallow some reform.

But how much reform? With hundreds of thousands of teachers facing immediate layoffs, speed was essential, as David Obey reminded everyone. Obey was doing an amazing job juggling thousands of line items as he put together a balanced package, but he was quick to anger and often high-handed with the transition team.

The first number for education was $30 billion, mostly to avoid teacher layoffs. Duncan suggested to Obama and Rahm that they more than triple the figure, but only in exchange for serious reforms. Obama agreed. Obey was happy about the money but skeptical of the strings. He told the Obama transition team, Okay, you've got twenty-four hours to tell my staff how you would spend $100 billion on education. Heather Higginbottom, Obama's policy director during the campaign, thought the whole thing was surreal. *One hundred billion dollars! How could we possibly be talking about that much money?*

The next day Higginbottom went to the Hill for a meeting with congressional staffers and told them that Obama was a reformer. Duncan and his policy advisor, Jon Schnur, had come up with a plan to spend $15 billion for teacher innovation projects and what would soon be called the "Race to the Top" fund. The simple idea—never tried before—was to bypass the normal funding formulas and reward only those states that were showing success. The original pot was huge—$15 billion was ten times more than the Gates Foundation gave out for reform over two years—and Race to the Top represented policymaking at its creative best. States would get the money only if they invested in successful charter school models, allowed student performance to

---

* In 1972 President Nixon, a longtime anti-Communist, opened the door to Red China. Had a liberal Democratic president tried the same thing, he would likely have failed to change the policy. Similarly, Republican presidents were stymied when they tried to take on the teachers unions.

count in teacher evaluations, and introduced national standards. By making states compete with each other for the money, the government could spur reform much faster. Obama (backed strongly by Rahm) knew he had a rare moment of leverage, and he invested time in working the details.

Obey wasn't big on reform. He wanted to spend a good chunk of the $100 billion on bolstering the same aid formulas for poor schools that had been used for years. These funding streams each had some merit (for instance, special-ed requirements from Washington had imposed an intolerable burden on local school districts). But in total, the status quo had failed to improve education over the past quarter-century. The United States was continuing to slip behind the rest of the world in test scores, graduation rates, and other measures. Obey and his Senate counterpart, Tom Harkin, were undeterred. They insisted on operating under the outdated impression that the biggest problem with schools in poor neighborhoods was that they didn't have enough money.* More money, especially to pay teachers, was needed but the deeper problem was a lack of accountability.

Here George Miller proved pivotal. Miller and other reform "disrupters" wanted deep change that moved beyond just spreading education money around to the districts of powerful members of Congress (a practice called "peanut butter politics") or pouring it down the same old rat holes. The forces of the status quo met the reformers partway. After Obey and Harkin tried to kill the $15 billion Race to the Top altogether, they compromised with Miller and Obama on $5 billion. This was disappointing; it amounted to 5 percent of stimulus money for education. But it was $5 billion more than Washington had ever spent funding what works in student achievement, and it was destined to grow. Race to the Top became the signature education program of the Obama administration.

THE OBAMAS ARRIVED in Washington on January 5. Malia and Sasha needed to be at their new school, Sidwell Friends, for the beginning of the second semester.† To drive home his message of collegiality, Obama went almost immediately to the Hill to meet with the Repub-

----

* Per-pupil expenditures in many failing urban districts exceeded $10,000 a year, higher than in some wealthy suburbs.
† For inexplicable reasons, the Bush White House had arranged for the former prime minister of Australia to stay in Blair House, the house across Pennsylvania Avenue from the White House that has been used by incoming presidents for generations. So the Obamas had to stay for several days at the Hay-Adams Hotel. .

lican leadership. He promised that he'd work for a bipartisan stimulus package with hundreds of billions in tax cuts. Republicans made all the right noises about working with the new president to ease the economic crisis.

The minority whip, Eric Cantor, a rising young Republican from Virginia, told Obama that he could get further input from the GOP if he posted the bill on the Web. Obama chuckled. "I could feign surprise and play politics as usual," he said, before explaining that they'd already thought of the idea of Recovery.gov. "[But] we can call it the Cantor plan if you want."*

The Republicans' problem was that they had no alternative way to give the economy a boost. Although even conservative economists were telling the GOP leadership that a huge stimulus was necessary, the party was stuck in the old tax-cutting mind-set. The Senate Republican leader, Mitch McConnell, wanted to reduce taxes for the middle class from 25 percent to 10 percent and give strapped states loans instead of grants. The economists replied that such tax cuts would be used to pay down consumer debt, which, though desirable, wouldn't do much to stimulate the economy. And they patiently explained that making loans to states was impractical. McConnell simply went looking for new economists.

Beyond stimulating the economy, Obama had to focus on cleaning up the specific messes the Bush administration left. The first was TARP. It was clear by November that the TARP bill that passed before the election wouldn't be enough to rescue the banks. But instead of pushing Congress for more bailout money, Bush quietly requested the second portion of $350 billion, then left it up to the president-elect to lobby the new Congress for it. "[TARP] stuck in our throats," Joe Biden concluded months later, "but it worked." Its passage consumed a large amount of time around the first of the year, as the president-elect mobilized to win nearly simultaneous passage of two monster bills, the stimulus and TARP, that were each as expensive as any bill in American history. Only the entire annual budget itself was larger.

On January 14, six days before the Inauguration, Obama went to the Senate to meet with the Democratic caucus. Both male and female senators rushed Obama and began hugging him. One senator held back and decided to count the hugs; he got to forty before stopping. Obama spoke briefly, singling out only Dick Durbin by name, then

---

* Recovery.gov had growing pains, but by September 2009, as the funds began to flow, it was providing plenty of useful information about how the money was being spent, as well as a user-friendly way to report fraud and abuse.

took questions. Most were about TARP. Several Democratic senators thought they had been the victims of a bait-and-switch, with Paulson first saying TARP funding would be used to buy distressed assets from the banks, then changing course to lending money to the banks. Their constituents were anxious.

Obama agreed it had been mishandled. "I'm not so far in the bubble that I don't know what people are saying about this program and how unhappy it makes them," he told the senators privately. But then he made a soft-sell case for getting it done before he took office. It was all very casual. "I think we need to do it," he said finally, noting that he would fix it when he became president.

It wasn't "a Knute Rockne moment," Senator Ron Wyden recalled. "But we knew how he felt." Wyden remembered asking whether "the digestive tract could handle it all." Obama believed the time for cap and trade was far down the road: "We've got lots of fights before we even get to cap and trade," he told the senators. After the stimulus, health care would be coming, he said, as he calmed fears of another Clinton-style debacle.

In the days that followed Obama worked the phones and brought along all but one of the seven freshman Democrats on a bill that he later said he knew was politically toxic. It also helped that Tim Geithner made the rounds of the Senate Democrats and told them he had made mistakes in coordinating with Paulson while still in his job as head of the New York Fed. They found the humility attractive. The second bailout was approved 52–42 by the new Senate five days before the Inauguration. Even before becoming president, Obama was drawing down his political capital to win approval for Bush's bailouts.

———

OBAMA'S FIRST TRANSITION setback was caused by Tim Geithner's inexplicable lapse in paying his taxes. When contacted by vetters just after the election, Geithner said that after being audited in 2006 he paid $16,732 plus interest in self-employment back taxes from his days as a consultant to the International Monetary Fund. But Geithner paid only what he owed for the years that he was audited, 2003 and 2004. He had also worked as a consultant in 2001 and 2002 and knew perfectly well that he owed back taxes for those years too. (Other IMF consultants reported receiving frequent notification of taxes owed.) That he would continue to chisel even after being audited struck Obama transition officials as foolish; some thought it disqualifying. But by the time the vetters confronted him on it, and he quickly paid back another $25,970, he had already been announced with great fanfare as Obama's choice to be secretary of the treasury, the department that houses the Internal Revenue Service.

"The chief tax collector in America is going to be a tax evader?" one Obama transition official asked another in amazement, as cable news went wild with the same analysis. "I don't think so." But he was. Obama had believed from the beginning of his political career that no one except his family was indispensable. But at this moment Geithner became the exception that proved the rule.

The case for sticking with Geithner was both substantive and political. With the banks in crisis and several hundred thousand Americans losing their jobs each month, key financial decisions were coming at the team at a furious clip. Though dozens of people were qualified to be treasury secretary, Obama believed there simply was no time to get someone new. And putting Summers back at Treasury wasn't as simple as it sounded; his confirmation hearings would likely have been a messy rehash of the 1990s that consumed valuable time. More important, abandoning Geithner would make Obama look weak. Strong leaders stuck with their people. Or so the Obama team would believe for another month or so.

Geithner's tax problem had two major consequences: it dramatically slowed the vetting process for all appointees, and it raised new constraints on who could be hired. In November the informal rule was that no one from Citigroup or other failing firms would be offered a Treasury job. By December it was no one from a TARP-covered firm, whether failing or not. And by early in the new year no one could be hired at Treasury who had any tax issue of any kind, even if it would have been overlooked in the past.

The fallout continued through 2009. All that year hardly anyone with any real-world experience was hired for an economic post. Gary Gensler, the new head of the Commodity Futures Trading Commission, was a rare exception, and he made it only because it had been twelve years since he worked at Goldman Sachs and he had worked on the Obama campaign. The rest were overachievers with fancy degrees and some government experience who had never actually made anything, or even traded anything, for a living.

————

WITH A HUGE flow of plans cascading out of the transition, it looked as though most of the action in 2009 would be at the White House, not in the agencies. Energy policy, for instance, cut across the Departments of Energy, State, Defense, and Interior and the Environmental Protection Agency. For a time there was talk of establishing a national energy council like the National Security Council established under Truman and the National Economic Council that Clinton created. Obama said no. He wanted to upgrade energy without having daily briefings on it, the way he did on national security and the economy.

Browner was ensconced, but Rahm made a face when the "czar" system came up. "I don't like czars," he joked. "They weren't good to my people." Little did he know that conservatives, tanked up by talk show hosts like Glenn Beck, would by spring use *czar* as an epithet for every administration official who didn't require Senate confirmation, neglecting to mention, of course, that Republican presidents also had dozens of similar appointees in their own areas of policy interest.

While most of the Bush fiefdoms were still around, nobody was going to do any housecleaning. The White House under Obama would continue to be what Harrison Wellford, who consulted on Democratic transitions, called a "coral reef," where the crustaceans die but their remains cling to the reef. The classy Beaux Arts Eisenhower Executive Office Building, once the home of the Departments of State and War, would still be filled by the White House Office of this or that: drug policy, AIDS policy, urban policy. Even as the subject matter they handled faded from public debate, the people in these offices looked busy.

The same was true in the agencies, many of which had been fattened by post-9/11 budget increases. The bigger the executive branch bureaucracy, the more congressional oversight (a function that badly atrophied under the Republican Congress) was seen to be required. Every Democratic member wanted to pound the gavel as a chairman. The Department of Homeland Security, for instance, reported to no fewer than eighty-eight committees and subcommittees. The result was a tremendous quantity of make-work. Coordinating with the White House coordinators kept everyone in the agencies and on the Hill feeling well coordinated, while the president and a few others made all the big decisions.

The real impediment to government reorganization was the economy. Rahm said immediately that there was simply no time for rearranging the agencies; doing so would only bruise egos without getting much accomplished. Creative ideas for reinventing government would have to wait for a sunnier day.

In fact, creative ideas of all sorts were in short supply, partly because staffers were already working themselves to the bone playing defense; it was hard to find the time for innovative policymaking. And nobody wanted to be seen as floating some off-the-wall idea. This limited the universe of job creation proposals, which left White House aides scrambling later on. The more honest ones later admitted that the "jobs summit" held in December 2009 should have taken place nearly a year earlier.

———

WHEN HE WAS elected Obama said his greatest concern about the presidency was "living in the bubble." To venture out of it, he insisted just before the Inauguration that his security team fashion a special "fat" BlackBerry for him to wear on his hip that wouldn't betray his location or otherwise compromise national security. Among its special features was a built-in lock that prevented anyone from forwarding or copying the president's emails. "I've won the fight!" he said when they handed it to him.

But the incoming White House counsel's office convinced Obama that he should use his BlackBerry only to communicate with twenty-five to thirty people, including family, a few friends from Hawaii and Chicago, his lawyer, accountant, and former campaign manager (David Plouffe), and a small handful of incoming White House aides. Email contact with his Cabinet or any other government officials outside the White House was prohibited because the lawyers said it might be subject to Freedom of Information Act requests. Inside the White House, inclusion became the ultimate status symbol. Denis McDonough and Mark Lippert, two young aides who came with Obama from the Senate, were at first the only National Security Council staffers with the president's email address. Jim Jones, the incoming NSC advisor, was offered it but indicated that he didn't use email. Larry Summers was annoyed at not being included and complained to Rahm, who put him on the list. Other White House policy aides were left off because their memos were supposed to go through the office of the staff secretary for comment from other advisors before they reached the president.

The lawyers and paper pushers sought to control what reached the president—all for his own good of course. But this was a potentially harmful decision. It meant that Obama was deprived of the back channels to a couple hundred friends who, without abusing the privilege, had occasionally offered him useful email advice during the campaign. He could reach them anytime by phone, of course, but that wasn't the same. The bubble had won.

———

BY NEW YEAR'S Day, three weeks before the Inauguration, the mood in the Washington transition headquarters had gone from collaborative to wary and even poisonous, as old relationships ruptured over the unseemly scrambles for position. Early on it felt almost like an office party, with staffers wandering easily in and out of the offices of soon-to-be Cabinet secretaries. Now everything seemed to be going on behind closed doors, as those with even a small smudge on their records were bounced from their dream job. One transition official summed it up by saying that the Obama transition had "begun with 'Kumbaya' and ended with the music from *Jaws*."

Washington was a rough town, even for ex-presidents. In early January Obama joined Bill Clinton, George H. W. Bush, and Jimmy Carter at the Bush White House for a five-president lunch. Staffers noticed that President Bush and his father got along well with Clinton but that all the former presidents seemed to find Jimmy Carter annoying. It wasn't just that Carter had publicly attacked all of them except Obama at one time or another; he was apparently talking too much and too seriously at the lunch, getting in the way of the convivial advice the others wanted to offer Obama. In the group photo taken to commemorate the gathering, Carter stands at the far right of the group, alone. One of the president-elect's aides made a mental note: this place has a way of chewing people up.

History would now take a bite of Barack Obama. If the current furious pace of job loss (700,000 per month) were to continue through 2009, nearly 8.5 million more Americans would lose their jobs, meeting most economists' definition of a depression. The circulatory system of the economy, banking, remained in crisis, and the longtime engines of American manufacturing, automobile companies, faced bankruptcy. Bill Clinton had left office in 2001 with a $236 billion budget surplus; George W. Bush was leaving with a $1.3 trillion deficit, severely limiting the new president's options in the years ahead.* If health care costs weren't brought under control, there would soon be little money left for anything else. The nation was at war in two countries, with shadowy struggles against al Qaeda under way in a half-dozen more. Nuclear technology was spreading to unstable regions, and climate change threatened colossal disruptions. With all due respect to Franklin Roosevelt in 1933, the Obama team liked to say, he didn't face crises both at home and abroad. If Obama's predicament was less desperate than FDR's, it was also a lot more complicated.

During the campaign Obama liked to say in his stump speech that

---

* For the first time in American history a president didn't raise taxes to pay for an expensive war (total costs of Iraq and Afghanistan so far exceed $1 trillion). In fact Bush cut taxes for the wealthy, which blew a $2 trillion hole in the deficit without helping middle-class Americans, whose incomes fell. He added a $1 trillion dollar Medicare prescription drug benefit without paying for it. However one adds it up, Bush amassed more debt in eight years than all his predecessors combined.

he was running for president "because of what Dr. King called 'the fierce urgency of now.'" This rhetorical flourish was suddenly assuming a practical cast. As the Inauguration approached, the president-elect understood that all his cautious caveats about change being like "turning around an ocean liner" were obsolete. Dr. King's urgent "now" was, well, *now*.

7

Historic Inauguration

Only one day in Barack Obama's presidency was assured to be in history books a hundred years from now: his first. For months he had been making presidential-level decisions, but the ceremonial transfer of authority carried its own power as a symbol of the nation's inspiring capacity for renewal.

The founders of the United States and twelve of its presidents—more than one quarter of the total—had owned slaves; the Capitol where Obama would take the oath had been built mostly by slaves; the Mall where hundreds of thousands would gather was the site of slave auctions in the early nineteenth century; the District of Columbia had for generations been segregated, first by law and now by fact.

Obama is not himself a descendant of American slaves, but his wife and children are, and he had become a source of pride and redemption for African Americans. A descendant of African goatherds on one side and Jefferson Davis on the other would work to repair this deepest breach, if only by standing for the promise of a unified nation.

The last big inaugural extravaganza, Ronald Reagan's in 1981, had been a victory celebration for one party and one movement. While Obama's Inauguration had special meaning for one group of Americans, it unleashed a broader exuberance, at home and around the world. Even many Republicans who loathed Obama's politics (and would savage him soon) found it in their hearts to say that January 20, 2009, was a good day for America.

For two years Obama had shied away from direct allusion to the president he revered most for fear of seeming presumptuous about his own place in history. But now he used the same train route to the capital as Lincoln had, swore the oath on Lincoln's Bible, and made sure the luncheon in the Capitol served the same menu served at the Inauguration of 1861 (seafood stew, pheasant with sour cherry chutney, and sweet potatoes) on replicas of Mary Todd Lincoln's china.

The festivities began on Sunday at the Lincoln Memorial, where

Obama gave a short speech about unity that many in attendance or watching on HBO later found more inspiring than the Inaugural Address. "Yours are the voices I will take with me every day I walk into the Oval Office—the voices of men and women who have different stories but hold common hopes," he said. The emphasis on storytelling and hope had proven remarkably consistent since the beginning of the campaign.

The delighted crowd was so big that access to the Mall was blocked to anyone who failed to arrive very early, a foreshadowing of what awaited the throngs who would attend the Inauguration. At the concert that followed, dedicated to American ideals, the Obama family got up and danced when Usher performed with Stevie Wonder and Shakira, then joined in when Garth Brooks sang "Shout!" Michelle waved to Tiger Woods and the president-elect heartily sang "This Land Is Your Land" along with Pete Seeger and Bruce Springsteen (including rarely used protest verses like "And some are grumblin' and some are wonderin' if this land's still made for you and me"). With a visual tribute to the African American singer Marian Anderson, famously denied permission to sing in Washington in 1939 until Eleanor Roosevelt intervened, the afternoon managed to be both fun and redemptive. It was a happy, contented moment for Obama, who looked out over the vast crowd and thought about the spirit that his campaign had unleashed.

On Monday Obama spent the morning helping a community service project paint a local school and visiting wounded troops at Walter Reed Army Medical Center. In the evening he hosted dinners for Joe Biden, Colin Powell, and John McCain. At McCain's party Marty Nesbitt was struck by the easy banter of the two former rivals, who had spoken on national security several times during the transition. Obama spent time talking to McCain's 97-year-old mother, Roberta, which left the Arizona senator beaming.

Obama's bonhomie masked disturbing news he had received shortly before arriving at the bipartisan dinners. John Brennan, his counterterrorism chief, told him that sketchy reports over the weekend of a possible terrorist attack during the Inauguration were more serious than previously believed. The FBI and Department of Homeland Security were set to issue a bulletin warning that individuals connected to al Shabaab, an al Qaeda affiliate in Somalia, had slipped over the Canadian border and were planning to detonate a bomb on the Mall. The tip came from U.S. law enforcement, but international authorities were also on alert about the group. Kenya, ironically, had recently accused al Shabaab of threatening jihad against Nairobi. Now the African

American about to be sworn in as president of the United States had to worry about a shadowy extremist group in the land of his father.

By this time Obama had been briefed for months on all kinds of security threats, but this one left him subdued. He canceled a final rehearsal of his Inaugural Address at Blair House and focused on absorbing updates of the still raw intelligence.

INAUGURATION DAY WAS clear but bitter cold, and even those with tickets knew they had better rise before dawn if they hoped for a glimpse of the ceremony. Obama dressed in a blue suit and red tie and emerged briefly from Blair House on Pennsylvania Avenue at nine o'clock, the beginning of an eighteen-hour day. Two Secret Service agents held open the door of the new presidential limousine, dubbed "The Beast" and equipped with eight-inch-thick armor-plated doors, night-vision cameras, and tear gas cannons. A fourteen-car motorcade then made the two-minute ride to St. John's Church on Lafayette Square, where on ten previous inaugural mornings the nation's president-elect and his family had gathered to pray.

Inside the small church Michelle's brilliant yellow dress drew appreciative looks from the small gathering of family, friends, and dignitaries. The choir sang "He's Got the Whole World in His Hands" and Bishop T. D. Jakes from Houston read from the Book of Daniel: "In time of crisis, good men must stand up. God always sends the best men into the worst of times." Rabbi David Saperstein, reading from Psalms in English and Hebrew, noticed from the altar that the good men and women of the congregation that day, including the Bidens and other dignitaries, had not yet stood. Finally Bishop Vashti McKenzie of the African Methodist Church asked that everyone rise. At that moment Saperstein saw something from his angle of vision: "If I had seen it in a movie I would have groaned and said, 'Give me a break. That's so trite.' " A beam of morning light shown through the stained-glass windows and illuminated the president-elect's face. Several of the clergy and choir on the altar who also saw it marveled afterward about the presence of the Divine.

As the Obamas made their ceremonial rounds, the outgoing and incoming national security teams were summoned to the White House Situation Room for a morning meeting that lasted nearly three hours. The Bush forces, led by Condoleezza Rice and Bob Gates and including the heads of the CIA and FBI, were still in their official positions; Hillary Clinton, Rahm Emanuel, Jim Jones, and the rest of Obama's NSC were technically private citizens.* The two teams already worked well together. Just a week earlier, on January 13, many had gathered at the White House for a crisis exercise. In the scenario, the group was asked to imagine that bombs were exploding in several American cities at once.

After the FBI briefed the transition teams about the overnight threat, a discussion ensued over the contingency plan (one of seventeen prepared for the new administration for various crises).† According to Stephen Hadley, Bush's NSC advisor, Hillary Clinton asked the best question: "So what should Barack Obama do if he's in the middle of his Inaugural Address and a bomb goes off way in the back of the crowd somewhere on the Mall? What does he do? Is the Secret Service going to whisk him off the podium so the American people see their incoming president disappear in the middle of the Inaugural Address? I don't think so."

As it turned out, the threat wasn't significant enough to cancel anything; like so many other wispy plots, this one turned out to be the product of two different terrorist groups trying to pin blame on each other. All along Obama calmly agreed that he wouldn't let terrorists disrupt his Inauguration even if they exploded a bomb in the middle of it. He would proceed as planned as a sign of democracy's strength.

———

UNLIKE HERBERT HOOVER and Franklin Roosevelt in 1933, the outgoing and incoming presidents got along well that day, having morning coffee at the White House and taking their ritual ride together down Pennsylvania Avenue. Obama was grateful for the generous help extended by everyone in the Bush White House from the start of the transition through this latest security matter. Bush was in good spirits too, though he complained to Obama in the limo about Dick and Lynne Cheney hounding him for a pardon of Scooter Libby.

In an office at the Capitol, Joe Biden got a little powder from makeup maven Bobbi Brown, who was helping out most of the A-list crowd except the Obamas (they had their own makeup person). "I guess

———

* For every State of the Union Address, one member of the Cabinet stays home to preserve the continuity of government in the case of catastrophe. For the Obama Inauguration that Cabinet officer was Gates, who both knew the government intimately and was part of Obama's team.
† President Bush made a point of making sure that the Obama team was fully briefed on all national security matters. The result was a series of meetings, the first ever, between outgoing and incoming senior officials.

afterwards I'll call you 'Mr. Vice President,' right?" Brown asked. "Keep calling me Joe," Biden told her.

As he strode toward the west door of the Capitol, Obama handed his bottle of water to Reggie Love and entered a small, dark holding area. He later said it was only then that the magnitude of the moment hit him. He felt as if he were about to be "shot out of a cannon." On the podium family members and dignitaries gathered amid rising excitement. The image that many later remembered most clearly was not of celebrities or sight lines or even of the man of the hour, but of the cheerful, weeping crowd of more than a million stretched down the National Mall as far as the eye could see, Woodstock Nation grown to maturity, broadened and integrated by race, religion, region, age, and all the other conditions that so often divide Americans. In Washington that day the wind chill was 17 degrees but it felt like spring.

Those who couldn't make it to the Mall celebrated anyway. Inside Georgina's Restaurant in Southeast Washington, Joanne Fisher, age 61, sat down at a table and pulled out pictures of her deceased parents, African Americans who had fought their whole lives for civil rights. As the ceremony began, she stood, clasped the framed pictures to her breast, and swayed back and forth as she talked to the television and to her parents. "We made it," she said. "Mama, Daddy, we made it."

"I was in 9/11," said Angela Bokern, watching the ceremony from a local pub. "Second tower. Sixty-first floor. Morgan Stanley. This is what I wanted to see September 12. Responsibility. Action. Service. This was the America I wanted to live in. And I am a Republican."

"This is not Jesus," Octavia Stevenson, a 21-year-old at Florida State University told her friend Kristin Murray, as they waited for hours to get near the parade route. "This is not Jesus," Murray replied. "But this is something I may not ever see again."

Among those who couldn't get in were several Obama speechwriters who had worked on the Inaugural Address. They and thousands of other bearers of purple-colored credentials were trapped for hours in a traffic tunnel leading to the Capitol, later called "the Purple Tunnel of Doom."* A rumor, never resolved, was that a security threat shut the tunnel down. Speechwriter Adam Frankel was disappointed, but he knew that whatever happened he was destined to be at least a small part of history. He was writing speeches for a man whose portrait he thought would one day likely appear on U.S. currency.

Obama had carefully choreographed his Inauguration with an eye

---

* The author was also a purple-ticket holder, though he and his family left the futile line for the warmth of an office party in time to see the swearing-in on TV.

toward reconciliation. He selected Rev. Rick Warren, pastor of the immense Saddleback Church in Orange County, California, to handle the invocation, a gesture to conservative evangelicals who had mostly opposed his election.* Rev. Joseph Lowery, who had marched with Martin Luther King Jr., provided some welcome inaugural levity, envisioning a time "when brown can stick around, when yellow will be mellow, when the red man can get ahead, man, and when white will embrace what is right." Aretha Franklin's "My Country 'Tis of Thee" (complete with her magnificent hat) and the performance by Itzhak Perlman and Yo-Yo Ma (whose strings were so cold that the crowd heard a taped sync) ran long and sent the ceremony past noon, the point at which Obama officially became president.

At 12:05 p.m., Chief Justice John Roberts rose to administer the oath. "I, Barack Hussein Obama," he began. Obama jumped in early. "I, Bara—," as Roberts, rushing the oath, said, "do solemnly swear that I will execute the Office of President to the United States faithfully." Roberts had substituted *to* for *of* and put *faithfully* at the end of the sentence instead of just before *execute*. Obama tried at first to follow the chief justice's lead but then, recognizing the error, paused and nodded as Roberts once more mangled the sentence, and Obama once more repeated it, with *faithfully* again at the end. After the momentary awkwardness they moved through the remainder of the oath and shook hands.

Because Roberts botched the oath, the most unusual thing about it was overshadowed and barely mentioned: the new president had chosen to use his full name, Barack Hussein Obama. He told the press after the election that he would use Hussein at his swearing-in but added, "I'm not trying to make a statement one way or the other." He was, he said, merely "following tradition." But he wasn't. Neither Jimmy Carter nor Ronald Reagan used a middle name when taking the oath, and Dwight D. Eisenhower and Gerald R. Ford used only a middle initial. The mention of Obama's middle name had been so taboo during the campaign that when a right-wing radio host said it John McCain was forced to apologize. Now Obama was clearly trying to make a statement to the world while insisting that it was no big deal—a perfect illustration of his determination to have it both ways as often as possible.

---

* Warren's selection was controversial because of some disparaging comments he had made about homosexuals. The flap faded, but he raised eyebrows in his invocation by mentioning Jesus Christ. That would have been less problematic had he been joined by clergy of other faiths, as in previous Inaugurations, but for the invocation at what is supposed to be an ecumenical ceremony, it rankled some non-Christians.

The preparation of the Inaugural Address reflected the same casual calculation. Just before Thanksgiving Obama was ambling around his sparse Chicago transition headquarters, looking for someone to talk to. "What's going on, Favs?" he asked his 27-year-old chief speechwriter. "We should talk about the Inaugural soon, huh?" His favorites, he said, were Lincoln's Second ("With malice toward none") and Kennedy's ("Ask not . . ."). He found FDR's First ("The only thing we have to fear . . .") too detailed and harsh after the opening, though the comparisons between the state of the world in 1933 and in 2009 were unmistakable.

Obama's approach to speechwriting was to begin the process by speaking aloud at length, while Favreau or others took notes. He told Favreau that he thought the best Inaugurals describe clearly for Americans "the moment we're in, how we got there, and the best way out. [They] anchor themselves in that moment." "I'll feel that we succeeded," Obama concluded, if the speech can do that and leave the audience saying to themselves, "This is why I want to go into public service and be a better politician. This is why I want to go home and be a better parent, better worker, better citizen."

Favreau worked on a couple of drafts on his laptop at Starbucks, with help from Ben Rhodes and, for the big George Washington ending, Adam Frankel and Sarah Hurwitz. He sent it to Axelrod and Obama after Christmas and Obama said he would take it from there. Over the weekend of January 10–11 Obama holed up in the Hay-Adams Hotel, where he rewrote more than half of the text. The speech was intended to be sober and restrained, not a barn burner. When his speechwriters told him he wouldn't hear clapping because the audience would be wearing gloves, he said, "That's good. I'd rather not hear any applause and just speak to people." Having used his lyricism to get elected, he chose to set that instrument aside in favor of a more practical tool to present sober reality and lower Americans' expectations.

Ten days before the Inauguration the family visited the Lincoln Memorial around 7 p.m. and, mingling with tourists, read the Gettysburg Address and the Second Inaugural on the marble walls. "Is your speech going to be that long?" Sasha asked. "A little longer," her father replied. "First African American president," Malia said. "Better be good."

As he stepped forward to deliver his Inaugural Address,* Obama summoned the themes that had brought him this far: "We gather be-

---

* Obama made a historical error at the start. "Forty-four Americans have now taken this oath," he said, neglecting to account for Grover Cleveland's two nonconsecutive terms in the late nineteenth century, which left the real number of forty-three.

cause we have chosen hope over fear, unity of purpose over conflict and discord. On this day, we come to proclaim an end to the petty grievances and false promises, the recriminations and worn-out dogmas that for far too long have strangled our politics." Had the country truly "chosen" unity over conflict? Were petty grievances at an "end"? It was hard to see how, but 2009 would provide some answers to whether "the recriminations" could be held at bay long enough to get something done.

To do so, Obama was placing his faith in the men and women who had built the country, "the risk-takers, the doers, the makers of things." In a line he wrote himself and intentionally refused to strip of its colloquial quality, he said, "Starting today, we must pick ourselves up, dust ourselves off and begin again the work of remaking America." But the government would be there to help. Where Reagan said in his First Inaugural that "government is the problem" and Clinton said in a State of the Union Address that "the era of big government is over," Obama said, "The question we ask today is not whether government is too big or too small, but whether it works." That question, in all three forms, would be asked again and again in the coming debates over his ambitious program.

Obama's larger theme was "the new era of responsibility." He refused to scapegoat the Wall Street money changers, as FDR had done in his Inaugural. The bad economy was a "consequence of greed and irresponsibility on the part of some, but also our collective failure to make hard choices." Calling on Scripture (I Corinthians 13:11), as he had when addressing African American fathers on Father's Day, he admonished, "The time has come to set aside childish things." That sound bite from Saint Paul became among the most quoted in the Inaugural, which suggests that his allergy to easy applause lines carried a price. Among the "childish things" that Obama and his speechwriters had themselves apparently set aside were lines simple and catchy enough for a child (or adult) to commit to memory. There would be no immortal sentence to emblazon on every piece of Obama paraphernalia.

The speech was by turns conciliatory and muscular toward the rest of the world, though without JFK's "pay any price, bear any burden" grandiosity. On civil liberties he rejected the "false choice between our safety and our ideals," and he hinted at his new foreign policy of engagement with adversaries: "We will extend a hand if you are willing to unclench your fist." Obama was the first president to single out Muslims in an Inaugural Address, a taste of speeches to come. He tried to conjure optimism for the future of other countries by placing their fate in the context of the American journey: "Because we have tasted the bitter swill of civil war and segregation and emerged from that dark chapter stronger and more united," he told a global audience, "we cannot help but believe that the old hatreds will someday pass; that the lines of tribe will soon dissolve." But then he pivoted to a tough message to terrorists: "We will not apologize for our way of life, nor will we waver in its defense. You cannot outlast us and we will defeat you."

Above all, Obama captured the historic quality of the day. After celebrating the American character he moved toward his conclusion: "This is the meaning of our liberty and our creed—why men and women and children of every race and every faith can join in celebration across this magnificent Mall, and why a man whose father less than sixty years ago might not have been served at a local restaurant can now stand before you to take a most sacred oath."

Afterward Sasha Obama could be heard saying, "That was a pretty good speech, Dad." For the throngs in Washington and the millions watching on television around the world, pretty good was good enough.

The consensus was that the day was more about the man and the moment than any moving words. William Safire, the dean of presidential speechwriters, called the speech "solid, respectable, uplifting, suitably short, superbly delivered." But he added that in light of the "towering expectations" it "fell short of the anticipated immortality." That was a bar that not even Obama could clear, and he was smart not to try. Had he loaded up the address with high-flown language it would have felt overcooked. The people of the United States and the world didn't need fancy rhetoric to make them cry. They needed a dose of reality to make them think—and they got it.

At the congressional luncheon afterward in the Capitol's Statuary Hall, the new president, surrounded by sculptures of the great men of American history, many of them slaveholders, felt his debt to those who had struggled to make this day possible. John Lewis, the only speaker from the 1963 March on Washington still alive, approached for an autograph of a commemorative picture. The president wrote, "Because of you, John. Barack Obama."

Ted Kennedy, dying of brain cancer, suffered a seizure and was wheeled out on a gurney. Bob Byrd, frail at 91, soon followed. "This is a joyous time, but it's also a sobering time," Obama said after they left, summarizing the mood of the day. He would respect the seriousness of the nation's predicament but not refrain from celebrating and even taking prudent risks. The Secret Service, jumpy over the terrorist threat, hoped he would cancel his plan to walk part of the parade route. But he felt strongly that Americans wanted to see their new president among them, and so the Obamas emerged from the limo twice as it moved up Pennsylvania Avenue, walking the final block from 15th Street to their new home.

As the parade began Obama reviewed the troops and executed a crisp salute he'd been practicing for days. Later he flashed a pinkie and thumb salute, the "shaka sign," to the band from Honolulu's Punahou High School, his alma mater. By sundown Barack and Michelle, as those lining the street called them, were on their way to the first-ever Neighborhood Ball, scheduled to show respect for their new local community. Through nine more official balls they slow-danced to the fitting Etta James standard "At Last," executed a modest "bump" in one or two faster dances, and greeted guests as quickly as they could before hustling to the next venue.

The Obamas invited about fifty of their closest friends and supporters to the White House for a reception after the balls. This was the most exclusive party in a week of classy parties—no press, of course, and only a small handful of aides—but guests arrived expecting that the first couple had already gone to bed. Michelle was exhausted and didn't stay long. The new president tapped a late burst of energy and hung out, still looking fresh in his tuxedo and holding a glass of champagne as if he were lingering at a wedding. As Wynton Marsalis and his jazz quartet played in the East Room, Obama recalled the parade and the peacefulness of the huge crowds, complimented the women on their dresses, and caught up on the buzz from Chicago. When someone asked how it would feel to sleep in a new house, he replied, "I could be in a Holiday Inn, on a bus, standing up. I just need to sleep." But as the clock passed 2:30 a.m. he didn't yet know how to reach the family quarters.

"Where do I go now?" he asked no one in particular.

8

Sea Legs

Barack Obama would get no honeymoon from the GOP. The image he had of himself as a latter-day Lincoln, looking for the "better angels" in other people—the bridging of red state–blue state divisions that brought him to national prominence in 2004—would be tested almost immediately. He extended his hand to Republicans and they slapped it away before the Inauguration scaffolding had even been taken down. In that sense Inauguration Day was merely a twenty-four-hour cease-fire in the partisan wars that had consumed the capital for at least two decades.

Obama had come to Washington on a promise of easing the conflict; that was a big reason he had done so well with independents and even some Republicans in November. Every early gesture to Capitol Hill was meant to strike a bipartisan tone. This reasonableness would cause him trouble in his first hundred days, though he would get points for trying.

From the beginning the White House discouraged a hundred-day time line. Obama's political advisors thought it was, as Dan Pfeiffer later put it, "a Hallmark holiday" that boxed them in. What if they had a bad first three months? Pfeiffer and Robert Gibbs tried to spread the word that Obama should not be judged until after his first year.

But privately Obama set three message goals for his first hundred days, all patterned, at least loosely, on how FDR operated in 1933.

First, he wanted to be seen as breaking sharply with the past. If Roosevelt was everything Hoover was not, Obama must be "the un-Bush," as Anita Dunn called it. This contrast should be shown, not told, which meant no explicit Bush-bashing.

Second, the White House must show competence daily, which meant not just enacting a recovery bill by Presidents Day, February 16, but putting other "points on the board," with splashy executive orders, elaborate bill-signing ceremonies, frequent interviews, and the constant impression of a highly engaged and hands-on president. The line in

FDR's famous 1933 Inaugural that caught Obama's eye was not "The only thing we have to fear is fear itself," but his call for "action and action now," which the president repeated on CNBC.

Conveying that ceaseless activity was the key to Obama's third and most elusive goal: restoring public confidence. While markets and polls would respond in large part to what happened in the economy, the tone at the top was critical. As Roosevelt had shown, public confidence was connected to the president's personal confidence. Americans wanted to see their president enjoying the job and staying cheerful even as he told them the truth about the condition of the country. Calibrating the ratio of optimism to realism would be a daily challenge for Obama, and at the beginning he would sometimes tilt too far one way or the other. But overall he seemed up to the job from the start. He was comfortable in the role. "The suit fits, the chair's not too big," as Axelrod put it. Even the most antagonistic radio talk show hosts, the ones who thought he was destroying the country, rarely suggested the job was too much for him.

It helped that the new president loved what he called his new "home office." If Obama was often annoyed and out of sorts during the campaign, he felt much more content in the White House, where he got to eat dinner with his family several nights a week for the first time in a long time.* "Barack seemed more relaxed than he'd been in two years," said his friend Julius Genachowski. "He was finally doing the thing that he went through all that craziness to get to, which was to sit with some smart people and tackle some challenges."

THE FIRST ORDER of business was to make sure there was no doubt about Obama's legitimacy as president. During the campaign right-wing "birthers" had spread a canard that he was born in Kenya, not Hawaii, and was therefore constitutionally ineligible to take the oath. Greg Craig, the incoming White House counsel, figured it was only a matter of time before the oath itself was questioned by wing nuts.

The chief justice was mortified by his mistake on the Inauguration platform. Obama had voted against Roberts's nomination in 2005 and had now become the first president ever sworn in by a chief justice he

------

* In the 1990s Obama's job as an Illinois state senator often kept him in Springfield during the week. After he was elected to the U.S. Senate his family stayed behind in Chicago, and in 2006 he began campaigning for president.

had opposed. But there was no bad blood; Roberts had simply gotten nervous and goofed.

Craig knew there was no constitutional requirement to repeat the swearing-in, but he also knew that without a do-over the Internet would be churning by the end of the week. So out of what Craig called "an abundance of caution," Roberts was invited to the Map Room on the first floor of the White House on the evening of January 21. Sitting on the couch beforehand Obama kept the mood light. "We decided it was so much fun . . . ," he joked. When he rose, Roberts asked, "Are you ready to take the oath?" Obama replied, "I am, and we're going to do it very slowly." Twenty-five seconds later it was over. To keep it from becoming a spectacle, the event was covered by only four print reporters. Scratchy audio and still pictures by White House photographer Pete Souza were the only other record. Obama was undoubtedly president now, though the "birthers" and their allies in Congress would never admit it.

THE PRESIDENT'S FIRST week was meant to show real, immediate change. To set a new tone and reverse several unpopular Bush policies immediately, Obama signed executive orders restricting lobbyists, closing the detention center at Guantánamo Bay within a year, lessening secrecy (by shifting the burden of proof to those advocating the classification of documents), barring ex-presidents from restricting the release of their papers, and lifting the gag order on abortion counseling overseas. In between he signed the Lilly Ledbetter Fair Pay Act for women and made symbolically important visits to major departments.

Obama's most significant off-campus visit was across the Potomac to the Pentagon, where he met with the Joint Chiefs of Staff in the command post known as "the Tank." Contrary to popular assumption, the chiefs are not technically in the presidential chain of command. (After they refused to go along with too-low troop estimates for the Iraq War President Bush and Defense Secretary Donald Rumsfeld circumvented them to talk directly to CENTCOM, the Tampa-based command center for operations in Iraq and Afghanistan.) By visiting the brass on their turf rather than summoning them to the White House Obama was making a significant gesture. He was simultaneously restoring their status and showing respect from a Democratic president with no military experience.

From the time he was young Obama had immersed himself in different cultures. To him the military, so separate from American civilian society, was like Indonesia or Chicago's South Side: a place to study, understand, and search for common ground.* He resolved to be vocal on veterans' issues and to avoid Bill Clinton's early problems with the Pentagon in 1993.†

Obama's foreign policy was dependent on restoring America's prestige abroad. He surprised the global media by granting his first interview as president not to a major American network or favored pundit but to Al Arabiya, a moderate Arab satellite channel. He offered the Arab and Muslim world "a new partnership based on mutual respect and mutual interest." This was seen in the Middle East as a diplomatic masterstroke and in the United States as another early sign (like using his middle name for the oath) that Obama intended to shed his reluctance to talk about his Muslim roots. Reaching out to the Muslim world would turn out to be his most distinctive foreign policy initiative of 2009.

Reaching out to the congressional. world was a bit more frustrating. Obama was determined to pursue his agenda in close cooperation with Capitol Hill. "We've tried the stone tablet route of depositing a bill on the steps of the Capitol," Axelrod said drily, in reference to the Clinton health care plan. "It wasn't well received."

But the new Congress showed right away that it had no taste for raising revenue to pay for middle-class tax cuts, health care, or anything else. In budget documents Obama floated the idea of saving $125 billion by limiting the deductibility of charitable contributions for those making over $250,000 a year to 28 percent, the level of the Reagan years. Congressional Democrats, citing the impact on charities, didn't even wait for the debris from the Inauguration parade to be swept away before they rejected the idea out of hand.

At 6:30 p.m. at the end of his first week Obama sat in the Oval Office chatting with senior staff. "This could get to be pretty lonely," he said.

———

FOR A TIME it seemed as if health care reform would never get off the ground. Early transition meetings left advocates inside the Obama camp in near despair.

As a sign of commitment Tom Daschle wanted a full health care plan articulated in the president's first budget. Otherwise, he argued, it

---

* McCain clearly carried the officer corps in November, but Obama did surprisingly well among enlisted personnel, whose voting patterns generally track the population at large.

† Clinton's difficulties with the Pentagon ranged from the fiasco over gays in the military to outlandish but damaging rumors that young White House aides had asked uniformed officers to carry their bags.

would look like Obama wasn't serious about reform. At the other extreme were those who argued that the idea was dead for 2009.

Even before he formally became budget director, Peter Orszag had offered a compromise with what was called the "placeholder" argument, a statement of intent with numbers only in an attachment. He and Gene Sperling (a Clintonite with experience in health care politics) figured that attaching a high dollar figure to health care risked making it a fat target before the process had matured.

The intensity of Obama's support for health care reform had been hard to discern during the transition. Orszag argued that out-of-control health care costs were wrecking the economy. But he also explained what another trillion dollars in upfront spending would do to the deficit. The case for backing off was plenty strong. Bill Clinton had reneged on his campaign promise of a middle-class tax cut in 1993 and hardly anyone noticed. If Obama chose delay he had plenty of room to say that the economy should take precedence.

Three days after the Inauguration Obama asked a dozen or so policy people gathered in the Roosevelt Room how many thought that health care should be in the budget as more than a placeholder with a bunch of zeros. Whether out of uneasiness about the newness of being polled by the president or lack of enthusiasm, at first no one spoke or raised a hand. The younger aides who sat along the wall were appalled. "Massive backsliding," one called it. Clinton-era staffers, burned by the failure of Hillarycare in 1994, seemed to be winning the argument with their cautionary advice. They all insisted that they favored health care reform but wanted to see how things played out before committing to it.

Tom Daschle, slated to be health czar, was in North Carolina tending to his ailing brother, who was undergoing treatment for brain cancer. He trusted Mark Childress, his longtime deputy for health policy, to put his case to the president. Childress was the only one with his hand up. He spoke about the importance of moving forward aggressively before the end of the year. "Pretty good case," Obama responded. "Okay, I'll channel Daschle."

But when he got back to town Daschle wasn't sure he'd been channeled. The president had been cryptic and Daschle thought the signals on whether health care was going forward were still mixed. So did Childress and the rest of his staff. Whatever the intention of the budgeteers, their machinations and political analysis sent Jeanne Lambrew, the new deputy director of the White House Office of Health Care Reform, into a panic. Was it all coming apart before they even started? Neera Tanden, who had worked as Hillary's policy director before joining the Department of Health and Human Services, told friends it felt as if her world was ending. On the other side, the budget team saw the transition debate as an argument over tactics that had spun into a toxic misunderstanding. Colleagues were barely avoiding shouting matches. Friends were challenging each others' motives and their commitment to health care reform.

The Sunday after the Inauguration, January 25, fearing that health care was losing altitude, Daschle went to see Rahm Emanuel in his new West Wing office. Within minutes Obama wandered in and hugged him, asking after his brother.

When they sat down Daschle said, "I just need to know—you've said this is so important to you. Can you reiterate that face-to-face or have things changed?"

Obama was determined to calm Daschle and keep him on the reservation. "I'm going to tell you something here and now," he said, looking Daschle in the eye. "This is more important to me today than it has ever been before. It will stay that way. I need your help." The president made Daschle believe he meant it, and as it turned out, he did.

Obama then set to work forging a compromise. The health care reform line item would say 0.00 in the budget itself, with an attached "reserve fund" chart that Orszag designed referring to $634 billion in new health care spending, with the stipulation that it might be higher. The die was cast in Week One. The president was operating on history suggesting that big initiatives introduced early in an administration tended to have a better chance of passage than those put forward later, as a president's popularity declined.

During the transition Carol Browner had argued strenuously that cap and trade should come first, but the stimulus changed the calculations; it included so much money for energy that it took away the urgency to do more. Among long-term reforms health care and energy were meant to be pursued on parallel tracks, but now it looked as if health care reform would have primacy in the first year.

A few days later Obama's voice grew uncharacteristically soft as he spoke to a small knot of aides in the Oval Office. "Two years ago, hardly anyone thought I'd be here," he said. "Life's unpredictable and we're all living on borrowed time. Let's figure out how to get it [health care] done." With that, he strode out of his own office.

There was a long pause as the aides looked at one another. Finally Rahm, who strongly opposed tackling full health care reform in 2009 and would continue to oppose it all year, repeated the president's words: "Okay, let's figure out how to get it done."

The political advisors who almost unanimously believed that Obama was wrong—that pushing health care in 2009 would crash the system and risk defeat—were on board now. This was the new president's first major decision in office and even if they didn't agree, they devoted themselves to making it happen.

When reminded later that Axelrod had favored pushing energy first, Obama said he didn't recall that. "One of the things that you discover when you're president is that even with close counselors who are willing to tell you what you don't want to hear, a lot of their arguments may be outside of the Oval Office, as opposed to right in front of me."

Everything would be fine as long as he got a bill. If the president and Congress pulled it off, health care reform would be more than an achievement on its own terms; it would accomplish something that had eluded presidents for nearly a hundred years and help redeem the promise of the 2008 election.

The Republicans knew that too, and vowed from the start to kill it.

———

FOR WEEKS BEFORE the Inauguration Obama had been playing bad poker on the stimulus. Instead of holding his cards close, then sweetening the pot for the Republicans with tax cuts in the final negotiations, he offered more than $300 billion in tax cuts at the front end of the process, nearly three weeks before taking office. (The final bill had tax cuts worth $288 billion.) Marty Nesbitt said later that the Republicans obviously weren't negotiating in good faith, but he'd also seen his old poker buddy play better hands: "He should have said, 'Here's the thing, no tax cuts.' And then go, 'Okay, you make some solid arguments—Okay, I'll give you $280 billion [in tax cuts].' " It was a big bargaining chip he left off the table.

To make matters worse, shortly before the Inauguration Obama had said that he had "no pride of authorship" on the bill, which annoyed House Democrats. If he refused to take at least some ownership of the stimulus, how could he expect members to sell it in their districts? Obama had essentially said to Republicans, Your fight's not with me, it's with Nancy Pelosi. Just days after the swearing-in Pelosi fumed privately, "The president threw me off the truck."

Few economists saw the tax cuts as truly stimulative. Americans would use the extra money (if they felt it at all) to pay down debt, not spend. This would be one of the largest short-term tax cuts in American history, nearly twice as much in immediate tax credits as provided by Bush in 2001. The difference was that the tax relief went to the middle class and working poor to fulfill Obama's "Make Work Pay" campaign promise. Republicans were so wedded to Bush's idea of marginal-rate tax cuts that they didn't think Obama's version of relief even counted.

Obama knew Pelosi would be fine. But he later said he should have given the GOP "more skin in the game": "[The Democrats could have] started off with no tax cuts, knowing that I was going to want some, and then let them [Republicans] take credit for all of them. Maybe that's the lesson I learned." Of course that wouldn't have worked either. Nothing except the policies rejected at the polls would satisfy Republicans. When reminded of Obama's tax cuts, they replied that many were actually "tax credits," little better than welfare. When Democrats put money in for infrastructure, Republicans called it make-work for unions. When the bill included funds to hire hundreds of new scientists and buy American-made scientific equipment, the Republicans claimed that only contracts that involved pouring concrete actually created jobs.

Three days after the Inauguration Obama invited Republican leaders to a private meeting at the White House. His tone was warm but direct. "You can't just listen to Rush Limbaugh and get things done," he told them with a pointed chuckle. (Limbaugh had informed his millions of listeners that he hoped Obama would fail.) By mentioning Limbaugh, Obama was reminding Republicans that they had to choose between being a governing party and a talk show party. But most of them, either because they were authentically hard-right or because they were facing potential primary challenges from conservatives, had already made that choice. They would be "Foxulists," Fox News conservatives with a populist twist. This entailed ignoring any message sent by the voters in November. When Eric Cantor persisted in familiar GOP arguments about taxes, Obama shot back, "I won." The Republicans felt he was rubbing their faces in it.

But the president was intent on being (or at least looking) bipartisan. The following week he took the unusual step of traveling to Capitol Hill to meet with the other party's House caucus on its turf to hear their concerns. Biden was dispatched to the GOP caucus in the Senate. Nobody could remember the last time a president and vice president had gone into the lion's den this way. By now, a week in, Obama knew that he wasn't making any headway with Republicans, but he wanted points for trying. And maybe a few might change their minds about cooperating. Fat chance. Before the president arrived House Minority Leader John Boehner instructed his GOP colleagues not to vote for the stimulus no matter what Obama said. And not a single one did.

The GOP thinking was logical and cynical at the same time. If Obama succeeded in stabilizing the economy with the support of Republicans, he would get all the credit. If he failed with their support, they would share the blame. But if he failed without their support, they could say "We told you so" to voters before the 2010 midterms. That became their strategy for the first two years of the Obama administration.

In the meantime Republicans schemed to drive a wedge between Pelosi and Obama. *The president wants to work with us; it's the speaker who's standing in the way,* they said. This wasn't entirely inaccurate. Rahm had encouraged conservative Democrats to criticize the package as a way of pressuring Pelosi to take out controversial provisions that might delay final passage.

Obama thought it made political sense to keep trying to work with Republicans, even if it temporarily hurt his relations with fellow Democrats. Every time the cable news piranhas reported on something controversial buried in the stimulus, such as much-needed seeding and repair for the National Mall or funding for the prevention of sexually transmitted diseases, Obama was philosophical. He thought these were good ideas, but he wasn't going to hold up his recovery program by insisting on them. Get them out of the package, he said.

But appeasement wasn't working. Boehner was still talking on TV about condoms in the stimulus even after all mention of contraceptives was removed from the bill. "As soon as we take out contraceptives, they say, 'Take out the Mall.' When we take out the Mall, it's 'Take out the honeybees,'" said George Miller, chair of the Education and Labor Committee. "It's death by a thousand cuts. In sports and politics, you never give up momentum. Republicans tried to break Obama's momentum. They failed, but they broke his stride for seventy-two hours."

Those three days at the end of the second week of his presidency were a disappointing early experience for Obama, as Republicans decamped to cable news studios to attack the stimulus from whatever angle they could. The White House, which still didn't have its email and computer systems properly connected, was caught off guard and had to play defense. It lined up only a few effective surrogates, and the president got sliced up in the usual cut and thrust of Washington politics.

For Obama the emphasis was on *usual.* He later said that although he expected plenty of partisanship, he was taken aback by the GOP's response to the stimulus, which with all the money flowing into the country should have been an easier yes vote. "I have to say it took me by surprise. There's a sense on the part of a big chunk of the Republican Party that they have no responsibilities to govern right now," he said. "From their perspective, they may just see this as payback."

He gave them more tax cuts than they had ever seen before—several times more than Bush for their middle-class constituents—and what did he get? No support on the House side and maybe two or three, if he worked them hard, in the Senate. He chose a bona fide conservative, Senator Judd Gregg, for an important economic post (commerce secretary), and what happened? Instead of viewing the choice as a gesture of bipartisanship (as Democrats did when President Bush chose Democratic congressman Norman Mineta as his transportation secretary), the Republicans hounded Gregg as a traitor until he dropped out of the Cabinet. "This place is insane," Obama told Nesbitt with a can-you-believe-it? grin.

———

THE MOST HELLISH part of the Seventy-two Hours from Hell involved Tom Daschle, whose dual nomination to appointment as HHS secretary and White House health czar was in trouble after revelations that he had recently paid $128,000 in back taxes on a car and driver provided for him by a big Democratic donor, Leo Hindrey.* Daschle's larger problem was that he was now the Washington archetype of the decent man who came to town to do good and stayed to do well. Though he wasn't technically a lobbyist for the law firm of Alston and Bird, the strategic advice he provided health industry clients (from whom he also accepted honoraria for addressing their meetings) and his frequent contacts with his former Capitol Hill colleagues amounted to the same thing.

Obama had campaigned hard against lobbyists and had just signed an executive order preventing them from serving in government. But he'd already granted a waiver allowing a lobbyist for the defense contractor Raytheon to become deputy secretary of defense, and now the Daschle publicity was making the president look like even more of a hypocrite.†

Coming less than a month after Tim Geithner's tax woes, the timing of the chauffeur story was fateful. If Daschle's problems had surfaced first, during the transition, he might well have survived and Geithner

———

* White House aides later said that Daschle's mistake was using his South Dakota accountant, who was too willing to say he owed the back taxes. A Washington accountant, they argued, would have known how to properly claim the car and driver as a deductible business expense. Daschle rejected this reasoning and blamed himself.
† Deputy Secretary of Defense Bill Lynn was only one of several former lobbyists who managed to make it in. Mark Patterson, a lobbyist for Goldman Sachs, became chief of staff to Geithner, and several White House aides had been registered lobbyists as recently as 2006. Even reformers considered the Obama standard to be arbitrary. The important reform, they said, was the one preventing government officials from lobbying their old colleagues after they left government. Barring lobbyists from serving, in this view, was merely cosmetic.

gone down, with significant consequences for the shape of Obama's domestic program. This was cold comfort to Daschle, who knew how to count Senate votes in a poisonous environment. He figured he could get confirmed, and the White House agreed, but only at a high cost for the president.

Daschle pondered his fate all night on February 2 and called Pete Rouse in the morning. When Obama came on the line and Daschle told him he was withdrawing his name from nomination, the president asked if he had given it enough thought, but didn't try to talk him out of it. Some hard-boiled White House aides reproached themselves for not pushing Daschle out weeks earlier, before the chauffeur story broke publicly, with his brother's brain cancer as a convenient excuse. Obama was more charitable but agreed now that he needed to go. Daschle remembered it as a warm conversation with none of the I-hope-you-have-a-good-rest-of-your-life sentiment that often characterized such partings. Obama called Daschle several times over the next few weeks to keep him informed and intermittently sought his advice on health care for the rest of the year.

That day Obama was already scheduled to sit for back-to-back interviews with five TV networks about the stimulus. Now the questions would be about Daschle. Obama despised prep sessions before debates and interviews, and he was in no mood for this one. As soon as Robert Gibbs started firing questions, the president put up his hand and said, "Wait. Let me tell you what I'm going to say, and you tell me why I can or can't say it." He then took responsibility for the whole mess and explained how sticking with Daschle would have sent the wrong signal. "I screwed up," he said in the prep session and then on camera before the world. "We can't send a message to the American people that we have two rules, one for prominent people and one for ordinary people."

Obama's press aides saw this as an early example of how the boss could defuse a political crisis by saying something that made perfect sense to ordinary people—"I screwed up"—even as it appeared revolutionary in Washington, where the most apologetic that previous presidents ever got was to assume the passive voice and tepidly allow that "mistakes were made." A trace of contrition was also good politics; Obama's approval ratings ratcheted even higher afterward. If he had failed to take responsibility, they said, he might have genuinely screwed up his first month and been on course to a disastrous debut.

But if Obama's response to the Daschle flap was effective and refreshing, it also had negative consequences for the staffing of his administration. The same day Daschle went, Obama decided that consistency required him to accept the resignation of Nancy Killefer as chief perfor-mance officer in the Office of Management and Budget. Back in 2005 Killefer paid $948 to settle a local tax lien stemming from her failure to pay enough in unemployment compensation tax on her household help, a relatively common oversight that had never jeopardized a nomination before. According to the "Zoe Baird standard" (named for Clinton's first nominee for attorney general, who was forced to withdraw), nannies were a problem only if they were illegal immigrants or had been paid entirely off the books. In any event Killefer's fate now became a prec-edent and several other talented nominees were disqualified for minor tax mistakes.*

Over time vetting became the most irritating headache of Obama's first year.† With 500,000 résumés for 7,000 positions, it should have been easy to fill all the personnel slots. But the intrusions into one's personal life required for public service kept multiplying. Vetting had become like airport security, where more precautions were added after every incident because no politician could risk being seen as doing less. The Obama administration, like those before it, didn't dare rein in the process for fear of seeming ethically challenged or insufficiently aware of the political costs of humiliating publicity.

The list of questions kept growing with every flap. Ever since dia-ries were subpoenaed in one of the pointless Clinton Whitewater inves-tigations, potential nominees were asked if they kept journals. Con-gressman Mark Foley's sexual emails led to new questions about email pseudonyms. Eliot Spitzer's problem with prostitution ensured that the question of whether one had ever paid for sex moved up higher on the list. Many nominees were asked point-blank if they had been disloyal to the United States, used illegal drugs since college, been unfaithful to their spouses, watched pornography online at work, or argued so loudly at home that the neighbors could hear. The security clearance applica-tion for summer interns was shorter; it ran to only forty-four pages.

Not every wrong answer was disqualifying, but the Torquemadas of the FBI wanted to know it all. The vetters sometimes ended the in-terviews by explicitly invoking one widely publicized case, informing nominees that Martha Stewart went to jail not for stock manipulation but for lying to federal investigators. By the time the vetting process was over, many of the president's choices, once so eager to go to Wash-ington, felt more like public enemies than potential public servants.

---

* The administration's chief tormenter on small tax matters was talk show host Glenn Beck, whose production company experienced its own small tax matter that was reported in 2010.
† The hassles began on Day One, when the White House computers couldn't import the transition's personnel system.

The process took months and backed up every decision in official Washington. The details of, say, structuring bank rescue plans at Treasury or assembling shovel-ready projects at Transportation were monstrously complicated. The paperwork would eventually stack several feet high; civil servants in the agencies could not get through it all before Obama's appointees were in place. Many of the career people were smart and dedicated and worked overtime, but many others caused traffic jams at the elevators at 4:30 p.m. as they raced to get home.

Much of the early anguish could be traced to the powerful Senate Finance Committee, which was holding up dozens of nominees who hadn't crossed their *t*'s and dotted their *i*'s. When Jim Messina was Max Baucus's top aide in 2005 he had arranged for a hardworking IRS agent, Mary Baker, to be detailed to the committee. Now Messina's old hire was helping to throw a wrench into the Obama works.

Baker answered not just to Democrats but to a group of minority staff aides known as "the Grassleys" for their tireless dedication to pursuing the idiosyncratic interests of their boss, Senator Charles Grassley, the ranking Republican on the committee. Unlike many committee chairmen and the top-ranking member from the other party, Baucus and Grassley were friendly and prided themselves on working closely together. When Republicans controlled the Senate and he was the chairman, Grassley had been solicitous of Baucus. Not surprisingly, Baucus was careful to return the favor when Democrats regained control in 2006. Their relationship would prove central to the Washington drama of 2009. Together they would have major influence, even veto power, over two of the major issues that would make or break the Obama administration: health care and energy.

So it was hard for the White House to raise too big a stink when the committee moved from vetting nominees to *auditing* them. Baucus and Grassley insisted that they had applied the same standards to Bush nominees, but it sure didn't feel that way at the White House. Where was the common sense? When audited, more than three-quarters of all American tax returns reporting more than $200,000 in income are found to have irregularities. Different auditors usually find different minor problems in the same set of returns. In the old days the individual would be told there was an issue, he'd pay the disputed amount, and the problem would quietly go away.

Instead of a quiet phone call, the Senate Finance Committee began issuing short public reports on individuals. To avoid humiliating its nominees, the White House felt obliged to bring in several volunteer tax attorneys to scrub three years of tax returns for every nominee before the names were sent to the Hill. This slowed the process to a crawl. After two months of the Obama administration, seventeen major positions at Treasury remained empty—positions at the heart of frantic efforts to keep the United States out of a depression. With the economy still in collapse, a visitor to the hulking Treasury Building next to the White House found it virtually empty at 6 p.m. This went on all spring.

It seemed as though everyone Obama knew complained about it. Penny Pritzker weighed in privately; Paul Volcker spoke out about the process in public. Republican Senator Lamar Alexander went on the Senate floor to blast his own committee for "the maze of forms and onerous reviews for nominees," to which Grassley replied that the only form in question was IRS Form 1090. Eric Cantor referred to Geithner and Daschle and quipped, "It's easy for [Democrats] to sit here and advocate higher taxes because—you know what?—they don't pay them."

Cantor had a point, but the vetting logjam was beginning to harm the quality of Obama's appointees. The process was skewed toward people who had led simple, cautious lives. Sometimes those people were terrific, but sometimes they were drones who added nothing to their agencies. Swashbucklers need not apply. If you'd shown some entrepreneurial moxie, say, and made your living as an independent contractor, you got a special form with twenty-one additional questions, each one a potential time bomb. Any red flag could mean asking for tax returns that went back a decade or more.

Dozens of potential nominees took themselves out of the running rather than risk public humiliation. This was especially true of nominees who came from outside of Washington and had not led the past twenty years of their life preparing to quit their jobs to work in the government. If they paid a housekeeper for a couple of hours every other week, they hadn't worried about a potential "Zoe Baird problem." By contrast, Washingtonians had been generally keeping their noses clean for years; there were so many officials-in-waiting that services sprang up to guarantee that nannies or gardeners were legal and on the books.

When you discourage or eliminate anyone with nanny problems, tax problems, lobbyist associations, Wall Street associations, complex personal finances, difficult family situations, and other miscellaneous concerns, the short lists get a lot shorter. The Obama administration's choices soon consisted mostly of the usual suspects from Washington: Clinton administration veterans eager to go back into government as the fourth or fifth choice for the job.

Hillary Clinton thought the vetting process and lobbying standards were getting "ridiculous," as she later put it, to the annoyance of the White House. Her choice to head the Agency for International

Development, Paul Farmer, a renowned medical anthropologist and humanitarian, withdrew in part because he couldn't account for every one of thousands of foreign friends he had made in recent years.* Tom Malinowski, in line to be assistant secretary of state for human rights, saw his nomination scuttled because he'd been a lobbyist for Human Rights Watch. The State Department was only one of several departments that had filled fewer than half of its political positions by summer.

White House aides could blame the rules of the Senate, which allow a single senator to put a hold on a nomination. But it was their own strict rules that caused much of the problem. In retrospect perhaps Obama should have used some political capital to push a new "rule of reason" standard for selecting his team. Instead he was caught between his idealistic notion of legions of ethically pure public servants and the grubbier reality of human nature and life in Washington.

————

AMID THE DASCHLE mess and caustic cable news, Obama stayed focused on getting the stimulus passed by Presidents' Day. As he studied his potential pressure points in the Senate, his attention soon turned to Arlen Specter, the ornery moderate Republican from Pennsylvania. Specter's big issue was cancer. Having survived two bouts with Hodgkin's lymphoma he was appalled that, for several years, fewer than 40 percent of proposals from qualified cancer researchers had been funded by the National Institutes of Health. Thousands of "beaker-ready" projects were turned down, which meant many potential cancer treatments, even cures, never surfaced. Specter resolved to use his status as a swing vote on the stimulus to remedy the problem, and on January 27 he introduced an amendment to the appropriations bill that would add $10 billion to the NIH budget, a 34 percent increase.

Early on Obama decided to hold a Super Bowl party in the White House movie theater to create some goodwill with members of Congress. But the new president wasn't yet of much use as an advocate for his program. He mingled amiably, clowned with 3-D glasses (passed out for viewing a Super Bowl ad), and when a young boy asked in front of the group where the bathroom was, Obama laughed and said, "I don't know. I just got here."

Fortunately for Obama, his friend and former Illinois colleague Dick Durbin, the Senate majority whip, was working the party. Durbin promised Specter that he would make sure the $10 billion for NIH was

————

* Farmer was the subject of Tracy Kidder's classic book *Mountains beyond Mountains.*

in the stimulus. Knowing that Specter felt he was above crude deals, he didn't extract a commitment then from Specter to vote for the whole package.

For the next two weeks Specter was his usual difficult self. When he met one-on-one with the president he predicted (accurately, it turned out) that if he sided with Obama on the stimulus, then Pat Toomey would run for his seat in the Pennsylvania Republican primary. Toomey, founder of the Club for Growth, a conservative tax-cutting organization, suddenly became a hot topic inside the White House, as aides and the president himself spent valuable time war-gaming the other party's prospects in the Keystone State.

This was not what the White House high command had in mind for the president's opening month. "We had a good plan for the first three weeks, then all of this shit happens," Jim Messina lamented. Axelrod found himself surprised that Washington was even worse than he expected. In Chicago he had always pitched clients that he was a better political consultant because he "lived in America, not Washington." Now he felt that line was truer than he knew.

Ax liked to tell the story about going to his favorite restaurant, Manny's, a cafeteria-style deli in Chicago, when Bill Clinton faced impeachment. "The cashier said, 'You know, I need this job—my husband is on disability. This guy Clinton has helped us in the last six years and I don't care about his personal life.' " That was when Axelrod realized that Clinton would not have to resign. "It helps to be from somewhere," he said. In February, having just arrived in Washington, he felt like a guy who needed a Manny's fix.

Obama's challenge, Axelrod thought, was to stay in touch with what the American people were thinking, not just what the cable pundits were yakking about. Axelrod was determined to keep his head "out there," past the Potomac. He referred to himself as "a Chicagoan on assignment" who was "renting, not buying" in Washington. This mentality, shared by Obama, wasn't peripheral; it was central to everything they were about. "Our greatest challenge is not economic or the threat from overseas," Axelrod said when the stimulus was under attack. "We'll handle that okay. It's how to avoid being lost in the bubble." They were two weeks in and the bubble was already growing, bloblike. "We were so focused on process that we failed to use the greatest tool we have—the bully pulpit," Axelrod said a couple of weeks later.

So Obama picked up the tool, first in private, then on the road. On February 4 he met with Democratic senators at the Newseum. (Although the museum is dedicated to press freedom, it was closed to the press that day.) Obama was confident and in total control. "Don't bet against me," he told the senators, who had been grumbling on TV about the details of the stimulus almost as much as Republicans had. "You can run away from me but you can never run far enough." He defended the contraceptives and other controversial provisions on the merits but explained why he backed off: "We can't lead with our chin."

Don't bet against me carried two potent meanings that would shape Obama's first year. The first referred to Obama personally: he was the new president signaling that he was tough and had won against stiff odds in the past. The black grandson of Kenyan goatherds had run against the most potent political machine in a generation and become president of the United States. Underestimating him, he was saying, was irrational.

And dangerous to the political health of Democrats. That was the second message. The big political question early on for moderate Democrats was the same as it would be in the fall on health care: Should they show independence from the president? Was it smart? Senator Jack Reed reminded his colleagues of the motto of the French Foreign Legion: "March or die." Paul Begala, a political consultant, informed the gathering that "the politics of differentiation" no longer worked. Scoring points at home by standing up to the president of your own party was yesterday's game: "If you go through a car wash with Barack Obama, you're the only one who's gonna get wet." In words that many would recall months later Begala told them, "Barack Obama is going to get re-elected. The question is, will you?" He thought of it as Tammy Wynette time: "Stand by your man."

Two days later Obama went to the House retreat in Williamsburg, Virginia. His aides later said that this was the day he got his presidency back on track, though many of the problems of the first month (a disciplined conservative message, poor use of Obama surrogates) would persist. Shortly before boarding Marine One Obama brought a draft of his speech into Axelrod's office, crossing out paragraphs and telling Ax he intended to "ad-lib" in places. The House had already passed the stimulus, but members feared they would be left hanging if the bill went down in the Senate. They wanted to see some backbone in their new president.

That night Obama used sarcasm and ridicule to lash the Republicans. "What do you think a stimulus is?" he asked in a mocking tone. "It's spending—that's the whole point!" He was just warming up. "When you start hearing arguments on the cable chatter, just understand a couple of things. Number one, when they say, 'Well, why are we spending $800 billion [when] we've got this huge deficit?'—first of all, I found this deficit when I showed up. Number two, I found this national debt, doubled, wrapped in a big bow waiting for me as I stepped into the Oval Office." By the end he was so pumped that he went back to his old "Fired Up! Ready to Go!" call-and-response from the campaign. The House Democrats were thrilled. He had his mojo back.

When they found their way out of the cable fog members decided that it wasn't such a bad bill after all. Steve Ballmer, the CEO of Microsoft, told the retreat he heartily endorsed it. He recounted getting off the red-eye from Seattle groggy that morning and encountering Pelosi, who told him, "Our priority is science, science, science, and science." By the fourth *science,* he said, he was awake and fully on board.

The next day Obama headed to Elkhart, Indiana, and Las Vegas for town hall meetings. He vowed that never again would he try to sell legislation from the confines of Washington. A new pattern was set: when trouble hits, get out of Dodge. Getting out in memorable visual style—appearances that would stick in the minds of the public—was a harder challenge.

When he returned he began turning the screws on the swing voters in the Senate, who now included a balky conservative Democrat, Ben Nelson of Nebraska. Nelson, Olympia Snowe, and Susan Collins had offered a plan to cut $50 billion and were summoned separately to the White House to discuss it with Obama.

In private Obama struck the swing senators as a welcome change. Under Bush, Nelson felt, the White House was always working *on* him, not with him. Meetings with President Bush were invariably in groups, so he was surprised to learn that when this president shouted a hearty "Hey, Ben!" as Nelson entered the Oval Office, no aides stood behind him. They were alone, and after some small talk about hunting (the president didn't hunt but was happy to chat about it with those who did), Obama was blunt: "Are you trying to torpedo it [the stimulus]—or me?" Neither, Nelson replied. He was just trying "to fix it." After the meeting the Nebraskan backed off his push to cut billions for health and education.

The two moderate Maine Republicans, Snowe and Collins, each had her own charming presidential one-on-ones, with the senators in the unusual position of asking for less spending on their states, not more. Snowe wanted reductions in stimulus money for national parks, the Census Bureau, and the Bureau of Mines; Collins had a couple of her own home state projects she wanted funded but was especially adamant that $870 million to prevent a flu pandemic be deleted, a position that embarrassed her three months later when swine flu was in the headlines and the money had to be restored. Of greater consequence,

Collins was among those insisting that $16 billion in school construc-tion and weatherization be removed. This was a blow to the longer-term popularity of the stimulus because the "Green Schools" effort championed by Kentucky congressman Ben Chandler and others would have been a tangible sign of the recovery in thousands of communities; parents taking their children to school would have seen where some of the money went. In contrast, such items as energy tax credits, scientific research, and averted teacher layoffs were largely invisible. The middle-class tax cuts were mostly pocketed without being credited politically. The only evidence of the stimulus that many Americans saw personally in late 2009 was road construction, and the motorists who connected that to Obama and the Democrats were as likely as not to be muttering about the traffic it caused.

Many economists thought the stimulus was too small, not too big. The bill funded only a fraction of the infrastructure projects listed by the American Society of Civil Engineers as in need of construction or repair. Worse, the projects did little to stir the imagination of the pub-lic. Some of this was inevitable; necessary repairs of sewage systems would never be sexy. But with the exception of $8 billion for high-speed rail, the first such investment ever (placed in the package by Rahm at the eleventh hour), and perhaps some science projects that bore great fruit, it was hard to think of projects that historians would look back on in twenty years and say, "*That's* what Obama got for his trillion dollars in 2009."* He would have to settle for preventing an-other Great Depression.

For the president concerns about his legacy were an unaffordable luxury. First, he needed to get the recovery bill passed. A measure they expected to be a relatively easy sell was going to be touch-and-go. Rahm, Orszag, and Durbin set up shop in the back room of Harry Reid's Capitol offices. All one hundred senators had sent letters to Reid with what they wanted in or out of the stimulus, and those wishing a personal audience were allowed to make a strict five-minute pitch to the majority leader. Rahm took calls from Pelosi, Obey, and other for-mer colleagues as they moved into the short strokes. The hyperkinetic chief of staff's shuttle diplomacy between the House and Senate went beyond the specifics of the recovery package; it set a precedent for how House and Senate conference committees would likely function in the big legislative battles to come.

---

* Even the logo for the Recovery and Reinvestment Act, attached to every project, was dif-fuse and forgettable. By contrast, the symbol of the National Recovery Act of 1933 was a handsome blue eagle.

In the end it was Nelson, a Democrat, who held up the bill. Rahm wouldn't tell the press what he gave Nelson in exchange for his vote; that would be bad form. But soon enough Nebraska community and rural hospitals quietly learned that their federal funding formulas had been slightly adjusted in a way that netted them $30 million extra. Good old Ben had gone to bat for them. Nelson had threatened to torpedo a $787 billion recovery bill, aimed at preventing millions of Americans from losing their livelihoods, over a spending item that amounted to less than half of one one-hundredth of one percent of the total package. He would be back when the health care debate ripened, angling for much more.

Finally, on the eve of Valentine's Day, the stimulus bill cleared the sixty-vote threshold necessary to avoid a Senate filibuster with one vote to spare. The American Recovery and Reinvestment Act of 2009 (ARRA) was law. Obama signed the bill in Denver, far from the madding crowd. This made symbolic sense but it also reflected his consistent underselling of his recovery program, as if it was a dog's breakfast concocted by someone else. Later, when he struggled to convince voters that the bill was good for them, he wished he had launched it better.

On the day after final passage Obama told a group of liberal columnists aboard Air Force One that he'd try to work with congressional Republicans in the future, but he had clearly been chastened by their obstructionist tactics. "I'm an eternal optimist," he said. "That doesn't mean I'm a sap."

Ten months later Obama said that the unanimous House vote against the Recovery Act "set the tenor for the whole year": "That helped to create the tea-baggers and empowered that whole wing of the Republican Party to where it now controls the agenda for the Republicans." For Obama this was the greatest surprise of 2009. "[It wasn't that] I thought that my political outreach and charm would immediately end partisan politics," the president said. "I just thought that there would be enough of a sense of urgency that at least for the first year there would be an interest in governing. And you just didn't see that."

In fact Mitch McConnell, the Senate minority leader, had made it clear that any cooperation with Obama was prohibited. According to Specter, who changed parties in April in a bid to save his seat in 2010, Senators George Voinovich, Lisa Murkowski, and Mel Martinez had wanted to join him, Snowe, and Collins in working with the Democrats on the stimulus. That would have made six Republicans willing to govern in a bipartisan way. But McConnell wouldn't hear of it. Specter wasn't the only one who would face a stiff primary challenge for stepping even a bit out of line.

All year Obama watched in amazement as the GOP swung even further to the right. The sensible conservatives he expected to do business with were in a tough spot, he told aides, when a third of the voters in their party—the ones who would dominate the GOP primaries—were not sure if the president was born in the United States. He'd won the election handily, but much of the opposition didn't believe he was legitimate. That was hardly a recipe for bipartisanship.

———

OBAMA KNEW HE had stumbled in his handling of the stimulus, and for reasons beyond his mishandling of taxes. He said later that he failed to properly exploit the support he received on the bill not just from GOP Governors Arnold Schwarzenegger of California and Charlie Crist of Florida but from every Republican governor not running for president in 2012. He'd spent time courting the wrong Republicans.

He would continue to try to score political points by stressing bipartisanship, particularly on health care reform, but he would no longer shape his strategy around it. Given the big Democratic majorities, Republicans were close to irrelevant in the House and of tactical use in the Senate only on votes where regional interests came strongly into play. (For example, McCain and a few other deficit hawk Republicans helped sustain Obama's veto of the F-22 fighter, a weapon so bloated and useless that even the Pentagon didn't want it.) On votes requiring spending, only Snowe's and Collins's among Republicans were usually up for grabs.

Otherwise, the game would mostly be played inside Obama's own party, where the addition of Specter and Al Franken (who was seated in June after an almost endless fight in the Minnesota courts) gave the Democrats the sixty votes necessary to shut off debate and get anything accomplished. This left zero margin for error. All year the GOP would try to block progress long enough to catch a break on the sixty; maybe that break would come when Bob Byrd or Ted Kennedy was too ill to vote, or when something happened that no one could predict. Eventually Reid came to see his sixty-vote majority as a burden. It empowered every member of the Democratic caucus to stick him up.

Nonetheless the political shift on Capitol Hill—and the reliable support of Pelosi and Reid—seemed to be a stroke of political fortune for Obama. Through a combination of the past two election results and increasingly clownish leadership, the Republicans were marginalizing their own party. They hadn't forfeited, exactly, but they hadn't shown up to help chart a new course either. The GOP was becoming the Party of No at a time when Americans were looking for some answers, or at least claimed to be.

Those answers began in the Recovery Act, a grab bag that would never get proper credit for being one of the most important pieces of legislation in a generation. Along with the bank rescue, the ARRA kept a recession from becoming a depression. The extension of unemployment benefits for thirty-three weeks, expansion of food stamps, and $50 billion in stabilization funds to states and localities (which prevented hundreds of thousands of layoffs) all kept the economy from cascading downward.

Michael Waldman, Bill Clinton's former chief speechwriter, believed Obama's big political misfortune on the stimulus was that budget rules required putting everything in one big package. In fact, it was five landmark pieces of legislation in one. If the bill had been split into the biggest tax cuts for the middle class since Reagan, the biggest infrastructure bill since the Interstate Highway Act in the 1950s, the biggest education bill since Lyndon Johnson's first federal aid to education, the biggest scientific and medical research investment in forty years, and the biggest clean energy bill ever, then Obama would have looked like Superman, or at least more like FDR.

But Obama believed all along that breaking up his recovery package was a recipe for failure. He was more interested in speed than credit. A congressman approached the first lady at a White House reception after the bill's passage and told her the stimulus was the best antipoverty bill in a generation. Her reaction was "Shhhh!" The White House didn't want the public thinking that Obama had achieved long-sought public policy objectives under the guise of merely stimulating the economy, even though that's exactly what had happened. This approach might have been expedient in the short term, but it robbed Obama of what should have been seen as a historic victory.

In truth the bill was a tremendous boon to the working poor, starting with an expansion of the Earned Income Tax Credit. Begun under Reagan and bolstered under Clinton, the EITC proved to be the greatest poverty fighter since Social Security ended destitution among the elderly six decades earlier. But because the name was so boring and fewer than half of those eligible applied for it, the program never got much attention for pulling more than four million people out of poverty each year. Under the stimulus, EITC eligibility was permanently expanded. Millions of families were set to receive wage supplements of up to $6,000 a year from Washington—enough to prevent them from slipping back into poverty. To Paul Krugman and other critics, the stimulus was an underfunded Band-Aid. They sold it short. For all its flaws, it was a generous and compassionate bill that set a new direction in American social policy.

Shortly after ARRA's passage Obama attended an event in Ohio where the point was to highlight that because of the new money seventeen police officers weren't laid off. This was small-ball and not worth the president's time, Anita Dunn realized. Besides, the public was more worried about whether the Recovery Act money was being wasted than eager to receive gift-wrapped presents from Washington. So Obama deputized Biden as his "Sheriff Joe" to bust stupid stimulus projects before the Republicans and the press did, a time-consuming task that he and a special inspector general performed well.

Ron Klain, Biden's chief of staff, developed a crack team that carefully tracked the $787 billion and pounced on any projects that looked like trouble. They missed a few but did better avoiding wasteful projects than FDR and the New Dealers in the era when the term *boondoggle* was coined. The danger was that the administration would get so cautious that the new money wouldn't be felt quickly enough on Main Street.

Biden himself said there was only "a 30 percent chance" that the economic program would be successful. At his first press conference as president, on February 9, Obama said, "I don't know what Joe was talking about."

ON JANUARY 30, ten days after being sworn in, Obama called Bruce Riedel at home. Riedel, a former CIA official, had begun advising the Obama campaign in 2007. Now the president asked him to conduct a review of the progress of U.S. military efforts in Afghanistan, where the Bush administration's neglect over the previous seven years constituted foreign policy malpractice. For months Riedel had told Obama that this would be the single most important foreign policy issue he would face, and Obama didn't disagree.

The reasons weren't hard to figure. The Af-Pak border was the most likely place where American soldiers would die on this president's watch; it was al Qaeda's safest safe haven and thus the source of the most serious national security threat against the United States.

Or was it? Joe Biden took a trip there just before the Inauguration at Obama's instruction and reported back to the president that if you asked ten people on the ground what we were doing in Afghanistan, you got ten different answers. Counterinsurgency. Nation-building.

Protecting population centers. Routing the Taliban. Helping the Kabul government. Building democracy. And so forth. "We got to decide why we're there," Biden told the president when he got home. "It's al Qaeda." Biden figured, "If there was no Al Qaeda, we would not be there. Period."

The war wasn't going well. Emboldened by the inept and breathtakingly corrupt government of Hamid Karzai, Taliban fanatics intimidated villagers into complying with their bloodthirsty and often inhuman demands. The U.S. military was hobbled by bureaucratic impediments. Army officers tipped off to the whereabouts of dangerous Taliban fighters found that they had to receive more than a half-dozen clearances (including from Pentagon lawyers) before they could go try to kill or capture them. By that time the enemy had often escaped. The Bush-era commanding officer, General David McKiernan, wasn't getting the job done in a war that had long been an afterthought to Iraq.

Accustomed to dealing with Bush, the Pentagon kept it real simple for the new president. It offered three options for Afghanistan: a large footprint, a medium footprint, and a small footprint. Afterward the White House realized that the military had created a phony large footprint that no one actually considered an option, and that the medium footprint should have been called the large footprint. One staffer said that all the talk of footprints made him want to go out and walk in the snow.

At first Obama sent the NSC back for more information, but the deliberations didn't take long. Gates, Clinton, and the rest of the national security team agreed that the twelve thousand additional troops authorized by Bush in December wouldn't be enough to secure enough polling places in Afghanistan to allow a fair election to take place later in the year. So on February 17, after a pair of meetings in the Situation Room, Obama approved the medium footprint, seventeen thousand more troops, with an emphasis on protecting the integrity of the election. Upon arriving at the NATO summit in Strasbourg on March 27, he added four thousand more for training the Afghan security forces. That brought the total since December to thirty-two thousand new troops.

When he got home from Europe Obama told his team that after the Afghan election he wanted to go back and revisit whether those thirty-two thousand troops were still needed. He was looking to get them out, not send more. Gates nodded his head. "I'd be reluctant, Mr. President, to suggest any additional troops," he said.

One official in the room with more experience in government than the president wondered whether Obama knew "just how full of shit" the Pentagon was on the subject of more resources. If the president believed that Gates and the rest of them wouldn't be back for more troops, the official thought, he had a bridge he wanted to sell him.

———

RIEDEL'S FORTY-PAGE REPORT recommended that the United States reverse the progress of the Taliban, convince Pakistan to pursue terrorists along the border, secure Pakistan's nuclear arsenal, and engage with India to lessen tensions with Pakistan. All were undertaken except the last. After a series of ten deadly bombings in Mumbai in November 2008 were linked to Muslim militants, India was in no mood for détente with Pakistan. In fact India moved into Afghanistan with billions in development aid, which greatly complicated efforts to get Pakistan to focus on al Qaeda.

Beyond securing the Afghan election, the decision to send more troops to the region was as much about Pakistan as about Afghanistan. Obama had long harbored a strong interest in Pakistan; he had traveled through the country for three weeks during college and stayed with the family of a Pakistani friend.* By the time of the transition he was admitting privately that the "dysfunction" there was the only issue keeping him up at night. Upon taking office he was surprised to learn that while Bush had authorized dozens of CIA-backed Predator drone attacks in Iraq and Afghanistan, he was so anxious to stay on good terms with the government of Pervez Musharraf that he approved only five or six that targeted the tribal areas harboring Osama bin Laden and other key al Qaeda operatives. Obama doubled the number of drone attacks on the Pakistani side of the border. "The CIA gets what it needs," he said.

By doubling drone attacks and doubling troop levels in Afghanistan from a year earlier, Obama saw himself as trying to make the best of a deteriorating situation. The alternative to bolstering Karzai was an Afghanistan once again controlled by the Taliban, which would like nothing better than to restart terrorist training camps that would teach young Muslims how to kill Americans.

But the expectations were unrealistic from the start. The White House, said one official, had put a gun to its own head by setting a mid-2010 timetable for measurable progress. Everyone familiar with the situation knew it was going to be a much longer slog than that.

———

* During the 2008 campaign critics tried in vain to make this seem nefarious. The American friends Mohammed Hasan Chandoo and Wahid Hamid are now, respectively, a financial consultant and a vice president of PepsiCo.

Biden wasn't convinced that adding resources would address that dysfunction, but he was quickly outflanked. The new troops approved by Bush were already in the pipeline. Iraq was ratcheting down and Afghanistan was ratcheting up. Antiwar liberals may have forgotten, but that's what Obama had promised again and again in the 2008 campaign.

When he was asked at the end of his first hundred days to name his toughest decision so far, Obama didn't hesitate before saying "Afghanistan." At the time he thought the big decision on sending more young Americans into harm's way was behind him. He was wrong. The Pentagon would be back with a request for a lot more troops. In December, asked the same question about his toughest decision of 2009, he gave the same answer: "Afghanistan."

———————

IN LATE FEBRUARY Obama displayed his pragmatism. Before getting to its own budget, the White House had to deal with Bush's leftover 2009 budget, now nearing completion in the new Congress. That bill had nine thousand earmarks in it, the special favors for individual members that McCain, in his words, had "made famous" during the 2008 campaign. Obama had joined him during their debates in slamming pork.

"How can we sign a bill with nine thousand earmarks in it?" Axelrod asked. Phil Schiliro said that he and the congressional relations team had cut the number of earmarks down from more than twenty thousand, a more than 50 percent reduction. "Nine thousand or two—earmarks are earmarks," Ax replied. He was the protector of Obama's change message. Now he and Gibbs wanted to make sure they didn't send an early signal of politics as usual.

The Hill veterans argued the other side. Pete Rouse pointed out that giving the president a two- or three-point boost in popularity at Congress's expense wasn't worth it. He and Rahm didn't see the point in ticking off Congress just before critical votes.* Harry Reid had said publicly that the earmarks were last year's business and should be treated that way by the White House. They should use "Bush's budget" as a fig leaf to let members have their goodies and then move on.

It was a tough call for Obama, who wasn't oblivious to the danger of drifting too far from the themes that had brought him this far. But

———————

* When Jimmy Carter tried to kill nineteen pet water projects shortly after becoming president in 1977, the Democratic Congress was furious. The same thing happened in 1993 when Bill Clinton tried to introduce grazing fees on Western lands. Both were stymied.

he swallowed Rahm and Rouse's argument. Earmarks went into the same category as gays in the military, special prosecutors for Bush-era crimes, gun control, and many other lower-priority issues. The mantra of the Obama White House for 2009 would be *No distractions.*

"We got big stuff going on here," the president said. For now, anyway, the potential for transformational change would trump immediate symbolic change in the Washington culture, a decision that would prove fateful. The earmarks stayed in the old budget but would not be allowed in the new one.

This was fine with Congress, which gave Obama a tumultuous welcome when he appeared before a joint session on February 24, just a little over a month after he took office. On the eve of the address Bill Clinton, reflecting the conventional view, suggested publicly that Obama wasn't being optimistic enough about the economy. Obama had already planned to be more upbeat and, as at other big moments, he delivered when it counted. "We will rebuild. We will recover," he said convincingly, before unleashing a string of promises, some of which might be kept (reforming health care) and some of which almost certainly could not ("a cure for cancer in our time," leading the world again by 2020 in the percentage of college graduates).

Obama was now fully committed to what some White House aides called the "big bang" strategy of using the economic crisis to confront long-festering problems in health care, energy, and education that were preventing the United States from achieving greatness in the twenty-first century. It was either visionary and long overdue or reckless and radical, depending on one's perspective. The latter view required critics to ignore that each of the policy proposals was centrist, pragmatic, and nonideological. (The stimulus contained GOP economic ideas and health care was endorsed at the outset by Bob Dole and Howard Baker.) Whether the timing was right for such political risk taking was a much closer call.

The reaction to the speech underscored how quickly Obama had established that he was moving beyond words to bold action. David Broder, the dean of political reporters, called the size of Obama's gamble "simply staggering." The speech, Broder wrote, was "a reminder of the unbelievable stakes he has placed on the table." Broder's colleague Tom Shales raised the issue of overexposure: "We've seen him in just about every framework but sitting in his pajamas at the breakfast nook." Now at least the White House would know that a joint session, where a dynamic young president dazzled official Washington and the 50 million people watching at home, was the best framework of all.

Even with the prime-time buildup Washington was stunned when the details of Obama's first budget came out. It marked a sharp shift in priorities across the board.* Congressional aides, sounding as if a bomb had hit the Hill, asked one another in amazement, *Did you read the thing?* (They didn't mean *actually* read it. Almost nobody had time to read the budget beyond the cheat sheets.) *Can you believe it? The guy is trying to do what he said he would!* This counted as heresy in a capital conditioned to believe that campaign promises are, in Ron Ziegler's immortal argot, "inoperative" the day after the election.

The president had his sea legs and was running a tighter ship. In March his 2009 budget passed 244–188 in the House and 55–43 in the Senate. (Sixty Senate votes aren't required for budgets.) Obama didn't have to make a single call to lobby for passage. He was in a new place with a new stature. "It's kind of like he decided, 'I'm the boss,' " Republican Senator Johnny Isakson said.

This widespread impression proved misleading. No president can wave a magic leadership wand and compel independent-minded members of Congress to fall into line. The boss of this enterprise had no influence beyond his ability to persuade others to go along with him. He would have to put together ad hoc coalitions and earn new support every day. "This isn't going to be easy," he said repeatedly of economic recovery, but Barack Obama might as well have been talking about his own new job.

Republicans and many Democrats thought the system was overloaded and the president too active. Senator Mary Landrieu spoke for her moderate colleagues when she said with a mixture of awe and worry, "Every time I think he's gonna step on the brake, he hits the gas." TARP, the Recovery Act, equal pay for women, children's health, Afghanistan, bank bailouts, auto bailouts, national service, the new ambitious budget—when would the fire hose get turned off? Not soon.

---

* Over the course of the year the administration was surprisingly successful in imposing budget cuts that eluded Bush. A study by the *Washington Times* showed that Obama got 60 percent of his proposed cuts approved by Congress, compared to 15 percent for Bush in 2007 and 2008. Obama saved more than $7 billion, though that constitutes less than one half of one percent of the budget.

9

Zen Temperament

In March 1933, only a few days after he was sworn in as president, Franklin D. Roosevelt went to Georgetown to celebrate the 92nd birthday of retired Supreme Court Justice Oliver Wendell Holmes Jr. The small group of revelers enjoyed a little bootleg champagne as the old jurist advised the new president, "Form your battalion and fight." After FDR left, Holmes rendered a judgment that was seen as capturing Roosevelt: "A second-class intellect but a first-class temperament."*

Barack Obama came to office with both a first-class intellect and a first-class temperament. Even his fiercest critics in Congress didn't try to deny that he was smart and had an easy rapport with people he met personally. The question for him was about his *public* temperament—the way his character and style connected to the American people. Temperament is the "great separator," as the legendary political scientist Richard Neustadt put it. "Experience will leave its mark on expertise; so will a man's ambition for himself and his constituents. But something like that 'first-rate' temperament is what turns know-how and desire into his personal account." In an age when the public gets to "know" the president so intimately through the media, those with temperaments that don't wear well—Herbert Hoover, Jimmy Carter, George W. Bush—have a harder time when things go badly.

A fine temperament is not the same as a winning personality; it denotes a particular mixture of ease, poise, and good cheer. That combination is necessary for great success in the presidency, but it's not sufficient. The office offers even the most temperamentally well-suited person a hundred ways to fail. All that Obama's easygoing temperament could do was improve his odds of handling the ongoing challenges and unpredictable events that would determine his fate.

Temperaments come in different shades. Lincoln's was funny and

---

* Some historians believe Holmes was referring to Theodore Roosevelt, who appointed him to the Court, but the assessment fits Franklin better.

wise, with a melancholy streak; he made other people feel good with his earthy stories. FDR's was airy and effervescent; Winston Churchill compared meeting him to "opening a bottle of champagne." Kennedy's was bad-boy ironic and Reagan's congenial with a theatrical touch. Clinton's was protean, by turns explosive, impulsive, wonky, folksy. Bush Senior had a country club affability and his son a fraternity rush chairman's charm.

Obama wasn't ebullient or a memorable raconteur. His cool, wry temperament—his moods famously never seemed to go too high or too low—could be perplexing. It had a mellow yet restless cast, a peculiar mix of calm, confidence, and curiosity. If the effect could sometimes be too professorial and disconnected from human hurt, the package was nonetheless impressive. With his high-wattage smile, elegant carriage, and a commanding baritone that could make his most ordinary utterances sound profound, Obama inhabited the role of president. Soon enough, his graying hair would add another touch of seriousness to a man who looked even younger than 47 when he took office.

It was this very seriousness that stood between him and certain elements of the American middle class that felt he didn't fully connect with them. Ironically, that gibe had arisen early in his political career when some black Chicagoans found Obama too "bourgeois" for their tastes—too middle-class. Rev. Jeremiah Wright's Trinity United Church was dedicated in its founding documents to rejecting "middle-class values" in favor of authentically African American ones. (This was partly a pose; a large percentage of the congregation was black middle-class.) By the time he won the nomination for the U.S. Senate in 2004, the perception of Obama as temperamentally diffident and detached from the real concerns of African Americans gave way to great pride. Many white liberals in Illinois, meanwhile, supported him in part because of his race; voting for him was an affirmation of themselves and their own open-mindedness. The same coalition powered him through the 2008 Democratic primaries.

But the rap that Obama lacked a common touch reappeared in that campaign. The only reason Hillary Clinton hung on so long in the primaries was Obama's weakness among white working-class voters who resented not just his claim that they were "bitter" and "clinging to guns and religion" but the whole Obama package. The attitude of these white voters was sometimes tinged with racism but had more to do with class anxieties. Obama was so obviously intelligent and well-spoken that he reminded them that a class of well-educated elites had left them behind. The Obama campaign worried that this vulnerability would hurt him in the November election, but the candidate deployed kitchen table issues (though he could never bring himself to call them that) and the financial crisis put a premium on brains and calm competence, which trumped class resentment. In any temperament contest with hotheaded John McCain, Obama won in a landslide.

With Obama, it was all about equipoise. "If I had to use one word to describe his temperament it would be 'consistent,'" Axelrod said. "He's a tremendously centered personality." The calm had a paradoxical cast. "He has great self-assurance without being egotistical and he's totally Zen-like without being arrogant," said John Podesta. "It's a very odd combination." The only other people so relaxed and intense at the same time are certain professional athletes.

Obama's temperament was also unusual because it was linked to his intellect. The two are normally more separate dimensions of personality, as Holmes's line about FDR suggests. Some Americans found Obama pedantic. But most of the time his refusal to be conspicuous about his superior intelligence lent modesty to what might otherwise have been an impression of cockiness. Pete Rouse said that in thirty years on Capitol Hill he had never seen anyone with more faith in himself. And the only one he had seen anywhere close to Obama in pure intellect was Maine Senator George Mitchell, a former federal judge. What separated Obama from other smart senators, Rouse concluded, was that he was so confident he didn't need to show it.

Obama's disciplined insistence on giving rationality and open-mindedness pride of place kept him from being swept away by emotional currents. A bemusement about the phoniness of politics and the bloated egos it produces—plus a hardheaded wife—protected him from hubris, at least for now. And like FDR and Reagan (who patterned his style on Roosevelt's), Obama's winning smile obscured a layer of self-protective ice, a useful combination in a chief executive.

The tricky part was calibrating his detachment. Standing slightly apart from the action offered perspective and insulated him from the partisan clatter; standing above renewed charges that he lacked the human touch. Axelrod and other aides paid attention to this difficult balance but not enough. Already vulnerable with white middle-class voters, Obama needed to spend more of his first year compensating with emotional connections to the lives of workers and small business people. Once in the White House, Obama didn't seem to grasp the psychological point that logic can convince but only emotion can motivate.

Part of this was a matter of public style. FDR and Reagan were better actors, an asset of special importance in the theater of the presidency. Obama won a Grammy Award for the audio version of his book *Dreams from My Father.* He could lovingly mimic even the female voices in his family saga and slipped easily into the accents of the black church. But his act was based on its never looking like an act. He knew that with one false and showy move he could crack the foundation of trust on which his public persona rested. "The core is authenticity and realness," said his friend Marty Nesbitt. And so he resisted role-playing, which was commendable but limited his options.

As did his pride in his probity. He was properly insistent on separating friendship from business, but he lacked (and was proud to lack) Roosevelt's manipulative streak, which he used during the New Deal and World War II to deceive people on occasion and play his advisors off one another. This might have made Obama a more admirable person than FDR, but it gave him one less tool for governing.

As his popularity fell in 2009 Obama stayed cool, in both senses of that overused word. He was comfortable in trying circumstances and still unmistakably hip, especially in the eyes of young people. Their ardor for politics dimmed as the prosaic presidency replaced the excitement of the campaign, and if he failed to deliver they might tune out Washington altogether. In the meantime Obama remained a figure of fascination, even awe, for those in their teen and twenties. Even when he disappointed them, the way he looked, sounded, and chose to relax were the coolest they had ever seen in a president.*

Cool also conveys effortlessness, which is appealing at first in a politician but can also be off-putting. He learned early in the 2008 campaign that Americans also like to see their public figures grapple and sweat; it makes them more human. Obama didn't mind being seen losing a few rounds; he knew that toughened him up in the eyes of voters. But sweat? It often seemed as if his abstract political understanding of the need to emote was in tension with his instinctive desire to master those emotions. Paul Volcker was among those impressed that nothing ever seemed to bother him, though he said that sometimes he wanted to shake the president and say, "Goddamn it! Get excited about this!"

Obama was often compared to the levelheaded Mr. Spock on *Star Trek* because of the way he chose reason over emotion and used logic to enter the minds of other people. Spock was born of a Vulcan father and a human mother but never seemed troubled by his mixed parentage. When the *Star Trek* movie came out in early 2009 the president

---

* It was not entirely a coincidence that applications for the Peace Corps and City Year tripled in Obama's first year. Nearly 20 percent of seniors at Ivy League schools applied to one program—Teach for America—and the figure was 40 percent at historically black colleges, a reflection of both a tight job market and rising idealism.

had it screened at the White House and got a kick out of flashing the Vulcan salute.

Obama's unflappable nature may have hindered his ability to forge an emotional connection with the public, but it proved a distinct asset in decision making. "He has the calmness of a deliberate mind," as Valerie Jarrett put it. His people were relieved and a little amazed that he never yelled at them, as Clinton and their other bosses routinely had. Rouse had frequently seen Obama irritated, critical, even furious, but not once over five years in the Senate and White House did he see his boss rip into someone; Jarrett said the same applied to the eighteen years she had known him. If Obama said something insulting to your face he was almost certainly teasing, which meant he liked you.

Otherwise his anger was short and understated, with a "C'mon, guys" or "Get control of this" or "I want you to take personal responsibility for it." His reputation for staying calm made even the mildest verbal slight or passing glance sting all the more. (The public got a glimpse of this the first week of his presidency, when he stared at Joe Biden and even touched his coat for joking about John Roberts's flubbing the oath.) Some aides came to fear Obama's dropped smile, his way of beaming broadly and insincerely before reverting instantly to a frown and a penetrating glare.

Of course no "purple fits" (as Bill Clinton's blowups were called) meant the staff also missed the warm Clintonian forgiveness that came after the storm, the little compliment or hand on the shoulder that told you everything was fine again. Aides often knew Obama was satisfied only when he said "What's next?" He didn't embarrass people with his outbursts, as both Bushes and Clinton sometimes did. But the temperature in the West Wing always felt like it was in the low 60s—not chilly, exactly, but cool.

———

MICHELLE OBAMA ONCE told a friend that as a child "Barack spent so much time by himself that it was like he was raised by wolves." She meant no disrespect to his mother and grandparents, who always wanted the best for him. Her point was that like the mythical founders of Rome and other children of legend, Obama's superior strength and resilience were in part the products of his instinct for self-creation. The same would hold true of his presidency.

Obama's character and talent were built on a more solid foundation than might be suggested by his exotic and often solitary upbringing in Indonesia and Hawaii, now the stuff of legend. His inheritance was formidable: the confidence and superior IQ of his absent Kenyan father;

the inquisitive and cheerful nature of his idealistic Kansas-born mother; the efficiency and unsentimental pragmatism of his hardheaded grandmother; and even the dreamy restlessness—"the possibility of remaking the world from whole cloth," as Obama put it—of his troubled grandfather, the outsider of the family.

Despite the pain of his father's abandonment when Obama was an infant, he did not have a conspicuously unhappy childhood. It featured an exotic blend of race and geography but also an unusual, even paradoxical combination of unconditional love and bracing independence. This helped protect him from the approval-seeking neediness that afflicts so many politicians. His mother never made him feel as if he wasn't good enough. And yet by sending him back from Jakarta to live with his grandparents in Honolulu, which must have been a wrenching separation for a 9-year-old, she forced on him a sense of responsibility for himself that many indulged and overprotected Americans now lack.

From adolescence on Obama felt compelled to figure out who he was and where he belonged. His racial identity issues were a potential barrier to advancement. But like so many people who succeed, he persevered through personal confusion and developed a sense of self that was larger than his cramped circumstances. Over time that brought self-assurance, perspective, stability, and possibility. He invented himself anew in each of the different worlds he entered, then took something from his surroundings for use in later life.

In Indonesia, where he lived as a pudgy and happy boy from age 4 to 10, his mother roused him at dawn for extra reading, writing, math, and appreciation of his black heritage. His Indonesian stepfather taught him how to box and fed him exotic local cuisine, including dog meat. He absorbed less Muslim culture than the dominant Javanese, which emphasized agreement and cooperation.* His mother, Ann, a secular humanist, studied Javanese peasants as an anthropologist and later said that while her husband became more American, she became more Javanese. The impact on a young child of his mother's devotion to a nonjudgmental people is hard to calculate, but Obama's younger half-sister, Maya, later said it was central to understanding him. Growing up

---

* Clifford Geertz, a legendary anthropologist at the University of Chicago, wrote, "Emotional equanimity is the mark of the truly *alus* [Javanese] character." Javanese culture emphasizes an aversion to conflict; if you think someone will say no to a question, you don't ask. The Javanese language has as many as seven or eight ways to express favor, each having a slightly different gradation of agreement. Indonesians are famous for their ability to interact with people from different backgrounds, which helps in a country where three hundred languages are spoken by 228 million people living in crowded conditions.

outside the continental United States, Obama developed unusual open-mindedness and curiosity.

As one of the only black kids at the elite Punahou School in Honolulu, he was a casual student and popular basketball jock who told off the white coach when he wasn't getting enough playing time. His confidence was bolstered by knowing he was as smart as the wealthy kids, though that had no immediate effect on his motivation. He read Malcolm X's autobiography ("His repeated acts of self-creation spoke to me") and was confused and depressed when Gramps unhelpfully told him that even his beloved grandmother, Toot, had been afraid of young black men who looked like him, an experience he would relate during the campaign in his famous Philadelphia speech on race. "The world shook under my feet, ready to crack open at any moment," Obama wrote in *Dreams from My Father*. "I stopped, trying to steady myself, and knew for the first time that I was utterly alone." He would either crumble and become isolated and embittered or emerge stronger and more self-aware.

His surroundings helped. Eric Whitaker, a Chicago friend, thought the origins of his temperament could be found in Hawaii, whose laid-back culture is more than a travel promotion. It's said that the only drivers there who honk horns are from out of state. Obama's 2008 blood pressure of 90/60 was statistically low, but less of an aberration in Hawaii, where stress is almost a sin, even in hard times.*

At Occidental College, where he dropped "Barry" in favor of "Barack," he devoted himself to understanding "how people learn to hate"; as a black man in a white world, he believed, "My life depends on it." Because that sounded melodramatic, even to his African American classmates, he settled on a more clinical approach to the world around him. "That's the only way to cure an illness, right?" he told a friend. "Diagnose it." Over time he trained himself to analyze rigorously. Transferring to Columbia University, he ran three miles a day, fasted, and impressed professors as a student of international relations.

In 1984 he moved to Chicago, convinced that "change will come from a mobilized grassroots." He later described his work as a community organizer as "the best education I ever had." The experience left him frustrated over his lack of success but also newly appreciative of politics—at any level—as a worthy vehicle for change. He revered Harold Washington, Chicago's first African American mayor, but harbored

---

* Researchers at Hamilton College in 2009 found Hawaii was the second-happiest state after Louisiana.

no illusions about the mayor's ability to bend the city's white power structure beyond a certain point.

The story of his election as the first black president of the *Harvard Law Review* in 1990 foreshadowed the way he operated later. At the time, the law school was practically a battle zone, with intense racial and ideological divisions. Besides Obama, the candidates for president of the *Law Review* included another African American and a white male conservative.* "Barack said, 'Look, we gotta be grown-ups,' " one of his professors, Martha Minow, now the law school dean, remembered. "To emerge as a leader with the respect of both blacks and conservatives was extraordinary." However, the triumph may have led to overconfidence in his ability to bridge wide divides and bring warring factions together.†

After graduating Obama turned down glittering career opportunities, a sign that he would consistently choose his own path over doing what was expected of him. Abner Mikva, the former Chicago congressman who became a judge on the U.S. Court of Appeals in Washington, offered him a clerkship, which would have led to a powerful clerkship the following year on the U.S. Supreme Court, where Obama would have been drafting major, even historic opinions before age 30. He wasn't interested.‡ He also rejected high-paying jobs with corporate firms in favor of returning to Chicago to work for a small civil rights firm and eventually to teach at the University of Chicago Law School.

Until he fell in love with Michelle and with her rooted black working-class family in Chicago, Obama's restlessness threatened to send him on a quest that would never satisfy him. Writing *Dreams from My Father* was by his own account cathartic: "It was into my father's image, the black man, son of Africa, that I'd packed all the attributes I sought in myself, the attributes of Martin and Malcolm, DuBois and Mandela." Upon learning that Barack Obama Sr., whom he met only once (in 1971, when he was 10 years old), had become an angry and drunken failure in Kenya, Obama was freed to live his own life.§ In the book he searches for his father and for himself and manages to find both. He

---

* Brad Berenson, who later became one of prosecutor Kenneth Starr's biggest boosters during the Lewinsky trial.
† Minow recommended him for a job as a summer associate to her father, Newton Minow, a senior partner at the Chicago firm of Sidley Austin. That's where Barack met Michelle, who was his supervisor at the firm.
‡ The plum went to his classmate Julius Genachowski, now the chairman of the Federal Communications Commission.
§ Barack Obama Sr. died in a car accident in Kenya when Obama was in college.

emerges a more patient and evolved person, completing a lyrical journey from a boy who thinks he belongs nowhere to a man who feels comfortable almost everywhere.

As a child Obama aspired for a time to be an architect, and his tiny, perfect handwriting reflected the careful artistry of a draftsman. He was a dreamer and planner by nature, possessed of a hard-earned discipline and fierce ambition. As early as 1991, before the publication of his book, he confided to his future brother-in-law, Craig Robinson, that he might want to run for president someday, an outlandish aspiration for a young black man in a strange city. In 1992 he rehearsed for his own grassroots career by spearheading Project Vote, a voter registration drive that broke all local records.

In politics Obama was always tougher than he looked. To get elected to the Illinois State Senate in 1996 he challenged the petitions of the incumbent, Alice Palmer, and rudely forced her and the other candidates off the ballot, allowing him to run unopposed. In Springfield the statehouse hacks found him arrogant at first, but even the Republicans warmed to him over time, partly through poker and golf. His reception in Chicago's black community was harsher. The thrashing he received in a 2000 primary campaign against incumbent congressman Bobby Rush made him humbler.

Only in the last two of his eight years as a state senator, when the Democrats took control, did he win passage of meaningful legislation, most notably a bill requiring the videotaping of police interrogations (a win-win for prosecutors and civil libertarians). He won a reputation as a nuts-and-bolts legislator who would compromise, and compromise again, to get something done. On some issues, such as campaign finance reform, this strategy brought tangible if watered-down results; on others, such as health care, his ambitious plan was reduced to almost nothing. As a self-described "extreme pragmatist" he was philosophical about it. He began quoting Martin Luther King in his campaigns: "The arc of the moral universe is long but it bends toward justice."

In 1997 he foreshadowed his talent for running a meeting. Harvard's Robert Putnam, author of the bestseller *Bowling Alone,* invited Obama to participate in the Saguaro Seminar, an elite forum on civic engagement with everyone from Christian-right activist Ralph Reed to *Washington Post* columnist E. J. Dionne in attendance. The group kicked around ideas ranging from establishing better relations with the Muslim world to finding common ground on abortion. From the start Obama, the least well-known participant, was recognized as a master at summarizing the views of each side of the debate better than the advocates themselves, then working toward the center—a trait he would bring to

White House meetings on some of the same subjects. Members of the group asked the obscure state senator if he was running for president.

His long-shot 2004 candidacy for the U.S. Senate, launched after he rejected suggestions from political consultants that he change his name, was a reminder of the importance of fortune in politics. He ran a skillful campaign but won the primary mostly because of the fortuitous release of the frontrunner's damaging divorce records. Then his likely GOP opponent in the general election dropped out after custody records revealed that his TV actress wife had accused him of dragging her to sex clubs. In the White House, Obama referred often to how lucky he was.

Upon arriving in Washington as a celebrity in early 2005 Obama worried about what politics was doing to him. "The longer I served in Washington, the more I saw friends studying my face for signs of a change, probing me for a newfound pomposity, searching for hints of argumentativeness or guardedness," he wrote in *The Audacity of Hope.* "I began examining myself in the same way; I began to see certain characteristics that I held in common with my new colleagues, and I wondered what might prevent my own transformation into the stock politician of bad TV movies." He bought a mansion in Chicago with the proceeds of book sales but even after becoming president would continue to remind people that as recently as 2004 he and Michelle had been paying off student loans.

By then Obama's enormous self-assurance was finally bolstered by success. Shortly after arriving in the Senate in 2005 Newton Minow asked him over lunch where his confidence came from. He said that when he arrived in Cambridge he didn't think he was up to the level of his classmates. "But when I was elected head of the *Law Review* I figured I was just as capable. And now that I've been in the Senate a month I realize the same thing." Within a year and a half he would extend the point to potential rivals for the presidency. In less than four years he could hold his own with anyone in the world.

———

THE COOL DEMEANOR that had helped bring him so far applied even to that most uncomfortable of subjects: race. In November 2006 he hosted a three-hour meeting in Washington to discuss a possible presidential campaign with a group of his closest supporters. After two hours an African American lawyer named Broderick Johnson said, "We haven't talked about race yet." Obama's answer was simple. "I've thought about it and I think the country is ready," he said. "We'll find out soon enough."

If it weren't for the intense pressures of the presidency, Obama's famously unflappable temperament wouldn't be seen as unusual. As his African American friends noted, they too had to stay cool to succeed. Ambitious black men are especially conscious of their need to contain their anger in order to prosper. It is practically a job requirement for them in the upper reaches of white-dominated professions. Growing up in the 1970s, this "Joshua Generation," as Obama called it in 2007, viewed poise and modesty as standard equipment for advancement. As much as they admired Malcolm X and Muhammad Ali, angry and cocky behavior wasn't going to get them ahead.

Obama managed to float easily between different worlds without seeming to "wear the mask" of the black man, as the poet Paul Laurence Dunbar memorably put it a century ago. Of course he wore multilayered masks of race consciousness that will keep historians busy for decades, but he kept the deeper questions of race at bay, at least for now. The president was determined that questions of personal identity, though fit subjects for literary introspection, not shape his approach to his presidency.

That hardly meant he ignored his racial heritage. In his first week as president he found a bust of Martin Luther King near a landing in the East Wing and put it in the Oval Office. A framed flier from the 1963 March on Washington that had hung in his Senate office also went near his desk, amid other relics of American history with no connection to race. When Michelle was given the task of deciding which artists' works should be sent over from the National Gallery for display in the White House, she chose many by African American artists, though there was still a broad mix of backgrounds and styles in the selection. Obama made a point of having jazz musicians to the White House, but he hosted nights featuring Latino and country music too.

New presidents always set a new social tone in the salons of Georgetown. Panic set in among Democratic Washington hostesses, most of whom had supported Hillary in the primaries; they had made sure to contribute to Obama in the general election, but weren't sure that was sufficient. One called up a friend to say she was planning a dinner party and needed at least a couple of African Americans to invite. Did her friend have any suggestions? She did, but wondered what the urgency was. The answer: "If there's no one African American there, everyone will know I have no contacts in the new administration."

After two months in office the president was asked by Ann Compton of ABC News at a news conference whether his early days had been a "color-blind time." He responded, "At the Inauguration I think there was justifiable pride on the part of the country that we had taken a step to move us beyond some of the searing legacies of racial discrimination in this country. But that lasted about a day."

The dry "about a day" comment reflected his utter confidence in handling racial shoals that had never been navigated before. As president he would continue to adopt some of the cadences of the black church before African American audiences, throw in a little street lingo ("We straight?") when paying a black cashier, and saunter across the South Lawn after descending from Marine One in a way "that left no doubt he's a brother," as the author Michael Eric Dyson put it.

Even so, some whites from a different era said that Obama "simply doesn't read black," as Ben Bradlee put it, in the same way that Bradlee said his close friend John F. Kennedy didn't "read Catholic." Both JFK and Obama, said Bradlee, are "just different than other people. They're 'stand out' people, with that mixture of self-confidence and ease." It was the ease with which he crossed dozens of invisible social, racial, and political borders that proved so compelling. Obama himself had long said this was his strong suit. And he managed to pull it off without seeming like a chameleon. There's only one side to him, his friends said. If he was no more "authentic" than the average person, he was discernibly more authentic than the average politician.

IN OBAMA'S CASE, his surface calm didn't seem to be shrouding deep inner turmoil. His aides from the Senate, the presidential campaign, and the White House routinely described him with the same words: "psychologically healthy." This was as much a comment on the other politicians they had worked under, men and women who ran the gamut from passive-aggressive to narcissistic to deeply insecure, as it was a diagnosis of Obama. He had a rich inner life; his demons might yet surface. But to many people who knew him, Obama seemed like an especially smart and capable version of a normal human being, whatever that was.

At the beginning of the campaign Axelrod's biggest worry was that Obama was *too* psychologically healthy. "I didn't think he was pathological enough to be president," Axelrod remembered, echoing the common view among reporters and handlers that you have to be a little crazy to run for high office. Obama had a big engine of ambition, but he didn't seem to Axelrod to require victory for his self-worth the way others did. There just wasn't anything needy about him, or if there was, it lay buried deeper than anyone other than perhaps Michelle could see.

Anyone who has ever worked in a large organization (or a small one, for that matter) knows the importance of a fundamentally sane outlook on the world. Unhealthy leaders create unhealthy cultures that produce not just bad karma but bad decisions. Bosses who are insecure and feel obliged to prove they're smart or tough or always in the right never seem to learn anything and, not surprisingly, have a worse batting average on the big questions that cross their desk.

Obama could occasionally seem cocky to even his most ardent supporters from Chicago, especially when he tilted his head up and bragged that he knew more about organizing, media, political strategy, domestic affairs, and foreign policy than the people around him. "I'm the best retail politician in America," he told a core of his early fundraisers at a dinner in Washington in July 2007. On the night he won the Iowa caucuses he told everyone within earshot, "I'm gonna win this whole thing!"

But, critically, his cockiness wasn't the product of insecurity. He listened more closely than other politicians—a trait that was mentioned again and again in interviews—and he leavened his enormous self-confidence with an acute self-awareness of how a reasonable and wise person should act. He could be intimidating, but he didn't make other people feel small. His psychological health might not lessen the number of errors he made, but it gave him a better chance of compensating for them.

Obama calculated without seeming calculating. In late 2006, when he was just amassing support, some big-money guests at a fund-raiser asked him whom he turned to for advice. The safe and proper answer would have been Tom Daschle, who by that time was supporting him, but instead Obama mentioned Vernon Jordan as an example. This was arguably ill-advised because Jordan was African American, and the last thing Obama wanted was to be seen as the black candidate. More important, Jordan was at that time (and for more than a year afterward) telling anyone who would listen that Obama wasn't ready to be president and that he was for Hillary Clinton. When, after the event, one of the men at the fund-raiser called up Jordan and heard that message about Obama's inexperience, it actually made the donor like Obama more; his naming Jordan now seemed all the more authentic and unpremeditated. Obama had the talent to make straight, nonpolitical-sounding answers into what the advertising industry once called a "unique selling proposition."

There weren't many one-faced politicians around. Whatever happened in the economy or abroad, however low his job performance ratings went, his character might offer him some political protection.

Jon Favreau argued that the president's temperament and his political fortunes intersected: "The most dangerous thing to him would be anything that starts exposing hypocrisy in him, or erodes trust in the president himself."

This did not happen in 2009. In his State of the Union Address at the end of his first year, Obama referred to a "deficit of trust" in all institutions, including the presidency. But through a bruising first year, that distrust never soiled Obama personally. Strong majorities still respected his character.

The willingness to take responsibility—most conspicuously in 2009 for his handling of the Daschle nomination, his inability to better articulate health care reform in the summer, and what he acknowledged as the "systemic failure" of intelligence agencies in the Christmas Day terrorism incident—contributed to the perception of authenticity. He understood that the old infallibility model of presidential leadership was obsolete and that some sense of humility and appreciation for human frailty would trump the old artifice any time.

Of course this was its own kind of artifice. One of his most loyal aides said that he had never received a single apology from him: "He'll change his mind but [in private] he'll never admit he was wrong."* Like many people, Obama was temperamentally unsuited to apology. He just knew it made good sense politically. It had worked for John McCain, who charmed the press for years with his consistent contrition. For Obama, the test would come when the screwups were bigger than bad-taste jokes and botched appointments. It would take time to know if he had failed on the big substantive questions of his presidency, and if he would cop to it.

He despised fake humility. During a campaign debate the Democratic candidates were asked for their biggest personal faults. Obama answered first and said he was sometimes disorganized and lost papers handed to him (no longer a problem once he went into the bubble of the campaign and presidency). Hillary Clinton and John Edwards gave phony answers that amounted to "I care too much sometimes." When Obama was asked about it later, he chuckled, rolled his eyes, and said that he should have said he was "too kind to animals" or "liked to help old ladies across the street when they don't want help."

For all the joshing, Obama prided himself on being empathetic, and with good reason: he had a knack for getting inside the heads of

---

* In his book *The Audacity to Win* David Plouffe disagreed and credited Obama with privately apologizing to him for his campaign gaffe about Americans who "get bitter, they cling to guns or religion."

others and seeing things from their perspective, even if that perspective (whether it was Tom Coburn's or that of an anti-Obama protester at a town meeting) struck his friends as irrational. This was the impression he sought to convey, and it contained plenty of truth. Much of the time he looked for the good in people.

Obama was usually charming and relaxed in his personal interactions, a fun guy to hang out with on the weekend. Everyone concurred that he was moved by stories of suffering and death and would often need a little time to compose himself after visiting soldiers in the hospital or meeting the survivors of war dead. He was silent the entire trip back from Dover Air Force Base, where he traveled in October in the middle of the night to salute the flag-draped coffins coming off the plane from Afghanistan. He cried when he missed his family during the campaign and was compassionate toward aides whom he had to fire.*

———

YET THERE WAS a hardness beneath. Not cold, but serious and often impatient. Along with "psychologically healthy," many described him as "unsentimental." One advisor described him as "the most unsentimental man I've ever met." This obviously didn't apply to his family; shortly before the Inauguration he told the press pool aboard his plane that on the night before leaving for Washington he was home alone when a friend of Malia's brought over a photo album of pictures from preschool and he found himself choked up as he looked at them. Nobody was suggesting he was uncaring; to a person, the advisors making the *unsentimental* point thought him decent. They were talking about his capacity to set feelings aside when confronting daily decisions, the emotional buffer zone that sometimes made him seem aloof to people he didn't know well. Jarrett put a positive spin on it: "He has an ability to emotionally detach in order to think clearly." Penny Pritzker called it "compassionate dispassion." Rouse referred to him as "a step removed from most people."

Most of the men who become president desperately value human approval. "If a staff member was upset, Clinton cared. If there was a chance to receive public approbation, that was good," recalled one aide who served both presidents. "Best I can tell, Barack Obama doesn't

———

* For example, Obama gave a consulting contract in 2005 to the aide who recommended his disastrous run for Congress in 2000, and an ambassadorship in 2009 to the only senior aide from his Senate office who wasn't brought to the White House.

give a shit. He is supremely serene in his own self." In this he resembled Reagan, who was often described as emotionally detached from everyone around him except his wife.

Obama could be cutting. After a senior official called him one day and talked his ear off without allowing the president to even ask a question or two, he told aides, "I never want to talk to that guy again." He didn't mean it literally, but he also didn't suffer fools or blowhards gladly, no matter what their station and reputation. Besides, presidents had to be that way about people sometimes. To him it was just part of the job description.

This unsentimental quality could make him bloodless in his assessments of situations and people, but it also let him see them more fully. He viewed even his inspirational abilities coolly and from a distance. "You know, I'm just thinking. It's pretty hard to campaign against hope," Obama told Marty Nesbitt one day in early 2007. Nesbitt saw his friend's logic immediately. "I thought, yeah man, if one guy is talking about hope, it jams you up. What are you going to say in response? 'Don't be hopeful!'?" The thinking wasn't cynical, just practical.

As a politician, it helped to be indifferent, or at least thick-skinned, about personal slights or past attacks by opponents. Just as he had little patience for "relitigating" issues, he disliked revisiting old grievances that had no clear bearing on the present. "I've never seen anyone so grudge-less," Jarrett said. This was unsatisfying for his liberal base, which wanted to see him thump Republicans and recalcitrant Democrats, but on balance it proved to be an asset.*

By looking beyond his own emotional reaction the president often saw something good in adversaries that his friends and aides missed. It offered him an instrumental empathy that was politically useful. In noticing how this annoying Republican or that disloyal Democrat was interesting on such-and-such an issue, and really not such a bad guy, he gave himself more options to bring them around on other issues. He complained often when people or media outlets were "unserious," a character flaw in his book. If he thought Eric Cantor was acting smug or Joe Lieberman sanctimonious, he didn't hesitate to say it privately. But he found venting about adversaries to be a waste of time. Having avoided expending the emotional energy on disliking someone, he

---

* Richard Nixon wasn't the only president crippled by his grudges. So was Jimmy Carter. Ted Kennedy wrote in his memoir, *True Compass,* that without Carter's insistence on holding a series of grudges, he might never have run for president against him in 1980. Kennedy, of course, held his own grudges against Carter.

was free to think more creatively about how to bend him or her to his purposes.

Some friends said that after the pain of the Jeremiah Wright episode he would never again let himself get emotionally bound to anyone beyond his family and oldest nonpolitical friends from Hawaii and Chicago. Aides and Cabinet members were almost all dispensable, though his basic sense of decency didn't allow him to cut off old friends who worked for him without long discussions to try to work something out.

The president was also unsentimental about himself. *Dreams from My Father* was introspective but hardly written with a rosy hue. His second book, *The Audacity of Hope*, an unpretentious look at his life in politics, lacked the moments of drama and touching anecdotes so many politicians favor. He read history and no doubt had his eye on writing some of his own, but much of the raw material was missing. When reporters went looking for his papers from his years in the Illinois State Senate they found that his schedules had been lost, destroyed, or, most likely, never kept in the first place, as he insisted was the case. Conservatives charged that he was covering something up; more plausibly, he had always traveled light. It was part of his restless makeup.

In the fall of 2009 University of Chicago officials approached the White House about housing Obama's presidential library. They were told it was too early. To the extent that he had thought about a library, he mused to a friend that maybe it should be an "online library," not bricks-and-mortar. This almost certainly won't happen; the demand for a splashy museum will likely be too great. But it said something about his state of mind.

———

OBAMA HAD ONE pet peeve that could make him lose his cool. It was a common source of anger for presidents: leaks.* Complaints about loose lips became a constant theme of Obama's early presidency. At his first Cabinet meeting he made a point of saying that he didn't want to see his Cabinet "litigating" policy through the *New York Times* and the

---

* Lyndon Johnson was known to withdraw appointments if their names leaked. Richard Nixon authorized "the Plumbers," a secret White House unit that broke the law while tracking leaks. Ronald Reagan got so angry that he said, "[I've] had it up to my keister [with aides talking out of school]." George H. W. Bush fell out with one of his top aides, Richard Darman, over leaks, and Bill Clinton was so perturbed about unauthorized disclosures that he shuffled his White House staff after Bob Woodward's book about his administration came out. (His aide Bruce Lindsey used to go over newspaper and magazine stories with a yellow highlighter and challenge aides, asking, "Did you say that?")

Washington Post. At a Blair House retreat for the Cabinet and senior staff at the end of July he devoted about a quarter of his comments to urging his people to keep their disagreements within the family: "We should be having these debates on the inside, not the outside." And during his twenty hours of deliberations over Afghanistan in the fall, he returned repeatedly to the theme. Naturally in Washington nearly every time he got upset about leaks it leaked.

For all his claims that he didn't want yes-men around him, no one on his staff was brave enough to tell the president that obsessing over leaks was a colossal waste of time. (Aides should have recognized that the age-old problem in Washington isn't managing leaks, but managing the president's fury over them.) But it wouldn't have mattered: leaks offended Obama's sense of discipline and reminded him of everything he disliked about the capital. He was fearsome on the subject, which seemed to bring out his controlling nature to an even greater degree than usual. When he thought Carol Browner had been leaking information during the transition, he told aides he was going to call her and make her knock it off. They convinced him to let staff handle it. In April Obama phoned EPA Administrator Lisa Jackson directly to ask how she thought an EPA "endangerment finding" about the perils of greenhouse gases had leaked. When word spread that David Souter was stepping down from the Supreme Court, the president opened the first meeting to consider his replacement not by musing over his historic opportunity to change the high court but by acidly complaining about the leak. When a senior staffer realized he'd spoken indiscreetly to a reporter, he sent an email around before the story even appeared in print, saying, "I shouldn't have said it," as if he were a confessing defendant in a Soviet purge trial.

Beneath his contempt for leaks lay a futile hope that the "No Drama Obama" world he had created for his 2008 campaign could somehow be replicated in the White House. In truth, the campaign had the usual share of staff drama, but it was repressed in the interest of winning. Now Obama sought the same in the interest of governing. He made it clear that he drew a bright line between expressing policy differences, which he liked, and breaking into factions, which he loathed.

Every Cabinet member and senior advisor who worked for Obama was terrified of acquiring a reputation as an infighter. It was inevitable that someone would lose his or her job over squabbling or leaking and no one wanted to be first. The policy stakes and sense of being part of history hardly meant the end of strong egos, but it drove those egos underground, which was no doubt a good thing for the administration.

Where earlier presidents found it necessary to mollify high-maintenance officials who threatened to resign over turf encroachments,* Obama didn't need to. The Cabinet and staff knew that playing that card with him would surely fail. He'd let them leave without the slightest hesitation.

Of course it was impossible to avoid bruised feelings, real or imagined. When the long-awaited campaign documentary *By the People* included extensive footage of Axelrod and Gibbs but nothing about Jarrett and Nesbitt, though they were interviewed, the explanation that the latter pair had been less involved in the campaign didn't convince everyone. "For them to exclude her [Jarrett] is a false reflection of reality," said one of the president's African American friends. "Some of us were almost physically sick watching it." Obama was sensitive to such exclusions.

The easiest way to make the president angry was to leave one's fingerprints on a story that reflected staff strife. After a front-page story in the *New York Times* reported on mild tension within the economic team that reflected some criticism of Larry Summers—a leak so innocuous that it would have been ignored in the Clinton administration—Obama came into the morning meeting quietly livid. He said he'd read the article and didn't want to see anything like it again. Then he paused and glanced around the room. Aides had long since learned to fear these silences, when he stared everyone in the eye without saying anything, as if each person there might be the guilty party. "Okay, that's all I'm going to say," he finished. His long pause said the rest.

This approach was effective in the short run, but potentially hazardous over time. Paranoia about leaks had a way of corroding modern presidencies, from Nixon on. The Obama model for plugging leaks was George W. Bush's first term, which was tightly run. But how about Bush's second term? Worry about unauthorized disclosures could harden into hostility toward the beneficiaries of the criticism: the news media. That hostility, though emotionally satisfying, had no upside over time.

Obama worked on the theory that being so accessible at the top—he was on TV more than any of his predecessors—compensated for his tight control over those under him. But history suggested that whenever the White House battened down the media hatches, water eventually came through anyway, and with much greater force.

---

* Nixon and Kissinger, Carter and Brzezinski, Reagan and Haig, Bush and Rumsfeld are only a few examples of the practice.

OBAMA'S SMILE COULD light up a room, but he also possessed a more subtle social skill often lacking in politicians: the ability to accept a compliment without looking like it was his due. When people at events shouted, "We love you, Barack!" he got in the habit of playfully shouting, "I love you back!"

He was canny in the use of his stature. During a meeting with Bill Gates, the Microsoft billionaire mentioned that his 6-year-old daughter, Phoebe, prayed every night for the president. Obama pulled out a pen and paper and wrote her a gracious note on the spot. This was obviously politically advantageous, but keeping the empathy genuine was important to him. Whether it was Tom Daschle, old friends and acquaintances, or lower-level aides, he was unfailingly thoughtful when someone he knew was sick or had experienced a death in the family. When Ted Kennedy lay dying, the president showed devotion far beyond what the Kennedy family expected.

Even so, gratitude was one of the few qualities that didn't come naturally to Obama; it was learned behavior. Michelle, who earlier in their marriage felt that he didn't appreciate her, readily acknowledged there was room for improvement here. Well into the campaign staffers had to twist his arm to write notes to big supporters or call the local precinct coordinators in Iowa. Even in the White House his daily political correspondence and call lists were chores he neglected more often than he liked to admit. He could multitask by signing photographs and writing thank-you notes while watching sports on TV, but he sighed wearily at the drudgery of it.

With those he favored Obama was a friendly guy. He made a point of celebrating the birthdays of people around him, often carrying in cupcakes and a candle himself. (On his own 47th birthday he also celebrated longtime reporter Helen Thomas's 89th.) He tried to stay chummy with aides, inviting them to play golf or basketball if they were good enough. But he wasn't one for morale-boosting compliments. Often, the most effusive he managed to be with staff was "I think that went pretty well." (Nervous outsiders brought in to brief at a big meeting were more likely to get a "That was perfect" or some other accolade.) Fixing a problem was not usually an occasion for thanks. Informed early on that Geithner had just been confirmed after an exhausting nomination fight, Obama nodded curtly and said, "What's up with Daschle?" After stories appeared in the press about aides who routinely worked past 1 a.m., Obama's first reaction was "You think it's bad for you—how about for me?"

Over time he had disciplined himself to say "I appreciate that" more often. After warming to it, he even sometimes said "I appreciate you" when meeting people for the first time, including foreign heads of state he had known only on the telephone. It was a greeting and a thank you in one, a little different, and it worked for him.

With his senior staff he tried to remind himself to be more thankful. The president's small meetings were generally divided into those clearly devoted to one topic and those in which he went around the room to get reports on initiatives and troubleshooting. A couple of days before the House passed health care reform Rahm Emanuel asked, "Is this a 'theme day,' or are we going around the room?"

"My theme is, 'You're doing a great job,'" Obama told his senior aides. "I just wanted you to know that because I don't say it enough."

When Obama's own temperament wasn't to his liking, he tried to adjust the thermostat. But there were limits to what any person, or president, could do to change his own nature.

Optimism is an essential trait in a successful American president. It's what gave the temperaments of FDR and Reagan their lift. This president shared their confidence in the future. And yet Obama had been so lucky in his personal life and political career that it bred a faith in himself that might not withstand the vicissitudes of the presidency. His first year would test when confidence became overconfidence, and if the president, so proud of his self-awareness, could distinguish between the two.

10

Rahmbo

The constant motion of the early Obama administration reflected the restlessness of not just the president but his chief of staff.

A few weeks after the first family finally got a dog, Rahm Emanuel ripped into Bo, whose household accidents were consuming valuable presidential time in cleanups. "I'm going to kill that fucking dog," the chief of staff barked, only half-joking as usual. "He's off message! They said he'd be trained and they lied." Now Rahm was warming to his own pique over the last-minute switch from the promised "shelter dog" mutt, on-message for a mixed-race president, to an effete purebred. "I told the president, 'You can have your Portuguese water dog, but you've also got a pit bull and his name is Rahm.' "

Rahm was more than a pit bull. And he was more than, as the nameplate he kept in his fastidiously tidy office had it, "Undersecretary for Go Fuck Yourself." Those were merely part of the legend he nourished to power his rise. A better analogy was to the thirty-sixth president of the United States. Rahm Emanuel was Barack Obama's own personal Lyndon Johnson, a shrewd legislative tactician with a ferocious will, an abrupt manner, and a proven ability to Get It Done where others couldn't, whether it was hammering out a thorny compromise on the stimulus or arranging for Bruce Springsteen to play "Hava Negila" at the Verizon Center. When he couldn't get it done and his boss landed in trouble, his rude behavior brought all his enemies out of the woodwork to trash him.

At only five-foot-eight and 150 pounds, Rahm hardly towered over people LBJ-style, and he didn't judge his success by whether he had another man's "pecker in my pocket," as Johnson put it. It would be hard to imagine Rahm showing reporters his gallbladder surgery scar, or LBJ doing yoga and ballet. But Rahm swore as much and stood just as close, jabbing his finger in anyone's chest to make a point and give them an urban Jewish version of Johnson's famous "treatment." Nobody in the world was exempt from his peerless effrontery. When British

Prime Minister Tony Blair arrived at the Clinton White House in 1998 amid the Lewinsky scandal, Rahm, not yet 40, put his finger in Blair's face moments before he went to the podium and said to the prime minister, "This is important. Don't fuck it up."

A decade later he was more sophisticated but just as tough and profane. When Jon Kyl of Arizona, the Senate Republican whip, criticized the stimulus, Rahm called him on it by arranging for a letter to be sent from the federal government to Arizona Governor Jan Brewer asking which billions in stimulus spending the state chose not to receive. When the liberal group Moveon.org sponsored radio ads attacking blue dog Democrats on health care, he told liberal activists that the ads were "fucking stupid" and they were "fucking retarded" to run them. (After the latter characterization was published in the *Wall Street Journal,* he apologized and hosted an event for the mentally disabled.) And when AIPAC, the Israel lobby, started complaining about the White House's firm language on Israel's settlements policy in the occupied territories, Rahm bluntly told the lobbyists and the Netanyahu government to get used to it. The message was unmistakable: President Barack Hussein Obama had a chief of staff named Rahm Israel Emanuel and he would use his knowledge and credibility for a new level of candor in U.S.–Israel relations, no matter how much the Israeli press screamed about it or Netanyahu himself called Rahm and Ax "self-hating Jews."

Rahm developed a strong relationship with the president—not a friendship, exactly (Rahm didn't play basketball or golf or get invited for weekends at Camp David), but a partnership that worked. Even when Rahm screwed up, Obama continued to dread the day he would leave the job. Some analysts said he needed a chief of staff who was an expert manager and stayed above the fray, like Jim Baker under Reagan or John Podesta under Clinton. Rahm's relentlessly Congressional focus, they said, made Capitol Hill too prominent in Year One, to the detriment of the president. Obama saw the logic but still believed he had made the right choice.

Rahm played by his own rules, scrolling through BlackBerry messages while the president talked, something no one else would dare try in the Oval Office. Most mornings he got up and worked the phones, a popcorn popper of new ideas and initiatives. Within the space of five minutes, he might be demanding that an economist be more creative in thinking about job creation; reaming out a congressman for missing a parliamentary maneuver; and insisting that the president and everyone else read a certain book, even if they were sure that his own notoriously short attention span prevented him from reading it himself. Obama loved his coiled energy, and Rahm was in awe of the president's equanimity. "How can he be so fucking calm?" he asked Gibbs one day early on, when it seemed as if the White House had no economic plan. Sometimes Obama had to hose him down with a firm "This is gonna get done, Rahm. It will."

Rahm, said one colleague admiringly, was "a respecter of no one." His preference for being feared was less Machiavellian than instinctive. Fear plus fearlessness equals power. He was fearless not just in personal relationships but in making and executing decisions. Most people have trouble either starting something or shutting it down when it isn't working. Rahm did both with dispatch. If someone thought he was abrasive and obnoxious, which everyone did from time to time, he shrugged and moved on. He occasionally admitted error and he didn't get defensive when confronted with superior facts (as long as you could spit them out in under ten seconds); he was merely exacting, exasperating, and frighteningly energetic.

On close contact, of course, he was an acquired taste. Those who didn't hate him, the line went, loved him a lot. Some subordinates (mostly male) found him bracing, funny, and refreshingly free of the usual passive-aggressive manipulation they had experienced in previous jobs. When he called them (men and women) "princess," they loved it. Others were repelled. Rahm was a walking repudiation of the soothing, "no drama" style they adored in the president, and even if they understood Obama's yin-yang reasons for hiring him, they chafed under his command. Reports that he'd mellowed over time were untrue. When an aide came to his office and stammered nervously on a difficult topic, Rahm barked at him, "Take your fucking tampon out and tell me what you have to say."

Some aides found his senior staff meetings unpleasant or even toxic. Rahm would snarl and snap his fingers "Let's go! Let's go! I don't want to wait. I've got shit to do," as if he were Ari Gold, the superagent on the HBO series *Entourage,* conspicuously based on Rahm's brother Ari Emanuel, the CEO of a big Hollywood talent agency. On the series Ari's much-abused assistant is a gay Asian American character named Lloyd. "He treats us all like we're Lloyd," said one fed-up aide.

For years Rahm cultivated his cinematic profile. He was still often called "Rahmbo," after the Sylvester Stallone action figure of the 1980s. In the film the protagonist pursues his mission of freeing American POWs in Vietnam with astonishing intensity. Stallone's John Rambo was by turns compelling and repellent and about as subtle as a hand grenade in the face. Even Rahm's mother, Marsha, a retired psychiatric social worker, liked the nickname. His grandfather, Herman Smulivitz, with whom Rahm had been close, was a boxer and hard-boiled union organizer in Chicago. That figured. But it also fit that his father, Benjamin, a pediatrician, was a *sabra,* a native-born Israeli (as distinct from a Diaspora Jew who settled in Israel). The word comes from the Hebrew for "prickly pear cactus," a desert plant with needles on the surface and sweet fruit within. Sabras are thus known for their abrupt and aggressive personalities, which, in the telling, mask sensitive.souls.

The Emanuel men all fit the sabra profile. Before caring for children, Benjamin had served with the Irgun, the right-wing Jewish underground fighting for independence in 1948. (His brother Emanuel was killed in a skirmish with Arabs in the 1930s, prompting the family to change its name from Auerbach.) The oldest son, Ezekiel, an oncologist and brilliant bioethicist now working on health care policy in the White House,* admitted to being frighteningly intense in college. Rahm, the middle son, born in 1959, had always been brusque but as a young man was such a good ballet dancer that he was invited to join the Joffrey Ballet. Even the youngest and arguably most brutal, Ari, had a soft spot for those, like him, who have battled dyslexia.

Rahm had his own struggles as a reckless 17-year-old growing up in Wilmette, Illinois, a prosperous suburb north of Chicago. Working the meat-cutter at an Arby's restaurant, he sliced his finger and it became infected. On prom night he went swimming in Lake Michigan and the infection spread wildly. With a temperature of 105 degrees he hovered between life and death for four days. As gangrene set in, the finger was partially amputated and he spent two sleepless months in the hospital, where he watched five roommates die. "It was a terrible time for me and worse for my parents," he told the 2009 graduating class at George Washington University. "But to be honest, I'm glad I went through it, because a funny thing happened along the way back from the precipice: Nearly losing my life made me want to live my life."

After Sarah Lawrence College and a master's degree from Northwestern in communication, he set out to work in Illinois progressive politics, eventually winning favor with the Daleys, who recognized in him the same make-something-happen qualities they saw in themselves. He was an observant Jew who traveled to Israel at a moment of danger during the 1991 Gulf War to work with a civilian unit repairing trucks on an army base. By 1992 he had shown great talent as a local fundraiser and went to work on Bill Clinton's presidential campaign, where he set records for hauling in contributions and developed a reputation

---

* Opponents of health care reform dug up old articles by Ezekiel Emanuel and cherry-picked them for quotes that could be taken out of context to harm the White House.

for bluntly telling wealthy Democrats that they better pony up—or else. Most of the most familiar Rahm legends date from this period, like the time he sent a dead fish in the mail, mafia-style, to a pollster who displeased him in a 1988 upstate New York race that he and Axelrod were handling, or the pleasure he took on the day after Clinton's 1992 victory in plunging a steak knife into the table of Doe's Restaurant in Little Rock and shouting "Dead," "Dead," "Dead" at the mention of each person he believed had betrayed the campaign. He loved it when the press retold the irresistible "ballet dancing enforcer" stories and knew that being feared in Washington enhanced his power.

Clinton asked Rahm to handle the logistics of his inauguration and he landed the job of political director in the White House. But as he later admitted, the position went to his head. When Hillary passed the word that Rahm had to go, he told his colleagues that before he vacated the West Wing, President Clinton would have to fire him directly, which he never did. He hunkered down in his office, resolved not to pick unnecessary fights, and grabbed an issue no one else wanted: the crime bill, then languishing. Within a few months he worked his way back in and in 1997 replaced George Stephanopoulos as Clinton's closest political aide.

From the start Rahm was a Democratic Leadership Council moderate, always reminding Democrats that the country wasn't Martha's Vineyard or Manhattan's Upper West Side and it made no sense to look soft on crime and terrorism. But even when he felt strongly about something, he remained an uber-pragmatist. Paul Begala recalled that in 1993 Rahm helped engineer the iconic image of Clinton convincing Yasir Arafat and Yitzak Rabin to shake hands at the White House. Begala, whom Clinton described as a "Catholic Likudnik," called his friend and shouted at him. "I hope your father is proud that his son brought a terrorist to the South Lawn," he told Rahm. "Did you wipe the blood off your hands?" Rahm responded with his default expletive. He didn't like anyone's questioning his devotion to Israel, but he would do what was necessary to help the boss. The same thinking applied in 2009, when he pressured the Israelis.

After Rahm took charge of the crime bill, the State Children's Health Insurance Program, and other successful Clinton initiatives, his legend grew. One Saturday morning in the 1990s he gave an aide, Dennis Burke (later the U.S. attorney in Phoenix), an assignment from his West Wing office. Burke walked across the driveway to his own office in the Executive Office Building and the phone was ringing. "Are you fucking done yet?" Rahm asked. "He was like your high school football coach,"

Burke remembered. "He'd yell at you every day, but deep down you knew he loved you."

Where someone else would have one Clinton announcement to make from Mark Penn's latest poll, Rahm would have three. When Attorney General Janet Reno, under prodding from FBI Director Louis Freeh, tried to slow something down, Rahm, much their junior in rank, would tell them, "Well, that's nice, but we're announcing it on Tuesday." Second terms usually induce torpor in federal agencies; Rahm almost single-handedly used the president's schedule to force his Cabinet departments to keep new initiatives coming.

During the Lewinsky scandal Rahm was out of the office on vacation and called in. "Can't you come up with a fucking hurricane or earthquake to get her off the front page?" he shouted. (Even as chief of staff he was considered harder to deal with when he was on vacation than when in the building.) Kris Balderston, a veteran of the Clinton White House, had a Wizard of Oz theory of the place: "You need a head, a heart, and courage. Rahm was always courage."

By the time he left Washington in 1998 to join the Chicago office of the investment firm Wasserstein Perella nobody was surprised to see him move from success to success.* He made a seamless transition to investment banking and pocketed more than $15 million in three years (mostly because the firm was sold to Lazard Frères). His service on the board of the mortgage giant Freddie Mac netted him at least $320,000 in 2000 for little work, one of those cozy deals for Washington insiders. He resigned to go into politics and won a tough race for the House. Rahm came back to Washington in early 2003 and within a mere two years was tapped to run the Democratic Congressional Campaign Committee, the same organization Congressman Lyndon Johnson used to power his rise. His mission in 2006 was to win back the Congress for the Democrats after twelve years in the minority, an intricate task (given the pro-incumbent gerrymandering in state legislatures) that he compared to "picking a lock." When the Democrats rolled, Rahm was elected chairman of the House Democratic Caucus, the fourth-ranking leadership position. A couple dozen freshmen knew that they wouldn't be there without him, which made for an impressive powerbase after only four years in the House. Nobody could say how long Nancy Pelosi would serve as speaker, but until he took the chief of staff job in 2008 the smart money was on Rahm as her successor.

---

* As a sign of how low the reputation of Wall Street had fallen by 2009, Rahm was forced to decline an invitation to speak to the board of directors of JP Morgan Chase.

INSIDE THE OBAMA White House Rahm wasn't always the slickest political tactician or the best policy analyst. It was the intersection of the two that got him going. Like scrawny Wayne Gretzky sensing where the hockey puck would go next, Rahm anticipated the action before it fully materialized. His instinctive sense of the flow of politics and policy wasn't unerring, but it allowed him to keep a balance between them. If the political or communications people wanted to move forward unharnessed to substance (a bill or policy announcement), he brought them up short. But if the policy shops (the National Economic Council and Domestic Policy Council) on the second floor of the West Wing, the area Rahm lampooned as "the Aspen Institute," lost sight of the fundamental political purpose of their wonkiness, he could be mercilessly dismissive.

In a 2007 book, *The Plan,* Rahm and his coauthor, Bruce Reed, divided Washington into "hacks" and "wonks." Readers assumed that Rahm was the hack and Reed, who was Clinton's domestic policy director, the wonk, but this was an oversimplification. "One of Rahm's greatest strengths is how he realizes that ideas can be a president's most powerful weapon," Reed said.

Because Rahm viewed ideas primarily as weapons, he was rarely wedded to them. To him they were interchangeable instruments of political will. He despised purists who couldn't see that something was almost always better than nothing, which left him open to charges from the left that he was too anxious to cut a deal on health care.

But Rahm also knew enough to understand when he was out of his depth. One day in May he started rewriting the Centers for Disease Control guidance on how many days the public schools should be closed after an outbreak of the H1N1 virus. Two weeks was too long; it would wreak havoc with the school year. Suddenly, as his kosher lunch arrived, he crunched up the paper in a ball, threw it in the trash, and said, "What the fuck do I know about this?" The closures were shortened to one week (and eventually one day), but with the close cooperation of CDC specialists, who were glad to have strong supporters of science back in the White House.

Rahm sent dozens of short BlackBerry emails a day, peppered with typos and misspellings that showed his haste. But his instrument of choice was the cell phone. In his twenty-five or so calls a day, he cut immediately to the point (usually to push a line or learn a precise piece of tactical information) and often hung up within a minute. He didn't appreciate it when he reached only voice mail or when someone failed to call back immediately. One day in early 2009 he left a message for

George Miller: "This is your best fucking friend, your *only* fucking friend in the world. Are you ever going to call me back?" No hello or good-bye. It had been two hours at most since Rahm called the first time.

Miller was one of the House members whom Rahm actually liked. But he got very good at pretending to like almost all of them, even the Republicans. Three mornings a week, when he wasn't swimming, he could be found using his privileges as a former member to work out at the House gym, where he rode the stationary bike and chatted patiently with even the most annoying of his former colleagues. He sometimes playfully greeted friends there by giving them the shortened middle finger. His injury was not a sore subject; even the president was known to curl his middle finger in imitation of Rahm's shortened digit and thrust it skyward with a laugh, like any guy making fun of a friend.

Having Rahm at the other end of Pennsylvania Avenue was a huge advantage to many House members. He didn't just know them; he knew exactly what they could get done and what they couldn't. This saved enormous time in the relationship between the two branches.

When it came to rounding up votes, Rahm's devotion to currying favor with members knew no bounds. "A man never stands taller than when he's down on all fours kissing somebody's ass," he liked to say, with only the trace of a smile. On the night before the key vote in late June on Henry Waxman's energy bill in the House, the Obamas held a Hawaiian luau on the South Lawn, complete with colorful leis, roast pig, and a dunk tank. Members of Congress and their families lined up to send Rahm (as well as Phil Schiliro and Robert Gibbs) plummeting into the water over and over. By the end of the evening he was wandering the lawn in his bathing trunks looking waterlogged. Asked afterward why he did it, Rahm said simply, "Anything to win."

But as the year wore on, strains developed with some liberal Democratic members. The oddest case involved freshman Eric Massa of New York, who called Rahm "son of the devil's spawn" shortly before resigning from the House amid charges of sexual harassment of male staffers. Rahm denied Massa's story that he had aggressively lobbied Massa while naked in the shower of the House gym and there were no witnesses. But the press never learned that Rahm had in fact cursed Massa out in a phone conversation. Rahm had better luck with the blue dog members he had helped get elected in 2006, but even they could be difficult for him. By the end of the year, he was caught between moderates who thought he was too aggressive and liberals who found him too passive, stretched between the president's sweeping vision and his own more realistic view of Congress's ability to get big things done.

Rahm maintained his clout in the House, but his connections to senators weren't as good; many in the upper chamber, especially early Obama supporters, preferred dealing with Rouse or Axelrod. But Rahm worked them too. To make up to Senate Budget Committee Chairman Kent Conrad, who had angered the White House by suggesting early on that health care wouldn't be in his budget, Rahm brought him a special dog food bowl and bone. Before Sonia Sotomayor's nomination for the Supreme Court was announced, the president consulted privately with senators, and Rahm called several to give them a heads-up once the decision was made. These common courtesies sounded like common sense but hadn't been extended in many years. Olympia Snowe was so grateful, she put it in a press release that Rahm had called. The "respecter of no one" had disciplined himself to remember the little things that can sometimes make a difference.

Everyone said essentially the same thing about Rahm: he was the go-to guy, often the *only* go-to guy, if you really needed something done. This was a pathetic commentary on what was supposed to be a community of doers. All across the city, well-meaning people sat in meetings and scheduled the next meeting before the meeting they were sitting in was even over. Rahm was often the one—in the Clinton White House, the House of Representatives, the Democratic Congressional Campaign Committee, and now the Obama White House—who made things happen, not with my-way-or-the-highway commands but with a relentless demand for action before his attention turned elsewhere. It was a strange but effective combination of intense focus and attention deficit disorder.

This bias for action made him popular with like-minded people in government who had spent their careers in search of anyone who could help them cut through all the talk and get something accomplished in their areas of expertise. It helped that he was loyal to the people around him and had their backs, would make any call to help them out, and knew whom to call. In both his first stint in Washington in the 1990s and more recently in Congress he identified hard-charging loyalists throughout the bureaucracy who could solve political problems and give him a critical heads-up on what was going on.

In Janet Reno's Justice Department, Eric Holder had been Rahm's back channel, but once he got the top job under Obama, Holder began acting more independently. When Holder gave a February speech on race saying that the United States was "a nation of cowards," Rahm was ticked. What part of "No distractions" did Holder not understand? He tried to place one of his people at Justice to help Holder politically, but the attorney general, knowing how Rahm operated, refused to take him. Only at the end of the year, after he had been bloodied on terrorism issues, did Holder realize that he should have coordinated more on the politics with Rahm.

———

FOR YEARS RAHM had played a strong outside game to match his skills as an insider. The fearlessness about life that began with his near-death experience in high school extended to the media. During the Clinton campaign in 1992 he learned to trust reporters and rarely complained about stories, figuring that a few dings were worth the ink. He was confident that the reporters knew that if they screwed him, they would lose a valuable source. So they would take care to keep him out of trouble.

Rahm also understood that a high public profile (and soon a powerful public myth) could offer a measure of protection in Washington. It didn't escape his attention that many powerful administration officials of the past—men like Bill Moyers, Richard Holbrooke, James Baker, Richard Darman, even his onetime boss George Stephanopoulos—had prospered by cultivating the press. When he got to Congress he often let selected reporters follow him around all day listening to his conversations. As late as the transition he would still be emailing financial reporters during Obama's announcement of regulators ("So what do you think?") or shooting down trial balloons on appointments ("If she gets the job, I go on a hunger strike").

Once in the White House he continued to give print reporters quotes for their stories but grew more discreet. He was furious when he learned that Axelrod had allowed NBC News (taping a special on life inside the White House) to place a camera crew in his office. He kicked the cameras out eight times on the day they tracked him. Nonetheless he was the most vivid, colorful character on the program.

Of course he couldn't say on TV what he really thought. His bottom line was too anti-Bush. "We have been left with a financial ruin, okay?" he said one day in February, exhausted by the daily fires he was putting out. "Let's not bullshit ourselves. We are limited by what George Bush's policies did to the fiscal condition of the country. Our options are capped, confined. Before we even get to health care, to cap and trade, we are dealing with Bush's legacy."

———

FOR ALL HIS history of self-promotion, Rahm was, as Rouse put it, "all about Barack Obama." At his 7:30 a.m. small meeting for the inner circle and 8:15 larger meeting for senior staff, Rahm's media and legislative strategy was focused intently on advancing the president's agenda and making him look good. That impressed Rouse and a lot of Rahm's subordinates.

Rahm's relationship with Jarrett was rockier. During the transition, when he tried to get her out of the White House, the two were on a collision course. They were learning to live together until July and the publication of a largely flattering *New York Times Magazine* cover story on her called "The Ultimate Obama Insider." The story, by Robert Draper, included quotes from Rahm, Rouse, and Axelrod (who was depicted as excluding Jarrett from a Wednesday night political strategy meeting at his house that Jarrett had in fact no interest in attending) that exacerbated internal tensions. Rahm's quotes, though friendly on the surface, made Jarrett sound personally close to the first family but peripheral to key decisions, which everyone denied. Obama, who loathed any sign of dissension, was furious about the story and banned cooperation with reporters writing profiles of White House staff, an overreaction reflective of his (and Michelle's) intense discomfort over the old Rahm-Valerie discord. When the *Times* ran a long profile of Rahm, neither the president nor his chief of staff gave interviews.

Rahm loyalists felt that Jarrett sometimes steamrolled them with the unstated assumption that her words were backed by her close friends Barack and Michelle. Jarrett loyalists, especially women and minorities, continued to feel that Rahm was insensitive, which was hardly the first time he faced that charge. They complained that they had trouble breaking into "the boys club" that had also largely run things during the campaign, when Obama first showed he was most comfortable with a tight circle of male advisors. Jarrett, Anita Dunn, Nancy-Ann DeParle, Christina Romer, and Carol Browner were proof that several women had real power inside the White House, and none believed Rahm was sexist. But other women and minorities felt the same subtle social exclusion that they often perceived in the workplace: that they were there to "fill a role" rather than for their true talents. They knew these attitudes were still present in the country at large but found it ironic to be confronting a boys club in the Obama White House.

Some of the grumbling involved race and gender, but most of it was about the White House being the White House and Rahm being Rahm. Veterans of the Obama campaign yearned for the ego-free days of Chicago; instead they faced the usual sharp-elbowed Washington narcissism, where every relationship was transactional and people felt their very identities threatened when they weren't invited to a meeting.

His management of the larger 8:15 senior staff meeting in the Roosevelt Room soon became legendary. Rahm's mantra to the thirty-five or so staffers was *No surprises,* which meant that the fastest way to get into trouble was for him to be blindsided in the press. The quality that impressed underlings most was his phenomenal ability to digest hundreds of bits of policy and political information and connect them to hundreds of other bits. Sometimes in the hall or on the phone, he'd say, "Hey, buddy, don't forget about . . . ," and it would be something the aides had, indeed, forgotten to attend to, even though they had much less on their plates than he did.

His colleagues and subordinates quickly concluded that Rahm was an accountability freak. Every Friday a dozen White House sections sent him a ten- to twenty-five-page report on their activities. Cabinet Secretary Chris Lu kept him abreast of initiatives out of the Cabinet; Melody Barnes, director of the Domestic Policy Council, tracked policy development (though Rahm wasn't much interested in the details); Phil Schiliro of legislative affairs kept score on what Rahm liked to call "the points on the board." Within twenty-four hours, by the time of the regular Saturday senior staff meeting at Rahm's house, he had skimmed and digested them all—a couple of hundred pages total. He would write blunt comments on each report (sometimes a simple "No") and begin firing questions about the content. Weeks later he could still remember details of the reports well enough to quiz the authors. *How about that story on C4 of the Wall Street Journal? How does that relate to what you told me last month?* If the Department of Energy was planning an announcement on energy labs, for instance, he could remember off the top of his head not just the policy issues involved but which members of Congress had labs in their districts and how they could be exploited politically.

Whether in the Roosevelt Room or off campus, Rahm's meetings were never just for show. If he went around the room asking "What's new?" and too many people said they had nothing to report, Rahm would say, "You know what? This is bullshit. If you guys have nothing to say, I'll just cancel these meetings. I can work out longer in the morning." He wanted to hear from every person there, on everything from the details of a Treasury initiative to the schedule for the Easter Egg Roll.

Rahm's screaming and swearing were easier to deal with than advertised, especially for those who were willing to push back. There was nothing out of control about his rages, perhaps because they were mostly connected to something else being out of control in the careful planning and execution he expected. His temper was just another weapon in his hyperorganized arsenal. Sometimes he'd curse just so he didn't disappoint visitors. Staffers who caught on to his act found him intense, sometimes annoying, and more than a little crazy, but not particularly scary, because they always knew exactly what they were dealing with: a constant demand for more. More early warning. More "top-line messages" for the press office to push. More announcements and concrete results to make the president look good.

Rahm's most memorable moments of sarcasm came when he was channeling the president's ire about leaks. "Any of you think you're smarter than the president, I got a suggestion for you," he told a staff meeting when word of a decision on the environment leaked earlier than the White House intended. "Go in there and tell him." At that moment the fuming chief of staff actually pointed from the Roosevelt Room to the Oval Office across the hall. "Go ahead, tell him."

In his own contacts with the press Rahm usually managed to sound candid without revealing much, and he was contemptuous of others who couldn't walk that line. He knew that the kinds of "process" stories that Obama found so irritating would have been considered decent press in the Clinton White House, but he convincingly laid down the law for his new boss. "This is it," he told the senior staff meeting after a colorful *New York Times* front-page piece depicted minor factionalism. "This is the end of it. If this ever happens again, I'm going to track down this person [the leaker] and fire him." Rahm knew perfectly well that it wasn't "this person" but many persons—that leaking was one part of Washington that would never change much. But he also understood that Obama was angry about it, and if the boss was mad, Rahm was mad. That was the deal he had made. He would subordinate himself to the president.

Of course that hardly turned Rahm into one of those aides FDR liked, the ones with a "passion for anonymity." Instead he quickly became the best-known member of the administration after the first family, Joe Biden, and Hillary Clinton. The main reason for the public notoriety was his reputation for profanity, which became some of Obama's most consistent comic material. On the eve of Mother's Day the president joked at the White House Correspondents Dinner, "This is a tough holiday for Rahm Emanuel. He's not used to using the word 'day' after 'mother.' " At another dinner Obama teased Rahm for riding a camel during the trip to Egypt: "This is a wild animal known to bite, kick and spit. And who knows what the camel could do?"

The real stories reinforced the myth. Harry Reid had an older secretary named Janice Shelton who kept a "cussing jar" and required a few coins every time someone in the office swore. In February, during the battle over the stimulus, she saw Rahm and said, "Oh, Congressman, now that you're in the White House, what do I call you? 'Congressman' or something else?"

"Just call me 'Shithead.' My wife does," Rahm said as he strode into the majority leader's office, oblivious to the jar on the table.

His obvious devotion to his wife let him get away with the Catskills spiel. During a budget meeting discussion turned to a program called "Abstinence Plus," a more comprehensive sex-ed curriculum. Rahm deadpanned, "Abstinence plus—is that the same as marriage?" For the first six months of the administration he lived alone in Washington while Amy and their three children stayed behind in Chicago. When the president said he wanted to make the White House a "family-friendly" place, Rahm replied publicly, "Yeah, for *your* family." At Penny Pritzker's pool one day during the campaign Rahm teased Marty Nesbitt's 3-year-old, "You're going to be working for me someday, Xeroxing all day, doing what I tell you." The little girl splashed him and replied sharply, "I'm going to put salt and pepper on you and eat you for lunch." Everyone roared, and thereafter Rahm was always in danger of being "salt and peppered" by the Obama family circle.

And by everyone else. The same enforcer who called to apply pressure was increasingly peppered by hundreds of calls and complaints from anyone who had ever known him. His old colleagues on the Hill were the worst. Many believed they were too important to contact someone lower down at the White House when a political problem arose in their districts. It had to be Rahm. That was fine with him, most of the time. It was the ideologues who annoyed him. He had long since given up on the hard-right conservatives, but by the spring of 2009 it was a small group of House Democrats who were causing problems. These weren't the moderate blue dogs from swing districts he had helped get elected in 2006 but members from safely liberal districts who owed Rahm nothing and were often suspicious of him. They insisted that they could not support any health care plan that didn't include a public option; they would sacrifice all the other gains in the bill to that one point. Democrats sabotaging health care! It was enough to drive any Democratic White House chief of staff crazy.

He liked the job and liked making history, but he was burning out and there was a good chance he would leave after the 2010 midterms. If Rich Daley, having broken his father's twenty-one-year longevity record, chose not to run for reelection as mayor of Chicago in 2011, Rahm would move home and jump into the race. Or maybe he'd try something outside of politics altogether, then run for governor or the Senate. One thing he wouldn't do is write a book. "I'm not capable of writing bad things about people I like," he said. And he liked a lot more people than anyone would ever know.

11

The Shovel Brigade

In the mid-1980s Donald Regan, who served as Ronald Reagan's chief of staff, described his job as "like a shovel brigade that follows a parade down Main Street cleaning up" after the elephants. First Lady Nancy Reagan didn't appreciate the job description and what it implied about her husband, and Regan was eventually forced out. But he was not far wrong in insisting that political life often consists of cleaning up someone else's mess.

Obama talked publicly and privately about the mess left him, and he wasn't referring just to the "poop," as he delicately put it to NBC's Brian Williams, that he scooped up after walking the family dog, Bo, on the White House Lawn. President Bush had, in fact, left a terrible pile of problems that would bedevil the Obama administration throughout. The new president was determined that he not let the cleanup overwhelm the other initiatives of his early presidency. That's one reason he rejected the advice of so many of those around him and pushed forward hard on health care reform.

Obama later said that one of his biggest political mistakes in 2009 was not focusing more on George W. Bush's legacy, the way Roosevelt savaged Herbert Hoover's record and Reagan kept punching Jimmy Carter long after taking office. He could have been more direct about Bush's failures but it probably wouldn't have made any difference. Linking the bailouts to Bush was useful for only a few months. Soon enough, Obama owned them.

Contrary to the Fox News chatter, Obama had no taste for socialism or even quasi-socialism, and he was hardly thrilled to have more power over the private sector than any president since Nixon imposed wage and price controls in 1971. He found the amount of time consumed mopping up after Bush the most exasperating part of the job.

The foreign policy legacy issues—from the prison at Guantánamo Bay to the war in Afghanistan to the Iranian nuclear challenge—were in a different category; national security was always on a continuum. It was on the domestic side where he believed Bush had let him down in his last months in office by failing to grapple better with the onrushing recession.

The mess that was easiest for the public to understand was the collapse of the American auto industry. Banking was wildly complicated (even for the bankers) and housing foreclosure something that (one hoped) happened to someone else. But practically everyone owned a car. Americans knew a lot more about PT Cruisers and Hummers than credit default swaps and mortgage-backed securities. And they had a good idea of what caused the reckoning: the auto companies let quality slip, built unsustainable health care benefits into the cost of every car, and failed to change their insular corporate cultures. Chrysler had been hollowed out by Daimler and was now in the clutches of Cerberus Capital Management, a private equity firm. GM was bloated and dysfunctional. Only Ford, under its talented new CEO, Alan Mulally, seemed capable of surviving.

As the recession worsened, auto sales dropped calamitously, from around 17 million cars sold a year to fewer than 10 million. This was a Depression-era decline and it sent the industrial heartland reeling. GM's CEO, Rick Wagoner, seemed oblivious; he went ahead with an expensive remodeling of his corporate kitchen. That tidbit didn't leak, but it was only a matter of time before the world learned that the auto companies' sense of PR was as weak as their balance sheets. When the CEOs, oblivious to symbolism, flew their corporate jets from Detroit to Washington in November 2008 to ask for a $25 billion bailout, public anger boiled over. The next time they made the trip they each made a point of driving hybrids all the way. But it was too late; their credibility was shot.

Over the course of the previous two years Nancy Pelosi and her lieutenants met privately three times with the auto executives. The congressional leaders found the automakers clueless, the worst group of executives they'd ever had in their offices in terms of "getting it." In late 2008, after seeing Paulson raid the treasury on behalf of banks, the car company CEOs figured they would too. They were walking advertisements for what economists called "moral hazard," the message that bailouts would send to other ailing companies that they could take huge risks without suffering the consequences. (Moral hazard applied to individuals too; if the government bailed out foreclosed-upon homeowners who took ridiculous risks, they might figure it was fine to take those risks again.)

The auto companies were almost comically irresponsible. They put nothing on the table and offered nothing by way of specifics or insights. They told the House leadership an old narrative based on a car market that no longer existed, as if they thought Congress hadn't noticed that car sales in the United States had been cut nearly in half. They apparently believed what they told one another at their Grosse Pointe country clubs about all members of Congress being idiots.

Pelosi was blunt with the executives: "When you show us the plan, we'll show you the money." Neither the automakers nor the Bush administration ever came up with a realistic plan. Liquidation wasn't much of an option; it would have created havoc in congressional districts across the country.

Obama claimed that Bush "kicked the can down the road" after the election. In truth, Bush made a few half-hearted attempts to address the problem and got no cooperation from Obama and the Democratic Congress. First Bush floated the idea of dropping the whole thing into the lap of a "car czar," preferably Paul Volcker. When Congress rejected that plan and new loans, the outgoing administration debated what to do. Paulson wanted to let Chrysler and GM go bust; he argued that unlike banks, saving the Big Three automakers wasn't systemically essential. Bush said "Not on my watch" and signed off on spending $17.4 billion in TARP money (which had been designated for financial institutions) to tide them over for a while. It was $17.4 billion in exchange for almost nothing: no realistic business plan and not even any collateral. The taxpayers had no hope of ever seeing that money again.

As the president-elect took control of the issue around the first of the year, he found himself in a squeeze. Bush's team had left him nothing, not even a memo on what they expected for the $17.4 billion. But the basic calculus was unchanged: balancing the interests of the auto companies and their employees and communities with the interests of taxpayers.

At first the public seemed on the side of bailing out the auto companies. Why were bailouts okay for rich bankers but not for hundreds of thousands of auto workers? Axelrod worried that a Wall Street versus Main Street story line could be damaging to Obama, so he and the rest of the political team argued that Detroit deserved one last chance to get it together. The economists inside the White House mostly countered that propping up "zombie" auto companies that deserved to die would bleed the government without fixing the problem and take the United States down the road to Japan's "Lost Decade."

Obama dove into the issue and applied himself to mastering as many of the details as he had time for in his daily economic briefings. He decided that he didn't want to off-load the problem on a big-name car czar, a term the press loved mostly because it rhymed. Health care and energy czars were bad enough; a car czar would have made for an especially juicy target.

Starting in the transition, Obama's point man on autos was Steven Rattner, a founder of the private investment firm Quadrangle (and a longtime Hillary supporter). Had he been officially crowned as czar, Rattner would have been eaten alive in the press for his Wall Street background and lack of familiarity with the auto industry. So instead Obama appointed a lower-profile twelve-person auto task force to provide some cover as his team tried to figure out the most complicated corporate restructuring ever attempted by Washington.

The task force was housed in the Treasury Department and reported to Larry Summers. It was run by Rattner and Ron Bloom, a banker-turned-labor negotiator with the United Steelworkers. Neither had any experience in the auto business, but that was the point: no conflicts. But they also had no experience working in government or at the top of a big American company, which was worrying for the business community. Chrysler and GM were hemorrhaging cash and would be back for another bailout at the end of March. Their fates and that of hundreds of thousands of workers were in the hands of neophytes.

The early months reminded Rattner of a video game: as you got to the next level, everything happened faster and faster. He remembered it as a rare period when big decisions could be made rapidly, often instantaneously. Looking back, he saw early 2009 as a scene out of Malcolm Gladwell's book *Blink,* where the task force's snap judgments eventually turned out just as well as if they had spent weeks or months making them, though it was impossible to know that at the time. The task force worked insane hours, with several young staffers routinely pulling all-nighters.

From the start Obama was determined that the government not run the auto companies, but Washington would decide who from the private sector would run them. The decision to fire Wagoner as chairman and CEO of GM didn't involve any long meetings with the president or decision memos for him to ponder. It was just assumed by everyone involved that a CEO who had blown through more than $13 billion in bailout money in ninety days would have to go. Paulson had pushed CEOs around (and fired the head of AIG), so it seemed natural to fire Wagoner, who had been at the helm for nine years and had presided over a 20 percent decline in market share and a stock price that fell from $70 a share to $3.

In late March, when Rattner did the deed in his spartan ground-floor office in the treasury, Wagoner was stunned. All that the GM chief could think to ask was whether the president of the UAW, Ron Gettelfinger, would also be terminated by the government. The answer from Rattner was no. Why should he be? For years the unions had simply asked for what they could get; it was up to management to hold firm. Besides, Gettelfinger had made major concessions already and would make more in the months to come.

Replacing Wagoner was harder than firing him. Rattner insisted that finding someone from outside GM would take six to nine months, though corporate turnaround specialists said it could be done much more quickly. With no time to waste, the task force decided to promote another GM executive, Fritz Henderson, from within. Henderson had spent his entire career inside the disastrous GM culture and made a less than stellar personal impression. As chief financial officer, he was implicated in GM's much criticized capital budgeting process. But he was ambitious and sounded game to make the tough decisions.

For the critical outsider perspective, Rattner began working on Ed Whitacre, who was revered in the business world for building a dinky regional telephone company into the modern AT&T, to come in as board chairman. Rahm knew Whitacre a bit and liked him; he figured Whitacre wouldn't hesitate to fire Henderson if necessary (as indeed he did, in December 2009, shortly before making himself CEO). Obama himself was kept informed but never got directly involved. Here was a momentous decision—the U.S. government sacking top management at one of the nation's largest and most venerable companies—and it was mostly handled by subordinates. With so much on his plate, the president didn't have time to get more deeply involved—and didn't think it would look right to directly fire Wagoner.

Saving GM was never debatable; letting it collapse and vaporize more than a million jobs would have sent the country into a depression. The big fight was over Chrysler. The task force debated giving Chrysler one more month to complete a deal with Fiat, the Italian automaker, then go through a bankruptcy reorganization with federal help. The alternative was liquidation. With as many as three hundred thousand Chrysler jobs on the line (if suppliers and dealers were included), Gene Sperling, a native of Michigan, argued passionately that this was almost a moral question. In the middle of such a big recession, no one could model or know for sure what such a sudden employment shock could mean to the economy. With the auto sector so central to Midwest communities, Sperling argued liquidation posed a type of "Lehman manufacturing risk"—the potential for a more rapid downward spiral than anyone was projecting. But there was another view at the Council of Economic Advisers, where Austan Goolsbee believed that Chrysler's huge overcapacity meant it couldn't be saved and that an effort to do so would just weaken a restructured GM and especially Ford, the only auto company not seeking a bailout. Goolsbee argued that the three hundred thousand figure was inflated and that liquidation would avoid the "zombie" problem. It was the least bad option.

As rumors of bankruptcy spread, the Michigan delegation went into high gear. Congressman John Dingell, 82, the longest-serving member of the House and still formidable, asked to see the president. Obama refused. With the bailout money already available through TARP, there would be no negotiations with Congress. And Dingell, whose wife, Debbie, was a longtime GM lobbyist, was the personification of the auto industry status quo. The president assigned Summers and Rahm to talk to the Michiganders. They learned that Dingell opposed not just liquidation but bankruptcy of any kind.

The task force was deeply ambivalent about which way to go on Chrysler. But before the big meeting with the president in late March, Summers, who by this time was setting aside his misgivings as an economist and reluctantly embracing much deeper government involvement, stifled dissent. Unlike earlier NEC advisors, he saw his role as giving Obama recommendations rather than options. More people at meetings meant more potential options, so Summers made sure to keep this one small. He told Goolsbee he couldn't attend.

Inside the Oval Office the president cut off Summers's recitation of the issues with a curt "I read the memo," then went around the room and asked his advisors if they were all on board with Summers's recommendation of a big Chrysler bailout, followed by a likely bankruptcy. Each said yes. But how about that paragraph of dissent buried on the sixth or seventh page of the memo? Obama wanted to know where it came from. Christina Romer said it was from Austan Goolsbee. "Where's Goolsbee?" the president asked, perturbed that he wasn't getting all the options. Moments later Goolsbee was summoned from the Eisenhower Executive Office Building, the Beaux Arts wedding cake next door where most of the White House staff works. He arrived, breathless, and sat in the only open seat, the vice president's customary chair (Biden was absent), right between the president and Summers, who gave him the fisheye.

Axelrod later said that day, Thursday, March 26, was one of the most eventful of Obama's first year. The president was simultaneously putting the finishing touches on the announcement of a new troop escalation in Afghanistan, preparing for his first European trip, and confronting flooding so severe that it would require the evacuation of Fargo, North Dakota. So it was no surprise when he cut the auto meeting short after twenty minutes and asked that it resume early that evening. "A half hour to decide the fate of the auto industry isn't enough," he said. In midafternoon he reviewed with Axelrod the highlights of what had been extensively debated over the previous three months and said he wanted to hear from more people.

When the group reassembled at 6 p.m. in the Roosevelt Room with several additional advisors who wanted to weigh in, Summers made his case: "You're going to pay a lot either way. [With liquidation,] you're paying for a funeral. At least in the other case, you might be buying something."

Rahm impressed the gathering with his detailed knowledge of which congressional districts in Michigan had which auto plants. Robert Gibbs pointed to the county-by-county breakdown of layoffs if Chrysler liquidated. "You're always explaining that things are bad, but it's not like the Great Depression," he told the president. "Well, in some of these counties . . ."

"I know what you're going to say," Obama interjected. "In some of these counties it *will* be like the Great Depression."

Obama mentioned Bush. Getting tough on the auto industry would go down better if Bush had taken a tougher line on banks. It could be justified only if Chrysler had a good chance of survival. Did it? To the dismay of the bailout advocates, Rattner wouldn't commit. He said the Fiat deal could still collapse; the task force hadn't yet completed due diligence (checking the financial condition) on the Italian automaker and they might be unpleasantly surprised. "In my experience," Rattner concluded, "deals get worse over time. It's a 51–49 call."

Brian Deese, the bearded 31-year-old assigned to handle the issue inside the White House, thought that the Fiat deal would work for Chrysler. Obama smiled mischievously. "I had a Fiat in college," he said. "It was in the shop all the time."

Deese said that though some doubted Fiat, the company was building a 40-mile-per-hour engine. Before he could say that he meant *gallon,* not *hour,* two or three people talked over one another amid laughter to say, "It's going to be that old Fiat you bought in college, Mr. President!"

At the end of the hour-long meeting Obama said, "I've decided. I'm prepared to support Chrysler if we can get the Fiat alliance done on terms that make sense to us." The task force, now informally known as "Team Auto," liked what the president said next: "I want you to be tough, and I want you to be commercial." He would give Chrysler thirty days and GM sixty days to reorganize with the help of the task force or face a cutoff of TARP money. He could live with the government's forcing a bankruptcy, but not putting Chrysler out of business altogether.

Goolsbee's argument hadn't changed his mind, but at least Obama had finally heard the full range of views. Veterans of the Clinton administration were impressed: here was a decision affecting the future of the industrial base of the country and this president made it crisply before a later than usual dinner. Their old boss would have been talking about it until 2 a.m. and still not have made a decision.

Obama knew that more government involvement with the auto industry would likely bring trouble. Bankruptcy was frightening. Many analysts insisted that Americans would figure that a bankrupt company could never be trusted to service their cars; they would desert Chrysler and GM in droves. Extending back a hundred years, there was simply no precedent for an auto company going bankrupt and surviving. And of course the politics of a government-backed bankruptcy were horrible, as all the polls indicated.

At 9 p.m. that Sunday Obama and Team Auto huddled around a speakerphone in the Oval Office to talk to the Michigan delegation. When the speakerphone malfunctioned, the president joked that it was "probably from a well-connected government contractor." Obama was calling not to consult with Michigan Governor Jennifer Granholm, Dingell, and the others, but to brief them on what he had decided. Congressman Sander Levin said he assumed all the bankruptcy talk was just to "bring the parties to the table." No, the president said. Bankruptcy was a "real possibility."

Obama now believed that the accountability provided by bankruptcy and reorganization was probably the only answer. Yes, he disliked cleaning up after Bush, but this, he said privately, was a perfect example of what he ran for president to do: confront problems rather than paper them over. He was proud of his bias for action and afraid that dithering would cause him to hate himself in the morning. He later told friends he didn't want to look back at his years in office and say he avoided tough decisions. So he'd take a bet even if the odds of success were only 50–50. "I feel lucky," he liked to say lightly after expending political capital. It reflected his faith in his skills as a prudent gambler.

But Obama was always game to draw some new cards. The Michiganders had stressed the need for the government to stimulate auto sales. After the conference call Summers recognized that they were right. In concentrating so hard on financial restructuring, the White House hadn't done enough to stir demand. Deese reminded him of an old "Cash for Clunkers" proposal (worth up to $4,500 toward a new car) that had originated in Europe and been pushed by Senator Barbara Mikulski and Representative Betty Sutton on Capitol Hill. Cash for

Clunkers had been killed during the stimulus debate by environmentalists, who thought it wasn't tough enough on gas guzzlers, and by the UAW, which implausibly insisted that it not apply to foreign-made cars. But Summers knew that neither interest group had time to press its case on a Sunday night. In an example of the nimbleness that the White House took pride in, he asked Deese and a couple of other caffeinated workhorses to get a coherent four-point plan (complete with IRS complexities) ready for the president within twelve hours. After an all-nighter, they did.

Word leaked on Sunday of the Wagoner firing, overshadowing Obama's big announcement the next day, March 30, that he would ask Chrysler and GM to "fundamentally restructure in a way that would justify an investment of additional taxpayer dollars." They would have thirty and sixty days, respectively, to develop plans. Did this mean some kind of speeded-up bankruptcy? Quite possibly, the White House confirmed. Within minutes something unexpected happened. After months of fearing that the b-word would kill all sales, the auto industry and Wall Street reacted positively. As long as there was a true restructuring plan, most of the stakeholders could deal with a quick bankruptcy.

It was a big leadership moment for Obama that at the time seemed akin to Ronald Reagan showing his toughness by firing the air traffic controllers in 1983. He was sending a message that the old days of being coddled by the government were over; the auto industry would have to truly change, not just pretend to. As it turned out, Obama won few points for this show of decisiveness. It was an early sign that Obama wouldn't get much credit for confronting what he inherited.

With the task force driving a hard bargain, the Chrysler negotiations were brutal. After thirty days it was still not clear whether Chrysler would file for bankruptcy. One key to the deal was getting GMAC (GM's finance arm) to merge with Chrysler's finance division, in essence a horribly tangled bank takeover. The other, related challenge was convincing Chrysler's secured lenders (the primary creditors) to take a "haircut" (a loss) that would eventually mean they got only twenty-nine cents on the dollar. Rattner had basically divided Chrysler in two, with the good assets to be owned mostly by the UAW and Fiat, which would try to use its cutting-edge technology (itself the subject of dispute) to revive the moribund company. The hedge funds and other lenders were left holding the bag on the insolvent part of the automaker. Jimmy Lee of JP Morgan, representing the secured lenders, told Rattner, an old friend, that the lenders were owed the full $6.9 billion they put up "and not a penny less." Rattner told him that was "ridiculous" because the liquidation value of the company was only $1 billion, according to Chrysler's own analysis.

It was the president's tough line that changed Lee's mind. When the lenders began complaining Obama blasted them publicly as "speculators" and made it clear that he would allow Chrysler to go out of business if they didn't negotiate. Lee left a message on Rattner's phone, saying, "We need to talk." After missing several deadlines Lee finally got the big lenders to sign on for $2 billion, which was less than they were owed but much more than they would have received in liquidation.

The Chrysler deal enraged many businesspeople far beyond the auto industry and Wall Street. Some argued loudly and sanctimoniously that in bankruptcy, secured lenders always get paid first, a hundred cents on the dollar. They muttered that in order to protect his union buddies, Obama was trampling on the hard-and-fast rules of capitalism. If secured lenders were screwed, who would ever lend again? Even some Democrats accused the president of assaulting the rule of law.

He hadn't. While a bankruptcy court would normally be required to pay secured lenders first and in full, the Chrysler deal was done prior to bankruptcy, where the biggest investor with the most leverage (in this case the government) always gets to call the tune. And the claims that Chrysler was being rescued by "Obama the socialist" because it was politically "too big to fail" were a tad hypocritical. The only reason many of the lenders had any money left was their connection to banks deemed by the government to be . . . too big to fail.

Despite the complaints from secured lenders claiming that capitalism was ending, the deal was logical enough. Parts suppliers got 100 cents on the dollar because they were so shaky that any haircut would kill them, costing thousands more jobs. Warrantees had to be paid off in full or reports of worthless warrantees would convince consumers not to buy any new cars. And at least some workers had to be protected or there would be no one on the assembly line. These were essential for the company to survive; making creditors whole was not. A splinter group of angry bondholders representing smaller institutions couldn't see this and sued. They appealed their case to the Supreme Court, which refused to hear it.

While he had his foot on their necks, Obama moved aggressively in late spring to force the auto companies to adopt fuel economy standards (35.5 miles per gallon by 2016, up from 27.5) that they had loudly resisted for decades.* Because he considered reducing dependence on

---

* The auto task force said it had nothing to do with this White House policy, which is a little like investment bankers who say they never talk to traders working for the same bank.

foreign oil to be a national security issue, Obama made an exception to his promise not to use his leverage to tell Detroit how to build cars. The CEOs came to the White House and acted as if they loved the idea.

Worried that Ford, the only company without a bailout, would suffer from the Chrysler and GM deals, Obama gave a casual-sounding but planned shout-out to the company as he left the podium. "By the way, I just want to mention, I think I still have my Ford parked in Chicago," he said cheerfully. "It's a Ford hybrid. It runs great. You guys [the media] should take a look."

The president's last (he hoped) big auto decision was on how to restructure GM. With 225,000 employees, 500,000 retirees, 11,500 suppliers, and 6,000 dealers, liquidation was never an option. But reshaping the vast company was maddeningly complex. After running and rerunning the numbers, the task force concluded that the only way to give the sprawling company a shot at long-term survival was to lift its crushing debt. So it recommended that the U.S. government take a majority interest in GM, making it in essence "Government Motors." That option upset Summers, who feared creeping socialism. But he knew it was necessary and sold it to Obama.

"This president was willing to do the right thing, as opposed to the expedient thing," Rattner concluded. "We could have put the money in as debt, taken no ownership, or very little ownership, and never had all this chatter about nationalizing a big car company. But it really would have been irresponsible. GM could not support this amount of debt. It would have had a very material chance of going bankrupt again." It might go bankrupt again anyway, but at least it wouldn't be doing so amid a depression that its collapse helped cause.

At any time during the negotiations the UAW could have scotched the whole deal. The widely circulated idea that Obama gave the unions a special break was wrong. Ron Bloom liked to point out that his old colleagues at the Steelworkers Union had done much better when their industry was restructuring. As Ron Gettelfinger contemplated a deal that would provide the UAW a 17.5 percent stake in GM in exchange for the closure of seventeen plants, massive new layoffs, wage freezes, cuts in retirement, vacation, and health care benefits, and a promise not to strike for six years, he walked the streets of Washington for two hours. On returning, he signed off on the deal and got his union to go along.

For years GM had survived partly by building cars offshore at lower cost; GM India was doing particularly well. It was hard to imagine that a company owned by the American taxpayers could continue adding jobs abroad while cutting them at home.* And yet the president, who had railed during the campaign at *private* companies shipping jobs overseas, was determined that politics not intrude. The challenge for Obama was to build a wall between ownership and management. Ironically this was the opposite of the shareholder democracy he favored for business in general.

Obama would have to develop a new definition of *public company.* He had begun musing about the problem a few weeks before GM's bankruptcy. At one of his daily economic briefings in May he turned to the larger question: What should the standards be for banks, car companies, and anything else? He told his advisors that this was a big deal, much bigger than any other president had faced in this area. The only time the U.S. government had ever before taken over private companies was during wartime. Obama liked the phrase *rules of the road* and had used it during the campaign to describe what Wall Street needed. Now he wanted the government to adopt some "reluctant shareholder" principles for these new public-private behemoths.

Diana Farrell, Summers's deputy and formerly the head of the McKinsey Global Institute, was assigned to head a committee to draft these guidelines. A few days before the scheduled GM announcement she delivered her confidential report to the president. The memo outlined the distinction between *ex ante* and *ex post* government involvement. In the ex-ante phase, when a failing company is being restructured, the government should be as heavily involved as any investor or lender. This would likely mean direct influence over selecting new management and new members of the board, though without demanding a seat for the government itself. But by the ex-post phase, when new management is in place, the government's role would be hands-off, like a private equity firm waiting to see if it had bet on the right corporate leadership. The Farrell report was a nuanced, sensible standard for the crisis management of American capitalism, but it was too early to know how well it would work, for car companies or any other enterprise.

On June 1 Obama made his dramatic announcement. As part of a "controlled bankruptcy" the U.S. government would pump another $30 billion into GM. But instead of more loans, the government would invest directly, bringing its ownership stake to roughly 60 percent. Taxpayers now owned more than 60 percent of GM! The figure stuck in

---

* The task force did eliminate the tax advantages of manufacturing car overseas, which led to GM's giving up control of its longtime German brand, Opel.

the mind as a sign of how much had changed in the country in just six months.

The president made a point of anticipating the critics. "What we are not doing—what I have no interest in doing—is running GM," he said. He knew that it looked bad for a president to be talking about warrantees and labor deals; these were private sector concerns. He vowed to sever the government from any decisions that related to the day-to-day operation of the company. To reinforce the point, Rattner insisted that the government would make "no plant decisions, no job decisions, no color-of-car decisions."

The bankruptcy of General Motors, once unthinkable, was now a fait accompli, and the government stake set off a round of wary analysis. "Just as George Bush spent much of his presidency seeking a way out of Iraq, Mr. Obama may spend much of his seeking a way out of the morass of new government investments in the private sector," David E. Sanger wrote in the *New York Times*. "The hardest part will be knowing how to time the withdrawal of government support—a balancing act between maximizing the investment of taxpayers and risking the company's fragile state."

In an industry famous for its pokey pace, everything was suddenly about speed. The task force designed a hurry-up workout and the bankruptcy judges went along. Chrysler's bankruptcy lasted only forty-two days, and the Fiat deal that induced such early skepticism seemed to have a fighting chance. GM's Chapter 11 restructuring was even shorter, though it would take months to sort out complications. In closing Pontiac and selling Hummer, Saturn, and Saab, GM was finally undergoing the radical surgery that should have been undertaken years, if not decades, earlier. The streamlined deals engineered by Team Auto were working better than anyone had dared hope.

In July, after the restructuring was mostly complete, Rattner returned to New York under a cloud. The investment business he founded was being investigated for its role in a pension fund scandal. Ron Bloom took over the task force, which began winding down its efforts. Obama was grateful to Rattner, but not grateful enough to put up with the political heat associated with finding him another high-profile assignment.

As the momentous auto decisions gave way to smaller ones, Rattner and Bloom had reason for pride in their intricate handiwork. They knew that even after all they had done, Chrysler and GM might yet go out of business; the outdated manufacturing systems of the American companies could make them easy prey for much healthier foreign automakers. But they also knew that the odds of survival were better with government equity, if the politicians could keep their hands off. That was a big *if.*

At a special Sunday briefing in June to give the congressional leadership a heads-up on the GM bankruptcy, Obama learned immediately that Congress hoped to take its new car company out for a spin. When pressed by the Michigan delegation for a commitment that GM's corporate headquarters wouldn't leave Detroit (a move that some analysts believed might help mend the broken corporate culture), the president was firm. That was a matter for the GM board, not the White House.

Of course it didn't take long for the casualties of the collapse to come protesting to the new owners. When two thousand GM dealers (about 40 percent of the national total) got the call in mid-June telling them that it was all over, many still couldn't quite process it. With at least one dealership in nearly every congressional district, the auto dealers had long been a potent lobbying force. Now they descended on Congress en masse. Many were angry that the president hadn't dropped everything to focus on the lost jobs. "It's much broader than the loss of sales and service," Congressman Bruce Braley of Iowa told Fritz Henderson and the other new auto company chiefs when they came to Capitol Hill. "It's part of the fabric of this country." Henderson was sympathetic to the tens of thousands who lost their jobs, but unmoved: "It's our last chance," he said.

As it turned out, the onslaught of favor-seeking was less than expected. About thirty or forty members of Congress and major community leaders called the White House, but most did so in a pro forma way; they knew the decisions wouldn't be reversed. Not everyone was so meek. Barney Frank threw his weight around as a powerful committee chairman to protect a few dozen auto industry jobs in Massachusetts. But even as Congress held hearings on the closing of dealerships, Henderson hung tough on almost every plea for mercy. Rahm too was determined to hold the line. He told his staff it was a "muscularity issue," a way to show the president's toughness while simultaneously keeping politics from overwhelming GM's recovery.*

The pain wouldn't go away for many months, maybe years. Obama appointed a special director of recovery for auto communities, Ed Montgomery, and he set about looking for ways to replace jobs. One GM plant in Pontiac became Motown Motion Picture Studio; Mont-

---

* At the end of the year, the GM car dealers convinced Congress to require GM to submit to arbitration on the closings of dealerships. In early 2010, with the business picking up, 660 dealerships were reinstated.

gomery was excited that the new project would bring three thousand jobs. But Michigan had lost eight hundred thousand jobs in nine years; its unemployment rate was over 12 percent and going higher. All the good ideas for the future, including worker retraining programs and $1 billion to make Michigan a center for battery development, would not rescue the state anytime soon. The carnage left by the collapse of the industry was heartbreaking on a human scale and hazardous to Obama's political health. Where were the new jobs for Michigan, Ohio, Pennsylvania, and all the other industrial areas of the country going to come from? No one knew.

One glimmer of hope came on the demand side. The Cash for Clunkers program, aided by a catchy name, proved so instantly popular in August that $1 billion in subsidies meant to last for ninety days were absorbed by auto buyers in only nine.* Congress was forced to immediately authorize $2 billion more (which lasted less than a month). The main beneficiaries were suburban families trading in their second or third car.

At first the logistics were a fiasco, as dealers complained angrily that the Department of Transportation was so disorganized that it couldn't answer calls, much less cut checks on time. But Ray LaHood's team responded quickly. By mid-September, after installing new software in record time and hiring nine thousand contractors almost overnight to process payments, Transportation officials straightened out the mess so well that they received rewards from grateful car dealers. On balance the program was a success, saving one hundred twenty thousand jobs and providing the only economic boost of the summer.† Ironically, one of the best-remembered Obama initiatives of 2009 was not a carefully organized initiative but a busted play.

Steve Rattner found himself surprisingly optimistic about the future of the American auto industry. At the beginning of the year he had put the odds at 10–1 against success. Either this president would join Bush in kicking the can down the road, or the bankruptcy process would somehow fall apart. Neither happened. By the third quarter of 2009, he gave the auto rescue an 80 percent chance of success. The restructuring of the industry had brought the break-even point down to 10 million vehicles sold a year, which was almost exactly where they were at midyear, with market share compared to Japanese manufacturers rela-

---

* Not a single person in government or industry came close to predicting Cash for Clunker demand. This should have been a lesson in the fallibility of the hundreds of longer-term projections by the Office of Management and Budget, the Congressional Budget Office, federal agencies, corporations, and think tanks. But of course it wasn't.
† After the program ended, September auto sales dropped sharply.

tively unchanged. Contrary to expectations, the b-word hadn't scared off anybody. And unlike, say, newspapers, there was no substitute for the automobile; Americans could put off buying a new car for a couple of years, but they would need one eventually. Would it be a Chevy or Chrysler instead of a Nissan or Toyota?* No one could say. But whatever happened to the American auto companies, the United States would have a new approach to troubled industries—a moderate, commonsense view, not the hands-off philosophy of conservatives or the heavily planned industrial policy of the left. Obama envisioned no fundamental shift in the role of government in business, and he believed that those who accused him of a power grab either weren't listening to him or were intent on distorting his views.

If so, there were plenty of Americans in both categories. White House aides always knew the auto bailouts were unpopular but they were surprised by the depth of the anger. The sacking of GM's CEO became a symbol of Obama's overreaching. "It was a seminal moment," a senior advisor lamented. "We knew everyone would hate us bailing out banks, but we thought they would like us saving auto jobs. It turned out they'd rather we hadn't." The episode was a powerful signal that the public's appetite for FDR-style bold intervention in the economy was limited. At the left-right fork in the road, the public went right.

Obama understood bailout fatigue, but he remained undeterred. His shovel brigade had become something more commendable—a fire brigade. In a sign of the times Austan Goolsbee summarized the administration's self-image on a comedy show, *The Colbert Report:* "Your house is on fire. A guy goes in and rescues your kid. Now is not the time to accuse him of kidnapping."

As 2009 wore on, kidnapping would be among the least of the charges the right leveled at Barack Obama.

---

* Toyota suffered a big setback in 2010 when millions of its cars were recalled.

12

Larry and Tim

Obama disliked bombast, so he developed little ways of bragging and seeming modest at the same time. He'd often say he was "pretty good" at something. He had a "pretty good speech" prepared for the 2004 Democratic Convention, he told friends. He'd had a "pretty good debate," he liked to say during the campaign after an especially effective performance.

On economics, he was more modest, allowing only that he had a "layman's understanding" of the subject, without the "pretty good" modifier. He meant that he could ask penetrating questions about, say, the toxic assets of banks or the churning of labor markets. The president was an exceptionally quick study, but he hadn't studied much economics and he didn't pretend to be an expert.

This made it all the more curious that he decided to keep his circle of economic advisors so small. Obama was unapologetic. The critics didn't get it. The guys they were trashing had stopped another Great Depression. But the same advisors had also failed to use the government's full leverage to prevent the *next* depression. A system where six "too big to fail" megabanks held 60 percent of the nation's assets remained untouched.

Obama's main tutors on the economy were Larry Summers, Tim Geithner, and Peter Orszag, with lesser roles played by Christie Romer, chair of the Council of Economic Advisers, and Jared Bernstein, a progressive economist on Joe Biden's staff. These experts plus Rahm Emanuel were the regulars in the President's Daily Briefing on economics, which would vary in length from a few minutes to more than an hour. It was a sign of the times that a meeting that in past administrations occurred roughly once a month (when economic data was released) was now daily.

The team shared certain assumptions beyond a general faith in pragmatic, nonideological solutions. Re-regulating the banking system was essential, the collection of economists thought, but first they had to save it. Early 2009 should be devoted to wrapping a tourniquet to stop the bleeding. This made sense, except that this period also represented a once-in-a-generation chance to cure the patient, or at least sharply increase the odds that the disease that had ravaged the American economy would not return anytime soon. That opportunity was largely missed.

———

THE DRIVING FORCE was Summers. He was director of the National Economic Council, which was designed in the early Clinton administration to be like the National Security Council, a neutral broker of competing views within the executive branch. Summers had said from the start that he didn't see the job that way. He would read across the ideological spectrum in economics journals, government reports, blogs, and the opinion press and filter everything for the president.* But he would also use his daily face time with Obama to push his own views.

"I'm what I am," he told Obama and Rahm during the transition. "Those who've watched me carefully over the years would say that I'm not without self-regard and I don't suffer fools or foolishness easily and that I'm not patient with the platitudinous and the content-free. It's not going to feel like a big mutual support session. But even people who don't like me or regard me as arrogant would say I'm pretty free of guile and duplicity and games. There will be no doubt of my team play. You're going to get a rigorous and serious argument. Think about whether that's what you want."

Obama decided that it was. He figured that he was intellectually curious enough, and Summers smart enough, to avoid the pitfalls associated with Summers being miscast in the NEC role. Summers's insecurities (and the sharp elbows that resulted from them) could be contained, Obama figured. Others with experience in government saw trouble ahead. In the early 1990s, Bob Rubin, the first director of the NEC, took his honest-broker role so seriously that he once sponsored a six-hour meeting with Clinton on the economy and said nothing the whole time. His job, he thought, was to make sure the president heard from a wide variety of sources. Rubin loved Summers but he made a point of asking Obama during the transition who would smooth out the natural frictions in the administration, the way Leon Panetta and

———

* Summers said he absorbed the thinking of the left by reading the *Washington Monthly*, *The Nation*, blogs by Brad DeLong and others, and the work of such critics as Simon Johnson and Paul Krugman.

later John Podesta had performed delicate bureaucratic diplomacy for Clinton. The president-elect replied, "I will."

Sometimes this smoothing took the form of wisecracks from the president. "I'm glad to see you're not rolling your eyes today, Larry," the president said one morning, his way of reminding Summers to behave himself in meetings. Obama enjoyed playfully slapping Summers down. "I don't want to belabor the point," Summers said one day. "Yes, you do," the president interjected with a smile. He teased Summers for repeatedly falling asleep in meetings, for sweating in winter, and for attaching probabilities to everything.* Summers's habit of finding a cloud around every silver lining led the president to privately dub him "Dr. Kevorkian." When the CEO of Freddie Mac said at a White House meeting that he needed to award retention bonuses because "some employees are uniquely qualified," Obama said lightly, "I guess you could say Larry Summers is uniquely qualified for his job, but I'm not sure he is." The line simultaneously conveyed his skepticism about the retention argument and about Summers's (or anyone else's) indispensability.

Summers was a drama guy in a no-drama White House, the exception that proved the rule. But like the other big egos in the administration (Hillary Clinton and Richard Holbrooke most conspicuously), he knew he would have to modify his behavior and show some self-effacement to survive. One day Summers was about to say, "That's the stupidest argument I've ever heard," but he caught himself midsyllable at "That's the stu—." He changed gears, smiled slightly, and said, "I'm trying to learn to be more constructive." He revived a bit of false modesty he learned from Rubin, prefacing some remarks by saying, "I may be wrong about this, but . . ." On his 54th birthday Geithner brought out a cupcake to celebrate. After singing "Happy Birthday," the group started in with "For He's a Jolly Good Fellow," which Summers amended to "For He's an Unpleasant Fellow."

Summers's larger view of his mission was best conveyed by a story he told about his daughter, a high school student preparing for her Advanced Placement test in American history. He noticed that her study materials contained plenty about the Great Depression but nothing about the short, steep 1982 recession, which featured 7.5 percent unemployment, 13 percent inflation, and 20 percent interest rates. His goal, he said, was to help the president make today's economic crisis

---

* At the 2009 White House Correspondents Dinner Obama, using a joke written by Axelrod, poked at a sensitive subject, Summers's unpopularity after he questioned the abilities of women in the sciences. He joked, "Larry Summers asked if he could chair the White House Council on Women and Girls."

as forgettable as 1982's, so that students who take AP history in 2030 or 2040 don't learn about this moment.

The man most responsible for the economy in 1982 was Paul Vol-cker, Carter's appointee to chair of the Federal Reserve, who made a series of gutsy decisions to raise interest rates and wring inflation out of the economy. Volcker had a different, more progressive analysis of the 2008–9 crisis than Summers and Geithner, and that difference would play out over the course of the year in ways that left Volcker frustrated. In the greatest economic crisis since the Great Depression, the new president left the greatest Fed chairman in history on the side-lines for most of 2009.

The chance that the 2008–9 recession might someday be a minor historical episode was due in large part to massive intervention by the Fed, which extended beyond its historic role in monetary policy to backstop the financial system by providing up to $13 trillion in guar-antees, with $2 trillion to $3 trillion actually spent (and most of that repaid). The fiscal policy of the last days of the Bush administration, TARP, and of the Obama administration, the Recovery Act, obviously helped. They worked essentially as triage to prevent bank runs (espe-cially on money market funds), massive layoffs of public employees, plummeting consumer confidence, and the other forces that might have turned a recession into a depression.

But the economic recovery would most likely be jobless and cheer-less, with little credit for anyone. White House aides and Treasury of-ficials labored eighteen-hour days, seven days a week for what seemed like no reward. From banking to bonuses, financial regulation to fore-closures, the administration was in a constant struggle to stay on top of economic developments. At Treasury, Gene Sperling thought that work-ing on a program as hated as TARP felt like being asked to do 'A' work under enormous time pressure just to convince the world to give you a 'C-plus' instead of a 'D'. When Sperling worked as a consultant on the TV show, *The West Wing* friends asked, "Is it realistic?" His answer was that on the show, nine months of work were condensed into a single hour. In the first three months of the Obama administration, he said, nine months of work were routinely condensed into a single week.

———

THE FIRST BIG economic debate of the new administration was over whether the government should use the leverage of TARP to force new behavior on lenders (credit was frozen) and on companies awarding outlandish bonuses. In a meeting less than two weeks after Obama took office, Axelrod argued yes, but Summers and Geithner opposed attaching big strings to bailouts. They thought it wrong to kick banks when they were down, not to mention violating their contracts.

Obama heard his political consigliere out, but sided with the guys who knew more about the subject. Axelrod tried to downplay the meeting's importance, but this was a fateful decision. If Obama had used the whip hand on banks early on, he might have pre-empted a brewing populist revolt and shown toughness that could make him more formidable in later tussles. Whatever he did, the right wing was going to call him a socialist (that had begun during the campaign with McCain surrogate "Joe the Plumber"). So he might as well have won more in exchange for the abuse. But he wasn't one for picking fights, at least not yet.

In the meantime, he needed to back up his treasury secretary. On February 9 Obama held his first press conference as president. "I am the eternal optimist," he said in arguably his most cogent description of his approach to public life. "I think that over time people respond to civility and rational argument." To that end, he sought to prepare the public for the unveiling of his much-awaited bank rescue plan. Obama said Geithner would be announcing the plan the next day. He added, "He's going to be terrific."

But Geithner wasn't terrific, to put it mildly. As far back as his days in the Clinton administration Geithner had been known as a poor speaker, prone to jargon and awkward word choice. (His fellow Fed governors once teased him for using *dimension* as a verb.) He had never been a professor and wasn't good at reducing complexities to their essence. He'd also never used a teleprompter before and chose the wrong moment to practice. The speech was a fiasco. Geithner scared the markets and the country by looking, as one aide in the White House communications office put it, "like a twelve-year-old playing treasury secretary."* The Dow dropped 382 points.

Worse, he didn't seem to have a coherent plan. The strategy cooked up during the transition was to confront home foreclosures first (to show Americans the new administration was working on things they could see), then decide how to spend the second $350 billion installment of TARP, then tackle the toxic assets of banks. But the pudding had no theme. Geithner didn't want to repeat Paulson's policy reversals, where one day TARP was about buying toxic assets and then—Never mind!—TARP would be lending money to the banks. So he thought he was acting in a principled way by being restrained and a little vague.

---

* Geithner was immediately sent to Democratic speech coach Michael Sheehan, who helped him bring up his game on TV.

He later said he was trying to buy time to defuse what he called "these big fucking bombs" left him by Bush, especially AIG, whose bailout was only beginning, and Fannie Mae and Freddie Mac, which suddenly needed another $100 billion each from the Fed.

Geithner's public belly flop was more conspicuous because no major figure other than the president was out there defending him. The perfect person to do so would have been Volcker, but Volcker hadn't been dialed into the policy, so he couldn't sell it. Jarrett rushed to tell the president that Volcker was being blocked by Summers. Obama wasn't happy and instructed Jarrett and Rahm to make sure Volcker knew that he could contact the president anytime. But you don't call the president; the president calls you. As a practical matter, Volcker couldn't easily end-run Summers; for months he would continue to be excluded from any major role in policymaking.

Nearly every day for the first two months, when it felt like water was constantly coming over the side of the boat, Geithner would ride over to the White House from the Treasury Building next door and join Summers for an hour, usually with Rahm, who would give the Treasury secretary explicit instructions on how to proceed. With so many decisions on so many daily developments, Rahm was acting almost as a prime minister on economic policy.

The discussions were often heated. At Treasury in the 1990s Summers and Geithner had become friends in part because they could argue viciously about economics without hurting each other's feelings. (They were even tennis buddies and vacationed together on occasion at Nick Bollettieri's Florida tennis camp.) When Pete Peterson, a New York billionaire, worried that Geithner might not be tough enough to be president of the New York Fed, Summers laughingly reassured him, "[Tim] is the only person who ever worked with me who'd walk into my office and say to me, 'Larry, on this one, you're full of shit.'" Now they quickly fell into a modified version of their old contrasting styles. Summers was not quite as obnoxious and Geithner was not quite as cutting; the long Geithner silences that had driven Summers to distraction in the old days had been replaced by a new self-assurance. They got along well enough, in part because there was plenty of power and work to go around.

Every idea they had for confronting the crisis faced huge constraints. Small businesses, for instance, were dying by the thousands, but helping them required excruciating policy choices. The $15 billion in new Small Business Administration loans contained in the stimulus was better than nothing, but it did little to leverage private lending. If the administration poured billions more into SBA loans, how much would end up as slightly cheaper loans to small businesses that would have gotten the capital anyway? And if there was a 25 to 30 percent chance of default by weaker companies, was it worth it? Massive defaults would punch another huge hole in the deficit and hurt confidence. On the other hand, when Americans lost their small businesses they couldn't reorganize or merge like large businesses; they lost everything, often merely because a bank's credit requirements had become irrationally tight overnight. The ten letters a day Obama read from ordinary people reflected the human carnage, and he tried to share it with his economic team. But there was not much more that any of them thought they could do about it.

IN THE EARLY days, Geithner often looked like a piñata. On Capitol Hill he got swatted when he met privately with the House Democratic Caucus in March. He cursed AIG (Geithner said *fuck* in private almost as much as Rahm did), but this was seen by Democrats as mostly a cover for what he had done on the company's behalf. He had a hard time explaining the government entities, dubbed "Maiden Lane I" and "Maiden Lane II," that the Fed had established to make AIG's investors whole, at a cost of $45 billion to the taxpayers. Back in the fall of 2008 Paulson and Bernanke had been running the show, but it was Geithner, as chairman of the New York Fed, who had structured the deals.

Most of the House members gathered in Room HC-5 of the Capitol knew few details about how a global meltdown was averted, but they were angry about AIG and let Geithner have it. His argument—that he had no statutory authority to restructure AIG since it wasn't a bank—didn't go over well. "I've been here a long time but have never actually seen a real lead balloon until you dropped one on us today," Charlie Rangel, chairman of the Ways and Means Committee, told him. Steve Kagen, a physician who represented Green Bay, Wisconsin, recalled the story of how former Packers coach Dan Devine's dog was shot by an angry fan as a way of chasing Devine out of town. "What kind of dog do you have, Tim?" Kagen asked to laughter. When Barney Frank warned against "de-Baathification," Kagen quipped, "Well, we have to kill *someone*." Kagen and the other Democrats didn't want Geithner fired, but they were insistent that he understand how angry their constituents were about the bailouts.

Summers wasn't in much better odor in the House. In late 2006 a large crop of newly elected House members had gathered at Harvard for a training session. Summers had already resigned as Harvard president, but he addressed the group and warned them that Washington allows only incremental change. One after another, the new Democratic members piled on. "We weren't sent here for incremental change!" they shouted, almost in unison. A little more than two years later, in early 2009, a group of twenty Democratic members gathered at Congresswoman Rosa DeLauro's house,* where Elizabeth Warren was the guest. Everyone agreed that night that President Obama had to start listening more to people like Warren, who came from outside the Summers-Geithner camp.

Obama already knew Warren, a professor at Harvard Law School who had become the scourge of the banking industry for her efforts on behalf of consumers. When they met at a Cambridge fund-raiser during his 2004 Senate campaign, his first words to her were "Predatory lending!" He had learned of Warren's work when legislating on behalf of credit card users in the Illinois State Senate. "He had me at 'Predatory lending,' " Warren later joked.

Once in the White House, the president wasn't much interested in hearing Warren's outspoken views on bailouts; he could read them in the reports she issued as head of a congressionally appointed panel reviewing TARP. But when it came time to re-regulate the financial sector, he made sure Summers met with her and incorporated her proposal for a new consumer financial protection agency, which became the centerpiece of the Obama financial reform package that Congress would still be fighting about in 2010.

A crackdown on credit cards, by contrast, was one of the president's early and almost entirely unnoticed victories. In May he signed sweeping legislation that limited fees, required disclosure of rate hikes before they were imposed, and ended the industry's practice of preying on college students before they were 21. But Congress erred badly in not making it effective immediately, which meant that Americans saw unconscionably higher interest rates on their credit cards until 2010.

Summers needed no convincing about the need to perfume the stinking bailouts with crowd-pleasing reform. In analyzing the events of 2008–9 he tried to take the long view. "The history of these things is that they were more expensive than anybody thought; they didn't usually happen as a single clap of thunder but with a number of different iterations; and that just as war had unintended victims, bailouts had unintended wealthy beneficiaries." he said. "There was no way it was going to look hugely attractive." Even when the bank bailouts proved

---

* Rahm Emanuel was living in DeLauro's basement apartment at the time but didn't attend the meeting.

much cheaper than expected, they still looked bad. Looking back on 2009, Summers admitted being surprised by the depth of the populist anger.

———

ON GOOD DAYS Summers was nearly as brilliant as he thought he was. He came from a family of economists (he had Nobel laureates on both sides),* entered MIT at 16, and became one of the youngest tenured professors in Harvard's history. Steve Levitt, the University of Chicago economist and coauthor of *Freakonomics,* remembered the first time he heard Summers speak, in 1988: "I'd never seen a performance like it in my life—a deep analysis with no notes." Senator Ron Wyden wasn't alone in his assessment: "When Larry's in the room it's obvious immediately who's the best read, most intellectually prepared person."

But by 2009 Summers's legacy was tarnished. With the deregulation of the Clinton years discredited, the 1999 *Time* magazine cover photo of Summers, Rubin, and Alan Greenspan as "The Committee to Save the World" now looked ironic, not iconic. As Treasury secretary in 1999 and 2000, Summers was famous for throwing his weight around, threatening to fire assistant secretaries and underlings for minor miscues. Routine meetings with officials from other agencies could grow heated. When talking with Clintonites Ira Magaziner and Derek Shearer in the mid-1990s Summers shouted, "You're protectionists!" A furious Shearer replied, "Walk down to the end of the table and say that to my face."

It wasn't true that Summers never listened to anyone. He would often listen just long enough to savage the other person's argument and prove he was right. But if that person made a convincing and logical point, he was willing to stand corrected. His style wasn't much different from the one he developed as a top-notch college debater at MIT. For hardy conversationalists, like the Harvard undergraduates who revered him when he was president, this was intellectually invigorating.†

But the tender egos of the Harvard faculty couldn't handle it. Summers's disdain for Cornel West's hip-hop CDs, which drove the African American studies professor to Princeton, was only the best-known example of his weak interpersonal skills. He would often begin

———

* Summers's father, Robert Summers, the brother of Nobelist Paul Samuelson, joined an older brother in changing the family name from Samuelson to Summers.

† The author, who met Summers at Harvard in 1978, was among those who found it stimulating.

his conversations with scholars in other fields by asking, "Why would you think that? What evidence do you have?" One might imagine the professors would enjoy the interaction but they didn't. He had little sense of his proper role as the university's president. When his political incorrectness led to his infamous comments about women having less aptitude in the sciences, his fate was sealed.

Summers's friends claimed he had mellowed by the time he entered the Obama White House, but that wasn't quite accurate. He was more politically shrewd and more aware of the consequences of his outbursts becoming public, but the old habits persisted. When Christie Romer was brought in to be the chair of the Council of Economic Advisers, Summers tried to exclude her from important meetings. Romer fought back, even suggesting to Summers that sexism might have played a role in her exclusion, a serious charge given his Harvard experience. "Don't you threaten me!" Summers yelled. "Don't you bully *me*!" Romer shouted.

Romer decided to make it clear early on that she wasn't going to be left out of meetings with the president. She went to Rahm, who promised it would never happen again, and it didn't.

When it came to access to Obama on the economy, practically everyone felt left out. Even some Obama supporters from Wall Street believed that the Rubin-Summers influence had grown too great. (Though Rubin himself was no longer in touch with Obama, his orbit still got the blame.) These members of his campaign's national finance committee wanted to tell the president that they thought so, but they weren't on his BlackBerry list anymore, and Reggie Love's BlackBerry address, a reliable way to contact Obama during the campaign, had now changed. The bubble that Obama claimed to dread was back.

It wasn't as if the president was entirely isolated from contrary ideas. At the Daily Economic Briefing, Jared Bernstein held up the progressive side of the argument, often with help from Romer and from noneconomists like Axelrod.* Robert Wolf of UBS weighed in from the other side. But, as one former Treasury official put it, Obama's economic team wasn't exactly Winnie-the-Pooh's Hundred Acre Wood, with Piglet, Eeyore, Kanga, and the rest, providing a diversity of backgrounds and perspectives. It ran the gamut from A to C, though hardly to F, much less Z. Obama's stated desire for lively debate ran straight up

---

* Bernstein was hardly a latter-day George Ball, the undersecretary of state in the Johnson administration who filled the role of house dove on the Vietnam War. He didn't have the bureaucratic heft to fight.

against his lack of tolerance for factionalism. It was hard to have both vigorous debate and no factions.

————

CAUGHT UP IN the stimulus debate, the wave of foreclosures, and a hundred other things, the administration seemed strangely detached from the banking crisis. Where was the focus? If, as the president kept saying, a lack of credit was at the heart of the recession, why couldn't the government act to unfreeze it? Why didn't the president drop everything and have round-the-clock Cuban Missile Crisis–style meetings to figure out what to do? The answer was that meetings on the banking crisis—and there were plenty of them—proved unsatisfying. Because the government and the banks couldn't agree on the value of the banks' toxic assets, there was no way to plug the gaping holes in their balance sheets.

The liberals had a way: nationalization. The fact that the government had no legal authority to selectively take over banks in the absence of ruinous bank runs didn't discourage them. For a time the idea seemed to be catching on, as Nobel laureate Paul Krugman used his perch from the op-ed page of the *New York Times* to advance it. But Geithner thought nationalization was folly. He explained that the U.S. government would want to sell the banks as quickly as possible after a takeover, but as the AIG mess showed, there would be no buyers for the suddenly wrecked financial giants. Nationalization would be like a roach motel, Geithner liked to tell his noneconomist friends. The government could check in, but it couldn't check out.

Summers was slightly to Geithner's left on reining in banks. But he too found the popular analogy to the nationalized Swedish banking system fallacious. He told Obama that Sweden nationalized its banks only after interest rates reached 100 percent and the nation had no other option. He argued that nationalization could set off a new round of devastating bank runs, which was exactly the panic they were all determined to avoid.

It was not entirely a coincidence that Summers detested the rival economists who most ardently advanced nationalization, especially Joseph Stiglitz, the Nobel laureate whom Summers had pushed out as chief economist of the World Bank in 1999. Stiglitz, arguably the most revered economist in the world, had been an early Obama supporter and Obama wanted to keep in touch. Summers didn't. During the transition, Stiglitz received a curt email from Summers: "I've been asked to get your views." Stiglitz took this as a bit of an insult, but he wrote a fifteen-page memo detailing how TARP should be restructured. Summers sent him back another one-sentence email that said only "Thank you very much." He never got around to responding to what Stiglitz wrote.*

The big dispute was over the size of the banks. Having pushed mergers to strengthen the big banks as recently as 2008, Geithner was not about to reverse course and let huge financial institutions founder, much less break them up. They didn't advertise it, but both Geithner and Summers were heavily invested in the idea of *too big to fail*. They pointed out that the United States had mostly small banks in the 1930s that offered no protection against widespread collapse. In fact, Canada's system of a few megabanks proved much more stable than the American system in both 1933 and 2008, which led to less suffering north of the border. Summers insisted that the United States—lacking a national bank—was actually the least concentrated banking system of any major nation. The true challenge, they thought, wasn't to break up banks but to regulate them and build in safeguards to prevent collapse.

The argument on the other side did not require an economics Ph.D., only an appreciation for when concentrated economic power threatens democracy. From Thomas Jefferson through Andrew Jackson, Theodore Roosevelt, Louis Brandeis, and on into the antitrust impulse that broke up AT&T in the 1970s, pro-democracy forces have always worried about the consequences of private institutions growing too large and powerful. Summers was right that the big banks were actually less of a political impediment to reform than the smaller community banks in every congressional district that swarmed Capitol Hill. But as Stiglitz testified in April, "We know that these too-big-to-fail institutions also have enormous resources to lobby Congress to deregulate. I think it would be far better to break up these too-big-to-fail institutions and strongly restrict the activities in which they can be engaged than to try to control them."

Summers and Geithner thought the banking system was too fragile to restructure and must be protected from ruinous bad runs. But at what price to the taxpayers? "Every plan we've heard from Treasury amounts to the same thing—an attempt to socialize the losses while privatizing the gains," Paul Krugman wrote. Jared Bernstein agreed that the Treasury might have overlearned the lesson of Lehman, bending

---

* The bad blood went back to the Clinton administration when Stiglitz wrote a memo highly critical of Summers and Rubin, and Krugman was upset that Summers got a job with Clinton and he did not.

over too far to prevent financial behemoths from suffering the consequences of their actions. Many conservative economists agreed with progressives that it wasn't Treasury's job to keep investors from taking big losses. And some libertarians were sounding more progressive than Obama. Even Alan Greenspan, the free-market apostle whose hands-off decisions as Fed chairman helped the bubble grow, now favored the government's breaking up the big banks the way Theodore Roosevelt broke up Standard Oil in 1908.

WHEN MARKETS WENT down after Tim Geithner spoke, the chatter began over whether he was the right man for the job. When markets rose on word of a new proposal, his prospects for surviving surged too. The tone of the entire Washington press corps began to resemble that of CNBC. This made no sense; the market verdict on how Obama and his people were doing should have been only one of many measurements. But it turned out the Big Casino still had plenty of clout, especially with Washington political reporters who were economically illiterate.

One day in late March Rahm used Geithner as an anthropological example of the capital's twisted culture. This is why Washington is so idiotic, he told the morning meeting. A week ago Geithner was hated and now he's loved. What changed? Nothing except the Dow and the silly cable pundits who increasingly set their fever charts by it. It was another example of why obsessing over who was up or down was just a waste of time.

Obama was steadfast in his private and public support for Geithner. In a speech in California he went so far as to compare him to Alexander Hamilton. After the treasury secretary's February fiasco Obama looked his senior staff in the eye and said, "Get this right." The scheduler, Alyssa Mastromonaco, was told to pencil in Geithner to join the president in showing his anger at AIG bonuses. The event may have helped, but Rahm was under no illusions. Geithner was secure because of some strange combination of the Dow and the peculiar folkways of Washington, where the fickle finger of blame shifted for reasons that defied explanation.

But the substance of Geithner's problem—the absence of a coherent bank rescue plan—remained. Developing a plan that could be taken seriously in the markets was a hugely complex undertaking, especially with so little staff at Treasury. The Fed's Term Asset-Backed Loan Facility (TALF) program, announced in November 2008 to back student loans, auto loans, and credit card debt, had taken months to get off the ground. Anything Treasury did about the balance sheets of banks would be the same.

They were six months post-Lehman and Obama was growing impatient. One morning Christie Romer told the president, "We have no plan." Obama sighed and said she was right.

Finally Geithner came up with a bank rescue plan called Public-Private Investment Partnerships. The idea was for the government to team with hedge funds to buy the toxic assets of ailing banks. But because neither the banks nor the government could properly price the assets, it didn't have much appeal. And by this time private investors battered by bad publicity wanted nothing to do with the government. "If we take part in the PPIPs and they work, we'll get called on the carpet for getting too rich," said one hedge fund manager. "If we lose the taxpayers' money along with our own, we'll be called on the carpet for an explanation. It's lose-lose." In either case, their bonuses would come under heavy scrutiny.

The program had few takers, in part because it was maddeningly complex. The Securities Acts of 1933 and 1934, which established the first regulation of Wall Street, were relatively easy to understand. Roosevelt and his team simply required companies to disclose publicly their financial condition before selling stock to the public. By contrast Obama's Wall Street proposals were so complicated that even his own Treasury Department didn't fully understand them. The documents outlining TALF and PPIP stood more than two feet high.

Summers was terrific at probing Geithner's proposals for their weaknesses, and the treasury secretary appreciated it. "On any problem, Larry will say, 'Here are the ten things I would worry about.' That's a huge value," Geithner said. But Summers didn't offer much of an alternative and it drove Geithner crazy that he analyzed everything to death. Geithner's mantra was simple: "Plan beats no plan."

Obama called a big meeting for Sunday, March 15, in the Roosevelt Room for everyone at the White House and Treasury involved in banking, plus the political and communications people. It went from 4 p.m. until past 11, and most of the discussion involved war-gaming various scenarios. What if the government poured capital into the banks and it didn't work? How should the banks' toxic assets be valued? (Book value? Market value?) Would revealing the true financial condition of banks lead to a bank run? The group hashed out all the contingencies.

At around 6:30 Obama broke into the discussion and said he had an announcement. "I'm going to get a haircut and have dinner," the presi-

dent said. "And when I come back I want you all on the same page."*
Summers and Romer had earlier been leaning toward a modified nationalization that involved taking over a couple of banks to make an
example of them (and thereby lessen excessive risk-taking in the future). But instead of devising their own plan, they kept analyzing the
pros and cons of different outcomes. Plan beat no plan, and the group
agreed to give Geithner's a chance.

On March 27, the CEOs of the thirteen largest banks came to Washington to hear directly from the president about the plan. They were
served only water, no ice or refills, which the bankers interpreted as a
Spartan symbol from an angry White House. Obama warned about an
onslaught of populism: "My administration is the only thing between
you and the pitchforks," he told them. Afterward, the bankers went
before the cameras on the driveway outside the West Wing and falsely
claimed that bonuses weren't discussed inside. In fact, they were already desperate to get out from under TARP, whose compensation limits were hurting their competition for talent. "Be careful how you make
those statements, gentlemen," Obama told them in the meeting. "The
public isn't buying that."

The president was frustrated that the banks hadn't done more to
extend credit and modify mortgages. The bankers pledged to do more
but Obama made no effort to get them to make firm dollar commitments. Summers thought that imposing lending standards and the like
in the American system was the role of regulators, not the president.
Obama did outline the conditions for escaping TARP. The banks would
have to pass stress tests designed by Geithner; raise private capital to
solidify their reserves equal to half of the money they borrowed from
TARP; and show more responsibility on bonuses. For all the tough talk,
Obama didn't want a fight. Geithner and Summers advised him that the
banks were too brittle to be asked to do more. The message of the day,
repeated by both Robert Gibbs and the bankers on the White House
driveway was: "We're all in this together."

Soon events began validating Geithner's approach. After the Financial Accounting Standards Board eased so-called mark-to-market accounting rules on April 2, the banks could consult their own esoteric
models and essentially value their bad assets however they wanted,
"mark-to-model." This didn't automatically make the nineteen struggling banks healthy again, but it helped, particularly on the credit
default swaps. The banking crisis began to ease with the use of the

---

* FDR did the same at a 1933 meeting with farm interests trying to agree on the details of
the landmark Agricultural Adjustment Act.

same magical valuations that had contributed to the problem in the first place.

An even bigger breakthrough came with one Geithner idea that turned out to be especially smart: stress tests. Because Geithner couldn't go to Congress for more money for banks, he figured he'd raise their valuations by showing they weren't as weak as Wall Street assumed. "It's a little like FDR's bank holiday in that it provided a way for people to differentiate between the strong and the weak," Geithner said later. By testing nineteen banks with the same standards and breaking precedent by publishing the results, the stress tests became central to Obama's rescue plan. Summers had been skeptical at first because, contrary to what Geithner claimed publicly, the tests were not designed with worst-case scenarios. But at least the bad-case assumptions were transparent and uniform across regional lines.

When the stress test results came back in May and the potential hole (trillions in losses) was much smaller than anticipated, Wall Street breathed a huge sigh of relief. With some generous assumptions about capital requirements, all but three of the nineteen largest institutions (Bank of America, Citigroup, and Wells Fargo) passed the stress tests and moved out of the government's intensive care unit.

This was one of the biggest events of the year, crucial to avoiding a depression. But it was too technical to get much public attention. Barack Obama noticed, though, and it made him even more partial to an economic team that he was sure had helped save the country from a far worse fate.

———

ON THIS, THE president was virtually alone. Wall Street traders thought Geithner knew little about markets. Left-wing bloggers thought Summers was Svengali. Nearly everyone found something troubling about the president's refusal to move beyond his heavy reliance on the pair. One senior aide tried to explain Obama's view this way: "If my car's broken, I'm going to take it to the best mechanic. And if he says it needs new sparkplugs, I'm not going to get a second opinion."

But what if the problem wasn't a broken car but a life-threatening illness? Wouldn't the president want a second opinion then? Summers argued that he exposed Obama to second opinions, and third and fourth. He claimed that it was faster for him to read those dissenting arguments and opinions and digest them than to have long-winded people meet with the president. Obama agreed. "The fact is that Larry Summers is very comfortable now making arguments, often quite passionately, that Bob Reich used to be making when he was in the Clinton White House," the president said later.

Of course none of this was a substitute for giving the president a range of views in person. (Reich, for instance, never got back in once the Obama campaign ended.) Even those fortunate enough to connect with Summers had no confidence that their advice was getting through to Obama. It was the difference, said one old friend of Geithner, between a "team of rivals" reporting directly to Abraham Lincoln and a team of rivals reporting to Edwin Stanton, Lincoln's prideful secretary of war.

PRESIDENT CLINTON HAD incorporated the concept better than Obama. When the stakes were much smaller, he would listen as Reich and Stiglitz on the left squared off for hours against Rubin and Summers in the center. And Clinton would call around to sample the opinion of others. Obama did a little of that, but as he acknowledged in 2010, not enough.

The failure to reach out more didn't apply just to liberal economists. Warren Buffett, who had been in touch with Obama every week as the economy collapsed in the fall of 2008, found himself mysteriously out of touch with the new president. Buffett didn't want to be a presidential advisor; he always preferred to work at arm's length. But in late 2009 the brilliant and commonsensical billionaire told a friend that he'd not had a single one-on-one meeting with Obama since he became president. They did speak once on the phone.*

The rising chorus of concern about lack of access eventually reached Obama's ears. One night in April, Summers had to endure a White House dinner with some of the people he had been blocking from the Oval Office. The president wanted to hear what other economists had to say. So Paul Krugman, Joe Stiglitz, Alan Blinder (a centrist from the Clinton administration), and Ken Rogoff (a more conservative economist and McCain backer) were invited to dine in the White House family dining room. Paul Volcker's plane was late, and when he finally arrived at the White House gate the Secret Service had already taken his name out of the computer and he was delayed even longer. He barely made it for dessert.

---

* In early 2010, when Ben Bernanke's nomination to a second term as Fed Chairman ran into trouble, Buffett was enlisted to help. But Obama was leery of spending too much time with anyone associated with large Wall Street firms, and Buffett's company had invested $5 billion in Goldman Sachs in 2008, a deal that turned out well for investors.

The dinner had been so hastily arranged that Stiglitz didn't even get invited until the morning of the event.* Over a lettuce salad from the White House garden and roast beef, the group held a spirited two-hour discussion. Obama grew slightly impatient when the conversation grew too technical or backward looking. He wanted to know what the economists would do if they were in his shoes. The answers from Krugman and Stiglitz—which amounted to taking over Citigroup and Bank of America for a brief time before breaking them up—hardly made Obama wish that he had hired these economists rather than Summers, who had considered the same idea but seemed more appropriately dispassionate in his analysis of it. If Obama had done what Krugman, Stiglitz (who had earlier said nationalizing the banks was the "only answer"), and plenty of other progressives wanted, it would have cost the government perhaps another trillion dollars and quite possibly caused a disastrous run on those banks.

Geithner and Summers took some satisfaction from the fact that history proved them and Obama right on avoiding nationalization. Within six weeks of the dinner it was clear that a collapse of the banking system had been averted without what Geithner called "the Old Testament" option: offering up a bank or two to satisfy the righteous anger of the nation. A few big institutions were still weak, but they were in no more need of a full takeover by the government than they were in 1933, when FDR rejected the nationalization pleas of New Dealers and left banking in private hands. Roosevelt adopted the bank rescue plan designed by Hoover's Treasury Department; Obama continued the TARP program begun under Bush. Both angered liberals with their initial caution when the financial system teetered but were vindicated by events.

The difference was that FDR's Treasury Department chose which big banks were healthy enough to reopen, whereas Geithner decided to save all twenty of the biggest. This could have severe consequences for a thousand smaller banks, hundreds of which would close in 2009, with more wreckage likely in 2010. There just wasn't enough money to go around. The FDIC, opposed for months to Geithner's approach, was suddenly swamped.

Any time Obama was accused of not having a wide enough circle of economic advisors, his aides mentioned the April dinner. Of course the dinner was, as the attendees noted, just one dinner, hardly sufficient to provide Obama with the diversity of economic opinions he needed.

---

* Obama, who said he read Krugman at least some of the time, had been asked by David Leonhardt of the *New York Times* why he didn't consult with Stiglitz and other critics.

As a result he never got a full argument for a third way between mild reform and nationalization that is sometimes called *conditionality:* using the government's leverage over banks receiving bailouts. Conditionality was the term the International Monetary Fund used when it was straightening out the finances of a developing country. It entailed giving the ailing banks a to-do list of conditions to meet. If the list wasn't completed, the banks didn't get the money. By dictating terms to banks in the developing world (sometimes too harshly), their messes were cleaned up quickly.

Simon Johnson, an MIT professor and former IMF economist who became a critic of the administration, didn't understand why mature banking systems that ran into deep trouble should be treated any differently.* He argued that the best chances for conditionality with the American banks were in September 2008, when the banks were desperate for government help, and in the spring and summer of 2009, when banks were desperate to get out from under TARP so they could resume paying monster bonuses.†

Geithner later pointed out that the government did attach some strings, such as changing the composition of the Fannie Mae and Freddie Mac boards, but that once Washington offered the banks the chance to recapitalize privately, which was much less expensive for taxpayers, it had no leverage. Summers said that demanding private recapitalization was itself a huge string, and that it worked. Banks raised much more in the private market to cushion themselves than anyone expected. "We treated this exactly as if we were a foreign country," he said. The IMF, he added, would have attached almost the same strings that the Obama administration did. The only way to include more conditions, Geithner and Summers insisted, was to go to Congress and seek legislation, which they didn't favor.

This analysis underestimated the power of the president in a major crisis. Early on, Obama could have gotten away with dictating terms to the banks. Flat on their backs, the banks were in no position to say no. Instead he was content to support temporary TARP restrictions on executive pay, stress tests, and recapitalization and leave fundamental restructuring for another day.

Reform would come, Obama said, pointing to his financial regulatory reform bill that was making it through committees chaired by Chris Dodd and Barney Frank. But by spring the bank lobbyists had

---

* Franklin Roosevelt's men applied a form of conditionality in 1933 in deciding the terms under which banks would be allowed to reopen.
† If the banks' short-term stability was in doubt, the conditions could have become applicable once they became healthy again—a form of triggered conditions.

descended like vultures to pick the package apart. With the crisis passing and the threat of TARP lifted, Obama's leverage was shrinking
every day. Hindsight suggested the president should have gone to the
nation and tried to push reform through at the beginning of the year,
when he had the most leverage with both the banks and Congress.
An early bank speech explaining why he intended to simultaneously
spend more money on middle-class Americans and restructure banks
might have taken some of the sting out of the bailout backlash—and
limited the dangers posed by financial institutions that were too big to
fail.

13

The Un-Bubba

During the 2008 primaries Hillary Clinton thought *she* was too big to fail—and Barack Obama too untested to succeed. She ran a powerful negative ad that began, "It's three a.m. and a phone is ringing in the White House." The red phone ad worked because it played into deep concerns about whether Obama was experienced enough to be president in a global crisis.

A year later some critics thought Obama was moving too fast, some thought too slow. But almost no one, least of all the Clintons, argued that he wasn't ready for the job. A senator with no management experience beyond sitting atop a brilliant presidential campaign (not always a good indicator, as the failed presidencies of Jimmy Carter and George W. Bush attested) turned out to be a natural executive.

Bill Clinton thought he knew why.

The relationship between the former president and Obama moved over the course of three years from frosty (when they barely knew each other and traded private insults) to chilly, to polite. A full three months passed after the Inauguration before the two men exchanged any words. In April the former president came to Washington for the signing of the Edward M. Kennedy Serve America Act, which nearly tripled the number of volunteers in Clinton's signature program, AmeriCorps, to two hundred and fifty thousand Americans, coincidentally the exact same size as Franklin Roosevelt's original Civilian Conservation Corps in 1933.

Obama, Biden, Clinton, and Kennedy sat in the Oval Office for a few minutes before heading for the local school where the bill signing would take place. The knowledge of Kennedy's terminal brain cancer eased the hard feelings of the year before, but the session remained full of awkward bonhomie. Kennedy laughingly told friends afterward, "[Clinton] practically pushed me over to Obama," as if to say, He's *your* guy. Someone had the bright idea of bringing around Bo, the Portuguese water dog, a gift from Kennedy to the Obama family, to the outer Oval Office, where Michelle Obama, Vicki Kennedy, Caroline Kennedy, and others had gathered. They all could agree on their love of dogs and how sad it was that the Clintons' dog, Buddy, had been run over in Chappaqua in 2002; it broke some of the tension.

Clinton still sniped at Obama behind his back, replaying the events of 2008, but he also appreciated how natural a president he turned out to be. Rather than analyzing the conventional attributes of good leaders, Clinton beamed in on Obama's skill at "laterally integrating" other people's experiences. No president can have enough of the right experience to be successful based solely on his own firsthand knowledge, Clinton told friends. The job is too big for that, which is why all of Dick Cheney's experience in different positions of government didn't make him a better leader. You have to have led multiple lives by absorbing the life and work experiences of others, Clinton argued. This was the only way to explain how someone like Obama, with no executive experience, could turn out to be a clear-eyed and effective leader. Here Clinton would splay the long fingers of each hand and join them together to explain the integration.

Obama's effectiveness at lateral integration was the result of more than just birth and experience; he possessed what psychologists sometimes call a fully integrated personality.* Despite scars he might bear from childhood, he wasn't usually working out ego issues in his relationships. This helped him move quickly to take the best of what other people offered. Homeland Security Secretary Janet Napolitano, a popular and effective governor of Arizona and not inclined to ingratiation, believed Obama was one of the most able executives she'd ever come across.

It remained to be seen if Obama had all the tools of a successful executive. Agenda setting didn't require major management experience, and the elixir of inspirational leadership lay in the realm of the gifted. But effectively running a bureaucracy with no preparation was difficult. Had he served even briefly in the executive branch of the federal government (as FDR did when he was assistant secretary of the navy), Obama might have been better equipped to manage the government. He was sophisticated enough to grasp the games that bureaucrats play to stymie presidents and their political appointees but not yet experienced enough to navigate expertly around the impediments.

At least he was decisive. Obama's decision-making style fell somewhere between Clinton's deep if gauzy discussions and Bush's snap

---

* Classic Adlerian psychology, named for Alfred Adler, a contemporary of Sigmund Freud, describes this favorably as "the unity of personality."

judgments based on instinct, which Obama had long believed was a recipe for failure. The more compelling comparison was to Clinton.

Both Clinton and Obama were left-handed (meaning right-brained),* highly pragmatic, extremely well-informed, and exceptionally bright—often the brightest in the room—but their minds and operating styles were sharply different. Clinton was volcanic and discursive; Obama cool and focused. Those who had worked for both presidents generally preferred Obama as a boss because he was less likely to bite their heads off. They noted that Obama arrived in the White House with an ability to avoid distraction and keep his eye on the big picture that it took Clinton four or five years in the White House to develop. They thought Obama was more disciplined, of course, but also better at channeling the policy process into concrete goals and long-term strategy. Several gave Clinton the edge on making creative intellectual connections between seemingly disparate points and on subtle understanding of the motivations of other leaders, at home and abroad. Clinton cared little for the balance-of-power stratagems that intrigued Obama, but his mastery of the human dimension of foreign policy gave Obama something to strive for.

Clinton had been a governor for twelve years before becoming president, but it was Obama, just four years out of the Illinois State Senate, who seemed to have innate executive ability. Clinton liked to ruminate; Obama liked to delegate. Clinton, especially at the beginning, would sometimes do the math himself on complex budget issues; Obama thought this was what his smart staff was for. Clinton was habitually late and let himself get fatigued from too much work; Obama was usually punctual and well rested, with a sensibly paced daily routine reminiscent of Reagan's without the naps. Both presidents drove their speechwriters crazy by rewriting their speeches at the last minute and not rehearsing. Clinton was superb at rhetorical riffing, Obama the more gifted wordsmith.

Clinton was more prone to self-pity, raging, "Who did this to me?" Obama wasn't immune to feeling sorry for himself; he told friends, for instance, that Clinton had it easier than he did because he could just be president and didn't have to clean up after the first Bush's messes. But Obama disciplined himself to power through recriminations and focus on getting things back on track. Aides often thought their meetings

---

* Until Harry Truman, only two U.S. presidents out of thirty-two, James A. Garfield and Herbert Hoover, were southpaws. But as Obama liked to point out, five of the last seven presidents—Gerald Ford, Ronald Reagan, George H. W. Bush, Bill Clinton, and now he—were left-handed.

with Clinton were too long; aside from the endless Afghanistan deliberations, Obama's aides often thought their meetings were too short.

Clinton was an inductive thinker with a horizontal mind. He talked
to people in wide-ranging college bull sessions (or late at night on the
phone) to establish a broad array of policy and political options, then
looked at them in context and fashioned a synthetic and often brilliant
political approach out of the tangled strands of his analysis. Aides were
not surprised to learn that he had cut most of his classes at Yale Law
Shool in the 1970s to work on campaigns. His connective intelligence
seemed untouched by narrow legal reasoning. When making policy
he favored decision memos with a range of options to be discussed
and often second-guessed his final choices. (One former advisor called
Clinton the "Second-Guesser-in-Chief.") The result was often positive,
but the process was invariably messy and wasted the energy of staff.

Obama was a deductive thinker with a vertical mind. He thought
deeply about a subject, organized it lucidly into point-by-point arguments for a set of policies or a speech, and then said, Here are my
principles, and here are some suggestions for fleshing out the details.
Obama's brain was more like Hillary's than Bill's, according to John Podesta. He favored decision memos that included options but contained
clear policy recommendations that would then be rigorously tested to
make sure they met his goals. He placed more faith in logic than imagination and insisted on a process that was tidy without being inflexible.
Tom Donilon described the president as a one-man energy conservation project: "There's not a lot of stray voltage."

Larry Summers didn't believe either approach was inherently superior to the other. As a professor he'd had some inductive graduate students who wrote their entire papers before figuring out their themes,
and some deductive thinkers who wrote from logical outlines. Some
aides who served both presidents thought the intense time constraints
of the early Obama presidency (Clinton didn't face a similar crisis) argued for the deductive approach.

The vice president was among those impressed by the president's
ability to avoid second-guessing himself. "The guy has a backbone
like a ramrod," Biden said. "Once he makes a decision, he's serene.
That's it."

––––––––

A NORMAL DAY in the White House began around 7:30 a.m., when a
dozen senior staff gathered in Rahm Emanuel's office; for many of them
and their subordinates it often ended at 11 p.m. The group included

Axelrod, Jarrett, Rouse, Messina, Sutphen, Gibbs, Dunn,* Donilon, Schiliro, Mastromonaco, and often a couple of policy people who were told to come around. At 8:15 the entire senior staff would assemble in the Roosevelt Room, where they were joined by another twenty-five or so people. At 8:45 Rahm would usually hold a legislative strategy meeting with Phil Schiliro and maybe Nancy-Ann DeParle (who had taken over for Daschle) if the subject was health care or Carol Browner on an energy bill.

Obama began his day by joining Michelle in the fitness room, where she often got going before 6 a.m. After seeing the kids off to school, the president read the *New York Times,* the *Washington Post,* the *Wall Street Journal,* and *USA Today* over breakfast and often caught up on other work. He walked downstairs to the Oval Office around 9:15, sometimes later. His wooden desk was the same one used by Kennedy and later Reagan, cut from the USS *Resolute.* He and Rahm would go over a quick to-do list, an exercise they often repeated by phone late at night.

At about 9:30 Obama received the Presidential Daily Briefing on national security (led by NSC advisor Jim Jones or his deputy, Tom Donilon). Later the name was changed to the National Security Session to reflect that the thirty- to forty-minute briefing had been broadened and extended to include not just terrorist threats but a daily policy discussion. At around 10:30 came the Economic Daily Briefing, led by Larry Summers. (This meeting sometimes slipped until the afternoon.) In between or after, Obama would meet with some of the same group that had gathered in Rahm's office earlier—"the Big Thinkers," Mastromonaco playfully called them—plus a speechwriter to go over last-minute changes in that day's public remarks.

Katie Johnson, the president's 27-year-old personal secretary, always had the day's "purple folder" ready for him, with ten letters received from ordinary Americans (out of forty thousand that arrived each day) to keep him connected.† He read the letters religiously, responded personally with handwritten notes to two or three a day, and often referred to them in public appearances. They were a lifeline to the world outside the bubble and they refreshed him. In 2009 at least three in ten were about health care, many relating tales of economic suffering

---

* Anita Dunn agreed to work only until the end of 2009 and left on schedule.

† The "red folder," by contrast, contained classified information or something that required the president's immediate attention, often a news bulletin so that the president wouldn't be caught unaware of events and have a "My Pet Goat" moment (named for President Bush's obliviousness on 9/11).

brought on by health insurance woes. Others referred to a specific problem in a government agency that Obama would follow up on. Jarrett pointed out that the lower-level staffers in the White House correspondence office who chose the letters had powerful jobs.

Obama worked in shirtsleeves and liked to lope through the first floor of the West Wing, maybe munching an apple he had grabbed from one of the fruit bowls placed on a table in the Oval Office. He would sit in a chair opposite the aide and often prop his feet up on the desk, as Lincoln did with his secretaries. This was almost unheard-of among recent presidents, who generally summoned underlings to the Oval Office. The White House had never before experienced what corporate gurus call "management by walking around."

Sometimes the drop-bys were calculated. Rahm's aide, Sarah Feinberg, would let Katie Johnson know that Rahm had a congressman in his office so that the president could amble by casually to say hello. It was a way of keeping the interactions easygoing and brief. But more often the drop-bys were spontaneous. The president didn't like sitting at his desk all day. It made him feel, Eric Whitaker said, like a bird in a gilded cage. If he had something to discuss with Rahm, he'd be as likely to wander down the hall to the chief of staff's office as to ask him to come to the Oval Office or to the small study where he often worked. If he was marking up a speech draft or otherwise wanted advice, he would walk a few feet past the small presidential dining room into Axelrod's or Rouse's office.* (Obama liked to tease Rouse, who rarely went on presidential trips, that he hated travel so much he wouldn't even travel down the hall to see him in the Oval Office.) First-time visitors were often amazed by how narrow the West Wing halls were; now they were much more likely to see the president himself squeezing past.

The Obama workday was brisk, with an occasional brief break for some jocular sports talk or a careful indoor toss with one of the footballs or basketballs that came across Reggie Love's desk.† (For weeks Obama twirled and spun the basketball Coach K of Duke left for him.) Obama liked to hear some of the milder staff gossip, whether it was about Reggie's fending off female admirers or Favreau's dating Quincy Jones's daughter. And he was thoughtful in asking aides he passed in

---

* The author had this experience while sitting in Axelrod's office one day. The president showed Axelrod some changes in a speech he was to deliver that evening, then paused to chat off-the-record on substance.

† When the president wasn't around, Love and Johnson liked to take the game outside, until one day in the Rose Garden Johnson missed a long pass from Love that was inches away from breaking a window.

the hall how they were feeling in a way that made them think he actually cared about the answer.

But the usual banter was kept to a minimum, often by the president's quick glance at his chronograph watch. Cabinet members, senators, and journalists got about a minute of charming pleasantries before the unmistakably clipped "Okay," which meant it was time to delve into the business at hand. Whereas Lincoln, FDR, and Reagan often perplexed visitors by telling long stories (usually as a diversion from discussing difficult topics), Obama surprised them with his low-key and straightforward focus on brass tacks. Rahm too had little patience for small talk; he made it clear through his sighs and glances that he didn't want anyone wasting a moment of the president's time.

When he was in Washington the president's schedule was a mix of public events, staff meetings, interviews, tapings, and sessions with foreign leaders and others. Bush's meetings usually included staff of the visiting official; Obama usually preferred that the sessions (especially with Cabinet officers and members of Congress) be one-on-one. Afterward Chris Lu (the Cabinet secretary) or Phil Schiliro (head of congressional relations) would ask the president for a very brief summary of what was discussed so they could follow up. (Less than half the time, staff would sit in to take notes). Like his recent predecessors, Obama reserved one day a week for lunch with the vice president. The afternoon was usually devoted to more meetings and four or five telephone calls, often with foreign leaders, capped by a casual review of the day's events with a few senior staff. He went upstairs for dinner with Michelle and the girls around 6 p.m., frequently followed by a drop-by at an evening reception.

For all his star power, Obama didn't enter the East Room with a large entourage and hush everyone with his presence. He materialized informally, often without "Hail to the Chief," and slipped out after a half hour or so. Unlike Clinton, he didn't exude the aura of the super-famous. Obama in person wasn't smaller than life, but his slender frame and easygoing manner made him smaller than the towering presence that so many of his guests expected. At six-one and 170 pounds, he was human-scale, without the celebrity sheen.

The president enjoyed the events well enough, especially when they included children and music. But with so many people to charm there was inevitably a dutiful quality to his socializing. One guest overheard a hushed conversation with Michelle in which the president sighed that he still had five or six couples to thank before he could make his escape. By 8 p.m. it was usually time to go back to his study in the residence for three or four more hours of work.

Obama thought of himself as a night owl. On most nights, after tucking in the girls and walking Bo on the South Lawn around 9:30, he would take a stack of papers up to the residence and work past midnight. The president was a diligent student; nobody could think of a time when he hadn't absorbed the briefing material before a meeting. He frequently called aides around 10 p.m. to frame the day's events in terms of what came next, but he didn't usually work the phones like Clinton or FDR. This was a man who in 1993 retreated to Indonesia for a few months shortly after getting married to labor on his first book alone, with no telephone.

The president enjoyed the solitude that evenings at home offered, but he paid a price. By checking in more often with power brokers in different realms, he could have simultaneously won new friends and picked up valuable intelligence. He did this sometimes, especially when he was on the road, but not enough. Longtime supporters, from CEOs to senior government officials, clergymen, and savvy local politicians with a common touch, complained that they didn't hear from him or, worse, had their calls returned by junior aides. They knew the president was extremely busy, but many felt the friend they still thought of as "Barack" wasn't reaching out enough for his own good. By the end of Year One, Obama agreed, and he asked Rahm to build in more unstructured time in his daily schedule for him to think and call people.

Nighttime was when he did most of his reading and regenerating. Sometimes he read a magazine article that he later recommended to everyone, like Atul Gawande's story in the *New Yorker* about two cities in Texas with dramatically different costs of delivering health care. He read newsweeklies, monthlies, and occasionally blogs but avoided cable news chatter ("WWF wrestling," he called it) because he didn't think he could learn much from even the friendly shows.

On many nights he pushed aside the briefing papers and stopped focusing on the immediate issues in front of him. He'd write on his desktop computer (or sometimes by hand) about things "down the pike," as he put it, that he wanted his people to think about. Marty Nesbitt said the president saw politics as a sequential puzzle: "He's always thinking, 'If I do this, then this could happen—or that could happen.' It's all in terms of cause and effect—like a Rubik's Cube." Anticipating events kept him from feeling swamped by them. Over and over, his friends and associates (including Henry Kissinger) described Obama's skill at what Julius Genachowski called "3-D chess" (an imaginary game played by Spock on *Star Trek*). As Nesbitt explained, "Before everyone else, he's already calculated the relative probability of several different outcomes, so when one of them happens—even though it may be a surprise to others—he's never really surprised." The great exception, of course, was the special election in Massachusetts in January 2010, which he didn't anticipate being a problem for Democrats.

At bedtime the president often read biographies of earlier presidents or a novel for a half hour or so before falling asleep. Among the novels he mentioned in 2009 were *Netherland* by Joseph O'Neill, *The Way Home* by George Pelecanos, and *Lush Life* by Richard Price. As an author he believed as a matter of principle in paying for books rather than getting them all for free. Obama sometimes said that what he missed most from his old life was browsing in bookstores. Now he browsed at night on Amazon.

THE PUBLIC ASSUMED that Obama was at his best giving a speech, but long before he mastered the art of oration his métier was the meeting. From his time as editor of the *Harvard Law Review* forward, people who knew Obama were struck by his ability to ask probing questions, listen politely to competing views, summarize those views better than those who expressed them, and render a logical and dispassionate decision. Whether the meetings were mere photo-ops or decisive turning points, Obama had somewhere acquired what the military calls "the habit of command."

Where Clinton would saunter into National Security Council meetings and sit in the middle of the table in the Situation Room, listening to the NSC advisor call on various subject experts, Obama would purposefully stride in and run the meeting from the head of the table. It was as if he had consciously decided to inhabit the role of leader. To do so he had to project not just great confidence but enough knowledge of the nuances of national security issues to justify that confidence in a room full of smart and experienced advisors. In that he unquestionably succeeded.

Mark Lippert, an aide from the Senate, noticed his command presence as soon as Obama arrived in the Senate in 2005. Obama had been there for two months when Bush nominated John Bolton, a right-wing UN hater, to be UN ambassador. As senators met to plot strategy for defeating Bolton (they ultimately failed), Obama, a freshman, took charge of the meeting. There was a pause, as if senators far senior to him were asking themselves, Who is this guy? Then, according to Lippert, they listened to him on the merits and followed his advice. Three years later, most Senate Democrats favored him for president over Hillary Clinton.

The flip side of that self-assurance was an occasional presumptuous certainty about his own views. Whether it constituted arrogance would soon be the source of whispered discussion. In a meeting of senators in 2006 to decide on the Democrats' message that year, Obama asked Hillary how she would distill Bill Clinton's message in 1992. Hillary explained that the message was "Putting People First"—a soft-edged populism that stressed an agenda for the middle class. "No, that's not what it was," Obama said. The other senators were shocked. This guy was trying to correct Hillary about what her husband's message had been!

When people got to know him better, they rarely saw seemingly arrogant comments as arrogant. That's because with Obama you were never quite sure when he was kidding, a useful trait for keeping other people off balance. Shortly after arriving in the Senate, Obama was asked to speak at the National Press Club. He thought it was too early to accept, but Gibbs and Rouse talked him into it. Afterward, they asked him how it went. "I thought I was excellent, but some people might have thought I was just very good," he said with a smile and a twinkle in his eye. (After later speeches, Gibbs and Rouse would joke, "Was he excellent? No, just very good.")

Most of the time, the self-assurance was a plus because it led to well-considered but crisp decisions. Denis McDonough, a deputy national security advisor, called him "a closer." McDonough or another aide would open up a subject and the president would settle it with dispatch. "The time from thought to action is very short," said McDonough. "He reads something and says, 'I want to change that' and 'I want a plan for this.'" He would sometimes deliberate for days, weeks, or, in the case of Afghanistan, months, but contrary to the gibes of Dick Cheney, there was nothing "dithering" about it. Obama would process a series of questions, facts, and insights that built on one another methodically. Penny Pritzker was struck by his capacity not just to absorb information but to use what he learned later. It was a subtle trait; unless you knew he was a good listener it might seem as if he wasn't registering what you were saying. "He doesn't respond with, 'Oh yes, you're right,'" Pritzker said. "But then he takes it in, and within a very short period you see action."

Obama operated with a small inner circle on politics and communications, and a slightly larger group on most policy decisions. The trick was getting into the room. Once there, he encouraged full debate. Joe Biden, who was often the person to see to get on the president's calendar, was struck by the president's inclusiveness: "The guy really does want intelligent input that disagrees with him." Reagan and the Bushes would often make big decisions with only a couple of advisors in the room. Obama generally widened the circle to at least a half-dozen depending on the issue at hand.

Larger staff meetings often followed a familiar format. The president might start out by saying something like: "Okay, guys, Here's what I'm thinking." Then he'd set the table for discussion with a quick recitation of key points before asking, "What am I missing?" His style of inquiry went back to his days as a law school professor. Sometimes it was a classic Socratic dialogue, with Obama asking all the questions; on other occasions it was more interactive. The president was determined to use the time to methodically develop his thinking on a subject, even if that meant finding out where he was completely wrong. Only rarely (as in the case of speech preparation) did he do all the talking.

Obama believed in the power of poking, prodding, and reasoning in a group. He felt that with enough applied logic it was possible to get to the nub of any issue; none of the matters before him was nuclear physics, after all, and he insisted that issues shouldn't be treated as more complicated than they really were. His approach was to drill down to the logical bottom of something, then build back up to a decision point.

He was fully aware of the habits of courtiers and subordinates everywhere to avoid being the bearer of bad news, to stifle their own dissenting opinions for fear of being in the minority, and—most important—to get the boss to do what they wanted while convincing him it was his idea. These age-old bureaucratic impulses, he told a friend, were particularly pernicious in Washington, city of yes-men.

His prodding, of course, could make the already intimidating experience of being in the president's company even more unnerving for all but his most trusted and self-confident subordinates, and even they often censored themselves. Obama wanted pushback and dissent. (Before his election, he had been on the selection committee for a prestigious State Department award given for "creative dissent.") But it was rare, precluded by reverence for the office and, too often, reverence for him personally.

His approach in meetings resembled that of a judge in a courtroom. The president, advisors said, was often like a swing-vote Supreme Court justice peppering the lawyers with questions during oral arguments without revealing which side of the case he would come down on. This was ironic considering that Obama had declined to apply for clerkships after law school and as a Chicago lawyer had almost no courtroom experience.* But he embraced legal reasoning instinctively and

---

* A week before the Inauguration Obama and Biden visited the Supreme Court and met privately for an hour with eight of the justices. Samuel Alito declined to attend. A year later, Alito mouthed the words, "Not true," when Obama criticized a Supreme Court decision in his State of the Union address.

would probe people in meetings for the weakness of their arguments. He didn't use legal language or debate fine points of law, yet meetings often felt like a series of polite but pointed cross-examinations. The only difference was that advisors were discouraged from being fierce advocates and encouraged to be more like Obama himself, carefully deliberating over complex and often contradictory evidence. Anyone adamantly locked into a position didn't last long.

Cabinet secretaries and other principals usually brought along deputies, assistant secretaries, general counsels, and other subordinates. Senior White House aides did the same with subject-matter experts who worked for them. Under earlier presidents, principals did most of the talking, with an occasional turn to a subject-matter expert for illumination. Obama, who disliked the stilted hierarchy of Washington meetings, frequently reversed this pattern; after opening comments from the principal he quickly beamed in on the experts, with senior officials interjecting only to point out areas of disagreement or to help bring a decision to a head. Per tradition, subordinates sat not at the big tables in the Roosevelt Room or Cabinet Room but in chairs along the wall. If Obama knew them, and he often did, he would frequently zing a question in their direction. He figured that these appointees must have an opinion that informed how their principals thought, so he might as well ask them directly, then, like an inquisitive judge, push the experts to the logical edges of their positions. At first those with experience in other administrations felt a little disoriented by Obama's style; just as past presidents didn't wander around the White House, they rarely recognized second-level officials. But the practice did more than expose Obama to a wider array of views; it also boosted morale. Some assistant secretary or middle-level staffer in a Roosevelt Room meeting got to dine out on what he told the president, instead of admitting to friends that he had been a wallflower. Subordinates soon learned that Obama didn't always agree with the loudest or even the smartest people in the room, which made the softer-spoken advisors feel more valued.

Obama managed to convey the impression that he viewed his people as colleagues. This lack of explicit power assertion in his relationships created its own power. It was about as far as possible from a line attributed to the Bush family: "That's why I'm president and you're not," both Bush father and son would occasionally tell subordinates. Obama's message was unspoken but quite different: *I may be president. I may give you unequivocal instructions. But that doesn't mean our long-standing relationship has to change.* Eric Holder told friends that he felt the president spoke to him as if they were Justice Department colleagues. Arne Duncan felt the same.

The main fear inside the White House was lack of preparation. If the president called on you, and he usually did, you had better bring something to the party. Obama liked to jump around the room with his questions rather than moving down a row. That meant there was often no time to collect your thoughts before weighing in. But when you did speak, he paid you the compliment of listening intently. The tone of his voice indicated that he expected you to be ready. And cogent. Obama always had his eye on the clock and would often say something like "Guys, we have twenty minutes left. Here's what I want to do with the remaining time."

If you were walking the president through an argument, he would often break in insistently with a "Wait a minute, tell me more about that" or, if you were foolish enough to lapse into confusing jargon, "Tell me that again, I didn't follow that." While he was never afraid to say he didn't comprehend something (a relief to others in the room who also didn't understand), he could be impatient when others were a little slow on the uptake, especially political aides who didn't absorb complex economic ideas. When he got the point quickly, as he often did, and someone was droning on as if he didn't, he would occasionally sharply interject, "I get it." When work didn't meet his standards he said so explicitly. Before the Cairo speech on relations with the Muslim world, one of the best of his young presidency, he reviewed a draft and said, "You know what? Not even close."

Obama was comfortable having his meetings be informal courtrooms, but he disliked retrials. As a candidate he had repeatedly expressed his objection to "relitigating" the Vietnam War and the 1960s. Now he carried into the presidency his distaste for revisiting settled questions. He infuriated some liberals by saying in a May speech at the National Archives that he didn't want long investigations of Bush and Cheney that would "relitigate the last eight years" (though they hadn't been litigated in the first place). Once staffers learned Obama's favorite pejorative, the narrow corridors of the West Wing could sound like a legal convention.

The refusal to relitigate became central to the speed of most decisions. Clintonian second-guessing was frowned upon. Obama's message to staff was: It's settled and I don't want to see it on my desk again. But the president was also determined to be flexible if new evidence was presented that was strong enough to reopen discussion and revisit prior decisions. So policy debates often revolved around the strength or weakness of such information. New evidence could take the form of new events on the ground in a foreign country, a new head count on Capitol Hill, or new economic data. But it had to be fresh and it better be compelling or it wouldn't be admissible. This approach was good for crisp decision making; not so good for innovative policymaking, which often emerges from unfocused Clintonian ruminations that were frowned upon in the Obama White House.

The president liked to make decisions at ten thousand feet, but his people knew that he could swoop down from that altitude and analyze an issue at what, in the lingo of the moment, was called "the granular level," as he did on Afghanistan. Peter Orszag recalled him poring over fifty or sixty riders to appropriations bills, deciding which technical amendments the administration should support. Most of the time he preferred staying higher up. "You guys are playing small-ball," he admonished aides. "Don't get down in the weeds."

Naturally everyone in the room with Obama (or in the presence of any president) wanted to be on the winning side of an argument. This created the familiar sight of aides and officials crafting their points to what they assumed Obama already believed. But the president's pragmatism made that harder to fathom. If Obama's Socratic questions seemed to indicate one view, the next two or three answers might conform to the assumption of the question. Then, when he approached the issue from the opposite direction, all the while maintaining a poker face, the same thing happened with the next several answers. The effect was a meeting that swayed back and forth as the participants attempted to weigh the facts and toady at the same time. It was often impossible to know if the president was sold on an argument or playing devil's advocate. One National Security Council meeting began with nearly every speaker leaning one way; after an offhand comment by the president, the next several speakers all leaned the other way. Obama hadn't made his decision yet, one participant remembered, but the Situation Room felt like the below-deck quarters of a listing ship.

As a meeting wound down, the president would succinctly summarize each side's most logical arguments. "It's not just a recitation of what they said," Rouse explained. "It's actually taking apart what they said, making sure everyone understands it, and thinking through certain aspects of it." For both outside advisors and close aides, the president's ability to extract meaning from a wide-ranging discussion was one of his most impressive qualities. "In an incredibly organized fashion he'll do an almost a, b, c, d recitation of an argument or a set of policies and it's almost like you've been given a road map to go finish your job," Heather Higginbottom said.

Occasionally the president would poll the room for a final sense of how everyone felt. He did this on one of his tougher early decisions, whether to release the "torture memos" written in Bush's Justice Department.* Because the narrow question was on whether to redact the details of the authorized interrogations, Obama went around the table asking, "Redact?" to each person in attendance. The polling was never binding; in fact much of the time he would ask for opinions after he had already made a decision. But it helped him bulletproof an argument and give him advance word of how it would be challenged once the decision was announced publicly.

Meetings usually ended with a refreshingly clear "takeaway"; the president would say, "Okay, guys, here's what I'm thinking and here's where I want to go," then enumerate ("One, two, three") exactly what he meant. As he wrapped up he'd often add, "Let me tell you five questions I want to address in the next session." Advisors almost never left the room wondering what the point of the meeting had been.

Sometimes he would announce his decision immediately, then adjourn the meeting. When it was a harder call he would say the subject needed more thought. He often wouldn't tip his hand until he'd had a chance to think about it for a day or two, late at night, or while working out in the White House gym. For the hardest calls of all, such as what to do in Afghanistan and Pakistan, the president would use his gift for running meetings to put his stamp on the presidency.

---

* Attorney General Eric Holder and White House Counsel Greg Craig were in favor of releasing the memos; CIA Director Leon Panetta and Director of National Intelligence Dennis Blair were opposed. After long consideration Obama decided that lawsuits had brought most of the details out anyway and he agreed to release the memos without heavy redaction.

14

Global Reset

When Joe Biden said, "We got the ticket in the right order," he was referring to the president's grasp of the economy. It was hard for Biden to give up the idea that his knowledge and experience would have made him a better foreign policy president than Obama. But eventually Biden conceded that point too. "He changed the equation overnight," Biden said. "We were *so* much better positioned in the world the day after he got elected. *The day after.*" Now Biden began musing about how it would have gone if the 2008 Democratic primaries had ended differently. "It would have taken me two years to do that," he said. "It would have taken Hillary four years to do that." Then he grew more modest. "I couldn't have done what he did—the way he won, his temperament and intellect, a sense of hope and expectation. I mean, he was the right guy at the right moment."

Even discounting for vice-presidential apple-polishing, there was truth in Biden's take. With his popularity over 70 percent in more than a dozen countries and over 50 percent almost everywhere, Obama had a once-in-a-generation opportunity. The whole world was anxious to see what he would do with it.*

Obama responded by traveling far more widely in his first year than had any previous president. In 2009 he made ten foreign trips to twenty-one nations (four of them twice). The next most frequent foreign traveler was George H. W. Bush, who visited fourteen countries in 1989.

Obama had loved studying international relations since the days when he aced a class on arms control as a Columbia undergraduate. In the White House he immersed himself in the details of intelligence and

---

* In eleven nations Obama's popularity in the middle of 2009 was greater than in the United States: Kenya, 94 percent; Germany, 93 percent; France, 91 percent; Canada, 88 percent; Nigeria, 88 percent; Britain, 86 percent; Japan, 85 percent; South Korea, 81 percent; India, 77 percent; Brazil, 76 percent; United States, 74 percent.

counterterrorism. His focus on the world had the intensity of a second-term president. (Two-term presidents traditionally devote most of their second terms to foreign policy, which they can control with less interference by Congress.)

Starting in July 2007 candidate Obama had pushed for a new policy of engagement. When he said during a YouTube campaign debate that the United States should negotiate with Iran, North Korea, and other thuggish regimes with "no preconditions," Hillary Clinton slammed him for being "irresponsible and, frankly, naïve." Some campaign aides, worried that he looked soft, wanted him to issue a clarification of his "gaffe." Obama refused. "Let me be clear about something: I didn't make a mistake," he said on a conference call with campaign staff. And he turned out to be right.

Positioned to the left of Clinton on Iraq as well, Obama needed to find the center if he wanted to be president. Out of a combination of conviction and political calculation, he compensated, fatefully, by striking a hawkish tone on the war in Afghanistan, going so far as to say he would bomb inside Pakistan to root out al Qaeda. This time it was the Pakistani foreign minister who called him "irresponsible," but he once again stood by his position. On several other occasions he said the United States had "taken its eye off the ball" and should step up the war against al Qaeda in Afghanistan.

As he settled into the White House the president was determined to stay consistent with those specific campaign promises, and to his broader goals of restoring American leadership and returning the nation to closer cooperation with its allies. Obama repeatedly described the essence of his foreign policy as "forging a new relationship with the world based on mutual interest and mutual respect." His strategy was to reinvigorate international organizations and establish breathing room for progress across a broad front.

Bush disparaged global forums; Obama put his chips on them. His success in foreign policy would depend largely on whether he could use NATO to help him in Afghanistan, the United Nations (through the Security Council and the International Atomic Energy Agency) to pressure Iran, and the Copenhagen summit to bring China more firmly into global efforts to combat climate change.

The first task was to change the tone. That's why the speeches he gave abroad in 2009—especially in Prague (setting the goal of a world without nuclear weapons), Cairo (reaching out to Muslims), and Oslo when accepting the Nobel Peace Prize (establishing the conditions that justified war)—were so important. Their purpose wasn't to solve problems, he told his foreign policy aides, but to create the space to solve problems. They brought him the credibility to move forward on specifics. They were necessary though not sufficient for real breakthroughs.

The two fundamental foreign policy priorities of Year One were restraining nukes—the most immediate threat to everyone's security—and improving relations with the Muslim world. Given the danger of loose nuclear materials falling into the hands of radical jihadists, these were related concerns. With the exception of climate change, all the pressing international issues—confronting Iran and North Korea, combating al Qaeda, withdrawing from Iraq, securing the Pakistan-Afghanistan border, advancing Mideast peace—fell into those two baskets. Scott Gration, a retired general who advised the Obama campaign and became special envoy to the Sudan, liked to call the policy "engagement with a purpose" or "dialogue for an outcome." After eight years of blustery condemnation that produced almost no results, it was time to send a message about a new American attitude.

"If people think you're at war with Islam, you're never going to succeed in Iraq or Afghanistan," said Ben Rhodes of the National Security Council. Rhodes said Obama believed the same logic applied to nukes. The United States, Obama thought, couldn't effectively pressure Iran until we unilaterally reduced our own stockpile of nuclear weapons and began pushing forward again on arms talks with Russia.

In that sense Obama's early initiatives were meant not just to mark a sharp break with Bush; they were intended to remove the hypocrisy argument that had long stood in the way of the United States advancing its interests. His humility was not preening or self-conscious but wielded as an instrument.

There was no Obama Doctrine in 2009, but he was feeling his way toward one. In his Nobel speech he took note of the long-standing tension in U.S. foreign policy between "idealists" and "realists" and said plainly, "I reject that choice." If he had a bias it was for a postideological world still struggling to be born, a world where people were sophisticated enough to hold seemingly contradictory ideas in their heads at the same time. Obama supported "an expanded moral imagination" and global human rights, but without "the satisfying purity of indignation" that often hindered negotiations with repressive regimes. His bold pragmatism, tempered by a Reinhold Niebuhr–style awareness of evil, would require new institutions and arrangements to supplement those that had prevented another world war for sixty-five years.* "This old

---

* Like Martin Luther King and Jimmy Carter, Obama repeatedly described Niebuhr as his "favorite theologian" or "favorite philosopher." Niebuhr, who died in 1971, articulated an American definition of just war and is credited with the first version of what became known

architecture is buckling under the weight of new threats," he said in Oslo.˙

The fresh architectural plans he had in mind included empowering the new G-20, revitalizing the 1968 Nuclear Non-Proliferation Treaty, jump-starting START talks with Russia on arms control, and moving toward global control of carbon emissions at the now yearly summits on climate change. The question was what would happen when engagement failed to produce progress. How would he react?

Above all, his foreign policy would seek to strike a balance. On the eve of his big speech at West Point announcing a troop escalation in Afghanistan, Obama's mind turned to President Eisenhower's famous Farewell Address in 1960. "Everyone quotes the 'military industrial complex' line," he said, trying out a theme he would articulate the next day. "But actually he [Eisenhower] has a very interesting passage where he talks about .the need to balance a whole host of considerations to maximize the pursuit of the national interest." Obama was determined that his foreign policy would always be broad-gauged and connected to what was affordable domestically, in both political and budgetary terms.

Was that wishful thinking? The new president could aim for balance, but world events had a way of upsetting even the best-laid plans.

———

BEFORE HE DID anything else internationally, Obama had to make sure the global recession didn't become a global depression. Upon taking office Franklin Roosevelt rejected the idea of coordinating with allies to confront the economic crisis. FDR chose not to attend the 1933 London Economic Conference and to look domestically for economic remedies. Obama didn't have that luxury at the April 2009 global economic conference also held in London of the twenty largest economic powers of the world (dubbed the G-20). With China and India now major players in the global economy, the smaller G-8 club (which met over the summer in Italy) was not enough anymore. At their June meeting in Pittsburgh, under prodding from the United States, the G-20 became permanent—a significant structural accomplishment for Obama's first year.

The emergency 2009 London meeting was the largest meeting of global leaders coping with an economic crisis (representing 80 percent of world trade) since that failed London conference seventy-six years earlier. The press didn't think much came of this one either because

———

as the Serenity Prayer: "Give us courage to change what must be altered, serenity to accept what cannot be helped, and the insight to know the one from the other."

most allies stiffed the United States on providing troops for Afghanistan and refused to emulate Obama's stimulus package.

It was true that the expansion from eight heads of state to twenty made supervision of the world economy more complicated. "If there's just Roosevelt and Churchill sitting in a room with a brandy, that's an easier negotiation," Obama said afterward. "But that's not the world we live in and it shouldn't be the world we live in."

Obama was nursing a head cold ("I feel like I have acorns up my nose"), and reporters were more interested in the stylistic impression he and Michelle left during the rest of the trip. This set the pattern of coverage for all the president's travels. Did Michelle breach protocol when she lightly hugged the queen of England? (No.) Was an iPod the wrong gift for a monarch? (Maybe.) Did the president bow too deeply to the king of Saudi Arabia? (No. It was mostly the camera angle). To the emperor of Japan? (Yes, though he's a powerless figurehead.) The fun stories obscured the substance. In London the G-20 agreed to spend $1 trillion to bolster one another's financial institutions and an additional $500 billion for the IMF to help stabilize the global economy. The biggest news consisted of what didn't happen: there was no squabbling, no fatal miscommunication, and, most important in a deep recession, no rush to protectionism.* The counterfactuals—what might have gone differently—had no immediate political significance but deserved a place on Obama's ledger.

The same was true of withdrawal from Iraq, which proceeded roughly on schedule all year long. This was mostly the result of the Bush surge that Obama and other Democrats opposed. American deaths in Iraq in 2009 were cut to 139, less than half of the 2008 fatalities in a war that had claimed about 4,450 American lives. Had the Iraqi withdrawal gone badly and Obama not been able to keep his campaign promise to begin rotating troops out, it would have been a tougher 2009.

———

IN LATE SUMMER Obama was holding a meeting with Hillary Clinton, Bob Gates, Jim Jones, and Joe Biden about the complexities of Iraqi governance. He suddenly turned to Biden and said, "So, Joe, I want you there once a month. You know the players. You take care of it." This was said to be no insult to Clinton, who, with all her globetrotting, hardly wanted to add a monthly visit to Baghdad.

Obama had changed his mind about Biden over the six months fol-

———

* It could have gone differently. The London Economic Conference of June 1933 was a fiasco and set back efforts to fight the Depression.

lowing the election. He went from not trusting him to keep his mouth shut about personnel decisions to trusting him fully to handle one of the biggest portfolios of his presidency.

From afar Biden looked like a windy, gaffe-prone glad-hander; up close he was still a filterless chatterbox. But for thirty-six years in the Senate he had used the long daily commute on Amtrak between Wilmington, Delaware, and Washington, D.C., to master the substance of government. His brainy staff always thought that he was smarter than his public image and now the president agreed. "Obama's idea of a blowhard is someone who talks but doesn't have anything to say," said Axelrod. "He thinks Biden has a lot to say, and a lot of wisdom." Once in office Obama quickly saw that his vice president was deeply knowledgeable about the nuances of foreign policy and surprisingly deft with foreign leaders, who, like American politicians, found him to be an irrepressible Labrador.

It was a sign of how busy the president was—and how surprisingly well Iraq went—that he never needed another meeting about Iraq for the rest of 2009. The president and vice president didn't even talk about it much at their weekly lunches.

———

AFTER THE PITTSBURGH G-20 Summit in June, Obama released a statement of principles on the global economy. The president's "Framework for Strong, Sustainable Balanced Growth" (that word *balance* again) began a regimen of capital and regulatory standards that would help prevent another meltdown. More important than the preliminary moves was a concept borrowed from the administration's education policy. The Framework formally envisioned a "regulatory race to the top" for nations that sponsored imaginative ways of regulating derivatives and other financial products that helped cause the crisis. This idea of generating healthy competition would move to the center of the administration's thinking.

Competition, the president believed, went down more easily if accompanied by new cooperation. Obama thought the highlights of his first presidential trip to Europe were the town meeting at Strasbourg, France, where he had wowed the global village the way he had American voters a year earlier, and his address to the Turkish Parliament, his first major speech abroad as president. Like his first TV interview, the first speech was devoted to Muslim outreach. "Many Americans have Muslims in their families, or have lived in a Muslim-majority country," Obama told the Parliament. "I know," he said, "because I am one of them." The comment was greeted by sustained applause.

Dating back to 2006, when Fox News morning anchor Steve Doocy first claimed that Obama had attended a Muslim madrassa, right-wing elements tried to depict him as a Muslim. (At various points more than a quarter of the electorate believed it, including Ross Perot.) Now, building on his use of "Hussein" in his Inauguration, Obama embraced the association. In Ankara the president was introduced as "Barack Hussein Obama" and he laid a wreath at the tomb of Kemal Ataturk, the founder of modern Turkey and a secularist. He figured he could deal with any political fallout at home; the next time he would face voters was nearly four years and a thousand turns of the screw away. So he put himself on the line to help secularists and other centrist Muslims build what the world arguably needed most: an influential moderate Muslim movement to offer hope to young alienated Muslim men who might be tempted to join terrorist organizations. In a world of a billion Muslims, it was the only way forward.

The president paid little if any attention to the right-wing attacks at home. "There have been times when America has shown arrogance and been dismissive, even derisive," he said in Strasbourg. If Fox commentators wanted to call that part of an "apology tour," then they were willfully choosing not to hear what Obama said next: "But in Europe, there is an anti-Americanism that is at once casual, but can also be insidious." The message was blunter than Europeans could ever remember hearing from an American president, and they loved it.

Ben Rhodes thought the "apology tour" critique had it exactly backward: "It's actually the opposite in the sense that by pointing out our capacity to make up for historical wrongdoing—be it slavery or torture—we're sending the same patriotic message that we did during the campaign, that our ability to perfect our union is what makes us an example to the world."

Obama thought his first session with Russian President Dmitry Medvedev in London went well. It was important to convince Medvedev and his patron, Vladimir Putin, to at least consider cooperating again. They got START talks, which had foundered under Bush, back on track, and when the United States later obtained Russia's support for a UN resolution rebuking North Korea for violating nuclear arms accords, Obama believed it was directly attributable to his reopening the subject of nuclear proliferation in London. Most important, Moscow began to toughen its line on Iran.

It would be months, even years before the labors of this trip or any of the nine other foreign trips Obama took during 2009 would bring major diplomatic breakthroughs. But after the fallow Bush years, at least he had planted some seeds.

THE PRESIDENT WAS, by several accounts, his own national security advisor, coordinating the different elements of foreign policy, intelligence gathering, and defense to suit his own needs. That was the way he wanted it, but the arrangement was also a function of the man with the actual job title, retired General Jim Jones, who took a modest view of his role. Bob Gates wished sometimes that Jones was more assertive. Gates had worked as deputy NSC advisor under Brent Scowcroft twenty years earlier and had strong ideas about how the job should be handled. Jones was smart and briefed well, but he didn't ride herd enough on the bureaucracy for Gates's taste.

Six months in, several senior domestic staffers had never laid eyes on Jones. He rarely attended West Wing meetings, delegated big logistical chunks of his job to his deputy, Tom Donilon, and rode home, sometimes on a bicycle, much earlier than everyone else, all of which fed rumors. But contrary to press reports, Jones's job was never in jeopardy. He became an example of someone derided by people who didn't know what was going on.

Jones was always in Obama's national security inner circle, which also included Clinton, Gates, Donilon, Leon Panetta, Dennis Blair (director of national intelligence), and John Brennan (assistant to the president for homeland security). The president appreciated that Jones was the only one in the White House who knew much about the military, a reflection of the gap between the civilian and military cultures in Obama's Washington and throughout the country. When it was time for Obama to decide in April whether to have Navy SEALs try to kill Somali pirates holding a commercial ship captain as hostage, it was Jones who handled the complex logistics. The story quickly faded but would have been one of the big events of 2009 had it gone badly.

Attendees at NSC meetings noticed that Obama often asked Jones's young deputies, Denis McDonough and Mark Lippert, to come upstairs and talk with him after the meeting in the Situation Room was over. They had been with him for much of the campaign and along with Donilon often had the last word with the president.* Because both McDonough and Lippert rarely spoke in meetings, their thinking was the source of great speculation—and some resentment—throughout the national security establishment.

---

* Lippert, who had been Obama's chief foreign policy aide in the Senate, missed most of the 2008 campaign while serving as a naval intelligence officer in Iraq. Inside the White House he clashed with his boss, Jim Jones, who thought he was using his close relationship with the president to trump him. In late 2009, Lippert left for another tour abroad, the first senior civilian aide in the White House to report for military service since World War II.

BOB GATES DIDN'T spend the most time of any Cabinet member at the White House; that was Geithner. But Gates was almost certainly the most influential member of the Cabinet. No one else in the room had anywhere near his experience in government, which offered him a natural advantage in any debate. And his pedigree as a Republican and former CIA director gave Obama political cover on controversial decisions. The same factors gave Gates virtual veto power on those decisions, though it helped that Obama genuinely wanted to hear what he had to say.

From the start Obama was inclined to back Gates against liberal critics. When photographs surfaced documenting the torture of detainees in Afghanistan and Iraq, the White House, responding to what it thought was an okay from the Pentagon, at first declined to block their publication. But after Ray Odierno, the commander in Iraq, told Obama directly that the pictures would lead to reprisals against U.S. soldiers, the president reversed his position. Many of the gruesome photos were autopsy shots not necessarily related to detainee abuse, but that distinction would be erased once they were released. When he finally focused on it, Obama didn't see it as a close call. He was fully committed to ending torture, but he didn't think the public would "learn anything new" from the photos. So why inflame the Arab street?

The decision on the photographs surfaced because of pending litigation. The same thing happened on deciding whether to redact portions of the so-called torture memos written by the Office of Legal Counsel in the Bush Justice Department. In February Obama overruled objections from the CIA and released some of the memos. He said that one of his biggest surprises on coming to office was how often he was crowded by court orders, Freedom of Information requests, and other legal points of decision. He preferred setting deadlines to responding to them.

THE PRESIDENT AND his secretary of state got along fine but still had some distance to go before they could be considered close. At first Clinton was often too deferential to Obama in meetings, just shy of obsequious. One assistant secretary of state described it as like a teenager trying too hard on a date. When she laid it on thick, the president, a bit embarrassed, would say little, which in turn made him seem a tad aloof. It was apparently better in private. Over time they recognized they had compatible senses of humor and made each other laugh with small observations about the people they met. Their staffs were terrified of detailing the relationship, but there wasn't much to say anyway. It was surprisingly unfraught. At their forty-five-minute meetings every Thursday in the Oval Office they covered a lot of business in a warm and professional way.

Obama had no self-doubt over who belonged at the head of the table. "I would put my judgments on foreign policy next to hers over the last four years on Iraq, on Iran, on how she would conduct diplomacy, on Pakistan," he said in a *Newsweek* interview during the campaign, and nothing happened in the White House to change that assessment. But he was careful as president not to rub it in. In meetings he made a point of complimenting her and he didn't tease her publicly. Before the White House Correspondents Dinner Clinton had slipped and broken her elbow en route to a meeting with Obama. Joke writers came up with a line for Obama about how she had "fallen again on her way to the White House." The president crossed it out.*

One reason the two got along was that Clinton was scrupulous in not undermining Obama. She sensibly decided to emulate what she did in the Senate and devote most of her first year to listening, learning, and, in the lingo of Washington, "checking the boxes" on the job, which meant trying to figure out the substance of what she was required to do. She went to school on the world, studying intensely, and struggled to manage the huge State Department bureaucracy. Like Obama, she had never run anything big before except a presidential campaign, which she managed poorly.

One of her top aides conceded that it would take several months before she was her creative self again, that she was burdened by the sprawling management challenge. So she would be dutiful for a while and avoid big strategic thoughts. (Her early bid to dub U.S. foreign policy "smart power" foundered when critics called it dumb.)

Obama's decision to designate special envoys for hot spots was first seen by the press as a blow to Clinton. With the exception of China, she wasn't given any country or region to focus on. But the use of envoys turned out to be a blessing for the secretary of state; it freed her to stay focused on the broader picture. (Condi Rice had been so burdened by inconclusive Middle East diplomacy that she accomplished little.) By not engaging in shuttle diplomacy herself, Clinton could bore in on such critical long-term issues as food security (the administration secured a landmark $20 billion deal to address world hunger), women in the developing world, unsafe drinking water (which kills more peo-

---

* Obama did joke at the banquet that just before the accident the Secret Service spotted Richard Holbrooke spraying WD40 all over the driveway.

ple than AIDS, TB, and malaria combined), and off-the-boil regional disputes where intervention by a secretary of state could make a real difference, including continued tension between Armenians and Turks.

Clinton wasn't above stunts. To drive home the new relationship of "mutual respect" with Russia, she posed with Russian Foreign Minister Sergei Lavrov and an oversize "reset" button. When Lavrov said that the Russian-language inscription on the button translated not as *reset* but as *overcharge,* Clinton laughed and said, "We won't let you do that to us."

Despite all the people she knew in politics, Clinton found herself unable to fill the posts at the department with people she trusted. "I don't know a lot of them. I'm taking a leap," she told a friend. This was an important advance, for her great shortcoming was in judging people. Some of her staff were first-rate but for years she'd had a weakness for toadies who outdid one another in proving their slavish loyalty to her, and for faddish experts. She might have won the nomination and been president had she surrounded herself with better people during the 2008 campaign. Now, by necessity, she would have to choose staff from outside her comfort zone, and it would be a good thing. Even though she didn't trust them yet, they quickly came to admire her, especially her ability to master complex issues quickly. The roll-up-our-sleeves ethic she brought was contagious. When she saw that the new people she had chosen respected her, she relaxed and grew into the job.

Clinton had the good sense to put some of her brightest people in jobs related to global partnerships and public diplomacy. She recognized that the old diplomacy, in which governments talked only to governments, had been replaced by many more people-to-people exchanges. In the past both terrorism and human rights abuses had been largely state sponsored. Now many of the most serious threats came from dangerous nonstate actors: tribes, factions, groups, and even individuals. Combating them—and building a more peaceful and prosperous world—required new thinking about nongovernmental organizations and going over the heads of local regimes to the people.

This was becoming much easier. Though Iranian state television refused to carry Obama's speeches, it no longer mattered much. With a hundred thousand Iranian blogs and near-universal cell phone usage in the country, the White House and State Department could post and text excerpts from any speech, ensuring that the president's words went viral. Even a less developed country like Afghanistan featured widespread cell phone usage. With each speech or crisis, the power of social networking grew. Alec Ross, who held the new State Department post of senior advisor for innovation, called it "twenty-first-century statecraft." A cyber arms race began, with Iran using Western technology to shut down dissidents and China harassing Google users to the point that the company left the country. In early 2010 Clinton gave notice that Internet freedom would become one of her major themes.

———————

MOST OF CLINTON'S foreign trips proved inspirational for the people of the host nations. Her decision to join forces with the man who defeated her in a presidential election spoke well of democracy and offered a model for peaceful power-sharing. After Madeleine Albright and Condi Rice, it was no big deal to have a woman as secretary of state, but Clinton was in a different league: she became a global symbol of women struggling and enduring. Her influence was especially great in developing countries, where most men contributed relatively little. Because women are the backbone of development—in agriculture, microfinance, and health—Clinton's immense popularity had a greater potential to leverage gains abroad.

Her style was a reflection of her high energy level and thirst to engage. Departing from the Eurocentrism of her predecessors, her first foreign trip was to Asia, which appreciated the gesture. In China she learned that thanks to Bush-era lack of interest, the United States would be the only country other than Andorra lacking a pavilion at the 2010 Shanghai Exposition, which the Chinese saw as a coming-out party as important as the 2008 Beijing Olympics. This posed a major embarrassment to both countries. Clinton spent months wheedling the necessary $60 million for the U.S. pavilion from private sources, a daunting task.

In early August she traveled to seven African countries in eleven days, including a visit to the conflict zone of eastern Congo, where no secretary of state had ventured since the widespread raping and killing had begun in the mid-1990s. The trip was reminiscent of one of her famous "listening tours" when she was running for the Senate from New York. Clinton would scribble notes and hold what her staff called "townterviews," combinations of town meetings and interviews by local journalists and officials.*

The pace was beyond grueling. When a Congolese student asked if she "channeled" President Clinton on issues, she snapped, "My husband is not secretary of state, I am." The video of her irritation played heavily in the United States, but it did nothing to diminish her im-

———————

* When Clinton landed in Kenya news broke that Bill Clinton was meeting with Kim Jong Il in Pyongyang to negotiate the release of two women journalists working for Al Gore's TV network. Her husband inadvertently upstaged that part of her trip.

pact. Having another high-level politician and celebrity to show the flag and troubleshoot was a great boon to Obama, and eventually to countries like Haiti that were desperate for her help, and that of her husband.

———

WASHINGTON WAS HARDER. Clinton played well with the other principals, but her staff chafed at having to answer to the White House. She bounced a few White House choices for assistant secretaries and needed a nudge from Obama directly before she accepted Jim Steinberg as her deputy.* When she insisted that a longtime aide, Capricia Marshall, be named chief of protocol, the president said fine, but he didn't want a Hillary person as part of his traveling party. It was a sign that some of the old tensions remained. Obama loyalists thought that Clintonites had received too many of the good jobs. To strike a blow for the Obama team, Denis McDonough, backed by Rahm (who wanted to do something for the early Obama loyalists), told Clinton she couldn't hire Sidney Blumenthal because he had spread dirt about Obama during the campaign.†

The White House could do nothing about Clinton's choice for her own chief of staff, Cheryl Mills, a longtime Clinton loyalist (and member of the defense team during Bill's impeachment). Mills was like one of those diehard Japanese soldiers who still wouldn't come out of the cave thirty years after the end of World War II. She was not just pro-Hillary, she was stridently anti-Obama until the fall of 2008, arguing not only that his candidacy was doomed but that it would set back the cause of her fellow African Americans. Even career diplomats with no allegiance to Obama complained that Mills was holding up personnel decisions.

Mills was right that during the transition Obama had told Clinton that she could name her own team, a fact that the White House often conveniently ignored. But he never meant to relinquish his power to appoint ambassadors, a traditional prerogative of presidents. After Clinton forces put out the word that Harvard professor Joseph Nye would be ambassador to Japan, the appointment was reversed. Obama, with the advice of UN Ambassador Susan Rice, decided that he preferred John Roos, a Silicon Valley lawyer and major campaign fund-raiser.

---

* Steinberg worked in the Clinton Administration but backed Obama in 2008.

† Among other calumnies, Blumenthal was accused by Obama loyalists of having given Matt Drudge a picture of Obama in Muslim garb, which was unlikely considering that Blumenthal had a few years earlier spent thousands of dollars suing Drudge.

Before he was elected, Barack Obama (right) took control of a "surreal" White House meeting on the economic crisis with (left to right) John McCain, John Boehner, Nancy Pelosi, President Bush, Harry Reid, and Mitch McConnell. Afterward he prevented a fistfight between Congressman Barney Frank and Treasury Secretary Henry Paulson.

2

In a quiet moment in his Election Night hotel suite with his mother-in-law, Marian Robinson. Starting the next day he made more big decisions than any president-elect in history.

Inside the Capitol, a last look before walking outdoors to take the oath. Amid a terrorist plot to disrupt the historic Inauguration, Obama urged the country to "put aside childish things."

In a freight elevator at an Inaugural Ball, the new president gave the new first lady his coat. Aides joked that Michelle Obama was "the Supreme Leader."

At play in the Oval Office. Obama was determined to "put points on the board" early and he did, with a string of legislative victories. The stimulus was greatly underappreciated but poorly framed by the White House.

Even the White House puppy proved controversial. "I'm going to kill that dog," Chief of Staff Rahm Emanuel barked. "He's off message!"

Obama leading his team out of the West Wing. "He's the most unsentimental man I ever met," said one advisor.

7

A burger with Vice President Joe Biden, who confided to an aide, "They got the ticket in the right order." Biden said Obama restored U.S. prestige overnight. "It would have taken me two years to do that."

8

9

At first Secretary of State Hillary Clinton related to the president "like a teenager trying too hard on a date." But they had compatible senses of humor.

Rahm Emanuel opposed major health care
reform in 2009: "I begged the president not
to do this." Then he worked frantically to
make it happen and developed a secret eight-
hundred-page plan.

Michelle Obama didn't want their "big sister" and advisor, Valerie Jarrett (left), to
take her husband's Senate seat.

12

David Axelrod (left) lampooned Larry Summers's "plutocrats." Summers (center) joked that Axelrod was "Che." Obama nicknamed Summers "Dr. Kevorkian."

13

Pete Rouse (right), the least known of the "Big Four," was likened to a sweeter version of Winston ("I Solve Problems") Wolf, the Harvey Keitel character in *Pulp Fiction.* Obama wanted Rouse and Jarrett (center) as "counterweights" to Emanuel and Axelrod.

With speechwriter Jon Favreau (left) aboard Air Force One. Obama's eloquent speeches opened "breathing room" for policy progress. But because the president loathed sound bites, the effect wore off fast.

In the outer Oval Office, Obama caught the coverage of Sonia Sotomayor's confirmation hearings. The president disdained most cable news and went to war with Fox, which he described as having a "talk radio format." Between the "tea parties," "birthers," and GOP hopes for his "Waterloo," the opposition was relentless.

"This whole thing about her not being up to the job is ridiculous," Obama said of the qualifications of Sonia Sotomayor (center) for the Supreme Court. "She's super smart."

16

Former Federal Reserve Chairman Paul Volcker, a "populist" on breaking up banks, was kept out of the loop for months. Volcker thought the White House viewed him as a "wax figure."

17

18

Obama pushed out loyalist Greg Craig over his handling of Guantánamo Bay detainees but quietly offered him a federal judgeship.

Obama presided over a seven-hour Sunday meeting about what to do with the banks. (Left to right) Gene Sperling, Larry Summers, Tim Geithner, and Christina Romer, who had earlier accused Summers of "sexism." "Don't you threaten me!" Summers shouted. "Don't you bully *me*!" Romer yelled.

(Left to right) Tim Geithner, Peter Orszag, Valerie Jarrett, Anita Dunn, Robert Gibbs, and Rahm Emanuel. The team helped prevent another Great Depression, but few noticed because unemployment was "much fiercer than we expected," Obama confessed.

Obama shooting hoops on the South Lawn between meetings (above), and trying to box out congressmen on the converted White House tennis court (below). With the game on the line, he always wanted the ball.

23

Before his landmark Cairo speech to the Muslim world Obama told aides, "We have to say in public what people normally only say behind closed doors."

Carla Bruni-Sarkozy (right) wanted to know if the Obamas ever kept a foreign head of state waiting while they finished making love.

24

25

In Oslo the president saw his Nobel Peace Prize for the first time.

At a New
Hampshire town
hall meeting
in August.
All year long
Obama failed to
find the "right
vocabulary"
to explain the
complexities of
health care.

26

Melody Barnes (left)
was the only senior
aide pushing health
care. In the Senate
Ted Kennedy's
absence was felt
acutely, and Max
Baucus (right) missed
crucial deadlines.
Congressional
"sausage making"
moved front and
center, harming
Obama and
Democrats.

27

28

Nurses hugged Obama
at a White House forum
on health care. Most of
the energy was with the
"tea party" movement
and other conservatives
who opposed reform.

(Above) Obama welcomed local children to the White House on Halloween with his mother-in-law and "Cat Woman" first lady. (Below) With daughters Malia and Sasha on the Colonnade. Eating dinner with his family almost every night kept the president in better spirits than during the campaign. The Obamas talked publicly about their daughters' grades and body mass indexes in order to lead by example: "I don't care how poor you are, you can turn off the television."

The White House worried that General David Petraeus (left, with General Ray Odierno) might be running for president. Obama confronted Petraeus over why his Iraq surge couldn't work in Afghanistan.

After General Stanley McChrystal (right) came across as insubordinate in a London speech, Obama told the Joint Chiefs in a cold fury that he was "exceedingly unhappy" and wanted to know "here and now" if they were onboard. Insiders called it the biggest confrontation with the military since Truman fired MacArthur.

Obama with (clockwise) Jim Jones, Admiral Mike Mullen, Robert Gates, and Hillary Clinton, en route to West Point to explain the expansion of the war in Afghanistan to 100,000 troops.

A special election to fill Ted Kennedy's seat in Massachusetts seemed to dash Obama's hopes for a first-year triumph on health care, creating a mood almost of mourning inside the White House.

Celebrating with staff in the Roosevelt Room on Sunday, March 21, 2010, as the House vote passes the magic number, 216, and his dream of health care reform is fulfilled.

At the end of Year One the president had fulfilled or made progress on nearly four hundred of five hundred campaign promises, but the road ahead was daunting. When an old friend asked about reelection, he said, "I have to run now otherwise it'll mean letting someone like Mitt Romney step in and get credit for the good stuff that happens after we've been through all this crap."

This went over badly in Tokyo, where the Japanese were accustomed to ambassadors with the stature of Walter Mondale or Howard Baker.

The sniping between the White House and State was hard to miss. When State Department sources alleged that the White House was "politicizing" the Foreign Service by naming campaign contributors to glamorous foreign posts (a long-standing tradition in Europe because so much of the cost of running embassies came out of the ambassadors' own pockets), White House operatives made sure reporters noticed that one of the Clintons' biggest fund-raisers, Hassan Nemazee, whom Bill Clinton nominated unsuccessfully for an ambassadorship in the 1990s, was indicted over the summer of 2009.

Dennis Ross became a symbol of the staff-level to-and-fro. Ross, who had served in Republican and Democratic administrations as the top Middle East expert, had never been close to Clinton, so when he arrived at the State Department to work on Iran policy he was given an office on the first floor, poor real estate by Foggy Bottom standards. (The power players are on the seventh floor, near the secretary of state's office.) Iran wasn't talking to the United States or welcoming visitors to Tehran, so Ross eventually became the department's Maytag repairman, waiting for something to do. Tom Donilon concluded that the Mideast peace process had stalled, and he arranged for Ross to come over to the NSC—more evidence of a power shift away from an uncoordinated State Department toward a dominant White House.

Then there was the case of retired Marine Corps General Anthony Zinni, who provided Democrats with critical early opposition to the Iraq War. He was summoned to the State Department and told by Clinton that he would be the next ambassador to Iraq. Biden called to congratulate him. But Zinni heard nothing for days and no one would return his calls. He finally reached Jim Jones, his friend of thirty years, who informed him that there had been a change and career diplomat Chris Hill was the choice for Baghdad. Zinni could be ambassador to Saudi Arabia instead. "You can stick that one up your . . ." Zinni told Jones, who just laughed.

―――――――

LIKE PREVIOUS AMERICAN presidents, Obama enjoyed his membership in the world's most exclusive club. He found that he often connected best with the new generation of world leaders about his age who regarded old rivalries and the cold war as little more than compelling museum pieces, to be studied perhaps, but not invoked as excuses, much less used as guides to the future. Dmitry Medvedev of Russia

(44), Felipe Calderón of Mexico (47), and Stephen Harper of Canada (50) were his closest contemporaries, but many of the others had also come of age in the new geopolitical system and were less burdened by the past.

The president had to tread carefully with important allies but he urgd them to focus on the future. In Ankara Obama predictably backed off his campaign promise to label the 1915 massacre of Armenians as "genocide." But he told the Turks that he had insisted the United States stop "relitigating the Vietnam War." Maybe it's because we're such a young country that we think this way, he said, but you guys let these problems go on too long. Why not move past them? Obama was about the only global leader who could get away with talking that way.

The early meetings were almost uniformly positive, as the heads of state basked in the glow of Obama's huge popularity in their home countries. And in private they appreciated his small touches. As he looked for ways to break the ice, Obama made a practice of memorizing greetings in the native tongue of most of his counterparts: "Hello," "Thank you," and "Good to see you" in French, Spanish, German, Russian, Chinese, Japanese, Korean, Arabic, and more.

Obama often used the early "bilats" (bilateral meetings) and social occasions as a way to satisfy his curiosity. Manmohan Singh, the prime minister of India, had unshackled the Indian economy in the early 1990s, a move that changed the world. Obama wanted to know all about it. He quizzed Danish Prime Minister Lars Løkke Rasmussen about Denmark's clean-energy policies before turning to his own aides to ask why the United States couldn't adopt some of them. He admired the life story of Chilean President Michelle Bachelet, a pediatrician, military strategist, and single mother of three, and enjoyed discussing Jorge Luis Borges's novels with her (even though Borges was an Argentine). When Dutch Prime Minister Jan Balkenende expressed disgust with depictions of Obama with a Hitler mustache, Obama told him not to worry; but he should know that it would take him all day to explain the strange perspective of the American right wing.

Obama's election by itself revived relations with European allies, but they didn't always go swimmingly. Great Britain fretted that its long-time "special relationship" with the United States wasn't so special anymore. After a candid assessment of Obama by the British ambassador to the United States leaked during the 2008 campaign (Sir Nigel Sheinwald called him "decidedly liberal" with "little track record"), the Obama transition team overreacted and decided to do no favors for the government of Gordon Brown, whom the Americans considered a lame duck. The president's first two one-on-ones with Brown, a fellow progressive, went fine, but when Brown requested a bilat in New York at the convening of the UN General Assembly in September, Obama declined, which Brown and much of the British establishment took as an insult. The White House realized it had erred and worked to reassure Brown. Clinton had to pay special attention to her good relationship with David Miliband, the British foreign secretary, to keep the close U.S.-British ties from deteriorating.

When German Chancellor Angela Merkel first called to congratulate Obama following the 2008 election, they bonded over a little story. After Obama first pronounced "Angela" with a hard *g*, Merkel gently corrected him by saying it was pronounced with a soft *g*, as in Angela Davis, the fiery African American revolutionary whom she remembered hearing about as a young girl growing up in Communist East Germany. Obama, who had read extensively about the black power movement, found this amusing. But the relationship foundered at first, a consequence of the squabbling between the German government and the Obama campaign over the logistics of his August 2008 trip to Berlin. The White House resisted inviting Merkel for a state visit, which the Germans resented. Merkel craved a good relationship with Washington, but, betraying her stiff Teutonic bearing, she didn't think Obama's rock star persona was good for the alliance. She backed his efforts to remove missile defense systems from Eastern Europe and came to like him as well as she liked Bush, who famously tried (and failed) to give her a backrub during a summit meeting.* They had differences on the financial crisis (Germans, worried about igniting Weimar-style hyperinflation, were wary of stimulus and favored a "Tobin tax" on all market trades), but the stories of ongoing tension were largely wrong.

Obama had a soft spot for French President Nicholas Sarkozy, whose considerable ego he took in stride. Obama considered him not just refreshingly pro-American but a forceful and creative ally, especially on pressuring Iran. Sarkozy was proud of spotting Obama's potential early (on a 2006 trip to the United States he had asked to see Obama and only two other senators) but a little insecure about their relationship, and not just because the lifts in his shoes did little to lessen the height disparity between them. In Pittsburgh for the G-20 summit Sarkozy felt as if Obama were using him as a prop on the final day. He refused for a time to go out onstage with the president.

Earlier Sarkozy was less than happy when Obama decided to spend

---

* Merkel's real issues were with Vladimir Putin. The Russian leader knew that Merkel had a lifetime phobia of dogs but allowed his two large Labradors to roam freely around the table in his Moscow office when the two had breakfast.

a free summer evening in Paris alone with his family instead of going out to dinner in public with their wives, where the cameras would record the foursome as the two most glamorous couples in the world. His Italian wife, Carla Bruni, the former model who released a CD in 2009 with songs about her "thirty lovers," delighted in telling friends that she shocked Michelle Obama at their first meeting. Bruni informed the first lady that the press of state business prevented her husband from making love to her as much as she would like, though in her telling they once kept another foreign leader waiting while they finished having sex. Bruni wanted to know if, like the Sarkozys, Michelle and the president had ever kept anyone waiting that way. Michelle laughed nervously and said no. .

Italian Prime Minister Silvio Berlusconi was the cause of some bemusement in the Obama camp shortly after the election when he told Medvedev in Moscow that the newly elected American president was "young, handsome and *bronzato,*" well tanned. At 72 Berlusconi didn't exactly connect with Obama, but the president found him to be an early help in upping Italy's contributions of troops to Afghanistan by a couple thousand. The Italian "Carabinieri surge" (one hundred crack police trainers) and French mountaineering units were a help there, though the German forces, restricted to daylight operations, were too greatly constrained to be of much use. The joke in Helmand province was that ISAF stood not for International Security Assistance Force but "Invited to See Americans Fight."

All the European leaders were sensitive to press reports that Obama was neglecting Europe. This became a common theme among certain heads of state, that the new American president wasn't fully respecting the "historic ties" between their country and the United States. The combination of the normal neediness of politicians everywhere, Obama's great stature, and his own shortcomings in showing gratitude led to claims that he was taking America's friends abroad for granted.

This became a particular problem with Israel, where Obama was at least 40 percent less popular than he was anywhere else in the world. From the start, his relationship with Israeli Prime Minister Benjamin Netanyahu was strained, and not just because the White House clearly favored the more moderate Tzipi Livni, the Kadima Party candidate, in the February 2009 election. Obama's push to limit settlements in the occupied territories was cited as the cause of the tension but in fact was no significant departure from the Bush policy.

The problem was more personal. Despite the best efforts of Rahm and Dennis Ross, the Israelis, like American Jews during the primaries, simply didn't trust Obama. They felt he didn't fully appreciate the emotional bond between the two countries and the special role of Israel in the world. It was hard to know how much of the distrust came from his outreach to Muslims and his policy of engagement with Iran, and how much from the same mistaken impression that took root among some Jewish voters during the 2008 campaign—that he had come of age as a radical Palestinian sympathizer, a familiar charge for which there was no evidence. In Chicago Obama, as usual, had liked to talk to all sides and was actually less critical of Israel than many of the liberal North Side Jews who bankrolled his early campaigns.

Over time American Jews had come around on Obama; 78 percent supported him in the 2008 general election, a higher percentage than backed Clinton, Gore, or Kerry (in part because so many were terrified of Sarah Palin). But it wasn't likely that an Obama boomlet would happen in Israel any time soon. Obama believed that he knew how to deal with Netanyahu, who reminded him of Chicago pols who would cut deals, play to their base, and otherwise do whatever it took to stay in power. But in 2009 and early 2010, he got nowhere with him, just as he hadn't with Chicago politicians for so many years.

Had they known Obama better, the Israelis would have learned that just because he was unsentimental by nature didn't mean he undervalued the alliance. In truth he was deeply concerned about Israel's security and said privately that the next decade could be a period of "maximum danger" for the Jewish state. The Israelis, he said, needed to recognize that without peace, time wasn't on their side.

In the meantime the White House was more annoyed at the Palestinians, who acted as if they could just sit back and offer nothing until the United States forced the Israelis to dismantle the settlements. The Palestinians knew they would never get a complete freeze on settlements or other unilateral concessions. As one senior White House official put it, they grew up in the Middle East, after all, where nobody thinks they're going to get the price they offer: "But they actually deluded themselves that they could get the camel at the price of a goat."

So it was not surprising that Obama considered the Israeli-Palestinian conflict the one area of "failure" in foreign policy in 2009. His special envoy to the region, George Mitchell, kept a low profile under the best of circumstances and now he went to ground almost completely. But at least Mitchell was traveling regularly to the region and working the problem. Bush had not begun the peace process early enough (in part because Yasir Arafat was still alive); Obama would lay as much groundwork as possible and hope for a favorable turn of events.

OBAMA'S STRATEGY FOR dealing with dictators was illustrative of his overall approach. The American right wing predictably attacked him for shaking hands with Venezuelan President Hugo Chavez at the Summit of the Americas in Trinidad in April, and for not bothering to respond to a long anti-American tirade there by Nicaraguan President Daniel Ortega. When asked what he thought of Ortega's diatribe, Obama said, "I thought it was fifty minutes long. That's what I thought."

He proved deft in depriving tiresome leftist demagogues of their ability to demonize the United States. The erratic Chavez found himself in the odd position of praising Obama, then calling him an "ignoramus." When Obama said that a coup against leftist Honduran President Manuel Zelaya was "not legal," it threw Chavez off balance, though the failure to restore Zelaya to power soon made Obama look ineffectual in Latin American affairs. Cuba was off balance too. It didn't know how to respond to Obama's relaxing travel restrictions, a move that was surprisingly popular in both Havana and Miami's Little Havana. The usual insults hurled at gringos seemed out of step with the new global reality shaped by Obama. Anti-Americanism had hardly disappeared, but it was showing signs of receding.

On several continents the same left-of-center nationalistic groups that had complained for years of U.S. imperialism and saw the CIA behind every plot now did 180-degree turns. They began sending letters to Human Rights First and other American-based human rights organizations asking how they could help. Because Europeans often proved unreliable allies to local dissidents, these activists suddenly began moving toward the United States again. There was something irrational about it: the same people who a year earlier saw the United States as the source of all evil now placed unrealistic expectations on Barack Obama.

NOWHERE WERE THE risks inherent in Obama's foreign policy more apparent than in Afghanistan. In March the president had signed off on an additional twenty-one thousand troops. Then he sent General Stanley McChrystal to Afghanistan to assess the situation. The results of that trip—a report of dangerously deteriorating conditions on the ground—would consume much of the president's time in the second half of the year.

In early May he hosted a trilateral meeting with Presidents Asif Ali Zardari of Pakistan and Hamid Karzai of Afghanistan. The group settled on a common goal: "Disrupt, dismantle and defeat al Qaeda." Nothing much concrete was accomplished, but the meeting showcased how interdisciplinary American foreign policy had become. The session was kicked off not by a military officer or a diplomat but by the secretary of agriculture, Tom Vilsack, who explained how progress on establishing water rights, slowing soil erosion, and planting new seeds could make a big difference in both nations. It was one example of the administration's new thinking. The new coin of the realm was COIN, which stood for counterinsurgency.

Af-Pak or "Pak-Af," as Biden sometimes called it, would become the test case of whether the West was capable of fighting a new kind of war. In September the president and his national security team would launch a thorough review that would ask every big question from multiple angles. The full answers wouldn't be available for many months or years, but they would help determine the fate of the Obama presidency.

15

Tyrannosaurus ℞

Reforming health care was always going to be hard. Obama constantly reminded people that there was a reason it hadn't gotten done in more than seventy years. He called it "a Herculean lift." To make matters harder, Obama's own top people—from Rahm Emanuel and David Axelrod to Joe Biden—were unenthusiastic at first. They felt that a big reform package would overload the circuits.

The president himself was under no illusions. He knew that unpopular bailouts and soaring unemployment had soured the public mood, but he pressed on anyway, largely because he was genuinely convinced that the status quo was financially unsustainable. "We knew that it would be all-consuming—in the midst of having to deal with this enormous economic crisis and two wars—and that it would take a lot out of us," he said later.

At a minimum, he accurately predicted, it would cost him ten to fifteen points in popularity before passage. And if it failed, he was in deep trouble. "I remember telling Nancy Pelosi that moving forward on this could end up being so costly for me politically that it would affect my chances if I were to run for reelection," the president said. But he told Pelosi that if they didn't get this done now, "it was not going to be done."

So Obama decided early to bet his domestic presidency on health care. It wasn't that he would face certain defeat in 2012 without it; unemployment and Afghanistan were much bigger issues for voters. But for greatness he needed health care, and he needed it soon. He concluded in November 2009 that trying to get Congress to sign on in the second, third, or fourth years was "just impossible to imagine." Six weeks after he said that, he would have to begin imagining.

Whether to pursue major health care reform in the first year had been a furious topic of debate going back to the transition. The first argument, in December 2008, had been over what to do with a pending bill to expand SCHIP, the children's health insurance program.

Tom Daschle and his team argued that it should be attached to a larger health care reform bill as a sweetener to draw votes. Rahm wanted it separated out and passed as a stand-alone measure to put some "points on the board," as he liked to say; he believed that pushing something too big on health care in 2009 was a mistake. Obama sided with Rahm, and the SCHIP expansion became law in early February, fulfilling a major campaign promise. But Rahm's tactical victory did nothing to slake the president's thirst for a bigger health care overhaul in Year One.

Axelrod agreed with Rahm on rejecting an ambitious plan, though he had a personal stake in reform. When his daughter Lauren was young, he had paid $8,000 to $10,000 a year in out-of-pocket expenses because his HMO wouldn't cover the full cost of the drugs she needed to treat her severe epilepsy; later Lauren's experimental brain surgery cost him much more.* But Axelrod was convinced that a recession was a "tough environment" for reform. The polls showed that people who have health insurance—voters—didn't place universal coverage high on their list of priorities. "They care more about energy," he said. He argued that energy and education were more compelling for the public and should be tackled first.

Joe Biden was on Rahm's side too. He said in a meeting during the transition that the Americans he and Obama had met on the campaign trail would understand if health care reform had to be delayed because the government was busy avoiding a depression. "They'll give you a pass on this one," he told the president. Liberal Democratic senators like Chuck Schumer and Byron Dorgan strongly urged Obama to hold off and focus on the economy. Anyone who knew Congress understood that getting a bipartisan bill would be difficult amid so much economic wreckage.

Christie Romer, speaking bluntly for the economists, harkened back to FDR, about whom she wrote her dissertation. After coming to office in 1933 he had postponed introducing Social Security for two years, until the economy began to revive. "Sometimes you face a war and that's what you have to fight," she told Obama. She recommended waiting on health care until the economy was in better shape.

Once the staff learned Obama's position, no one except Rahm made a persistent case for holding off. But among senior advisors only Domestic Policy Council Chair Melody Barnes, a former top aide to Ted

---

* Axelrod's wife, Susan, cofounded CURE, a nonprofit devoted to research on epilepsy. With the help of a new anticonvulsant drug, Keppra, Lauren Axelrod's seizures have stopped. Now 27, she lives in a group home in Chicago.

Kennedy, was an ardent proponent of moving forward with health care first, and she wasn't handling that issue. The portfolio belonged to Nancy-Ann DeParle, who was Daschle's replacement as director of the White House Office of Health Reform. DeParle, the Rhodes Scholar who had run Tennessee's health care system and later Medicare under Clinton, accepted the job in February without knowing for sure whether health care had been put on the back burner.

It didn't take her long to find out. If Obama had been as weak and overly conciliatory as some of his liberal critics believed, he would have decided during the transition, or after the Inauguration, or in the spring, or in the dog days of August, to hold off on major health care reform until later in his term. Delaying the bill would have been perfectly consistent with his campaign promise, which was merely to sign universal coverage legislation *by the end of his first four years.* Once he made up his mind, his dewy-eyed staff would back him to the hilt. But the reality was something that aides didn't much like to discuss: the president was moving ahead alone.

OBAMA'S DECISION, AS usual, reflected both strategic and tactical thinking.

His strategic view was that the health care system could no longer be·patched up, and that the recovery wouldn't last if it came without long-neglected structural changes. He believed that the health care status quo was unsustainable and would wreck the fiscal future of the country; it was almost a national security issue for him.

Without health care reform, he thought, the country would drown in debt, though of course he put it in wonkier terms: "[It was] very clear to us in the transition . . . that if we couldn't get a structure in place to start controlling health care costs, then it was impossible for us to find a pathway towards dealing with the long-term deficit numbers." He added that one of the most "eye-opening" conversations of the entire transition was when Peter Orszag explained to him that failing to control Medicare and Medicaid entitlements would make balancing the budget impossible without cutting nondefense discretionary spending (everything else in the budget) by 70 percent. "That's seven-zero," the president said in amazement.

Orszag was fine with health care reform as long as it didn't blow another hole in the budget. Since November he had been conducting a running tutorial for the president on a system careening out of control. Insurance premiums for individuals had more than doubled in a decade of low inflation (up 130 percent for small business), and the number of uninsured Americans would soon surge past 50 million with no end in sight. Even those with the most invested in the status quo, insurers and hospitals, knew that something had to change.

Then there was the moral question. Though the obligation to the uninsured and uninsurable didn't poll well, it weighed on Obama. After some coaxing from staff during the campaign, he had spoken often of watching his mother struggling with insurance forms as she lay dying of cancer. As he traveled the country in 2007 and 2008 hundreds of voters told him their wrenching stories of medical bankruptcy or shockingly callous treatment at the hands of the insurance companies. In the White House he received scores of similar letters every day. He promised he would help.

His tactical view was that success breeds success. Even with a big win on the stimulus, he figured that the what-have-you-done-for-me-lately political culture would demand something else major before the 2010 midterms. If he didn't use his political capital in 2009, he might very well lose it.

Once Obama's commitment was clear, consensus among Democrats on a framework followed. Amid surging deficits Obama and his advisors agreed that any reform would have to be "revenue neutral," meaning *paid for.* But how? During the transition Biden had weighed in strongly against paying for health care by immediately repealing the Bush tax cuts, which were heavily tilted toward the wealthy but also helped the middle class. That would be asking Congress to raise taxes in the middle of a huge recession, which Biden argued was a non-starter. Obama agreed. The same fate awaited the idea of raising revenue by reducing the deduction for charitable contributions.

To begin addressing the cost question, the transition team floated cutting Medicare Advantage, a giveaway to the insurance industry that Obama had criticized during the campaign. Everyone on the Obama team agreed that Medicare Advantage (a supplement to basic Medicare that wasn't cost-effective and benefited wealthier seniors) had to be cut; the numbers for achieving health care reform didn't work any other way. This reflected a blithe assumption that Obama was so popular with younger voters that he could take for granted the party's longtime base among the elderly, millions of whom were misled into thinking that their essential Medicare benefits were at risk. Democrats didn't bargain for the speed with which Republicans could execute a persuasive flip-flop. As recently as 2008 the GOP had supported Medicare cuts. Now Republicans began pandering to seniors with all the fiscally irresponsible enthusiasm once employed by Democrats.

For months Obama had been reading up on health care economics. The most sensible proposal for saving money involved offering incentives to health care providers to move from the old fee-for-service model for paying doctors to the system already used by the best hospitals, where all doctors were on salary. Shifting away from fee-for-service would save billions over time. The idea would become one of the most important, if least noticed parts of the bills in Congress.

Other cost-saving plans were much sketchier. Obama suddenly had a lot of time for Orszag's highly speculative claims that "comparative effectiveness" guidelines on medical treatments could save billions, though Orszag tried to explain away the fact that while head of the Congressional Budget Office he had released reports showing that beyond hospital infection control (a critical area), there were few cost savings from government experts' advising doctors on how to practice medicine. (Orszag thought many "game changers" for cutting costs didn't "score" in CBO's calculations.) The only potential savings in this area would come from *telling* doctors how to practice: withholding reimbursements for treatments that supposedly didn't work. Once doctors and patients got wind of this, it was bound to be wildly unpopular. The medical community had little consensus on what worked scientifically because study results often conflicted, and many "best practices" over the years later turned out to be ineffective or even harmful. Litigating those effectiveness studies before newly created federal panels would be an administrative nightmare and a violation of yet another solemn Obama promise: "I will not let the government get between you and your doctor." Even after a flap over a clueless panel recommending no routine mammograms for women under 50, Orszag clung to this paternalistic idea long enough to get it into the Senate bill. Cass Sunstein, by contrast, kept insisting that true behavioral economics called for people to be nudged, not pushed, in the right direction.*

The tension between the trillion-dollar upfront expenses of reforming health care and the potential long-term savings of "bending the cost curve" would animate the Washington debate all year. Obama continued to stress that reform was a fiscal sanity issue. With baby boomers retiring, deficits would be even larger without reform. The essential question, he thought, wasn't *Can we afford to?* It was *Can we afford not to?*

Health care had a thousand moving parts, and Obama was determined not to follow Hillary Clinton's course in 1994. He would not

---

* When Harvard Medical School professor Jerome Groopman eviscerated Orszag's view in the *New York Review of Books*, blogger Mickey Kaus called for Orszag to be fired, which was not Groopman's intention.

develop a big plan, drop it on the Capitol steps like "a stone tablet," and refuse to bargain.* That, he told aides, would be the worst of both worlds: "I'd get all the [political] pain for putting out all the details, but also hit for not fulfilling campaign promises." Most important, the barons of Capitol Hill would feel they had less ownership of the issue. As with the stimulus, if they didn't own it, they wouldn't move it.

This would mean that after many years of precut deals Congress would have to get back into the messy and often unseemly business of actually legislating, an ongoing and complex process that voters didn't comprehend and the press had trouble covering. It was more comforting, if less realistic, to believe, as many progressives did, that if Obama would simply lead, the docile Democratic Congress would follow.

Some argued that Obama overlearned the lesson of the Clintons' defeat and should have introduced his own bill earlier. Politically, he would have been better off doing so. Legislatively, he would likely have been worse off trying to circumvent the congressional committee process. The bigger challenge over time was the similarity to the 1994 bill. Both were enormously complex and unwieldy plans that no one in Washington—not to mention the American people—could possibly read in their entirety, much less understand. Obama anticipated this problem, which is why from the start he laid out a strategy that emphasized avoiding details and moving quickly.

The plan called for laying out broad principles shortly after the Inauguration, winning support—or at least neutrality—from the insurance and drug industries (compensated by the arrival of 30 million new customers), and letting the congressional sausage makers do their thing. Then he'd step in later in the process. By summer this strategy would be much maligned by progressives, who wanted him to stand up and fight.

But Obama wasn't into gestures. He wanted to win.

———

NATIONAL HEALTH INSURANCE failed in the United States over the course of the twentieth century because of the opposition of doctors and the GOP. Theodore Roosevelt's Bull Moose Party first called for it in 1912, but serious consideration of the reform didn't begin until the 1930s, when Franklin Roosevelt favored what he called "cradle to grave" coverage. The opposition of southern racists—and a family con-

---

* In a swipe at the Clintons, Obama told the author during the 2008 campaign, "If Daniel Patrick Moynihan or Bill Bradley or John Chafee come to me with the possibility of compromising, I'm not going to tell them, 'It's my way or the highway.' "

nection to a prominent doctor—convinced him it was unattainable.*
After World War II Harry Truman proposed the first serious national
health insurance plan, but the American Medical Association and Republicans depicted it as "socialized medicine" and killed it. In the
1960s Lyndon Johnson went the furthest, with Medicare (for seniors)
and Medicaid (for the poor). Beyond a stab at hospital cost containment, Jimmy Carter wasn't much interested (a big reason Ted Kennedy
challenged him for the 1980 Democratic nomination), and Bill Clinton's
1993 proposal famously foundered on its complexity and botched
politics.

After Clinton lost Congress in the 1994 midterms he resolved to
make progress on health care reform incrementally.† Despite two ve-
toes by President George W. Bush, SCHIP eventually reached about
5 million children nationwide, but that still left 47 million Americans
uninsured, a number worsening daily as unemployment surged.

To get moving, Valerie Jarrett's office organized a White House
Forum on Health Reform on March 5, with a large assortment of stakeholders, health care experts, and elected officials, including Ted Kennedy in one of his last public appearances. The main sessions, though
not the breakout panels, were carried live on C-SPAN and other networks, which was as close as Obama came in his first year to fulfilling
his campaign promise to conduct the whole thing in public.

At the outset the president said his goal was "comprehensive health
care reform by the end of the year." To appeal to the Republicans in attendance, he warned "liberal bleeding hearts" not to get too ambitious
about universal coverage and advised all sides to avoid "dug-in" positions. The only thing nonnegotiable was that he would sign no bill that
contributed to the deficit. Everything else (except a single-payer plan,
which he had ruled out in 2008 as politically impractical) was on the
table. The perfect, Obama said over and over in the months that followed, should not be the enemy of the good.

The president wasn't alone in wanting to be nonspecific. In 2008
Henry Aaron, a well-respected Brookings Institution scholar, went
so far as to tell the Obama campaign that he simply couldn't support

---

* Southerners thought national health insurance would lead to integrated hospitals. The personal connection involved FDR's son James who was married at the time to Betsey Cushing,
daughter of the famed Boston surgeon Dr. Harvey Cushing. As Roosevelt weighed extending
Social Security to medical services, Cushing visited him at the White House and told him
that doing so would wreck his profession. The president backed off.
† The Republican takeover in the 1994 midterms is usually attributed to Democrats looking
impotent on health care reform, but Clinton's support for gun control measures was likely a
bigger factor.

any plan that contained more than sketchy principles. He and most of his colleagues were so burned by the experience of 1994 that they didn't even want to see any numbers. The consensus among health reform activists was that the only way to win this time was to stay vague, defer to Congress, and buy off the powerful interest groups responsible for the infamous "Harry and Louise" ads that sank reform in 1994.*

Obama knew that Franklin Roosevelt's 1935 legislation creating Social Security covered fewer than 40 percent of senior citizens. Retired domestics, state employees, and farmworkers were excluded, which meant that few blacks were covered. Many New Dealers considered the bill too watered-down to be worth enacting, a sentiment that would be heard repeatedly in 2009. But Roosevelt knew that if he could get a bill through, it could be fixed later—and it was. Social Security was strengthened in every decade that followed. The same thing happened with civil rights. The Civil Rights Act of 1957 was followed by major bills in 1964 and 1965.

The point was that the process had to start somewhere. If the bill failed, it would be another generation before a Democratic president tried again. And what would happen in the meantime?

———

THE POLITICS OF health care had begun changing in 2006, when Andy Stern's Service Employees International Union (SEIU) struck a deal with its longtime enemy, Wal-Mart. Stern, a brainy former social-services worker, had built the SEIU into the fastest growing and most innovative union in the country. His dream was to unionize Wal-Mart but he would settle for enlisting it in a larger cause. The retail giant was fiercely opposed to unionization but sensible enough to join with labor as well as the National Federation of Independent Business (the small business lobby), the Business Roundtable (the big business lobby), the AARP, the American Medical Association, and other major players in the debate, most of whom had always been against reform in the past. Under the banner "Divided We Fail" the group issued a statement saying essentially that they could all continue to despise one another but agree on the need for major changes in health care.

In April and May 2008 the stakeholders held dozens of meetings, and the uneasy alliances almost broke up several times. America's Health Insurance Plans, the giant lobby for insurers, was headed by

———

* "Harry and Louise" were a fictional couple discussing over the dinner table how Hillary Clinton's plan would hurt them.

Karen Ignani, a savvy former official of the AFL-CIO, who, over the objections of some of the CEOs she represented, decided that insurers should position themselves as pro-reform. In meetings with her board she stressed the likelihood of major change and therefore the need for insurance companies to stay at the table and shape it. If they played their cards right, insurers could end up with millions of new customers in exchange for ending their rejection of people with preexisting conditions. It would require reworking their business model (which called for expensive cherry-picking of healthy customers), but that was preferable to more radical reform that would put them out of business. And mandates forcing businesses and individuals to buy insurance were their friends.

———

EVEN SO, MOST of the industry still preferred the status quo. It was a historic fluke that Ignani, a friend of Stern, was pro-reform. So was George Halvorson, the CEO of Kaiser Permanente, a large and influential insurance company. It also helped that Jeffrey Kindler, the CEO of Pfizer, the drug giant, happened to be a Democrat, still a rarity in the ranks of CEOs. Had others been in these positions, the health care interests might have gone into full-throated opposition in March instead of October. And had loud opposition from the right begun five or six months earlier, reform would likely have failed. "Thank God August didn't happen in March," Stern said.

Part of the deal was that the industry would pay for the media to build public support for the plan. It would have been preferable if the 13 million members of "Organizing for America" (formerly Obama for America) pitched in, as they did with hundreds of millions of dollars for Obama's 2008 campaign. But their response to David Plouffe's entreaties was underwhelming. So in April Jim Messina and Senator Max Baucus's chief of staff, Jon Selib, met with corporate, union, and public interest lobbyists at the office of the Democratic Senatorial Campaign Committee to create a new coalition, "Americans for Stable Quality Care," to sponsor a media campaign in favor of health care reform. The ads they produced didn't do much to cut through the clutter, but it was better than having the interests on the other side.

An important symbolic threshold was crossed on May 11 when Obama met in the Roosevelt Room with industry and labor representatives. All agreed to commit to cutting the rate of growth in health care spending by 1.5 percent a year for ten years. That still didn't pay for the move toward universal coverage but it helped nudge the process forward. So did support from retired GOP stalwarts like Bob Dole and

Howard Baker, who noted that the ideas being floated were strikingly similar to what they proposed in the early 1990s.

From there the White House began cutting its own deals. Some were relatively easy. Obama agreed to speak to the AMA convention—the first president to do so in a quarter century—and open the door to malpractice reform (loathed by trial lawyers and the Democratic Party) in exchange for doctors' not actively opposing him. Other negotiations fell apart. The Business Roundtable decided reform was too expensive (the Chamber of Commerce, of course, had been opposed all along), and the American Hospital Association retreated after member hospitals objected to the trade organization's concessions on reimbursements.

ALL THE CLAIMS of no quid pro quo couldn't obscure the major deal cut in the Roosevelt Room in July between Rahm Emanuel and Billy Tauzin, the colorful former Louisiana congressman representing the Pharmaceutical Research and Manufacturers of America, better known as PhRMA. Rahm had long championed bills to let Medicare negotiate for lower drug prices and allow for the reimportation of cheaper prescription drugs from Canada, both loathed by the industry. Television ads on those issues were a big part of how he got the Congress back for Democrats in 2006. Obama's 2008 presidential campaign even aired a commercial targeting Tauzin personally for preventing Medicare from negotiating for lower drug prices.

Now Rahm bargained his babies away to Tauzin and Big Pharma in exchange for $80 to $95 billion in drug-price discounts and rebates, plus $150 million in ads supporting reform (the latter being pocket change for the industry). More than a third of the money would go to fill the so-called donut hole in the Bush-era Medicare prescription drug benefit, a gap that required seniors to pay out-of-pocket when their drug costs totaled between $750 and $4,550 a year. Progressives were appalled that the drug industry, which stood to gain billions from the legislation, couldn't cough up more. Drug companies thought Tauzin had given away too much.* At the time, Tauzin, whose original offer was only $22 billion, bragged that he could "whip" the House (get it to vote against reform) if he didn't get what he wanted. Because Rahm believed him, he was at a disadvantage. In the end, the filling of the donut hole survived into both the House and Senate versions of the bill, but in the confusion few seniors heard the good news.

---

* Tauzin resigned in 2010 in part because of unhappiness on his board with his support for reform.

These deals, and more to come, were not what Obama supporters had in mind when they affixed "Change We Can Believe In" stickers to their cars. Rahm tried to keep the deals quiet, but he was unapologetic about his efforts to neutralize the interest groups. "The doctors fought [Truman's] Medicare, the hospitals fought [Carter's] cost containment, the insurance companies fought children's health care," he said, ticking off the Democrats' historical failures on health care reform. "The lesson is, you gotta get the constituency groups to participate in the reform process."

The good news was that the concessions from interest groups were adding up—$80 billion from PhRMA, $150 billion from hospitals, $100 billion from the insurance industry—to the point where more than half the total price tag was committed by the very interests that had opposed reform in 1994. Sure, they were getting 30 million new customers, but many of those customers would be over 50 and sick—bad bets. Many of the interest groups realized later that it would have been smarter for them to stick to the status quo.

In the short term the success of the backroom deals validated Obama's strategic vagueness. If the president had gone public early with his own detailed plan, as many critics suggested, he would have angered various players on the specifics and likely doomed the legislation. Making enemies of powerful interests early on would have been emotionally satisfying and politically advantageous for the president, who needed more ways to show he was fighting on behalf of the middle class. But the glow of a presidential speech attacking powerful interests would wear off and the whole thing would die. The hard Washington reality was that there wasn't enough public support to propel the bill without buying off special interests, which, in turn, had protected themselves for years by buying off much of Congress.

There was cunning here. The idea was to keep interest groups on board long enough so that when the president blasted them and they went into active opposition (as the insurers and hospitals inevitably did), it would be too late to derail the bill. Or so they thought at the time.

———

IN APRIL REPRESENTATIVE Henry Waxman, chairman of the House Energy and Commerce Committee, went over to the White House to talk with the president. Waxman had just knocked off John Dingell for the chairmanship. He looked like an accountant but wielded as much power as anyone in the House.

The question was which bill, energy or health, Waxman's committee should move on first. "It's like choosing between two of your children," Obama told him. "But I care about health care more."

Waxman believed that passing health care through his committee was easier, so in order to get both done he should tackle energy first. He thought he could get both through the House over the summer. "If you get both done this year, what will you have left to do?" Obama asked with a smile.

"We'll think of something," Waxman replied.

On the Senate side, Orrin Hatch wasn't nearly as optimistic. He thought Ted Kennedy's absence would doom health care reform altogether. Hatch had been elected to the Senate from Utah in 1976 by campaigning against Kennedy, but they had become good friends and worked together on bipartisan legislation. Kennedy, he believed, was the only senator who could temper the demands of the liberals while nudging conservative colleagues like him toward a workable compromise.

Where Kennedy's absence was felt most acutely was in the Democratic caucus. Many Democrats said privately that if Kennedy had been driving the process, the bill would have been more progressive, more bipartisan, and more on schedule. His committee was taken over by Chris Dodd, but most of the action moved instead to Max Baucus and the Senate Finance Committee he chaired.*

Baucus was an amiable Westerner of middling stature in the Senate who gave Bush crucial bipartisan support for his massive tax cuts in 2001. He issued a white paper endorsing health care reform in 2008 that got things rolling in the Senate at an important moment. Now he insisted that he and his pal Chuck Grassley, the ranking Republican, could work across the aisle with four other members of his committee to get something done. The moment the Big Six took control of the process, the White House knew it was going to be ugly. The six states represented—Montana, Wyoming, Maine, North Dakota, New Mexico, and Iowa—made up only 3 percent of the U.S. population, but this hardly deterred the senators from thinking it was fitting that the fate of health care rested in their hands.

Baucus and his staff did important work on the mind-bending details of the bill, but all spring he kept missing deadlines—May 15, June 15—and now he was going home for the July 4th recess without a bill. On July 14 Obama invited the congressional leadership and the committee chairmen to the White House for a status report. The House bills seemed to be moving, though even they were slowed by the immense

---

* In January 2010 Dodd, facing a tough reelection fight, announced his retirement.

complexity involved in reshaping an industry that constituted one sixth of the American economy. The president pointedly asked Baucus what the problem was in the Senate. Baucus stressed the importance of a bipartisan effort, which by this point was becoming a threadbare answer. The president seemed mildly irritated. "I got the sense that the urgency barometer is going up," Baucus said afterward. But Obama fatefully declined to change his strategy by leaning harder on Baucus to begin markup (the period in the legislative process where amendments are introduced and a "marked-up" bill gains momentum). He figured that would alienate the moderates in both parties whose support he would need for passage.

Inside the Finance Committee Grassley's foot-dragging was slowly killing the bill. Jim Messina, who had won his job as White House deputy chief of staff in part because of his longstanding relationship with Baucus (and his knowledge of Western politics), pleaded with his old boss to forget Grassley, secure the Democrats, and then do a deal with Olympia Snowe, a moderate Republican from Maine on the committee. Baucus was having marital troubles (he would file for divorce in August), and he was happy to have dinner with Messina nearly every week in the spring and summer. The senator always told his former aide, whom he described as like a son to him, the same thing in private that he said in public: he and Chuck would produce a better, more generally acceptable bill than anyone else. Some Democrats urged Harry Reid to sidestep Baucus and just take Chris Dodd's bill, which had won committee approval earlier, directly to the Senate floor. But Reid was old-school and deferred to Baucus. Had Tom Daschle, who centralized power, still been majority leader, he would have likely bypassed Baucus by this point. But passage would have been difficult at best, as it was when then–Senate Majority Leader George Mitchell got crushed when he tried to go to the floor with the Clinton proposal in 1994. The moderate Democrats on the Finance Committee would have felt disrespected and almost certainly voted against.

Among the Republicans, Mike Enzi of Wyoming was toying with Baucus, with no intention of ever voting for a bill, but Grassley seemed more genuinely torn. Grassley told colleagues that Arizona Senator Jon Kyl, the Senate minority whip, was being so nasty toward him that he was souring on the Senate and might retire. Rahm and Messina didn't believe that, and they thought the president was wasting his time by having Grassley over to the White House half a dozen times. They knew that Grassley—and their last shot at true bipartisanship—was lost just before the August recess, when Obama asked him a simple question: "If we give you everything you want—and agree to no public plan—can you guarantee you would support the bill?"

"I can't guarantee I would," Grassley said.

Baucus was nothing if not loyal to his friends. Even when Grassley went back for an August town meeting and started touting Glenn Beck's book and warning that "death panels" would mean "pulling the plug on Grandma," Baucus didn't give up on him. He figured that was just Iowa politics, that Chuck had to indulge the right wing. Finally Baucus saw a fund-raising letter from Grassley that ripped everything about "ObamaCare," including many of the features Baucus thought they had agreed on in committee. That—and a successful visit by the president to a Montana town meeting—finally got him moving. He returned from the recess committed to pass a bill out of his committee, which he did on October 13.

Just to be safe, Rahm had signed off in April on what he called "an insurance policy," a clause in the budget bill that allowed the Senate to pass provisions related to health care through the budget "reconciliation" process, which required only fifty-one instead of sixty votes. Under Senate rules only those parts of the health care bill specifically related to taxing and spending could be passed that way, which meant that any final product would, in the words of the Senate parliamentarian, "look like Swiss cheese." But it was something that might come in useful if all else failed. The *Washington Post* blogger Ezra Klein called the gambit "the equivalent of having your mean, heavily-tattooed older brother stand quietly behind you when you ask the kids down the street if you can play ball with them." But the older brother appeared too menacing to the bipartisan traditions of the Senate and the idea languished until 2010.

Harry Reid knew from long experience with the opposition that there would be no "Kumbaya moment" when the Republicans would concede error and convert to support for comprehensive health care reform. This was going to be a Democratic deal, with maybe Snowe and Susan Collins, just like the stimulus. By this time Democratic senators were starting to worry. Crucial time had been lost chasing a mirage. Baucus's dawdling had wrecked the president's timetable.

But the ultimate blame rested in the White House. "We should have taken the hit for ending bipartisanship early because it was never going to be bipartisan," a senior White House aide said later. "I love Max Baucus, but I wish we'd put our foot down harder and said, 'It's over, Max.'"

FOR A CERTAIN species of C-SPAN viewer, following the health care debate was like following sports. Fans paying especially close attention knew that all the bills working their way through Congress had basic elements in common: coverage for 31 million Americans out of 47 million uninsured (the Republican plans insured 3 million); mandates compelling employers and employees to buy insurance or face financial penalties; subsidies to help the uninsured buy policies on new "exchanges," like the one created in Massachusetts; generous help for small businesses that would be required to insure employees; Medicare cuts and industry givebacks for cost control; tough new regulations of the insurance industry, including bans on discrimination against those with preexisting conditions; and new incentives for preventive care. The bills had hundreds of other complex moving parts, but the big sticking points over time were how to pay for the upfront implementation of reform ($700 billion to $900 billion over ten years), how to contain costs long-term, and whether to include a public option.

The public option was originated in 2005 by a Berkeley professor, Jacob Hacker, as a compromise for progressives who preferred a single-payer plan but knew it had no chance of passage. The idea was to give people some choice other than the insurance company monopolies and to provide competition that would drive down costs. The concept polled well, but played into a narrative of coercive big government that was starting to get traction among independent voters. Liberals liked the public option for the same reason conservatives reviled it. Each side thought the plan was a nose under the tent, a way to bring on a single-payer system, which was either the commonsense Medicare-for-all approach adopted by most other industrialized countries or a nefarious "government takeover," depending on one's perspective.

The truth was that even the most "robust" (the latest buzzword) public option would not lead to single payer, if for no other reason than that the nation wouldn't stomach another big health care debate for at least a generation. A public option was to be available only to the uninsured, which meant that more than 90 percent of the liberal activists cheering for it would not be able to buy into it themselves. Even if it succeeded in driving down costs, no one knew by how much. (For all the publicity given to Congressional Budget Office projections, their fancy numbers were largely guesswork.) The White House saw it as merely "a means to an end," not the heart of the bill, and was skeptical all year that more than fifty-one or fifty-two senators would support it.

On one level the loud public option debate was good for the overall prospects of the bill because it distracted media attention from more divisive story lines, such as the mandates forcing individuals and companies to buy insurance. But the public option flap also crowded out discussion of the historic nature of the reform. Liberals lost perspective. The number of voters who in the 2008 campaign backed Obama explicitly because he supported a public option was tiny. How could it be otherwise? While there was plenty of talk about "choice and competition," the phrase "public option" wasn't used a single time in a single campaign speech, TV ad, or presidential debate in 2008 by any candidate in either party. But now it became a rallying cry for the liberal base.

This drove the White House around the bend. Were liberal Democrats really going to sacrifice universal coverage and ending discrimination against sick people—ideas for which they had been fighting for decades—for a public option? Messina met with progressive groups and put it to them: "Eighteen months ago you never heard of a public option and now you're willing to die in the streets for it?" Rahm thought they were "fucking crazy." He told anyone who would listen that a public option wasn't necessary. But with the president delivering another message, liberals began to feel they were getting taken for granted.

Reid's head count showed as early as May that there simply weren't enough votes in the Senate for a public option. And here the White House made a tactical mistake. Obama should have either acknowledged the death of the public option and explained why it wasn't essential—or dug in for a fight. Instead he chose to muddle through. Rahm's pique at clueless liberals who didn't know anything about getting legislation passed clouded his judgment about how to fashion a message for the Democratic Party. He thought he could satisfy the base by having Obama lash out rhetorically at insurance companies, but it wasn't enough. Liberals wanted to see their president fighting for them over something. Instead, the most enthusiastic proponent of health care in the White House—the one who insisted on it over the objections of his team—was made to look lukewarm about the whole thing.

Obama's view was that he needed to stay open to all ideas, so he listened to the proposal offered by Senator Kent Conrad for a series of health care cooperatives and asked Conrad to show him how it would work in practice on a national scale. Conrad never came up with anything real, and West Virginia's Jay Rockefeller and others derided co-ops as a joke.

The "trigger" for a public option, favored by Snowe and Rahm, offered better grounds for compromise. A trigger meant that the public option would only be offered if, down the road, there wasn't enough genuine competition in the exchanges to reduce costs. But the trigger was rejected out of hand by liberals. George Miller pointed out that triggers had never worked on other issues. "It's the equivalent of 'I'll still love you in the morning,' " he said. Baucus and Snowe argued that it would actually be more of a club over the heads of insurers than a public option, but by that time liberals were passionately committed. Many didn't seem to be familiar with any other provisions of the entire bill.

––––––––

ALTHOUGH THE PRESIDENT didn't want Waxman to move forward on energy first, he went all-out to win approval of the cap-and-trade bill, calling dozens of members of Congress.* Even so, Obama was shocked that Waxman managed to get an energy bill through the House on June 27. It was only Waxman's astonishing skill at putting together a 1,400-page bill that kept energy headed down the track.

Relations between the chambers, never warm, now took a turn for the worse. After the energy bill passed the House, Baucus informed Waxman that it was going nowhere in the Senate and that it wouldn't be revisited for "quite a while." This hardly discouraged Waxman or made him feel he'd made a mistake. He thought it worthwhile to have moved a bill just to "show the Senate how to do it." It was a marker, he said, the first ever price set on carbon, even though the bill wasn't likely to become law for the foreseeable future.

The White House political operation thought passing the energy bill through the House was one of the biggest mistakes of the year—a shock to the body politic. Having cast a tough vote for cap and trade and watched it languish in the Senate, plenty of House members would be leery of getting burned again on another big piece of legislation, namely health care.

More important, by holding back on finalizing his committee's version of the health care bill until July, Waxman lost track of time. Passing an energy bill meant that the House would miss Obama's deadline of getting a health care bill through the House by the August recess. Now both chambers were far behind schedule and about to face angry constituents. Instead of bringing home a completed bill that could be explained, members of the House would have to offer their constituents a work-in-progress. It didn't bode well.

––––––––

* Cap and trade, already at work in Europe, called for the creation of an administrative authority that would grant pollution permits that could be traded on an exchange. Because emissions would be capped—placing a price on carbon—the scheme would simultaneously reduce emissions and let the traders make money.

FOR MONTHS PETER Orszag and the president liked to tout research produced by the Dartmouth Institute that showed astonishing regional variations in per capita Medicare reimbursements. It turned out that more wasn't necessarily better when it came to health care in the United States. In fact areas of the country that spent more on health care often had worse results. Green Bay, Wisconsin, was a good example. While Medicare spent an average of more than $71,000 per end-stage patient in Miami and Los Angeles, it spent only $33,000 in Green Bay and hospital stays there were 25 percent shorter than the national average, yet with no worse outcomes.

Obama went to Green Bay to drive home the point. But confronting regional disparities was harder than it seemed. The government couldn't simply force local hospitals to conform to certain federal standards without eliciting cries of "rationing." Sure enough, at the end of the year new recommendations for women being screened less often for cervical and breast cancer, while independent of reform efforts, raised just such worries.

Meanwhile Obama seemed to have sided with Orszag over Sunstein. Appearing on *Good Morning America* on June 24 Obama dodged Diane Sawyer's question about whether his reform would require doctors using "best practices"—even if there was no consensus—"by law." The Senate bill would, and the House bill would not. This was potentially a far more critical piece of the package than the public option, abortion, or many other provisions. Health care reform would not include "death panels," but there would apparently be government panels, with power, on just about everything else.

Not that comparative effectiveness would necessarily save much money. The Congressional Budget Office, under Douglas Elmendorf, kept shooting down Orszag's cost savings, at one point issuing a report that Orszag's ideas would save a measly $2 billion. Then in mid-July Elmendorf shocked Washington by "scoring" the pending bills on Capitol Hill in such a way that they seemed unaffordable. "The curve is being raised," Elmendorf wrote, in a direct rebuke to his predecessor, Orszag. Elmendorf was summoned to the White House for what became known as the "Showdown of the CBO Directors," a wonkfest for those obsessed, as so many in Washington were just then, with the details of health care.

"Will it bend the cost curve?" in the capital was like "What were the weekend grosses?" in Los Angeles or "Who took a haircut on the deal?" in New York. You could often walk down Pennsylvania Avenue in front of the White House and overhear snatches of conversation about the nuances of health care economics as Washingtonians tried to show they were au courant.

————

IT WASN'T TRUE that the angry town meetings of the August recess were the turning point of the health care reform debate. The big swoon in Obama's approval ratings had actually come in May and June, before the town meetings, when Americans suffering under double-digit unemployment seemed to lose their appetite for social experimentation.

Andy Stern of the SEIU called all the bailouts a "dragging anchor" on Obama's progress on health care and other concerns. "Had he not inherited so much, the momentum of his election would have carried him further," Stern said. By summer Obama had lost the thread of the conversation with independents. Was he changing Washington, or was Washington changing him?

"Our success in stemming the panic in the first three months created huge political problems for us, because people started looking around and saying, 'Well, why are you bailing out the banks?' or 'What are you doing with the auto industry?' " Obama said later. "It's very hard to prove a counterfactual, where you say, 'You know, things really could have been a lot worse here.' "

Axelrod thought the political problems for Obama began in the spring, when the action shifted to the congressional "sausage factory" and the debate began centering on the public option. It took on "outsized significance" by "giving the left a rallying cry and the Republicans a wedge—an entry point—to start yammering about government-run health care," Axelrod said. "The coverage was largely about the sport of it, the point scoring—'Here's what the Finance Committee is doing' and 'Here's what CBO says.' It's a hard thing to manage even if you're president because a lot of the action is being driven on the Hill."

The president deserved his share of the blame for the flagging fortunes of his program. For months he had trouble locating what Jarrett called "the right vocabulary" on health care: "It was like he was trying to find the combination on a lock—how to say this in ways that people could understand." Obama later confessed that he said to himself over the summer, "I've got to step up my game. I'm not breaking through." Even though he avoided jargon, his town meetings and press conferences were too professorial and antiseptic.

The root of his communications problem in late spring and early summer was that Obama misunderstood the argument over *costs*. He believed that the original argument had to be focused on paying for the bill, but Americans were more interested in how to pay *their* bills. The more the public heard about confusing health care spending details, the less it liked the whole idea. Obama and the Democrats had to explain why the country needed to spend a trillion dollars today to save trillions of dollars tomorrow. It was a hard sell.

After cost didn't fly as a selling point, the president tried to stress improved quality. But most voters thought their doctors were pretty good, so they couldn't see backing the plan on quality grounds. That left "stability and security" as the message. It was accurate enough, but boring, not to mention smacking of poll testing. The Wednesday night meetings at Axelrod's apartment were attended by political and press operatives from the White House and the DNC who had almost unanimously opposed undertaking reform in 2009 because they thought the politics were so bad. So it figured they wouldn't be creative in reframing a debate they didn't really want to be having.

In retrospect Axelrod believed that the president should have shifted earlier to highlighting "insurance reform" as his theme. When rumors surfaced that he was wobbly on the public option, he sent a letter to Senate Democrats stressing his strong support for it. It would "keep the insurance companies honest," he said. But by then people were so dug in that few were listening.

The problem for the White House was that voters were dug in on the right but not the left. During the campaign Obama liked to say, "We are the ones we've been waiting for."* By the August recess it was clear that "we" weren't showing up at the town meetings or much of anywhere else. There were, in fact, thousands of small meetings in support of health care reform, but they hardly constituted the "wind at my back" that Obama had enjoyed in 2008, much less a mighty social movement for change.

———

"IF WE'RE ABLE to stop Obama on this, it will be his Waterloo. It will break him," South Carolina Senator Jim DeMint said in July. This intense personalizing of policy differences was both malicious and clarifying. For certain conservatives Obama was not an adversary; he was the enemy, and the forces arrayed against him grew rapidly, some from the genuine grassroots and some from "AstroTurf" lobbying, where powerful interests fund "spontaneous" demonstrations.

The "tea party" movement was born in February when a CNBC

———

* The line originated with the poet June Jordan in 1980 and was adopted by the group Sweet Honey and the Rock. Obama picked it up from the Rev. Jim Wallis of Sojourners.

reporter, Rick Santelli, a self-described "Ayn Rander," went on a rant against Obama on the floor of the Chicago Board of Trade.* "This is America," Santelli said over the din. "How many of you people want to pay for your neighbor's mortgage [when he has] an extra bathroom and can't pay the bills?" He promised a "Chicago tea party" for summer. Santelli quickly retreated from politics in favor of continuing his career as a business news correspondent, but the idea caught on, funded by a conservative AstroTurf coalition called FreedomWorks (headed by former House Majority Leader Dick Armey) and hyped by Fox and talk radio. A young conservative teacher in Washington state named Keli Calender was credited as the first Tea Party organizer, giving the movement some grassroots cred.

The crowds at the early tea parties were small, but they grew bigger for the tumultuous town meetings during the August recess (covered on cable only when there was angry shouting) and eventually drew tens of thousands to the National Mall on September 12.† The protesters marching on Washington were incoherent politically, but they were good at getting publicity. A noisy group of "birthers" got attention for claiming, with no evidence, that Obama wasn't born in the United States and thus was not legitimately president.‡ Others had ties to militia groups determined to challenge the legitimacy of the federal government. Long after press accounts proved that the bills contained no "death panels" to determine when to end life support for the elderly, Sarah Palin and her followers continued to peddle the canard.

The fraudulent "death panel" debate failed to change any minds, of course, but it did focus attention on the effect of the legislation on the elderly, which hurt Obama. And it highlighted how much simpler and more effective the Republican messages were, even if they weren't always true.

By not setting out his own specifics, Obama was staying flexible for the end game. But the gambit jeopardized a big chunk of the traditional Democratic base among the elderly. Even if they wouldn't be affected by the cuts in Medicare Advantage, senior citizens had genuine reason to fear that all the Washington talk of cutting costs might lead

---

* Rand, the author of *Atlas Shrugged*, was a libertarian and ardent capitalist.

† The organizer spread a photo on the Web purporting to show a crowd exceeding one million, but the picture was actually from a 1997 rally for the Promise Keepers, a Christian group.

‡ It was a mark of how far this lunacy had entered the mainstream of the GOP that Tom DeLay, the de facto Republican leader of the House for twelve years, demanded that the president produce his birth certificate.

someday to a reduction in their standard Medicare benefits.* Of all the communications failures of the health care debate, the inability of the White House to reassure seniors was the most inexplicable.

———

OBAMA HAD ENORMOUS confidence in his ability to sell something politically, and so he set out on a July tour. He began in Minnesota, with the "Fired up! Ready to Go!" chant. Everywhere he went he tried to turn up the heat on insurance companies, but they made a surprisingly elusive target. Some of these companies were sponsoring ads in favor of reform, which made them hard to attack by name. And it wasn't in Obama's nature to lash out anyway.

At first the president ignored many of the best arguments for reform. He didn't focus on people losing their insurance when they lost their jobs because doing so would shine a light on the fact that the stimulus hadn't fully kicked in yet and jeopardize his message of renewed confidence. So he lost a chance to connect health care to the recession. For similar reasons he didn't talk often about soaring "medical bankruptcies." Americans have an optimistic tendency to see illness and bankruptcy as things that happen to other people. They didn't want to think about it. And the president shied away from placing discrimination against the sick in the category of historic injustice, which would have turned health care into a civil rights issue. Polls suggested that connecting the debate to civil rights was a bad idea. People had enough troubles without worrying about someone else's right to see a doctor.

To make matters more confusing, Obama was still vacillating on the public option. Full-throated support wouldn't move any Senate skeptics, but admission that a public option was dead would infuriate liberals. Instead, as Senator Jack Reed noted, Obama took a leaf from FDR and decided to keep everyone guessing about his real views.

Why didn't he call lawmakers from both parties and both houses and flesh out on specifics instead of letting health care become a rugby scrum? When Obama looked back on it after the Massachusetts debacle, he conceded that this strategy—the one he finally implemented in 2010—would have been the best way to go in 2009, too. He had thought seriously about a British-style "Question Time" with Republicans as early as February 2009, but after his unpleasant experience with the GOP on the stimulus he decided against it. That, he later

———

* A disturbing number of angry constituents had no idea what they were talking about. Summer 2009 brought the spectacle of people getting up at town meetings and shouting to their hapless representatives, "Get the government's hands off my Medicare!"

concluded, was a mistake. Meeting with the Republicans on television would have kept the 2009 debate more civil. It was one campaign promise he should have kept earlier.

––––––––

INSTEAD, ALL OBAMA felt he could do at the time was stroke Congress and plan for the unexpected, which the staff did endlessly. Over the summer Rahm worked his aides to the bone by forcing them to write the White House's own secret health care plan, more than eight hundred pages of carefully crafted language that they hoped would pass muster among Democrats in both chambers if it had to be activated. The White House bill, which was never released, closely tracked what Obama later said in his speech before Congress: it taxed Cadillac plans, but with certain exemptions for labor; used tax credits (as favored by the Senate) to improve affordability; stayed neutral on the Orszag "best practices" debate; and included the kind of modest tort reform Obama was already on record supporting. It featured no public option because the White House knew that was a nonstarter.

Rahm insisted that every contingency be covered. If Baucus's bill fell short in the Senate Finance Committee, the White House would take its own bill directly to the floor. If it failed there, they'd come up with another compromise. If that deal didn't work, they'd move to reconciliation.

One day in August the president appeared at the morning staff meeting and quoted one of his favorite movies, *Apollo 13*. "Failure," he said, "is not an option."

16

Professor-in-Chief

Looking back over 2009 Obama felt he had "two fundamental obligations." The first was to rescue the economy from imminent collapse, to "pull it out of the ditch" and begin creating jobs. The second was to stop "papering over problems" and make long-term investments to strengthen the economy. He neglected to mention a third obligation that he embraced: to explain his progress to America and the world and try to bring the public along.

Obama was famous as a good explainer with a professorial air. On TV he was convincing, even compelling. Those who paid attention learned something (though not as much as they did from Bill Clinton, the master of the illuminating public policy explanation). Beyond responding to daily events, Obama saw his role as tying together the strands of his policy in a natural and comprehensible way. But as early as March the president thought his White House was losing the thread of the argument.

Over the course of the year the communications problem went from bad to worse. It was partly his fault and partly a function of the unwillingness—or inability—of the political culture to answer his Inaugural call to "put aside childish things." The net effect brought a surprising irony: before taking office, Obama was expected to ace communications and personal narrative and struggle in executive leadership; instead, the reverse happened.

In September 2008 John McCain had turned to Obama in their first debate and accused him of not understanding "the difference between a tactic and a strategy." This was rich coming from McCain, who was arguably the most tactical politician in Washington and whose campaign languished for lack of a strategy. But it was also 180 degrees wrong about Obama. The president had never been especially good as a tactician; his measured and wordy sentences—free of catchphrases—could leave him a step behind in the normal Washington tit-for-tat. Strategy was his strong suit, or at least he liked to think so.

That's what left him so frustrated now. After a brilliant campaign strategy, a good transition strategy, and a workable first-month strategy, the president felt he lacked a coherent idea of where to go from here. All the crisis management and Bush cleanup was just treading water. "We have to take this thing big," Obama told his senior staff in late winter.

With major victories on the stimulus and the budget, Obama was doing well, but restless. He kept saying publicly that the challenge was like "turning around an ocean liner, not a speedboat" (a rare memorable metaphor). But was the larger point sinking in? Rahm was brilliant, the president told aides, but his ideas were scattershot and too tactical. He would see something in the paper, jump on it as no one else could, and turn it to political advantage with a presidential announcement or event. Unfortunately the pudding had no theme.

God knows Obama had been trying to make his program hang together. At a press conference on March 24 he outlined what he called his "comprehensive strategy."

Step One was the recovery program, already in place.

Step Two was to stabilize the housing markets, which turned out, he said at his next press conference, to be harder than he had hoped.

Step Three was to start the flow of credit. He noted that the TALF program (begun under Bush, though that went unmentioned) had securitized more loans in the previous week than in the past four months combined.

Step Four he called "the most critical part of our strategy." That was investment in renewable energy, education, and reforming health care, while "reducing nondefense discretionary spending to the lowest levels since the 1960s."

All these steps sounded logical, and yet the stairwell didn't seem to lead anywhere. People were lost.

On his trip to Europe in the first week of April he and Axelrod talked about how events were moving at such warp speed that it was easy to lose the forest for the trees. The president thought that the public just wasn't getting the thematic relationship between his different proposals. "People want to know what's it going to look like on the other end of the recession," as Anita Dunn later explained it. "They've been patient through the rough times but need his vision of a better place."

This was the generous view of the American public, an assumption that voters had what Dunn called a "very sophisticated" understanding of how reducing our dependence on foreign oil, reforming our bloated health care system, and fixing our public schools were all connected to putting the economy on a sounder long-term footing. Dunn argued that the people understood that it was bad out there and weren't looking for miracles, only some signs of progress. "Timidity is the worst politics," she concluded. That in itself was a conceptual breakthrough for Democrats, who had reconciled themselves to a cautious and incrementalist approach the last time they were in power.

Obama's economic speech on April 14 at Georgetown University was his most significant attempt all year to paint on a larger canvas. First he outlined his rescue plan in detail, explaining to populist skeptics that a dollar of capital in a bank can result in eight to ten dollars of loans to families and businesses. To critics of his decision not to nationalize the banks he said, "Government should practice the same principle as doctors: 'First, do no harm.' " Nationalization, he noted, would cost a lot more money and undermine confidence.

It was the next part of the speech that marked a change in the scope of his argument. Obama described for the Jesuit university audience the parable at the end of the Sermon on the Mount about one man who built his house upon a rock and another who built on sand.*

Obama said his "new foundation" for the economy had "five pillars": new rules for Wall Street to reward innovation, investments in education to make the workforce more competitive, investments in renewable energy and green jobs, investments in health care reform to cut costs for both families and businesses, and deficit reduction to protect future generations.

At first glance the connective tissue seemed a little thin. Exactly how would he add all that spending but reduce the deficit? Calling it "investment" wouldn't do the trick, nor would limiting tax increases to those making more than $250,000 a year, as he promised during the campaign. He had said in a recent press conference that the aim of the package of large investments was "to ensure that we do not return to an economic cycle of bubble and bust." But what exactly was the connection between, say, better education and reducing volatility in the markets? Or green jobs and deficit reduction?

The answer was straight out of the song "Dem Bones" ("The knee bone's connected to the thigh bone, the thigh bone's connected to the . . ."), though no one in the White House put it that way. Obama believed that in the twenty-first century all the big problems were directly connected to one another. Education reforms (particularly community colleges, which he was bolstering) were connected to economic

---

* White House advance teams covered up monograms of Jesus that would have turned up in the shot.

growth, which was in turn dependent on reducing health care costs and transitioning to clean energy. A newly trained workforce in green jobs (that could not be shipped overseas) would give the American economy a broader and healthier base for growth than financial engineering. That new economy would, in turn, produce enough income to reduce the deficit if it wasn't swamped by rising health care costs. And all these connections applied globally, where the long-term prospects of the global economy depended on political stability, which was connected to education in the developing world (especially for women) and to confronting the destabilizing prospects of climate change, all in the context of an open trading system based on real productivity gains instead of bubbles. That was the theory, anyway.

But even then, there were problems with the message. Simon Rosenberg of the New Democratic Network, a think tank for the Democratic Party, saw immediately that Obama's recipe for long-term economic growth by cutting health care costs and moving off foreign oil, though commendable, was at odds with the conventional recovery that his own economic team sought, one that featured rising real estate prices and robust consumer sales. Reform, in that sense, was at odds with recovery. Obama, he said, was lacking a "holistic economic narrative," a strategy for bringing back the middle class. Long-term thinking was fine, Rosenberg and other prominent Democrats said, but it shouldn't come before more attempts at job creation. By the middle of the year some analysts had begun to think that no energy and health care bills would be preferable to the ones that seemed poised for passage.

Obama believed he could have a semiconventional recovery *and* reform. He had fashioned an overarching theme, a "new foundation," but would it register? Only if the jobs picture improved significantly. For many Americans the president was too airy, even pedantic, and not attentive enough to the heartache of the unemployed. Though he talked a lot in the abstract about empathy, he wasn't showing enough of it, which worried Axelrod's Wednesday night group.

But Obama thought that he couldn't plausibly talk about jobs yet, an omission that set him up for the anger to come. It wasn't until fall that he conveyed to the public that he was focusing daily on their number-one concern. "The truth is, without economic growth there was no way to stem the job losses," he said later. "So our first practical task was to make sure that this recession did not slip into a depression, and that we were able to get the economy growing again." To promise lower unemployment when the economy was still shedding four hundred thousand to five hundred thousand jobs a month, he said, "would have been building whatever house we built on sand."

Or perhaps on hope. Here Obama's political probity—his determination not to promise something he couldn't deliver—sent him off-message. Obama didn't want to talk about jobs until a real recovery began, and he knew the stimulus would be slow. But by letting the focus shift away from putting people to work his narrative became fuzzy.

He would pivot to jobs after Labor Day, he figured. When health care was done.

———

OBAMA'S SPEECHES SHOWED how his orderly mind worked. The process usually began with what Jon Favreau called the "download," when Obama would outline off the top of his head what he wanted to say and the speechwriters would take notes. It was intimidating to write speeches for a man they considered the best-writing American president since Lincoln, though Obama was generous with credit and he encouraged his writers to stretch themselves and take risks with turns of phrase.

Obama spoke publicly almost every day, and his aides preferred him to use a teleprompter. The prepared remarks went over better that way, in part because the president was a little farsighted and squinted slightly at the written text or talking points when he had no prompter. (Because his eyesight had not yet deteriorated to the point that he felt he needed reading glasses, no one seemed to have mentioned the squinting to him.) His use of the teleprompter was seized on by critics as evidence that he was overly scripted, which was ridiculous considering that he often made more off-the-cuff public remarks in a week than most presidents did in a month, and some (for instance, Reagan) in a year.

Prepared speeches were just part of the daily routine, but every so often the president would say, "I want to give a race speech." By that he meant that it was time to say something big and potentially important, like the one he gave on race in Philadelphia during the campaign. How important—and whether the words would someday end up on the wall of his presidential library—would not be clear for years. Almost all the rhetoric was destined to fade. It was the policy commitments that would loom largest. His description of Afghanistan as a "war of necessity" in an August 17 speech in Phoenix to the Veterans of Foreign Wars may have been his most fateful utterance of 2009.

Most of Obama's speeches followed a pattern. He favored what he and his speechwriters called "naming." Sometimes that meant literally naming names, as he did when he said something touching and specific about all thirteen Americans killed by an Arab-American army psychologist at the base at Fort Hood, Texas. More often "naming" meant identifying particular problems, challenges, counterarguments ("Now, some have argued that this recovery plan is a case of irresponsible government spending"). Naming was specific without being blunt, precise without being boring. It cut away the cloudiness of most rhetoric without losing all the poetry. Obama's Georgetown speech and his address at the National Archives on Guantánamo and the tension between freedom and security were good examples of the type.

This contrapuntal structure was unusual in that it risked giving some airtime to the other side's perspective. It trusted the audience to identify the superior argument he was making. When he said he was "not naïve" about Republicans, he exposed himself to the charge that he was. When he made a point of knocking down arguments that the CIA was involved in the Iranian street protests, he left room for "Obama Denies CIA Ties to Iran Dissidents" headlines all over the world. The straw man mode of argumentation worked better in private discussion than in public dialogue, and yet he seemed to get away with it most of the time.

A related quality of his speeches and impromptu remarks was their complexity. "We don't write sound bites," said Ben Rhodes, the foreign policy speechwriter. Obama's gift, he argued, was in "distilling complexity, explaining complexity, and respecting the complexity of the world." Ever since the Philadelphia race speech during the campaign was a hit without sound bites, Obama felt his rejection of sound bites had been validated. He loathed what he called the "talking points" of modern politics, the predictable one-liners.

This diffidence toward cogency was ahistorical. From Lincoln's "a house divided against itself cannot stand" to Reagan's "Mr. Gorbachev, tear down this wall!" handy encapsulations have helped presidents govern. Sound bites gave video editors and reporters a common hook for their stories, which made it easier to frame the president's message and imprint it in the public consciousness. Without them, speeches were like fast food that left you hungry again soon after the meal.

Obama prided himself on respecting the intelligence of the voters but he sometimes needed help connecting with the average person. During the 2008 Pennsylvania primary he claimed that the mistake he made in saying some voters "cling" to guns and religion (his only major gaffe of the entire campaign) was one of "syntax." Afterward Senator Claire McCaskill told him, "Barack, don't use that word 'syntax' again. In Missouri we think that's the tax we pay on beer."

Obama took the point about keeping things simple but he hadn't treated Americans like children in the 2008 campaign and he wasn't about to start now. The president thought that part of not talking down to people was skipping the usual chest-beating rhetoric. He generally avoided saying things just so Americans would feel good about themselves. It might be cathartic to attack the Iranian regime or inspirational to pledge (as Bush did in his Second Inaugural) to end tyranny around the world, but it wasn't productive. Bush's line "Either you are with us or with the terrorists" would have been unthinkable coming from Obama. He usually resisted the temptation to excoriate Republicans for the same reason: it substituted satisfaction for results.

But Obama believed that even a complicated speech should try to tell a story. A speech could enumerate points and lay out detailed policy ideas, but he insisted it not "sound like a laundry list." In 2009 the story arc was usually a variation of "how we got in this mess and how we will get out of it." This was where the artistry came in, as he connected tangled policy questions to the lives of Americans with the help of carefully chosen anecdotes about real people.

The naming, the complexity, the avoidance of feel-good sentiment, and the storytelling worked only if they rang true. In the hands of speechwriters these qualities of good writing had to clarify and illuminate his argument or they were pointless, in which case he would flip that page of the speech over and write out in longhand precisely what he wanted to say.

The president's assumption about the intelligence and common sense of his audience was optimistic, even Pollyannaish, but for most of 2009 it seemed to work even when his listeners didn't fully understand what he was saying. "He treats people like adults," Rhodes said. "He doesn't think they're not smart enough or can't handle someone explaining the problems—whether it's race in America or the problems of the Muslim world. He knows that explaining things to people like they're adults is a sign of respect. It's also a bit of a prerequisite for progress. He's telling people not to be afraid of what's going on in the economy, or differences we have with people around the world, or changes that are taking place in the twenty-first century. He's saying, 'If we talk through this, we can get through this.' "

But before long Obama began paying a price for favoring complex versions of policies over those with simple, elegant designs and colorful metaphors that were easier to sell. Even when he did come up with a catchphrase ("New Foundation"), he neglected to repeat it often enough for it to sink in. And for all his well-crafted tales of ordinary Americans, he neglected his own personal narrative. Hawaii, Harvard, Chicago, the campaign—then what? For many people, everything he did after arriving in the White House was a blur. His visceral connection to their economic hardship was still hard to feel.

Moreover, a lot of Americans weren't adults; they were more like the boisterous kids in the back of the car when Dad is trying to drive through a hurricane. And for at least a generation they had been more attuned to pictures than words. The White House had no stage manager, no one to do for Obama what Michael Deaver did for Reagan and Harry and Linda Bloodworth-Thomason did for Clinton. It was easy for Obama backers to laugh at that and call it superficial, but staging counted. Whether he liked it or not, Obama was a performer in the theater of the presidency. Axelrod was a wordsmith, not an expert on visuals, but the bigger impediment to changing the communications strategy was Obama himself.

"It can't be too staged," said Marty Nesbitt. "He's going to tell the truth even when it's the hard truth, and without tricky rhymes or slogans. It takes time for the realness to take root, but he thinks it will." Here Nesbitt quoted something Michelle said when they were first discussing running for president in 2006: "If we can't do this being ourselves, I don't want to win."

ALL WORDS, NO deeds. Both Hillary Clinton and John McCain tried to make that argument about Obama. It followed the classic advice offered by political consultants, to turn your opponent's strength into a weakness. (The most notorious example was the Swift Boat Veterans for Truth using John Kerry's greatest asset, his heroism in Vietnam, against him.) In Obama's case the idea was to use his great speechmaking skills to make him look like a vacuous celebrity.

The problem for the Republicans was that Obama wasn't an empty suit. The idea of targeting an opponent's strength made sense; the particular strength they went after did not. Obama was not all talk; he put a premium on getting things done. That meant that conservatives would have to change their line of attack.

They settled on depicting Obama as a "socialist" or a "fascist" or whatever charge seemed to resonate with the base. Jon Stewart told Bill O'Reilly when he went on his show that Fox News was committed to inducing "a full-fledged panic attack about the second coming of Chairman Mao."

Fox gave free rein to its newest star, Glenn Beck, who claimed Obama had a "deep-seated hatred for white people" and that more than a dozen "czars" (also known as White House aides) were a threat to the Republic. The network hyped stories about small rallies by right-wing "tea party" protesters and turned a minor aide with an embarrassing résumé into a crusade. Van Jones, a White House advisor on green jobs who barely knew the president, had been a radical in his youth and as an adult had signed a contemptible petition raising the possibility of U.S. involvement in 9/11. His resignation was inevitable (it came at midnight on a Saturday night). But the story was treated by Fox for weeks as a major top-of-the-news scandal. Afterward even the smallest details about the most obscure administration aides (including the sexual orientation of one) became fodder for Fox.

There was a history between Obama and the network. After he wrapped up the nomination in June 2008, Obama visited the News Corporation offices in New York with the intention of making peace. He chatted amiably with owner Rupert Murdoch, who openly admired Obama, but the conversation turned tense after Roger Ailes joined the group. Obama explained that he hadn't been granting interviews to Fox because the network was buying into bogus stories, like the one about his being schooled in a fundamentalist Muslim madrassa in Indonesia. Ailes responded huffily that Fox was just reporting the news. Murdoch, who was visibly embarrassed by Ailes's ungraciousness, extravagantly complimented the candidate, and the meeting ended with an informal agreement by Obama to resume relations with Fox. He granted a long interview to Bill O'Reilly, as well as one to the Murdoch-owned *Wall Street Journal*. But when Murdoch passed the word inside News Corp. that he was planning to endorse Obama, Ailes threatened to quit. Murdoch, knowing that Ailes was a cash cow for his company, gave Ailes a five-year contract, endorsed McCain early, and let Ailes move News Corp. even further right.* Obama placed a courtesy call to Murdoch during the transition but wrote Fox off.

By the time he was president he was in no mood for reconciliation. In a June CNBC interview with John Harwood, best remembered because the president swatted a fly on the air ("That was pretty impressive, wasn't it? I got the sucker"), Obama took off after Fox. When Harwood said some critics thought he was not being held sufficiently accountable for his policies, Obama bristled and replied, "It's very hard for me to swallow that one. First of all, I've got one television station entirely devoted to attacking my administration. That's a pretty big megaphone. And you'd be hard-pressed, if you watched the entire day, to find a positive story about me."

At a minimum the network had perfected a process of asking the White House about wild, often untrue accusations from Fox commenta-

---

* This didn't sit well with some of Murdoch's more liberal children, who despised Ailes.

tors, then claiming its White House reporters were merely "covering the controversy." For most of the late summer and fall the gambit worked. When Obama was scheduled to speak to schoolchildren in early September, Gibbs was questioned for three days at his briefing about outlandish charges, ginned up by Fox bloviators, that Obama was bent on spreading · a socialist message. After Fox launched wall-to-wall coverage of an amateur YouTube sting of ACORN, a community organizing group that received some federal money for census work, the mainstream media felt guilty for being slow to pick up the story.* Jill Abramson, managing editor of the *New York Times,* confessed that the paper had suffered from "insufficient tuned-in-ness to the issues that are dominating Fox News and talk radio" and assigned a reporter to monitor opinion media. That was exactly what the White House feared.

In late September Axelrod held a frosty meeting with Ailes, who told him that he thought Obama was a dangerous radical. On the basis of what? Axelrod wondered. A health care plan patterned on fifteen-year-old proposals by Bob Dole? A bank rescue plan that rejected nationalization and was being attacked from the left? An expanded war in Afghanistan? The conversation reminded Axelrod of the days when people thought fluoridated water was some kind of evil plot.

Fox's tone remained unchanged and the White House soon launched an unprecedented campaign against the network.† The goal was to interrupt Fox's ability to contaminate the media food chain. Anita Dunn got it going by saying on TV that Fox had become a "wing of the Republican Party." Axelrod and Rahm chimed in to push the line that Fox was "not a news organization," and Gibbs defended his colleagues for their "chin music," baseball lingo for throwing brushback pitches.‡ Obama, looking unperturbed by the whole flap, told NBC News that certain unnamed media were "operating basically as a talk-radio format."

The effort to bar Fox's White House correspondent, Major Garrett, from the press pool failed, as other reporters insisted to Gibbs that he be included. Even many Democrats thought it would have been

---

* ACORN is a nationwide network of community organizers that helped Obama in 2008, though not nearly as much as some claimed.

† John F. Kennedy ostentatiously canceled his subscription to the *New York Herald Tribune,* Richard Nixon put reporters on his infamous "Enemies List," and George W. Bush's White House refused to grant interviews to MSNBC, but an orchestrated boycott was something new.

‡ Rahm quietly called Murdoch three times to tell him he welcomed his ideas, a peace offering that Murdoch appreciated. The point was to maintain decent relations between the White House and the Murdoch-owned *Wall Street Journal.*

smarter to take the anti-Fox campaign "off campus," to let outside TV partisans like James Carville, not administration officials, lead the charge. But White House communications aides insisted that the only way to change the network's behavior was to elevate the confrontation. They saw it as "political malpractice" to treat Fox as a normal media outlet and felt vindicated when Garrett stopped asking them about anti-Obama slurs spread by the network's commentators. Within weeks administration officials and even the president himself resumed granting interviews to Garrett.

The episode was symptomatic of a communications team that was off its game. In going after Rush Limbaugh and Fox, the White House seemed to be punching beneath its weight class. It undermined Obama's message of reconciliation and looked small. The boycott, while good for rallying the base and distracting attention from concessions on health care that angered liberals, was ultimately counterproductive. Independent voters (more than a few of whom watched Fox) might reasonably conclude that a president who wanted to talk to Iranian thugs might at least be willing to sit down once in a while with his enemies at home. Even the urge to identify and combat the many lies told about the president could be taken too far. David Carr of the *New York Times* wrote that the "Truth-o-meter" on the White House website reminded him of "the blog of some unemployed guy living in his parents' basement, not an official communiqué from Pennsylvania Avenue."

Personal interactions worked better. Obama thought that answering questions from supporters on television was politically pointless, but he usually looked forward to conversing with the other side.* At an August town hall in Bozeman, Montana, a proud member of the NRA rose to ask a tough question about paying for health care. You could see Obama's eyes light up. The exchange was teed up perfectly for the White House: the confident young president taking the best shot from Fox Nation, then pushing back with a lucid and convincing answer.

Unfortunately for Obama, that was the exception in 2009. For a variety of reasons—lack of passion, complicated explanations, absence of catchphrases that penetrated the debate—Obama found himself outfoxed by Fox and the noisy yet disciplined cadres of the American right.

---

* When Bush ran for reelection in 2004 his town hall meetings were open to carefully screened supporters only.

THE MOST COMMON media criticism of Obama (even from supporters like Colin Powell) was that he was overexposed. He granted scores of interviews, issued op-ed pieces, taped weekly radio addresses and webcasts, popped into the White House briefing room for daytime press conferences, appeared on late-night TV, and held a televised town hall meeting outside of Washington on average once every couple of weeks. "You're the president, not a rerun of *Law and Order*," Bill Maher joked.

In the old media environment of three channels Obama would unquestionably have been wearing out his welcome. But technology was transforming what insiders called "the optics" of the presidency. If Americans felt overdosed on their president, they could change the channel to one of 450 others he wasn't on and decide later to experience him in their own way (YouTube, DVRs) and on their own time, which lessened any feeling of being bombarded.

In the new, fragmented media culture, the president believed he needed to be omnipresent or the vacuum would be filled by adversaries. Instead of being at the mercy of what the old broadcast networks chose to cover, the White House could now flood niche media markets with content via blogs, Twitter feeds, Facebook pages, and Flickr photo streams. With greatly shortened news cycles, the old notion of the "message of the day" was obsolete. Now the White House sent messages to reporters several times a day. Obama's media strategy was to follow bad news with more news (or at least more information). The idea was to put out any fire with the fire hose of his cascading initiatives and winning personality. The danger was that in becoming impossible to avoid Obama might "jump the shark" as a cultural phenomenon—cross an invisible line from hip to tiresome.*

However one viewed his ever-present persona, the use of technology to spread the president's message abroad represented an unheralded change in global communications. All year young White House and State Department social networking whizzes refined their approach. In March Obama made history by holding the first live Internet video chat by an American president, with more than a hundred thousand questions submitted on Whitehouse.gov.† In June his Cairo speech was spread via a text-messaging forum. In July his speech in Ghana

---

* The phrase "jump the shark" originated with a later episode of the TV show Happy Days in which the character called "The Fonz" (played by Henry Winkler) jumps over obviously fake sharks while waterskiing.

† The most popular by far was on whether legalizing marijuana would stimulate the economy and raise revenue by allowing the government to tax it. Obama said no and joked, "I don't know what this says about the online audience."

was disseminated on Facebook. And in December, when communications aides realized that 50 percent of Pakistanis and 30 percent of Afghans owned cellular devices, six key sentences from the president's speech sending more troops to Afghanistan (including "America seeks an end to this era of war and suffering") were translated into Arabic, Dari, Pashto, and Urdu and sent by compressed video to the region.

AT HOME OBAMA appeared on Jay Leno's show on NBC and in several *60 Minutes* interviews with Steve Kroft on CBS. He opened the White House for a day to NBC News, held a town meeting on health care with Diane Sawyer on ABC, and sat for dozens of one-on-one interviews with cable outlets and talk radio hosts like Ed Schultz (for liberals) and Michael Smerconish (for independents and Republicans). When he appeared on five Sunday shows on September 14—a first for a president—critics complained that it was overkill and he made no news. But to promote their own shows, all the networks covered him as if he had said something highly significant, thereby extending his impact.

Most of the time Obama was overexposed only to those who regularly watched Fox News, CNN, MSNBC, PBS, Comedy Central, or CNBC or listened to NPR. That sounded like a big audience, but in total it amounted to only around 10 percent of the electorate who voted in general elections. (The percentage of tuned-in primary voters was much higher.) These 12 to 15 million committed news consumers either loved Obama or hated him but they usually wanted to see and hear him. The other 110 million voters who were largely uninterested in politics were not being force-fed very often. They could go days without catching sight of Obama's picture, which was why the White House sent him into the anchor booth in St. Louis during the All-Star Game and ghosted articles on parenthood under his byline for *Parade* magazine. Even when his job approval ratings drooped, his personal ratings stayed healthy, if no longer spectacular (a standard he was never capable of sustaining). The Obama White House was the biggest, splashiest reality show ever—lacking in tacky or embarrassing drama, perhaps, but still entertaining.

To prove he wasn't overexposed, all the White House had to do was keep him off camera for two or three days. The yelps would begin almost immediately. Where's the president? Why isn't he taking part more forcefully in the debate? When he stopped holding full-dress news conferences in the second half of 2009 (substituting short "availabilities" before and after meetings) the White House press corps complained.

Obama was unmoved. If all they wanted to do was fling Republican talking points at him ("Are you dithering on Afghanistan?") or extend two-day stories into ten-day stories (the gate-crashers at the state dinner), he wasn't going to play. He had never shown much patience with what he considered the often trivial interests of the White House press corps, and his irritation grew over time. Instead his format of choice was the one-on-one interview. He sat for 152 interviews in 2009, far more than any of his predecessors.

After his Asia trip in November Obama vented about the media. It was bad enough that they misreported the bilaterals, wrongly assuming he got nothing in return from the Chinese. (In fact, he said, they had moved in his direction on both climate change and sanctions against Iran.) The trip reinforced his view that the American media was fundamentally unserious. He bowed too deeply to the figurehead emperor of Japan. So what?

The United States had big challenges ahead in staying competitive, and much of the media, he thought, was clueless about what was truly important. For instance, he noted that President Lee Myong Bak of South Korea, presiding over a "very competitive" economy, had said that his biggest problem in education was that Korean parents were too demanding and were insisting on importing English teachers so their kids could learn English in first grade instead of having to wait for second grade. This is what complacent America was up against. "And then I sit down with U.S. reporters, and the question they have for me, *in Asia,* is, 'Have I read Sarah Palin's book?' " At this point, the president shook his head, incredulous. "True. True story."

The president was doing his job in trying to prepare the country for a much more competitive future. The problem was that anxious Americans weren't necessarily looking for a professor, even a cool one, to lecture them about getting more serious. And the news business, a struggling industry desperately trying to cater to the appetites of its customers, wasn't going to change any time soon.

Moreover, the communications strategy of 2009 violated a lesson that Obama no doubt knew from his years as a fan of the Chicago Bulls. As long as Michael Jordan tried to win every game by himself, the Bulls fell short. They didn't begin to rack up championships until he let talented supporting players shoulder more of the load. The White House hadn't yet developed enough effective surrogates in the Cabinet and elsewhere to carry the administration message on the Sunday network interview shows and in other venues. Obama wasn't a ball hog on the basketball court but as president he was taking all the shots.

OBAMA'S ELECTION AS the first black president spoke louder about race than anything he might try to say about it to the country. An explicit national "conversation" on the subject would be stilted, but he was determined to use the bully pulpit to bolster a counternarrative to certain behavior patterns in the African American community: dropping out of school, committing violence, and fathering children without taking responsibility for them. This "cultural reformation," as the Harvard sociologist Orlando Patterson called it, was a long-term project, but both the president and the first lady were eager to tackle it in speeches and White House events. It dovetailed with the "responsibility era" Obama promised in his Inaugural Address.

From the start there were anecdotal signs of an Obama Effect, in which teachers found that invoking the president helped them inspire students to work harder.* Adults seemed open to behavioral changes, too. In June *Jet* magazine published a cover story titled "America's Family Man: How Obama Is Restoring the Image of African-American Males" that included a black lawyer who, after recognizing himself in Barack's initial hesitancy in marrying Michelle, got off the fence and proposed to his weeping girlfriend, offering the example of the first couple for the happy married life he now hoped for. In its November issue *Essence,* normally devoted to black women, included comments from black men about how Obama's success helped them stop making excuses and take more control of their own lives.

Obama disliked politically correct excuses. He didn't think much of the analysis offered by Jimmy Carter and others that suggested he was the victim of racism. If there was so much racism, he mused, then how did he get to the White House in the first place? "I was black before I was elected," he quipped to David Letterman.

In the meantime the president had concrete, if low-profile ideas for expanding opportunity: hundreds of new charter schools, the spread of Geoffrey Canada's successful Harlem Children's Zone (a holistic approach to poverty that produced terrific results), and a White House Office of Social Innovation to identify and provide seed money for successful model programs. But the funding levels were small and not likely to grow much any time soon; the power of the Obama example would have to do for now. Both the president and the first lady used

---

* Paul Vallas, the school superintendent in New Orleans, directed that the president's picture be hung in every classroom. But early research showing the racial achievement gap closing after students viewed an Obama speech didn't bear up under scrutiny.

their platform to reach out to the local Washington, D.C., community in a way no president had done before. They invited more than fifty thousand disadvantaged kids to the White House over the course of 2009. In a highly segregated city they took pains to visit a dozen schools and community centers in the three quadrants (Southeast, Southwest, and Northeast) that were mostly black, poor, and ignored by the white power structure. At the White House alone they hosted a poetry jam, a planting in the White House garden to encourage healthy eating, several master classes in music, and a Father's Day event that struck close to home for the fatherless president. Instead of gathering fathers and sons, the White House brought together fathers (some celebrity, some White House staff) with unrelated boys from single-parent families. Obama's goal was to model the importance of trying to break the cycle.

Exhortation had its limits; families wouldn't "stop eating that Popeye's chicken for breakfast" (as candidate Obama urged a black audience in Beaumont, Texas) just because the president said so. And Obama grew irritated when the media focused too much on his lecturing his own community. He was speaking to all kids, he said. On those occasions where he spoke to a black audience, he sometimes felt misinterpreted. After he addressed the NAACP in July he complained that the first half of the speech reviewing the history of discrimination and the continuing challenges of race had been ignored by the press in favor of the lines about "personal responsibility" and the need for kids to aim for something beyond being "rappers and ballers."

But it was that last message that was newsworthy because it could not have been conveyed by a white president. Obama knew that too many African American children had internalized failure. Among the most insidious forms of racism was the assumption that blacks simply weren't as smart as whites, and that including them might be necessary for the sake of diversity, but not for added brainpower or talent. Obama's superior ability and intelligence exploded that stereotype; even those who despised his politics had to admit he was smart. That offered the hope of diffuse social and psychological benefits that couldn't be easily measured but were unmistakably powerful.

Obama also accelerated the maturation of black politics, though in ways that sometimes proved uncomfortable for African Americans. A black president and his black political director (Patrick Gaspard) told one of only two black governors in America (David Paterson) that he should step aside and not run for governor of New York in 2010 because he would be a drag on the ticket. (Paterson, who had assumed the governorship after Eliot Spitzer resigned in a sex scandal, declined, though he later dropped out.) The African American chairman of the Republican National Committee, Michael Steele, called it "stunning" that the president would do such a thing. While Steele tried an improbable embrace of racial solidarity politics (the GOP had zero African Americans in Congress or statehouses), Obama was moving toward a true standard of political color blindness.

. Republicans responded by shouting about racism—black racism. Rush Limbaugh went straight for a racial pitch on his radio show: "Obama's America, white kids getting beat up on school buses now. You put your kids on a school bus, you expect safety but in Obama's America the white kids now get beat up with the black kids cheering." Later he flatly stated, "Obama's entire economic program is reparations." The goal of the new administration was clear to Limbaugh: "They want to use their power as a means of retribution," he told his listeners. "That's what Obama's about, gang." About a fifth of the American public basically agreed with Limbaugh, which was either a small or large number of people, depending on your perspective.

———

OBAMA HAD ALWAYS been skillful in maintaining his black identity in a white-dominated environment. Of course, now it was not just a majority white world he was living in, like Hawaii or Harvard, but a majority white country he had been elected to represent. He couldn't be "the black president" and didn't want to be, and yet he wouldn't relegate race to being a mere footnote either.

His black friends were sometimes unsure of whether to bother him on issues of race. When they socialized with the president, they didn't want to burden him with their worry that high-ranking African Americans on the White House staff like Gaspard, Mona Sutphen (deputy White House chief of staff), Melody Barnes (chair of the Domestic Policy Council), didn't seem to have influence commensurate with their positions. And the National Security Council staff of 240 was almost entirely white.

John Rogers, who declined a job in government to tend to his Chicago investment firm, wondered why the car companies and AIG and other recipients of bailout billions weren't being pressured by Capitol Hill to hire more African American executives and move beyond tokenism on their boards. That's what Harold Washington had done when he was mayor of Chicago and Maynard Jackson when he was mayor of Atlanta. Rogers, Bruce Gordon, former head of the NAACP, Charles Ogletree, an Obama mentor at Harvard Law School, and other of Obama's African American friends thought that most of Obama's aides didn't get the point.

But with a black man as president the pressure was off. The numbers of high-ranking African Americans in corporate America were actually shrinking; for all the growth in the black middle class, almost no blacks held senior management positions in hedge funds or venture capital firms. Perhaps out of fear of being associated too closely with the pressure tactics of the civil rights movement, now out of fashion in the age of Obama, almost no one seemed to be pushing to obtain something concrete on behalf of the president's base in the black community. Jesse Jackson said it was important to find more people like Rogers who wouldn't just preen because they got in the room with the president, but would try to get more African Americans in the room. Vernon Jordan, by contrast, argued that race consciousness was an impediment to progress for blacks at the upper reaches of the American power structure. He thought blacks should aim to be hired because they were qualified, not because they were African American.

In his books and speeches Obama had long been willing to explore what W.E.B. DuBois called the "double consciousness" of well-educated minorities who came to thrive in both black and white worlds. It was his self-aware but unself-conscious ease in negotiating the still treacherous waters of race that helped sell Obama to so many Americans in the first place. But where and when to explain race in the presidency became an issue.

———

IN LATE JULY Harvard professor Henry Louis Gates Jr., a distinguished African American scholar, was arrested for disorderly conduct in his home after a white Cambridge, Massachusetts, police sergeant, James Crowley, responded to a suspected burglary when Gates and another dark-skinned man (his taxi driver), just in from the airport, were seen by a neighbor pushing hard against Gates's own front door.* The professor and the police officer became engaged in a clash of egos. Gates angrily demanded Crowley's badge number. Crowley, feeling his authority challenged, arrested and handcuffed Gates even after he had ascertained that Gates was in his own home.

At the end of a long prime-time press conference devoted to health care, Lynn Sweet of the *Chicago Sun-Times* asked Obama about the incident. He couldn't very well avoid the question entirely, but he waded

———

* Gates had flown in from New York, not China, as widely reported.

too far into a case for which he didn't have all the facts. Obama wanted to show sympathy for other blacks who routinely faced such humiliations and for his "friend" Skip Gates.* The part of his otherwise nuanced remarks on the case that caused him trouble was the use of a single word, *stupidity,* in reference to the Cambridge police department making the arrest. This was a much more comprehensible and combustible story to cover than health care, and a distracting media frenzy ensued.

It took the president a couple of days to recognize, as he later said, that the "stupidity" line had itself been stupid. Heeding the advice of his wife, he made a Friday afternoon surprise appearance in the press room to "ratchet down" (though not apologize for) his remarks and embraced Crowley's suggestion that the three of them have a beer at the White House.

On July 31 the cable networks went crazy in anticipation of the event. In an afternoon of self-parody, the beer choices of each were endlessly scrutinized; CNN even posted a countdown clock on the screen. The president asked Joe Biden to join them, which balanced the tableau racially. Biden's history of good relations with cops was also a factor, though his sympathies lay with Gates. Greeting Crowley, Gates quipped, "You looked bigger the last time I saw you." (The following week he gave a speech in which he jokingly offered to help get Crowley's kids into Harvard, which didn't go over well.) Crowley described the meeting as "two gentlemen who agreed to disagree."

But there was more to it than that. After the photographers were escorted out, a fifth man secretly joined the "beer summit" under way on the Rose Garden patio: Sergeant Dennis O'Connor of the Cambridge Police Patrol Officers Association, the union representative. The union argued that because the president was an admitted friend of Gates, Crowley needed a supporter there too. The White House reluctantly agreed to O'Connor's presence but took pains to keep it quiet. O'Connor didn't say much in the twenty-five-minute conversation, which was a mix of polite discussion of the issues and forced conviviality. Both Cambridge police officers left with a much higher opinion of the president than when they arrived.

For Obama the beer summit was an attempt to salvage a story that had taken a toll on his approval ratings. He rationalized it as a "teachable moment," but this was clearly the wrong case to teach the country

---

* In fact they were more acquaintances than friends. Gates had joined Vernon Jordan, Andrew Young, and others in the African American elite in favoring Hillary Clinton in the Democratic primaries.

about racial profiling. Glenn Loury, an African American professor at Brown, wrote, "It is depressing in the extreme that the president, when it came time to expend political capital on the issue of race and the police, did so on behalf of his 'friend' rather than stressing the policy reforms that might keep the poorly educated, infrequently employed but still human young black men in America out of prison."

———

"POORLY EDUCATED, INFREQUENTLY employed." The president tried to reserve at least a little time for the issues that brought him into public life in the first place. Obtaining the education necessary to stay out of trouble and make a life for oneself was central to Obama's domestic agenda. He would use his personal standing with students, his policy creativity, and his willingness to buck conventional Democratic Party interest groups to move the debate forward.

But even innocuous efforts ran into strong opposition. On September 8 the president gave a speech that was meant to be shown in every elementary and high school in the country. It wasn't a new idea; Reagan and George H. W. Bush had done the same, warning against drug abuse. Their speeches had occasioned no controversy. But Obama had both more sway with students and less with their politically polarized parents. Fox News feasted on reports that some right-wingers kept their children out of school that day with the claim that the president wanted to indoctrinate schoolchildren into socialism. In the limo en route to an Arlington, Virginia, high school for the speech, Obama told domestic policy aide Heather Higginbottom sarcastically, "The president of the United States telling kids to work hard and stay in school? This is crazy!"

His unobjectionable message was skillfully delivered with personal details (about how his father had left when he was 2 years old) and memorable lines ("If you give up on yourself, you give up on the country") that made it accessible and relevant for students of widely varying ages.

———

"I DON'T GET all wee-wee'd up about cable news," the president said. Such nonchalance often left Obama flat-footed in the new hyperpartisan media environment. On big issues like the stimulus in February, health care in August, and Afghanistan in December, Obama as the patient professor-in-chief was no match for the ceaseless chatter. It added to the impression that the president was better on strategy than the tactical requirements of hand-to-hand cable combat. His equanimity amid heavy flack sometimes shielded him from harsh political truths he needed to hear. The cable anger was hyped but it reflected something real: a sense among beleaguered middle-class Americans that once again they were getting shafted. Obama ignored this at his peril.

On *60 Minutes* in September, Obama pointed to what he called "a coarsening of our politics that I've been running against since I got into politics." The challenge in the cable culture, where the loudest voices get the most attention, is "How can we make sure that civility is interesting?" Returning civility to politics, he admitted, "is still a work-in-progress."

American political rhetoric has always been brutal.* But now technology disseminated the old red-ribbon typewriter rants and smudged pamphlets globally. It was hard to see how things were going to get more civil when every loudmouth with a talk show or hatemonger with a laptop could mainline venom into the system.

In the meantime the modern media cacophony threatened to drown out Obama's agenda. The president understood that, as Roosevelt said in explaining why he delivered only two or three Fireside Chats a year, "public psychology cannot be attuned for long periods of time to a constant repetition of the highest note in the scales."† Obama knew his voice could wear out if he overused it. But he didn't seem to have much choice.

WHAT SAVED OBAMA from being too familiar was his ability to change gears rhetorically, aiming his words at different audiences in different, often unconventional venues. Whether he was taping an introduction for comedian George Lopez's new late-night show or giving an interview to *Men's Health* magazine, he managed to find a way to keep it classy. His friend Penny Pritzker, an art collector, said his ability to speak in such different languages reminded her of the art world, where work was sometimes divided into "high voice" and "low voice." Only the rarest artist, Pritzker said, could speak both.

Obama's high voice/low voice instinct was on display at the end of May, when a couple of days before leaving for his "high voice" speech to the Muslim world in Cairo, he stopped by the ground-floor White House library, where the comedian Stephen Colbert was waiting for

---

* Thomas Jefferson was attacked for having a slave mistress; Abraham Lincoln was depicted as a coward and a monkey; and Bill Clinton was maligned as a cocaine-dealing murderer.
† FDR operated in his own cacophonous media world. Big cities in the mid-twentieth century had five or six daily newspapers, many of them filled with venomous columnists spewing hate at the president. But with the exception of Father Charles Coughlin, the anti-Semitic "radio priest," the critics weren't usually on the air, which made them less noxious.

him. Colbert was planning to host his show in Iraq and wanted a "bit" involving the president and General Ray Odierno. At first the White House was skeptical about appearing with Colbert's loveable blowhard character. But when Axelrod saw the script, he walked it into the president, who loved it, especially when as commander-in-chief he orders Odierno, "Give that man a haircut!" (As it happened, Obama favored close-cropped hair and frequently complimented aides Jon Favreau and Mark Lippert on their buzz cuts.)

Obama's first take was fine, but Colbert quickly agreed when Obama said he would tape a second. The comedian later said he found the second take more "presidential."

"You're a good actor, Mr. President, Emmy-worthy," Colbert said.

"As long as I get to play the president," Obama laughed.

In fact his acting was so good that many viewers thought he had appeared live on the jumbo screen in Baghdad ordering Colbert's buzz cut. The soldiers in the live studio audience in one of Saddam Hussein's old palaces went wild. With fifteen minutes of his time and a willingness to risk a little criticism for being unserious, Obama showed support for the troops, rallied his young fan base, and won points with a chunk of the U.S. military that usually votes Republican.

———

AS 2009 WORE on, Obama learned what he always intuitively knew: that his charm and rhetorical skills had their limits. For all his words of bipartisanship, he failed to convert Republicans to his cause. They stayed disciplined and unified in their determination to obstruct most of his initiatives. This wasn't hard, because any GOP member of Congress who considered cooperating with the president knew what would come next: a primary challenge.

Other nations might listen more politely than Republicans at home, but they would go their own way too, on matters large and small. This came as a rude surprise to some Obama hands.

For years Chicagoans had carefully prepared a bid to host the 2016 Summer Olympics, designed to take place in an area, coincidentally, close to the president's South Side house. Obama led pep rallies and otherwise helped out wherever he could. But in early September he tried to beg off going to Copenhagen, where the International Olympic Committee was meeting to select the site. Even with the heads of state of the other finalists planning to attend, the president argued at first that it was enough for Michelle and Oprah Winfrey to represent him. He had the right instinct, but the whole matter was caught up in civic pride on steroids. Mayor Daley, who saw winning the Olympics for

Chicago as the capstone of his career, was furious that the president might not show up: Obama realized that if he didn't fly to Copenhagen and Chicago didn't get the Games, even his most fervent friends and supporters would blame him. And the U.S. Olympic Committee was telling Valerie Jarrett that one push from the president was just what the city he loved needed to get over the line. So he went, and Chicago lost to Rio de Janeiro, finishing an embarrassing third in the balloting. Back at the White House Obama shrugged and noted Michelle's heavy investment of time and effort: "Look guys, if I didn't go, my wife would have killed me."

———

OBAMA WAS OFTEN depicted as too timid in fighting back against Republicans, but he could be combative on occasion. In July he spoke at a community college in Macomb County, Michigan, a well-known swing area that had gone heavily for him in 2008 but was now part of a state where unemployment hit 14 percent: "I love these folks who helped get us into this mess, and suddenly they say, 'This is Obama's economy.' That's fine. Give it to me. My job is to solve problems, not stand on the sidelines and carp and gripe."

Here in one unscripted aside was Obama uncut. First, sarcastic "love" for the critics who drove the country into the ditch. Then an accurate summary of their line of attack ("This is Obama's economy") and a showy assumption of responsibility that encapsulated his view of the presidency ("My job is to solve problems"). And finally a Teddy Roosevelt–style blast at those who are not in the arena (implicitly suggesting that Republican politicians and cable analysts are equally irrelevant) and merely "stand on the sidelines" to "carp and gripe." What saved the comment from being over the top was that he accompanied it with the hardest of truths—that most of the lost auto jobs were not coming back—and with a promise (backed by $12 billion in his budget) of community colleges like Macomb's as the economic engines of the future.

At an October fund-raiser in San Francisco Obama stepped up the mocking language: "When I'm busy and Nancy [Pelosi]'s busy with our mop cleaning up somebody else's mess, we don't want somebody sittin' back saying, 'You're not holding the mop the right way.' 'That's a socialist mop.'" At that point the president pantomimed mopping and smilingly challenged the Republicans, "Why don't you grab a mop? Why don't you help clean up?" This had some of the playfulness that FDR brought to ribbing the GOP for mistreating his dog Fala and his joyful skewering of Congressmen "Martin, Barton and Fish." Before long "Grab a Mop" would become a theme at local Democratic dinners across the country.

But the time for blaming Bush and the Republican "Party of No" for his problems was rapidly expiring. It was beginning to sound like the excuse making that Obama said he abhorred. He could flay banks and insurance companies to score some political points, but by 2010 he would own the economy and own Afghanistan, and his new task would be to explain what he planned to do with his new possessions. Almost nothing else would stick.

Looking ahead, the roughest, most sobering domestic problem was that employment lagged behind recovery. That meant that the economy would be improving long before people felt better.

This was an obstacle that would challenge even Obama's greatest rhetorical powers. He could make all the arguments about unemployment being a lagging indicator, about the other "green shoots" showing some economic hope, about how he had always said it would take time. He could take solace from polls showing Americans had greater patience than anyone expected. But it was still a challenge to explain why joblessness seemed headed in the wrong direction. The curve of persuasion was growing steeper.

17

Off-hours

The occasional crankiness of candidate Obama receded in the presidency. Living "above the store," as he liked to say, brightened his mood. For all the strains of the job and weekly travel, Year One allowed for the most family time the Obamas had experienced since their children were born. If Obama's White House workday too often seemed disconnected from the concerns of the middle class, the pictures of him in his role as husband and father conveyed the right image of what an American family should be.

The image was authentic, which helped. From the start, the Obamas took pains to have as normal a family life as possible, with regular attendance at soccer matches, basketball games, and flute recitals. The president often worked his schedule around school events and was proud to have made all the parent-teacher conferences. The household staff was instructed not to make Malia's and Sasha's beds or perform other chores for them. At dinner nearly every night the family went around the table and reported on the "roses and thorns" of the day. Presidential trips to Africa and Russia doubled as family sightseeing excursions.

Two days after the Inauguration the new first lady invited all the ushers, electricians, housekeepers, and others on the permanent White House staff to a reception in the East Room with her own staff, where the two groups formed concentric circles and introduced themselves to one another. Michelle, whose father had worked his way up from janitor to water engineer, later told her aides that she expected them to learn the names of the household staff, not the other way around.

Starting in her first week, she visited federal agencies that hadn't seen a president or first lady in years, if ever. The response was overwhelming, as African American women on the rope line routinely burst into tears on her arrival. Like the president's signs of respect, it was hard to quantify the results. But having thousands of members of the "B Team" (as in, "We'll be here when you come and after you go") feel personally connected to the Obamas energized the agencies and made it harder, though hardly impossible, for bureaucrats to throw sand in the gears.

Whether she was displaying her hula-hooping skills (142 revolutions) and skipping rope as part of a Healthy Kids Fair or dressing as Cat Woman on Halloween, Michelle brought her own formidable charm to the White House.* She was a hugger with friends, acquaintances, and even the Secret Service, who, according to a book by conservative Ronald Kessler, found her considerate. Her informal, bare-armed J. Crew look went global, and she soon became more popular in opinion polls than her husband, which was quite a turnaround from the sustained right-wing attacks of the campaign. An appearance in $540 satin sneakers by the Paris designer Lanvin caused a stir, but more often she showcased less expensive American designers. (A $148 dress she wore on ABC's *The View* sold out immediately).

The first lady had never been political; her interests ran more to the nonprofit work she had done in Chicago. Her causes in the White House—childhood obesity, mentoring girls, balancing work and family—were things she had been talking about for years. It was easy to see her enormous impact in the shining eyes of her young listeners all over the world as she told her story of growing up as a black girl on Chicago's segregated South Side, going to Ivy League schools, then, like her husband, rejecting the life of a corporate lawyer in order to work in the community.

Michelle missed the simple things about her old life—driving to Target to pick up stuff; watching the girls at ballet class—and she had to stifle the caustic comments her friends had long enjoyed. She gave fewer than half a dozen interviews all year long, mostly softballs. Behind her warm personality she was a demanding boss.† Although things were going well in the East Wing, she quickly decided that her first chief of staff, Jackie Norris (one of those credited with organizing the Iowa caucuses), was the wrong fit and she brought in her old boss from the University of Chicago, Susan Sher. Any time "the Supreme Leader," as Axelrod called her, weighed in on a personnel matter, her husband and everyone else in the White House listened closely. When it came time to pick a Supreme Court justice, she strongly favored Sonia

---

* Sally Quinn, a longtime social arbiter in Georgetown, has known every first lady since Mamie Eisenhower and said Michelle was her favorite. She found her the most natural and authentic and the least guarded and bored.

† Vanessa Kirsch, founder of Public Allies, a nonprofit group that placed young people in service organizations, hired Michelle to run the group's Chicago office in the 1990s but quickly felt as if it was Michelle who had hired her.

Sotomayor, whose experience as an isolated minority student at Princeton mirrored her own.

It frustrated Michelle that she couldn't be more overtly involved in policy matters for fear of arousing opposition that would undermine her husband's efforts. So she worked quietly. When George Miller told the president over lunch that Michelle had expressed an interest in his national service expansion bill, Obama told him, "Sounds like you better get that bill out of committee."

In the beginning Michelle's priority was to make Malia and Sasha's midyear adjustment to their new private school, Sidwell Friends, as seamless as possible.* In Chicago, Obama had driven his kids to school when he was home. That was impossible now, and the girls were embarrassed by the presidential motorcade. But Michelle insisted on as much normality as could be arranged. The self-described "Mom in Chief," who readily admitted to being influenced as a child by *The Brady Bunch*, took off most of the summer of 2009 to be with her daughters. The girls liked sightseeing in Washington, especially riding the elevator up the Washington Monument. (When a park ranger declined to tell them the secret of how he knew the elevator would open onto the observation deck at the precise moment he snapped his fingers, Malia said merrily, "My daddy can make you tell me." The president laughed and said he wouldn't.) Both girls loved having sleepovers at the White House, where a new swing set was positioned within sight of the Oval Office. Sasha and her friends from second grade would sometimes play on the Truman Balcony or troop down to the White House physician's office on the ground floor, calling out, "Doctor! Doctor! I hurt my finger!"

The presence of Michelle's mother, Marian Robinson, the first mother-in-law to live in the White House since the Truman administration, added to the homey feel. Over Thanksgiving her son, Craig Robinson, brought the Oregon State basketball team he coached to town to play George Washington University. The president sat beside her. "She kept punching me every time it got close," he chuckled the following week in the Oval Office. "I had to remind her that, first of all, the Secret Service could arrest her for that. And secondly, it's not my fault."

In Chicago Michelle, who hated to cook, had befriended a young University of Chicago graduate and chef named Sam Kass, who became the family's personal chef and educated them about food. Kass

---

* Republican Party Chairman Michael Steele criticized the Obamas for choosing to send their children to a private school. In Chicago they had gone to the Lab School of the University of Chicago, also private.

came along to the White House as assistant chef and helped plant the first White House vegetable garden since Eleanor Roosevelt's Victory Garden in World War II. It provided food not just for the Obama family and state dinners, but for local soup kitchens. The idea was to spur a major national shift toward nutritious eating, which health policy advisors considered essential to the long-term success of health care reform. Within weeks reports filtered back to the White House of kids in other cities wanting to start gardens.

When entertaining, the Obamas managed to be down to earth without seeming unpresidential. The White House mixed performances by contemporary groups like the Foo Fighters and Los Lobos with Stevie Wonder, Tony Bennett, and Yo-Yo Ma. There was fencing and Frisbee on the South Lawn, a poetry jam and *Mad Men*–themed party in the East Room, and more than a dozen parties for children. As he handed out candy to hundreds of local public school kids on Halloween, the White House swathed in cobwebs and bathed in orange light, a beaming president told social secretary Desirée Rogers, "I could do this all day!" By the end of the year, when the White House hosted seventeen Christmas parties featuring tens of thousands of guests and requiring the first couple to spend at least twenty hours posing for photographs, the president wasn't saying that anymore. At some 2009 parties the Obamas skipped the receiving line and guests were disappointed not to have their pictures taken with the president and first lady, which they had come to expect. Eventually the White House Social Office inserted a notice in invitations informing guests that a receiving line would form only if time permitted.

Rogers, a onetime Mardi Gras Zulu Queen and Harvard Business School graduate who became a Chicago executive and socialite, worked closely with her friend Valerie Jarrett to turn social events into public outreach and political events like bill signings into constituency celebrations. This was a new twist on White House entertaining. The coordination between the West Wing and the East Wing was closer than in any recent administration, with a member of the first lady's staff sitting in on most White House meetings. Rogers and Jarrett launched two mentoring programs, one for boys and one for girls (Michelle took on fifteen mentees she saw regularly), and dispatched celebrities and White House staffers to local schools. The president himself didn't have much time for social planning, though when he saw them at a Hispanic caucus event he did personally convince Marc Anthony and Jennifer Lopez to perform at the White House on Latin Night.

The first state dinner, for the prime minister of India, was famously marred by a pair of gate-crashers named Salahi, which led to calls for

Rogers to testify on Capitol Hill over her failure to post a staffer with a clipboard by the entrance.* Rogers, already a target for having posed amid a recession for glossy magazine covers, stood accused of wanting to attend the party rather than secure it, which was not accurate. White House aides rashly invoked the separation of powers to prevent Rogers from testifying, in part because they feared how she might come across. This overreaction, which further hurt Rogers's reputation and likely hastened her exit, reflected the Obamas' attitude about the whole kerfuffle.† Because every visitor to the White House (including the Salahis) goes through a magnetometer, they felt there was little more danger to them than at any event and that the responsibility for screening guests resided with the Secret Service, not the social secretary's office. When asked on television if he was angry over the security lapse, the president felt obliged to say yes. But mostly he was annoyed at the press for its failure to find an exit strategy from the story.

BY ALL ACCOUNTS the Obama marriage was much improved. Around 2000, when Obama lost an impetuous race for Congress, Michelle wanted him to leave the state senate and begin catching up financially with his successful law school classmates. She grew sullen and resentful over her husband's unwillingness to shoulder more household and child-rearing duties. It was a measure of the importance that Obama placed on seeming normal that he shone a light on his shortcomings as a husband. "I wouldn't gloss over the fact that that was a tough time for us," the president later said. "There were points in time where I was fearful that Michelle just really didn't—that she would be unhappy."

But Michelle eventually found that she could lean on others for help and that expecting Barack to be home every night for dinner, as her own parents had been, was unrealistic. Just as he inoculated himself on youthful drug use by writing about it in *Dreams from My Father,* he laid out their marital problems in his 2006 book, *The Audacity of Hope.* (" 'You only think about yourself,' she would tell me. 'I never thought I'd have to raise a family alone.' ") It worked again, and their bumpy patch became just another part of the Oprah-ready narrative they were building together.

Michelle was a tiger when it came to Barack and other women. After he won Iowa the actress Halle Berry was quoted saying, "I'll do what-

---

* In fact, such a staffer had been posted, but to no effect. A third crasher who wore a tuxedo and blended in with the Indian delegation was later identified.

† In early 2010, Rogers quit in frustration, another example of a president's hometown friend being chewed up in the capital. She complained that no one would publically defend her.

ever he says to do. I'll collect paper cups off the ground to make his pathway clear." When Barack reported with a smile how eager Berry was to campaign with him, Michelle told him only half-jokingly that she didn't care if it was an event for starving children in Africa, he couldn't appear with her—or else. In the White House she enjoyed teasing him about what he was missing: "I get to go to this fun event today and you have to work on health care."

As a candidate and then president, Obama was constantly besieged by attractive women, which naturally caused the international press to manufacture stories. When he went to Italy for the G-8 in July a mischievous photo editor at Reuters sent around the world a picture of him and French President Sarkozy admiring the derriere of a 17-year-old Brazilian woman. But when the video came out, it was clear that the president was merely turning to help an older woman down the steps. As much as the media wanted to find some juicy vice, it eluded them. Perhaps one day a crippling personal shortcoming would surface, but it wasn't likely.

———

JUST BECAUSE OBAMA usually stayed outwardly calm didn't mean he wasn't peeved. The causes of his ire weren't hard to figure out: petty politics, insipid journalism, people who disappointed him (by leaking information or proving incompetent), and nasty surprises. In Chicago early in his career he would occasionally ream out reporters when they wrote something he considered unfair. (Later he learned that was what press secretaries were for.) His irritation when blindsided could cause him to lose his cool. Early on, he let loose when he heard that Louis Caldera, the head of the White House Military Office, had terrified New Yorkers by authorizing Air Force One and an F-16 fighter to fly low over Manhattan as part of a photo shoot. (After a short investigation Caldera was fired). When Obama picked up the *New York Times* and learned that Justice Department lawyers had invoked the Bush-era "state secrets" privilege when contesting a lawsuit alleging torture, he was livid. He exclaimed angrily to aides, "What the fuck? This is not the way I like to make decisions."

Obama had his share of what Jim Jones, a former marine, called these "Whiskey Tango Foxtrot" moments. As a child, he wrote, he had learned to curse from watching Richard Pryor movies. It was a generational thing; even women swore much more than they used to. And while some older Americans surely objected, at least the milder profanity humanized Obama, as when he was overheard by ABC News saying off the record that hip-hop artist Kanye West was a "jackass" for disrespecting Taylor Swift at the Video Music Awards. Ever since Nixon, campaigning against Kennedy in 1960, tried to make an issue of Harry Truman's cursing (before being caught on the Watergate tapes uttering hundreds of expletives), presidents have tried to hide their profanity like a bad habit.*

Obama's other bad habit, of course, was smoking. In June, after years of debate, Congress finally passed a bill that allowed the FDA to regulate tobacco for the first time. This made it possible for the executive branch to crack down on tobacco industry abuses with rule making rather than legislation. When Obama signed the landmark bill in a June 22 Rose Garden ceremony, he referred in a half-sentence to the fact that he had begun smoking in high school, but said nothing else about his own vice.

At a press conference the next day he tried to control his defensiveness as he answered the predictable question: "I don't do it in front of my kids. I don't do it in front of my family. I would say that I am ninety-five percent cured, but there are times when I mess up." Once again the honesty, the sense of *This is who I am, flaws and all,* contained any damage; indeed for many voters living in Oprah's America, the confession of a common failing may even have drawn them closer to the president.

His awareness that the habit humanized him didn't mean he wasn't serious about quitting, though for many years he clearly wasn't serious enough. Reporters in the pressroom of the Illinois State Capitol remember his often dropping by to bum a cigarette and talk. During his 2004 Senate campaign he tried to keep his addiction a secret, but afterward Michelle made it clear in magazine stories that she was not above using the press to curb his habit. "Print that he promised me he'd quit," she told one reporter. When he started his presidential campaign Michelle told him he "couldn't be a smoking president."

But the vice proved difficult to shake. He had snuck a cigarette from time to time on the campaign (for instance, just before the 2008 Al Smith Dinner in New York, a high-stakes humor event) and admitted after the election that he had occasionally "fallen off the wagon." When questioned in December 2008 by Tom Brokaw on *Meet the Press,* he had been careful to promise only that he wouldn't smoke "in the White House," which is a smoke-free zone. He rarely complained about how hard it was to quit; Marty Nesbitt said he'd never heard him discuss it. Instead he responded to cravings with Nicorette gum and the

---

* When Nixon piously attacked Truman's swearing, JFK laughed and said, "We had best leave that to Mrs. Truman."

occasional smoke in a grove near the White House tennis court, though no one ever got a picture of it.

A picture of him smoking was about the only image that the White House didn't allow in Year One. The unprecedented openness to official White House photographer Pete Souza began right away, with a romantic picture of the new president and new first lady, wearing his jacket to protect her from the cold, leaning into each other in a service elevator on the night of the Inauguration. A few days later Souza photographed the new president wearing goofy 3-D glasses while watching the Super Bowl and, soon enough, tossing a football in the Oval Office.

On his trip to Egypt Obama posed wearing an Indiana Jones hat, an echo of a college-age picture of him looking suave with a Panama hat pulled over his eyes. For seventy years after Calvin Coolidge was photographed wearing an Indian headdress, presidential headgear of any kind was nearly verboten. Bill Clinton made wearing baseball caps acceptable again, but the candid shots of him and later George W. Bush in the White House were more circumspect than Obama's. Thousands of Souza's pictures were posted on Flickr, where they could be downloaded for free. Obama was sensitive about the size of his ears, but he was photogenic and never seemed to look ill at ease.

During the 2008 campaign the Obamas were ambivalent about how much to let their daughters be photographed, but the need to craft a family-friendly image won out. On the Fourth of July 2008 in Butte, Montana, Malia's tenth birthday, he let the whole family talk to a camera crew from the tabloid TV show *Access Hollywood*. The children were impossibly cute, with Sasha opening and closing her hand while saying "Blah, blah, blah" to imitate her father talking too much.

In the White House he and Michelle barred interviews with the children but allowed plenty of pictures on certain occasions, like the day their new dog, Bo, arrived. It was obviously useful politically to let the whole family become part of the story but the Obamas were also intent on leading by example. Obama even added a spontaneous section to a November 2009 speech in Wisconsin on education that mentioned how Malia scored a disappointing 73 on a science test at school before buckling down and earning a 95 on her next test. "Malia will tell you, my attitude was if she came home with a B, that's not good enough because there's no reason she can't get an A," Obama told *Essence* magazine in an interview on the importance of education. "So those are things any parent can do. There's no doubt that Michelle and I have more privileges compared with a lot of parents. We understand that. But I don't care how poor you are—you can turn off the television set during the week." Michelle got personal when it came to health. She said she had changed the family diet after a report on the kids' body mass index from their doctor. Using their platform to do good trumped privacy.

———

OBAMA JOKED DURING the campaign that he was saving string for a book called "This Is Ridiculous" that would chronicle all the concessions to the process that he was forced to make, from attending silly events to telephoning people he couldn't stand. In the White House he found many more stories that would fit easily into the book. The pack mentality of the press always made for good material. The president was especially annoyed when his "date night" with Michelle in New York was criticized in the media as a waste of taxpayers' money. Bush had flown repeatedly to Crawford, Texas, with no criticism.

Obama often walked the line between irritated and wry. When told, for instance, that Bush's former White House chief of staff, Andrew Card, had made plans for a new fleet of twenty-eight presidential helicopters at the unimaginable cost of $11 billion, Obama scotched the program and deadpanned, "The helicopter I have now seems perfectly adequate to me. Of course I've never had a helicopter before, you know? Maybe I've been deprived and I didn't know it."

The president was at his most playful when he got together with his closest friends and aides, three or four of whom were on familiar enough terms to call him Barack when no one else was around. Where Bush favored belittling nicknames (like calling Karl Rove "Turd Blossom"), Obama went in for good-natured razzing. "We've been here forty-five minutes and Ax has talked for thirty-five," he said one afternoon. "Aren't we paying you enough to get a decent bag?" he kidded Cassandra Butts, an old Harvard friend working in the White House, when she spilled papers. During his European trip in early April Obama was awakened in Prague and informed that the North Koreans had launched a long-range missile. As Ax, looking disheveled, was joined by Lippert in gym shorts in a secure location of the hotel, Obama joked, "I don't know which is more frightening—your hair, Lippert's legs, or this launch."

His friends were prime targets. If you were with him on the basketball court or even fooling around playing water basketball in the White House pool, he would trash-talk good-naturedly after scoring. ("This is *my* court. I own this *whole* court.") Aides got the treatment a little less often, but enjoyed it when they did. When the household staff brought Axelrod and Ben Rhodes water one day during a speech preparation session in the Oval Office, Obama looked up and said with a straight face, "Don't bring out water for these guys. They didn't do anything to deserve water." Then came the patented "Heh, heh, heh." Sometimes Obama was teasing aides and looking out for their health at the same time. He was so anxious to get his portly senior advisors, Axelrod and Rouse, to work out with his personal trainer that he offered to pay.

Just about anyone was fair game for a little ribbing, from the wife of a congressman who wanted three pictures taken with the president to the chairman of the Federal Reserve. "Ben, first of all I want to thank you for the service you've performed," the president said one day when Ben Bernanke appeared at his daily economic briefing. "No one else is going to thank you, so this is about as good as it's gonna get."

Obama liked *Seinfeld* moments. On a trip with GOP Senator Richard Lugar in 2005 to the former Soviet Union, the Americans were served an array of inedibles, including a fish encased in gelatin. Ever after, any unappetizing dish on a foreign trip might prompt the president to whisper in mock horror, "The fish Jell-O! The fish Jell-O!"

His wry side usually got him in trouble when it surfaced publicly. He apologized to Nancy Reagan just after the election for saying at a press conference that she engaged in séances,* joked before the Super Bowl that Jessica Simpson was "in a weight battle, apparently," when Matt Lauer pointed out that a dieting Simpson had bumped him from the cover of *US Weekly,* and apologized for comparing his own lack of bowling prowess to the Special Olympics when he appeared on *Jay Leno.* These gibes were all unpresidential, but they didn't hurt him because they were human and normal and the public was a little tired of the Gotcha! games of modern politics.

Even so, he learned to keep his public quips cautious and thus not terribly funny. After the Leno interview Steve Kroft of *60 Minutes* asked the president if he had been "punch drunk." It was probably not a coincidence that in a prime-time news conference the following week Obama barely cracked a smile and didn't engage in what Chris Matthews called "towel-snapping" with the press. When he went on *Letterman* in September he was affable but wary. Handed a heart-shaped potato, all he could manage was "That's remarkable."†

While Obama loved a huge megaphone, he was frustrated (though not surprised) by the scrutiny of his every word. He had long since

---

* In truth, Nancy Reagan consulted her astrologer on her husband's schedule. It was Hillary Clinton who reportedly took part in a séance in the White House solarium, where a new age mystic made contact with the spirit of Eleanor Roosevelt.

† Obama's jokes for formal speeches were prepared by a "Humor Cabinet" consisting of Axelrod, Favreau, John Lovett, and a rotating collection of guest writers, including Seth Myers of *Saturday Night Live.*

trained himself to pause and think before speaking in public. It usually worked fine in preventing the gaffes that afflict most politicians, but it kept him from being his normal self, and this left him in a bit of a rhetorical bind. If he spoke too honestly, he would get in trouble and commit the sin of distraction. But he knew the bigger danger was in becoming too cautious and platitudinous; that would mean losing the authenticity that had brought him this far.

OBAMA WAS DETERMINED to stay as normal as possible for as long as possible. Well after he was elected, he was still in the habit of leaving phone messages in which he slowly said, "This is Ba-rack O-bama," as if his name was still hard to remember. Even with his closest aides the president identified himself on the phone as "Obama": "Gibbs. Obama. We need to think about . . ." Or "Pete. Obama. Remember when we talked about . . ."

He didn't feed off the crowds like so many politicians; he found working the rope lines tiring, and he often laughed about the public adulation. In early 2008 a middle-aged African American woman was so overcome with emotion at a rally in Cincinnati that she collapsed in rapture. When a reporter showed him the video on her laptop, he exclaimed in mock horror, "It's a cult!"

His mother was an atheist, and though he had found God in Chicago he was never a regular in the pews at Trinity. When speculation arose about where in Washington the Obamas would regularly worship, the answer was nowhere. "Let's be blunt," Obama said. "We were pretty affected by what happened at Trinity and the controversy surrounding Reverend Wright. That was disturbing to us. It made us very sensitive to the fact that as president, the church we attend can end up being interpreted as speaking for us at all times." To avoid that, the Obamas sometimes attended services at a tiny chapel at Camp David run by the military and used by a few military families.* The navy chaplain there, Carey Cash, whose great-uncle was the singer Johnny Cash, was known for his compelling sermons. He had witnessed a lot of action in Iraq and spoke often of how a "wall of angels" protected the soldiers around him. The president found special comfort in church when responding to tragedies or weighing matters of war and peace,

---

* Obama liked Camp David, but because of his children's school activities, went only occasionally. And he only rarely went home to Chicago. By contrast, George W. Bush spent 977 days at either Camp David or his Crawford ranch, more than a third of his presidency.

but like other presidents he attended services irregularly, in part out of concern about the inconvenience it caused other worshippers.

He was a committed Christian but his spiritual life had an ecumenical cast. He thought the Muslim call to prayer a beautiful sound and held the first Passover Seder ever in the White House. Jim Wallis, a pastor and social activist who had met Obama at the Saguaro Forum at Harvard, emailed him after his grandmother died that he would need some spiritual counseling as president, preferably from someone who (unlike Wallis) had no political interests. But Obama didn't find such a person, or kept him a secret if he did.

While he didn't readily share his fears, there were no taboo subjects with Obama. Even assassination threats, which surged 400 percent at the time he took office before settling back to historical norms, weren't out of bounds. Michelle was always concerned about safety, but the president was fatalistic and occasionally looked to make light of the macabre. In the press conference where he stumbled over the encounter between an African American Harvard professor and a Cambridge police officer, he joked about what would happen if he tried to jimmy his way into his new home, the White House: "Here, I'd get shot." When a slender male African American friend went out on the Truman Balcony with him, he gestured to the tourists behind the South Lawn fence and joked, "If you wave to them they'll think you're me and you might get shot."* When a visitor made the faux pas of commenting that Reagan's tax and budget proposals went sailing through Congress in 1981 in large part because he was wounded in an assassination attempt, the president cheerfully replied, "If it's okay with you, I'd rather not get it done that way."

———

MOST PRESIDENTS AREN'T as well-read as they claim; they're outer-directed people, and the lists of their favorite books are often concocted. Obama's list, compiled at the request of the *New York Times* just before the election, was no doubt political too. It omitted *The Auto-biography of Malcolm X,* which he admitted in *Dreams from My Father* had a profound influence on his life. But because Obama came to office as a conspicuously intellectual president, it may offer some clues.

From the eighteenth and nineteenth century, Obama listed Thomas Jefferson, Adam Smith, Ralph Waldo Emerson, and Mark Twain, as well as Lincoln of course. Among the works of African American writers he

---

* There was no danger. When the Secret Service is alerted that the president is on the Balcony, the crowds are moved across Constitution Avenue, away from the fence.

cited W.E.B. DuBois's *Souls of Black Folk,* Martin Luther King's *Letter from a Birmingham Jail,* and Toni Morrison's *Song of Solomon,* the last of which he referred to several times on the campaign. Other novelists who influenced him were John Steinbeck (his favorite was *In Dubious Battle*), Graham Greene, Alexander Solzhenitsyn, Doris Lessing, and Robert Penn Warren, whose *All the King's Men* has long been required reading for anyone interested in politics. He cited philosophers and theologians Friedrich Nietzsche, Reinhold Niebuhr, and Paul Tillich and rounded out the list with Chicagoan Studs Terkel's *Working* (an oral history of working people) and Robert Caro's classic, *The Power Broker,* which contains useful advice on how to get things done in government. Obama neglected to mention the reading material he devoted special attention to as a child: comic books.

On TV the president liked *Mad Men* and *Entourage,* but his viewing habits ran more to basketball, football, and sometimes golf, as well as a regular fix of *SportsCenter* on ESPN. His iPod contained all of Stevie Wonder's work and at least thirty Bob Dylan songs, plus plenty of Bruce Springsteen, Sheryl Crow, and Jay-Z. He liked August Wilson plays and knew a few Shakespearean soliloquies by heart. His all-time favorite movies included *The Godfather, Casablanca, One Flew Over the Cuckoo's Nest,* and *Lawrence of Arabia,* and there were memorable lines from other films that became running jokes. When something went wrong in the national security bureaucracy, aides could usually get a presidential laugh by quoting Ed Harris's character in *Apollo 13:* "Tell me this isn't a government operation." Obama was fond of pointing out that he too had to operate in an imperfect world. He recalled the sequence in the film when Mission Control uses duct tape and a few odds and ends the astronauts have on board to fashion a makeshift solution to save the crew. The movie was about using American ingenuity to solve a big problem, and he thought it resonated.

AS PRESIDENT, OBAMA had more time than during the campaign to indulge his love of basketball. On weekends the onetime high school player could often be found on an indoor gym court at Fort McNair or Camp David or, weather permitting, shooting hoops with a couple of friends on the South Lawn's hard-surface tennis court, where he ordered two baskets installed and lines painted. (He and Michelle still used the court for tennis too.) He played the UConn women's basketball champions in P-I-G and won, but the real action was in the pickup games, where the president's secret weapon was always choosing Reggie Love for his team.

Obama liked playing with young locals (including a software engineer and a juvenile corrections officer) unconnected to government, but he also used the games for some politics. With four good players in his Cabinet (Duncan, Donovan, Geithner, and Salazar) and lots of eager players on the Hill (including North Carolina Congressman Heath Shuler, a former quarterback for the Washington Redskins, and in 2010 "Downtown Scottie Brown," as he was called in high school, the new GOP senator from Massachusetts), these games were the hottest ticket in town. There were even reports of a brisk business in private basketball lessons in Washington for those angling for an invitation.

Arne Duncan believed that how you played basketball revealed your character. He had started playing with Obama in the early 1990s, mostly at the Field House at the University of Chicago, where street hustlers and Nobel laureates mixed it up. As a one-time professional, Duncan was several cuts above Obama, of course.* But from the start, when Obama wasn't anyone important, Duncan noticed his intelligence on the court. He was slowed a bit by age and tendonitis in his knee but proved strong, agile, and especially good at anticipating the flow of the game. As a left-handed guard with a decent jump shot, the president could be tricky to cover. He'd pass well, cut sharply, and drive to the basket. Chris Duhon of the New York Knicks played with the "Baller-in-Chief" and reported back that he was a surprisingly good player. His one criticism echoed the GOP's: "He can only go left."

One weekend, Duncan set up a game with five college players, not big stars but plenty good. He assumed they would pick up sides but the president said he wanted to play them all. So it was Obama, Duncan, Marty Nesbitt, Eric Whitaker, and Reggie Love (the only one under forty) against the college players half their age. Love was having an off day but the president's team still narrowly took three out of five short games. "See, Arne, you always underestimate us," the president said. "We *always* overachieve."

In Chicago in the 1980s Obama watched Michael Jordan and the Bulls struggle for a few years before beginning their run of championships. When asked during the primaries when he was going to fight back against Hillary (a question similar to the one posed in 2009 about his Republican critics), Obama invoked "the Jordan Rules," the Detroit Pistons' strategy for bottling up Jordan and the Bulls in the late 1980s.

---

* After returning to Chicago to work in finance and later in education, Duncan traveled all over the country with Craig Robinson and John Rogers (ex-husband of Desirée), playing tournaments. When Michael Jordan was making his comeback in the 1990s after his first retirement, Duncan practiced with him often.

"It wasn't a pretty sight. But until the Bulls learned to push back, it was going to be hard for them to win," Obama said.

Duncan liked to compare Obama to Jordan, not as players but in the spirit they brought to the court. "What they both possessed was this instinct of being a killer," Duncan said. "Nice guys, great smiles, they seem relaxed—but the same mental toughness and relentless desire to win." Late in the game Obama could be heard confidently telling his teammates, "We got this," just as he had right before the election. In Duncan's experience, most players, even terrific ones, run and hide when the game is on the line; they don't want the ball. But Jordan famously won big games at the buzzer. Obama didn't sink as many, but he was game to try, or at least pass for the key assist. "At the end of the game, Barack always wants the ball," Duncan said.

Obama thought of himself as a clutch performer, holding back a bit in the second and third quarters and letting the tension build until the climactic moment. His closest advisors first noticed the trait when preparations for his announcement speech in Springfield, Illinois, in 2007 went poorly. Obama stayed up writing until 4 a.m. and barely bothered to rehearse.* After the speech scored big, Axelrod said to Gibbs, "He's obviously a game player and not a practice player." Gibbs replied that now he knew why Obama hadn't been a starter on his high school basketball team.

Over time his staff got used to it. As president he routinely rewrote speeches at the last minute, skipped rehearsal, and assumed the best. With the game on the line, he hit the three-pointer with nothing but net. His aides had faith he would, but worried still; even Michael Jordan missed sometimes.

———

OBAMA LEAPT INTO any competitive challenge. Over the summer of 2009 he decided to take up fly-fishing in Montana. It rained the day that he and Jim Messina went out on the river, but the president was completely hooked on the sport and happily soaked. After being humiliated at a Pennsylvania bowling alley during the primaries, he worked hard on his game in the White House bowling alley that Nixon installed, plotting his public return to the lanes in 2012.

On weekends the president looked forward to competing in any game available, including Scrabble, pool, and poker, usually Texas Hold 'Em or a game called 727. Beginning with his poker nights in

* Michelle Obama was the opposite. Before her speech to the 2008 Democratic Convention, she practiced endlessly.

Springfield, he was a cautious player with a good poker face and a habit of growing exceptionally quiet when the hands were dealt. He'd peer at his cards and glance up, totally expressionless. When he won he wouldn't gloat or say anything bombastic, just take his winnings; when he lost it would be the same. But if someone else won or lost a big hand he'd crack a joke, often a little friendly trash talk. His game was serious and no-nonsense when it involved him, and full of humor when it came to anyone else.

Like JFK, he had downplayed his love of golf during the campaign for political reasons (it's seen as a more Republican sport) and had little time to play. But as president he golfed about twice a month, usually at Fort Belvoir or Andrews Air Force Base, less than Clinton but much more than Bush, who played little after 9/11. Obama barred cameras from the course when he played, as Kennedy did. Wrong image.

Obama wasn't nearly as good at golf as he was at basketball, which might be one reason he worked so hard at it. He labored diligently on his lefty swing, which still wasn't much to look at (another reason he allowed no pictures). The president shot in the 90s, which, when he partnered with Marvin Nicholson, was often good enough to collect on friendly bets, a dollar a hole. He was the first president who played golf routinely with young staffers, who enjoyed the chance to play hooky from work.

He asked Joe Biden to play once. When the vice president beat him with a 77, it was the last time they played together, which became a running joke between them. Al Gore got upset in 1993 when the Clintons didn't invite him for movie night in the White House theater, but Biden told aides he "didn't give a shit" whether Obama included him in social and recreational activities, and the president usually didn't. Biden prided himself, he told them, on not being a "pain in the ass," and thought Obama liked him better because of it.

From the start Obama was indisputably the First Fan. When he appeared on television to talk knowledgably about "March Madness" college basketball brackets or the minutiae of the Super Bowl, sports fans knew instinctively that he wasn't faking it.* The president understood the code of loyalty under which real fans are never neutral in their choice of favorite teams and players, so he wore his Chicago White Sox cap on weekends and his Sox jacket as he threw out the first pitch at the All-Star Game in St. Louis. When he was asked on TV in Los Ange-

---

* When John Kerry referred in 2004 to Manny Ramirez of the hometown Boston Red Sox as "Manny Ortez," he lost votes among sports fans everywhere. So did Cubs fan Hillary Clinton when she moved to New York in 2000 to run for the Senate and wore a Yankees cap.

les who was the greatest NBA star of all time, Kobe Bryant or Michael Jordan, he blurted out, "Oh, Michael!" This was a departure from the practice of his predecessors, who mostly felt obliged to represent all teams.

Obama was the first president to have a team (the Bulls) over to the White House when it hadn't won a championship, and he made sure Jarrett's Office of Public Engagement included a staffer assigned to coordinate appearances with teams. Not surprisingly Obama was intrigued with Tiger Woods, whom he invited over for a West Wing tour and a chat when he was in Washington in April for a charity golfing event. In December, when Woods was exposed as a philanderer, he was sympathetic to the Woods family ordeal at the hands of the press. LeBron James, an Obama campaign contributor, also visited the White House, though Jordan, who had no interest in politics, did not.

Complaints arose that Obama's sports mania had created a testosterone-heavy staff at the top. This was annoying to the White House but hardly politically damaging. In fact the masculine temperament Obama conveyed through his genuine love of sports was at least a modest plus for Democrats, long derided as the "mommy" party, though there was no evidence anyone ever polled responses to his recreation choices, as Dick Morris had done in the 1990s for Clinton. But it helped that his off-hours image was closer to Reagan clearing brush than to Carter struggling with a killer rabbit in his pond.

After learning that the *New York Times* was at work on a story about the president's recreational activities being all male, Obama scheduled domestic policy chief Melody Barnes for eighteen holes. He also decided to host a dinner in the residence for senior women staffers. He had hired more women for powerful White House positions than had any of his predecessors, yet several of them felt marginalized, not by the exclusion from his recreation but by their treatment at the office. The discussion at the dinner focused on what one woman in attendance called *de facto* as opposed to *de jure* sexism—that women members of the staff seemed to get the last word with the president less often than the men did. They groused that Rahm Emanuel and Larry Summers too often excluded them from meetings, though as one pointed out, they did that to men too. The overall tone was pleasant and everyone present found Obama a good listener. Afterward the women dubbed the dinner "our basketball game with the president."*

---

* The dinner went so well that the women decided to have their own regular monthly "basketball game" at a local restaurant without the president. The group included Valerie Jarrett, senior advisor to the president; Mona Sutphen, White House deputy chief of staff; Anita Dunn, director of communications; Carol Browner, director of the White House Office of

Not much changed around the office—Obama was just more comfortable most of the time with guys—but at least he recognized it as a problem to work on.

————

OBAMA SOMETIMES HAD trouble relaxing. He had asked his friends Marty Nesbitt and Eric Whitaker to hang out with him in Washington on the first six weekends of his presidency, and they came plenty of times through the year. Once, after playing golf, Whitaker asked if the game had cleared his head. Obama said no, he was thinking about Guantánamo. When he was under pressure he could be found sometimes with his head tilted back, sighing and rubbing his temples. But most of the time he left the problems—and workday emotional detachment—behind for a few hours. "When you have dinner with him, he's not objectively 'participating' in the dinner," said Marty Nesbitt. "He's all there, arguing about who's going to win the NBA championship. We have a lot of laughs about the kids and the funny things they do."

Even as his approval ratings on handling his job waned in his first year, Obama's personal popularity remained healthy by historical standards. The American people took the measure of Obama the man and decided they liked him fine, though they might have warmed up to him more after a little P-I-G or two-on-two on the White House basketball court.

———————————————————————

Energy and Climate Change Policy; Nancy-Ann DeParle, director of the White House Office of Health Reform; Melody Barnes, chair of the Domestic Policy Council; Christina Romer, chair of the Council of Economic Advisers; Nancy Hogan, director of presidential personnel; Susan Sher, the first lady's chief of staff; Alyssa Mastromonaco, director of scheduling and advance; and Lisa Brown, staff secretary.

18

The Skinny Guy and the Fat Cats

From the beginning Wall Street compensation was a big headache. The same firms that had driven the country into a ditch were still lavishing billions in bonuses on their employees, with the excuse that this was necessary for retention of valued executives. The American public wasn't buying it, especially from those banks receiving taxpayer money through TARP. Obama wasn't either. Nine days after entering office, he blasted the 2008 bonuses as "the height of irresponsibility."

But it was hard to tell where the tongue-lashing ended and the true crackdown—if there was to be one—began.

Inside the White House Axelrod was among the few representing the so-called populist side of the argument, and a joshing debate broke out. Axelrod asked Summers, "So, what does your plutocrat constituency make of this, Larry?"

"It's good to be hearing what Che thinks," Summers replied.

Axelrod wasn't excluded from economic policy discussions, but it was his judgment on how to frame the message and the political implications of the bonuses that Obama sought. When political advisors pushed crowd-pleasing ideas, they were usually shot down by the economists.

Summers and Geithner were driving the policy. One of Obama's closest allies and friends in the Senate, Claire McCaskill, found she was no match for them. McCaskill had a bill to limit executive compensation to the president's salary, $400,000, for executives of firms receiving federal money. She got some rhetorical support from the president, who agreed with Axelrod that he needed to be out front on the issue. But Geithner pushed back hard, arguing that the bill would make it difficult to get banks to cooperate with the administration's plans.

The treasury secretary later described himself as "stunned" by the "deeply offensive" suggestion that he was doing the bidding of Wall Street. He had never worked there, never had a house in the Hamptons, and didn't socialize with bankers, he said. "It's not my world, I'm not close to that world, and I spend a huge amount of my time listening to academic arguments against the financial community." He claimed he was looking at the issues on the merits and wasn't carrying water for anyone. Why didn't the press ever report that many of the big financial players were angry at him for the new transparency requirements? But there was little doubt that Geithner had absorbed the values of bankers "by osmosis," as Paul Krugman put it.

Mark Patterson, Geithner's chief of staff and among those who made the most strenuous argument against curtailing bonuses, had been a Goldman Sachs lobbyist before joining the administration.* In the first seven months Geithner's calendar included at least eighty phone calls or meetings with Goldman Sachs's Lloyd Blankfein, JP Morgan's Jamie Dimon, and Citigroup's Richard Parsons and Vikram Pandit, among others. Geithner argued that it was the treasury secretary's job to talk to the financial community and he insisted that those eighty calls were a "tiny fraction" of the calls received by his predecessors. He said of the bankers, "They spend all their time complaining that I'm not spending enough time listening to them." Geithner wanted to hang a big sign in his office that said "No Whining."

Those contacts were not evidence of any conspiracy. But you didn't have to consider Goldman a "great vampire squid wrapped around the face of humanity," in the words of Rolling Stone's Matt Taibbi (a latter-day Lincoln Steffens with a Gonzo twist), to believe that moneyed interests were looting the treasury. When Warren Buffett bought $5 billion of Goldman stock in October 2008, he got a good price. Why couldn't the taxpayers get the same? Why did Goldman get 100 cents on the dollar—more than $13 billion—from the government through AIG? It was done in November 2008 on Bush's watch, but Geithner, in his role at the New York Fed, was the one who handled the deal.

Geithner's explanation was that the liquidation of AIG would have disastrous global consequences. "You either prevent default, because default would be cataclysmic, or you don't," he said. "And when you prevent default, you're doing so to make sure they can meet their contractual obligations."

Some experts on corporate shenanigans, such as former prosecutor Eliot Spitzer, said that all the complex explanations were specious. Beyond the AIG deal and TARP, Goldman was benefiting from tens of billions in Fed guarantees. So when the firm became hugely profitable again and handed out $23 billion in bonuses, Joe Nocera of the New York Times rightly asked, Where is the taxpayers' bonus?

Geithner didn't believe in punishing Goldman or anyone else. And

* Patterson received a waiver to work at Treasury.

he didn't back fundamental restructuring of the banking industry because, at bottom, he didn't think the system was broken. The real problem in 2008, he thought, was old-fashioned risk in the real estate sector and not the exotic financial products or proprietary trading.*

Before long Geithner would see that Paul Volcker took a rather different view of the "Big Casino" that Wall Street had become.

EARLY ON OBAMA announced a proposal to cap compensation for top executives at TARP-supported companies, but McCaskill soon learned that the president wasn't going to push it. The same thing happened to Chris Dodd, who attached restrictions on compensation to the Senate's stimulus bill. Geithner and Summers asked Dodd to delete a provision making the bonus restrictions on TARP-backed firms retroactive. After first claiming that he didn't know who arranged for the change, Dodd later admitted it was the administration. In the no-good-deed-goes-unpunished department, Dodd's high profile on restricting bonuses later left him open to the charge that he'd known about the AIG bonuses for weeks and done nothing to object to them.

For those who were outraged by the bonuses, Dodd's amendment, which became law, was better than nothing (the position of many Republicans), but it brought unintended consequences as companies found ways around the restrictions with delayed compensation.

In mid-March the bonus story suddenly got hotter. New documents showed that four hundred AIG executives received $165 million in bonuses even as the collapse of their company was taking the global economy over the cliff. Members of Congress outdid one another in heaping scorn on the firm. Summers made a tone-deaf appearance on the Sunday talk shows arguing that AIG's conduct had been "outrageous" but that the "sanctity of contracts" meant that nothing could be done about the bonuses. Afterward he and Geithner admitted that they had put the president in a box politically.

Obama tried to bust through his inner calm and get himself worked up about bonuses, at least on television. "I don't want to quell anger—I think people are right to be angry. I am angry," Obama said. But was he? At a White House briefing on March 16 to announce that he had instructed Geithner to pursue "every single legal avenue" to getting back the bonuses, Obama got a frog in his throat and coughed. "Excuse me,"

---

* Proprietary trading occurs when financial institutions trade not only for their clients but for . themselves.

he joked. "I'm choked up with anger here." The audience laughed because it knew he wasn't.

In truth he was appalled and philosophical at the same time, listening with an annoyed expression to the tired "retention" argument peddled by bankers and their apologists. This view held that the only bankers who could "unwind" AIG's toxic derivatives were some of the same geniuses who had caused the mess in the first place. A more plausible argument, offered by Summers, was that all the wailing about AIG was destroying its brand and its "market cap" (value) and thus making it much less likely that the company would ever pay back what it owed the treasury. Every slap at AIG was arguably costing the taxpayers tens of billions of dollars, he argued.

Within hours of the AIG firestorm the House, with some Republican support, rushed through a bill that taxed bonuses for executives at bailed-out companies at 90 percent. Some argued that the bill was flatly unconstitutional; others weren't sure. But it was hasty and irresponsible populism. Obama thought the pitchfork fever was out of control and there was little support for it in the Senate. The idea quickly died.

As the spring wore on, the president knew that he had to revisit the issue of bonuses. Geithner, again at odds with Axelrod, didn't think they should be regulated at all, but he ended up digging into the question of "alignment." For years CEO pay had not been aligned with performance; everyone knew that. But Geithner and Summers now understood that compensation wasn't aligned with "sound risk management" either. Individual greed was destabilizing the system. What Summers had earlier denigrated as a "populist" argument was gaining some traction with him. And the political need to address obscene corporate pay was undiminished.

So on June 11 Geithner sounded tough on camera talking about new "principles" that would crack down on golden parachutes and pay that was unconnected to performance. He proposed that companies shift bonuses into three years of restricted stock, the idea being to discourage reckless decisions to inflate short-term profits and boost bonuses. And he chose a "special master for TARP compensation," Ken Feinberg, a lawyer who had worked out compensation after 9/11. It was a good choice. Over the next six months, Feinberg managed to cut executive pay at TARP firms roughly in half.

But once again the government's bark was worse than its bite. Obama decided to use the Securities and Exchange Commission and the Federal Reserve to regulate the true villains of the tale: the compensation committees of corporate boards. Shareholders were to be given some new rights to review compensation packages (called "Say on Pay"), an important advance. But those rights were nonbinding and they didn't apply to traders, which was where a lot of the real money was anyway. All in all, Obama's response was hardly Rooseveltian. Neither Theodore nor Franklin would likely have thought it ambitious enough.

The bottom line was that Washington would largely rely on companies to curb their own greed, unless they were wards of the state. This meant that corporate America could hunker down and wait for the storm to pass. When it did, Wall Street was unlikely to go all the way back to the bad old days of obscene compensation totally unconnected to performance. Too much had happened. But they would go at least partway back, for that was the world they knew.

Obama's refusal to position himself as a full-throated populist on compensation hardly dampened the growing anger that corporate chieftains felt toward him. Wherever they gathered, even the Democrats among them spoke of how "scared" they were of new federal power to meddle in what they considered to be their private affairs. When Geithner addressed the Economic Club of Chicago, the business executives at the tables, many of whom knew Obama personally and supported him financially, had to be convinced in the question-and-answer period that the president wasn't moving in a "socialist" direction.

It was no surprise when some big investment banks insisted on returning their TARP money as quickly as possible. These firms were eager to escape government protection so they could resume using 40 to 50 percent of their revenues to enrich themselves. Meanwhile the banking industry wasted no time unleashing its army of lobbyists to water down Barney Frank's re-regulation efforts, aimed at preventing another meltdown. Having been saved by the government, they now turned on it.

Wall Street's boundless ingratitude toward a Democratic president who (along with his Republican predecessor) had rescued them from ruin was reminiscent of a story FDR liked to tell. A lifeguard saves a rich man from drowning. Afterward the rich man returns to the beach and yells, "Hey, lifeguard, you lost my silk hat!" The metaphor popular in the Obama White House was that bankers were like Doberman pinschers who had been hit by a speeding car and were whimpering by the side of the road until a man came along and rescued them, at which point they bit him.

Geithner knew the populist anger was rising and wasn't sure how to cope with it. Bill Clinton had him up to Harlem for a two-hour lunch and told him there was little he could do. "You could pull Lloyd Blankfein into a dark alley and slit his throat and it would satisfy them for about two days, and then the bloodlust would rise again," Clinton told him.

By mid-2009 Geithner and Summers believed they had been proven right on the retention issue. The angry liberal argument about highly paid executives denied their bonuses—Where are they gonna go?—had been disproven by events, they said. Stars at TARP-backed firms were being lured away by hedge funds not connected to the government. Penalizing TARP-backed firms on compensation, though politically satisfying, was proving problematic. It gave incentives to institutions to get out from under TARP protection before some of them were healthy enough to do so.

Obama found that argument irritating and he was glad to see Feinberg take a whack at compensation. In June the *New York Times* reported that big bonuses were back at Goldman Sachs and other banks. Obama later told a friend that the angriest he got as president in his first year was when he heard Blankfein say that Goldman was never in danger of collapse. That was flatly untrue, he said.

"Let me get this straight," the president said in a meeting one day when the subject turned to Wall Street. "They're now saying that they deserve big bonuses because they're making money again. But they're making money because they've got government guarantees."

"These guys want to be paid like rock stars when all they're doing is lip-synching capitalism," Austan Goolsbee chimed in. "They're the financial version of Milli Vanilli!"

———————

To give himself a broader range of high-level economic advice, during the transition Obama had cooked up the idea of a "President's Economic Recovery Advisory Board" modeled on the President's Foreign Intelligence Advisory Board, an influential panel in every recent administration except George W. Bush's. When he asked Paul Volcker to chair it, Volcker said he'd do so only if it was going to be real, not a "show thing," like when he was called in for a photo-op during the campaign, then sent home. Obama gave him the right assurances, but he either didn't know or didn't tell Volcker that under sunshine laws, every meeting of the board would be a matter of public record. To Volcker this defeated the whole purpose of the panel, which was to provide confidential advice to the president.

Summers and Volcker viewed each other warily. Predictably Summers reacted badly to the Volcker board and Volcker, who expected that his advice would reach Obama unfiltered, reacted badly to Summers's interference. Summers claimed that he was willing to let

Volcker offer independent advice, but he exercised veto power over every board appointee (to prevent conflicts of interest, he said), tried to hold down the number of meetings, and insisted that Volcker and the assembled CEOs, venture capitalists, and labor leaders send their reports to the president through him. To get around the sunshine laws, Volcker set up a series of subcommittees that met privately. But, he was unhappy to learn, even the subcommittee memos were modified by Summers before reaching Obama.

Volcker could always go through Valerie Jarrett if he needed to see Obama, but he didn't want to abuse the privilege. After hearing from Obama often during the campaign, Volcker's phone stopped ringing. He wryly told friends he was nothing more than a "wax figure" for the White House.

It wasn't that Volcker was somehow unimpressed with Obama. He thought he was better informed on the economy than any other president he had met, and he had known all of them going back to Lyndon Johnson. But on critical structural questions, he argued that the administration wasn't being nearly tough enough.

On most economic issues Volcker's advice was unexceptional. The advice his advisory board provided the president on climate change, health care reform, and small business largely reflected what Obama already believed anyway. Everyone agreed on the need to avoid bank nationalization, but the Volcker board was split on the essential question of financial re-regulation, with Volcker cast in the unusual role of progressive, well to the left (on treatment of Wall Street) of the others. Paul Volcker, principal author of what was once thought of as heartless Reaganomics, was now the most populist of the bunch!

Volcker believed that the Fed had gone to "the very edge of its lawful and implied powers," but he wasn't hugely interested in the raging debates over the overlapping roles of the Fed, the SEC, the Commodity Futures Trading Commission, and other agencies in regulating potentially explosive financial products. (When regulators started complaining on the Hill about their jurisdictions being rearranged, Geithner summoned them to the big conference room at the Treasury Department. "This is fucking ridiculous," he said. "You've all got to look past your own institutional interests.") For Volcker these were bureaucratic, not philosophical differences.

The more important question went much deeper: What was to blame for the crisis: lax supervision or the very structure of Wall Street? The bankers themselves and just about everyone connected to the administration except Volcker believed the blame for the bubble-and-bust economy was inadequate regulation (by the Fed, the SEC, Clinton,

Bush, Congress, whoever). They tried to avoid the question of whether the very idea of five megabanks controlling $9 trillion in assets was a threat to the economy.

Dodging the central issue was itself a critical decision. The essence of the Obama regulatory policy was based on the hope that the government could muddle through by *supervising* systemic risk instead of *ending* it. The notion that some firms were "too big to fail" was never addressed squarely. One nervous regulator compared the policy to France's famous Maginot Line against Germany before World War II. If we just build the fortifications thicker, the French said, we can keep the Nazis out.

Of the major players, only Volcker (who didn't consider himself a player because he didn't hold a government job) thought the whole financial system was conflict ridden and dangerous. Contrary to much reporting, he did not advocate reinstating the Glass-Steagall Act. But he did favor segregating commercial and investment banking from proprietary trading.* Advising clients while trading in one's own accounts, he felt, was an obvious conflict of interest (the laughable claims of bankers that they had internal "Chinese Walls" notwithstanding) and an inherent source of instability. Why should core banking operations be subjected to such risk? Under his plan, some new marriages would break up. Bank of America and Merrill Lynch would have to separate; same for JP Morgan Chase and Bear Stearns (which had merged in 2008). Goldman Sachs would have to sell off GS Capital Partners (its trading subsidiary) or stop benefiting from all the privileges of being a bank holding company.

Volcker was a droll character, but the idea that speculative trading would be backed by the federal government because these firms were "too big to fail" offended him. It was like Washington propping up huge casinos. As for the claim by Blankfein that Goldman was doing "God's work" by making capital available to businesses, well, that was preposterous. Volcker had never seen any evidence that the financial engineering of Wall Street contributed in a meaningful way to the GDP. He was fond of saying half-facetiously that the only financial innovation he could think of that had improved society was the ATM machine.

This wasn't the auto industry, Volcker said, with millions of jobs and a direct connection to growth (and the bailouts there were bad enough), but a bunch of extremely wealthy traders whose larger eco-

---

* The 1933 Glass-Steagall Act, repealed in 1999, separated commercial and investment banking. Volcker's reform idea would allow commercial banking and investment banking to be housed under one roof but required the separation of most trading operations.

nomic justification—reducing risk—had now been exposed mostly as a shallow excuse for sucking billions of dollars out of the economy and into their own pockets.

Volcker rejected the administration's premise for financial re-regulation. The idea of the government trying to keep an eye on so-called systemically important institutions struck him as both impractical and unfair. How do you determine which financial institutions are systemically important? (No one would have guessed it about AIG.) And when you do identify such institutions, and they think they're protected, doesn't that give them an unfair advantage? Why should certain favored nonbanks be treated like banks? And why should they be so big? Volcker was impressed by a new book by Henry Kaufman, one of Wall Street's genuinely wise men. Kaufman pointed out that over the past two decades, the number of American banks fell by half, with the ten largest now holding more than half the financial assets of the entire country.

To the policy mandarins, who believed from the beginning of their academic training in the merits of financial engineering, Volcker's argument wasn't serious. "Too big to fail" and moral hazard were real problems, Summers and Geithner acknowledged, but they could be contained with the proper regulatory tinkering. They figured the president had enough on his plate without assaulting the megabanks the government had just helped survive the crisis.

Obama respected Volcker and asked to see his memo on the subject. Just before the announcement of his financial regulatory reform package in June, Obama called Volcker and confessed that he hadn't taken his advice. Volcker was surprised. He thought the president would see that the U.S. Treasury and the taxpayers should not be standing behind companies engaged in speculative trading.

––––––––

OBAMA WASN'T WRONG that the banks had to be saved first. They provided the lifeblood of the economy. But there was something unseemly about the way the rescue of the economy was designed. If massive federal aid was good enough for greedy bankers, the logic went, why not for needy homeowners? Millions of Americans, disproportionately black and Hispanic, were about to lose their claim on the American Dream.

Obama agreed in principle, and he pushed Geithner, Summers, and the others to confront the foreclosure crisis. Bush's "Hope for Homeowners" plan had been a total failure, designed so badly (it made lenders eat most of the losses) that fewer than five hundred loans had been modified under it. Obama was determined to do better, but when it came down to choosing between banks and homeowners, he was sticking with the banks.

Obama's earliest Senate supporter and close friend, Dick Durbin, felt differently. Just below Harry Reid in the Senate leadership and popular with his colleagues, Durbin passionately favored so-called cram-down legislation (the shorthand of critics that eventually got picked up by the press) that would allow bankruptcy judges to renegotiate the terms of homeowners' mortgages, as they often did in commercial real estate transactions when borrowers went bust. Like McCaskill, Durbin won Obama's lukewarm support for his bill, but the president and Rahm wouldn't lift a finger to help.

Despite the support of some large banks, Durbin's bill lost by a surprisingly wide margin. The White House wasn't willing to take on regional and community banks, whose executives were among the most generous contributors to their local members of Congress. Durbin fumed that "the banks own this place." He found it ironic; political support for the banks increased at the exact same moment that public support for the banks evaporated. How could that be?

The answer lay in the composition of the Democratic majority. To win back control of Congress in 2006, Rahm had recruited many moderate Democrats from conservative districts who would be vulnerable in the 2010 midterms. So whereas FDR had a strong faction of his party that treated banking and regulation as an ideological issue (led by Wright Patman of Texas), Obama did not.

The pressure on banks also lessened as most paid back their TARP loans with interest. Obama later said that this was one of the biggest surprises of the year. Instead of being $700 billion in the hole, the government was owed less than $100 billion. "It turned out better than any of us could have expected at the time," he said later.

———

THE BIGGEST PROBLEM on Main Street was real estate. Obama's housing policy was an improvement over Bush's, but that wasn't saying much. In February Obama and Secretary of Housing and Urban Development Sean Donovan announced a $75 billion plan to help the nine million homeowners facing foreclosure. The plan led to unrealistic expectations among strapped homeowners.

By spring it was clear that the government's efforts were aimed at only about three million of the nine million, the ones the Obama administration figured had a reasonable claim to stay in their homes.

These were the responsible people living full time in their house, not speculators or second-home buyers. Most had received subprime mortgages and just needed a little help with loan modifications to prevent or at least delay foreclosure. The plan was not directed at potential "walkaways" (whose homes were worth so much less than they paid for them that it made more sense financially to walk away), at the foolhardy (who had bought, say, a $600,000 house on a $60,000 income), or at the unemployed (whose unemployment compensation was not counted by the banks as income when renegotiating, so they usually couldn't be helped).

But even those who qualified for government help often had big trouble refinancing, as banks went from being absurdly loose to absurdly tight with credit. For years refinancing was like a lottery prize you didn't deserve to win; now it was like painful kidney stones that you couldn't find a doctor to remove. While more than a million homeowners had their favorable terms extended, only about one tenth of that number permanently refinanced their loans.

The White House and Treasury fretted over what to do. Rescuing everyone from foreclosure was impossible; it would create huge moral hazard, not to mention costing taxpayers another trillion dollars. But even the Obama plan required exquisite fine-tuning or it would be horrifically expensive as banks dumped their worst mortgages on the government. Summers designed an inventive provision that incentivized banks to find responsible borrowers. "This is where Larry showed he was a virtuoso policymaker," said Goolsbee. But Elizabeth Warren's congressional oversight panel was scathing in an October report. Warren said the administration's plan didn't keep pace with the huge flow of foreclosures and did little to help the recession's biggest victims: the unemployed and those with subprime mortgages.

After some jawboning by the president, the banks reluctantly began to process more loan modifications. The White House knew the program was working a little better when powerful hedge funds like BlackRock and Fortress began calling up and screaming that the loan servicers they owned were modifying too many loans. But conversions to a permanent new rate remained slow. By the end of his first term Obama would likely be able to say that he helped a few million Americans avoid foreclosure. Of course it wouldn't be much to brag about because millions more would be forced from their homes.

Like the trillions in Fed guarantees to banks, housing policy was a long way from the Fed's traditional bread and butter of regulating the money supply. But injecting massive liquidity into the system (mostly by bolstering Fannie Mae and Freddie Mac) was its own form of Milton Friedman–esque monetary policy, and it worked. In the same way that Volcker, more than Reagan, was the key to saving the country from inflation in the early 1980s, it was Bernanke, more than Bush and Obama, who saved it from deflation. The events of 2009 proved anew that no American president has as much direct power over the economy as the chairman of the Fed.

It was no surprise when Obama announced in August that he would reappoint Bernanke as Fed chairman, a position that many had once expected for Summers. Bernanke screwed up badly in 2007 and 2008, but since then the Fed had moved boldly to stabilize the economy. Of course plenty could still go wrong in banking, autos, and especially commercial real estate, where plummeting asset values would wreck havoc when thousands of mortgages came due in 2010 and 2011. The system that would handle these and other challenges was structurally unchanged from when Barack Obama took office.

————

WHEN IT CAME to structural reform, the devil was in the details, and those details were in the hands of Congress. Obama's best idea was a proposal for a new Consumer Financial Protection Agency to crack down on predatory lending. (The agency would likely start by requiring the terms of loans to be written in plain English.) Wall Street lobbyists, whose salaries had until recently been paid for with taxpayer money, went to work watering it down. The financial services industry spent $344 million in the first three quarters of 2009 lobbying against regulation, a pittance for bankers but enough to weaken the bill. Despite a new chairman at the Commodity Futures Trading Commission, Gary Gensler, who became a tiger for regulation, the derivatives market that had brought so much woe would remain lightly supervised.

This time Obama fought for his progressive reforms, though not always to great effect. When the Chamber of Commerce ran misleading ads alleging that butchers and other small businesses would be harmed by the new consumer agency, the president called the Chamber out by name (rare for a president) and departed from his prepared speech to remark archly, "I don't know how many of your butchers are offering financial services." In his December 12 radio address he attacked a "pep rally" of Republicans and financial interests dedicated to beating back reform with "phony arguments" meant to maintain the "bad habits of Washington." Just as in the stimulus and health care debates, the GOP would unanimously line up against doing anything.

On the larger issue of whether banks could be too big to fail, the president remained unwilling to adopt a harder line. The banks were still brittle, Geithner argued, and in some cases too quick to get out from under TARP. But the concerns of people like Paul Volcker and Henry Kaufman about excessive concentration of wealth in a handful of megabanks were beginning to get more of a hearing inside the Oval Office.

In the fall big financial institutions were again taking excessive risks. Having learned little, they apparently figured that they would keep the profits if their bets paid off and could saddle taxpayers with huge costs once again if they did not. Bonus levels returned nearly to their 2007 highs.

Obama knew he had to start catching up to the public outrage. On December 13 he went on *60 Minutes* to castigate "fat cat bankers on Wall Street" who had not shown "a lot of shame" and "still don't get it" about why the public was angry. He warned the bank lobbyists not to water down his financial reform package. But it was too late to back up the point with much muscle. All but two of the nineteen biggest banks had already repaid TARP.

The following day the chairmen of Goldman Sachs, Morgan Stanley, and Citigroup were supposed to join other bankers at a meeting with the president in the White House but were fogged in at LaGuardia Airport and had to take part by speakerphone. "Well, I appreciate you guys calling in," Obama said, though he was clearly peeved. The speakerphone conference symbolized the administration's impotence. The time when the government had leverage over Wall Street had passed.

As Christmas approached, the president believed the big banks had regained enough health that he could begin to confront them directly. He was finally eager to find a way to make them pay. He rejected a bonus tax as too easy to get around (by boosting salaries or deferring compensation) but settled on another approach that could both raise revenue and, he hoped, work politically in the midterm elections. "We are not going to let Wall Street take the money and run," he said in an early 2010 Saturday radio address. His answer was a steep bank tax that would confiscate about 5 percent of bank profits to be used to pay off the rest of TARP. "We're going to collect every dime," he said. The proposal was cleverly constructed. Community banks were untouched by the tax, which meant that the banks with the greatest clout in Congress wouldn't be lobbying against it. And if the big banks that would be hit by what Obama tactfully called "the fee" (those with more than $50 billion in assets) tried to pass along the cost to their customers, they were sure to lose market share to smaller banks. The Republicans were silent for once. They hated taxes but weren't eager to be seen siding with Wall Street.

Even so, the financial regulatory reform package continued to languish in Congress. Rahm thought that if the administration had given the Hill more ownership of the issue, as it did on health care, the remedies for preventing another economic collapse would have been approved more quickly. But the bigger problem was that for most of the year Obama bought the Geithner-Summers argument that the banks were fragile and couldn't be confronted while they remained in peril.

By late 2009 Obama was looking for a way to jump-start the bill. He began to have second thoughts about rejecting Volcker's idea of separating commercial and investment banking from proprietary trading. Biden pushed him to revisit the idea, and on October 28 Obama met with Volcker and his economic team to discuss it. Volcker had been to only a couple of small meetings with the president before (never one-on-one), but this one felt different. And the idea was beginning to pick up steam elsewhere, with Mervyn King, director of the Bank of England, and several former CEOs and former treasury secretaries from both parties now in support. When Goldman was revealed to have secretly shorted the very stocks it was recommending to clients, more momentum built.

Geithner and Summers continued to resist. Both had backed the big financial deregulation bill of the 1990s. Their explanation for the crisis had always been that most of the remaining regulations on the books were plenty strong but hadn't been enforced under Bush. They argued that proprietary trading had little if anything to do with the 2008 meltdown. In 2009 they favored certain reforms, but not major restructuring of the financial sector. Siding with Volcker would mean admitting that the critics were right—that Clinton and Rubin had erred in allowing the old New Deal regulatory architecture to be repealed.

Rubin, now retired from Wall Street, worried about the president's tone. Obama was right to push back, he thought, but would the populist rhetoric spook markets, short-circuiting recovery? Even progressive economists inside the White House shared the concern. "It's a balance," Jared Bernstein said. "You don't want to kill the golden goose, but you don't want it to crap all over you either."

In December the president overruled Summers and Geithner and endorsed what he came to call the Volcker Rule. Volcker discussed it with a wary Geithner on Christmas Eve, and Summers reluctantly agreed to fashion a plan. In January Obama, with Volcker towering over him, unveiled the idea publicly with a blast at the banks. Simon Johnson and other critics were delighted that the financial restructuring they had long advocated was finally on the table. If Congress passed the president's bill, banks would no longer be able to make risky trades that were, in a crisis, backed by the full faith and credit of the United States.

———

BY THE END of the year the big tension in the economic realm was between job creation and deficit reduction. Summers, Romer, Sperling, and the political team were on the job creation side, with Geithner and Orszag hoisting the flag for fiscal responsibility. Obama grew frustrated that the two sides couldn't reach a consensus that balanced the two.

When it came to jobs, there wasn't much out-of-the-box thinking in the Obama administration. Little ideas like employing the inner-city jobless to tear down abandoned buildings and replace them with pocket parks (originated by former treasury secretary Paul O'Neill) slipped through the cracks. Big ideas like slashing the payroll tax and replacing it with value-added taxes or carbon taxes (advocated by Bill Drayton, founder of the Ashoka Foundation, among others) never got a full review. Some of the more innovative ideas were pushed by John Doerr, the Silicon Valley venture capitalist who served on the Volcker panel. Doerr won approval of a "cash for caulkers" plan, plus other incentives for weatherizing and retrofitting buildings, that could create jobs, cut carbon emissions, and reduce dependence on foreign oil all at the same time.

Rising foreclosures, surging demand for food stamps, huge state budget gaps—they all had their origin in the lack of jobs. By the end of 2009 more than seven million jobs had been lost in the two years since the economic crisis began. Just as the investor class breathed easier and the president declared the economy "back from the brink," unemployment hit double digits. At 10 percent, it was the highest since 1982, and that didn't even count more than twenty million Americans who were underemployed and thus depressing the living standards of their families. .

White House advisors could rationalize that joblessness was a lagging economic indicator. They could explain that the Recovery Act was only now kicking in. And they could insist that things could have been much worse. But no argument had the power to change the harsh political reality—everything the president hoped to do was dependent on getting that number down. If it was below 7 or 8 percent and heading lower, he would be fine. If it wasn't, he would be in deep trouble, with steep losses in the midterm elections and an impression of political impotence. He could push tax credits for small business hiring and incentives to create jobs in weatherization and a dozen other ideas, but none was a silver bullet. Like so many of his predecessors, Obama was the prisoner of developments that were largely beyond his control.

As 2010 began, the White House was staring at a jobless recovery with plenty of pain ahead. Summers could not yet be sure that his grandchildren in 2040 would avoid studying the Great Recession of 2008–9.

19

Modus Obama

As political staffers got to know him better, they learned what Jarrett, Axelrod, and Rouse had long known: that Obama was not a conventional politician. He didn't care much about presidential precedent and liked to operate a little differently than expected. But the system kept sucking him into some of the same old ways of doing things.

"Donor maintenance," for instance, at first didn't seem presidential to him and, not coincidentally, it bored him. Most members of his campaign's national finance committee didn't hear from Obama at all in the first several months of his presidency. Remembering the perception that Bill Clinton had "rented out the Lincoln Bedroom" to big donors, the Obamas closed the Lincoln Bedroom to any overnight visitors, preserving the site of the signing of the Emancipation Proclamation as a second-floor shrine.

But the president, conscious of the need to preserve a Democratic Congress, hardly ignored fund-raising. Because campaign finance rules had been rewritten to end large individual contributions to the party, Obama had to work harder for a much smaller haul than Clinton or Bush. In the second half of his first year he hosted two or three fundraisers a month, held mostly on the road.* It was the most time he had spent with wealthy Democrats since the earliest days of his campaign and he found it a chore. With the exception of a few ambassadorships (especially to large countries requiring wealthy envoys to cover for inadequate entertaining budgets) and a handful of the usual commissions and boards, contributors didn't seem to get much in return from Obama. If you were rich and didn't think you had been treated right, no one in the White House was going to lose sleep over it.†

---

* After the landmark Supreme Court decision in the case of *Citizens United v. Federal Election Commission,* fund-raising for the 2010 midterms promised to be entirely different, with unlimited independent expenditures sure to influence the process.

† This was bound to change in 2010 with the appointment of Julianna Smoot—finance director of Obama's campaign—as White House Social Secretary.

Inside the White House it was a fast and slippery track. The president wasn't one to trash people, but his aides chuckled over those clueless colleagues whom some of his younger staffers derisively called "mouth breathers," the ones who stood around with their mouths half-open, always a step behind, not sure what to do or say. Obama liked hard workers who took care of business. He sometimes recalled a scene from the movie *The Departed* in which Mark Wahlberg's character says, "I'm the guy who does his job. You must be the other guy." At a party to thank his campaign workers just after the Inauguration, the president said that David Plouffe reminded him of that character: "Always working, always doing his job, never hobnobbing with the big shots." He would never have told the director of FEMA after Hurricane Katrina, "Heck of a job, Brownie," unless it was true.

Obama had little tolerance for toadies. "His basic view is, 'Don't tell me I'm wonderful, tell me what's going on out there,' " said Claire McCaskill. All that insincere flattery was part of the Washington he disdained, though he was shrewd enough to know that it was also part of the job description. He felt the same about the waves of criticism in the second half of the year. It was important to listen to it but not let it throw you off course.

One of the big surprises for Obama at the beginning was how much he had to deal with the petty egos of Congress. As the health care debate heated up after Labor Day he spent dozens of hours in meetings with members. But because he lacked the elemental neediness of most politicians, he could never fully relate to their desire to be stroked. For the president, schmoozing members was like raising money or working a rope line. He didn't loathe all the gripping and grinning and chitchat; often he'd pick something up, the way Lincoln did in the 1860s when he took his "public opinion baths." But he didn't savor it either, as many politicians did. All things being equal, he would rather be upstairs reading a tome on nonproliferation or watching ESPN. And so he had to work at the part of being president that required being an actor. When he attended an event that didn't particularly interest him, he wasn't playing himself. He was playing "Barack Obama" in a costume he had carefully pasted together with the glue of self-interest, and he was playing him well.

The question was how long he could keep it up. He had convinced himself that charming members of Congress with room-temperature IQs was an important part of the presidency; his success depended on it. Or did it? Somewhere along the line the dimension of the job that he liked the least—dealing with Congress—had come to define his first year. In the name of getting things done, he had lashed himself to another branch of government—a broken branch.

The problem with the Senate, as he knew from experience, was that everyone there was an independent operator. Even ostensible allies could turn against you. Kent Conrad, for instance, was the second senator to endorse Obama (after Dick Durbin), and he could have been the head of OMB if he wanted, but in mid-March he said publicly that health care shouldn't go in the budget. This was viewed in the White House as "next to treachery," in the words of one aide, who forgot that a mere two months earlier this had been the view of so many of the senior staff that Daschle felt obliged to complain directly to the president.

The senior staff wanted to cut Conrad off at the knees, show him and everyone else that Democrats couldn't publicly defy the president and get away with it. But when they began to outline to the president how they planned to make Conrad sorry he'd ever lived, Obama said calmly that he'd already had a different, more conciliatory conversation with him. This worked better. Conrad scampered back into line and, though he continued to speak his mind, he was careful not to blindside the White House again.

This pattern was repeated again and again in 2009, as Max Baucus, Ben Nelson, Olympia Snowe, and other senators tried the patience of the White House staff. But the president remained unfailingly genteel. He believed there was one sure way to alienate members of Congress and that was to throw one's weight around. Rahm might intimidate a few Democratic congressmen, with greater or lesser success, but the days of President Johnson sticking his finger in the chest of Rhode Island Senator Theodore Green were long over. Even FDR learned that attempts to purge or even discipline fellow Democrats almost always ended badly.*

So Obama ultimately didn't think he had much choice but to throw in his lot with the congressional leadership. Even when he disagreed with Harry Reid's tactics on health care, the president liked his old-school, low-ego style. (He couldn't have cared less about Reid's "Negro" gaffe, and thought the media attention to it was stupid.)† Nancy Pelosi got over her pique at the way the stimulus was handled and also became a valued ally. Obama knew that Reid and Pelosi were colossally

---

* Roosevelt campaigned against six conservative Democrats in the 1938 midterms and five of them won.
† Reid was quoted in John Heilemann and Mark Halperin's book, *Game Change,* as saying that Obama was a "light-skinned" African American with "no Negro dialect unless he wanted to have one."

unpopular, but the three of them would need to stick together to get anything done.

The problem with the inside game was simple: it angered a good chunk of the American public. The Obama operating style that played well in Washington (especially for those officials and advocates who had personal contact with him) didn't translate nationally. He seemed to be settling in as a congressional player, a global statesman, and a dedicated family man—but not as the job-placement-officer-in-chief that so many Americans wanted.

––––––––

ONE BIG JOB Obama did get to fill was Associate Justice of the Supreme Court. The search typified Obama's methodical approach to decision making. After his first Court vacancy in 1993 Clinton drove his staff crazy with three months of countless meetings in which he reversed himself several times before finally choosing Ruth Bader Ginsburg. She was a good pick, but the obsessive process was beyond messy. At the other extreme, Bush aides couldn't believe how cavalier President Bush had been in nominating his lightly qualified counsel, Harriet Miers, to the high court. (Miers ultimately withdrew in favor of Samuel Alito.)

Obama's process was thorough, well-organized, and it took less than a month. Greg Craig and Ron Klain led a large team of lawyers that parsed every utterance the candidates made in their whole lives. When he heard their detailed reports Obama joked, "It's pretty clear there's no way I could be a candidate for the Supreme Court."*

An early list of twelve was quickly reduced to six and finally to four women: Sonia Sotomayor, a judge on the U.S. Court of Appeals in New York; Homeland Security Secretary Janet Napolitano; Diane Wood, a federal appeals court judge whom Obama knew as a part-time professor at the University of Chicago Law School; and Harvard Law School dean Elena Kagan.†

Sotomayor, a Princeton summa and graduate of Yale Law School, had developed a reputation in some legal circles as a mediocre legal thinker. Obama scanned about a dozen of her opinions and was

––––––––

* The idea that Obama was a "constitutional scholar" was, according to his former colleagues at Chicago, a bit of a myth. He had taught a class on race and the Constitution, an important but small slice of constitutional law, and he knew the precedents on other big legal issues, such as the separation of powers and the commerce clause, better than most presidents, but he wasn't an expert.

† For appearances' sake, the name of Judge Merrick Garland was briefly included to suggest that males were also being seriously considered. They were not.

greatly impressed when he interviewed her. "This whole thing about her not being up to the job is ridiculous," he told aides. "She's super smart." In the end she beat out Wood and Napolitano (Kagan had already been eliminated) on the basis of what Obama described as "her heart." He was "comfortable" with her—high praise in his book—and especially struck by how active she remained in the community after going on the bench, delivering dozens of inspirational speeches at local high schools in New York. He wasn't concerned about her reputation for scolding the lawyers who appeared in her courtroom. This reflected a double standard, the president thought, because men with a similar judicial temperament were invariably described as "firm." It impressed him that the vetting process produced friends who described her as an exceptionally warm and considerate person, the first to help at any sign of trouble.

Obama realized that nominating Sotomayor would raise the same racial issues he had spent so much time during the campaign attempting to avoid. She had been involved in a controversial affirmative action case involving firefighters and made the mistake of saying on more than one occasion that a "wise Latina woman" could "more often than not reach a better conclusion than a white male who hasn't lived that life."* One former Clinton aide said his old boss would never have nominated Sotomayor after that comment, but Obama didn't seem concerned; he said publicly that she had used "a poor choice of words" and left it at that. When Rush Limbaugh and Newt Gingrich called her "a racist" Obama waved it away. The president was obviously conscious of the political advantages of naming the court's first Hispanic, but he brooked no explicit discussion of politics during the selection process.

At first White House aides fretted over how Mexican Americans would react to a Puertorriqueña. Just as Asian Americans often dislike being lumped together, Latinos are highly conscious of their differences from one another. But it turned out that all Latinos were proud of Sotomayor; she reflected well on them even if they were of a different nationality. And when the "She's a racist" talk began, large numbers of Latinos took it as an insult to them all. First a Democratic president made them proud; now the Republican opposition was assaulting their pride. Of all the demographic setbacks suffered by the GOP since 2006, this was arguably the worst, for everyone in politics knew that

---

* In *Ricci v. DeStefano,* Sotomayor refused to overrule a decision against a white New Haven firefighter who qualified for a promotion based on an exam but was turned down for the job.

if the Democrats could solidify their Latino support they could stay in power for years, even decades.

Conservative critics pounced on Obama for stressing "empathy," and Sotomayor herself, under questioning from Senator Jon Kyl in her confirmation hearings, said she disagreed with Obama's 2005 statement that "what's in a judge's heart" is sometimes the "critical ingredient." But Obama never backed away from his "heart" standard. For a president who made a point of stripping every decision of emotion and sentiment in favor of reason, it was a revealing preference. Obama saw his job and that of his appointees as being self-aware enough to keep the mind and the heart in proper alignment.

Even as he applied that standard to the Supreme Court, he was falling short of it himself. Polls showed that growing numbers of Americans felt he was disconnected from the pain they were feeling in the recession. He hadn't shown enough empathy on the job, but he wasn't prepared to admit it yet.

———

THE PRESIDENT WAS a clever politician and he surrounded himself with the most politically sophisticated aides he could find. But his perception of the presidency was that the president should stay above politics as much as possible. Or at least try to look that way. If he were governing by polls, he liked to say, he never would have bailed out banks and auto companies, insisted on health care reform amid a recession, and sent sixty-one thousand more troops to Afghanistan.

Of course Obama's communications strategy was driven by politics, from holding presidential town hall meetings in swing states to choosing the day that he was being followed by crews from NBC News to duck out to a hamburger joint like a regular guy.* And the very structure of the administration, which further centralized decision making in the White House to the point where many Cabinet secretaries had their chiefs of staff appointed by Rahm Emanuel's shop, was built to advance the president's political interests.

Even so, former Clinton aides were struck by how much less Obama talked about the political angles than had Clinton. Unpopular decisions were made largely without reference to how the politics would work out. He didn't spend much time worrying about, say, conservatives who screamed about his canceling Reagan's missile shield in Eastern Europe

———

* According to a poll of Chinese youth, the fact that the president paid for his own hamburger was the second best-known fact about him in China, after his receiving the Nobel Peace Prize.

or liberals who complained that he was going slow on gay marriage or wouldn't investigate the abuses of the Bush administration.

The president disliked the Washington ritual of interest groups visiting the White House and telling the press afterward how much they agreed with the president. He considered it phony. "Don't go out there and say I'm endorsing your policy on travel," he told travel and tourism executives who came in after Obama created a flap by saying TARP money shouldn't be used for fancy corporate retreats. "We disagree on some issues and you can say it." When a credit card company CEO started in on what a boon credit cards were to small business, Obama cut him off: "Wait a minute, you should know how you are perceived." He was polite but unyielding. As the meeting ended he used almost precisely the same words he had with the tourism lobby: Don't say we agree. While this may have left the participants feeling disappointed that they didn't get more, they could at least say that the president dealt with them straight.

Obama often paid a price for underplaying the politics and overestimated his ability to reason with people. For instance, the administration's budget originally included a plan to shift the costs of treating certain service-connected disabilities from the Veterans Administration to veterans' private insurers, saving more than half a billion dollars a year. This was a big change, but Obama figured he could convince veterans' organizations that "third-party billing" was a fair trade for his 20 percent increase in the VA budget. In March he met with the heads of a dozen veterans' groups in the Roosevelt Room, including several amputees. The vets didn't appreciate it when the president told them, "No one in Washington ever tells you guys no." They had just been through plenty of *no* under Bush. Then, speaking of their sacrifice, Obama said, "Nobody feels this more than I do."

The veterans looked at one another in amazement. "Our jaws dropped," remembered one. *Nobody feels this more than I do?* How about us? The president, they concluded afterward, was overworked; he was on autopilot and off his game. They left the meeting and went to the press to blast the outsourcing to private insurers. Jon Stewart joked about "the Frito-Lay Medal of Honor." Two days later Obama not only reversed the policy but covered his retreat by ending the Pentagon's notorious "stop-loss" orders that involuntarily extended active duty service. He appointed a special veterans' coordinator in the White House to tend to the veterans' groups. And he learned a lesson about anticipating the political reaction before he injected himself into the process.

VETERANS AFFAIRS WAS a 2009 concern; gays in the military was not. The White House was all too familiar with the way the issue had blown up in Clinton's face in 1993, breaking his first-year momentum. Fifteen years later, the compromise that emerged from that controversy—the military's don't ask–don't tell policy—was a failure. Exemplary soldiers, including much-need Arabic translators, were routinely expelled from the armed forces based on flimsy gossip. (Most of those thrown out were women.) Obama knew all this but had no appetite to distract Washington from health care with a messy fight over an emotional issue.

After news stories reporting that the Justice Department had filed a brief arguing that the 1996 Defense of Marriage Act (DOMA) was constitutional, gay and lesbian leaders let Obama have it. He was defending a law that equated gays to pedophiles, they said. At a hastily organized White House event on June 29 commemorating the fortieth anniversary of the Stonewall Uprising, Obama renewed his campaign promise to repeal DOMA and end don't ask–don't tell.* The latter issue affected relatively few people but for many voters it became emblematic of whether Obama was keeping his campaign promises. Most were under the mistaken impression that the commander-in-chief could end the don't ask–don't tell policy with a stroke of the pen, just as President Truman did when desegregating the armed forces.

In fact, it would take an act of Congress to change the law, which as a practical matter would mean getting the Pentagon to sign on. In March, as Bob Gates, Admiral Mullen, and Jim Jones were getting up to leave a meeting on Afghanistan in the Oval Office, the president casually remarked, "I just want you to know I'm serious about repealing don't ask–don't tell and I want to get to it when we're done with some of this." The message was that the military should prepare to move on the issue in 2010. But Obama wanted to avoid a brawl on Capitol Hill. At the end of the year, the White House privately informed a half dozen leaders of gay rights organizations that the deal was this: Gates and Mullen (who proved to be eloquent on the subject) were on board for a gradual change in the policy as long as the Pentagon could control how it got done.

———

SOMETIMES THE CHICAGO boys were not Chicago enough. Self-styled tough-guy supporters were always urging Obama to coldcock someone. The pattern was set as early as February 2008, when frustrated backers wanted him to punch back hard at Hillary Clinton. Combative

———

* A third promise, to sign hate crimes legislation, was fulfilled in October.

Democrats felt the same in September 2008 about Sarah Palin and in February 2009 about House Republicans who were pummeling him on the stimulus. It happened again in the summer of 2009, when right-wingers concocted the threat of "death panels" for seniors if health care reform was enacted. Every time Obama was attacked, his liberal critics said, he held off until the pressure built and he could rush to the rescue with a big inspirational speech. Frank Rich of the *New York Times* argued, "This repeated cycle of extended above-the-fray passivity followed by last-minute oratorical heroics has now been stretched to the very limit." Gibbs was only one of several political advisors who agreed. They wanted Obama to pick more fights.

In truth, Obama wasn't shy about occasionally stepping into the fray when he thought the timing was right. He lambasted Wall Street "speculators" and "fat cats," mocked conservative critics for accusing him of "trying to pull the plug on Grandma," and flayed insurance companies and the Chamber of Commerce for their "bogus" ads attacking health care reform. Most of the time he tried to respond in a light, dismissive way rather than with roundhouse punches, which he believed were counterproductive. Civility, he believed, was just good politics.

But by the end of the year he was caught between his growing and no longer contrived anger at Wall Street and his understanding that populism would rattle markets and slow the recovery. In that sense, his political interests (bashing banks) were not aligned with the country's economic interests (stable markets), except to the extent that a rising economy would ease the anger and help Democrats in the 2010 midterms. He hadn't yet found the right balance between voicing public dismay with Wall Street and promoting economic growth.

As far back as the stimulus, Obama was prepared for the Republicans to be nasty and obstructionist. But by mid-year, Democrats were starting to get under his skin, too. He wanted liberals to stop questioning his motives when he kept trying for some bipartisanship. "It's easy to say this stuff in theory about how we must do this or that, but we actually want to change people's lives," he told a visiting union leader one day. "We need to be nimble and work with the other side, and that frustrates liberals."

The president also believed that many liberals didn't pay enough attention to the details of governing to notice how aggressively the administration was pushing a progressive agenda. Obama and his Cabinet quickly made enemies among the entrenched corporate interests accustomed to working hand in glove with the Bush administration. Powerful lobbies for oil and gas, banking, chemicals, sugar, and more were thrown on the defensive by new regulations. At the Pentagon Bob

Gates killed the F-22 and began making progress on Obama's promise that the era of no-bid contracts on bloated weapons systems was
over.* EPA chief Lisa Jackson didn't wait for Congress and began on her
own to regulate greenhouse gas emissions under the Clean Air Act; she
also enraged the coal industry by reviewing permits for the destruc-
tive "mountaintop mining" ravaging the landscape of Appalachia. Julius
Genachowski, chairman of the FCC, took on Internet service providers
by enforcing the pro-consumer principle of "net neutrality," and Tom
Vilsack at USDA began enforcing new food safety standards and angered the timber industry by protecting 58 million acres of roadless
forests. Eric Holder's Justice Department restricted the abusive applica-
tion of the state secrets privilege, under which "national security" had
become an all-purpose excuse to classify virtually anything.

Obama wasn't always comfortable with what his Cabinet was doing;
he would have preferred, for instance, that Holder not move toward
prosecution of U.S. government employees for committing torture, a
decision that the CIA argued was terrible for morale. Obama believed
that banning torture on his first day in office was a critical part of restoring American prestige in the world, but he wasn't eager to drag the
country through trials of CIA interrogators who exceeded their authority, and such trials grew less likely over time.

Whatever his own views, Obama refused to interfere with Holder's
decision in November to try Khalid Shaikh Mohammed, the master-
mind of the 9/11 attacks, in federal court in New York City instead of
before a military tribunal. Holder had already opted for military tribunals in other cases and hadn't been sure which way to go on this one
until the last minute, when he was convinced that enough evidence existed to convict the terrorist known as KSM without resorting to whatever information had been illegally obtained through waterboarding.
KSM had said so many incriminating things in public that prosecutors
wouldn't need to use his interrogations, and attempts by the defense
to do so were likely to be barred by the judge. By turning to federal
prosecutors in New York who had long experience in terrorism cases,
Holder increased the odds of a speedier resolution than if the case had
been handled by military tribunals, which had been bogged down for
years in complicated appeals. Even so, the civilian trial was also likely
to be delayed for many months, even years.

Holder was determined to establish his independence from his friend
the president. His greatest regret in public life was doing Bill Clinton's

* Military reformers nonetheless complained that, like Donald Rumsfeld, Gates was still
more talk than action when it came to reforming procurement.

bidding when Clinton wanted to pardon fugitive financier Marc Rich just before leaving office in 2001. So it wasn't a surprise that he kept at arm's length from the White House and didn't tell New York Mayor Michael Bloomberg of his plans until the eve of the announcement. Police Commissioner Ray Kelly, who was responsible for defending the city, was kept entirely in the dark. Bloomberg was furious with the administration for being blindsided and tried to appeal to the president. But Obama was in Asia and the announcement was scheduled for the following morning. The mayor was told there was no time to discuss it further.

At first, Bloomberg and Chuck Schumer felt they had no choice but to say they accepted the decision. In their public statements, they said only that they wanted to make sure New York would be reimbursed for the cost of the extra security, then estimated at $75 million. When the politics went bad and the community in Lower Manhattan rebelled against holding the trial there, Bloomberg raised the cost to $200 million and finally to $1 billion, at which point it was clear the idea was dead. Its abandonment by Obama was only a formality.

Wherever the trial was held, trying KSM in civilian court was bound to be a campaign issue for years. Even though acquittal was an extremely remote possibility (the conviction rate for terrorists is 100 percent in the United States), a difficult judge could prove embarrassing for the government. Holder literally crossed the fingers of both hands when discussing his hopes for randomly drawing the right judge, a gesture that did not inspire confidence that he had thought through the politics of his decision.

But Obama didn't second-guess himself. He had repeatedly promised during the 2008 campaign that his attorney general would be the people's lawyer, not the president's. The decision on KSM was consistent with a speech that Obama gave at the National Archives in May, in which he said that detainees would be treated in one of three ways: tried in federal court or military tribunals, sent back to their country of origin, or, if there was no evidence against them but they remained dangerous, held without trial. The last option enraged civil libertarians, but Obama wasn't about to risk freeing dangerous terrorists.

Of course the president's argument at the National Archives—"We cannot keep this country safe unless we enlist the power of our most fundamental values"—would sound reasonable right up until the next major terrorist attack in the United States, when the recriminations previewed by Dick Cheney would explode. Whatever the sincerity of Cheney's dark convictions, his attacks on Obama were part of a deadly serious political setup aimed at a huge "I told you so" if things went badly. In that sense the Obama presidency was coming to depend on the very security that the right accused him of undermining.

THE RETURN OF terrorism as a central issue in American politics began on Christmas Day, when Umar Farouk Abdulmutallab, a 23-year-old Muslim Nigerian, tried to ignite explosives hidden in his underwear on a Northwest Air flight from Amsterdam to Detroit. The president and his family had just arrived in Hawaii that day for a week-long stay, and were singing Christmas carols when they heard the news. Obama waited three days before responding and, with too little information, announced that the suspect was "an isolated extremist." This was not accurate. He was, in fact, a trained agent of al Qaeda. It was soon pointed out that after Richard Reid, the "shoe bomber," tried to blow up an airliner at Christmastime in 2001, a vacationing President Bush took six days to respond, prosecuted Reid in civilian courts, and suffered no political attacks from anyone over it. The double standard did nothing to tamp down the story.

The press leapt on the incident in part because it played into a narrative that the president had slow political reflexes. Didn't he realize that the American people were frightened? If he was going to be the adult in the relationship with the public, he needed to recognize when to calm the country. The level of vulnerability that the incident exposed was terrifying to millions of people and it angered Obama.

The president was disciplined about self-correcting, especially if there were errors to account for. Obama stepped forward to say that allowing the Christmas Day terror suspect to board an airliner reflected "systemic failure."* He returned to Washington and made up for lost time with a thorough investigation designed to show hands-on management of the story and a new clarity about what he now called "the War on al Qaeda." The incident, in which no one but the terror suspect was injured, was arguably a blessing in disguise because it gave the government a chance to diagnose problems at the National Counterterrorism Center, which had plenty of information about Abdulmutallab (his father, a banker, had warned the U.S. embassy in Nigeria that his son had become a jihadist)but failed to connect the dots.

The long-term fallout revolved around the FBI reading the suspect his Miranda rights, after which he stopped talking until the FBI (in

---

* Homeland Security Secretary Napolitano didn't help the administration's cause when she said in the aftermath that "the system worked." She said she was referring to what happened after the terror attack was foiled and that she had been quoted out of context, but the damage was done.

a smart move that military interrogators likely would have shunned) flew his father over, at which point he provided valuable intelligence. After a January 5 meeting in the White House, the press was told that Robert Gates had no problem with the FBI handling the case. In fact, Gates had not been consulted. If he had been, he would have told the White House about an exception in U.S. law to reading Miranda rights in cases of national security.

Obama saw the incident as a learning experience and was philosophical about the political hit he took. "If he'd come out two hours after the incident they [Republicans] would have said he was responding too quickly without knowing the facts," said Marty Nesbitt, who was with Obama in Hawaii in the days following Christmas. "They were going to criticize him either way." And keep the heat on him. By the new year, the story of the Miranda rights had been lumped in with the decision to try Khalid Shaikh Mohammed in civilian court to make Obama look as if he wanted to treat all terrorists like common criminals. This was a distortion of the careful distinctions the president had laid out in his National Archives speech, but there wasn't a lot Obama thought he could do about the feverish new politics of national security. He vowed to stay focused on his job.

———

FOR ALL THE accusations of softness, Obama could be a hard-nosed president. The best example on the domestic side was in education. Looking ahead, he feared that the future workforce of the United States would be unable to compete internationally. A study by McKinsey and Co. put the cost to U.S. productivity of the international achievement gap at $1.3 trillion to $2.3 trillion a year. The American education system's poor results became a top-line issue inside the White House.

Obama believed that the economic future of the country was at risk if serious reform—including national standards—didn't begin immediately. His education program included establishing more charter schools (and closing down failing ones), focusing intently on the few dozen urban schools that produced the most dropouts, bolstering community colleges (which trained the workforce of the future), and expanding and simplifying student loans. But the key was developing a new generation of highly effective teachers (not "highly credentialed," because the teachers-college sheepskin often bore no relationship to their skills in the classroom), so the president pushed hard for career ladders and master teacher programs. To identify the good and bad teachers, he and Arne Duncan believed it essential to tear down what Duncan called the "firewall" between student achievement and teacher evaluation.

For decades teachers unions had insisted that the consistent failure of students to improve even slightly over the course of the school year (as measured by tests and other forms of evaluation) could not be held in any way against their teachers. Because the unions obstructed the use of any September-to-June student evaluation in judging teacher performance, the whole system had zero accountability—almost unimaginable to professionals in any other part of the economy.

It was time to press the issue. Obama and Duncan, showing a little Chicago-style muscle, gave states a "choice" right out of *The Untouchables:* Lift your caps on the number of charter schools you allow and your prohibitions on holding teachers accountable for whether kids learn anything, or lose access to a piece of the $4.5 billion "Race to the Top" fund. Duncan considered the idea to be the centerpiece of the administration's education reform efforts.

And it worked. By the end of 2009 more than a dozen states were scampering to comply, with some state legislatures even going into special session. Major reform was under way without a penny having yet been spent. Meanwhile, the education accountability issue was cleaving the Democratic Party, with creatively disruptive reformers like Duncan and big-city mayors on one side and teachers unions and their incrementalist supporters on the other. To the surprise of the education establishment, Obama rejected temporizing and threw all his weight behind the reformers.

By not going into open warfare with the teachers unions Obama kept the issue under the radar. But he was especially proud of what he was accomplishing. "We've done as much on education reform as any administration in the last twenty years, and nobody knows it," he said.

———

OBAMA'S RELAXED MANNER and willingness to delegate and improvise kept him from being a control freak. But he was committed to exercising as much control as possible over everything he touched. One of his agency heads said that on a scale of one to ten, with ten being obsessive control, the president was an eight or nine.

Obama had long been a student of management. In the 1980s Gerald Kellman, who hired Obama to be a community organizer in Chicago, introduced him to the work of Peter Drucker, still the best commonsense yet deep thinker on the subject. Obama saw that the business guru Drucker and the radical community organizer Saul Alinsky both rejected the idea of charismatic but meddlesome leaders taking everything on their own shoulders in favor of dispersing responsibility throughout the organization. And as Obama studied up on modern presidents, he preferred the Republican corporate style of running the White House to the more chaotic atmosphere when Democrats were in charge.

Some of Obama's management ideas sounded smart but could be self-defeating if carried too far by disciples. The campaign injunction "Swim in your lane," designed to hold down turf struggles, was frequently used to expand them. (One aide was overhead saying, "I'm going to tell Rahm that guy is out of his lane!") Worse, the concept reflected a preference for bureaucratic peace over originality. Sometimes, as Obama knew, the freshest ideas come from people who swim sideways.

The subject experts and policy mandarins tried to hold their "best and brightest" arrogance in check, but it didn't help that in the four decades since David Halberstam's landmark book by that name, the words had somehow lost their intended irony. And some of the people around Obama didn't seem familiar with what the experts on expertise called "confirmation bias," whereby even researchers with the best intentions analyzed data without the true disinterest that faith in research required. Their conclusions, supposedly "based on the data," were suspiciously close to where they would have ended up without all the graphs and statistics.

The most glaring example of the limitations of policy mandarins, especially the academic economists, was job creation. Late 2009 featured major struggles within the economic team over how to balance jobs with deficit reduction. Tensions rose on December 13 when Christie Romer said on *Meet the Press* that in her mind the recession wouldn't be over until unemployment fell to "normal levels," which she defined as around 5 percent. Larry Summers was on record saying the recession was already over. Obama was less concerned with the semantics than with finding the right balance between deficits and jobs; he felt his team had failed him on that.

One big source of dispute was over whether to use billions in leftover TARP money to help small business. Peter Orszag, who wanted more deficit reductions in the 2010 budget, always had some argument about how this or that creative idea was "flaky" or didn't fit OMB's macroeconomic models. Larry Summers's staff did the same. If, say, a small business loan program might lose 20 cents on the dollar to default, it was immediately scotched. But that was only a problem in the abstract world of economists, where government programs were judged by the same standards they would apply to banks. Government, arguably, had a responsibility to help struggling small businesses, and an 80 percent success rate would help real small business people in real American towns that didn't much care about OMB's "theory of guarantee" models.

This disconnection from the world was the malign consequence of the American love of expertise, which, with the help of citadels of the meritocracy, had moved from a mere culture to something approaching a cult. Obama was skeptical of cant but still in thrall to the idea that with enough analysis, there was a "right answer" to everything. But a right answer for whom? Obama felt he had to reach out beyond his staff for answers, so he hosted a few dinners with business leaders. By the end of the year he overruled the economists and moved forward with ideas for job creation that he had rejected before.

———

MOST OF THE time Obama seemed to fit commonly accepted notions of what makes a good manager or leader. "Exemplary leaders know who they are and what their deficiencies are, and who they can have around to compensate for their weaknesses and complement their strengths," said Warren Bennis, an authority in the field. "They know their limits and blind spots. They're aware of people they hit it off with and those they don't—and why. They can answer the question: How do you abandon your own ego to the talents of others?" Bennis said he was thinking of Obama.

The great exception to the argument for Obama as a good manager came in the case of one of his oldest supporters. Most presidents eventually face painful decisions in this area; they find they have trouble balancing short-term political needs with loyalty to longtime advisors.

Greg Craig was a widely admired Washington attorney and friend of Bill and Hillary Clinton going back to Yale Law School. He was Clinton's lead White House lawyer in the Monica Lewinsky case and seemed firmly inside their orbit. But in 2006 Craig was so impressed by Obama that he betrayed the Clintons (their description) and defected, the first major Clintonite to do so. At the time the move helped Obama immensely inside the Washington establishment. Then, during the primaries, Craig burned the last of his bridges by publicly attacking Hillary's lack of foreign policy experience and inability to control her husband.* He served as an Obama counselor on foreign policy and legal matters and played the role of John McCain in debate prep. After the election Hillary could barely stand to be in the same room with

———

* The author was surprised when Craig went on the record with him to make that charge in January 2008, a pivotal point in the campaign.

him, which meant that he couldn't be national security advisor or deputy secretary of state or hold any other big foreign policy position.

So Craig became White House counsel, a job he didn't really want. He and Rahm Emanuel had never seen eye-to-eye in the Clinton White House, and before long Rahm concluded without much evidence that he was a poor manager who focused on a few pet issues and could never get on top of all the detainee cases and court dates (often involving ACLU lawsuits) that bore down on the president. The real issue was the difference between a political perspective and a legal one. Rahm wasn't a lawyer and he had little patience for tangled legal issues that become political headaches. Why couldn't the counsel's office figure out some way to keep those pesky resettlement questions and lawsuits out of Obama's face while he was trying to fight two wars and prevent a depression? Rahm thought Craig was constructing a mini-NSC in the counsel's office—empire building—instead of sticking to the White House's legal business; Craig, not surprisingly, thought that Rahm was sliming him.

The backdrop to the Craig story was the administration's failure to fulfill one of Obama's most widely publicized promises: closing the prison at Guantánamo Bay by January 1, 2010. During the 2008 campaign both Obama and McCain said the prison had become a recruiting tool for al Qaeda and should be shuttered. Press reports later suggested that White House aides needed a fall guy for breaking the promise and settled on Craig.

As with most personnel matters, the truth was more complicated. White House aides readily admitted that Craig bore no blame for Gitmo's not closing. Early in the transition Harvard Law professor Martha Minow and a group of lawyers wrote a report for Obama explaining how legally and logistically complex shutting the prison would be. (Bush had promised to do so in 2007 but made little progress.) After the Inauguration the Pentagon reported that finding a site in the United States for the prisoners was difficult. When the government finally settled on an underused federal prison in Thomson, Illinois, planners learned that it would take many months to renovate. The original deadline had never been realistic.

Without sustained presidential attention and someone assigned exclusively to Gitmo, closing the prison would be tough. Obama asked Holder and Gates to focus on Gitmo detainees but neither they nor Craig nor the Pentagon's general counsel, Jeh Johnson, nor anyone else was given responsibility for handling the many complexities of actually closing the facility. For months, Obama simply let one of his signature campaign promises slip between the cracks. Only after Craig flamed out were Pete Rouse and David Rapallo, an NSC official, asked to supervise the issue. In the meantime the Bush administration's decisions on which prisoners to release into their countries of origin were turning disastrous, as two Gitmo prisoners sent back to Yemen were reported to have returned to terrorism.

Beyond the legal issues, closing Gitmo was largely a political problem. It involved getting Republican Senator Lindsey Graham to give the administration some political cover. The deal required making sure that none of the detainees were put in the U.S. Naval Brig in Charleston, South Carolina, his home state. Before the Christmas-day bombing attempt, when the politics of terrorism changed almost overnight, this deal could have been cut. But Gates was lukewarm and neither Holder nor Craig was as politically sophisticated as the president expected. The independence that Obama granted Holder and the Justice Department meant the president needed a White House counsel to represent his political interests more directly. Craig seemed more focused on advancing his liberal arguments. According to one of Craig's adversaries, the president often agreed with the arguments but didn't appreciate Craig, a litigator by profession, belaboring his points. He preferred advisors who expressed their opinions strongly and cogently, then gave them a rest. The worst way to win over Obama was to lobby him and "relitigate." Craig denied that this was a problem.

The flashpoint (or perhaps it was merely Rahm's pretext) came over Craig's plan to bring four Chinese Muslim Uighurs from Gitmo to resettle in northern Virginia. It didn't seem like a big deal at first. Like Bush, Obama favored transferring certain detainees out of the facility. In December 2008 a federal judge had found that seventeen Uighur prisoners, who had been swept up in the post-9/11 fever without any link to terrorism, posed no danger. Rahm quickly signed off on letting two of the men settle in the United States; even he didn't anticipate the congressional reaction. But within days of the announcement in April that the Uighurs were being sent to Virginia, the story blew up in Obama's face. Congress was suddenly gripped by NIMBY fear. The Senate voted 90–6 to prevent any Guantánamo detainees from coming to the United States—the first congressional setback for the Obama administration, and the beginning of the GOP's campaign to stoke fears about Obama's toughness on terrorism.

Craig came up with a sensible Plan B, which called for resettling the Uighurs in Bermuda. Obama thought it was a good compromise. But Craig didn't tell the president that he was actually going to fly with the prisoners to Bermuda, almost as if he were their attorney. Denis McDonough had cleared the trip, but it enraged Rahm and apparently displeased the president, who agreed that Craig had lost his perspective and was tone-deaf to the politics of a senior White House official riding around with Gitmo detainees. It didn't help that Craig was caught in powerful interagency crosscurrents with the Justice Department on a legal appeal involving the State Secrets Act and with the Pentagon on the decision over releasing photographs of torture.

Obama liked Craig personally; in meetings they had an easy rapport that made unsuspecting observers think he was securely in the inner circle. But the president was clinical when it came to separating friendship from business. He finally agreed with Rahm that Craig wasn't right for the job, though it took him months to make a change. When stories began appearing in the press during the summer that Craig would be gone by the end of 2009, the president refused to tamp down the speculation. If people wrongly thought he was scapegoating him for Gitmo, that was their problem. Craig played for time. His early, ardent support for Obama's 2008 campaign counted enough to give him a few extra months to save himself.

Obama delegated the task of nudging him out to Rouse, who tried to suggest an evasive if technically accurate cover story—that Craig had never wanted the job in the first place. Craig didn't take the hint, and he turned down Obama's offer of an ambassadorship or a prestigious appointment to fill a vacancy on the D.C. Circuit, just a step down from the Supreme Court. After some thought, Craig decided he didn't want to be a judge. Even though it would have made the president seem less cold, the White House was anxious that the offer not leak, for fear it would look as if Obama were offering judgeships as consolation prizes.

Craig vowed to stay until at least the end of the year, but one day in November someone in the White House leaked that he was being fired, a "drive-by shooting," Craig called it. He read in the *Washington Post* that he was out, replaced by Bob Bauer, Obama's personal lawyer. Obama had the decency to talk with him about the situation three or four times and to call in sympathy after the *Post* story. He wasn't as heartless about his loyal supporters as the Georgetown gossip had it.

But the residue of the story was harmful. Obama and Rahm had badly mishandled the case, and it hurt their reputations inside Washington. Rahm was supposed to have grown up since the Clinton days, but after this and the "retard" quote in the *Wall Street Journal,* it wasn't hard to find people who thought he simply didn't have the maturity for the job. Greg Craig thought he had been mistreated. Yet even after what happened to him, Craig still had nothing critical to say about the president, on the record or off.

———

EARLY ON, OBAMA tried to lay out an operating principle for his administration. It was, not surprisingly, a character trait rather than an ideological idea: "That whole philosophy of persistence is one that I'm going to be emphasizing again and again as long as I'm in office. I'm a big believer in persistence."

He was also a big believer in the related quality of patience—on the part of others. He was impatient in private but would push back at critics who wanted his reaction on their timetable. Reporters always seemed eager to test his media reflexes, as if they were doctors pounding a little hammer on his knee. Obama liked to hammer back. When he was asked at a news conference why it had taken so long to respond to news of the obscene AIG bonuses, he replied tartly, "It took us a couple of days because I like to know what I'm talking about before I speak." In June he came under the same pressure for taking his time before speaking out against the Iranian regime for its postelection crackdown. When Chuck Todd of NBC News asked what the consequences would be for his diplomatic initiatives with Iran, the president dodged, then said sharply, "I know everybody here is on a twenty-four-hour news cycle. I'm not."

This would become a constant refrain. The president had no beef with the news media in general, but he loathed its rhythms and its obsession with what he called "the circus." He saw its inability to resist the latest superficial story as contributing to the "coarsening of our politics."

Obama was convinced that all the cable noise was just another part of "the bubble," the chatter of elites with little connection to real Americans. The reason presidents failed, he believed, was patently obvious: they lost touch. That explained why he traveled outside Washington about once a week and made sure to read those ten letters from average Americans each day. "I worry about him getting information," Eric Whitaker said. "I worry about people not telling him the truth." So did Obama.

One of the reasons they didn't tell him the truth was that many of his appointees and staff revered him too much. Axelrod described some in the White House as being willing to "walk through a wall" for the president. This wasn't so healthy. Loving the boss can be almost as harmful to an enterprise as loathing him. No matter how often the president said that he wanted people disagreeing with him in meetings, few did.

So little by little in the second half of the year Obama lost much of his connection to the American people. Some voters felt he wasn't expressing their anger; others just thought he was talking at a level over their heads. He could be folksy, but he didn't have Bill Clinton's gift for making complex subjects fully accessible. In fact the two presidents' relationships with the public were the inverse of each other. During the late 1990s Americans didn't trust Clinton personally, but they trusted his ability to deliver for them on pocketbook issues; in 2009 the public trusted and admired Obama personally, but not his approach to the issues that affected their lives.

The bailouts and big ambitious ideas took their toll, especially with independents, who in November voted Republican in gubernatorial elections in New Jersey and Virginia.* The White House could rationalize those defeats by saying that the Democrats were bad candidates and that Obama's popularity remained at over 50 percent in both states. But the political climate was changing faster than almost anyone expected. The cable noise that the president disdained was drowning out some of what Obama was trying to say. As he lost the narrative thread—the story of change—his magic began to dissipate.

Much of the Democratic base wanted Obama to repudiate the conciliatory themes of the campaign. Liberal supporters urged the president to deck somebody—anybody—on the right. They figured that he had proven in the past two years that he could take a punch; the question now was whether he could throw one. (The red Muhammad Ali boxing gloves that he treasured apparently weren't enough to convince them.) By this theory, adversaries of any kind respond only to strength. It was the old James Carville approach: if they think you won't hit them, they'll keep hitting you. It was human nature and elemental politics, according to most political consultants.

Obama's way around this bit of received wisdom was to pay lip service to it in public ("I'm skinny but I'm tough"), to take on big, fat, easy targets in the right-wing media, but not to fully engage with his Republican critics. He thought that if he sounded too partisan, he would lose the quality that had propelled him in the first place. He figured that his moral authority, like Lincoln's, rested on some empathy for his adversaries. But by the end of the year he still hadn't reconciled the tension between his short-term need to overpower the opposition and his long-term interest in floating above the circus. And perhaps he never would.

His friends thought the public should stop waiting for him to change. To them, it was about the audience changing its perspective. "When

---

* Jon Corzine lost in New Jersey and Creigh Deeds lost in Virginia.

20

"Don't Blow It!"

As the year wore on, Obama inhaled anything to do with foreign policy and national security, and he proved to be surprisingly tough-minded. Liberal constitutionalists like Garry Wills, who had hoped the former law professor would stop presiding over a national security state and unconstitutional war-making powers, were severely disappointed. Obama was acutely conscious that protecting the country was his first responsibility, and he devoted more time to confronting al Qaeda and other terrorist groups than to any other challenge in his presidency. That was the main focus of his daily National Security Sessions, his deliberations on Afghanistan and Pakistan, and, in a longer time frame, his attention to nuclear nonproliferation and public diplomacy.

One irony of the Christmas Day "underwear bomber" episode was that the president had just been briefed on Christmas Eve about more classified attacks by CIA-run Predator drones against al Qaeda targets in Yemen. He was trying to wipe out some of the same terrorist leaders who were sponsoring the airliner attempt.

Obama was intently focused on killing al Qaeda's "high-value targets." The volume and geographic scope of the effort was greater than under Bush, in part because of the evolution of the threat. The president sat down every Tuesday and went through "threat charts" that detailed where the enemy was most active. His policy called for staying on the offensive. At the end of the first year, Joe Biden gave the score—twelve key al Qaeda targets and one hundred "associates" killed. Obama was determined to nail terrorists but careful not to seem proud of making war. Decisions that he knew would lead to the deaths of American forces and innocent civilians weighed on him every day. "It's the hardest part of the job," said his friend Marty Nesbitt.

Dick Cheney could say what he wanted about Obama's weakness in fighting terrorists; Peter Bergen, the terrorism expert who once interviewed Osama bin Laden, obtained classified information showing that the Obama administration conducted more Predator strikes in its first year, fifty, than during Bush's entire presidency. Not once in the first year did the intelligence community believe the president had withheld resources.

What changed most in Obama's war on terror was the language, including use of the phrase "the war on terror" itself. Obama, who considered terrorism a tactic, thought the Bush administration had framed the struggle in an overly broad and inflammatory way. Early on, the linguistic adjustments went overboard, as Janet Napolitano was ridiculed for a reference to "man-caused disasters," a phrase that was never heard again. But Obama was a man of precision and the clarity helped. He was fighting al Qaeda, a deadly terrorist organization. He wanted to keep the focus there, not slip into easy talk of "Islamofascism" or other phrases that might inflame a billion Muslims against the United States.

———

THE MAIN TENET of Obama's foreign policy remained engagement. But as he stepped up the tempo of negotiations, a foreign policy mantra emerged among critics. Where were the "deliverables"? Where were the concrete concessions, the evidence that the United States had not been played for a sucker?

The White House's answer was to point to relations between the major powers. Obama's engagement with Russia and China, aides argued, led both nations to rethink their alliance with Iran. The foreign policy team was especially proud of Obama for driving a stake between Russia and Iran by "flushing out" each nation's position on Russia's reprocessing of Iran's uranium. When Russia, backed by the international community, made a real offer to Iran on reprocessing and Iran rejected it, relations between those two countries suffered. In November both Russia and China voted to back more vigorous International Atomic Energy Agency inspections of Iran's nuclear sites. Obama immodestly believed the strategy on proliferation had been "pretty flawless," which was a premature assessment—both Russia and China often took two steps backward for every one forward—but at least something was happening to step up the pressure.

The critical challenge with Iran was balancing the promise of engagement with new global support for economic sanctions. It reminded one Obama advisor of Yitzak Rabin's old maxim: "Fight terror as if there's no peace process, and negotiate peace as if there's no terror." That subtle strategy couldn't begin, of course, until events in Tehran clarified.

In the meantime Obama was convinced that foreign policy couldn't be conducted through blustery condemnation. Even positive language about American values failed to resonate anymore. It might have sounded good to American ears, but soaring talk of freedom did nothing to advance the nation's interests abroad. It was time to try a dramatically new approach to public diplomacy. Granting the Arab satellite channel Al Arabiya his first interview as president was only the beginning. For the rest of the year he delivered special video messages to commemorate practically every holiday with meaning in the Middle East. On March 20, for instance, Obama delivered a special holiday message to the Iranian people via the Voice of America. He used Nowruz, the Persian New Year, to tell Iran that the United States was "now committed to diplomacy that addresses the full range of issues between us." He was candid about the "strains" in the relationship but upbeat and friendly. Before signing off with a bit of Farsi, he quoted a Persian poet: "The children of Adam are limbs to each other, having been created by one essence." It may have sounded hokey to the few Americans listening, but it played well in Iran.

The full rollout of the new approach came on June 4 at Cairo University, arguably the most important speech Obama gave all year. The risk was that he would just raise expectations for progress that could not be met. The potential reward was the chance to move a dysfunctional region beyond emotion to some realistic assessment of its own self-interest, a long-term process, but one that Obama was uniquely qualified to begin.

Like most Obama speeches it was a last-minute affair. The process always began with Obama talking out loud for an hour as the speechwriters took notes. "This doesn't work," he told them after the first draft. "This is a speech where we have to say in public what people normally only say behind closed doors." The night before the speech Denis McDonough and Ben Rhodes were working past midnight in the King's Palace in Riyadh when they got an email from Reggie Love: "Hey, are you guys still up?" Obama, who had to leave the palace at 5 a.m. to fly to Cairo, wanted to come by with what he said were some final edits.

But there were more changes to come. On the flight to Cairo the president called Rhodes to the front of Air Force One and told him to insert a strong paragraph about the Holocaust: "We need to call out Holocaust denial and say this is baseless and ridiculous and it prevents the future we're trying to get to." This was the first time an American president confronted the issue, which in the past was thought best ignored. Rhodes was still working on the speech on his laptop when Obama had his "bilat" with President Hosni Mubarak of Egypt.

From his opening *Assalumu Alaikum* ("Peace be upon you"), the traditional Arabic greeting, Obama signaled that this would be a different kind of speech than anyone had ever heard before from an American president, or any other American official for that matter.

The speech was aimed at "hearts and minds," a concept that had been discredited during the Vietnam War.* Now the idea was back in a big way. Every time Obama quoted from the Quran or drew a lesson from history, the target of his speech was clear: the average Muslim trying to lead a normal life but tempted by his diet of anti-American hate speech to side with the extremists.

Obama never said the words *terrorism, terrorist,* or *war on terror,* but his purpose was to subvert the Islamic extremism that breeds terrorism. The t-word had become inflammatory to Muslims, who were tired of being lumped in with terrorists in their depictions in the West. A faster way to the hearts and minds of a Muslim audience was to talk about the tensions between Islam and the West in a different key.

Ayman al-Zawahiri, Osama bin Laden's number two, warned in an audio message released at the time of the speech, "America has put on a new face but its heart is full of hate." But the president of the United States whom Muslims in more than a hundred countries now saw on state television, the one whose middle name was Hussein, did not appear to hate Islam or anything else. He talked of "listening to each other" and "common principles of justice and progress, tolerance and the dignity of all human beings." He challenged Muslims to live up to the tenets of their faith.

The seven themes of his speech all held together like an especially lucid lecture by a history professor: confronting violent extremists, devising a two-state solution for Israelis and Palestinians, preventing a nuclear arms race in the Middle East, promoting democracy, respecting religious freedom, securing women's rights, and promoting economic development. The tone was understated and respectful.

But Obama could always sell in a big moment, and he did so again as he reached his peroration:

> There is also one rule that lies at the heart of every religion—that we do unto others as we would have them do unto us. This truth transcends nations and peoples—a belief that isn't new; that isn't black or white or brown; that isn't Christian or Muslim or Jew. It's a belief that pulsed in the cradle of civilization, and that still beats

---

* The filmmaker Peter Davis made a famous antiwar documentary in 1974 that he titled *Hearts and Minds.* He meant the title ironically.

in the heart of billions. It's a faith in other people, and it's what brought me here today.

The address was greeted warmly, especially in Europe. Polls showed the American president was more popular than Merkel and Sarkozy in their own countries, and in some especially relevant places. On the outskirts of Paris, in public housing projects full of immigrants whom the French interior minister had described as "scum," young Muslims wore T-shirts emblazoned with Obama's image. His approval rating in Great Britain surged to 86 percent, compared to 16 percent in 2008 for President Bush. The approval numbers were over 60 percent in most other countries in the world—a huge turnaround. The only place the president's numbers dropped after the speech was in Israel.

But the Cairo speech wasn't aimed at any nation. "Our objective was not to get some signed agreement from the Muslim world that they were all going to align with us against terrorism. They had already pledged to do that," Obama said later. "The question was, are you starting to affect the Arab street in a way that creates a different environment?"

The answer wasn't immediately clear, but there were encouraging signs. Within three days a pro-American coalition in Lebanon came from behind to win an election against a party backed by Hezbollah; a preelection visit by Joe Biden had helped. It was impossible in the tangled world of Lebanese politics to prove cause and effect, but Obama's speech was seen throughout the region as a healing balm. On those rare occasions over the next year when something good happened in the Middle East, some analysts would cite the "Cairo Effect," whether justified or not.

Alyssa Mastromonaco had the inspired idea of taking the president from Cairo to Buchenwald, the site of the Nazi concentration camp near Weimar, Germany. Accompanied by Elie Wiesel, who had been in the camp as a 16-year-old when it was liberated, Obama gave an eloquent speech. But it was the symbolism of the trip that mattered. Weimar had been the capital of Germany's prewar republic and was now host to Chancellor Merkel and other representatives of the nation's vibrant democracy. Its juxtaposition with Buchenwald reinforced the message of Cairo that societies could descend into the darkness of hate and murder and emerge as a new people with values of tolerance and respect.

The concentration camp visit was also politically shrewd. Israeli commentators prepared to slice up the Cairo speech and the newly tough Obama line on West Bank settlements were forced to muffle their attacks. Most checked any inclination to renew campaign canards that Obama bore animus toward Israel. Some American Jews were critical, but many fewer than expected.

After Cairo, Obama was determined to stick with his engagement of the Muslim world. On August 22, the eve of Ramadan, he delivered yet another five-minute message of greeting. The speech went beyond the usual ceremonial words and showed signs of behind-the-scenes work to advance what he called "this critically important dialogue." He mentioned that the H1N1 virus (swine flu) was a particular concern for those Muslims about to undertake the hajj (the annual pilgrimage to Mecca). He added that U.S. embassies had been instructed to undertake outreach to the Muslim communities in their host countries, and he touched again on the need for a two-state solution in the Middle East.

———

FOR YEARS OBAMA had believed that the greatest national security threat facing the United States and the world was the spread of nuclear weapons. He couldn't understand why the issue wasn't higher on the agenda. Preparing for his April speech in Prague devoted to the subject, he told his foreign policy team, "In my mind, if we can do this and we can do health care, we will have made a huge difference."

The speech, which was more widely covered abroad than in the United States, envisioned a world without nuclear weapons. "I'm not naïve," he told the cheering throng. "This goal will not be reached quickly—perhaps not in my lifetime. It will take patience and persistence. But now we, too, must ignore the voices who tell us that the world cannot change. We have to insist, 'Yes, we can.' "

Six months later the secretary of state delivered a speech at the United States Institute of Peace in which she gave the world even more leeway. The goal might not be met "in our lifetime or successive lifetimes," Clinton said. The extension from Obama's forty or fifty years to Clinton's skepticism about ever ridding the world of these weapons did not escape notice in the White House. She was backing the president's policy, but not with the same nuclear-free vision he possessed.

In September, when Obama became the first American president to chair a session of the United Nations Security Council, he devoted the session to winning passage of a resolution supporting a long arms control agenda. The UN had no particular clout on these issues, but the event laid down a symbolic marker and elevated nonproliferation from the ministerial level to a priority for heads of state.

Obama used the nuclear issue to find areas of agreement with China. In December 2008 the increasingly erratic Communist regime in North

Korea quit the six-party talks on nuclear weapons; in April North Korea fired a missile over Japan (and threatened to hit Hawaii); and in May it conducted an underground nuclear test. Every effort to resume negotiations, including the delivery of a letter from Obama to North Korean leader Kim Jong Il, was coordinated closely with the Chinese. Obama's first year brought no progress with Pyongyang, but at least the world was united in how to confront it.

Obama's nuclear agenda was ambitious. After a new START treaty with the Russians he envisioned ratifying the Comprehensive Test Ban Treaty rejected by the Senate in 1999; he figured that improved monitoring stations made the treaty more workable and thus possibly more acceptable to Republicans. He also sought to strengthen the Nuclear Non-Proliferation Treaty (which provided the basis for limiting membership in the nuclear club) by negotiating a verifiable treaty reducing nuclear fissile materials.

After years of Bush's disdain for international treaties these were all tall orders. Approval of treaties in the Senate required two thirds of the body to vote aye, sixty-seven votes, so Obama moved forward simultaneously on a voluntary, nonbinding track. He announced that he would sponsor an April 2010 summit in Washington where every country in attendance would be asked to come with a tangible sign of national progress on nonproliferation.

Obama's most important short-term goal, established in the Prague speech, was to "secure all vulnerable nuclear material around the world in four years." Upon arriving in the Senate in 2005 he had traveled to the former Soviet Union with Senator Richard Lugar and seen many poorly secured weapons sites. In the White House his daily intelligence briefings told him that al Qaeda was actively seeking access to fissile materials in Pakistan and elsewhere. This was the biggest danger in the world, "a race between cooperation and catastrophe," as former senator Sam Nunn put it, and it dismayed the president that it didn't have a higher profile in the United States. Ignoring the nuclear threat was more evidence of what he considered a flight from seriousness.

While achieving his four-year goal was technically doable and entirely affordable, it would be yet another tough deadline for Obama to meet. Most countries were distressingly complacent about terrorists' making a nuclear bomb. Some officials even went so far as to tell arms controllers that this was a problem primarily for the United States and Israel because that's where any bomb would likely go off. They generally didn't recognize the danger to the world. The point of pushing hard on unilateral arms control was to argue that the United States was beginning to do its part, so other countries should also secure their highly enriched uranium.

When it came to warheads, the president believed in what's called an "existential deterrent," in which having one hundred or fewer nuclear weapons is just as effective as having ten thousand. But he also knew that such reductions weren't likely, considering that everyone from Robert Gates to the Russians opposed them. The bureaucratic impediments to a new nuclear policy were formidable. At the Pentagon nukes were the province of the Acquisitions Department, which naturally always wanted to acquire more. Nonetheless, Obama pushed forward to unilaterally reduce American nuclear stockpiles, and he cancelled the nuclear bunker-buster bomb developed under Bush. To the dismay of liberals, he stopped short of renouncing first-use of nuclear weapons, the centerpiece of the decades-old policy of deterrence.

To give himself some cover on nuclear weapons, Obama called in heavyweight alumni. In May he met with Nunn, former secretaries of state Henry Kissinger and George Shultz, and former secretary of defense William Perry to discuss proliferation policy. "I don't think anyone would accuse these four gentlemen of being dreamers," Obama said afterward.

Shultz spoke for the group when he praised Obama's eloquence in Prague: "We all noticed on your website that the first sentence is, 'We will work for a world free of nuclear weapons.' That's the vision." But Shultz hastened to add that he noticed the *second* sentence too: "As long as nuclear weapons are around, we will be sure to have a strong deterrent ourselves." He and the other Republicans were happy to be included in a nonpartisan effort, but he wanted to make sure everyone knew they weren't going to back unilateral disarmament.*

Kissinger, a master flatterer who hadn't ingratiated himself (yet) with Obama, laid it on thick when they met; he gave Obama high marks as a strategist. But by November he was looking for a quick checkmate. "He reminds me of a chess grandmaster who has played his opening in six simultaneous games," he told a reporter over dinner. "But he hasn't completed a single game and I'd like to see him finish one.'"

That wasn't strictly true. Among the most skillful moments of the year for Obama was his handling of the removal of Bush's missile defense system in Eastern Europe, a major impediment to improved U.S.-Russian relations. At first Poland and the Czech Republic were upset, but they felt better when they learned that they would soon receive

---

* The Senate reinforced the point in a resolution just before Christmas.

more modern and mobile SM-3 interceptors (sea-based antiballistic missiles). Their attention, like the world's, was refocused from Moscow to Tehran, whose missiles were in range of Europe. Obama had killed Ronald Reagan's "Star Wars" dream and almost no one noticed.

By may 2009, in advance of Iran's June 12 election, American policy toward Iran had undergone a quiet but profound shift. Whereas for years the United States had unrealistically called on Iran to end its entire nuclear program, Obama now sought only to prevent it from weaponizing its nukes. Because the country contained no oil refineries, it possessed a legitimate need for nuclear power. Obama argued that the world could accept this as long as the reprocessing of the enriched uranium was handled outside Iran, most likely in Russia. With even Iranian liberals unwilling to see the nation abandon its nuclear program, a policy of "limitation with inspection" made more sense than ultimatums for total dismantlement.

Before the June Iranian elections the White House, in realpolitik mode, had mixed feelings about who should win. The challenger, Mir Hossein Mousavi, was clearly preferable to President Mahmoud Ahmadinejad, but if Mousavi beat the Holocaust-denying demagogue it might set back progress on negotiating for inspections of nuclear facilities. A new Iranian president would take months to settle in and would likely feel obliged to prove his toughness by pushing forward on nuclear development. Sanctions against a new moderate government would be harder to enforce.

After the mullahs stole the election for Ahmadinejad, Obama was cautious. He avoided full-throated support for the dissidents, which would give the regime the excuse to say that the revolt was inspired by the United States. Conservatives attacked the president for holding back, but it made sense. He argued plausibly that given the history of U.S. meddling in Iran, loud support for the protesters would just give Ahmadinejad and the mullahs a propaganda tool. After the crackdown and bloody pictures of a young Iranian woman shot dead by the authorities spread around the world, the president toughened his rhetoric, which was translated into Farsi and Arabic by the U.S. government. But by waiting a few days before speaking out on the side of the demonstrators, he kept the focus on where it belonged: Ayatollah Khamenei and his thugs. The demonstrators seemed to agree and expressed no concern about the American president's tardiness in speaking out.

HAD IT COME in any other context, Iran's admission that it was developing a nuclear reprocessing facility near the holy city of Qom might have prompted Israel to launch a bombing campaign. But the Israelis now seemed to understand that this would do more than anything else to bolster the Iranian regime. It seemed as if the mullahs were hoping for Israeli bombs; if they had to lose part of their nuclear program, better to have it taken away by the Israelis than the International Atomic Energy Agency. In any case, most of the facilities were secure in underground tunnels that Israeli bombs and missiles couldn't penetrate.

Thanks to the election aftermath, Israel was willing to give sanctions a try. "Before the elections, the sense was that if a taxi driver in Tehran ran out of gas, he would blame America, the Zionists and the West," Michael Oren, Israel's ambassador to the United States, told *Newsweek*'s Lally Weymouth. "Now, that same taxi driver runs out of gas, he gets out of his cab and starts cursing his own government."

But Israel's patience wasn't endless. Arguably the top diplomatic priority for the U.S. government in the second half of the year was to build support around the world for harsher sanctions against Iran that would bite the regime without hurting the people too much. Obama decided to retain a tough-minded Bush Treasury official named Stuart Levey to pressure governments and companies to stop doing business with Iran's Revolutionary Guard Corps, the nexus of finance and military in the regime.

On his China trip in November Obama spoke at length to Chinese President Hu Jintao about Iran. The Chinese leader waited several days after Obama left (so as not to be seen making a concession), then signed on to tougher IAEA inspections. After years of Chinese unwillingness to endorse international inspections, this counted as a real step forward.

Even so, neither sanctions nor pressure for inspections would yield much until the political situation clarified. The mullahs were content to offer bogus concessions and stall for time with diplomatic hints and feints. But the indirect impact of Washington's new policy was considerable: it ended a thirty-year era in which any time the Iranian regime got in trouble, it simply played the "Great Satan" card. By extending a hand to the clenched fist of Tehran, Obama helped expose the bankruptcy of the regime to its own people.

"Bush would have made this about us—all about what the U.S. has done to promote freedom," said a senior NSC staffer. "It's not about us. It's about them." Even though the Cairo speech didn't air in Tehran, the message was getting through online and through cell phones—a positive message praising the Iranian people that worked much better to disorient the regime than any of the usual bashing.

SHORTLY BEFORE 6 A.M. on October 9 Robert Gibbs awakened Obama by phone to tell him he had won the Nobel Peace Prize. The president was greatly surprised. As word spread by BlackBerry, some aides at first thought it was an out-of-season April Fools joke. When Obama got downstairs he called the Norwegian ambassador to express his thanks and to say that he didn't deserve to be in the company of past recipients. He recounted that Malia had come in that morning to say, "Dad, you won the Nobel Peace Prize and it's Bo's birthday. Plus we have a three-day weekend coming up." Axelrod and Ben Rhodes heard that end of the conversation and told Favreau to put what he'd said to the ambassador in the draft of the president's speech.

Obama and his staff knew the award was awkward. Lech Walesa, who won the Nobel for leading the Polish Solidarity movement against communism, spoke for most people when he called it premature. When aides congratulated the president, he shrugged and said, "I just want to pass health care." They knew some blowback was on the way. "In all of your years as a political consultant," Rhodes said to Ax, "I bet you never thought you'd have to advise a client on how to defend himself against winning a Nobel Prize." Obama's speech that morning struck the appropriate tone. He said he was "humbled" and described the prize as a "call to action" on moving toward the elimination of nuclear weapons and other global objectives.

It was just one more event in a busy day. The president went from the Nobel remarks to a meeting on job creation and then to a three-hour session in the Situation Room on Afghanistan. In both meetings, he was greeted without the slightest acknowledgment that he had just won the most prestigious prize in the world. That was as he wanted it. His advisors knew by then that he had no use for flattery and might well hold it against anyone who made a fuss over a prize he had just got done saying on television that he didn't really deserve.

For more than five years, going back to his convention speech at the 2004 Democratic Convention, Obama had faced sky-high expectations. Each time he cleared the bar. The Nobel Peace Prize was another spur to perform, another way of setting him up to be a great president or a historic flop, though he betrayed no concern that it could be the latter. The singer and activist Bono described it as a warning: "The Nobel Peace Prize is the rest of the world saying, 'Don't blow it.'"

Because he hadn't yet earned it, the award fed a meme (begun the week before on *Saturday Night Live*) that he hadn't yet accomplished anything as president. This was as false abroad as it was at home. As State Department spokesman P. J. Crowley said, it's better for the national interest "when the United States has accolades tossed its way rather than shoes."*

But the meme continued. Obama's trip to China in November 2009 was derided by the American media as a failure. Analysts charged that he didn't stress human rights (as President Clinton had by raising Tiananmen Square in the 1990s) and returned empty-handed on curtailing currency manipulation. The Chinese authorities decided at the last minute to pull the plug on his town hall–style meeting, so the Chinese people never saw it. "No, we haven't made China a democracy in three days—maybe if we pounded our chest a lot that would work," Gibbs emailed a reporter from China. "But it hasn't in the last 16 years." Obama figured that the satisfaction that would come from calling out the Chinese was less important than building goodwill for future progress, particularly on climate change issues, where he held productive talks with both Hu Jintao and the Chinese premier, Wen Jiabao. The leaders were also in accord on handling North Korea, an important advance in convincing China to take more responsibility for its region.†

Moreover, it was inaccurate to say that the president hadn't raised touchy issues. Standing next to Hu at a joint press conference, he tackled a question about "the Great Firewall of China" (Internet censorship) and suggested that the government should talk to the Dalai Lama, a more sensitive subject in 2009 than the massacre twenty years earlier in Tiananmen Square. With plans underway for Obama to meet with the Dalai Lama in the United States in 2010 and continue arms sales to Taiwan, American officials prepared for a rough patch in U.S.-Chinese relations. Despite the great age and glory of Chinese civilization, Beijing was now like a strapping adolescent ready to sit at the big table. The regime's erratic temper made the nations that thought of themselves as adults nervous, but they knew they had better get used to it.

———

IT WOULDN'T BE until the end of the year, in Copenhagen, that the outlines of future U.S.-China relations came into fuller view.

For months the big climate change conference looked like it was going to be a bust. With the Senate blocking action on the cap-and-trade program that had passed the House, Obama was faced with the prospect of going to Copenhagen empty-handed. After all the hype

———

* In 2008 an Iraqi man at a press conference in Baghdad threw a shoe at President Bush.
† The communiqués from both sides after the summit set off a frenzy in India, which felt the United States had acquiesced in greater Chinese involvement in South Asia.

about the conference being the successor to the landmark 1997 Kyoto Protocol (which established the first legally binding international restrictions on carbon emissions), this wouldn't do. So White House aides passed the word that the president would stay home. Copenhagen wasn't a meeting for heads of state anyway, they insisted.

The blowback was immediate: Obama would fly to Copenhagen for Chicago's Olympics bid but not to try to save the planet? So for a time the plan was to hop over to Copenhagen from Oslo after Obama picked up his Nobel Prize. Then it turned out that the president had to be back in Washington immediately for the final Senate negotiations on health care. With expectations for the conference suddenly lowered—any treaty, the Danish prime minister announced, would not be legally binding—Obama resolved to board Air Force One and return to Denmark toward the end of the conference to see if he could complete a last-minute deal. He and Premier Wen had a good conversation on climate change in November in Beijing. Maybe the world's two biggest carbon emitters could get something accomplished.

But when he arrived in Copenhagen at 9 a.m. on December 18 the president found a chaotic international conclave that had achieved almost nothing in eleven days. Low-lying island states facing extinction were pleading tearfully for the rest of the world to help. European states that grandly committed themselves to emission caps and couldn't understand why America didn't join them in making legally binding commitments (the answer was that doing so without Congress would set up another Kyoto situation, in which the United States couldn't back up its pledges) now blithely subcontracted the hard work of negotiating to the United States. And rapidly developing states like China, India, Brazil, and South Africa were upset about the double standard of an emissions agreement that would restrict their growth. That was unfair, they said; the United States and other developed countries hadn't had to worry about dirty energy when they were building their economies in the nineteenth and twentieth centuries.

Hillary Clinton had been in Copenhagen's Bella Center (an abandoned shopping mall) for days, negotiating hard but getting nowhere. Beyond progress on establishing a $100 billion "green fund" for developing countries paid for by wealthier ones (the U.S. contribution would come to $30 billion by 2020), the conference seemed hopelessly deadlocked. Obama gave a short speech to the plenary session aimed at salvaging something. He stressed the need for all nations to set goals, create a mechanism for measuring progress, and help the most vulnerable countries adapt to climate change. America's own commitment, he reiterated, was to cut carbon emissions 17 percent by 2020 and 80 percent by 2050, a goal that would require the conversion to a clean energy economy he had pledged to begin. He turned on the star power as he mingled with the delegates, but his appearance had a dutiful quality to it. With the conference draped in failure, the only hope for a breakthrough lay in bilaterals with the leaders of developing countries. But things had deteriorated so badly that the Americans heard Indian Prime Minister Manmohan Singh had already gone to the airport.

Obama met with Russia's Medvedev in an effort to speed progress on START. All day he tried to nail down a time to meet again with Premier Wen and, separately, with the leaders of India, Brazil, and South Africa, who were representing the developing world. The president had been in Copenhagen for only a few hours and the chaos of the conference was already beginning to wear on him. "I don't want to mess around with this anymore, I just want to talk with Premier Wen," Obama told his team. Finally a session was scheduled for 7 p.m. in a hotel conference room, though the American advance team reported back that the room was occupied. With dozens of emails going back and forth, nobody was quite sure of the arrangements. As Denis Mc-Donough and other aides walked ahead of the president toward the room, they saw that the Chinese were already inside, conferring with the three other world leaders Obama had been hoping to meet with.

Instead of waiting for that meeting to end, Obama decided to crash it. He casually strolled in to find Wen meeting with Singh (who hadn't gone to the airport after all), Lula da Silva of Brazil, and Jacob Zuma of South Africa. The Chinese director of national energy, a feisty hard-liner named Xie Zhenhua, yelled "Out!" at Obama in some mixture of Chinese and broken English, but the president didn't understand it or chose to ignore it.

As the other heads of state rose to greet him, Obama motioned for them to sit and said cheerfully, "There aren't any seats." When functionaries scrambled to find some, the president noticed one on the other side of the table and said, "No, no, don't worry, I'm going to go sit by my friend Lula." He walked over, said, "Hey, Lula," and pulled up a chair. Obama liked Lula personally, even though old-line leftists in Brazil were resuming anti-Americanism there and he knew the Brazilians felt obliged to side with China in the negotiations. Within moments chairs were provided for Clinton and two American advisors, Todd Stern and Michael Froman.

There ensued a ninety-minute closed-door negotiation that ended the deadlock and salvaged something of the conference without producing a major breakthrough. Obama and Clinton passed each other notes and assigned Stern and Froman to move off to the side and negotiate particular points. The Americans knew that China wouldn't agree to international limits on carbon emissions or intrusive inspections, but believed that establishing some transparency was worth the effort. So the conversation focused on convincing China to voluntarily list its targets and emissions in an international registry. This sounded disappointing to environmentalists who had hoped for years for binding agreements, but it would represent the first time China subjected itself to global norms of transparency of any kind.

The Chinese were already producing cleaner cars than the United States and they were converts to cutting emissions. But as in other areas, they had their own way of doing things. Instead of broad emission caps, they tracked what they called "carbon intensity" (as measured by CO_2 per unit of gross national product) and had recently pledged to cut it by 50 percent below 2000 levels by 2050. Even if they fell short and continued to resist inspections (which they considered encroachments on their sovereignty), the establishment of a registry would at least allow other nations to hold them accountable for their pledges. So Obama and Clinton dug in to press hard for a commitment to the registry.

Wen seemed to be negotiating in good faith, but Xie clearly resented the pressure from the United States. When the parties neared an agreement Xie began screaming at Wen, who instructed the translator not to translate. "Internal discussion only!" the translator said. "I'll take that to mean that we have a successful agreement," Obama said, and moments later rose to leave the room.

Because Wen was a no-show at that evening's plenary session, a few influential reporters thought he hadn't truly endorsed the deal. The sincerity of the Chinese commitment would depend on their opaque internal politics and take time to ascertain, though of course the same could be said of the United States.

The Copenhagen conference provided a glimpse of what former national security advisor Zbigniew Brzezinski called "the G-2," the United States and China, alone at the top. Both countries disliked the idea. The Chinese preferred to keep a low international profile as they focused on sustaining their miraculous growth; the Americans weren't willing yet to share superpower status, and they were more comfortable dealing with China in the company of allies. The jostling in the meeting was a preview of the challenges of twenty-first-century global politics. For now Obama was proving that personal, even ad hoc diplomacy was better than none at all.

Back in the plenary session, reaction to the agreement was mixed. It was a bit like health care at home at the end of the year, with some angry and disappointed and others gratified that any progress at all had been made. "It adds up to a significant accord—one that takes us farther than we have ever gone before as an international community," Obama told the delegates. "Here is the bottom line: We can embrace this accord, take a substantial step forward, and continue to refine it and build upon its foundation. We can do that, and everyone who is in this room will be a part of an historic endeavor—one that makes life better for our children and grandchildren."

The nonbinding Copenhagen Accord was ratified. If the American Congress could get its act together, the agreement would give the world something to work with at its next climate conference, in Mexico City in 2010.

21

Chaos-istan

The autumn of 2009 was when Afghanistan became Obama's war. The whole world knew that after endless deliberation with his advisors he decided to send forty thousand more troops, bringing the total commitment to around a hundred thousand. But the hundreds of news accounts missed a deeper and more personal story of conflict at the highest levels of the U.S. government. For months, the military brass tried to box in and manipulate the young Democratic president with no military experience. Finally, he asserted his authority as commander-in-chief to dress down his commanders and impose his will.

Obama wasn't prepared to lie about the military's efforts to manipulate him. When asked if he had been "jammed" by the Pentagon, the president hinted at the test of strength he had just been through. "I neither confirm nor deny that I've gotten jammed," he said in the Oval Office on the day before his December 1 speech at West Point outlining what he considered to be the biggest and thorniest decision of his presidency so far.

For two years Obama had been jamming himself on Afghanistan. Every time the subject of Iraq arose on the campaign trail, he responded by saying that the real war was in Afghanistan. He promised repeatedly to pursue al Qaeda along the border with Pakistan. By the time he reached the point of decision, his lack of room to maneuver was mostly of his own making.

In truth Obama had come into office knowing little about the situation on the ground in Afghanistan and he received advice from Bush holdovers that he wasn't prepared to resist. The result was that he stumbled into a large commitment without fully realizing what he was getting into. When he saw what had happened, he slowed everything down in August and September and launched the most detailed presidential review of a national security decision since the 1962 Cuban Missile Crisis.

IN EARLY SPRING Dick Durbin asked his friend how it was going. The president said he was grappling with a lot of issues at once: "[But] there's only one that keeps me awake at night. That's Pakistan." Obama told Claire McCaskill that figuring out what to do about Af-Pak might be the most important decision of his presidency. Everything about the policy and the events on the ground suggested trouble ahead.

The big fear was nukes. Pakistani authorities claimed they had firm control of their arsenal; that agents of the ISI, the Pakistani intelligence agency that maintained ties with Islamic militants, could not compromise the nation's nuclear program. The U.S. government wasn't so sure. "It's very fucking difficult to stabilize a country that's dysfunctional—that doesn't want your help but knows it needs your help," said one senior official.

The CIA tried hard to interview A. Q. Khan, the Pakistani nuclear scientist suspected of transferring nuclear technology to Iran and North Korea, among other irresponsible parties. But the Pakistanis, who freed Khan from house arrest in early 2009, wouldn't hear of it. U.S. authorities rationalized their failure to interrogate Khan by saying his information was too old to be of major use. In other words, no one, perhaps not even Khan himself, knew how far fissile material and the technical know-how to make a nuclear weapon had spread.

In the meantime the Pakistanis came to the Pentagon looking for helicopters and other advanced weaponry that they claimed would be used to fight al Qaeda. But the United States knew perfectly well that the Pakistanis would take these American-made weapons and send them directly to their other border, the one with India. If the United States meant to take the battle to the terrorists, as Obama promised, it would have to stay intently focused on the region.

Since late spring Obama had been impatient with the Pentagon's pace in Afghanistan. Why, for instance, did it take six months or longer for the additional twenty-one thousand U.S. troops to even arrive there? The answer involved a bewildering discussion of logistics, not to mention the increasing complexity of deployments in a military that now overwhelmingly involved families, many of whom had been worn down by multiple tours of duty. (In the past that number of troops could have been inserted in a month.) This meant a long delay in implementing the March strategy for taking on the Taliban.

IN THE MODERN-DAY American military, wars in the Middle East weren't run from the battlefield or even the Pentagon but from the Tampa, Florida, headquarters of Central Command, or CENTCOM. The four-star in charge since late 2008 was General David Petraeus, fresh off his triumph envisioning and then executing the surge in Iraq, which succeeded so well that it took the top foreign policy headache of the previous decade and rendered it nearly a nonstory.

Petraeus knew how to handle himself in diplomatic and media circles; his sophisticated and persuasive PowerPoint presentations were legendary. It didn't take long to figure out that he was, quite simply, the smartest general most people inside and outside government had ever met. And ferociously ambitious. The White House worried that he was running for president, but his real ambition was to be his era's Carl von Clausewitz or Alfred Thayer Mahan, the dominant military strategist of the twenty-first century.

Petraeus had first become famous inside the military for rewriting the army manual to incorporate new ideas for counterinsurgency (COIN), the strategy of fighting guerrillas begun by the British in Malaysia just after World War II and mangled by the Americans in Vietnam. When Petraeus made the concept work in Iraq he became a hero inside the government and the best-known general since Norman Schwarzkopf.

But the application of Iraq-style COIN to Afghanistan didn't seem to be working. As a sign of the confusion at the top, no one told the president that the twenty-one thousand new troops he approved in March would not be enough to mount a renewed counterinsurgency campaign. It was Jim Jones's job at the NSC to inform Obama that COIN in rural areas requires large numbers of troops and costs a fortune. By the time he did so, Obama was already feeling boxed in, the victim of a textbook case of "mission creep," whereby the mission expands without an explicit policy decision.

Then the Afghan elections were delayed once more. In 2008 Bush had acceded to President Hamid Karzai's idea of letting the date of elections, originally scheduled for April 2009, to slip, then slip again. Now they were scheduled for late summer. Nothing could improve on the ground, Obama believed, until the political situation was clarified.

All the while the war had to be paid for. In April Obama asked Congress for an $83 billion supplemental appropriation for Afghanistan and Pakistan. It was his roughest sledding so far in the House. David Obey, the key congressional appropriator, informed him that he would support it now, but that was it. He was done with Afghanistan after the supplemental; any further escalation would be funded over his objections.

Steve Kagen, also from Wisconsin, told the president aboard Air Force One that a veteran who lived in his district had said, "This is 1964 when I went to Vietnam. I've seen this movie before."

"And it doesn't have a happy ending," the president replied.

All winter senior State Department officials worried that the Pentagon was getting it wrong, that it viewed this as another war of attrition, the kind the U.S. military had been trained to fight from the Civil War on. The brass seemed to think that if somehow we could kill all the bad guys, the problem would go away. Richard Holbrooke had a different view: "If this becomes a war of attrition against the Pashtun, we're in trouble."

Soon even the most conventional Pentagon planners got the point. On May 4 a B-1 bomber dropped a two-thousand-pound bomb on a building in the Afghan city of Farah, killing dozens of civilians. At first the United States tried to quibble over the death toll, which just made matters worse. Whatever the number of Taliban dead compared to civilian dead, the incident was a reminder that, unlike in Serbia, the United States was not going to bomb its way to victory. It was suddenly clear to everyone in the government that weapons like the B-1 had little if any place in this war. For years the dark joke had been that Afghanistan couldn't be bombed into the Stone Age because it was already in the Stone Age. This now became policy.

Bush and now Obama moved toward the heavier use of pilotless Predator drones in Somalia, the Sudan, Afghanistan, and increasingly across the unmarked border into Pakistan, where the Pakistani government pretended not to notice. Although the drones often killed bystanders along with the terrorists, the death toll of innocent civilians was lower than with conventional bombing.* These classified missions marked a big improvement in the war against jihadists—the Predators nailed several "high-value terrorist targets" in Obama's first year—but he knew they weren't a real answer for Afghanistan. Biden disagreed. He felt a sharply focused counterterrorism plan featuring Predators, CIA operations, and ten thousand to fifteen thousand additional troops could do the job.

The president was under no illusions about the place. When Obama attended Occidental College in the early 1980s he was friends with Steve Coll, who went on to edit the *Washington Post.* In 2004 Coll wrote *Ghost Wars,* a book that captured the tortured history of the CIA's role in Afghanistan. Obama read it and absorbed its point about the limitations facing any outsiders trying to negotiate the country's complex tribal politics. Every briefing after he was elected president reinforced the message. But liberals who assumed that in his heart

---

* By mid-2009 the air force had fewer pilots flying airplanes than remotely controlling the drones from the ground.

Obama was for withdrawal were mistaken. The president genuinely believed that national security interests—namely, preventing another attack on U.S. soil—were at stake. He had promised repeatedly during the 2008 campaign that he would step up U.S. efforts in Afghanistan, and now he was doing so.

———

IN MAY BOB Gates sacked General David McKiernan, the top U.S. commander in Afghanistan, after less than a year on the job. This action was extremely rare in the U.S. military. Generals had been relieved of their command only a handful of times since World War II. Gates and Admiral Mike Mullen, the chairman of the Joint Chiefs of Staff, convinced the president that McKiernan, who commanded armored units in Iraq, wasn't nimble enough to accelerate the critical nonmilitary parts of the mission, such as building local militias. Gates and Mullen didn't want to repeat the mistake of the Bush years, when the Pentagon and the president acted as cheerleaders for any commander in the field. They had to face facts squarely: the policy was failing and it was time for a change.

Besides, Mullen was eager to promote his intense protégé, General Stanley McChrystal, who had handled "black ops" (spying, sabotage, assassination) in Iraq and Afghanistan before returning for a stint in the Pentagon, where Mullen put him on the fast track. McChrystal was a smart and especially gung-ho officer with not an ounce of body fat that anyone could see. He insisted that most of his officers live in forward base camps rather than comfortable billets.

His record was hardly spotless. In 2004 McChrystal had helped cover up the death by friendly fire of Army Ranger and former NFL player Pat Tillman and, according to Tillman's mother, lied about it. But the incident didn't seem to impede his promotion to four-star general. At his confirmation hearings he apologized to the Tillman family and said he had made a "mistake."

The change in commanders would have a big influence on the course of events in 2009. Because dismissals were so unusual in the military—and so disruptive to the culture of the armed forces— McKiernan's firing meant that all the other generals in the U.S. military were now fire-proof, safe in their jobs for the foreseeable future. That freed the military to toy with the civilian leadership without fear of the consequences, a point that wasn't lost on Joe Biden. Moreover hiring McChrystal meant that instead of Obama getting a plan in May from McKiernan, he would get one in September from McChrystal, when the situation was more difficult politically both in Washington and

Kabul. By then congressional support had dwindled and Karzai had less legitimacy.

———————

AS THE MILITARY writer Tom Ricks never tired of reminding his readers, Biden had been wrong before. He opposed the Gulf War in 1991, which turned out well. He supported the Iraq War in 2003, which turned out badly. And he opposed the Iraq surge in 2007, which turned out well. Of course everyone made mistakes. Gates, as head of the CIA, didn't believe the Soviet Union would collapse; Hillary Clinton supported the Iraq War and opposed the surge; Obama got the Iraq War right but the surge wrong. And that's not even mentioning the Bush crowd.

So the Pentagon's quiet efforts to discredit the vice president because of his track record didn't work. Biden might have a problem with his mouth, but at least what came out of it was consistent. All year long he wanted a lighter footprint. At a March meeting in the Situation Room he had argued that a heavy concentration of U.S. forces simply made the United States a bigger target and a source of recruitment for the Taliban. Clinton and the military countered that the situation had to be stabilized before true political reconciliation could have any hope of working.

In truth the political situation on the ground, though dysfunctional, was not hopeless. American officials were impressed by the native political smarts of the Afghans; the local chieftains reminded them of ward heelers in Chicago, the metaphor of choice for conveying toughness in Obama's Washington. These tribes hadn't forgotten the depredations of the Taliban, and they could now be reached more easily because the United States had ended its senseless policy of burning poppy fields, which did nothing but alienate the local populace and drive many villagers into the hands of the Taliban. The Obama team chose instead to focus on big-time drug traffickers, some of whom had close ties to Karzai's brother.

Karzai himself felt disrespected by Obama. Under Bush he had enjoyed a twice-monthly videoconference with the president. A pattern developed: Bush would read from a list of things that needed to be done and Karzai would solemnly promise to address each item, "lying through his teeth the whole time," as one official put it. This undermined any leverage the U.S. ambassador in Kabul might have. Shortly after taking office Obama was unanimously advised to drop the teleconference, which he did. In May he invited Karzai and Pakistani President Asif Ali Zadari to Washington for a trilateral conference—useful for breaking the ice—and avoided one-on-ones with Karzai.

———

THE TENSION ON Afghanistan between the White House and the Pentagon began in the summer, when Jim Jones traveled to the region with Bob Woodward in tow. "This will not be done by the military alone," Jones told Woodward during the trip. "We tried that for six years." He stressed economic development, not more troops, as the answer and made the same point to the commanders he met in Kabul.

When the traveling party landed at Camp Leatherneck in Helmand province, Jones heard that commanders in the field already wanted more troops. Most of the twenty-one thousand approved in March had yet to arrive, but the situation on the ground was deteriorating quickly. Woodward reported in the *Washington Post* that Jones warned Marine Brigadier General Lawrence Nicholson that new troop requests would likely be met by the president having "a Whiskey Tango Foxtrot moment." The story landed hard in Washington in early July, and not just because it confirmed the president's favorite expletive. It played into fears at the Pentagon that went back as far as the Vietnam War. A 1998 book by West Point graduate H. R. McMaster, *Dereliction of Duty,* was practically required reading in the U.S. military. The book showed how the Joint Chiefs of Staff acquiesced in the lies and deception of Defense Secretary Robert McNamara and the Johnson White House. (The military's own lies at briefings in Saigon were downplayed.) McMaster's lesson was that military commanders should always be willing to speak out about what they thought it took to win a war.

Again during the Iraq War the uniformed military felt it had been pushed around. Unfortunately for Obama the events of 2009 were colored by those of 2002 and 2003, when General Tommy Franks's troop requests for the invasion of Iraq were scaled back sharply by Secretary of Defense Donald Rumsfeld, and General Eric Shinseki's congressional testimony accurately estimating that "hundreds of thousands" of troops were needed in Iraq was so embarrassing to Bush that Shinseki was encouraged to retire early. (No one from the White House or secretary of defense's office bothered to come to his retirement ceremony at West Point, a major snub in the military.) The brass, which was still upset over being rolled by Rumsfeld and his theory of a "light footprint," resolved that it would never again stand by as a president ignored its troop requests. Gates, in turn, was operating under the shadow of Rumsfeld, who would always be remembered as the defense secretary who underresourced a war.

Petraeus's take was characteristically nuanced and scholarly, though it ended up in the same assertive place. In 1987 he had written a 328-page PhD dissertation at Princeton, *The American Military and the Lessons of Vietnam*. The war, he noted, "was an extremely painful reminder that, when it comes to intervention, time and patience are not American virtues in abundant supply." This would seem to argue against open-ended commitments. But in the same thesis he offered another "painful reminder," this one specifically for his own breed: it's the military, "not the transient occupants of high office, [who] generally bear the heaviest burden during armed conflict." Twenty years later Petraeus wasn't about to let one of those "transient occupants" unfairly burden the institution he loved.

Meanwhile Obama and his senior White House staff had their own Vietnam book, Gordon Goldstein's *Lessons in Disaster*, an account of McGeorge Bundy's role in embroiling the United States in the war. Tom Donilon read it twice, recommended it to Rahm Emanuel, and it became must-reading in the NSC and the political shop. The book, Donilon thought, was about a thoroughly failed process in which none of the assumptions was challenged. Goldstein explained that Johnson had bumbled into war without understanding the true nature and ambitions of the communist insurgency in Asia and the fallacy of the so-called domino theory. Reading Goldstein encouraged the Obama team to broaden its questions about the complex interactions of al Qaeda and the three separate tribal insurgencies in Afghanistan and Pakistan. It helped force the president and his people to confront which Vietnam analogies they thought were relevant and which were not.*

Obama's conclusion was that the differences outweighed the similarities. The most salient difference involved what, after 9/11, the foreign policy mandarins liked to call the "existential danger." As Richard Holbrooke, who had served as a young diplomat in Vietnam, pointed out, the Viet Cong never posed a direct national security threat to the United States. Al Qaeda did.

But the quagmire comparison couldn't be dismissed. David Obey, who was against the war, told the president on the phone about a recent Bill Moyers documentary he'd seen that featured archival footage of LBJ wrestling with Vietnam. "It is stunning to listen to Johnson talk to Dick Russell [a wise conservative senator from Georgia]," Obey told Obama. "It is terrible, gut-wrenching to listen to them both say, 'Well,

---

* Shortly before he died Robert McNamara told Walter Pincus of the *Washington Post* that although he was hopeful about Obama's progress on nuclear weapons, he was worried that Afghanistan was another Vietnam fiasco.

we know this is damn near a fool's errand, but we don't have any choice.' "

———

AFTER MCCHRYSTAL GOT the job in June, Gates said casually at a White House meeting, "By the way, Stan thinks he should do a reassessment. He thinks he should do a full-blown report and tell you what's happening because things are worse than Stan thought they were." Obama just listened.

But Biden said, "Whoa. Whoa. Whoa." He was chomping at the bit, practically jumping out of his chair as he told the group that he had an old story to tell from the Senate of the 1970s. It was about Senator John McClellan of Arkansas, who had taken part in the Army-McCarthy hearings and later chaired the first committee investigating organized crime.

As a freshman senator in his early 30s, Biden went to see McClellan to try to win a spot on the criminal law subcommittee. "Mr. Chairman, should I send you a letter?" Biden asked. McClellan took out a cigar, and now the vice president was mustering his best imitation of an Arkansas drawl: "A bit of adviiiiice. Nevuh send a chairman a lettuh he doesn't want to receive."

Biden's view was that McChrystal's report was a letter they didn't want to receive, especially since it would be submitted before the Afghan election. It made no sense: conditions would be different after Karzai won or lost. Why do this now? He had warned the president in March that the Pentagon was going to figure out a way to get more troops, and now he was being proven right.

With all his experience, Gates should have seen bureaucratic trouble ahead that would complicate his relationship with the president. Reports from the field are meant to fill in the details so that policymakers have enough information to make a decision. The worst outcome would be to have the commander-in-chief and top general out in public with differing views, which is essentially what happened in 2009.

Obama was good at getting people to give him their honest opinions, but he lacked any experience in managing bureaucratic conflicts across distances of thousands of miles—and it showed. The president later admitted privately that his administration had handled the assigning of the McChrystal Report "stupidly." Instead of simply asking him for a status report on the deteriorating situation on the ground, he let Gates and Mullen dispatch McChrystal with a vague assignment that included making recommendations. Obama always liked to define his terms and the parameters of any debate, and that hadn't happened. And he figured he should have known that any report would inevitably get out if put on paper.

————

ON AUGUST 17 Obama flew with Michelle and Biden to Phoenix, where he addressed the Veterans of Foreign Wars. This wasn't Obama's natural habitat, but he won a polite reception for his muscular speech defending the rights of veterans. Most significantly he called Afghanistan "a war of necessity." Biden made little secret of his dislike of that formulation. As far as he was concerned, the only place the United States had to fight "by necessity" was where al Qaeda had a significant presence. And at the moment that wasn't in Afghanistan.

McChrystal was a necessity man and now sounded the alarm. His soon-to-be-legendary sixty-six-page report went to Gates on August 30, with interagency distribution in the days that followed. It warned of "mission failure" among "serious and deteriorating" conditions if more troops were not sent. The report concluded that widespread official corruption was as much a threat as the insurgency (actually three different insurgencies by different jihadists) to the mission of the U.S.-led NATO coalition. The report acknowledged the military's shortcomings in the region: "Pre-occupied with protection of our own forces, we have operated in a manner that distances us—physically and psychologically—from the people we seek to protect. . . . The insurgents cannot defeat us militarily; but we can defeat ourselves."

It was a potent and accurate critique. The question was what to do about it. Confronting the deep-seated problems of Afghan society required not just counterinsurgency but an ambitious nation-building campaign. That, in turn, meant at least another eighty thousand troops and an open-ended commitment lasting ten years or more. At a million dollars per soldier, fully implementing McChrystal's plan would mean spending another trillion dollars on top of the trillion the United States had already committed in the region. Even the middle option he recommended, forty thousand troops, would mean a hundred thousand American troops in a country with only one hundred al Qaeda fighters altogether. Did that really make sense?

Such questions were soon to receive an extraordinarily thorough airing. The first of ten Af-Pak meetings came on September 13, when the president gathered sixteen advisors in the Situation Room in the basement of the White House. This was to be the most methodical national security decision in a generation. Beyond the twenty hours of meetings with the full group, policymakers spent hundreds of hours in smaller meetings at the White House, Pentagon, State Department, and CIA.

At the first session Obama told the group to forget about the debate over troop strength for the moment and see if they could reach a consensus about the essential facts on the ground. After that would come a full two-hour meeting devoted to defining the mission. Each principal had read the McChrystal Report and a lot else and now settled in for a semester's worth of classes with Professor Obama. Unlike the usual seminar, though, this teacher didn't know the answers to the questions discussed in class.

Tom Donilon commissioned research that backed up an astonishing historical truth: that neither the Vietnam War nor the Iraq War featured any key meetings where all the issues and assumptions were discussed by policymakers. In both cases the United States was sucked into war inch by inch.

The Obama administration was determined to change that. "For the past eight years, whatever the military asked for, they got," Obama explained later. The structure of military decision making "presupposed sign-off without rigorous debate." Obama now acted to change that structure. "My job was to slow things down," he said. Under McChrystal's own request, no more troops would go to Afghanistan before January 2010 at the earliest. So the president had something precious in modern crisis management: time. "I had to put up with the 'dithering' arguments from Dick Cheney or others," Obama said. "But as long as I wasn't shaken by the political chatter, I had the time to work through all these issues and ask a bunch of tough questions and force people to sharpen their pencils until we arrived at the best possible solution."

Obama established a methodical process: first the policymakers developed a strategy, then they assessed the resources necessary to implement the strategy, and finally they discussed how to get out. The president later said his "logic chain" was meant to avoid making decisions based on faulty premises. He insisted on "testing all of the assumptions" before sending more soldiers to risk their lives.

From the start Obama was eager to do something he generally liked to avoid on the domestic side: get "down in the weeds," as he put it. He spent the first several meetings posing a series of pointed questions: Is an effective partnership with Pakistan possible? Was COIN even workable in Afghanistan? In Pakistan? What does "defeat the Taliban" mean? (They spent hours on how to measure defeat.) What is the likelihood that al Qaeda would return to Afghanistan in the event of a Taliban takeover? (High.) Does the Taliban have to be routed in both Afghanistan and Pakistan in order to keep al Qaeda from threatening U.S. national security? (Not necessarily.) If the Taliban took Kabul and controlled Afghanistan, could it link up with the Pakistani Taliban to threaten the command and control of Pakistan's nuclear weapons? (Quite possibly.)

The Pentagon and State Department assigned hundreds of people to answer all the group's questions, only to find that at each meeting the president and his advisors had even more: Could the Kabul government eventually carry the burden of its own security? Could the United States work with provincial governments as well as Kabul? Could Taliban fighters be "reconciled" instead of killed? How exactly could the U.S. government force Karzai to reduce corruption and replace ministers? Why had the Afghan police force actually been shrinking after eight years and tens of billions of dollars in aid?

It was a sign of how out of touch the Pentagon had been with realities on the ground that only now did the government learn that the Taliban offered the seventeen thousand freelance militia in the country a third more in pay each month than did the Afghan security forces. No wonder the much-despised Taliban recruited better from the pool of young Afghan men trying to feed their families. "You know what?" Obama said. "We gotta pay them more." He issued an immediate order for a pay increase, and in December the Afghan army had its highest recruitment success in years.

Early on, the president eliminated withdrawal as an option, in part because of a new classified study on what would happen to Pakistan's nuclear arsenal if the Islamabad government fell to the Taliban. The United States, he concluded, simply couldn't do without a substantial military presence in the region. He was never in any doubt that there was, in his words, a "fundamental strategic interest in making sure Afghanistan doesn't revert to being a safe haven for al Qaeda."

With so much terrorist incitement in other nations and in cyberspace, who was to say that Af-Pak was the locus of the threat? The answers were in the "threat charts." Officials pointed to the FBI's finding that the two biggest terrorism conspiracy cases it cracked in 2009, one in Colorado and one in Chicago, both featured trips back and forth to the border between Pakistan and Afghanistan. Sophisticated terrorist plots required training in person, which was much easier in failed states or lawless border regions. Or so most experts believed.

———

OBAMA'S APPROACH IN the meetings was the same as always. He was, according to one participant, "clear-eyed, hardheaded and demanding."

More than once the president felt obliged to remind those briefing him that it wasn't 2001 anymore. The United States had been in Afghanistan for eight years and doing more of the same wasn't going to cut it. The war in Afghanistan was destined soon to pass Vietnam (eleven years) as the longest war in American history.

Some of the questions were rhetorical. "Are we getting results commensurate with the enormity of the investment of troops, their families and the taxpayers?" Obama asked. The answer was obviously no, which meant that before sending more troops, he needed a series of detailed responses. "Show me strategies to transfer to a post-American presence," the president said. (The phrase *exit strategy* had been tossed out because everyone knew the United States wouldn't be fully exiting any time soon.) He drove the military and the CIA hard, requesting precise accountability metrics. When military planners couldn't provide clear ways of measuring success, he sent them back to the drawing board, which contributed greatly to the length of the process.

The president had problems with the "product" he was getting from the intelligence community and the Pentagon. CIA Director Leon Panetta found himself on the defensive over faulty projections of Taliban advances. The Defense Department had weak answers on budget questions. Obama complained that despite hundreds of budget planners working in the Pentagon, no one there could tell him what the various plans would cost. How could that be? So he brought Peter Orszag into the Sit Room, a place budget directors had rarely, if ever, ventured before, and OMB ended up handling the numbers. Obama ordered thirty new intelligence products (answers to big questions). This helped him open up each session by saying, "Okay, here are the facts . . ."

Amid all the requests for specifics was the most basic question of all: Will the policy make the United States safer? With al Qaeda already operating in the Sudan, Somalia, Yemen, and the northwestern frontier of Pakistan, would securing Afghanistan genuinely enhance U.S. national security? Here the effect of a Taliban-controlled Afghanistan on the security of Pakistan's nuclear arsenal became a big issue, though most of these conversations remained classified.

The early deliberations showed a split between two essential positions: counterinsurgency, under which Afghan population centers would be defended and developed by American troops, a process of nation-building that would take many years; and counterterrorism, Biden's view, which called for Predators and special forces to root out suspected terrorists but gave up on nation-building. Biden's aim was to avoid making Afghanistan a "permanent protectorate," but even his strategy would require bases inside the country and up to fifteen thousand additional troops. He worked to build some breathing room between large-scale escalation and withdrawal.

COIN was aimed at creating conditions of security that a strong government could then build on. But if the government was corrupt, even the best COIN would be for naught. And Obama thought a national COIN was unsustainable. "I am not going to do a ten-year, one-trillion-dollar Afghan plan," he said at one meeting. "It's not required and not in the public interest." So the conversation kept coming back to the Karzai government. It wasn't just that Karzai's brother was widely believed to be an opium dealer (and on the CIA payroll to boot); most major ministries were dysfunctional.

In building the Afghan security forces, the cultural gap was immense. The *New York Times* reported that after coalition forces constructed new barracks for the troops they were training, the Afghans often ripped out the sinks and put them on the floor to wash their feet before prayer, leaving gaping holes in the walls. New kitchens went ignored as Afghans cooked over fires on the floor. The meetings featured extensive conversation about the illiteracy and poor training of the Afghan officer corps, though no consensus on what to do about it.

Like other presidents, Obama believed it was wrong to bring up politics in the Sit Room. So one of the critical factors in his eventual decision—the level of American public support required to sustain a major commitment—was left unspoken. The need for public backing for any war was one of the most important lessons taught at the Army War College, but no one from the Pentagon wanted to talk about it. Of course Rahm and Axelrod and the rest of the White House political team talked about it upstairs all the time. They worried that Obama's presidency would run aground in the mountains of Afghanistan.

———

UNLIKE PRESIDENT KENNEDY'S thirteen days of meetings during the Cuban Missile Crisis, the existence of the Af-Pak sessions wasn't secret. That meant an explosion of unauthorized disclosures, spin, and cut-throat bureaucratic gamesmanship. The most spectacular leak came on September 21, when Bob Woodward revealed the McChrystal Report in the *Washington Post*. The White House was predictably furious. It went without saying that the leaker, who the White House suspected came from the office of the Joint Chiefs of Staff, would be fired if caught.

The flap over the leak did nothing to chasten the Pentagon. In fact the military, practiced in the ways of Washington, now ran PR circles around the neophytes in the Obama White House, leaking something to the Pentagon reporters nearly every day. The motive for all the leaks seemed clear to the White House: to box the president into the policy that McChrystal had recommended.

Admiral Mullen, the son of a Hollywood publicist whose clients included Bob Hope and Jimmy Stewart, looked unassuming but knew how to handle himself in the press. Mullen was an unimpressive briefer in the Sit Room, yet he understood all the right sensitive things to say in public ("Lead quiet. Lead listening"), and he effectively conveyed that he was a nonpartisan voice of reason in Washington. Petraeus of course was a pro at cultivating reporters. Their man McChrystal had avoided reporters while working black ops and serving in the Pentagon; he was inexperienced with the media. So now Mullen convinced Rear Admiral Greg Smith, who had coordinated communications for Petraeus in Iraq, to come out of retirement and manage McChrystal's image.

Even before the leaking of the report, McChrystal, working with Mullen's approval, made himself shockingly accessible to the press. He sat for a long, colorful interview with *60 Minutes,* appeared on the cover of the *New York Times Magazine,* and dismissed the Biden plan to *Newsweek:* "You can't hope to contain the fire by letting just half the building burn." Mullen himself began to tout what was supposed to be internal advice. He invited the bureau chiefs of the five TV networks to the Pentagon for a background lunch, where he told them that the McChrystal Plan had to be adopted in full, including a five- to eight-year commitment of forces, maybe longer, or the United States faced defeat.

Mullen dug himself in especially deep at his reconfirmation hearings for chairman of the Joint Chiefs when he made an aggressive case for a long-term commitment. Rahm was enraged at his public testimony and let the Pentagon know it. When Petraeus gave an interview to *Washington Post* columnist Michael Gerson on September 4 calling for a "fully resourced, comprehensive counterinsurgency campaign," the chief of staff was even angrier. The Pentagon said Petraeus hadn't even realized that Gerson was President Bush's former chief speechwriter, which had contributed, of course, to the impression that Petraeus was a Republican.

Mullen and Petraeus thought the whole thing was a big misunderstanding. Most of McChrystal's interviews had been arranged to coincide with McChrystal taking command—not the new policy deliberations—and any impression that the Pentagon was advancing McChrystal's report at the expense of the president was inadvertent. Mullen and Petraeus claimed that they were doing nothing more than dutifully reiterating the full COIN policy that had been established by the president in March and fleshed out by Jim Jones in an NSC planning directive sent to the Pentagon in July. They said that once they heard the policy was under review, they stopped talking. "Hey, Denis, don't worry," Petraeus told Denis McDonough of the NSC, "I get it."

If so, apparently McChrystal didn't get the word. Scheduled to give a speech on October 1 before the Institute for Strategic Studies in London, McChrystal wasn't sure if he should make the trip, but Mullen told him he should definitely go; it would help the alliance. The speech was unexceptional until the question period, when McChrystal let loose. He referred derisively to a "plan called 'Chaos-istan,' " which he described as a strategy for making Afghanistan a "Somalia-like haven of chaos that we simply manage from the outside." The Chaos-istan plan, depicted as some out-of-left-field idea, turned out to be taken from a CIA report that McChrystal had no authority to declassify. Then the general crossed his commander-in-chief in ways that would have consequences. When a questioner asked if he could support a presidential decision to fight the war with drone aircraft and special forces that focused on defeating al Qaeda (the Biden plan), McChrystal replied, "The short, glib answer is no."

If the president sided with Biden, the commanding general *couldn't support it?* This was insubordination, and the White House was livid. Was McChrystal out of control or just naïve? (The consensus was: naïve.) Obama and his senior staff believed this had Mullen's and Petraeus's fingerprints all over it. They were using McChrystal to jam the president, box him in, manipulate him, game him—use whatever verb you like. The president had not yet decided on a policy and didn't appreciate the military sounding in public as if he had. Some aides worried at least briefly that Petraeus was politically ambitious and was making an implied threat: Decide Afghanistan my way or I just might resign my command and run for president in 2012. It wasn't a crazy thought. Representative Peter King and various blogs were promoting him for high office. Although he insisted he was uninterested, Petraeus was a registered Republican in New Hampshire and well positioned to run as a Colin Powell–style alternative to Mitt Romney, Sarah Palin, or anyone else in the 2012 presidential primaries. When asked about it, Petraeus was, as he later put it, "Shermanesque." Not interested. "What part of *no* don't you understand?" he said.*

On the day after the London speech McChrystal was summoned to Copenhagen to meet with Obama, who was trying—and failing—to lure the Olympics to Chicago. They talked alone for twenty-five minutes while Air Force One sat on the tarmac. It was only the second time the two had met since McChrystal took over in June. The president wasn't happy but he held his temper in check, as usual. By this

---

* Civil War General William Tecumseh Sherman famously said in 1884 that if nominated for president he would decline and if elected he would not serve.

time the White House had concluded that McChrystal was simply in over his head in the media world, a pawn in Mullen and Petraeus's game. Obama found that he liked McChrystal personally and thought he had the right approach for completing the mission. *Of course* he wanted more troops, Obama figured. All battlefield generals do.

But Obama was perfectly aware of the box he was now in. He could defer entirely to his generals, as Bush had done, which he considered an abdication of responsibility. Or he could overrule them, which would weaken their effectiveness, with negative consequences for soldiers in the field, relations with allies, and the president's own political position. And how was he going to fire someone so soon after he fired General McKiernan? There had to be a third way, he figured, and he set to work thinking his way out of the predicament.

In the meantime it was important to remind the brass who was in charge. Inside the National Security Council, advisors considered what happened next historic, a presidential dressing-down unlike any in the United States in more than half a century. The commander-in-chief now undertook the most direct assertion of presidential authority over the U.S. military since President Truman fired General MacArthur in 1951.

In the first week of October Gates and Mullen were summoned to the Oval Office, where the president told them that he was "exceedingly unhappy" with the Pentagon's conduct. He said the leaks and positioning in advance of a decision were "disrespectful of the process" and "damaging to the men and women in uniform and to the country." In a cold fury Obama said he wanted to know "here and now" if the Pentagon would be on board with any presidential decision and could faithfully implement it.

"This was a cold and bracing meeting," said an official in the room. Lyndon Johnson had never talked to General William Westmoreland that way, or George H. W. Bush to General Norman Schwarzkopf. Presidents Kennedy, Carter, and Clinton had all been played by the Pentagon at various points but hadn't fought back as directly. Now Obama was sending an unmistakable message: Don't toy with me. Just because he was young, new, a Democrat, and had never been in uniform didn't mean he was going to get backed into a corner.

Mullen described himself as "chagrined" after the meeting. He had always felt strongly about the importance of civilian control of the military and in 2008 had delivered a message to the armed forces reminding all service personnel to stay out of politics. No one intended to box the president in; of that he was certain.

Now he and Gates pledged support and told the president that the conduct would change, and it did. On October 5 Gates said in a speech to the Association of the U.S. Army that it was "imperative" that generals provide their advice "candidly but privately."* (He felt the White House was just as guilty of damaging leaks as the Pentagon, and he hoped his message of discretion was heard there, too.) Jones reinforced the discretion point in interviews. Mullen and Vice Chairman of the Joint Chiefs General James Cartwright stopped selling the McChrystal Plan and told Petraeus and McChrystal to stop talking publicly until the policy deliberations were resolved. "They swore loyalty," said one senior civilian official. "And we chose to believe them."

––––––

WHEN THE AFGHAN elections were finally held in September they were marred not by violence (the State Department's fear) but by theft. The Karzai forces stole a million votes, which was "fraud even by Illinois standards," as Bruce Riedel put it. Unlike Ahmadinejad in Iran, Karzai would almost certainly have won without stuffing the ballot boxes; that made his corruption all the more exasperating. It took weeks to sort out the returns, convince Karzai to approve a runoff election, and move forward when the runoff was canceled after the leader of the opposition withdrew amid charges that the process was rigged. The election, said one advisor, was "about as bad an outcome as we could have hoped for."

The election mess had the effect of lengthening the deliberations in Washington. Richard Holbrooke was among those arguing that nothing could be decided until the outcome of the election was determined. It was partly a matter of appearances; headlines reading "More Troops" wouldn't look good next to ones reading "Chaos in Kabul."

For the avid students of the Vietnam War gathered in the room, the Karzai government looked suspiciously like the hapless Saigon regimes of the 1960s. One of the great ironies of global politics was at work again: in any relationship between a major power and a client state, it's the weaker party that calls the tune by threatening to collapse or otherwise resist its patron. This was a familiar paradox in the region. Here "the Great Game" of nineteenth-century imperialism was playing out again, with exasperating local regimes empowered once more to yank the chains of empire.

––––––

* Gates had an interest in clashes between presidents and generals. On his flight back from Pakistan in January 2010 he watched the 1964 movie *Seven Days in May,* which depicts an attempted military coup.

IF NOTHING ELSE, the autumn meetings were a direct rebuke to the Bush decision-making style. Dick Cheney's complaints about "dithering" set a new high in chutzpah (as they call it in Wyoming): here was the architect of the policy that ignored Afghanistan for eight years complaining about Obama's careful attention to it. Donald Rumsfeld meanwhile claimed to the press that commanders in the field hadn't requested more troops for Afghanistan on his watch. Mullen shot him down—a rare public rebuke.

Politically Obama was already getting boxed in on the Hill, as John McCain and Joe Lieberman praised his "courage" in advocating a robust commitment, a not-so-veiled threat that they would raise hell should he decide not to accede to McChrystal's request, whatever it might be. On the liberal side Nancy Pelosi and David Obey argued that every foreign occupation of Afghanistan had ended in disaster and that the United States risked the same humiliation experienced by the Soviet Union in the 1980s. This was true enough as a debating point, but the historical references did little to address the security situation inside the country. Afghanistan was shaping up as a political loser—another example of Obama making tough decisions that would win him no points.

FOR ALL THE leaking and staff squabbling, there was always a gravitas inside the Sit Room befitting the seriousness and complexity of the decisions. It was an adult group. The average age of the military men was well over 60, whereas plenty of Obama's domestic advisors were in their 40s, 30s, or even 20s. Policymakers with some mileage on them knew better than to be too adamant about the cases they were making. There was a tentative quality to almost every conclusion reached. Several of the key players went through what Jones called a "metamorphosis" during the meetings. In truth it was more like a return to their roots. Almost everyone in the room, including the president, ended up framing the issue based on their own experience.

Jones, who had been skeptical at first of a larger footprint, came around to troop escalation. He was, after all, a retired four-star marine general, "a Semper fi guy," as one participant put it. As NSC advisor he might not champion the military perspective, but he sure as hell wasn't going to sandbag his old colleagues. Jones's service as supreme allied commander in Europe shaped his Sit Room contributions. Under Bush the "Coalition of the Willing" in Iraq had been something of a joke; for Obama it was central. He needed to get eight thousand to ten thousand European troops and make international cooperation real. That required help from Clinton, Holbrooke, and others, but Jones would be the point man on winning the cooperation of his old NATO friends.

Gates was arguably the most important player in the room, but he said contradictory things. At first he argued that McKiernan's request for more troops in March should be the end of it. A large footprint, he noted, would only make the United States into an occupying power like the Russians he had spent years studying. In October he was still skeptical. When McChrystal's face on the videoconference screen in the Situation Room was replaced by a mission statement on a slide reading "Defeat the Taliban. Secure the Population," Gates was cutting. "We don't need to do that," he said. "That's an open-ended, forever commitment." But by the middle of the process Gates had abandoned his comparisons to the Soviets' disastrous experience in Afghanistan. The Soviets killed more than a million refugees and terrorized the country, he said. The United States shouldn't "just automatically say that because they lost, everyone loses." Now he readily embraced the recommendation of forty thousand troops, which was hardly a surprise. Cabinet members almost always back up their own people.

And yet "there was more ambivalence in Bob Gates than anyone else in the room," said one participant. It may have been that he was just more willing to show how uncertain he felt. By several accounts, not once did anyone in the meetings say, This *will* work. That's because no one, including the president, was sure what would.

———

GATES AND CLINTON got along famously. "For most of my career, the secretary of state and defense weren't speaking to each other," Gates liked to joke. The key to making the relationship work, he thought, was to allow the secretary of state to speak for American foreign policy. By letting Clinton be Madame Outside, he could be Mr. Inside, with the secretary of state usually deferring to him on national security issues. Together they made a formidable pair.

Clinton was less conflicted than Gates; she was game for a larger and more open-ended commitment. Part of the explanation went back to her experience on the Senate Armed Services Committee, where she forged close relationships with several members of the Joint Chiefs, including Mullen. She wanted more troops to protect vital State Department personnel on the ground, but also because she was simply more hawkish than Obama. During her husband's presidency she had watched military intervention in the Balkans bear fruit when everyone said it would fail.

Clinton would go for long periods in the Af-Pak meetings without saying anything. Then, at critical moments, she would offer penetrating comments, especially on the links between the various branches of the Taliban along the border. This was the nub of it, she felt. The United States simply needed a larger presence in the most dangerous territory in the world. Whatever one thought of her military judgment, these words carried great political weight. It didn't escape notice that Clinton was the second most powerful Democrat in the room. Her strong belief that a reluctant Democratic Party should be dragged along into an expanded commitment in Afghanistan trumped Biden's misgivings.

Several people in the Sit Room couldn't help wondering what it would have been like with Hillary Clinton at the head of the table. She sounded like the general election candidate she promised to be if she won the nomination in 2008—the toughest guy in the room. Her sense of urgency and mission was greater than the president's; her force field had more energy. But she would not likely have been as sensitive as Obama to the domestic costs of a long commitment in Afghanistan.

When they imagined Biden as president, they chuckled. "Heads [in the Pentagon] would have rolled and we would have had a different policy," said one. "But no one would have been able to figure out what the policy was." Biden's idea for ten thousand to fifteen thousand more troops never got much traction because it didn't cohere as a concrete proposal. He couldn't say exactly how a counterterrorism strategy would actually work, perhaps because, unlike Dick Cheney when he was vice president, Biden did not have a large national security staff to prepare elaborate plans.

Even so, the longer the process went on, the better Biden got. He asked question after question, particularly about police and army training, and the answers from the Pentagon were clearly inadequate. Obama asked a lot of his own questions, but Biden's were often more biting. The president privately encouraged the vice president to play the bad cop. His queries made the process longer but also deeper, as Obama and Biden worked in tandem to send the brass back to the Pentagon again and again to fashion better plans to bolster the Afghan military and police.

———

ON OCTOBER 26 Obama met with the civilian leadership without the military. By this time he had received an NSC "consensus memo" summarizing the direction of the meetings. For the first time the Pentagon and other agencies contributing to the memo concluded that degrading, but not destroying, the Taliban would satisfy U.S. security interests. It was also critical, the memo said, to accelerate the transfer of authority to the Afghan security forces. The size of those forces, the group concluded, was less relevant than the quality of those enlisted.*

Gates had been involved in the consensus memo and now he and Jones worked together on a compromise of thirty thousand troops with ten thousand more obtained through NATO. Rustling up the additional forces in Europe would still be tough, but they believed it would be easier than in the Bush years, in part because of Obama's stature abroad.

The final plan was beginning to take shape, but the president had two big worries if the United States committed more forces. First, what would happen if in two years the Karzai government collapsed? The answer was to emphasize relations with regional and tribal leaders. He would do what he could to avoid putting all his chips on Karzai and what Petraeus called Karzai's "crime syndicate."

But was that possible? Paul Begala, a close friend of Rahm and former political advisor to President Clinton, noticed that ninety-nine times in sixty-six pages the McChrystal Report mentioned something called GIRoA, which stood for Government of the Islamic Republic of Afghanistan. It was a sign that the entire fate of the endeavor was tied to the effectiveness of the Kabul government, just as in Vietnam, where the Saigon regime proved so impotent. "If GIRoA is FUBAR [military lingo meaning "fucked up beyond all recognition"], then all the American soldiers are for naught," Begala told Rahm. Obama knew this and spent hours in the Sit Room discussing how to make better use of local tribal leaders and other forces outside of Kabul.

The president's second big concern was: What if in two years the military insisted that the United States stay with a full force? "A lot of my questions had to do with the pace in which troops were arriving and the pace in which the troops would be leaving," Obama recalled. The bell curve the Pentagon presented him was fat: troop strength ramped up slowly and drew down slowly. "My whole point was, 'How do you move that bell curve to the left?'" the president said. His metaphor of choice on Afghanistan was the same one he made popular on health care ("bending the cost curve")—a graph.

He told the group his reasons for doing so were largely economic. This wasn't 2001, when the budget was in surplus. A bigger, longer commitment might have been possible if the nation hadn't just spent

---

* Thousands of Afghans had routinely been enlisting in the U.S.-backed police or army, deserting with a weapon, then reenlisting and beginning the cycle again.

$1 trillion in Iraq and hadn't just gone through the worst financial crisis since the Great Depression.

———

JUST BEFORE 4 A.M. on October 29 Obama stood silently in the predawn darkness at Dover Air Force Base and saluted as the flag-draped coffins containing eighteen servicemen killed in Afghanistan were removed from a cargo plane. They were among the fifty-five dead in Afghanistan in October, the bloodiest month for Americans since the war began in 2001. The family of one soldier, Sergeant Dale R. Griffin, asked that the media be allowed to cover the transfer of Griffin's remains, which gave the world the first look at the solemn arrival since President Bush banned coverage eight years earlier. Obama decided that it was a symbolically important moment for reconnecting the country to the great sacrifices of the military. After consoling the families, the president rode in silence back to the White House.

At the Sit Room meeting the next day he asked the generals for a "surge" similar to the one Petraeus had executed in Iraq, with a fixed date for withdrawal. Obama had been among the Democrats who opposed the surge in Iraq, but he knew he'd been wrong and Petraeus right about that strategy, and it was time to see if it could be applied in Afghanistan.

Two weeks later, on Veterans Day, Obama walked through the section of Arlington National Cemetery reserved for the war dead from Iraq and Afghanistan. The way things were going there would be many more casualties as the war in Afghanistan dragged on. When he returned to the Situation Room, the president was in a pensive mood.

The November 11 Veterans Day meeting, the eighth on Af-Pak, would prove pivotal. "I don't want to be going to Walter Reed for another eight years," he told the group. He acknowledged that he was more annoyed than at any of the previous seven meetings. "I'm usually more sedate than this," he said.

His unhappiness reflected news that day of two dissenting cables from Karl Eikenberry, a retired general and now U.S. ambassador to Afghanistan, leaked to the *Washington Post*. It was a good thing for the Pentagon that the *Post* didn't possess the memos themselves, because the language was scathing.* Eikenberry, who had once commanded U.S. forces in Afghanistan, wrote, "President Karzai is not an adequate strategic partner." He "shuns responsibility" for defense, governance, and development and has a "record of inaction" on corruption. But

———

* In January 2010 the *New York Times* obtained them.

Eikenberry went further. Like Matthew Ho, an experienced civilian affairs representative who provided a devastating ground-eye critique of
the war when he resigned in protest from the Foreign Service in October, Eikenberry argued that more troops might actually weaken the
U.S. mission in Afghanistan:

> The proposed troop increase will bring vastly increased costs and
> an indefinite, large-scale U.S. military role in Afghanistan, generat-
> ing the need for yet more civilians. An increased U.S. and foreign
> role in security and governance will increase Afghan dependency,
> at least in the near term, and it will deepen the military involve-
> ment in a mission that most agree cannot be won solely by mili-
> tary means. Further, it will run counter to our strategic purposes
> of Afghanizing and civilianizing government functions here.

If Obama's escalation ended in more failure, he couldn't claim that
he wasn't warned. Here was a man who had seen Afghanistan from
both the military and diplomatic sides and seemed utterly pessimistic.
But a closer reading of the cables suggested that what made Eikenberry
despair was the idea of an "indefinite" U.S. role that "increased Afghan dependency." If a policy could be fashioned that wasn't indefinite
and didn't increase dependency, then perhaps he could sign on. The
memos eventually helped Obama fashion a short leash for Karzai as
part of the new policy.

Eikenberry's memos infuriated the McChrystal crowd. There was no
love lost between the two generals, who later rode back from the region together in virtual silence. The cables were assumed to have been
leaked from the White House, perhaps as retaliation for the disclosure of the McChrystal Report and all the other Pentagon leaks. White
House officials, knowing firsthand the president's intense feelings about
leaks, claimed otherwise. "What I'm not going to tolerate is you talking
to the press outside of this room," Obama told the group sharply. He
was back on his antileak jihad, which itself leaked.

That day the president gave preliminary approval to the plan presented to him by the military, which called for forty thousand more
troops to be sent to Afghanistan over twenty-one months. But the timetable stuck in his craw. Already in a snappish mood, he found it ap-
palling that in the world of modern military transport it would take
nearly two years to get those boots on the ground. In the Gulf War
in 1990–91 the military got half a million troops to the region in less
than six months. "I don't know how we can describe this as a surge,"
Obama said sharply. The president then turned to Petraeus. "Am I mis-

taken in remembering that the thirty thousand troops in Iraq arrived in a six-month window in 2007?"

"No," Petraeus said, "you're not." The president was treading in a sensitive area. "Any time Iraq was mentioned it was like putting a hot rod under Petraeus. He would practically levitate," said one person in the room.

Obama bore in: "So why is this surge taking place over twenty-one months if that one was done in six months?"

Petraeus replied that the Afghanistan surge was not modeled on Iraq.

"Well, your presentation earlier was on Iraq," Obama reminded him.

The general always threw in the caveat that Iraq and Afghanistan were very different countries. Afghanistan would need new runways, ammo storage, billets, and other military infrastructure before many more U.S. troops could arrive. But the whole thrust of his analysis, the basis of his prestige, was that what he learned in Iraq could be applied to Afghanistan and other nations. They had talked about this for hours in previous meetings and now the president was calling Petraeus's bluff, as one note taker at the meeting put it.

"The only way we'll consider this is if we get the troops in and out in a shorter time frame," Obama said.

The president might have been annoyed at Petraeus for the foot-dragging approach to Afghanistan, but he owed him a debt of gratitude for Iraq. A combination of Petraeus's COIN program and a clever diplomatic approach to the factions and militias helped reduce the level of violence in Iraq to the point where Obama could begin to fulfill his campaign promise of a phased withdrawal. During 2009 more than thirty-five thousand troops rotated out of Iraq. The president's goal was to do the same for Afghanistan starting in 2011.

OBAMA WAS MOVING out of his probing mode and toward conclusions and eventually presidential orders. This would not be a five- to seven-year nation-building commitment, much less an open-ended one. The time frame the military was offering for both getting in and getting out must shrink dramatically, he said. There would be no nationwide COIN; the Pentagon was to present a "targeted" plan for protecting population centers, training Afghan security forces, and beginning a real—not a token—withdrawal within eighteen months of the escalation. He asked Mullen to establish a workable schedule for him to present at the next meeting. To make sure everyone got the message, the White House issued a statement that day: "The president believes that we need to make clear to the Afghan government that our commitment isn't open-ended."

The McChrystal Plan was now as dead as the Biden Plan. For all the talk of the impossibility of splitting the difference, the policy would be a speeded-up combination of the two. The McChrystal team had won on troop strength, but Obama and Biden won on narrowing the mission. Having thinned the bell curve and moved it left—into 2010 and 2011 instead of later—the president was now more comfortable with where he was headed.

The ninth meeting, on November 23, took place at night. This was when the president circulated a preliminary document outlining his "shaped option," which was titled "Max Leverage." The name referred to leverage on the Taliban and al Qaeda, but it might just as well have applied to leverage on Hamid Karzai and the Pentagon. Even General Cartwright, who had favored a large troop buildup, now argued that short timetables might focus Karzai's mind.

Mullen had returned with a timetable that was much more to the president's liking. It called for sending thirty thousand American troops, with ten thousand more from NATO; added to the troops already there, this brought the total to about a hundred thousand. The new troops would arrive by mid-2010 and their progress would be evaluated at the end of the year. By July 2011 a significant number of troops would begin to come home. At Mullen and Gates's insistence, the plan included a caveat: conditions on the ground permitting.

As usual Obama went around the room testing the reaction. All but Biden were supportive. The vice president continued to make no secret of his objection to such a large buildup of troops. But even when the meeting ended after 10 p.m. it wasn't clear to everyone that a final decision had been made. The president was still playing it close.

The day after Thanksgiving, November 26, was devoted to fine-tuning the decision. From 10:30 a.m. to 9:15 p.m. Obama and a small group of White House staff took various drafts of the eight-page, single-spaced consensus memos floating around the bureaucracy and shaped them into a policy. Tom Donilon, Denis McDonough, Doug Lute, and other NSC deputies ran through the complex decision trees, as Obama said yes or no to a long series of detailed policy options. Rahm Emanuel, David Axelrod, Jim Jones, John Brennan, and others wandered in and out, offering recommendations. Rahm complained that Ax had tried to relitigate the decision at the eleventh hour, but by now everyone was on board with the new plan. The president phoned Gates and Clinton, who tweaked specifics but raised no new major issues.

Later Obama offered clues to his thinking at the moment of decision.

He had worried that, at any troop level, even well over a hundred thousand, he might face what he called "a flat line." By this he meant that troops would prevent Kabul from being overrun but not accomplish much else. They'd be "hunkered down" for the long haul. In that case, he said, "there's no point at which we can say conditions have changed sufficiently so that we can start bringing our troops home." Instead he sought what he called "an inflection point" (more lingo from the world of policy mandarins) by which progress could be measured, not by the number of enemy killed but by the strength of Afghan security forces. "The strategy that I'm pursuing is designed to say, 'Let's see if we can change the conditions on the ground in a certain time period.' There are risks associated with that, but in the absence of that push, we are in a situation that doesn't change. There are big costs associated to troop presence, to casualties, to a slowly deteriorating situation over a course of years that is at least comparable and probably worse than us going ahead and making this big push now."

On Sunday, November 29, having made his decision, the president decided to hold a final Oval Office meeting with the Pentagon brass and commanders in the region who would carry out his orders. He wanted to put it directly to the military: Gates, Mullen, Cartwright, Petraeus, and Jones, without any of the others.

Obama asked Biden to come back early from Thanksgiving in Nantucket to join him for the meeting. The vice president had prepared a thirty-page memo for how to make the new policy work. It mostly consisted of advice on how to navigate around the Karzai government to achieve the mission's objectives. Biden later told a friend that as they were walking near the Rose Garden, Obama started smiling and said he wondered what the meeting would be like if the roles were reversed, with Obama as vice president and Biden as president: "It would be worth it to see what happens when we walk in that room." Obama laughed when he thought of the looks on the generals' faces. "I would really enjoy that."

Biden didn't know exactly what he would have done if he were president, but he was sure it wouldn't have been as wise. "Mr. President," he said, "that's why you're president and I'm not."

As they walked along the portico toward the Oval Office, Biden asked if the new policy of beginning a significant withdrawal in 2011 was a direct presidential order that couldn't be countermanded by the military. Obama said yes.

The president didn't need the reminder. Obama had already learned something about leaving no room for ambiguity with the military. He would often summarize his own meetings in a purposeful, clear style by saying, "Let me tell you where I am," before enumerating points ("One, two, three") and finishing with, "and that's my order."

Inside the Oval Office, Obama asked Petraeus, "David, tell me now. I want you to be honest with me. You can do this in eighteen months?"

"Sir, I'm confident we can train and hand over to the ANA [Afghan National Army] in that time frame," Petraeus replied.

"Good. No problem," the president said. "If you can't do the things you say you can in eighteen months, then no one is going to suggest we stay, right?"

"Yes, sir, in agreement," Petraeus said.

"Yes, sir," Mullen said.

The president was crisp but informal. "Bob, you have any problems?" he asked Gates, who said he was fine with it. The president then encapsulated the new policy: in quickly, out quickly, focus on al Qaeda, and build the Afghan army. "I'm not asking you to change what you believe, but if you don't agree with me that we can execute this, say so now," he said.

No one said anything.

"Tell me now," Obama repeated.

"Fully support, sir," Mullen said.

"Ditto," Petraeus said.

Obama was trying to turn the tables on the military, to box them in after they had spent most of the year boxing him in. The "logic chain" was now in his favor. If, after eighteen months, the situation in Afghanistan had stabilized as he expected, then troops could begin to come home. If conditions didn't stabilize enough to begin an orderly withdrawal of U.S. forces (or if they deteriorated further), that would undermine the Pentagon's belief in the effectiveness of a hundred thousand troops. The commanders couldn't say they didn't have enough time to make the escalation work because they had specifically said, under explicit questioning, that they did.

It wasn't a secret that someone in the military would likely have been fired had Biden been president. But the vice president admitted to other advisors that it was better that Obama was in charge and showing more mercy toward the Pentagon. The generals thought they were working him over, Biden said privately, but the president had the upper hand. He was a step ahead of them, and as much as some of them thought they had obliterated the July 2011 deadline for beginning a withdrawal, they were mistaken.

When he spoke to McChrystal by teleconference Obama couldn't have been clearer in his instructions. "Do not occupy what you cannot transfer," the president ordered. In a later call he said it again: "Do not occupy what you cannot transfer." He didn't want the United States moving into a section of the country unless it was to prepare for transferring security responsibilities to the Afghans. The troops should dig wells and pass out seeds and all the other development ideas they had talked about for months, but if he learned that U.S. soldiers had been camped in a town without any timetable for transfer of authority, he wasn't going to be happy.

———

THE PRESIDENT'S DECEMBER 1 speech at West Point struck a decidedly un-Churchillian tone, and there was no Bush-style language about the glory of the cause. When he spoke of "the price of war," Obama wasn't talking just about the price in human lives; he was referring to the hundreds of billions of dollars it would cost. At the president's request Ben Rhodes inserted a section that explicitly rejected the Vietnam analogy, which was the first time anyone could remember a president's disputing historical parallels rather than invoking them. The most striking omission in the speech was any definition of victory. This was wholly intentional. Fighting al Qaeda would be an ongoing struggle with no surrender papers signed aboard an aircraft carrier, as Bush liked to put it. And once the president allowed cost into the equation, he had to leave himself room to exit before victory—whatever that meant—was achieved.

Critics panned the speech as one of his flatter efforts, which the president found ironic; more than any other he had delivered all year, he said, this one "hit [him] in the gut." As he peered out at the audience of young cadets, he thought about how his decision would mean that some of them might not be coming home alive.

Bruce Riedel, back at the Brookings Institution and well positioned to assess the policy, thought Obama had selected "the best of a lot of really bad options. The alternatives—cutting and running or staying at current levels—were even worse. They guaranteed defeat."

But the public seemed confused by the subtle new policy. "The cavalry is coming—but not for long," was David Gergen's summary. Howard Fineman of *Newsweek* said it reminded him of the Marx Brothers song "Hello, I must be going."

It didn't take long for Clinton, Gates, and Petraeus to begin endorsing nation-building and exploiting their "conditions on the ground" loophole. Testifying on the day after Obama's speech, Gates told a House committee, "I have adamantly opposed deadlines. I opposed them in Iraq and I oppose them in Afghanistan." At the Pentagon the message coursing through the building was that the summer of 2011 didn't really mean the summer of 2011. The president was unperturbed. Obama's attitude was "I'm president. I don't give a shit what they say. I'm drawing down those troops," said one senior official who saw him nearly every day.

Two days after the West Point speech Obama met with his speechwriters to discuss his December 10 speech in Oslo. The timing was awkward. How do you accept the Nobel Peace Prize just after committing to war? He disliked their draft and cleared part of his schedule for time to think. The night before leaving for Oslo he stayed up most of the night writing a rough draft by hand. After a full day at the office he boarded Air Force One for the overnight flight and slept only an hour as Jon Favreau and Ben Rhodes took drafts back and forth to the forward cabin. The arrival ceremony was delayed as the president held Air Force One on the tarmac and scribbled out changes. After a meeting with the Norwegian prime minister he focused on the end of the speech but had to leave for the award ceremony before the last-minute revisions were inserted in the text, which he read in final form for the first time onstage.

Obama made sure to open on a note of humility. "Compared to some of the giants of history who have received this prize . . . my accomplishments are slight," he told the Norwegian dignitaries, before launching into a deep and, considering the haste of the preparation, carefully argued case for distinguishing between just and unjust wars. "Instruments of war do have a role to play in preserving the peace," he said. "A nonviolent movement could not have halted Hitler's armies." He stressed the importance of diplomacy and sanctions in dealing with Iran and North Korea but noted, "Negotiations cannot convince al-Qaeda's leaders to lay down their arms."

At the small private dinner afterward he dined with the Nobel Selection Committee, which consisted of four women and one man, all Norwegian public servants. Any concern that they may have been disappointed by Obama's Afghan policy or speech was quickly dispelled by the effusive toast of Sissel Marie Ronbeck, the senior member, who harkened back to the selection of Martin Luther King in 1964 to explain that the award is sometimes given for great promise as well as results. The women of the world revered Barack Obama, she said, and "women know best."

BACK HOME THE president had no way of knowing whether his Af-Pak gamble would work, but he was going to make damn sure this war wouldn't be another Vietnam. The Pentagon and the critics could think whatever they wanted; he would start a partial but real withdrawal in July 2011. By the summer of 2012—not coincidentally, the middle of his reelection campaign—the public would know that the American commitment in Afghanistan was winding down. The logic was clearer than the pundits realized: if the situation improved on the ground, it was time to begin leaving; if it didn't, that meant the escalation had failed and adding more troops wouldn't fix anything. The reporters who were so sure that Obama would be manipulated into staying needed to understand, said an NSC official, that the decision in 2011 would not be made at the Pentagon: "This will be a presidential order."

At the conclusion of an interview in his West Wing office, Biden was adamant.

"In July of 2011 you're going to see a whole lot of people moving out. Bet on it," Biden said as he wheeled to leave the room, late for lunch with the president. He turned at the door and said once more, "Bet. On. It."

Of course betting on developments halfway around the world was always hazardous. A thoughtful American president can deeply analyze a problem in order to arrive at the "right" solution, or the least wrong one. But Obama's insistence that he could shape the right side of the bell curve reflected his confidence—or overconfidence—in the power of any president to control his surroundings. "Events are in the saddle and ride mankind," Ralph Waldo Emerson wrote. Now they would begin to ride Obama.

Just three days after the president's West Point speech a suicide bomber killed thirty-six, including many Pakistani military officers, at a mosque near the army garrison in Rawalpindi, the latest in a wave of terrorism that had left more than four hundred dead in Pakistan since summer. It reflected a so-called unholy alliance between al Qaeda, the Taliban in Afghanistan, and the Taliban in Pakistan, the last of which had become a major concern to Islamabad.

Hamid Karzai continued to be a problem. He told Senator Mark Warner that the Americans were there to help themselves, not Afghans. Then, reversing course, he said the Americans might have to stay twenty-five years. At Christmas, when U.S. forces killed ten Taliban soldiers assembling IEDs, Karzai echoed local complaints that the men had actually been civilians.

That week a Jordanian doctor, Humam Khalil Abu Mulal al-Balawi, betrayed his case officers and turned into a suicide bomber, killing eight CIA employees and wounding six more at a border outpost near Khost, the greatest blow to the American intelligence services since the 1980s. The attack, al-Balawi said in a video released after his death, was revenge for one of the Predator drone's most successful operations of 2009, the killing of Pakistani Taliban leader Baitullah Mehsud.

The Taliban weren't indigenously popular. Even in the most dangerous parts of Helmand province, the desire to return to the twelfth century was limited. But as 2009 drew to a close the Americans who labored faithfully on policy in the region sometimes found it hard to avoid feelings of futility. More than one recalled a story told by Zalmay Khalizad, a former U.S. ambassador to Afghanistan, who once received a direct message from the Taliban: "You have all the watches, but we have all the time."

22

The Perfect and the Good

During the 2008 campaign well-wishers along the trail gave Obama little good luck charms to carry in his pocket. He wasn't as superstitious as Roosevelt or Reagan, but the president was a big believer in the power of luck.

When informed in June that his poll numbers were sagging, Obama first snapped, "You had to call nine hundred people to tell me that?" But then he suddenly grew chipper about health care. "I know, I know, but I feel lucky. It may not be the optimal time, but I think we can get it done."

Rahm Emanuel wasn't so sure. He thought proceeding in 2009 with universal health care coverage was too big a political risk. "I begged him not to do this," Rahm said later. For the better part of a week in August Rahm made the case aggressively. Obama had said clearly that he welcomed dissenting views and Rahm was the only one gutsy enough to comply.

Rahm's sharply reduced plan would insure more than 10 million Americans (sometimes he said 20 million) and could attract bipartisan support. The idea was to expand coverage for children further than Congress had in February, bolster Medicaid (increasing the number of single mothers eligible), regulate the insurance industry more heavily, add a couple of other crowd-pleasers for seniors, and call it a day.

One advisor called Rahm's approach "the *Titanic* strategy": insure women and children first. Later, aides were less comfortable with the *Titanic* metaphors.

At the end of a meeting in the Oval Office with a half-dozen senior staff just before the August break, Obama stood up suddenly and said, "I understand what Rahm is saying and maybe we'll have to scale back, but we don't have to do that now. Remember, if we do, twenty-two million go uninsured." With that, he walked out of his own office, which was becoming a familiar flourish when the subject was health care.

Obama concluded that it was time to go "big" again in support of his plan. Once he settled on that course, Rahm used every ounce of his considerable energy to execute the president's wishes. The question was how. The White House megaphone wasn't as powerful as the one Obama had wielded on the campaign, when the media waited to see how each side framed its message of the day. In the presidency the coverage was as intense but harder to control.

Sometimes, just after he made an announcement in the Rose Garden, Obama would walk inside and watch the immediate cable commentary for a few moments on a small television on Katie Johnson's desk, then mutter a bit as he reentered the Oval Office. By June he was frustrated with the messaging and ordered his staff to include in his public events more real people with real health care problems, the kind who wrote him every day. It didn't help much because he was trying to fight for a plan that didn't exist yet. That's why the schedule was essential to the strategy. The White House bet that it could let the smelly congressional process play out and then "sell" the bill. But for months there was nothing solid to sell.

So rumors filled the vacuum, some of them true. Obama tried to shut down any concern that people would lose their insurance by repeating his mantra: "Under our proposals, if you like your doctor, you keep your doctor. If you like your current insurance, you keep that insurance. Period, end of story." But it wasn't the end of the story. The reality was that a lot would change, and the public knew it. By 2013, the year of implementation, the system would be transformed in ways that were impossible to predict.*

———

MID-2009 WAS A tough time for the president politically. As fear of economic collapse eased, the public grew more demanding. People tended to pocket their gains, or their smaller-than-expected losses, rather than crediting them. So if you didn't lose your public sector job because of the stimulus bill's aid to states, it was not something to celebrate. If you lost your job and, thanks to the stimulus, paid $400 a month for interim COBRA insurance instead of $1,200, you might not be sure why you were paying less. And if your company laid off your friends but not you, it was still hard to feel cheery about the future.

Moderates and independents, more than a third of the electorate,

* Some critics wondered if Obama intentionally delayed implementation until after the 2012 election. But experts said that any change affecting a sixth of the U.S. economy could not easily begin before then.

didn't welcome aggressive moves from Washington. Their skepticism about government made it difficult for them to see what all the spending would do for them. These weren't tea-party types or right-wing crazies biting fingers off at town meetings (as happened in southern California) or comparing the president to Hitler (as people did in Virginia, Texas, and the sidewalk in front of the White House, among other places). These were average people worried about deficits and hanging on to what they had. Obama's deference to the wildly unpopular Democratic Congress in formulating legislation struck many of these independents as weak. A powerful anti-incumbent mood—partly left over from 2008, partly a reaction to the still sour economy—took hold.

On Capitol Hill, the House Democratic leadership was angry too—at the Republicans. Nancy Pelosi thought the president just didn't understand the GOP caucus in the House the way she did. These people were extreme, she said. She accurately predicted that health care would be the stimulus all over again, with no Republican votes. She gave Rahm (who sometimes playfully called her "Mommy") an earful: "Does the president not understand the way this game works? He wants to get it done and be beloved, and you can't have both—which does he want?"

Eventually Obama got the point. Bipartisanship wasn't working. The Republicans, as the president told Michael Smerconish's radio audience on August 19, were trying to stop health care in order to win at the polls in the midterms, as they did in 1994. It was as simple as that.

Obama realized it was time to get more specific, or at least thematic, while leaving himself room to maneuver on the details. "I'm getting guff about my plan doing X or Y and I don't even have a plan," he told aides. After a series of meetings over the summer he had a better idea of what to push at the staff level on Capitol Hill. Much of the Senate bill would be written with the help of OMB. It would reflect the cost-containment ideas of Peter Orszag.

———

To sell the plan required a big speech. The White House knew, as Dan Pfeiffer put it, "This was our best card to play." The question was when. David Gergen, who had experience in White House communications under five presidents, urged Obama to deliver it in early summer, before opposition set in. But the White House thought the timing was wrong. Speeches were like junk food; the effect wore off quickly. Had Obama delivered a major speech in June, aides figured, it wouldn't have influenced Senator Max Baucus's dawdling or the town hall meetings. Then the White House would have had no weapon in the fall.

Remembering that Bill Clinton's health care speech to a joint session of Congress in September of his first year hadn't worked, Rahm suggested a daytime speech followed by a seven-minute Oval Office address to the nation. But Obama opted in early summer for a primetime address to Congress just after Labor Day, the same venue that had succeeded so well in March. He envisioned talking not just to the folks at home—the conventional target audience—but directly to Congress on behalf of the American people.

———

JUST AS THE obstructionists found their groove, Obama's fabled ground game stalled. The campaign structure, "Obama for America," had become "Organizing for America"; David Plouffe and company had 13 million names of Obama supporters in the computers at the DNC. The size of the list dwarfed anything seen before in American politics, but they didn't know what to do with it. After a couple of early efforts to rouse the base fell short, they realized they couldn't go to the well too often.

It wasn't enough to say that the Obama team had mastered social networking. Marshall Ganz, the Harvard professor who started the "Camp Obama" training sessions for campaign organizers in 2007, had not been consulted by Plouffe since then, and even during the campaign Plouffe had been a little standoffish about traditional community organizing techniques. It was as if the political operatives had forgotten most of what they learned during the campaign about the grass roots. They neglected the months of training local organizers that was necessary to lay the groundwork for a successful effort. Organizing for America passed petitions and hosted thousands of meetings and house parties, but the overall impact was underwhelming. The community organizer president didn't seem to have the time to organize effectively for the largest nonelectoral campaign of his presidency.

Jim Messina and Axelrod visited the Senate just before the August recess to brief Democrats on health care. It made the members feel better. The moderates seemed capable of grasping the core political reality. Evan Bayh of Indiana, who voted with the Republicans on everything from Bush's tax cuts to blocking Obama's budget, was adamant. "We're all screwed if you don't get something real on health care," he said. Democrats realized that their base would be totally demoralized without it. The only way Obama had carried Indiana or any other state was with the intensity of core supporters; that would evaporate if health care lost. Jim DeMint, the South Carolina obstructionist, was right. It would be Obama's "Waterloo."

House Democrats were more restless. After Health and Human Services Secretary Kathleen Sebelius admitted on the Sunday shows that the public option was "not an essential element," liberals went nuts. The White House had to back off and pretend that it was still fighting for the provision, even though Rahm had known for weeks that the public option lacked the votes in the Senate. Pelosi decided to assume for the time being that the other chamber didn't exist. With liberal fever spiking, she announced that any bill coming out of the House must contain a public option.

When Democrats started grumbling that his magic had worn off, Obama was unconcerned. He figured it was like a close basketball or football game: whoever had the ball last usually won. There was plenty of time to go. In late August he reminded a gathering of Organizing for America of where he had been a little less than a year earlier, when Palin-mania had swept the media and his numbers dipped. "Everybody was, you know, obsessed with it," the president said. " 'Obama has lost his mojo' —and cable TV was twenty-four hours a day. Do you all remember that? There's something about August going into September—where everybody in Washington gets all wee-weed up." It was Obama's way of telling liberals to relax and stop peeing in their pants.

"You should exercise your authority and cancel summer," Dan Pfeiffer told him.

At a meeting in the Oval Office on September 1 Robert Gibbs made a joke about bad poll numbers on health care. "Guys, this isn't what we're here to do," the president said. "It's not about 2010 [midterms] 'crippling my presidency,' quote unquote. This is about whether we're going to get big things done." He took a little shot at Clinton: "I wasn't sent here to do school uniforms."

Rahm asked the president, "Are you still feeling lucky?"

"My name is Barack Hussein Obama and I'm sitting here," the president said. "So yeah, I'm feeling pretty lucky."

———

THE SAUSAGE WASN'T made yet, but the customers were already sampling it and retching. Even if the August recess brought no decline in the polls for Democrats, it was painful. Members of Congress faced angry, often ill-informed constituents all across the country. Only the most raucous town meetings made the news, but almost all of them were well-attended and tense. Members were forced to defend a bill that hadn't been written yet, which was hard to explain to voters who had accessed one of the committee versions online.

If "we are the ones we've been waiting for," as Obama said during the campaign, the "we" had been otherwise occupied since the Inauguration. The Obama masses were tired of politics for now, and few showed up in support of health care reform at the town meetings. Pastor Jim Wallis had emailed Obama when he became president that he needed not just the wind at his back but "the wind in front of you," clearing a path for social change.

With the wind blowing in the wrong direction, the president had to come in off the bench and save the game.

Jon Favreau knew that this speech, scheduled for September 9, was a big deal—the biggest speech of Obama's presidency so far. And he knew he had to work in Ted Kennedy somehow.

As a young man, Obama, unsentimental as always, had never been particularly taken with the glamour of Camelot. Born in 1961, the year JFK was inaugurated, he was too young to be enchanted. His relationship with Ted Kennedy got off to a rocky start in 2003 when he said, while still in the Illinois State Senate, that Kennedy was "getting old and getting tired" in pushing a prescription drug bill. (Kennedy let Obama off the hook because in 2004 he had been mangling his name as "Osama.") But Kennedy provided wise counsel when Obama arrived in the U.S. Senate, and after the freshman admired a seascape Kennedy had painted, Kennedy had it taken down from his wall and sent it to Obama as a gift with the inscription "Barack, I love your audacity."*

Kennedy's endorsement of Obama's candidacy at American University after the South Carolina primary moved Obama to tears. It also strengthened his resolve to achieve health care reform in 2009. While Kennedy didn't explicitly make his endorsement contingent on it, Obama knew what the lion of the Senate expected. He also knew that watching two of his own children, Teddy Jr. and Kara, go through cancer had made the whole thing intensely personal for Kennedy, who couldn't get over meeting other families in the cancer wards who were bankrupted by the ordeal. Beyond their increasingly close friendship, Obama believed that Kennedy stood for an idea that had been out of fashion but was essential to the success of his presidency: that government could be made to do something right for people.

After Kennedy's funeral on August 29 his widow, Vicki, told Obama that she had a letter from Ted that she wanted to send him. Favreau learned of the letter and asked Axelrod if Vicki could fax it to the White House earlier than she planned. The big speech on health care was only days away and he needed all the material he could get. Ben Rhodes's wedding happened to be the weekend before the speech, in

---

* The painting now hangs in the president's private dining room.

California; Obama told his speechwriters they shouldn't cancel plans to go. But it left Favreau even more frazzled than usual as he penned a long speech in just a few days.

Obama usually worked on a computer, but this time he handwrote nine pages of a new version, the bulk of the speech. The rest he marked up with his tiny architectural lettering, complete with neat arrows and blocks of inserts. As usual he had the best sense of how to make the argument progress logically. And he knew just how to use Kennedy's letter for the simple peroration, which he wrote himself.

The president had become a bit cavalier about preparing for big events, too cavalier for Rahm, who was annoyed that Obama would give such an important speech without a run-through beforehand. The conventional "stakes are high" line was in this case true. The White House saw the speech as the last big barrier to passing some kind of bill. If the president blew it, the bill would die, and with it his best chance to build a big domestic legacy. Nailing the speech would make passage in some form all but inevitable—or so they thought. Of course Obama had no intention of blowing it. As in Cairo, he was confident he could hit the jump shot at the buzzer without an extra practice day.

———

JUST AS HE had in March, Obama used the House chamber and assembled guests to superb effect. He somehow managed to turn a complex and often boring set of details into a comprehensible and reassuring story of how he and his allies in the room proposed to fix a system that had broken down. He explained that the mandates were not much different from mandatory auto insurance and that 95 percent of small businesses would be exempt from them. And while he plainly told the health insurance industry that he had no intention of driving it out of business, he warned, "If you misrepresent what's in the plan, we will call you out. I will not accept the status quo as a solution. Not this time. Not now."

The audience hushed as he quoted from Kennedy's letter describing health care as "above all, a moral issue," with "the character of our country" at stake. Now came what was arguably Obama's most direct description of his governing philosophy: "I've thought about that phrase quite a bit in recent days—the character of our country. One of the unique and wonderful things about America has always been our self-reliance, our rugged individualism, our fierce defense of freedom and our healthy skepticism of government."

Then he pivoted to the Kennedy legacy and named all the Republicans in the room—McCain, Hatch, Grassley—who had worked with

Kennedy on health legislation. "That large-heartedness—that concern and regard for the plight of others—is not a partisan feeling. It is not a Republican or a Democratic feeling. It, too, is part of the American character. Our ability to stand in other people's shoes. A recognition that we are all in this together; that when fortune turns against one of us, others are there to lend a helping hand. A belief that in this country, hard work and responsibility should be rewarded by some measure of security and fair play; and an acknowledgment that sometimes government has to step in to help deliver on that promise."

By this point Democrats in the chamber knew that if they could set aside their old habits of paralysis they would be part of a historic Congress. "We did not come to fear the future. We came to shape it," Obama said as he sailed to the end, secure that, for now, anyway, he was on his game.

But any hope of detailed coverage of the president's message was quickly dashed when the big news out of the speech was that Representative Joe Wilson, a backbench Republican from South Carolina, shouted, "You lie!" at the president at the moment he referred to illegal immigrants.* After the speech Wilson's own wife called him on his cell phone and asked who "that nut" was who shouted at the president. Obama barely noticed, but Pelosi, sitting behind the president on the rostrum, glared at the Republicans. This sort of epithet in the Capitol against a sitting president was unprecedented.

Rahm was apoplectic. Afterward he told GOP Representatives Roy Blunt and Paul Ryan, "No president has ever had that happen. My advice is he apologize immediately. You know my number." John Boehner directed Wilson to call Rahm and convey his apology to the president, which he did. But the next day Wilson told the press that he had done so at Boehner's request, lessening any impression of genuine contrition. Predictably Rush Limbaugh and other radio talk show hosts said Wilson shouldn't have apologized, which emboldened him to raise money and revel in his new status.

In 2009 heckling the president had become a career move, though the behavior didn't stop Wilson and his wife from lining up in December to have their pictures taken with the president at the White House Christmas Party for Congress. Pelosi, responding to a question about whether the tone of the times was as vitriolic as in 1993–94, got emotional at her weekly news conference. "I have concerns about some of the language that is being used because I saw this myself in

---

* Obama had not lied, but it was true that on a party line vote the House had rejected barring undocumented workers from buying insurance in the exchanges.

the seventies in San Francisco," she said tearfully.* "This kind of rhetoric was very frightening. It created a climate in which violence took place."

Ironically Obama had addressed the temper of American politics in his speech to Congress. "When we can no longer even engage in a civil conversation with each other over the things that truly matter," he said, "we don't merely lose our capacity to solve big challenges. We lose something essential about ourselves." The Wilson outburst may have exposed his critics as boorish extremists, but no one with a trace of seriousness could be happy about losing "something essential" right there in the Capitol on national television. It was a shocking symbol of the demons let loose by Obama's ascension. His presidency had brought new hope and new hate at the same time.

————

EVEN AFTER THE September speech the president was still vague about what he wanted. When senators urged him to focus on the economy, his response was, I *am* focusing on the economy—the *long-term* economy, which won't work if we can't "bend the curve" on health care costs. His insistence on this dry business school rationale for action did little to stir the soul.

Would the bill control costs? Not as much as the Democrats (with the backing of the nonpartisan Congressional Budget Office) claimed. But the status quo definitely wouldn't control them. If the legislation failed it would be many years before a president tackled the issue again. At least with a bill, even a flawed one, the process of reining in costs could begin. One thing Obama insisted on was the Senate language that gave the government huge new powers to regulate the marketplace. If the bill passed, the days of wasteful "fee for service"—doctors charging for each procedure—were numbered.

Senator Ron Wyden, a wiry former college basketball player from Oregon, knew as much about health care as anyone in the Senate. One day at the White House Wyden told Obama he didn't want to talk about the "horserace," the prospects for a bill. He wanted to talk about what would happen *after* a bill passed. If you don't introduce real choice and competition, he said, premiums will go up. He reminded the president that during the campaign he had repeatedly pledged to bring down premiums by $2,500 for the typical family, a promise he couldn't possibly keep.

————

* Pelosi was referring to the murder of San Francisco Mayor George Moscone and Supervisor Harvey Milk, the subject of the 2008 film *Milk*.

Wyden asked the president if he had heard recent testimony by the CBO's Douglas Elmendorf, who said that 90 percent of Americans would not get the chance to enroll in a public option. In other words, the vast majority of folks screaming for a public option would have no option of using it. "Mr. President, what's going to happen when people find out they can't get it?" Wyden asked. "If Democrats force Americans to buy unaffordable coverage from monopolies, people will come after the party with pitchforks."*

By this time, early autumn, the White House was coming to the realization that this was not just about getting a win, any win, to brag about. The old view that anything was better than the status quo was giving way to the understanding that if the bill wasn't structured right, it could blow up in their faces.

———

OBAMA'S POLITICAL TEAM, bolstered by polls, had argued for months that the president should lacerate the unpopular insurance industry, and he had done so intermittently. But on October 17 Obama used his Saturday radio address to call out the industry in the strongest terms a president had used about the private sector since FDR.†

The insurers, Obama said in a tone of outrage, were making a "last-ditch effort to stop reform." Their revenues "actually go toward figuring out how to avoid covering people," and health care dollars "continue to be poured into their profits, bonuses, and administrative costs that do nothing to make us healthy." An industry study (the Pricewaterhouse report) showing that premiums would surge after the bill's passage was "bogus," the president told his audience.

Obama was probably wrong about the bogus part; health insurers were already using the years before the bill would take effect in 2013 to jack up their rates, just as credit card companies did before the crackdown on them took effect in 2010. But the president believed he had to strike back. Americans would never support a bill that they thought would make their insurance more expensive. The attacks didn't register because they included no memorable invective and at first seemed inauthentic from the normally even-tempered president. But as he kept up the attacks into the new year they began to sink in.

———

* The pitchfork metaphor for populism, which went back to angry farmers spearheading revolution, had been revived by Pat Buchanan in 1996 when he was running for president. It got a good workout in 2009.
† Truman's criticism of coal operators and JFK's barbs about steel executives weren't as fierce.

ON THE WAY back to Washington from a speech he gave on Wall Street in September, Obama fell into a heated exchange with Queens Representative Anthony Weiner and Barney Frank aboard Air Force One that highlighted the liberal grievances. Weiner and Frank complained about Obama's speech to a joint session, which progressives on the Hill liked less than the general public. "When you said, 'If you like what you have, you can keep it,' you tied our hands," Frank said, arguing that this gave insurers a tool to resist reform. Weiner was angry that the president stigmatized the single-payer system by saying it would be "like in Canada," when Weiner's single-payer proposal was different. The least the president could do, Weiner said, was stop kissing up to moderate Republicans.

"What does Snowe get you?" Weiner demanded.

"Snowe gets me Snowe and Collins," the president said. He thought the moderate Republicans would also give him cover to nail down moderate Democrats like Ben Nelson, Mary Landrieu, and Blanche Lincoln.

Weiner was unimpressed. "Bipartisanship should be a means to an end, not the end in itself," he said, which was precisely the president's position, though the congressman didn't seem to realize it.

Then Weiner went on a tear about how the president should have started with expanding Medicare, a popular program.

"Now you're changing the argument on me!" the president interjected sharply, as the conversation turned testy.

The Queens congressman was just getting warmed up. "The fact that we've lost seniors is a sign of how badly we've messaged the bill," he said. "We did a terrible job reminding people that we're the party of Medicare." On this one, Weiner scored.

Obama was sore at Weiner for leading a group of liberal members still touting a single-payer plan, which fed the argument that the public option was just a Trojan horse for a total government takeover of health care. Weiner, in turn, felt that Obama had never truly been committed to a public option. "They messaged the public option like *Sybil,* with a different face every day," he said later.

Weiner knew he'd gone over the top with the president. "This is my first trip on Air Force One," he had told Obama when they boarded an hour earlier. When they got off at Andrews Air Force Base, Obama teased, "This was your *last* trip on Air Force One."

The president, who enjoyed a good argument, didn't mean it. A few weeks later Weiner was back on the presidential plane, and the congressman still felt free to speak his mind about the White House.

"They have an exaggerated sense of their guy's ability to come in and save everything at the end," Weiner said. "One of these days he's going to miss the jump shot at the buzzer."

_____

IN EARLY FALL Pelosi was worried about where the process was going. "What if it doesn't work?" she asked the White House. "What if we tell them [insurance companies] that they have to insure thirty-five million new sick customers and they send premiums through the roof? What happens to us then?" Her zeal for a public option was born less of liberal ideology than self-preservation; if increased competition through a public option didn't drive down costs, she might not be speaker much longer. To protect Democrats in the 2010 midterms she built into the bill some instant political winners like a $250 drug rebate for seniors.

There were still lots of ways for the whole thing to come apart. As he worked to blend his committee's bill with the other two in the House, George Miller, who marked up the bill for twenty-one straight hours in his committee, called it the most complex and compelling domestic issue he had confronted in thirty-five years in Congress.

Health care was like an ecosystem, each part dependent on the other. So the "step by step" approach favored by Republicans didn't take into account this interconnectedness. If you required insurers to stop discriminating against people with preexisting conditions, you needed to expand the risk pool with mandates compelling employers and employees to buy insurance. If you imposed a mandate, but the fines for noncompliance were too low, there wouldn't be enough healthy young people buying insurance to cover older, sicker patients. If you increased subsidies to low-income recipients to make the coverage they were forced to buy affordable, you did nothing to incentivize insurers to hold down costs. If you dropped the public option and let the state insurance monopolies continue, the lack of competition would make premiums rise. But if you added a public option without increasing Medicare reimbursements, then hospitals would revolt. And this was just scratching the surface of the complexity.

Before they could get the bill through the House, Pelosi and the relevant committee chairmen—Miller, Waxman, and Charlie Rangel—had to make concessions to the so-called blue dog coalition, a collection of fifty-two frightened white moderates, most from districts that Obama had lost.* Many had come to office on a pledge of independence from

_____

* The "blue dog" name came from paintings by Cajun artist George Rodrigue that hung on Billy Tauzin's office when he was in the House. It was also a play on "Yellow Dog Democrats," who had been "choked blue" by liberal extremists.

national Democrats; many didn't seem to understand that the worst thing for them politically was for the president to fail. The blue dogs were conflicted on health care. As bring-home-the-bacon politicians they hoped to win expanded breaks for rural hospitals and small businesses in their districts. But as deficit hawks they felt beat up by TARP, the stimulus, energy, and now this. How much more change could they take?

Rahm, who had recruited most of them to run in 2006, liked to say there was no such thing as blue dogs, only Democrats who wanted to get to *yes* on health care and Democrats who didn't. He worked hard addressing their specific concerns and kept them quiet about the mandates, the only provision that could kill the whole thing if a public outcry developed. But the blue dog Democrats were nervous. The only way to get their votes was to give them something that would allow them to say they had proven their independence from Obama and shown their credentials as cost-cutters. So Pelosi, Miller, Waxman, and Rangel held dozens of meetings, most designed to let a member (often a blue dog) claim he or she had influenced the bill.

Liberals, meanwhile, kept complaining that Obama wouldn't come forward and say forthrightly what he was for. The White House thought this critique was laughably naïve. "Do these guys really think that the president saying what he wants is the best way to get what he wants?" asked one senior aide. "Do they understand politics at all?" His point was that skillful politicians have always exercised strategic vagueness in tacking toward their objectives.

When certain liberals, imitating tea-party conservatives, floated the idea of running TV ads against foot-dragging moderates they considered DINOs ("Democrats in name only"), Rahm was vicious (that's when he made the "fucking retarded" comment). But even mild efforts to make the bill more progressive brought out the ward heeler in him. "Let's be honest," he said. "The goal isn't to see whether I can pass this through the executive board of the Brookings Institution. I'm passing it through the United States Congress, with people who represent constituents."

Rahm's voice dripped with disgust for those dainty Democrats who imagined they were above politics. "I'm sure there are a lot of people sitting in the shade at the Aspen Institute—my brother being one of them—who will tell you what the ideal plan is," he said. "Great, fascinating. You have the art of the possible measured against the ideal."

In the clash of the perfect and the good, Obama and company figured good was plenty good enough.

THE TEA PARTIES and tumultuous summer town meetings were grass-roots or Astroturf affairs, but on November 5 Michele Bachmann, a right-wing congresswoman from Minnesota, sponsored an official rally in front of the Capitol. This one included speeches by John Boehner and others in the House GOP leadership.

The crowd of five thousand gathered under banners of the now familiar image of Obama as the white-faced Joker from *Batman* and Pelosi as "Weasel Queen." Protesters were happy to see their movement's new celebrities, like Congresswomen Virginia Foxx of North Carolina, who had said that the health care bill was "more dangerous than terrorists." Signs reading "Waterboard Congress" and "Stop Obamunism" could be chalked up to the American tradition of vigorous debate, but the rally also included a pair of gruesome five-by-eight-foot photographs of Holocaust victims, many of them children, under the line "National Socialist Health Care, Dachau, Germany, 1945." No one in the Republican caucus made any effort to distance themselves from the Nazi comparison.

For the GOP the afternoon was marred only when a man in the crowd suffered a heart attack. His life was saved by the government-run health care personnel who work at the U.S. Capitol.

———

SUDDENLY ABORTION, A long-dormant political issue in the mainstream, came back to the fore. At Ted Kennedy's funeral service Cardinal Sean O'Malley of Boston managed to work in a little lobbying on health care. O'Malley pulled the president aside and told him that the Catholic bishops were eager to back the bill but couldn't support anything that would open the way to abortions. Listening patiently, Obama had no idea how actively the Church was about to flex its muscles.

Shortly before the House bill reached the floor, the U.S. Conference of Catholic Bishops rejected a compromise worked out by Congresswoman Lois Capps that would have segregated private funds for abortions from public money in a future health exchange. The bishops called that "money laundering" and weighed in heavily behind Congressman Bart Stupak's amendment, which prevented abortions funded even by private insurers. Women's groups called passage of the Stupak Amendment the worst setback for the pro-choice movement in a generation.* But after they expressed their outrage, every pro-choice

* It was more restrictive than the Hyde Amendment, which barred any use of federal money for abortions (although seventeen states allowed their Medicaid programs to fund it). As a practical matter, the vast majority of women paid for abortions out of their own pockets so as to leave no record of it.

Democratic congresswoman voted for the bill, with the demand that the abortion language be removed in the conference committee. These members knew that Republicans were just using abortion to kill reform, and they wouldn't fall for it.

The Stupak Amendment was a good example of why it made some sense for the White House to let Congress take the lead. If it had been Rahm Emanuel asking women members to pass a White House bill containing language so objectionable, they would likely have refused. Pelosi herself would have no doubt complained about being pressured by the White House, and the entire bill might well have died. But with her strong pro-choice past and leverage as speaker, she was able to hold the women on board. The politics of the Stupak Amendment were sure to reappear any time health care came before the Congress.

House Republicans complained that, after offering an alternative that contained almost no expansion of coverage, they were excluded.* Had they chosen to take part, they could have passed many amendments and wielded considerable power over the final shape of the legislation. Over on the Senate side Mitch McConnell vowed to use any rules he could find to delay the Senate's business. John McCain, who had called for deep cuts in Medicare during the 2008 campaign, suddenly emerged amid a tough primary fight against an Arizona right-winger as the champion of profligate spending on behalf of well-off seniors, a breathtaking reversal of the fiscal discipline on which he had built his career. Several Republicans brought printouts of the two-thousand-page bill to the floor, as if the bill's length by itself was an argument. (The bill was so long in part because, in the archaic traditions of Congress, every change in the law required reprinting much of the old law.) Finally Democrat Sheldon Whitehouse pointed out on the floor that the legislation actually contained fewer words than a Harry Potter novel.

OBAMA PUT IN dozens of hours with members of Congress in the White House and on Air Force One. His style was neither to twist arms nor butter them up but to engage on the issues. John Adler, a New Jersey Democrat from a swing district (who ended up voting against), described it as a "comfortable, soothing, soft approach." In November Hillary Clinton got back in the health care game. The president had her over for lunch to talk about the issue and later asked her to work the Arkansas delegation.

---

* The GOP version would insure about three million of the forty-seven million uninsured and allow insurers to sell across state lines in states with the weakest regulation.

With only two votes to spare, it helped that Bill Owens had just won a special election in New York's Twenty-third District. The overreaching by Palin-style conservatives, who knocked a moderate Republican out of the race, was now proving important in the House as Owens voted yes. Representative Anh Cao of New Orleans, a Vietnamese American pro-lifer elected from a heavily Democratic district, became the only Republican to vote for the House bill.*

On Saturday night, November 7, Obama went to the Cannon Caucus Room and told the Democratic caucus that together they had made more progress on comprehensive health care reform than any administration and any Congress in seventy years: "When I sign this in the Rose Garden, each and every one of you will be able to look back and say, 'This was my finest moment in politics.' " As the president left some Democrats began chanting, "Fired Up! Ready to Go!"

After the bill passed that night by a 225–220 vote, Obama called the House leadership to thank them for their hard work, as well as the heads of the AARP, the AMA, and the American Nurses Association, without whose support in the last week the bill would have failed. The evening felt historic, as member after member insisted there was no turning back now. Or so it seemed at the time.

————

ON THE SENATE side Harry Reid stepped to the fore. Just when everyone assumed the public option was dead, Reid staked out a position on the left that created a public option but allowed states to "opt out." This was Reid's attempt to shore up his liberal base in Nevada, where he faced a tough reelection fight. By throwing a bone to what some Senate staffers called the "FireDogLake crowd" (after a fierce left-wing website written by Jane Hamsher, a former Hollywood producer), he had slowed the bill. After the Massachusetts debacle, some senators would privately argue that it was here, when progressives insisted on one last try for the public option, that the crucial delay took place. "This whole thing could have been done by Thanksgiving if we had been willing to make FireDogLake very angry," said one Senate staffer.† As it was, the bill passed the Senate Finance Committee on October 13 and wasn't voted on before the full Senate until Christmas Eve.

The White House was irritated by this delay and let Reid know it.

————

* Cao filled the seat held by William Jefferson, who was convicted after the FBI found bricks of cash stored in his freezer.

† FireDogLake was already very angry. Hamsher promoted a campaign called "Kill the Bill."

With sixty Democratic senators and sixty votes required to move a bill to the floor, the party had zero margin for error. When Reid and Senators Dick Durbin, Charles Schumer, and Patty Murray went to the Oval Office on the evening of October 22, they found a skeptical president. Obama was on record favoring a public option, but his first priority was a bill. And he still thought the best way to get one was to win over Snowe, who had just finished telling Reid on the phone how mad she was at him for endorsing opt-out instead of the trigger. If Reid had stuck with Snowe—or simply brought the Baucus bill directly to the floor—the bill would have moved through by Thanksgiving.

Instead, after blending the Dodd and Baucus bills, Reid submitted his handiwork to the referee, Douglas Elmendorf of the CBO, and held his breath waiting for the "scoring." If CBO said the bill was too expensive, it would derail the bill. The wait while CBO scored the Senate bill was excruciating for Obama.

"I mean, Lyndon Johnson did not have to go check with the CBO before he passed Medicare," Obama said later. "From the time that Harry Reid put his bill out until we actually were able to move the process was three weeks just waiting for CBO."

Baucus and Reid had added broad new powers for the government to hold down costs by limiting fee-for-service medicine. By eventually putting most doctors on salary (like those at the Cleveland Clinic and Memorial Sloan-Kettering), the reform package would finally tackle "overutilization" and at least a few of the other big cost drivers that the politicians had been ignoring for months. It was here that the policy transformation was baked into the process. The bill scored beautifully.

Moderate swing Democrats were still on the fence even if the bill contained no public option. With every vote needed, each was milking the moment. One by one, Obama and Reid moved toward closing the deal. First came "the Louisiana Purchase": Mary Landrieu received $100 million to help with health care costs associated with Hurricane Katrina. Then Ben Nelson got to work. The former Nebraska insurance commissioner excised the provision that lifted the antitrust exemption enjoyed by the insurance industry, but hinted that he might be pro-reform—for a price. Blanche Lincoln, who was heavily lobbied by the Clintons, held out for changes when the bill reached the floor.*

---

* No matter how popular Obama was, members of Congress saw no advantage in being seen as loyal. When Obama went to Arkansas to campaign for Lincoln in March, his approval ratings were still over 60 percent. Beforehand Lincoln told White House aides, "I want him to say that I'm independent and call 'em as I see 'em."

When they rewind the clock to figure out what went wrong, some Obama aides settle here. What if Obama had stood up and said no to these individual senators who were sticking up the country for their state's selfish interest? What if he had said, "Okay, it's C-SPAN time"? The public might have felt that Obama was finally being true to the spirit of his campaign. And, had their bluffs been called, no Democratic member wanted to go down in history as the one vote that killed health care.

At the time, transparency seemed a lot less important than results. Rahm was extremely nervous about the bill's prospects. If it didn't pass the Senate by Christmas, he said, they were fucked. The bill was unpopular enough without giving senators another chance to get an earful from constituents over the holidays. Obama had to sign it by the State of the Union in late January or look like a crippled president, he said. Every day in late November Rahm would ask Pete Rouse, who was talking regularly with Reid, whether the bill was going to get done. He even called him on Thanksgiving.

"I did this crap in the Senate for ten years," Rouse told Rahm whenever he seemed to be freaking. "Ultimately you get there."

Day after day the principals worked on Senate moderates. Obama made a special project of Snowe, bringing her to the White House for pleasant one-on-one conversations, during which she explained that a Maine public option had been a horrible failure and soured her on the concept. Biden constantly spread the message with his old colleagues that it was fine to vote against the bill—he understood the politics back home—but they had to be with the White House on cloture.* "Don't snatch defeat from the jaws of victory," the vice president told them. With progressives, he used what he called the "Don't bullshit me" conversation: "I've known you for twenty years and talked health care with you endlessly in the gym, and never once until this year have I heard you mention the words 'public option.' Now you're telling me it's the most important thing in the world? Please."

On Sunday, December 6, Obama went to the Senate, where Harry Reid was using the only effective strategy to move legislation: weekend and holiday sessions.

"We're going to be in television commercials together next fall,"

* Cloture is the procedure for ending debate and proceeding to a vote on the bill. Under Senate rules, it requires sixty votes.

he told the senators. "The only question is whether those ads will be about accomplishments, or about failure."

He mentioned laid-off plant workers he'd just met in Allentown, Pennsylvania, and how uncomplaining they were about losing their health insurance. All these folks want, Obama said, is for someone to stand up for them. More than one person in the room thought he was successfully channeling Martin Sheen from *The West Wing*.

"Decades from now," the president said, "this will be the kind of vote you remember. It will be written in the faces of children and families who are relieved of the burden of anxiety and sorrow."

––––––––

SUDDENLY JOE LIEBERMAN decided to hijack the process for a little star turn. The source of Lieberman's overnight opposition to the bill was some combination of insurance companies in Connecticut (whose stock prices rose sharply after Lieberman helped kill the public option) and a consuming hatred for liberals that he had developed after going nowhere in the 2004 presidential primaries and losing the 2006 Senate primary in Connecticut to antiwar challenger Ned Lamont. Lieberman won reelection that year as an independent, endorsed McCain (and vouched for Palin) in 2008, and began voting more often with Republicans.* Behind the good cheer was a bitter man.

When he announced he couldn't support a public option in any form as "a matter of conscience," Democrats of all stripes, even those who opposed a public option, were dismayed by his sanctimony. The chatter in the Senate cloakroom was all about Joe, which is the way he usually liked it. But he was lucky that he didn't hear more of exactly what his Democratic colleagues were saying about him. Democrats everywhere now moved from dismay to apoplexy. When Lieberman went to get his hair cut in Georgetown, even his longtime barber, Renato, wouldn't let him out of the chair until he'd given him an earful on health care.

To appease Lieberman in a way that would also please liberals, Reid amended the bill to expand Medicare eligibility down to age 55 (from 65), a proposal that doctors and hospitals loathed but that Lieberman was on record as firmly supporting in a September 2009 video interview with the *Connecticut Post*. But on December 11 Lieberman told Reid that this was a deal-breaker too, and he wouldn't even wait to find

––––––––

* Lieberman even hired a veteran of the Heritage Foundation and the Christian Coalition, Marshall Wittmann, as his communications director. Wittmann was no longer hard-right but he remained a conservative.

out how the CBO scored the idea.* Reid, who had been patiently listening to Lieberman's patter for months, felt Lieberman had stabbed him in the back. Two days later, to the shock of the White House, Lieberman made it clear on *Face the Nation* that not only was he flip-flopping on expanding Medicare, but he would filibuster any bill that contained it.

Rahm, dressed in his casual weekend clothes, went over to Reid's office for an emergency meeting with Jim Messina, Nancy-Ann DeParle, Chris Dodd, and Chuck Schumer. If they had Snowe in hand, they could afford to kiss off Lieberman, but Snowe was playing hard-to-get with the president, and Reid thought courting her was a waste of time. Nelson, still negotiating over abortion and anything else he could win, wasn't quite nailed down either. The wily Nebraskan always had to be the last holdout, just as he was on the Recovery Act in February.

Reid's skill was counting heads, and he agreed with Rahm that they had to have Lieberman. So they dropped the Medicare expansion, the last shred of something that might be called a "public option." Doing so was painful, but it won Lieberman, who knew that if he found yet another reason to torpedo the bill he would be stripped of his committee chairmanships. To soften the blow the leadership committed to permitting the uninsured to select from the same menu of private plans offered federal employees and members of Congress. This fell in the better-late-than-never category. Allowing Americans "to get the same health care as Congress gets" had been one of Obama's biggest promises in the 2008 campaign.

———

FOR WEEKS, FIVE progressive Democrats and five moderates, the "Gang of Ten," worked to keep lines of communications open. Reid asked Schumer, the only one with the energy and savvy to whip the caucus, to help him get to sixty votes. He now reported that progressives like Sherrod Brown, Jay Rockefeller, and Tom Harkin—who were strongly for a public option and felt aggrieved at progressives being taken for granted—were on board for passage. They weren't happy, but they remembered Ted Kennedy's advice, that half a loaf is better than none. And this bill was more than half of what they had been fighting for all these years. With passage, flaws could be fixed down the road.

The Democratic base didn't fully agree. To the chagrin of the Senate progressives, Howard Dean, former party chairman, now said it was

———

* Although Medicare was in financial trouble, the expansion would have been less expensive than subsidizing expanded private insurance.

time to "kill the whole bill."* ("I'll kill Governor Dean," Reid said when he heard the news.) The fact that Dean's 2004 presidential platform included no public option and was far less progressive than the 2009 Senate bill apparently had no bearing on his thinking. Liberal Democrats convinced themselves that if insurance and pharmaceutical stocks surged on news that the bill advanced without a public option, that must mean the bill was terrible. They couldn't accept the idea that the interests of 30 million uninsured Americans and the interests of companies eager for 30 million new customers might overlap. Axelrod, reflecting Obama's view, warned that killing the bill was "insane" and would have "tragic" consequences.

The stench from the spectacle was overwhelming. Cable news cameras were now inside the congressional sausage factory, watching the ugly process up close. So it was no surprise that Obama's poll numbers fell lower each day, which in turn made Democrats even more nervous. "[Health care has so] overwhelmed the debate," the president said in November, "that people have sort of forgotten what we've done [on a dozen other issues]."

Reid was a tough bird, but the man who didn't flinch in 1981 when a bomb was placed under his car now admitted that he wasn't sleeping at night. Chairing the Nevada Gaming Commission in a mob-infested state was easy compared to this, he said. Here he was engineering the greatest social legislation since Medicare in 1965, and no one seemed to give him much credit. In January 2010 his historic work was overshadowed by dumb (though hardly racist) remarks he made to the authors of a new book about the 2008 campaign. The U.S. Senate was broken, but the majority leader used some masking tape and baling wire to make it work again.

After all Obama's patient meetings with her, Snowe decided that the bill was being "rushed" and announced that she would join her fellow Republicans in a filibuster. This shocked DeParle, who had been meeting with Snowe's staff every day and thought she would end up in support. Word spread quickly on Capitol Hill that Snowe understood that if she voted with the Democrats she would lose her spot as the ranking Republican on various committees. Snowe's aides denied this; she had been faced with the same implicit threat before the Finance Committee vote and nonetheless voted aye. But her excuse that she hadn't had time to absorb the bill rang false. "That's hardly a reason," Arlen Specter said. "She's had plenty of time to read the bill now." Snowe

---

* As did Keith Olbermann, who carried considerable weight with liberals.

had caved, though she knew the existing system was far worse than a flawed bill.

Max Baucus, who had often voted with the GOP, went to the floor just before Christmas to call out the Republican leadership for "forcing" his committee's Republican members to abandon their bipartisan efforts. Grassley, Snowe, and Enzi wanted to work across the aisle but were told they could not, Baucus charged. The proof of the GOP leadership's bad faith, he said, was that they never even offered an alternative. Matt Drudge posted video purporting to show that Baucus was drunk on the floor. Angry and frustrated were more like it. For months on end he had been played for a fool.

So it would be all Democrats. The GOP appeared to have lost its gamble that Reid could not hold all fifty-eight Democrats (plus two independents). On December 18 Nelson came to terms. He settled for some compromise language on the Stupak Amendment (allowing states to ban abortion coverage by insurance companies, which none likely would). Most conspicuously he got Reid to agree to have Washington pick up all of Nebraska's $100 million tab for expanding Medicaid, a soon-to-be-legendary concession known as "the Cornhusker Kickback."

But this time Nelson had outfoxed himself, as even Nebraskans overwhelmingly thought the deal stank. The blowback was so intense ("He got the corn, we got the husk," said California Governor Arnold Schwarzenegger) that after the first of the year Nelson wrote to Reid withdrawing his personalized provision. But by then, fatefully, the Cornhusker Kickback was already in the bill that passed the Senate. In the past, this was just how things were done; now the deal became a symbol of how Obama and the Democrats were playing the same old Washington games.

McConnell used all the parliamentary tools at his disposal to prevent passage before Christmas, his last best chance to kill the bill. By now the courtly traditions of the Senate club lay in tatters, as Tom Coburn went to the floor a few hours before the key vote and asked for an unusual moment of prayer. "What the American people ought to pray is that somebody can't make the vote tonight," Coburn said. This was clearly a reference to 92-year-old Senator Robert Byrd, who lay at home ailing. Coburn's prayer went unanswered. Not long before 1 a.m. on December 21, Byrd was wheeled in to vote. After three more days of pointless wrangling the Senate went into session early on Christmas Eve morning and shortly after 7 a.m. approved the bill, 60–39.

Obama called Vicki Kennedy, Harry Reid, and a dozen Democratic senators to thank them for their help and wish them a Merry Christmas. The consensus was that it was a good and historic thing for the country, but that it shouldn't have been so hard.

After the holidays Obama was preoccupied dealing with the fallout from the Christmas Day bombing attempt. Then, on January 12, an earthquake destroyed much of Haiti, eventually killing at least two hundred thirty thousand. On hearing the news Obama ordered the entire U.S. government to mobilize. He was visibly moved by the suffering and vowed that the United States would not forsake the Haitian people after the cameras left. He told the twenty-five officials from different agencies who met in the Situation Room until 1 a.m. that this was "an important leadership moment for the country."

Between terrorism and Haiti, Obama still found time to work out the differences in the House and Senate versions of the health care bill. For nearly three weeks the president became enmeshed in the complicated negotiations. Labor was furious about the Senate's tax on so-called Cadillac plans; over the years unions had sacrificed pay increases in exchange for lavish benefits and they didn't see why they should be heavily taxed. Obama worked out a compromise that satisfied the unions, though it required the Democrats to find more sources of revenue. Big Pharma suddenly withdrew its support for the deal over the president's insistence that the terms of patents allow cheaper generic drugs to come on the market more quickly.

Through endless meetings Obama stayed patient. With another week or two of talks, his aides thought, he would have a final bill approved. Then he could pivot fully to jobs in his State of the Union Address.

NINE DAYS BEFORE the January 19 special election in Massachusetts to fill Ted Kennedy's seat, two public polls landed like grenades in the White House. The first, by the *Boston Globe,* had the Democratic candidate, Attorney General Martha Coakley, up by seventeen points. This was consistent with earlier surveys that showed her cruising to victory. But a second poll, by Public Policy Polling, showed a dead heat between Coakley and Republican Scott Brown, a state senator best known for having posed nude for *Cosmopolitan* as a young man and for being the father of an *American Idol* contestant. Senate staffers later said that had they known earlier that the race was going to be close, they would have worked right through Christmas and New Year's to finish the bill.

Pollsters in Massachusetts began picking up some of the highest anger levels they had ever seen. Coakley had fought banks and insurance companies as Massachusetts attorney general and should have been in tune with the public mood, but it was Brown, crisscrossing the state in his truck, who had the momentum. He exploited anger over the underwear bomber being read his Miranda rights. Supporters began chanting "Forty-one! Forty-one!" in reference to Brown being the forty-first GOP vote, enough to beat health care in the Senate. David Axelrod immediately offered to send reinforcements—seasoned political operatives—from Washington. At first, the Coakley campaign said no.

Coakley had taken a six-day vacation in the Caribbean three weeks before the election—an unforgiveable sin in politics—and with a week to go compounded the error by traveling to Washington for a fundraiser hosted by K Street lobbyists (immediately exploited in a TV ad by Brown). On January 13, after a televised debate in which Brown scored points by describing the open Senate seat as "the people's seat," not the Kennedys', a quote appeared in the middle of a *Boston Globe* story that would soon be remembered as one of the great gaffes of modern American politics. The Brown campaign had posted video of its candidate shaking hands outside Boston's Fenway Park, a shrine in Massachusetts. A *Globe* reporter asked Coakley why she was in Salem at a rally of the Salem School Committee instead of meeting voters. "As opposed to standing outside Fenway Park? In the cold? Shaking hands?" Coakley said dismissively. "I now know the members of the [Salem] School Committee, who know far more people than I could ever meet."

The next morning, Obama, who had been keeping up with the race since the first disturbing poll, wandered into Axelrod's office as usual. When Axelrod told him the Fenway story, the president reached out and grabbed his shirt.

"No! No! You're making that up! That can't be right! Tell me she didn't say that!" Obama said, with a few obscenities tossed in. That was the moment the full weight of it hit him. Health care was in deep trouble. So was his presidency.

Even before setting off for Massachusetts for a futile final weekend of campaigning, Obama knew Coakley was finished. He summoned David Plouffe to the White House to accelerate planning for how to hold the Congress for the Democrats in 2010. The president was not despondent but he found the situation "incredibly aggravating," as one aide put it. As the returns on January 19 showed Brown winning handily, Obama, calmer now, found himself thinking about Nancy-Ann DeParle and the other staffers who had been working endless hours on the bill. He'd need to figure out how to lift the sense of mourning that had descended on his White House.

Massachusetts offered a trifecta of bitter irony. Ted Kennedy had devoted his storied career to achieving universal coverage and pleaded for it on his deathbed; now the man who won his seat represented the decisive vote against it. Massachusetts had been the first in the nation to enact health insurance for all its residents, a plan overwhelmingly supported by Bay State voters, including Brown; now those voters, worried about being taxed twice, had acted to deprive the rest of the country of what they enjoyed. The streets of Boston had erupted in celebration on November 4, 2008, as Barack Obama's election redeemed the promise of progressivism; now it looked as if the most consistently liberal state in the country would capsize the Obama presidency and block the most significant piece of social legislation in nearly half a century.

For all that, Obama should have seen it coming. Independent voters who went for Brown in Massachusetts represented millions of angry Americans in other parts of the country. Over and over, Brown voters in focus groups brought up not Massachusetts but Nebraska and the smelly deal for Ben Nelson's vote. They complained about the negotiations being held behind closed doors. In 2008 Obama had promised a cleaner, more transparent process that brought people together across party lines. In 2009 he failed to deliver it. The president was so confident that he could work the levers of government to bring believable change that he misjudged the depth of the public's scorn for the old politics in both parties.

Even so, it was hard to say that Biden, Rahm, Axelrod, and the others who had wanted him to avoid tackling fundamental health care reform in 2009 had been right all along. Obama had come tantalizingly close to making his gamble pay off, closer than any president in seventy-five years. He had driven to the five-yard line only to be stopped on a fluke play. And so he would resist the temptation to view every decision of the past twelve months through the lens of one election in Massachusetts.

Inside the White House there was plenty of talk about the "political malpractice" of the Coakley campaign.* The president couldn't get over what a pathetic effort it was. But the returns contained a message they couldn't ignore. Soon enough Obama began, as usual, to analyze the results from a dozen different angles. He turned to what he called their big "tactical mistakes" of 2009. The whole thing had gotten too congressional and too focused on Democrats, he said. If the American people don't see us working together, we'll all get thrown out. In

---

* The bulk of the blame fell on pollster Celinda Lake, Senator Bob Menendez (chairman of the Democratic Senatorial Campaign Committee) and his staff, and the candidate herself, who had compounded her Fenway Park gaffe by calling Red Sox great Curt Schilling "a Yankee fan."

the meantime, the White House hadn't been clear enough about the mess that was left them. We should have explained better who was responsible for all these problems, he said: "We rolled up our sleeves and drove out of the ditch instead of pointing fingers, and now, nine months later, people don't remember who's to blame."

In the days that followed, the president conceded publicly that the communications effort in 2009 wasn't what it needed to be, especially on health care. His team agreed. Somehow the "vocabulary" that Jarrett said Obama was looking for in the summer had remained elusive. Small business didn't know about the subsidies in the bill for them; seniors didn't know that the bill closed the "donut hole"; young adults didn't know they would be able to stay on their parents' plans until age 26—no one knew anything!

The day-to-day messaging was miles behind the disciplined Republicans, who always appeared to be working off snappy talking points. Democrats from Obama on down seemed faintly embarrassed about repeating a party "line." Coordination between the DNC and the White House was weak and it cost them. More broadly, the message of the Democratic Party was cloudy. As the prospects of health care reform faded, Senator Al Franken said of the Republicans, "Their bumper sticker has one word: 'No.' Our bumper sticker has—it's just way too many words. And it says: 'Continued on next bumper sticker.' "

Rahm and Ax (who was responsible for communications) grimly joked to Rouse that he was lucky he didn't have a higher profile. They had been feted as strategic geniuses and would now be derided as incompetent fools. That was Washington. Obama wasn't the type to look for scapegoats but major adjustments in strategy and tactics lay ahead. Long before Massachusetts, the White House political staff knew that it was losing the political wars of Washington. The passage of health care through the House and Senate was more ugly than uplifting. So some new strategy was required. Maybe something could be negotiated by spring involving use of the complex "reconciliation" process, which required only fifty-one votes in the Senate. Or maybe not. In January, the only thing Obama and his senior staff knew for sure was what they weren't going to do—move right and go small, with bite-size initiatives that could be dressed up as real change. It wasn't 1995 anymore and he wasn't Bill Clinton.

In his campaign ads Scott Brown had neither run against Obama nor identified himself as a Republican. But after his victory Democratic Washington descended into chaos. Of all the lessons offered by pundits, Democratic members of Congress from swing districts learned only one: *You're on your own. Obama has no ability to save you.* Even

Barney Frank said publicly that health care reform was dead, and he had a lot of company.

For the Obama White House the last week of its first year was by far the worst week. Besides the Massachusetts fiasco the week had brought an ominous Supreme Court decision that empowered corporations to flood American politics with money, guaranteeing not just Republican advances in the 2010 midterms but an uneven political playing field for the foreseeable future. The Citizen's United case, the White House knew, could make the other political problems they faced look small.

After saying at the hundred-day mark in late April that they preferred to be judged at the one-year mark, Obama aides were in no mood for scorecards. At his daily briefing a glum Robert Gibbs was asked what the president was doing to mark the anniversary. "Nothing special," Gibbs said. "It's a date on a calendar that denotes he's been here a year."

The president wasn't feeling so lucky anymore. Even before the 2008 election, he had told aides that he might be a one-term president. Suddenly that was looking less like false modesty and more like a plausible outcome, though one they would start working hard to avoid. He had achieved many successes in 2009 but come up short, his political capital depleted.

And yet the president was unbowed. On the last Sunday of his first year in office, January 17, 2010, the day before Martin Luther King Jr. Day, Obama spoke from the pulpit of the Vermont Avenue Baptist Church in Washington, where King had appeared in 1956. The president knew by then that Scott Brown would win two days later, but he was taking his own advice from his Inaugural. It was a moment to "pick ourselves up and dust ourselves off."

"There are times when I'm not so calm. Reggie Love knows. My wife knows," he told the congregation. "There are times when the barbs sting." His voice began to lift: "It's faith that keeps me calm. It's faith that gives me peace."

Now Obama's soft voice gave way to a thundering delivery. "The same faith that leads a single mother to work two jobs to put a roof over her head when she has doubts. The same faith that leads an unemployed father to keep on submitting job applications after he's been rejected a hundred times. . . . A faith in things not seen, in better days ahead, in Him who holds the future in the hollow of His hand. A faith that lets us mount up on wings like eagles; lets us run and not be weary; lets us walk and not faint."

Here was the old Obama, the one who believed in what he called a "philosophy of persistence." He was back, and for a moment at least, anything was possible again.

Epilogue

Eleanor Roosevelt liked to tell a story about her husband's funeral. When Franklin Roosevelt died in 1945 and a crowd surged down Constitution Avenue to witness his funeral cortège, a man collapsed to the ground in grief. After he regained his composure, the man standing next to him asked, "Did you know the president?" As he got to his feet, the first man replied, "No, but he knew me."

As he began the second year of his presidency, Obama understood that he had to work more on conveying that he *knew* the people and what they cared about. He had governed well but bloodlessly, and with less to show for his first year than he and his supporters had hoped. Obama acknowledged in end-of-the-year interviews that he'd focused too much on policy and not enough on connecting. As usual, he was acutely self-aware and detached enough from what he called his "remoteness and detachment" to admit it was a mistake.

Many Democrats worried that it was too late—that he'd had his one bite at the apple. The health care debate was so bollixed up, they said, that even a victory on the bill would prove Pyrrhic. They forgot that presidents have multiple chances to revive themselves. Whatever his shortcomings, Obama hadn't had as bad a first year as, say, Abraham Lincoln (who lost a major battle at Bull Run and couldn't motivate his generals) or John F. Kennedy (who was humiliated abroad and ineffective with Congress). Democrats would have to learn to adjust their expectations and conquer their sense of despair—their feeling that if Barack Obama and big majorities in both houses of Congress couldn't change the world, nothing could. In 1961, even before Kennedy (with sixty-four Senate Democrats) ran into early trouble, Richard Neustadt told the historian William E. Leuchtenburg, "The Kennedy presidency will be many things, but the New Jerusalem will not be one of them."

The White House knew that a successful 2010 would require adjustments. Its communications strategy worked fine, said one Obama friend with a mordant sigh, unless you included communicating on jobs, health care, autos, banks, spending, and terrorism. Axelrod was in charge of the message but the real blame rested with Obama, who, from the first days after the election, retained too much control. He resolved in the new year to widen his circle of advice and trust his Cabinet and other surrogates to speak for him. He had failed, he knew, to "flood the zone" with a consistent, memorable message.

In the 2008 campaign, Obama had one strategy and one goal. The challenge was to stick with the strategy through the flak and execute it. The presidency proved much more complicated. Instead of one or two rivals, Washington presented a confusing array of interest groups and competing power bases. And Obama had been naïve about the brazenness of the opposition. In early 2010 it turned out that ninety-three Republican members of Congress cut ribbons or put out press releases claiming credit for stimulus spending in their districts that they had voted against. Eight Republican cosponsors of a bipartisan Budget Commission to tackle entitlements (the deadweight sitting on the future of the economy) suddenly decided they couldn't support any commision that might endorse tax increases. So they voted against their own idea and the bill was defeated. (Obama set up his own bipartisan commission, but its findings won't be binding.) The president would have to find a way to expose the opposition and make his gibes stick, as Roosevelt did when he said, "I welcome their hatred," or Reagan, when he told Democratic critics to, in the words of Clint Eastwood, "Go ahead, make my day."

Even before Scott Brown won in Massachusetts, the White House began devising a new strategy. Thank God, one advisor said, for the State of the Union Address, which was quickly moved up from early February to January 27. That would let the president push the reset button for his second year right away. Besides, preparing for the speech would take everyone's mind off the White House's self-inflicted wounds.

By now the speechwriting team was confident that Obama would once again hit the three-pointer. The speech had plenty about jobs, jobs, jobs, the mantra of the hour. It had the requisite tax credits for small business and child care credits for middle-class families and even a gimmick—a one-year budget freeze that would do nothing to curb the big-ticket entitlement programs—for the deficit hawks who had forgotten that the recession wasn't over yet.

But no one knew until the day of the speech what the president would say about health care. Democrats were hearing from some constituents that they should just drop the whole thing. The mood was so bad on the Hill that Phil Schiliro, the best vote counter around, said the bill had no better than a 40 percent chance of passage. Obama gave an interview to George Stephanopoulos in which he seemed to be backing off from the major reform he had so long envisioned. In truth, Obama never wavered in his desire for a bill, but he got crucial assurances from Pelosi that she could pull House Democrats out of their funk if they passed a small business jobs bill first, which they did. Together the president and the speaker settled on a strategy of buying some time, then moving forward. Persistent progressivism.

Obama went before Congress amid great suspense. It took him more than a half hour to shift from jobs and the economy, but when he got to health care he doubled down on his proposal, dared Republicans to come up with something better, and reminded fellow Democrats, "We still have the largest majority in decades, and the people expect us to solve some problems, not run for the hills."

"We don't quit," the president said. "I don't quit."

AFTER THE MASSACHUSETTS debacle, Joe Biden suggested that everyone in the White House "take a deep breath." It was good advice. On reflection 2009 didn't look so bad after all for the Obama administration even without health care.

PolitiFact.com, a database of the *St. Petersburg Times* that won a Pulitzer Prize for its fact-checking of the 2008 campaign, had catalogued 502 promises that Obama made during the campaign. At the one-year mark the totals showed that he had already kept 91 of them and made progress on another 285. The database's "Obameter" rated 14 promises as "broken" and 87 as "stalled." With promises ranging from "Remove more brush and vegetation that fuel wildfires" to "Establish a playoff system for college football," PolitiFact selected 25 as Obama's most significant. Of those, an impressive 20 were "kept" or "in the works."

Because he had more latitude on foreign policy and national security, Obama kept almost all his promises there. He pledged a sixteen-month withdrawal of most forces from Iraq and, despite renewed violence in Baghdad, stayed on schedule. As promised he gave a speech at a major Islamic forum (the Turkish Parliament) in his first hundred days; canceled the F-22 fighter; made U.S. military aid to Pakistan conditional on antiterror efforts (previously the $5 billion came with no strings); required that Homeland Security funding be allocated on the basis of risk, not regional politics; fulfilled his many commitments to veterans; and banned torture, though not the practice of "extraordinary rendition" that allowed detainees to be shipped back to their countries of origin to be tortured there.

Obama promised an investment in high-speed rail and delivered, though only enough for a down payment on a new rail system. He was ahead of schedule on his pledge to invest $150 billion over ten years for renewable energy and was already providing money to convert factories to "clean technology centers" and weatherize millions of homes, though progress on the ground was very slow. Cap and trade seemed to be fading on Capitol Hill but other ideas for putting a price on carbon had new life. Symbolic energy promises, such as a full fleet of plug-in hybrid cars at the White House within a year, proved unrealistic.

Some of the kept promises sounded cosmetic, such as creating the government's first chief technology officer and establishing a White House coordinator for nuclear security. But staff is power in Washington, and attention and funding come with turf.

For most of 2009, the Pentagon wasn't ready yet to abandon the don't ask–don't tell policy. But at the end of the year, Obama told Bob Gates and Admiral Mike Mullen that it was time to move more rapidly toward ending the policy because "it's just wrong." After undermining the president on Afghanistan, Mullen now made it possible for him to fulfill an important promise. The admiral's passionate and historic congressional testimony in early 2010 changed the terms of the debate and all but ensured an end to discrimination against gays in the military.

Among less noticed promises, Obama kept his commitment to expand AmeriCorps; begin a social investment fund (similar to the Corporation for Public Broadcasting) to stimulate nonprofit growth; increase funding for national parks and forests; boost crime prevention in New Orleans; and enhance earth mapping from space.

If anything, Obama overperformed on education. He quickly fulfilled his pledge to recruit more math and science graduates to teaching and to create an "artists corps" of young artists to work in low-income schools. He focused intently on closing poorly performing schools, something no other president had tackled. Most important, Arne Duncan's "Race to the Top" competition was leveraging reform across the country. The idea of rewarding only success (instead of using the same old funding formulas) was soon extended not just to the overhaul of No Child Left Behind but to realms unrelated to education, such as regulatory reform and energy policy. The U.S. government report issued out of the G-20 meeting in Pittsburgh envisioning a "race to the top" in regulating global financial institutions was only one of several new efforts to create healthy competition. The concept offered the first glimmer of an Obama governing philosophy.

To the president the basic challenge was to fund what works. He was committed to expanding Geoffrey Canada's Harlem Children's Zone, which provides comprehensive services to more than eight thousand children in a ninety-seven-block area of Harlem. A Harvard study showed astonishing results, as Canada's intense program raised the scores of black children thirty-five points on math tests, greatly reducing the achievement gap. Obama's first budget contained only $10 million for planning, but the administration expected to start accepting applications in 2010 for twenty "Promise Neighborhoods" around the country, funded by public-private partnerships. If other cities could replicate Harlem's success, the former community organizer's promise of change might yet be redeemed. It was his best—maybe his only—chance to do something about the grimmest reality of the African American community—that one third of black males in their twenties have been caught up in some way in the criminal justice system.

———

MOST OF OBAMA'S "broken" promises were more about the White House's not pushing Congress on an issue rather than Obama's breaking a pledge, though they often amounted to the same thing. Others were in the "incomplete" category. Path-to-citizenship immigration reform was still stuck in line behind health care, energy, financial regulation, and of course jobs.

The most glaring shortcomings were in the area of process, which turned out to be of much greater concern to voters than most analysts predicted. Obama spoke up for transparency but the agencies were slow to comply in making more records available. And he set the ethics bar too high by promising to hire no lobbyists in his administration, which proved unrealistic. The White House did launch a website to track stimulus projects, Recovery.gov, and a new center to release documents that had been needlessly classified, a boon to historians. Eventually logs of all White House visitors were released. And despite the waivers Obama gave to several lobbyists, they did not have much influence with his administration, a huge change from the Bush years.

In the "broken promises" category, Obama refused to push Congress to prevent bankrupt corporations from awarding fat bonuses or to allow judges to "cram down" new terms on home mortgages. The Justice Department kept Obama's pledge to begin reforming "mandatory minimum" sentencing but dragged its feet on filling scores of judicial vacancies (fearful of distracting the Senate from health care), a decision which could have long-term consequences for the bench. Nor did anyone in Washington encourage states to require that interrogations and confessions in homicide cases be videotaped, the signature issue a decade ago of an Illinois state senator named Obama.

THE PRESIDENT COULDN'T help it: he was annoyed by the lack of credit for what he had accomplished. "I don't think people fully appreciate the degree to which, prior to health care, we had twelve straight victories in a row," Obama said. He reeled off six of them, bills he signed that regulated tobacco, cracked down on predatory lenders, reined in credit card companies, expanded national service, financed health insurance for millions more children, banned pay discrimination against women. "These are pieces of legislation that in any normal year would be considered huge accomplishments."

Obama believed the financial system stabilized more quickly and at lower cost than he expected. "That was a big positive because during the transition, frankly it was touch-and-go [whether the crisis would deepen]," he said. On the negative side the president added, "The contagion shifted from Wall Street to Main Street in a way that was much fiercer than we had hoped."

So it was a good news/bad news year in the economy. Obama and his economic team had prevented a depression—no small accomplishment. The recession was officially ending. All but $80 billion of the $700 billion in TARP spending had been paid back, and in 2010, if a proposed new fee on banks was enacted, the government's bank rescue plan would actually go into the black. After six major federal interventions, housing prices, which were expected to drop another 20 percent or more, were up 5 percent in 2009. That still left millions of homeowners underwater but in early 2010 the administration responded with more assistance for those facing foreclosure. "We have the right people in Washington," Warren Buffett concluded, "If we'd had a group that behaved like a deer in the headlights, that deer would've gotten run over."

Even so, the underlying economy remained fragile and unemployment disturbingly high, which was why so much of the stimulus was scheduled to take effect after 2009. "We anticipated [in late 2008] that in 2011 you were still going to have some significant unemployment problems and that they might even bleed into 2012," the president said.

Even as he succeeded substantively, Obama was struggling with his tone. The economic crisis inevitably pulled the White House away from the themes of the campaign. Axelrod always argued that Obama's change message was based on three pillars: bringing the country together, moving toward bipartisanship, and confronting the special interests. The bruising events of 2009 had prevented the president from succeeding at any of them. The country wasn't unified, to put it mildly; he had tried bipartisanship and been rebuffed; and, while bashing banks and health insurance companies rhetorically, he downplayed confronting the special interests in favor of getting things done.

Obama said he anticipated that the bailouts and the preoccupation with health care would take a political toll. "I said during the transition that my political capital would go down pretty rapidly," the president said in late November.

The president was proud—maybe too proud—of his record abroad. He described what he called "a pretty flawless execution of what our strategy was at the beginning of the year. . . . We said very early on that we had to get all the nations of the world to cooperate around the financial crisis—and to a remarkable degree, they have. . . . We said we wanted to take an engagement approach with Iran and North Korea [so that] we could guarantee international consensus if they reacted badly—and we have."

The country's relationship with Russia, he said, was yielding "unprecedented levels of cooperation," not just on containing Iran but in Afghanistan. Russia was even letting the United States fly over its territory with weapons bound for the region. Most significantly, in March 2010 Obama signed an arms control treaty with the Russians. If ratified by the Senate, START would lead to the largest reduction in nuclear arsenals in two decades and advance efforts to pressure Iran to curtail its own nuclear program.

Obama was concerned that Iran was continuing to stiff the IAEA and that North Korea was not about to return to the six-party talks, but he thought the world was now properly positioned to respond with sanctions and other forms of isolation.

In the long term, the president believed the rogue states and terrorist groups could be contained. It was America's competitors he worried about, the ones who were educating their children, training their workforce, and rushing to dominate world trade in the new clean energy economy.

"People don't grasp the gravity of what we're up against in terms of maintaining America's primacy in the world," he said with the sober look that presidents once reserved for discussing the cold war. "My challenge over the next several years is to see if I can inject that sense of seriousness—as well as hopefulness—in the American people, if not in some of the folks on Capitol Hill."

OBAMA WAS A competitive guy and wanted to get reelected as much as any president. Around Thanksgiving, when things headed south, he said to an old friend, "Who would really want this job for more than one term?" Then he added, "But I have to run now, otherwise it'll mean letting someone like Mitt Romney step in and get credit for the good stuff that happens after we've been through all this crap."

Winning reelection was important, but less critical to Obama than accomplishing big things no matter how long he stayed. His friends were emphatic on this point. "He knows he will have to spend a lot of his life after age fifty-four living with what he accomplished or failed to accomplish as president," Julius Genachowski said. "It's unimaginable to him to have to live in his fifties, sixties, and seventies without having made the most of it."

The way to make the most of it, the old friends agreed, was for him to stay who he is. "The core is the authenticity, the realness," said Marty Nesbitt. "He's going to tell us the hard truth without a lot of tricky rhymes or slogans. There will be better communication but I wouldn't look for a more 'staged' process.

Axelrod figured there were only two issues that could stop him: unemployment and Afghanistan. Obama had more control over the latter, but maybe not for long. At a dinner for historians, Robert Dallek reminded the president that the rule of thumb in American history was that wars distract presidents from their domestic priorities. This was true for Wilson, Roosevelt, Truman, Johnson, George H. W. Bush, and his son.

Sure enough, it was only a matter of weeks before the bureaucratic tensions over Af-Pak resurfaced. By the first of the year the Pentagon was saying that it couldn't get thirty thousand troops to Afghanistan by summer of 2010 as promised. Lieutenant General David Rodriguez, the deputy commander in Afghanistan, told reporters he wasn't even sure all the troops could arrive by the fall. On a December trip to the region Mullen claimed to be "reasonably confident" of staying on schedule but added blithely, "Life doesn't always work out."

This went over badly in the White House. Biden and Rahm, backed up by Jim Jones, now argued that the military had misled the president about its ability to meet the rapid deployment schedule that was at the heart of Obama's strategy.* The brass had rolled the new president in March with the request for the original twenty-one thousand troops, jammed him with the McChrystal Report, and was now trying to game him on the pace of the escalation.

McChrystal was angry too. He insisted that he had never thought it realistic that thirty thousand troops could arrive so quickly. This was

---

* While the United States was spending hundreds of billions fighting a war, China was spending huge amounts extracting raw materials from Afghanistan for its economy.

news to Obama, who had explicitly outlined the rapid deployment to McChrystal in a teleconference call on November 29.

The Pentagon began to argue privately that the White House was "playing politics" with the deployments, aiming to withdraw troops from Afghanistan in time for Obama's 2012 reelection campaign. This was true, but hardly a secret: the president had signed off on the troop increases only after "moving the bell curve to the left"—a rapid escalation and a rapid withdrawal. He didn't think the American public had the stomach for a long commitment. The first key moment would come in December 2010, when the Pentagon would review its progress.

The stage was now set for a serious bureaucratic clash in 2010 and 2011 over the "bell curve policy," with the Pentagon, backed by the State Department, on one side and the president and vice president on the other. By all odds, it wouldn't be pretty.

THE START OF Obama's final push on health care came at the beginning of February when he went to the House Republican caucus in Baltimore to answer questions from GOP members of Congress. John McCain first proposed the idea (borrowed from Great Britain's *Question Time*) during the campaign, and Obama had been thinking seriously about letting cameras into one of these sessions since his first month in office. When he thought he could pass a bill in 2009 without Republican support, he made the mistake of putting the notion aside.

Now he ventured into Republican territory to great effect. Obama's habit of doing his homework paid off. He showed the Republicans the courtesy of reading their proposals before politely eviscerating them. When he chuckled that they were treating his centrist health care proposal—the same ideas endorsed by Bob Dole and Howard Baker—as if it was a "Bolshevik plot," he owned the event.

The president followed up on February 25 with a bipartisan summit on health care at Blair House, the prototype of a new democratic institution that Obama will likely use again. The seven hours of discussion showcased Obama's great skill at leading a meeting but, as expected, brought no bipartisan agreement. It did, however, have the effect of reminding House Democrats that their real enemy was the GOP—not fellow Democrats in the Senate they had resented for nearly a year. Republicans were now irrelevant, as the fate of the bill rested entirely on whether House Democrats could unify.

Under the byzantine rules of Congress, the only way for Democrats to salvage health care reform was for the House to swallow the already approved Senate bill whole, otherwise it would have to go back to the

Senate, where, with only fifty-nine Democrats, it would die. Then the Senate would adopt certain agreed-to amendments to the financing of the bill under the rules of reconciliation that required only a simple majority—fifty-one votes (the House demanded this "sidecar reconciliation" in writing before voting for the Senate version). Allowing reconciliation to be used for health care was the "insurance policy" Rahm had made sure was in the April budget bill. Republicans acted as if Democrats were doing grave damage to the system by using reconciliation, but the GOP had in fact employed it more frequently over the years, most conspicuously for its $1.8 trillion tax cuts in 2001.

The Senate was now easier than the House, where a combination of abortion opponents (led by Bart Stupak) and nervous blue dogs made Pelosi's work especially challenging. But after a period of despondency, the bill miraculously revived, in part because one insurer, Anthem Blue Cross of California, announced a 39 percent rate hike in the middle of the debate. In early March, Obama began intense lobbying, saying he would do "everything in my power" to get a bill passed. He minced no words in explaining to Democrats that the fate of 31 million uninsured Ameicans wasn't the only thing on the line. So was his presidency, not to mention the future of the Democratic Party.

The endgame provided the highest drama of the Obama administration to date. On March 12, Pelosi sent a memo to the House Democratic caucus insisting that "we have to just rip the Band-Aid off and have a vote." Some members were so afraid to vote for any bill with the "Cornhusker Kickback" in it (even though it was obviously being deleted in reconciliation) that they urged the use of a parliamentary fig leaf called "deem and pass." But this was for what David Plouffe called "bed wetters." The leadership decided on up-or-down votes, no gimmicks.

The most inspired move was the House's insistence that the Senate include its college loan expansion in reconciliation. By cutting out the middlemen lenders, the government saved more than $60 billion, about half of which was used to help pay for health care. The math of the bill wouldn't have worked without it.

For six weeks Pelosi had been promising she could get the votes, even when it looked like she would have to rustle up a daunting sixty-eight of them. Now the tenacious speaker began to prove it, as each day in the last week before the scheduled March 21 climax brought a few more private commitments. Obama delayed and then postponed until June his trip to Indonesia in order to lobby. All told, he met with or telephoned all sixty-eight, some more than once. Many of the conversations had a ritual quality; the members were going to vote yes but wanted to be able to brag about their face time with the president.

Even so, the nervous White House and speaker's office went into the final weekend a half dozen votes short. Obama spoke eloquently to the House Democratic caucus, quoting Lincoln on the need to stand for truth. The liberals (most conspiciously Dennis Kucinich) were coming home but a group of thirty moderates from the Midwest and Pacific Northwest felt their states had been badly harmed by the reimbursement formulas in the Senate bill, which had deleted more than $8 billion in regional adjustments. This Quality Care Coalition was also concerned that the Senate bill didn't move fast enough from fee-for-service medicine to "value-based reimbursement," a collection of ideas that experts (benefitting perhaps from wishful thinking) believed could slash costs.

At 11:30 P.M. on Friday March 19, Congressman Ron Kind of Wisconsin, one of the coalition's negotiators, stormed out of the speaker's conference room. He was unhappy with the White House's position and was taking the American Medical Association with him. The negotiating ploy worked and by 3:00 A.M. the holdouts had a deal with Nancy-Ann DeParle. It had to stay secret before the vote or the regional adjustments HHS Secretary Sebelius agreed to in writing (the Senate bill gave HHS wide latitude) would smack of "Cornhusker" giveaways. Just as with the stimulus a year earlier, the short strokes were all about funding formulas. The final deal, brokered mostly by Congressman Bruce Braley, was $800 million in regional adjustments that benefited a dozen states (including Nebraska) and the promise of a "reimbursement summit" in September 2010.

Stupak, meanwhile, had been losing leverage all week. Twice, he insulted nuns on television for defying the bishops and moving in favor of the bill. The support of nuns and Catholic hospitals gave a few prolifers cover to side with Pelosi. To salvage something, Stupak settled for an executive order reaffirming the Hyde Amendment banning federal funding for abortions. After the new White House Counsel, Bob Bauer, banged out the new language on his computer on Sunday morning and brought it to the Oval Office, the president knew he had clinched the deal. In a sign of the times, Stupak's reward was to be heckled by Congressman Randy Neugebauer as a "baby killer" on the floor of the House, just one of several ugly epithets directed at Democrats. Barney Frank was subjected to antigay taunts by protesters and John Lewis, Emanuel Cleaver, and Jim Clyburn to racist slurs.

Even with the outcome clear, the final vote played on TV like a cliffhanger. An emotional John Boehner said the bill "disgraced the Founders." Pelosi, amending one of her predecessors, Tip O'Neill, argued that "all politics is personal." As the electronic scoreboard neared the magic 216 votes, Democratic members began chanting, "Yes we can!" Outside the Capitol, Organizing for America and MoveOn.org volunteers, in a counterdemonstration against Tea Party activists, chanted "Yes we did." At the White House, the Roosevelt Room was packed with staffers in jeans watching C-SPAN. It felt like Election night though Obama said he was even happier now. The president came in ten minutes before the vote, bringing cheers. Afterward he gave everyone in the room a hug: "Thanks so much. Great work."

Shortly before midnight, Obama appeared in the East Room with a teary Joe Biden at his side. "After nearly a hundred years of talk and frustration," the president said, "we proved we are still a people capable of doing big things." With a glint of triumph in his eye he added: "This is what change looks like."

The next morning, David Axelrod spoke movingly in a senior staff meeting about what the bill meant for people like his daughter Lauren. In the Situation Room, the president and Hillary Clinton hugged each other tight. Just before signing the bill on March 23, Obama hugged Biden, who whispered, "This is a big fucking deal." After the gaffe was picked up by a microphone, Gibbs tweeted: "And yes, Mr. Vice President, you're right." With twenty-two pens the president signed the bill. Later he summarized the ambitions of his presidency. "We don't fear the futute. We shape the future!" he exulted.

A relieved and happy president knew that the stench of the process would soon fade and that within a few years Americans would shake their heads in amazement that we had lived for so long in a country that forced people into bankruptcy to pay medical bills. He had won ugly—without a single Republican—but won all the same. Whatever happened next—however bad it got—Barack Obama was in the company of Franklin Roosevelt and Lyndon Johnson now in terms of domestic achievement, a figure of history for reasons far beyond the color of his skin.

Acknowledgments

Some books are marathons; others are sprints. This one felt like both. I started work in earnest in November 2008 and finished in March 2010. Along the way, I had little idea where I was going because the story hadn't happened yet. The impetus for the book came from my mother, Joanne Alter, who died just after the election. She was always eager for me to write books, so plunging into this one right after her death seemed fitting. My father, Jim Alter, has been a source of wise advice throughout, as have my siblings, Jennifer Alter Warden, Jamie Alter Lynton, and Harrison Alter.

I live in Montclair, New Jersey, but spent many days in Washington interviewing sources at restaurants and coffee shops, which usually proved better for loosening tongues than getting together in their White House offices. At night I would often stay on the third floor of the lovely Georgetown home of Joan and Ev Shorey, old family friends who first came to Washington in the early 1960s and have great historical perspective. They lived this book with me, evoking memories of Mom and cheering me on. I'm grateful for their hospitality and friendship. My other gracious hosts in Washington were Alexis Gelber and Mark Whitaker (now Washington bureau chief for NBC News), who were *Newsweek* colleagues for twenty-five years and offered their usual trenchant advice.

I continued writing my *Newsweek* column throughout, with the help and indulgence of Jon Meacham, Dan Klaidman, Bret Begun, Debra Rosenberg, Mark Miller, and Devin Gordon. I'm especially grateful to Howard Fineman, Michael Hirsh, Jeff Bartholet, Evan Thomas, Michael Isikoff, Darren Briscoe, Fareed Zakaria, Chris Dickey, Jacob Weisberg, and John Barry for their terrific insights around the office. Don Graham and Ann McDaniel continue to make The Washington Post Co. a hospitable place to work in a tough media environment. Special thanks to Daniel Stone and Ben Adler. Before joining *Newsweek* Ben provided important early research and reporting, as did the irrepressible Dayo

Olopade and Rob Grabow. Throughout the process Judy McGhee offered crucial help keeping me organized and moving forward.

My agent, Amanda Urban, took care of me as usual, though I can't say she turned out to be right when she told me at the beginning of the process, "This will be easy for you." Michael Waldman and Jeff Toobin, great friends and editors in a crunch, were kind enough to read the entire manuscript beforehand and offer shrewd comments on a tight deadline that spared me many problems. Jerry Groopman called me a few times a week to put in his brilliant two cents on health care and keep me focused.

At Simon & Schuster, which also published *The Defining Moment* in 2006, my thanks to Carolyn Reidy, David Rosenthal, Aileen Boyle, Jackie Seow, Lisa Healy, Jonathan Evans, Judith Hoover, Irene Kheradi, Elissa Rivlin, Victoria Meyer, and Julia Prosser. The indispensable Roger Labrie made sure the book got done (a close call), and Alice Mayhew, my editor, is the reason for it in the first place. Alice remains the gold standard in nonfiction book editing for good reason. Her careful attention and encouragement kept me going.

At MSNBC, thanks to Chuck Todd, Keith Olbermann, Rachel Maddow, Ed Shultz, Chris Matthews, Andrea Mitchell, Joe Scarborough, Mika Brzezinski, Phil Griffin, Izzy Povich, Jon Larson, Katy Ramirez, Amy Shuster, Greg Cockrell, Natasha Lebedeva, Lisa Nelson, Sheara Braun, Jennifer Kay, and many more.

From outside the government, special thanks to Michael Lynton, Rob Warden, Molly Lazar, Paul Begala, Mark Knoller, Simon Rosenberg, Michael Kinsley, Walter Isaacson, Cliff Sloan, David McKean, Andy Stern, Larry Coben, Jim Fallows, Phil Keisling, Charlie Peters, Gregg Easterbrook, Nicholas Lemann, Alan Brinkley, Bill Drayton, Don Epstein, Marty Nesbitt, Eric Whitaker, Joel Benenson, Jon Schnur, Doug Band, Margaret Carlson, Bobbi Brown, Norman Atkins, George Hackett, Keith Ulrich, Bob Shrum, John Rogers, Bettylu Saltzman, George Haywood, George Stevens, Jr., Newt Minow, Martha Minow, Abner Mikva, Richard Lazar, John Podesta, Fred Krupp, Jeff Berman, Steve Richetti, Stephen Colbert, Evie Colbert, Arianna Huffington, Harry Smith, Cassandra Butts, Ted Marmor, Richard Danzig, Bruce Riedel, Larry Korb, Garry Trudeau, Walter Shapiro, Nora McAlvanah, Susan Thomases, Josh Gotbaum, Flora Greenhouse, Lee Greenhouse, Vanessa Kirsch, Hillary Rosen, Alan Khazei, Michael Ryan, Bob Rubin, Josh Steiner, Josh Beckenstein, Harrison Wellford, David Sanger, John Harwood, Maureen Dowd, Joe Nocera, Andy Rosenthal, Christina Bellantoni, Major Garrett, Kati Marton, Robert Draper, Ron Suskind, Dennis Burke, Alan Fleischmann, Jesse Norman, Jonathan Schorr, Jon Schnur,

Sidney Blumenthal, Bill Daley, Mandy Grunwald, Tamara Luzzato, Tammy Haddad, Rick Hertzberg, Phil Bennett, Robert Dallek, Ben Bradlee, Sally Quinn, Donald Katz, Leslie Katz, Derek Shearer, Jamal Simmons, Warren Bennis, Brian Mathis, Tom Hamburger, Bob Drogin, Jim Johnson, Bob Boorstin, Roger Altman, Larry Korb, Joe Rospars, Dan Esty, Geoff Stone, Elizabeth Warren, Joel Motley, Betsey Myers, Peter W. Kaplan, and several others who might be compromised by inclusion or whom I have inadvertently omitted.

Scores of people I interviewed inside the executive branch and Congress—the critical sources for the book—are not listed here or in the Note on Sources. Several are quoted by name in the text but the vast majority are not. It pains me not to be able to acknowledge those working for the government, but I know that doing so would set off the usual guessing game about who told me what. It's inevitable, but why offer clues? My deepest thanks to all of you.

This book has not been easy for my family. Our three kids have been a great source of strength and amusement. When she was home from college, Charlotte offered sound judgment on our jogs together. One of the great pleasures of the project was the time I spent with Tommy, who goes to college in Washington. Our third child, Molly, and my wife, Emily Lazar, bore the brunt of it. They called me "Nessie" after the Loch Ness Monster because of the rare sightings when I would venture out of my home office. Molly, still blessedly at home, put up with all the time I spent in "the salt mine" on the third floor. And Emily balanced a tough day job with doing much more than her share around the house while remaining a great source of love, comfort, and good advice throughout. This one's for you.

Note on Sources

This book is based largely on interviews I conducted between mid-2008 and early 2010 with more than two hundred people inside and outside government. I also consulted the official White House transcripts that record everything the president says in public statements, White House visitor logs and schedules, White House press pool reports, contemporaneous accounts of telephone conversations, and personal notes kept by attendees at important meetings. On those few occasions where exclusive material or quotations have been drawn from newspaper and magazine articles, I've cited the sources in the endnotes. *Newsweek,* the *New York Times,* the *Washington Post,* the *Wall Street Journal, Politico, Politifact, Politics Daily, Atlantic Media, Slate, TalkingPointsMemo,* and *RealClearPolitics* have all been especially helpful for insight into the complex events of Obama's first year. Google has been indispensable for fact-checking.

My reporting in this book drew on more than a quarter-century (!) of covering politics for *Newsweek.* It also benefited from longtime connections in the city of my birth, Chicago. I first met Barack Obama there in January 2002, when he was an Illinois state senator and unsuccessful congressional candidate. My aunt died and he came by my cousin Bob Rivkin's house to pay his respects. We chatted briefly about what he might do next with his life. In the years since, I have interviewed Obama a half-dozen times and talked with him occasionally off the record. The first interview was in 2004, when I wrote the first cover story about him to appear in a national magazine; the most recent was on November 30, 2009, in the Oval Office.

With a few notable exceptions, I've been able to interview anyone else I wanted in the White House, including Vice President Joe Biden and the president's four top aides: Rahm Emanuel, Valerie Jarrett, David Axelrod, and Pete Rouse. All were extraordinarily busy but informative and I'm grateful to them for their time.

Dozens of other members of Congress, administration officials, advisors, aides, and other sources were extremely helpful. Most, though not all, of the interviews were conducted on background, which means that I could use what they said but not attribute it to them. These arrangements are regrettable, but nowadays they're often the only way that people in Washington will utter an interesting word. Sad to say, books like this one would simply be impossible without background sources. I agreed to check back with sources before using any direct quotations obtained from the interviews. Several of these sources were gracious enough to put up with my endless questions on more than one occasion. In a few cases, I interviewed sources more than a half-dozen times.

This book largely reflects the direct observation of Obama and his circle by the people who know them best. If I use quotation marks around something that Obama said privately, it comes from a source who actually heard it. On the few occasions in the book where sourcing might be secondhand, I paraphrase the comments unless the source has consulted contemporaneous notes.

Because I wasn't present at internal White House meetings, I depended on note takers and on the memories of participants. I believe that when the president is talking, that occasion is so memorable that eyewitnesses can be trusted to remember what he said, especially if the quotations are short. Longer quotes from the president are either from his public statements as released by the White House or from my interviews with him, the latter being cited in the endnotes. When quotations from sources are obtained by other reporters, I've tried to cite those reporters in the endnotes. Otherwise, readers may correctly assume that any fresh material I present without citation comes from my own reporting.

I learned something about the intersection of journalism and history that I should have known long ago: sources aren't willing to talk much when their subject areas are in the news; it's only weeks later that they open up. My hope was that I could use some of the material I gathered for the book in *Newsweek*. But it turned out that sources were wise to this and almost uniformly stipulated that I could not use what they were telling me in the magazine, only in the book.

A journalist or historian is no better than his sources, but any mistakes herein are entirely my responsibility.

Notes

PREFACE

xvii Arthur M. Schlesinger Jr.'s cycles: Arthur M. Schlesinger, Jr., *The Cycles of American History* (New York: Mariner Books, 1999).

xviii "This is not a normal presidential situation that I find myself in: Author interview, President Obama. November 30, 2009.

CHAPTER 1

5 "I was impressed": Henry Paulson, *On the Brink: Inside the Race to Stop the Collapse of the Global Financial System* (New York: Business Plus, 2009), 14.

8 "I think this is absolutely nuts": David Plouffe, *The Audacity to Win: The Inside Story and Lessons of Barack Obama's Historic Victory* (New York: Viking, 2010), 339.

8 "Playing with dynamite: Paulson, 291.

8 "almost apologetic": Ibid., 341.

9 "TARP Is Total Abdication of Responsibility to the Public": Andrew Ross Sorkin, *Too Big to Fail: The Inside Story of How Wall Street and Washington Fought to Save the Financial System—and Themselves* (New York: Viking, 2009), 488.

9 "We may not have an economy: Evan Thomas and Michael Hirsh, *Newsweek,* May 25, 2009.

11 "because it's pretty hard: Paulson, 303.

CHAPTER 2

17 "Most of my good friends: Darren Briscoe, quoted in Evan Thomas, "A Long Time Coming," *Public Affairs,* 2009, 195.

17 "vintage college dorm: *60 Minutes,* CBS News, November 17, 2008.

18 David Plouffe joked: Plouffe, *The Audacity to Win,* 291.

20 "I told you: Richard Wolffe, *Renegade: The Making of a President* (New York: Crown, 2009), 410.

23 Fritchey said no: *Chicago Tribune,* February 1, 2009.

30 Summers was a consultant: Louise Story, "A Rich Education for Summers (after Harvard)," *New York Times,* April 6, 2009.

30 the running mates had a chilly conversation: Mark Halperin and John Heilemann, *Game Change* (New York: HarperCollins, 2010), 413.

31 "Barack says, well, folks: Jonathan Alter, *Newsweek,* October 13, 2008.

CHAPTER 3

38 "You are the forty-fourth president: *60 Minutes,* CBS News, November 16, 2008.

38 watching her daughter become first lady: Ibid.

40 "never imagined: MSNBC, November 4, 2009.

41 "The world got so messed up: *The Colbert Report,* November 5, 2008.

CHAPTER 4

47 "You never want a serious crisis: Gerald Seib, "In Crisis, Opportunity for Obama," *Wall Street Journal,* November 21, 2008.

55 The Clinton retread story was true enough: Al Kamen, "Like It's 1993," *Washington Post,* April 6, 2009, online.
64 Eventually a full quarter of Obama appointees: Ibid.
65 frighteningly prolific law professor: Richard H. Thaler and Cass R. Sunstein, *Nudge: Improving Decisions About Health, Wealth and Happiness* (New Haven: Yale University Press, 2008).

CHAPTER 5
72 Obama and Bill didn't have a proper one-on-one meeting: *Meet the Press,* NBC, September 30, 2009.
72 "Philippe, that is ridiculous!: Jonathan Van Meter, *Vogue,* December 2009.
73 Reines and her foreign policy advisor: Ibid.
74 The Clintons still considered him a traitor: Jonathan Alter, *Newsweek,* January 28, 2008.

CHAPTER 6
77 "If we had played games: Author interview, President Obama.
81 In the Federalist Papers: Thomas Geoghegan, "Mr. Smith Re-writes the Constitution," *New York Times,* January 10, 2010.
83 That didn't even include the $8 trillion: Mark Pittman and Bob Ivry, "U.S. Taxpayers Risk $9.7 Trillion on Bailout Programs," Bloomberg.com, February 9, 2008.
87 "some tail" on the Recovery Act: Author interview, President Obama.

CHAPTER 7
101 It was a happy, contented moment for Obama: Wolffe, *Renegade,* 306.
103 "So what should Barack Obama do: Peter Baker, "Obama's War over Terror," *New York Times,* January 17, 2010; Martha Joynt Kumar, "The 2009 Presidential Transition," *Presidential Studies Quarterly* 39, no. 4 (2009); Spencer Hsu, *Washington Post,* January 20, 2009.
103 Bush was in good spirits too: Wolffe, *Renegade,* 305.
104 "shot out of a cannon": Ibid., 306.
104 "I was in 9/11: Sheryl Gay Stolberg, *New York Times,* January 21, 2009.
104 "This is not Jesus: Ibid.
105 "I'm not trying to make a statement: Mike Allen, "Swearing In: 'Barack Hussein Obama,' " Politico.com, December 10, 2008.
108 "solid, respectable, uplifting: William Safire, *New York Times,* January 20, 2009.
108 "Because of you, John: David Remnick, *The New Yorker,* February 2, 2009.

CHAPTER 8
111 "action and action now: CNBC interview, January 7, 2009.
116 "One of the things that you discover: Author interview, President Obama.
129 "set the tenor for the whole year: Author interview, President Obama.
134 "The CIA gets what it needs: Baker, "Obama's War over Terror," *New York Times Magazine,* January 4, 2010.
136 "a reminder of the unbelievable stakes: David S. Broder, *Washington Post,* February 26, 2009.
136 "We've seen him in just about every framework: Tom Shales, *Washington Post,* February 25, 2009.
137 A study by the *Washington Times: Washington Times,* January 14, 2009.
137 "It's kind of like he decided: Scott Wilson, *Washington Post,* April 29, 2009.

CHAPTER 9
138 the "great separator: Richard Neustadt, *Presidential Power and the Modern Presidents: The Politics of Leadership from Roosevelt to Reagan* (New York: Free Press, 1991), 172.
141 When the *Star Trek* movie came out: Jon Meacham, *Newsweek,* May 25, 2009.

143 "Emotional equanimity is the mark: Clifford Geertz, *The Religion of Java* (Chicago: University of Chicago Press, 1976), 240.

144 Researchers at Hamilton College: *Yahoo! News,* December 17, 2009, online.

144 "change will come: Barack Obama, *Dreams from My Father* (New York: Three Rivers Press, 2004), 133.

145 "It was into my father's image: Ibid., 220.

146 he confided to his future brother-in-law: Ryan Lizza, *The New Yorker,* July 21, 2008.

147 "The longer I served in Washington: Barack Obama, *The Audacity of Hope* (New York: Random House, 2006), 104.

151 Plouffe disagreed and credited Obama: Plouffe, *The Audacity to Win,* 216.

CHAPTER 10

160 "fucking retarded: Peter Wallsten, *Wall Street Journal,* January 26, 2010.

162 "It was a terrible time for me: *The University Hatchet,* George Washington University, May 17, 2009.

164 His mission in 2006: Jonathan Alter, *Newsweek,* March 27, 2006.

169 *New York Times Magazine* cover story: Robert Draper, "The Ultimate Obama Insider," *New York Times,* July 21, 2009.

CHAPTER 11

180 "probably from a well-connected government contractor: Steven Rattner, *Fortune,* October 21, 2009.

183 As Ron Gettelfinger contemplated a deal: Micheline Maynard and Michael J. de la Merced, *New York Times,* July 26, 2009.

185 "Just as George Bush spent: David Sanger, *New York Times,* June 1, 2009.

187 But Michigan had lost eight hundred thousand jobs: Bill Vlasic and Nick Bunkley, *New York Times,* June 10, 2009.

CHAPTER 12

191 "For He's an Unpleasant Fellow: Jackie Calmes, *New York Times,* June 7, 2009.

194 "[Tim] is the only person: David Wessel, *In Fed We Trust: Ben Bernanke's War on the Great Panic* (New York: Crown, 2009).

200 "We know that these too big to fail institutions: Testimony of Joseph Stiglitz before the Joint Economic Committee, April 21, 2009.

200 "Every plan we've heard from Treasury: Paul Krugman, *New York Times,* March 3, 2009.

203 "The only thing between you and the pitchforks: Eamon Javers, Politico, April 3, 2009.

204 "The fact is that Larry Summers: David Leonhardt, *New York Times,* May 3, 2009.

207 Simon Johnson, an MIT professor: See Simon Johnson and James Kwak, *13 Bankers* (New York: Pantheon, 2010).

CHAPTER 14

224 In eleven nations: Pew Global Attitudes Project.

227 "Everyone quotes the 'military industrial complex' line: Author interview, President Obama.

233 "I would put my judgments on foreign policy: Jonathan Alter, *Newsweek,* February 4, 2008.

237 Zinni heard nothing for days: Barbara Slavin, *Washington Times,* February 4, 2009. Laura Rozen, ForeignPolicy.com, February 4, 2009.

240 "young, handsome and *bronzato:* Jo Steele, Metro.co.uk, November 6, 2008.

CHAPTER 15

244 "just impossible to imagine: Author interview, President Obama.

246 "it was clear to us in the transition: Ibid.

248 highly speculative claims that "comparative effectiveness: Jerome Groopman, "Health Care: Who Knows Best?" *New York Review of Books,* February 11, 2010.

253 the major deal cut in the Roosevelt Room in July: Alicia Mundy, *Wall Street Journal,* July 7, 2009.

262 "Our success in stemming the panic: Author interview, President Obama.

262 "I've got to step up my game: *Good Morning America,* ABC News, September 20, 2009.

CHAPTER 16

270 "The truth is, without economic growth: Author interview, President Obama.

275 "It's very hard for me to swallow that one: CNBC, June 17, 2009.

276 "insufficient tuned-in-ness: Jim Rutenberg, *New York Times,* October 22, 2009.

276 "operating basically as a talk-radio format: Savannah Guthrie interview, NBC News, October 22, 2009.

277 "the blog of some unemployed guy: David Carr, *New York Times,* October 17, 2009.

278 "You're the president: Bill Maher, *Real Time with Bill Maher,* June 12, 2009.

281 Black lawyer recognizes hesitancy: *JET Magazine,* "America's Family Man: How Obama Is Restoring the Image of African-American Males," June 2009.

281 normally devoted to black women, includes comments from black men: *Essence,* November 2009.

281 "I was black before I was elected: *Late Night with David Letterman,* September 21, 2009.

282 After he addressed the NAACP: Gene Robinson, *Washington Post,* July 19, 2009.

283 "Obama's America, white kids getting beat up: Quoted in Jonathan Chait, *The New Republic,* November 2, 2009.

286 "It is depressing in the extreme: Glenn C. Loury, *New York Times,* July 25, 2009.

287 "a coarsening of our politics: *60 Minutes,* CBS News, September 13, 2009.

287 "public psychology cannot be attuned: Jonathan Alter, *The Defining Moment: FDR's Hundred Days and the Triumph of Hope* (New York: Simon & Schuster, 2006), 271.

CHAPTER 17

292 even the Secret Service: Ronald Kessler, *In the President's Secret Service* (New York: Crown, 2009), 223.

293 "kept punching me every time it got close: Author interview, President Obama.

295 an exit strategy from the story: Kristina vanden Heuvel, *This Week with George Stephanopoulos,* ABC, December 6, 2009.

295 "I wouldn't gloss over: Jodi Kantor, *New York Times Magazine,* October 26, 2009.

295 "I'll do whatever he says: Lisa Lerer, *Politico,* February 20, 2008, online.

296 "Whiskey Tango Foxtrot" moments: Bob Woodward, *Washington Post,* July 1, 2009.

296 he had learned to curse: Barack Obama, *Dreams from My Father,* 78.

297 "Print that he promised me: Jonathan Alter, *Newsweek,* December 27, 2004.

297 he wouldn't smoke "in the White House: *Meet the Press,* NBC, December 7, 2008.

298 "Malia will tell you: "America's Teachable Moment," *Essence,* March 2010.

299 The president was especially annoyed: Jodi Kantor, *New York Times Magazine,* October 26, 2009.

301 "Let's be blunt: Jacqueline L. Salmon, *Washington Post,* October 19, 2009.

301 The navy chaplain there, Carey Cash: *Washington Post,* October 19, 2009.

304 a brisk business in private basketball lessons: Wright Thompson, "The Power Game," *ESPN Outside the Lines,* 2009, online.

305 "It wasn't a pretty sight: Jonathan Alter, *Newsweek,* February 4, 2008.

CHAPTER 18

310 "by osmosis: Quoted in Evan Thomas, *Newsweek,* March 28, 2009.

310 In the first seven months Geithner's calendar: Daniel Wagner and Matt Apuzzo, *Washington Post,* October 9, 2009.

310 "great vampire squid: Matt Taibbi, "Inside the Great Bubble Machine," *Rolling Stone*, July 2, 2009.

310 "You either prevent default: Jackie Calmes, *New York Times*, December 10, 2009.

310 Where is the taxpayer bonus? Joseph Nocera, *New York Times*, June 18, 2009.

317 over the past two decades, the number of American banks fell by half: Henry Kaufman, *The Road to Financial Reformation: Warnings, Consequences, Reforms* (New York: Wiley, 2009), 97.

318 "It turned out better than any of us could have expected: Author interview, President Obama.

CHAPTER 19

330 According to a poll of Chinese youth: *New York Times*, November 18, 2009.

333 "This repeated cycle: Frank Rich, *New York Times*, September 12, 2009.

337 A study by McKinsey and Co.: Kevin Huffman, *Washington Post*, January 2, 2010.

338 "We've done as much on education reform: Author interview, President Obama.

339 "Christie Romer said: *Meet the Press*, December 13, 2009.

339 "Larry Summers was on record saying: *This Week*, ABC, December 13, 2009.

CHAPTER 20

351 His approval rating in Great Britain surged to 86 percent: Brian Knowlton, *New York Times*, July 24, 2009.

351 "Our objective was not to get some signed agreement: Author interview, President Obama.

354 "He reminds me of a chess grandmaster: Roger Cohen, *New York Times*, November 23, 2009.

355 "Before the elections: Lally Weymouth, *Newsweek*, October 12, 2009.

357 "The Nobel Peace Prize is the rest of the world: Bono, *New York Times*, October 17, 2009.

358 "No, we haven't made China: Helene Cooper, *New York Times*, November 17, 2009.

CHAPTER 21

363 "I neither confirm nor deny: Author interview, President Obama.

369 Pentagon's Vietnam book: H. R. McMaster, *Dereliction of Duty* (New York: HarperCollins, 1997), 370.

369 "a Whiskey Tango Foxtrot moment: Bob Woodward, *Washington Post*, July 1, 2009.

370 White House Vietnam book: Gordon Goldstein, *Lessons in Disaster: McGeorge Bundy and the Path to the War in Vietnam* (New York: Holt, 2009).

370 "It is stunning to listen to Johnson: Sheryl Gay Stolberg, *New York Times*, December 12, 2009.

373 "For the past eight years, whatever the military: Author interview, President Obama.

374 the president eliminated withdrawal as an option: Peter Baker, *New York Times*, December 6, 2009.

374 classified study on Pakistan: Ibid.

376 the Afghans often ripped out the sinks: Thom Shanker and John Cushman Jr., *New York Times*, November 5, 2009.

376 when Bob Woodward revealed the McChrystal Report: Bob Woodward, *Washington Post*, September 21, 2009.

377 "You can't hope to contain the fire: Evan Thomas, *Newsweek*, September 26, 2009.

377 Petraeus gave an interview: Michael Gerson, *Washington Post*, September 4, 2009.

378 a "plan called 'Chaos-istan: Mark Hosenball, *Newsweek*, October 10, 2009.

378 "The short, glib answer is no: Tom Bowman and Mara Liasson, interview, NPR, December 3, 2009.

381 what Jones called a "metamorphosis": Anne E. Kornblut, Scott Wilson, and Karen DeYoung, *Washington Post*, December 6, 2009.

382 "We don't need to do that: Ibid.

384 "A lot of my questions: Author interview, President Obama.

385 "I'm usually more sedate than this: Anne E. Kornblut, Scott Wilson, and Karen DeYoung, *Washington Post,* December 6, 2009.

385 Karl Eikenberry, a retired general: Greg Jaffe, Scott Wilson, and Karen DeYoung, *Washington Post,* November 12, 2009.

389 "there's no point at which we can say: Meeting with columnists, November 9, 2009.

391 As he peered out at the audience of young cadets: *60 Minutes,* CBS News, December 13, 2009.

CHAPTER 22

397 He wants to get it done and be beloved: Vanessa Grigoriadis, *New York,* November 1, 2009.

402 "No president has ever had that happen: Dana Milbank, *Washington Post,* September 10, 2009.

406 "What if we tell them: Vanessa Grigoriadis, *New York,* November 1, 2009.

407 "I'm sure there are a lot of people: Sheryl Gay Stolberg, *New York,* November 9, 2009.

408 a man in the crowd suffered a heart attack: Dana Milbank, *Washington Post,* November 6, 2009.

411 "I mean, Lyndon Johnson did not have to: Author interview, President Obama.

413 Lieberman was on record as firmly supporting: *Connecticut Post,* September 8, 2009.

415 "[Health care has so] overwhelmed the debate: Author interview, President Obama.

418 "As opposed to standing outside Fenway Park?": David Filipov, *Boston Globe,* January 13, 2010.

EPILOGUE

423 "remoteness and detachment": George Stephanopoulos interview, *This Week,* ABC News, January 20, 2010.

425 "the core elements: Ibid.

426 "it's just wrong: Elisabeth Bumiller, *New York Times,* February 1, 2010.

428 "I don't think people fully appreciate: Author interview, President Obama.

428 "We have the right people: *Charlie Rose,* PBS, November 13, 2009.

Index

About the Author

Jonathan Alter, a Chicago native, is the author of the bestseller *The Defining Moment: FDR's Hundred Days and the Triumph of Hope* and *Between the Lines: A View Inside American Politics, People, and Culture.* He is a national affairs columnist for *Newsweek* and an analyst for NBC News and MSNBC. Alter lives in Montclair, New Jersey, with his wife, Emily Lazar. They have three children, Charlotte, Tommy, and Molly.